THE ROUTLEDGE HANDBOOK OF POSITIVE COMMUNICATION

The Routledge Handbook of Positive Communication forms a comprehensive reference point for cross-disciplinary approaches to understanding the central role of communication in the construction of hedonic and eudemonic happiness, or subjective and psychological well-being. Including contributions from internationally recognized authors in their respective fields, this reference uses as its focus five main scenarios where communication affects the life of individuals: mass and digital media, advertising and marketing communication, external and internal communication in companies and organizations, communication in education, and communication in daily life interactions.

José Antonio Muñiz-Velázquez is a teacher, researcher, and head of the Department of Communication and Education at Universidad Loyola Andalucía. He is the author of several publications about positive communication.

Cristina M. Pulido is a teacher and researcher at the Department of Journalism and Communication Sciences of Universitat Autònoma de Barcelona. Her PhD in communication, art, and education is from the University of Barcelona. Her main research interest is in the promotion of social change through media, especially overcoming sexual abuse. She has participated in diverse competitive research projects and published in the main international scientific journals.

ROUTLEDGE HANDBOOKS IN COMMUNICATION STUDIES

THE ROUTLEDGE HANDBOOK OF POSITIVE COMMUNICATION

Contributions of an Emerging Community of Research on Communication for Happiness and Social Change

Edited by
José Antonio Muñiz-Velázquez and Cristina M. Pulido

Routledge
Taylor & Francis Group

LONDON AND NEW YORK

First published 2019 by Routledge

2 Park Square, Milton Park, Abingdon, Oxfordshire OX14 4RN
52 Vanderbilt Avenue, New York, NY 10017

Routledge is an imprint of the Taylor & Francis Group, an informa business

First issued in paperback 2020

Library of Congress Cataloging in Publication Data
A catalog record has been requested for this book

ISBN: 978-1-138-63327-8 (hbk)
ISBN: 978-0-367-65968-4 (pbk)

Typeset in Bembo
by Apex CoVantage, LLC

CONTENTS

Contents

Contents

ILLUSTRATIONS

CONTRIBUTORS

Tamara D. Afifi is a professor in the Department of Communication at the University of California-Santa Barbara. Her research focuses on communication patterns that foster risk and resiliency in families and other interpersonal relationships, with particular emphasis on how people communicate when they are stressed and the impact of these communication patterns on personal and relational health; and information regulation (privacy, secrecy, disclosure, avoidance, stress contagion). Her work centers on families as communicative systems of stress and resilience.

Mel Ainscow is a professor of education at the University of Manchester, UK. His work focuses on ways to make schools more effective for all children. A long-term consultant to UNESCO, he is currently working on international efforts to promote equity and inclusion globally.

David Alameda is a marketing research consultant (CIM) at AEDEMO and previously held positions at GECA Consultants and CIMEC. He is also currently a professor at the Pontifical University of Salamanca in brand management, marketing and advertising research. He belongs to the research groups Brand Management and Communication Processes (Complutense University of Madrid) and the Group Management of Advertising and Brand Communication (Pontifical University of Salamanca).

Purificación Alcaide-Pulido is a researcher and professor in the area of communication. Her research areas of interest are university image, the application of social media tools and social networking sites in HEIs, and student' satisfaction. Alcaide-Pulido has published papers and participated in international conferences in business communication. She is also working on various projects in England and Portugal.

Ángel Alloza Losana is currently CEO of Corporate Excellence–Centre for Reputation Leadership. Prior to this position, he worked at BBVA as the global director of strategy for communications, reputation and brand. He is also co-author of *Atrapados por el consume* and *Corporate Reputation*.

Antonio Ariza-Montes is a professor of human resource management at Universidad Loyola Andalucía, Spain. His interests include organizational behavior, human resources management, volunteerism and social innovation. He has published a large number of papers in relevant international journals.

Rafael Araque-Padilla is an associate professor of marketing at Universidad Loyola Andalucía, Department of Management (Spain).

Gary A. Beck is an associate professor of communication at Old Dominion University. He co-edited *Communicating Hope and Resilience Across the Lifespan*, as well as chapters in multiple volumes on positive communication across the lifespan. His research has been published in *Communication Monographs*, *Personal Relationships*, *Journal of Family Communication*, and *Communication Quarterly*.

Erica C. Boling is an associate professor of literacy education at Rutgers, the State University of New Jersey. She conducts research on teacher education and the impact of student-created digital stories on teaching and learning.

Cátia Branquinho is a PhD student at Lisbon University (FMH) and is also a clinical and health psychologist, national researcher of the HBSC/WHO study in Portugal, and psychologist at OPP (Portuguese Board of Psychologists).

Emma Camarero is a lecturer in the Department of Communication and Education at Universidad Loyola Andalucía. Her area of expertise is in media literacy for social change and documentary film. Dr. Camarero has written around 70 publications including articles, books and book chapters, and as a filmmaker has created several institutional videos and documentaries.

Mariano Carbonero-Ruz was a lecturer at University of Cordoba from 1987 to 2013 and at the Universidad Loyola Andalucía since 2013. His current research interests include computational intelligence and theoretical researches as an application of methods to problem-solve in different areas of economics.

Pilar Castro-González is an associate professor of marketing at Universidad Loyola Andalucía, Management Department. She has more than 11 years of professional experience as marketing director, consultant, analyst and member of board of directors in different companies (private and public). She was visiting scholar in Loyola University Chicago-Quinlan School of Business and has published some journal articles and books about business internationalization and international marketing strategy. Her research interests include gamification, e-commerce, brand relationship, gender ideals in advertising and teaching innovation.

Covadonga Chaves completed a PhD in Experimental Clinical Psychology at Complutense University of Madrid (2013) and holds a master's degree in Clinical and Health Psychology (2009). Her doctoral dissertation got the 2015 International Positive Psychology Association (IPPA) Award to the Best Dissertation.

Alice Chirico has an MS degree in psychology from Catholic University of the Sacred Heart, and she is a PhD candidate at the same university. Her main research interests concern optimal experiences and complex emotions conveyed through virtual reality and music.

Catherine A. Coleman completed her PhD at the University of Illinois, Urbana-Champaign, and is currently an associate professor of Strategic Communication at Texas Christian University. She researches advertising and marketing, transformative consumer research, and consumer culture. Her research is published in the *Journal of Advertising, Consumption, Markets & Culture*, the *Journal of Public Policy & Marketing*, as well as other journals and books.

Francisco Cuadrado is a professor of music, education, and communication at Universidad Loyola Andalucía. Apart from his academic career, he has worked as composer, sound designer and music producer for more than 20 years.

Andrés del Toro is a PhD professor from Universidad Loyola Andalucía (Seville). He specializes in corporate communications, strategic planning and social media and is currently researching the opportunities that social media provides to companies and professionals.

Alexander Fedorov is a scientist, teacher, media education specialist, film critic, deputy director of the Anton Chekhov Taganrog Institute and main editor of the journal *Media Education*. He is the author of 20 books on media education and media literacy and more than 500 articles in media studies and media literacy education journals.

Celestino Fernández is Distinguished Professor Emeritus in sociology at the University of Arizona (UA), where he continues to teach a highly popular course on happiness. At UA, he also served in several administrative positions, including as vice president for academic outreach and international affairs. Dr. Fernández has published more than 50 academic articles and book chapters on various topics, including popular culture, higher education and Mexican immigration; he has served on about 50 international accreditation visits and has composed 50 corridos (Mexican ballads)—several have been recorded. Prof. Fernández has lectured internationally for 40 years.

Jessie K. Finch is an assistant professor of sociology at Stockton University in Galloway, NJ. She studies migration, deviance, social psychology and health. She has published in peer-reviewed journals such as *Teaching Sociology* and *Sociological Spectrum* and has received grants from the National Science Foundation. She is the co-editor of *Migrant Deaths in the Arizona Desert* from the University of Arizona Press (2016) and teaches courses on research methods, popular culture and happiness.

Clara Fontán Gallardo is intelligence and knowledge senior manager at Corporate Excellence–Centre for Reputation Leadership as well as Adjunct Professor at Universidad Loyola Andalucía.

Megan Fromm is an assistant professor at Colorado Mesa University in Grand Junction, Colorado, where she teaches media law, design, multimedia, writing, media theory and media literacy and also advises the student-produced *Horizon* magazine. Fromm is the curriculum lead and faculty for the Salzburg Academy on Media and Global Change, a summer study abroad program. She is also the educational initiatives director for the Journalism Education Association. Her first co-authored textbook, *Student Journalism and Media Literacy*, was released in November 2014. Fromm has recently authored chapters on media literacy pedagogy and social media and youth empowerment. She also writes for PBS' MediaShift website, EducationShift, on topics such as media and journalism education.

Andrea Gaggioli is an associate professor of psychology at Catholic University of Sacred Heart and coordinator of the Research Unit in Psychology of Creativity and Innovation. His main research focus is positive technology, which investigates how emerging ubiquitous technologies, such as virtual reality, mHealth and personalised e-health tools, can be used to promote psychological well-being and foster positive change.

Fernando Galindo Rubio is a professor and researcher at Pontifical University of Salamanca (Spain). His main research interest is the development of audiovisual communication products aimed at mobile devices.

Tania Gaspar is an associate professor at and president of the School of Psychology of Lusíada University and also serves as a clinical and health psychologist, national researcher of the HBSC/WHO study in Portugal and also coordinator of several research projects. Gaspar is also an author and coauthor of several national and international papers, books and chapters and psychologist at OPP (Portuguese Board of Psychologists).

Margarida Gaspar de Matos is full professor at Lisbon University (FMH) and also serves as a clinical and health psychologist, PI of the HBSC/WHO study in Portugal and also coordinator of several research projects and several PhD and Postdoc researches. Gaspar de Matos is the author and co-author of several national and international papers. She is also a chartered psychologist at OPP (Portuguese Board of Psychologist), a psychotherapist and representative of OPP in EFPA, serving as convenor of the Board of Prevention and Promotion.

Jane E. Gillham is full professor in the psychology department at Swarthmore College. Her major research and clinical interests are at the intersection of clinical psychology, developmental psychology, and education, particularly the ways in which schools can promote well-being in children and adolescents.

Diego Gomez-Baya is an assistant professor in the Social, Developmental and Educational Psychology Department at the University of Huelva (Spain). His research is mainly focused on psychological adjustment and healthy lifestyles during adolescence and youth from a developmental and educational perspective.

Inmaculada Gómez-Hurtado is a teacher of social sciences and inclusive education at the Department of Integrated Didactics, Universidad de Huelva (Spain). Her research areas include attention to diversity (inclusive education), teaching of social sciences and school organization and leadership.

Belén Gutiérrez-Villar is a professor at Universidad Loyola Andalucía in the area of communication and marketing. Her research areas are branding and marketing in higher education.

Annabell Halfmann is a research assistant at the Institute for Media and Communication Studies, University of Mannheim, Germany. Her research focuses on computer-mediated communication and on aspects of media use and well-being. She is specifically interested in how social norms and self-control influence media uses and effects.

Susan Hallam is emerita professor of education and music psychology at the UCL Institute of Education. She was awarded an MBE in the 2015 New Year's Honours list. She joined Oxford Brookes as professor of education in January 2000.

Don Heider is executive director of Markkula Center for Applied Ethics (Santa Clara University). He was also a founding dean and professor at the School of Communication at Loyola University Chicago, until summer 2018, and founder of the Center for Digital Ethics and Policy. He is a multiple Emmy-award-winning journalist.

Paula Herrero-Diz teaches courses on digital journalism and journalism genres at Universidad Loyola Andalucía. Her research focuses mainly on digital contents created by children, communication and social change, young empowerment and media literacy.

Gonzalo Hervás is an associate professor in Complutense University of Madrid. In 2004, he was a visiting scholar in the Positive Psychology Center of the University of Pennsylvania. Currently, he is the president of the Spanish Society of Positive Psychology (2016–2019) and coeditor of the *Journal of Happiness Studies*.

Matthias Hofer is a senior research and teaching associate at the University of Zurich, Institute of Mass Communication and Media Research. His main research areas are entertainment, emotion and well-being research, presence and embodiment in virtual environments, and social capital in new media. His research also focuses on media use and effects throughout the human lifespan.

Jian Jiao is a master's student and teaching assistant in the Department of Communication at the University of Arizona. His interests focus on interpersonal communication and relationships, especially romantic and family relationships.

Susanne M. Jones is an associate professor of communication studies at the University of Minnesota, Twin Cities, MN. Her research focuses on supportive communication processes and emotion regulation. Her research has appeared in *Communication Monographs*, *Communication Research*, and *Human Communication Research*, as well as in interdisciplinary journals, such as *Sex Roles* and *Mindfulness*. She is an associate editor for *Mindfulness*.

Sara Kim is a PhD student and a teaching associate in the Department of Communication at the University of Arizona. Her research focuses on international students' cultural adjustment and their communication and identity management on social media.

Antonio L. Leal-Rodríguez holds a PhD with international mention in economic sciences and management from Universidad de Sevilla. His research interests include knowledge management, innovation, sustainability and organizational culture. His research has been published in a variety of leading scientific journals.

Dawn Lerman is professor of marketing and executive director of the Center for Positive Marketing at Fordham University's Gabelli School of Business, where she also serves as associate dean of graduate studies. Her primary research interests include social responsibility in the marketing and consumption of brands and the impact of words and other aspects of language on brand perceptions, consumer-brand relationships and memory for brands.

Anastasia Levitskaya is a scientist, teacher, media education specialist and docent of the Taganrog Management and Economics Institute. She is the author of books and more than 100 articles in media studies and media literacy education journals.

Isabel Lopez-Cobo is a lecturer in education at Universidad Loyola Andalucia. She develops her work in the field of improving the effectiveness of schools and the development of emotional education in primary school. She participates actively in research projects (European and national) related to diversity, skills assessment of the university professorate and the creation of learning communities in disadvantaged environments.

Javier Lozano Delmar is an associate professor in the School of Communication and Education at Universidad Loyola Andalucía (Loyola University Andalusia) in Spain. His research work focuses mainly on television studies, analyzing new narrative strategies such transmedia content, social television, active audiences and fandom-generated content, and television promotional strategies. He is currently working on a new project about happiness and media, analyzing how participative audiences and the consumption of TV programs and films can be seen from the perspective of positive communication.

Timothy de Waal Malefyt is clinical associate professor at Gabelli School of Business, Fordham University, in NYC. For 15 years he led strategy and brand development as VP, director of cultural discoveries for BBDO Worldwide advertising in NYC, and D'Arcy, Masius, Benton & Bowles in Detroit, at which produced a breakthrough campaign for Cadillac. Dr. Malefyt holds a PhD in anthropology from Brown University and he is co-editor of *Advertising Cultures* (2003), *Ethics in the Anthropology of Business* (2017) and co-author of *Advertising and Anthropology* (2012). He is frequently cited in *Business Week, New York Times, USA TODAY*, and *BrandWeek*, among other media.

Galit Marmor-Lavie teaches at the Stand Richards School of Advertising and PR at University of Texas, Austin. Her publications focus on spirituality and advertising. She was a spokesperson, has done some public speaking, and teaches courses in the fields of strategic communication and campaigns.

Irene Martín is adjunct professor of the Faculty of Communication, Pontifical University of Salamanca. She is the author and coauthor of different publications in recent years, such as articles, reports and chapters of books within the research line of marketing and communication. She is a member of research teams in funded research projects, all related to the field of communication and marketing. She has developed research work in corporate communication, strategic management of knowledge and intangibles, CSR, as well as in the study of new business models.

Juan-Ramón Martin-Sanromán holds a PhD in communication and works as professor and researcher at Pontifical University of Salamanca Communication School (Spain). In 2014, he founded @DesignOnScreens and believes in the use of design and beauty to improve happiness.

Santiago Mejia is assistant professor of law and ethics at Fordham University's Gabelli School of Business. His research interests span normative ethical theories of businesses, organizational behavior, moral psychology and virtue ethics.

Rosa Melero-Bolaños is professor at Loyola Andalucía University in the area of communication and marketing.

Holman Meyerhoffer is a master's student and teaching assistant in the Department of Communication at the University of Arizona. Holman studies positive interpersonal communication, mindfulness, and neuroscience to promote personal and relational growth, inclusive of feminist, intercultural and egalitarian considerations.

Paul Mihailidis is an associate professor in the school of communication at Emerson College in Boston, Massachusetts, where he teaches media literacy, civic media and community activism. He is founding program director of the MA in Civic Media: Art and Practice, and is principal investigator of the Emerson Engagement Lab as well as the faculty chair and director of the Salzburg Academy on Media and Global Change. His research focuses on the nexus of media, education and civic voices.

Julien C. Mirivel is interim dean of the College of Social Sciences and Communication and professor of applied communication at the University of Arkansas at Little Rock. He is the author of *The Art of Positive Communication: Theory and Practice* and *How Communication Scholars Think and Act: A Lifespan Perspective*.

Horacio Molina-Sánchez holds a PhD in accounting and finance and a degree in law. His research focuses on corporate governance for ideological institutions. He is a member of the board of directors of the Spanish Association of Accounting and Business Administration.

María José Montero-Simó is associate professor of marketing at Universidad Loyola Andalucía (Spain) and Chair of the Department of Management.

José Antonio Muñiz-Velázquez is a teacher, researcher, and head of the Department of Communication and Education at Universidad Loyola Andalucía. He is the author of several publications about positive communication.

Elizabeth A. Munz is an assistant professor in the Department of Communication Studies at West Chester University. Her research examines parent-child communication during times of transition. Specific transitions for her research program include the transition to kindergarten and the transition to grandparenthood.

Sean Murray is a graduate student in the master of communication and culture program at Ryerson University. Her master's thesis surveyed Canadian edible campuses with the intention of understanding their diversity and relevant best practices. She created the first comprehensive Canadian database of edible campuses.

Javier Nó-Sánchez is a professor of information technology at the Universidad Loyola Andalucía. He is dean of the Social and Human Sciences School and director of the Teacher Training and Innovation Center.

Catherine O'Brien has been actively engaged in sustainability efforts locally, nationally and internationally for more than 25 years. Catherine is an education professor at Cape Breton University, Canada, where she developed the world's first university course on sustainable happiness based on the pathbreaking concept she created.

Mary Beth Oliver is Distinguished Professor and co-director of the Media Effects Research Laboratory at Penn State University. Her research examines emotion, social cognition and media, with an emphasis on media entertainment. Her recent work focuses on the role of meaningfulness and media in enhancing feelings of well-being and the experience of connectedness with humanity.

Joshua R. Pederson is an assistant professor in the Department of Communication Studies at the University of Alabama. He specializes in research and teaching about communication in close relationships. His specific research interests include understanding how personal networks shape processes of coping and repair during challenging life experiences.

José Javier Pérez-Barea is assistant professor and researcher at Universidad Loyola Andalucía, Department of Management (Spain).

Margaret Jane Pitts is associate professor and director of graduate studies in the Department of Communication at the University of Arizona. Maggie uses qualitative inquiry techniques to examine positive interpersonal communication processes and outcomes.

Juan F. Plaza works as a professor at the Faculty of Social Sciences of the Loyola Andalucía University, in Sevilla (Spain), where he teaches a range of courses in written communication.

Cristina M. Pulido is a teacher and researcher at the Department of Journalism and Communication Sciences of Universitat Autònoma de Barcelona. Her PhD in communication, art, and education is from the University of Barcelona. Her main research interest is in the promotion of social change through media, especially overcoming sexual abuse. She has participated in diverse competitive research projects and published in the main international scientific journals.

Jesús Ramírez-Sobrino is a doctor in economic and business sciences who specializes in market studies and opinion and data analysis. His research focuses on the strategic analysis and planning of organizations. He received the National UNICAJA Award for Economic Research (2007).

Mimar Ramis is a former postdoc researcher on the FP7 IMPACT-EV project working on the evaluation of scientific, political and social impact of SSH research. She has promoted different initiatives on scientific communication at the university level and has published in several scientific journals with international impact.

Marina Ramos-Serrano works as associate professor at the Communications School of Universidad de Sevilla, where she lectures on advertising creativity and new media technologies. Her main research fields are communication and advertising in the digital age, and branded content.

Arthur A. Raney is the James E. Kirk Professor of Communication at Florida State University. His research examines how and why we enjoy media entertainment, with specific attention to the role of morality in those processes. Recently, his work has focused on the relationships between media consumption, self-transcendent emotions, well-being and prosociality.

Daniel Raposo is a professor at the Polytechnic Institute of Castelo Branco and a researcher dedicated to visual identity design.

Diana Rieger is a professor in the Department of Communication Science and Media Research at LMU Munich. Her main research interests concern the effects of entertaining narratives in movies and social media, as well as the ubiquity of mobile communication and its effects on well-being and interpersonal relationships. She further investigates the effects of extremist internet propaganda and potential counter-voices.

Giuseppe Riva is Director of the Applied Technology in the Neuro-Psychology Lab at Istituto Auxologico Italiano, Milan, Italy, and full professor of general psychology at Catholic University of Sacred Heart, Milan, Italy. His main research focus is the use of immersive and distributed technologies, such as virtual reality and augmented reality, to promote psychological well-being and foster positive change.

Luis Rivas is lecturer in economics at Pontifical University of Salamanca (UPSA) and IE University, Spain. He is Head of the Transference of Research Results Office, UPSA, and has published books and articles on economics of happiness, growth and economic development, international economics and globalization.

Jose Luis Rodriguez Orjuela completed an MS i Computer Science at Loyola University Chicago and is currently a data scientist at Quinlan School of Business at Loyola University Chicago. His research is in user experience, sentiment analysis and behavioral economics. As part of his role as data scientist, he supports faculty research and develops applications for the CME Group Business Analytics Lab.

Milagrosa Sánchez-Martín is lecturer on psychology in the Department of Psychology at Universidad Loyola Andalucía, Spain. She teaches methodology and data analysis. From 2013 to 2014, she has been working as technical staff in methodology and statistics applied to biomedical research in the Andalusian Public Health Service. She is also a founding partner of the company Metodik, which was awarded as one of the best business ideas of 2013 from the University of Seville. It is dedicated to providing methodological advice for data analysis in research projects. Her field of interest is the application of statistical and methodological innovations to studies related to the social sciences and health. Dr. Sánchez-Martín has intensively participated in several projects, one of which is related to happiness and media.

Frank M. Schneider is a post-doctoral researcher at the Institute for Media and Communication Studies, University of Mannheim, Germany. His research interests include digital communication, entertainment, political communication, communication processes and effects, and research methods.

Silvia Serino is a post-doctoral researcher at the Catholic University of the Sacred Heart of Milan. Her approach is multidisciplinary, investigating how the brain represents the body. She has published more than 90 papers on international scientific journals.

Thomas J. Socha is professor of communication and director of the graduate program in Lifespan and Digital Communication at Old Dominion University in Norfolk, Virginia, USA. He was the founding editor of the *Journal of Family Communication* and currently serves as the series editor of the Lifespan Communication: Children, Families and Aging book series published by Peter Lang. His publications include seven books, more than 50 chapters and articles and 75 conference papers about positive interpersonal communication, family communication and children's communication.

Elias Soukiazis is Lecturer in Applied Econometrics and Economics, University of Coimbra, Portugal. He has published books and articles on happiness, economic growth, international trade, regional economics and human capital.

Fernando Suárez Carballo is a PhD professor at the Faculty and faculty of Communication of the Pontifical University of Salamanca (Spain). He is also a member of the research group Business Innovation and Creativity and has written several articles and book chapters related to graphic design and visual communication, his main lines of investigation.

Linda Tuncay Zayer is associate professor of marketing at the Quinlan School of Business at Loyola University Chicago. Her research lies in the areas of gender, transformative consumer research and consumer culture. She has published in the leading journals of her field and is co-editor of the book *Gender, Culture and Consumer Behavior*.

Beatriz Valverde is lecturer in the bilingual double degree of early childhood and primary education at Universidad Loyola Andalucía, Spain. Her research interests are twofold: she conducts research on TEFL in primary, secondary and higher education, and also publishes on English literature in the 20th century, specifically on the work of Graham Greene.

David Varona is a researcher a teacher of digital journalism and design as well as production of digital contents at the Universidad Loyola Andalucía.

Beatriz Villarejo-Carballido is a post-doctoral researcher at the University of Deusto. Her research line is focused on the use of "language of desire" in audiovisual alternative products as way to overcome gender violence. She has led the ICT and Media Education topic at the Multidisciplinary Educational Research International Conference for two years. She has also participated in competitive researches and has been published in several international scientific journals.

Peter Vorderer is professor of media and communication studies at the University of Mannheim in Germany. His research focuses on users' interest in entertainment and new media, as well as the consequences of using them. He is a fellow of the International Communication Association, for which he served as president from 2014 to 2015.

Mathew A. White is an associate professor and director of the master of education program in the School of Education at The University of Adelaide. He is a principal fellow in Melbourne Graduate School of Education at The University of Melbourne.

Steven R. Wilson is professor in the Department of Communication at the University of South Florida. His research focuses on influence and identity management within close relationships. His recent research explores how US military families navigate communication challenges when service members deploy to a warzone and then return home.

Ashley Woodfall is senior lecturer in media theory and practice as part of the faculty of Media and Communication, Bournemouth University, UK. Ashley worked in the television industry for many years before joining the teaching and research community at Bournemouth University. His research interests cover the lived media experience of children in a cross-platform world and creative research methods.

Lucas J. Youngvorst is a doctoral candidate at the University of Minnesota, Twin Cities, MN. His research focuses on the intersection of supportive communication and computer-mediated communication. His research has been presented at various regional, national and international conferences and has appeared in *Communication Quarterly*.

Nicole N. Zamanzadeh is a PhD student at the University of California, Santa Barbara (UCSB). Her research interests include technology use, stress and family resilience. Her current work investigates questions about technology use habits as a potential source of stress or resilience within the family system.

ACKNOWLEDGMENTS

As we say in the introductory chapter, this book is a dream—a dream shared by many people. We would like to express our most sincere gratitude to all the people who have dreamed that this book was possible, as well as necessary, and have consequently worked to make it a reality. Thank you, therefore, to each and every one of the authors of the insightful texts that make up this volume, for their valued time and good work. In particular, we would like to thank Carmelo Vázquez; first, for his generous words in his preface to this volume. Second, and more important, because he has been, is and will always be a source of inspiration, not only from a scientific and academic point of view, but also as an ethical and human bulwark.

This volume is rooted in the Conference of Positive Communication held in 2016 at the Seville headquarters of Universidad Loyola Andalucía. For this conference and for this volume to become a reality, we always counted on the enthusiastic support of our vice-rector for research, Carlos García Alonso. To him, and to all the participants in that exciting conference, including our students who volunteered in its organization, we want to show our profound gratitude.

Thanks also, naturally, to Routledge publishing house, which supported this project from the beginning. We would like to express our appreciation especially to Felisa Salvago Keyes, who, after the reception of our proposal, immediately opened up the doors for it to be carried out. In addition, special thanks to Christina Kowalski, who has provided us with precious assistance in the arduous process of publishing a book like this.

We cannot fail to extend our recognition to each and every one of the teachers and mentors that we have had in our life, academic and personally. Without them, we would not be here. In every sense of the word *here*. If we had to name them all, however, we would have to go back to the ancient Greece; fortunately, the list would be virtually infinite.

Finally, we want to thank you, the reader of these words. If you continue reading the book you have in your hands, we guarantee that when you finish it, you will be convinced that communication, in all its human dimensions, makes it possible, despite the ups and downs, to create a better world. In this sense, there is still so much work to do: our task has only begun.

José Antonio Muñiz-Velázquez and Cristina M. Pulido
Seville and Barcelona (Spain)
April 2018

PREFACE

As the so-called rational optimists tell us, the world is now in the best place in terms of material elements, and we live in a more luminous era compared to any previous time of humanity.[1] However, at the same time, unexpected challenges and risks present themselves, and many of these new challenges are related to the flow of information. Up until the time of Galileo, it was believed that the universe was filled with a subtle fluid called "ether," which was responsible for the movement of all things. In a certain sense, the small-and large-scale dissemination of information (e.g., from our genetic code to "Big Data") has been transformed into a modern-day ether. This so-called "fifth element" has been described in both Western medieval and Eastern cosmologies as supplementing the four basic elements: earth, water, fire, and air.

The *Routledge Handbook of Positive Communication*, which has been brilliantly edited by José Antonio Muñiz-Velázquez and Cristina M. Pulido, precisely captures some of the effects of this new fifth element; however, the book's contributors uniquely perceive this element by elucidating the positive effects of communication. While apocalyptic messages concerning the development of technology and communication are as commonplace, it is rare to find an academically sound view about the positive aspects of these new developments. The aim of this book is not to propose a naively positive vision by offering a sweetened "Disneyfied" vision but rather to complement our outlook with a perspective that *also* considers the positive aspects of communication. This work arrives timely to offer an excellent complementary understanding that is led by a long list of reputable academics.

In 1966, American psychologist Earl Carlson published a nearly unknown article titled "The affective tone of psychology."[2] Carlson had the fortunate idea to analyze how thematic contents and emotional terms changed in university psychology manuals that were published in the United States from 1875 to 1961 (approximately 100 years). He found that, from the beginning, there was a linear rise in the coverage of issues related to human suffering (e.g., stress, depression, anxiety, and anger) and a decrease in the coverage of themes related to positive emotions (e.g., happiness, love, passion). This unbalanced view toward negative emotions was taught for at least one hundred years to psychology students, and a similar view likely occurred within other disciplines of the social sciences. Fortunately, since the late 1990s, the emergence of the positive psychology movement has been effectively contributing to reverse or at least correct the negative bias that was initially described by Carlson. Understanding the positive aspects of human interactions is equally as important as analyzing the negative side in understanding human nature.

The historic imbalance in representing the good and bad aspects of human nature in academic psychology has been notorious even to this day.

Communication is not merely the aseptic exchange of information between a sender and receiver. Norbert Wiener (1942), the great pioneer of computational theories of communication, said that cybernetic systems were teleological systems. That is, their operation can be described as being oriented to an end that is programmed by humans, as in the case of language with machines. Wiener's ends-oriented idea, which was initially developed to understand man-machine communication, seems essential to understand communication between humans. In addition to tangible effects, as noted in the title of this book, all communication involves an intention, desire, and ultimate function. Furthermore, understanding these aspects, apart from the more instrumental elements analyzed by communication experts, is essential. Undoubtedly, positive psychology can potentially offer a useful theoretical framework to analyze the functional and teleological aspects of communication. This academic approach to the study of positive functioning makes it possible to identify not only the aspects related to enjoyment (e.g., from essential mother-child communication to the entertaining elements of mass media) but also the subtler aspects related to growth and personal development. All of these aspects are amply approached in this opportune book.

The structure of this book is personally satisfying in that the authors dedicate space to reflect on the ethical aspects related to communication. Naturally, communication aimed at increasing well-being (i.e., hedonic or eudaimonic) without attending to a moral commitment to respect dignity, foster critical thinking, and care for the common good, would be morally abject. This phenomenon obviously occurs in totalitarian political systems as well as in domesticated democracies; additionally, it occurs in the economistic practices of social communication firms that are focused on modern appearance and is shaped by purely commercial interests. These delicate and exciting aspects of communication have only recently been studied in academia. One senses growing tensions between free information *versus* economic interests, the human desire to communicate *versus* the spurious incentive of that desire, and the increasingly blurred discernment between truth and reality. We are witnessing an epic change in which human consciousness begins to become configured with never-before-known parameters that are characterized by having almost instantaneous access to information without geographical limits and a growing sense of belonging to a common humanity. We live in a hyper-communicated world in which we have to fight to make communication more effective but also truer and more subject to human values. This is the framework within which positive communication can be understood, and in this sense, this book is a pioneering work that is sure to elucidate both known and unknown domains.

Without a doubt, this book arose from the editor's and author's deep desire to communicate; furthermore, their desire is adorned with commendable optimism and deeply ethical appreciation. The prevailing message throughout this book is that there is an ethical requirement to promote communication that helps us become better people. This meliorism is based not on a naïve assumption but on the solid support provided by positive psychology and modern information science. It is possible to create a better world, and communication is a powerful tool to do so. One cannot be distant or cynical about these issues, and the authors are not.

Despite the international nature of this book, a local reflection can be made given that this issue has a more universal scope. Dreaming of a better life and society does not seem very typical of the Hispanic character. Lord Byron said that Spain had had the misfortune to have as a literary myth the shadow of Don Quixote, a dreamer whom everyone mocks merely for dreaming and fighting admirably to achieve his dreams. According to the English poet, that mockery toward those who dream has shaped a national character given to daydreaming, fear of social punishment, and avoidance of the corresponding planning that allows those dreams to become reality.

Fortunately, this book escapes this literary *fatum* and is a book of dreamers who, with the best conceptual tools in their hands, intend to contribute to the psychological science and practice reflected in achieving the Aristotelian wish for the best and most virtuous life possible.

I have probably exceeded the space granted by the generosity of the editors. A well-meaning reader might think that talking about positive communication is redundant; however, in a world filled with an abundance of noise and fury, to critically raise the positive aspects of communication requires both academic value and ethical impulse. This pioneering book accomplishes this task with a vengeance.

Carmelo Vázquez
Professor of Psychopathology
Complutense University of Madrid
President, International Positive Psychology Association (2013–15)

Notes

1 Pinker, S. (2018). *Enlightenment now: The case for reason, science, humanism, and progress.* London, UK: Penguin.
2 Carlson, E. R. (1966). The affective tone of psychology. *The Journal of General Psychology*, 75(1), 65–78.

Introduction

1

THE FLOURISHING SIDE OF COMMUNICATION EFFECTS

José Antonio Muñiz-Velázquez and Cristina M. Pulido

We had a dream—a dream to create a book like this one, a book as a framework for future research for those who want to go beyond the common perspective of someone from the academic field who usually observes the effects of social communication. Traditionally, in scientific observation focused on the sociological and psychological effects of communication, the point of view has almost always been from the negative side, namely, the danger and abuse regarding the well-being of people. Indeed, this perspective was and is absolutely enriching and necessary, but it is incomplete.

Fortunately, beginning a few years ago, from several corners of the research community, in geographical and disciplinary terms, things have been changing. Indeed, it is important to underline the adverse consequences of a communication that does not respect others and their well-being. However, it is also important to carry out communication studies to point to the possible positive effects of communication. In physics, we find the so-called *observer effect*, which refers to changes that the act of observation of a phenomenon will make on the phenomenon itself. Mutatis mutandis, we think that a similar effect can be found in communication studies. Therefore, if we focus our research on positive communication effects, maybe we can help to increase them. For example, if we can demonstrate that adding positive values to the content of a commercial is good for the advertising brand in terms of marketing, in addition to being virtuous in ethical terms, other brands could follow in the same vein, and thus, little by little, positive communication would be an increasing reality. Such an outcome is one of the ultimate goals of this volume.

Welcome to the Marvelous Adventure of Positive Communication

With the aim of collecting the main perspectives in the increasing scientific corpus about how communication can help us to improve our well-being, this new handbook seeks to set a comprehensive starting and reference point for theory, research, and practice with regard to the relationship between happiness and communication. In other words, to build the fundamentals of positive communication. Including contributions from internationally recognized authors in their respective fields, this Routledge Handbook of Positive Communication that is before you has been written from a wide international and multidisciplinary viewpoint with diverse approaches. Two main fields, however, stand out in this integration: communication studies and positive psychology.

The diverse chapters of this handbook strive to demonstrate the strengths of this emerging cross-disciplinary approach to understand the central role of communication in the construction of hedonic and eudaimonic happiness, or subjective and psychological well-being, whether we are talking about individuals or societies.

In the next chapter, Beatriz Villarejo-Carballido, Cristina M. Pulido, and Mimar Ramis aim to drive deeper into the discussion about the main concepts and perspectives in positive communication and the importance of strengthening the links between academic and social impact in this field and beyond.

In Chapter 3, Gonzalo Hervás and Covadonga Chaves seek an answer to a dual question: what is the extent and depth of the current scientific description of human happiness, and how important is the means and magnitude of the dissemination of this scientific knowledge about happiness throughout society. In their pages, we find, apart from a complete overview of what we scientifically know about happiness, a description of the differences between a hedonic concept of happiness, or the so-called subjective well-being (satisfaction with life, positive emotions, etc.), and a eudaimonic concept of happiness or psychological well-being—that is, the conception of happiness based on human virtues and character strengths. The authors end with a warning that although happiness studies currently have a large and strong framework, human happiness remains one of the most complex phenomena of human existence.

Once we share what science says and what it does not say about happiness, the book moves ahead with the analysis of positive communication, clustering into six main scenarios where human communication appears in the life of the individuals: interpersonal communication in daily life interactions, specially, in the private sphere; communication in conventional mass media; advertising and marketing communication; public relations and communication in companies and organizations; digital communication; and finally, communication in the field of education. Following is a brief overview of what we are going to find in each scenario.

When Happiness Can Be Spread With a Simple Word

The first section focuses on positive interpersonal communication, meaning that type of communication that works toward increasing happiness or well-being through interpersonal interactions within all those scenarios that form our everyday life. The section starts with a clear warning by Thomas J. Socha, who states that the word "positive" is not a simple addition but "a clarion call to communication scholars of all stripes to join the study of communication's higher purposes." In this line, Socha's chapter offers a reinforcement of the evolving conceptual framing of positive interpersonal communication, which will finally be considered as a metapattern for studying those interpersonal communication patterns that facilitate (or inhibit) the satisfaction of human needs, among other aspects. Socha states that positive interpersonal communication is a complex episodic process with several levels of analysis, of co-construction of participants' well-being in terms of mutual needs-satisfaction and benefit, as well as reinforcement of relationships and character strengths of senders and others.

After Socha's introductory framework for the study of positive interpersonal communication, Jessie K. Finch and Celestino Fernández offer a more anthropological perspective. In their chapter, they place the emphasis on cultural differences and the importance of social and cultural context regarding the concept or idea of happiness itself, for example, and how its conception can be influenced by the level of individualism, as opposed to collectivism. Close to this, the authors also stress how verbal and nonverbal communication elements and styles, such smiling and laughter, the role of inequality, the prominence of listening and sharing, etc., can be changed culturally. Thus, in this way, they try to demonstrate the importance of cultural conditioning in experiencing and communicating happiness.

Going ahead with the importance in the realm of interpersonal interactions of even a simple word for our well-being, Julien C. Mirivel focuses his analysis on the nature of peak communication, which is defined by him, following Gordon (1985), as those moments of interaction between individuals that bring a deep sense of joy, fulfillment, or happiness. It is a kind of moment or communicational behavior that, moreover, can appear at any time, as the author says. His contribution also offers an overview of his reach model of positive communication, which is for him "any verbal and nonverbal behavior that functions positively in the course of human interaction" (Mirivel, 2014, p. 7). He narrows in, specifically, on six of those possible behaviors: greeting, asking, complimenting, disclosing, encouraging, and listening. Undeniably, as the author says, each one of us can make a difference in our lives and the lives of people around us by making simple communicative choices in those six situations described and beyond, "transforming any ordinary moment of human interaction into an extraordinary one" (Mirivel, 2018, p. 58).

In Chapter 7, we find the work of Nicole N. Zamanzadeh and Tamara D. Afifi, who focus on communication in families. They affirm that, against the majority of scholars that approach communication within families and couples from a negative point of view, it is very important to study the positive effects of a communicational family interaction, specifically in two relevant aspects of our well-being: resilience and thriving. For this, they underline the usefulness of the new theory on stress and resilience in close relationships, the Theory of Resilience and Relational Load (TRRL). This theory examines the role of certain communication patterns in creating stronger families and therefore stronger individuals in psychological terms.

Chapter 8 by Steven R. Wilson and Elizabeth A. Munz also addresses family communication. The authors explore the main theories addressing this communicational realm, as well as their relation to positive communication. Thus, they offer a deep and rich theoretical review of the main concepts that help us to understand to what extent we can conceptualize the power of positive family communication.

Next, we find Gary A. Beck and Joshua R. Pederson's contribution. In Chapter 9, they address another main scenario in which our well-being is closely related with our relational nature: romantic relationships. Their chapter provides a research frame into the process of cultivating various positive contributors toward effective relational functioning. After providing a summary of the nature and experience of relational flourishing or thriving, the chapter underlines the importance of communication in facilitating the development of these flourishing experiences into a romantic relationship. Only then will we be able to build a meaningful relationship that will become a real optimal experience for our lives.

The following chapter, written by Susanne M. Jones and Lucas J. Youngvorst, asks to what extent supportive and mindful communication is also good for our physical health, as the authors say, in good times as well as in bad times. They focus on what they call enacted support, which they closely relate with concepts as mindfulness, present-centered awareness, compassion, empathy, emotion acceptance, etc., all of them as essential tools for building a real person-centered message behavior that provides receivers' emotion regulation abilities, coping, and eventually well-being.

Going beyond mindfulness, the first part ends with a chapter by Margaret Jane Pitts, Sara Kim, Holman Meyerhoffer, and Jian Jiao dedicated to another of the perhaps deeper positive psychology constructs, namely, savoring. This concept refers to a person's capacity to recognize, appreciate, and elevate pleasant life experiences (Bryant & Veroff, 2007). In other words, it speaks to the process of mindfully attending to a moment to enhance feelings of pleasure associated with that experience, which also entails a social dimension. The fact of sharing those amusing experiences will be important. Thus, for the authors, this savoring experience must also be considered a positive interpersonal communication. In addition, several communication practices, such as recognition and acknowledgment, can be considered savoring experiences themselves, as Pitts and Socha (2013), or Pitts (2016) have noted. Savoring is amply described in the field of positive psychology, but it is a relatively new construct in the field of interpersonal (positive) communication. This chapter tries to bridge both scientific fields to draw attention to the potential savoring has to increase quality of life and well-being through its practical application in interpersonal communication contexts.

Mass Media Discourse, Values, and Human Happiness

After the first part of the book centered in interpersonal communication and several of its possible positive effects, the second part focuses on social and mass media communication. As Mary Beth Oliver and Arthur A. Raney affirm in their introductory chapter, most of the scholarship on mass communication studies and media psychology has often been focused on the variety of harms that mass media consumption can inflict on individuals and society, such as aggression, stereotyping, health issues, less than fully positive values, such as materialism, sexism, etc.

Indeed, as the authors recognize, it is absolutely important to research those negative effects. However, at the same time, it is also indispensable to observe, analyze, and describe the numerous positive effects. Thus, over the years, we have found a growing body of scholarship that recognizes the positive sides of media consumption: the improvement of feelings of purpose and meaningfulness, connectedness with others, compassion for oppressed individuals, altruism, etc. Their chapter provides a clear overview of the importance of the evolving scholarship in positive media psychology by illustrating its relevance across television, film, news and journalism, games, etc., without forgetting newer media formats, such as mobile communication, social media, or user-generated content.

Following the framework by Oliver and Raney, Chapter 13 offers an analysis of the different forms of positive experiences that can be obtained through the consumption of media entertainment. Its authors, Matthias Hofer and Diana Rieger, show that apart from the media entertainment offering fun, thrilling, pleasurable, or suspenseful experiences (hedonic experiences), human beings also consume sad, serious, poignant, and thought-provoking entertainment, which would be closer to eudaimonic experiences. In this sense, their research review suggests that eudaimonic and hedonic entertainment experiences could be the result of two different processes: the first one is slow and deliberate (eudaimonic), and the second one is automatic, fast, and intuitive (hedonic). Without doubt, both of them are interesting and important for the construction of a complete framework for positive media entertainment consumption that feeds the well-being and happiness of spectators.

The main theme of the following chapter is a very specific kind of spectator: the fan. Javier Lozano and Milagrosa Sánchez-Martín explore the eudaimonic dimension in the consumption of fictional entertainment as a fan, which is defined by them as a spectator who creates a deep emotional and cognitive bond with the product, carrying a very large social facet, as usually he or she participates in groups, online communities, etc. Many character strengths are present in fan consumption, as the authors state; they especially highlight love and sense of belonging as well as the sense of engagement in a rich cognitive and intellectual activity. Indeed, these are two great ways to grow eudaimonically, leading humans to flourish.

This second part, focused on the positive effects of media communication, ends with Chapter 15, written by Margarida Gaspar de Matos, Cátia Branquinho, and Tania Gaspar. Their approach is more transversal in terms of life development, laying stress on childhood and adolescence as key periods of our formation as individuals as well as on media consumers. Specifically, they reference the importance of "screen time activities" for young people in terms of using media not only while avoiding harm but also in promoting health, increasing family and community attachment, etc. In short, media can act as a protective agent of social and cognitive flourishing for people beginning at early ages.

Marketing Communication, Advertising, and (What Kind of) Happiness

Beginning a few years ago, content related to happiness has been increasing in our countries not only in certain kind of media and bookstore shelves but also on walls, billboards, and showcases and in ads announcing all sorts of products, services, initiatives, and events. In other words, happiness as brand communication strategy, which is the issue described in the third part of the book.

In this section, the chapters explore advertising speeches and marketing communications and the extent to which we can call them "positive" in the scientific sense proper of this qualifying adjective. In other words, how brands, through their advertising and marketing campaigns, can improve consciously or unconsciously not only consumers' hedonia but also their deeper happiness, that is, real flourishing or psychological well-being. A priori, this seems to be difficult task, but the seven texts of this part of the book show that it is not too difficult.

Positive marketing is currently a reality. We insist once more in using "positive" in its absolutely scientific meaning, as Dawn Lerman and Santiago Mejia demonstrate in Chapter 16. The authors, who are members of the Center for Positive Marketing at Fordham University, define positive marketing as marketing practices that impact positively the well-being of society and the happiness of individuals. Furthermore, they ask to what extent this objective can be taken as the ultimate goal of marketing itself.

After Lerman and Mejia's framework, José Antonio Muñiz-Velázquez and Juan F. Plaza ask in Chapter 17 whether advertising can be really a friend of authentic happiness (Seligman, 2002). This extends not just to advertising in general but to great advertising, in terms of effectiveness. Indeed, needless to say, we are talking about advertising, which means a business investment that must produce results. Therefore, it is necessary to analyze what kind of happiness is being transmitted in successful brand campaigns, what type of values accompany brands and products, whether these values are closer to hedonia or eudaimonia, and whether they are based on virtues and character strengths or not (Peterson & Seligman, 2004). After the analysis, the authors conclude that this confluence between advertising effectiveness and eudaimonic discourse is not only possible but also growing.

In Chapter 18, David Alameda and Irene Martín address the same idea from the brand engagement perspective. The main objective of the chapter is to research positive brand communication from the two paradigms, the hedonic and eudaimonic construction of brand values, for which they use a sample of advertising speeches of different big brands. In their results, they coincide with other researchers in affirming that we are witnessing a new value-oriented marketing, a marketing and a brand communication with an ultimate goal: making this world a better place, a truly happier world.

A great example of this is the case study that Timothy de Waal Malefyt shows us in Chapter 19. He explores the positive aspects of consumer relationships with products, brands, and services from a qualitative ethnographic perspective. Malefyt presents a study about the company FedEx and its relationship with small business managers, in which he underlines the importance of having an "insider view" to produce truly positive communication for both agents, that is, brands and consumers.

In the middle of this journey focusing on the relationship between brand communication and consumer happiness, Chapter 20, by Belén Gutiérrez-Villar, Pilar Castro-González, Rosa Melero-Bolaños, and Mariano Carbonero-Ruz, looks back to the happiness indexes that social scientists are using to rank countries; these indexes and rankings have been increasing in popularity in the last years and have been adding increasingly richer indicators. One second objective of their chapter is to evaluate the relationship between the level of people's happiness and the sense of well-being that brands provide, trying to prove the existence of a positive relationship between those two facts. The authors end their contribution by remembering that the task of brands is to build a relationship with consumers that convey positive values and to contribute to this growing demand of improving the well-being of society.

The third part closes with two chapters that describe very specific examples of how to conceive of positive advertising. First, in Chapter 21, Linda Tuncay Zayer, Catherine A. Coleman, and José Luis Rodriguez Orjuela focus on so-called femvertising, a possible form of positive marketing communication defined by Castillo (2014) as those advertising campaigns that, apart from pursuing its commercial goals, use pro-female talent, messages, texts, and imagery to empower women and girls. In short, femvertising is advertising that strengthens the subjective and psychological well-being of the female half of the population.

Finally, Chapter 21 brings the section to an end by linking advertising with spirituality, perhaps one of the more difficult character strengths to relate to contemporary commercial communication. The author, Dr. Galit Marmor-Lavie, states that although advertising is perceived as one of the most materialistic industries, it is also true that there is an increasing requirement to understand how spirituality, beyond religiosity, and advertising might live together and help one another. Marmor-Lavie also explains why introducing spirituality into the core of advertising and business could build a true connection between consumers and advertisers/companies.

In conclusion, these seven chapters try to demonstrate that a positive advertising, one sustained in values related with authentic human happiness and endorsed by positive psychology, can not only be possible and desirable but also necessary for brands, given the change of certain values of the society we find ourselves in (Angus, 2018).

New Public Relations for New Corporations for a New Economy

Very close to positive marketing communication, the next section focuses on public relations and corporate communication. First, we find an introductory framework in which Luis Rivas and Elias Soukiazis describe and lay out the fundamentals of a relatively new concept called the economics of happiness, in which companies and corporations develop their activity and existence themselves. They point to several examples of how the paradigm is actually shifting in many economic sectors, in which we can be witnesses of the strong link between ethics, successful business, and human happiness.

On the other hand, one of the first factors of happiness at work is the social environment of the company, much like one of the main reasons for unhappiness at work is a bad social atmosphere (REF). Therefore, in this sense, management of internal communication must be directed to boost not only business effectiveness but also employees' well-being. If it is true that, in addition to a new "happiness economy" we are in a "reputation economy" or an "intangible assets economy," employees play a key role. This is affirmed by Ángel Alloza and Clara Fontán, the authors of Chapter 24. Companies are concerned with the support of their key stakeholders, and above all, the main voice of a company comes from its employees. In this sense, building, and sharing with employees a corporate purpose beyond identity, mission, or vision is essential. For this purpose, positive internal communication has a major role in performance.

Chapter 25, written by Antonio Ariza-Montes, Antonio L. Leal-Rodríguez, Horacio Molina-Sánchez, and Jesús Ramírez-Sobrino, reiterate the line above. These authors examine within non-profit public service organizations the link between well-being and authenticity, understanding the latter as a key enhancing factor of organizational communication that may lead to the attainment of competitive advantages and superior performance in addition to employees' well-being, at least their subjective well-being. Their empirical results link authenticity and well-being more strongly, underlining that there is a positive relationship between these two variables.

In Chapter 26, the final chapter of this fourth section, Rafael Araque-Padilla, María José Montero-Simó, and José Javier Pérez-Barea propose socially responsible consumption as an alternative. Through values and concepts related to eudaimonic well-being, such as social contribution or responsibility, a kind of consumption could be fostered where the individual achieves greater happiness levels than with just a hedonistic or even hedonic consumption. Thus, consumers could use this type of consumption as a *vehicle* to achieve his or her desired (real) happiness.

When (Digital) Technologies Provide Us With Real Happiness

After looking at interpersonal communication, media, advertising, and corporate communication, it is time to hone in on another growing and increasingly complex field: the digital environment. Thus, the fifth section focuses on the Internet ecosystem, emphasizing several important aspects that characterize the so-called positive digital technologies, that is, those digital technologies that can help us to improve our level of subjective or psychological well-being. As Riva (2012, p. 37) states, the result of combining "the objectives of Positive Psychology with enhancements of Information and Communication Technologies" can occur both at the hedonic level and at the eudaimonic level.

The first of the seven chapters of this section offers a general framework, described by Giuseppe Riva, Silvia Serino, Alice Chirico, and Andrea Gaggioli. As the authors show, the current human communicative experience depends increasingly on some kind of interactive device or digital service. The implications of this for our well-being are therefore indisputable. Therefore, this requires an interdisciplinary approach that integrates the scientific principles of positive psychology to understand how interactive technologies can be used in evidence-based well-being interventions. The chapter bases the concept of positive technology on the analysis of the theoretical and conceptual frameworks, showing how interactive technologies can be used to help individuals achieve greater well-being. The chapter ends with a presentation of different practical examples of this emerging concept.

In the chapter that follows, Paula Herrero-Diz, Marina Ramos-Serrano, and Ashley Woodfall show a fantastic example of the possibilities of using digital technologies in a real positive sense. Specifically, they propose a review of the ways in which social media networks, particularly YouTube, can also act as a channel for the diffusion and spreading of happiness, not only in terms of hedonia but also of eudaimonia. In addition, they observe this "positive infection" especially among young people, children, and teenagers. In short, the authors present clear cases in which young prosumers may be developing, through video blogging practices, certain character strengths in themselves and in the rest of users.

Also interesting are the links that the authors of Chapter 29 build between variables as diverse as usability, beauty, happiness, and the digital divide. Juan-Ramón Martin-Sanromán, Fernando Suárez Carballo, Fernando Galindo Rubio, and Daniel Raposo point that, although there is still a long way to go, it seems clear that in terms of beauty, usability, and user experience, digital design has an important responsibility regarding the subjective as well as psychological well-being of those users. Beauty matters for our happiness in the digital sphere as well.

Chapter 30, by Frank M. Schneider, Annabell Halfmann, and Peter Vorderer focuses on the so-called salutogenic side of being permanently online and permanently connected (POPC), mainly thanks to ubiquitous mobile devices. Regarding the polemical question of whether the POPC lifestyle benefits or damages our life, the position of the authors is clear. Without denying the dangers of excess, they posit that the POPC mindset may also facilitate the fulfillment of basic human needs and may help individuals to experience a more flourishing life in terms of meaningful connections with others, for example. After adding some key factors to those potential salutogenic outcomes of POPC, the authors encourage future studies focusing on how mobile media users with a POPC lifestyle may gain salutary benefits from it.

However, apart from the ubiquity of mobile media, beginning a few years ago, other kinds of digital devices have been making it possible for us to live in a continuous state of connection. Those devices are the so-called wearables, the central topic in Chapter 31 by David Varona and Javier Nó-Sánchez. Specifically, they write about the possibilities that wearables, together with the concept of the Internet of Things, can help us have a more flourishing existence. For example, these devices enable us to practice many character strengths and, let us not forget, many hedonic skills.

Varona and Nó-Sánchez finish their contribution by discussing ethics. Part five ends with this subject, and it is the subject of its last couple of chapters. First, in Chapter 32, Andrés del Toro and Purificación Alcaide-Pulido discuss altruism in the digital and social age. They explain how the ethical principle of being "good" toward others in "real" life is perfectly transposed to digital networks or the so-called social media. This applies to both companies and individuals. For this reason among many others, the authors are able to affirm that social media can also be an excellent example of positive technology.

Effectively, without ethics, we cannot talk about positive digital technologies at all. This idea is highlighted in Chapter 33 by Don Heider. The author points to several key ethical issues regarding our online behavior, reminding us that happiness and ethics are intimately related, extending to the digital environment as well. To learn and to interiorize this as soon as young people access digital reality must be a priority for the digital literacy of future generations of users, that is, future adult citizens. However, this is a question related to the next and last section of our book, namely, education. Let us delve into this topic.

Communication, Schools, and Human Flourishing

The last part of this volume highlights positive communication in the large and complex field of education. Thus, positive education would be education whose ultimate goal is the well-being and happiness of children and students. This form of happiness, however, is based on personal and intellectual development, growth, and human flourishing, without forgetting academic goals in traditional skills (Seligman, Ernst, Gillham, Reivich, & Linkins, 2009).

Along these lines, once we have seen positive communication in a variety of scenarios, we see it also has much to contribute to the happiness-education binomial. Specifically, these chapters approach several relevant issues within this wide area, such as the so-called curriculum of happiness, music, and positive communication in education, audiovisual literacy, the role of expectations at school, online and offline education and character strengths, rethinking sustainable happiness in schools, and ethics.

This section begins with the deep review of positive education by Diego Gomez–Baya and Jane E. Gillham. In their contribution, Chapter 34, we learn the extent to which positive education has reached an important presence among scientists and practitioners of education, in all senses. As they highlight, the positive education paradigm affects all aspects of education: interactions between teachers and students, classroom interventions, school building level policies, public policy, etc. Along these lines, positive communication skills have an important role both inside and outside the classroom. They complete their contribution by describing several examples of successful intervention programs. Any of these programs can serve as a great model for schools aiming to promote not only academic performance but also the well-being of children and adolescents and help them flourish fully as human beings.

Along these lines, it is very important to clarify what happiness actually means in the context of schools, as we run the risk of confusing the real significance of a "happy student" or "happy curriculum" in schools. This is a point made by Isabel Lopez-Cobo, Inmaculada Gómez-Hurtado, and Mel Ainscow. They also point to another important issue in the field of a real positive communication in education: the inclusive curriculum. After explaining the main components of an inclusive education, in which differences and diversity must be a real source of growth, they also highlight the role of school leaders and their communication skills to promote this inclusive culture. A culture of inclusion that, as the authors say, is useful not only for improving academic performance but also in helping students live a full life.

On the other hand, it would be very difficult to live a flourishing life without one of the main and purely human dimensions of our species: the arts. Chapter 36, by Susan Hallam and Francisco Cuadrado, focuses on one of the arts: music. Specifically, they underline the importance of music education in a positive education model, given the deep relationship between music and happiness. In this sense, it is worthy to recall the words by Nietzsche, when he said that *life without music* would be an "error" because it would be robbed of its chance to be most truly itself (Came, 2014). In addition to all its attributes, music also has a communicative dimension. The authors appreciate that music increases the capacity of humans to exercise a broad number of character strengths.

Another important issue in positive communication in education is media literacy and digital literacy. Indeed, over the years, this is something increasingly relevant the students' curriculum, not only in terms of avoiding dangers, disorders, or threats, especially among young users, but also because of its power for positive social change and the empowerment of individuals. Chapter 37, by Emma Camarero, Alexander Fedorov, and Anastasia Levitskaya, provides a deep discussion of this issue.

The following contribution, Chapter 38, continues to delve into media literacy practice but from a perspective focused in ethics. Specifically, Megan Fromm and Paul Mihailidis argue for an approach to media literacy that embraces an ethics of care, focusing on its relational aspects. Thus, the authors propose a normative approach to include the ethics of care in media literacy. Their concern is that while conventional media literacy has been focused on media civic responsibility in its care for truth, for example, they add an ethics of care that focuses on those who have not yet been so fortunate to be able to have direct access to media literacy.

The Internet and the whole digital reality is another scenario where communication and education are connected. Thus, there are many opportunities for human flourishing through online education. Beatriz Valverde and Erica C. Boling focus on this in Chapter 39. They show the possibilities of online learning experiences in creating spaces that also promote students' well-being. In addition, they offer ideas and suggestions to successfully surmount the challenges faced in the promotion of well-being in online education. In this sense, they underline the importance of an heutagogical approach to online teaching, and show how with this approach we can understand the promotion of Eudaimonia through online learning. Recall that the concept of heutagogy refers, in brief, to the capacity that a learning environment has to facilitate the development not just of learner competencies but also the learner's capacity to learn (Blaschke, 2012). Indeed, this ability is closely related to several character strengths.

Education and communication, as Catherine O'Brien and Sean Murray remind us in the following chapter, are key in establishing "new narratives that support individual and collective transitions toward healthier, sustainable lifestyles and livelihoods." Starting from this general premise, the authors propose that to talk about positive education and happiness, we must also consider the dimension of sustainability in regards to our environment. As Williams (2017) notes, while nature can make us happier, if we turn our backs on nature, complete happiness becomes more difficult to attain. Not for nothing, our emotions, especially positive emotions, are associated with a connection between nature and ourselves (Capaldi, Dopko, & Zelenski, 2014). Thus, nature's "happiness" is also essential for us. Therefore, the "happier" and healthier our planet is, the happier we will be. In the penultimate chapter, Catherine O'Brien and Sean Murray provide an extensive review of the so-called Living Schools model, in which educational programs integrate sustainability education with "new" pedagogies focused also on health and well-being. In this model, positive communication in the classroom, at school and with the whole community has a featured role. The results of this model can be observed more and more, but as the authors recognize, it would be enriching to support further research in this area.

Finally, the section ends with a chapter dedicated to an overview of character strengths in schools and how positive communication influences them. In these pages, Mathew A. White closes the entire volume with the concept of flourishing, offering us an exploration of two approaches to character strengths in educational settings. The first approach involves a theoretical framework, and the second approach involves integrated educational programs across a broad variety of subject areas. As a final summary, White reminds us of the importance for teachers to focus not only on the contents of lessons but also on the teaching process and of the way in which both the content and the process contribute to a more flourishing life for students.

This Dream Has Only Just Begun

After this brief review of the main content of the rest of the chapters of the book, which lies somewhere between a collective monograph and a handbook, we can see that this project is unprecedented. It is true that there are a few similar publications in the communication field, even publications by Routledge. Such is the case for *The Routledge Handbook of Health Communication*, *The Routledge Handbook of Environment and Communication*, *The Routledge Handbook of Family Communication*, *The Routledge Handbook of Emotions and Mass Media*, *The Routledge Handbook of Language and Intercultural Communication*, *The Routledge Handbook of Public Communication of Science and Technology*, *The Happiness Illusion: How the Media Sold us a Fairy Tale*, and, more recently and perhaps most similar to our case, *The Routledge Handbook of Media Use and Well-Being*. This book, in turn, attempts to cover communication from a wider and more integrated view by including social, media, business, corporate, and educational perspectives. For this reason, the contents may be of interest to scholars from several academic fields, including graduate and postgraduate students and researchers who are interested in the (positive) effects of social communication on individuals as well as on society as a whole. However, this book is also addressed to practitioners of communication who are concerned with their social responsibility and their role in people's psychological well-being and personal growth.

Last, communication, in all kind of human interactions, can be a very powerful tool to improve the world in astonishing ways. We agree with Socha and Beck (2015) that communication has the potential "to go far beyond lower level needs-satisfaction and into moments of communicative perfection: the stuff of dreams." As we said at the beginning of this chapter, this book was our dream, but more precisely, our dream is the change that this book could trigger by demonstrating how far communication in all its grounds can go in making us authentically happier.

References

Angus, L. (2018). *Top 10 global consumer trends for 2018 emerging forces shaping consumer behaviour*. Euromonitor International. Retrieved from https://blog.euromonitor.com/

Blaschke, L. M. (2012). Heutagogy and lifelong learning: A review of heutagogical practice and self-determined learning. *The International Review of Research in Open and Distance Learning, 13*(1), 56–71. http://dx.doi.org/10.19173/irrodl.v13i1.1076

Bryant, F. B., & Veroff, J. (2007). *Savoring: A new model of positive experience.* New York: Psychology Press.

Came, D. (2014). *Nietzsche on art and life.* Oxford: Oxford University Press.

Castillo, M. (2014). *These stats prove femvertising works.* Retrieved from www.adweek.com/news/technology/these-stats-prove-femvertising-works-160704

Capaldi, C. A., Dopko, R. L., & Zelenski, J. M. (2014). The relationship between nature connectedness and happiness: A meta-analysis. *Frontiers in Psychology, 5,* 976. https://doi.org/10.3389/fpsyg.2014.00976

Gordon, R. D. (1985). Dimensions of peak communication experiences: An exploratory study. *Psychological Reports, 57*(3), 824–826.

Mirivel, J. C. (2014). *The art of positive communication: Theory and practice.* New York: Peter Lang.

Mirivel, J. (2018). On the Nature of Peak Communication: Communication Behaviors That Make a Difference on Well-Being and Happiness. In J. A. Muñiz-Velázquez & C. Pulido (Eds.), *The Routledge handbook of positive communication* (pp. 50–59). New York, NY: Routledge.

Peterson, C., & Seligman, M. E. P. (2004). *Character strengths and virtues: A handbook and classification.* Oxford: Oxford University Press.

Pitts, M. J. (2016). *Communication savoring.* Presidential Address at the 15th International Conference on Language and Social Psychology held in Bangkok, Thailand, June 22–25, 2016.

Pitts, M. J., & Socha, T. J. (Eds.). (2013). *Health communication: Vol. 3. Positive communication in health and wellness.* New York: Peter Lang.

Riva, G. (2012). What is positive technology and its impact on CyberPsychology. *Studies in Health Technology and Informatics, 181,* 37–41. doi:10.3233/978-1-61499-121-2-37

Seligman, M. E. P. (2002). *Authentic happiness.* New York: Atria.

Seligman, M. E. P., Ernst, R. M., Gillham, J., Reivich, K., & Linkins, M. (2009). Positive education: Positive psychology and classroom interventions. *Oxford Review of Education, 35*(3), 293–311. https://doi.org/10.1080/03054980902934563

Socha, T. J., & Beck, G. A. (2015). Positive communication and human needs: A review and proposed organizing conceptual framework. *Review of Communication, 15*(3), 1–27. http://dx.doi.org/10.1080/15358593.2015.1080290

Williams, F. (2017). *The nature fix: Why nature makes us happier, healthier, and more creative.* New York, NY: Norton.

2

RESEARCH ON POSITIVE COMMUNICATION AND SOCIAL IMPACT

Beatriz Villarejo-Carballido, Cristina M. Pulido, and Mimar Ramis

The value of science is currently addressed depending on their contributions to improving living conditions and societies (Soler-Gallart, 2017). There are some of science disciplines where their contributions are not questioned—for instance, the advancement of medicine to obtain better illness treatments or to find solutions for eradicating some type of virus. For instance, describing the Zika virus (Zanluca & dos Santos, 2016) is not enough, although it is a necessary previous step. It is easy to measure if this type of research achieves or does not achieve in its research results. But in the case of social sciences, there are some doubts about their utility for contributing to improve societies. One of the ways to face this situation is precisely to demonstrate that research linked to social sciences is contributing to improving living conditions and social improvements with evidence (Flecha, Soler-Gallart, & Sorde, 2015).

Communication research is a discipline inside of social sciences with one characteristic: its nature is interdisciplinary (Craig, 1999; Jensen, 2012). Thus, positive communication as a field inside of communication research that also has an interdisciplinary approach. This particularity is a strong characteristic that could be helpful for doing research with a better understanding of research goals. But definitively it will be useful if the research on this field goes one step further, contributing to research results that guarantee improvements and not merely descriptions of social phenomena. In fact, the evaluation of the research measures the impact of research results in three mainly areas; scientific, political, and social impact (Reale et al., 2017). Scientific and political impact already had different ways to measure them. The way to measure social impact is still discussed in the academic area. In this sense, one of the contributions is the notion of social impact as evidence of social improvements or living conditions (Flecha et al., 2015) that has obtained recognition. In fact, Flecha (2014) illustrated the difference between scientific, political, and social impact and the interrelation among them. Social impact occurs when the implementation of the research results obtains evidence of social improvements in relation to the stated goals of society. Considering this contribution, this chapter aims to reflect on the need to address positive communication research to the stated goals of society for achieving social impact. In addition, this reflection takes the example of the sustainable development goals elaborated by the UN for illustrating how positive communication research can contribute to them.

The Sense of Positive Communication Research

Positive communication research is an emergent field that can contribute to goals that society needs. Furthermore, the transversal nature of positive communication indicates its relevance for different study areas of human needs. Authors who wrote about positive communication defined the influence of positive psychology in this field (Socha & Beck, 2015). Even so, positive communication also has particularities. Previous works on positive communication focused more on interpersonal communication than other fields. But recent advances in this area open other possibilities, such as the role of mass media and social media in the promotion of positive communication (Garde-Hansen & Gorton, 2013). However, the relevance of collecting previous research agenda on positive communication is a basic step for going further.

Considering the contributions of Socha and Beck (2015) the topics of the agenda on positive communication are: to examine the vital role positive communication plays in needs-satisfaction and to understand that needs-satisfaction approach is heuristic and raises important questions about common collective goals and values. In this sense, Socha highlights that "we desire communication which is efficient, intelligible, creative, artistic, as well as ethical, and don't value communication that is inefficient, garbled, boring, unethical, or worse, violent and hateful" (Socha & Beck, 2015, p. 190). And the third topic for them is to research how communication can improve relationships for living happily. Concluding, the communication has the potential to build communication perfection for achieving the stuff of dreams in authors.

The question that remains is do these topics answer a society's needs? Could they achieve research results that evidence social improvements or better living conditions? it depends on the ability to connect with the stated goals of society, and of course, if the research can bring evidence of social impact (Soler-Gallart, 2017). Positive communication includes in its own definition of the improvement of the well-being and happiness of humans; therefore, this definition contains the perspective of improving human lives, but it is necessary to provide scientific evidence that positive communication is already achieving this impact. This is the challenge, and this is the sense of positive communication.

Listening to the Needs of Society and Working to Address Them

One of the tasks of the researchers is to listen to the needs of society. And how this can be done? Easy—we should pay attention to the demands asked by citizens or goals developed by different institutions (Flecha et al., 2015). We can make a big list of describing all the needs expressed by citizens. We can work with the goals expressed by social movements that connects with demands of citizens or capturing those goals expressed by international institutions, for instance the UN. As we said in previous sections, we do this reflection considering the sustainable development goals (SDF, hereinafter) defined by the UN. In addition, to think about the social impact of the positive communication research, it is better to specify goals and think about examples that can achieve concrete evidences.

Reviewing the SDG, not all could be addressed from positive communication research, but some of them could be. There are 17 SDF defined by the UN: 1) No Poverty, 2) Good Health and Well-Being 3) Zero Hunger, 4) Quality Education, 5) Gender Equality, 6) Clean Water and Sanitation, 7) Affordable and Clean Energy, 8) Decent work an economic growth, 9) Industry, Innovation, and Infrastructure, 10) Reduce inequalities, 11) Sustainable cities and communities, 12) Responsible consumption and production, 13) Climate Action, 14) Life Below Water, 15) Life on Land, 16) Peace, Justice, and Strong Institutions, 17) Partnerships for the goals. Some of these objectives have a strong link with positive communication research, and we reflect how some of these objectives could be worked on from positive communication research.

Good Health and Well-Being

This goal is addressed to promote healthy lives and well-being for all at all stages. In this sense, the field of health communication has a large trajectory in crossing fields of health and communication areas for promoting a better health care for all (Freimuth & Quinn, 2004; Parrott, 2004; Ratzan, 2001; Tulsky et al., 2017). One of the main areas of the health communication is how to improve communication between health professionals and patients for improving their health and assistance. Other research areas are more focused how to improve this health communication through the use of social media (Heldman, Schindelar, & Weaver III, 2013) or through the use of artificial intelligence for giving a better e-health service to the patients (Kreps & Neuhauser, 2013). Likewise, positive communication has a prominent presence in this research area. In fact, this presence is transversal. For instance, research focused on health literacy usually focuses on the model of patient-centered communication (Roberts, Morgan Roberts, O'Neill, & Blake-Beard, 2008), which means that caregivers and health professionals should pay attention to improve their communication skills for being helpful for patients, to take care the way that they communicate and how they follow-up their patients, being understandable for them. Results on health literacy also give recommendations on how communication should improve for being more effective. In short, good communication is a crucial element (Mirza & Zaidi, 2015), and this fact could be linked with positive communication research. Next steps are to research more profoundly these findings under positive communication research and extracting specific evidences of health improvements of patients.

Quality Education

This SDG goal is crucial for improving people's lives and sustainable development. In this sense the research on successful educational actions has contributed to guarantee quality education for all (Flecha, 2015). These types of actions are successful because they obtain the best results on learning and well-being in different contexts. Nevertheless, the interpersonal communication between students and teachers has also a trajectory in this field for building a positive environment to learn as indicated in research on positive education (Seligman, Ernst, Gillham, Reivich, & Linkins, 2009).

On the other hand, an emerging field that is taking more relevance is the use of audiovisual resources for promoting a better education and communication. This is the contribution of Karlin and Johnson (2018). These researchers affirm that documentary films could be useful for education, because they could promote social change, impact of ways to look the social reality, more awareness regarding some social issues, etc. But one of the obstacles is that there is scarce data to provide the evidence of this impact. The authors suggested in their paper that it would be necessary to collect evidence of the documentary films through different types of impact measurements to guarantee the data collection of the impact. And what is the relation with positive communication? Communication and education are two different fields but at the same time are interrelated. Positive communication research could focus on collecting data evidence of the impact of positive communication in educational contexts for guaranteeing quality education, this means that students can learn more and better while they are happier to do that in a secure environment.

Gender Equality

This SDG goal addresses the challenge of overcoming gender discrimination and the violence than girls and women suffer every day in all parts of the world. Gender equality is not only a fundamental right in the words of the UN, but it is also a requirement for building a peaceful and sustainable world nowadays. Research on positive communication should focus on how it can contribute to overcoming gender violence and gender discrimination. These two specific objectives are essential in contributing to this SDG goal.

Regarding gender discrimination, it is relevant to remember that not all girls and women in the world have ICT and Internet access, and it is necessary to overcome the gender digital divide (Singh, 2017). This contribution focuses on the relevance of promoting ICT use by the girls and women overall in the developing countries. Singh (2017) highlights the need to strengthen women's capabilities to create communities of knowledge exchange through ICT use. Women can promote social change also if they have this access. There are different studies and initiatives that are promoting the entrepreneur's ability through the use of ICT (Hashim, Amir, & Razak, 2011). Considering these contributions, it is very important to focus positive communication research on what type of interpersonal communication engages more women and girls to obtain their empowerment. The other specific goal is to overcome gender violence. This goal is crucial. As we know, there is a global movement for eradicating sexual harassment and gender violence around the world, for instance with the global campaign under the hashtag #metoo or the initiative of Time's Up. One of the possibilities to address the positive communication linked to social change is to study how types of media campaigns could be successful in contributing to eradicating sexual harassment and second sexual harassment (Vidu, Valls, Puigvert, Melgar, & Joanpere, 2017). The need to collect evidence of behavior change through actions of positive communication campaigns could be one of the research lines that contributes to this SDG.

Climate Action

Climate change affects the lives of people of every country. For this reason, one of the goals of the UN is to address climate action to overcome the negative effects of this climate change. There are different types of research addressing this goal from different disciplines of science. The contribution of positive communication could focus on how to communicate to address social change in this matter. For instance, research by Altman shows how the use of participatory media could be useful for communicating the impacts of climate change on cultural heritage and human rights in Asia and the Pacific, and thus this communication has an impact on the behavior change (Altman, 2008). During this research, the communication process involved all community members affected by this social climate change, and promoted access to knowledge of how to improve these effects. This helped the community members affected to plan for the future to avoid more drastic climate change effects. This example could also be analyzed under positive communication research, how interpersonal communication is applied in this process, and if this type of communication does or does not have elements of positive communication that guarantee people will feel involved in this goal. In fact, expert scholars in this field highlight the contribution of communication in addressing climate change (Ballantyne, 2016) is very relevant. Positive communication has another role here to collect evidence of the social impact of positive communication strategies for addressing behavior change that at least improve the effects of climate change.

Conclusions

The examples provided are focused on these four SDG to try to illustrate how we can address our interests in positive communication research linked with the society goals. Of course, researchers on positive communication could address other goals not limited to these. The common element that we need to guarantee is precisely that our research can improve the lives of people or the whole society in specific fields. In this sense, positive communication research could be complemented by contributions of communication for social change. In fact, both fields are complementary. This is useful for overcoming research based on descriptive approach and searching the impact of these contributions. In this sense, the contributions of Jacobson are so useful. He did a review of the theory of Amartya Sen's Capabilities Approach and Communication for Development and Social Change (Jacobson, 2016). He found that the crossing of both disciplines can be positive for building a theoretical framework that can explain better a at macro sociological scope integrating into a conceptual framework that also includes economics, democratic politics, human rights, and so on. In this sense, if we add also the contributions of positive communication research, it could contribute to understanding more the human nature.

Years ago, Paulo Freire explained in books such as the *Pedagogy of Oppressed* (1970) that human nature is dialogic. And this means that communication is a basic need, not only a desirable element. If we do not communicate, we cannot survive in good conditions. Our nature is dialogic. The challenge is how this type of communication could be the best one for us, providing well-being, happiness, and awareness for the common good. Each day, millions of interactions affect in the lives of the people in a positive manner or the opposite. This has a real impact for the good or for the bad. The responsibility of giving evidence of how positive communication could offer a better human experience in different senses is from the researchers. On the other hand, editors of mass media have also a responsibility to guarantee a better positive media environment, avoiding fake news, sexism or racism, sexual harassment, or other type of offensive messages. Spreading this type of message usually has a negative impact on our common public sphere. Social media also has a prominent role in this public sphere. But in this case the responsibility for publishing offensive messages is not solely on the media editors. Here, all of us are responsible to take care of this public sphere and to create a secure online environment characterized by positive communication that promotes a better understanding and a desirable world to live in.

Thus, this field is other research line that we would emphasize before ending our paper. Research on the role of media in promoting positive communication that achieves better understanding could be linked with the SGD of Justice and Peaceful Societies. This contribution could improve societies because if we have a secure, positive media environment, it directly impacts our common public sphere. We have here another research area for analyzing profoundly. We have a horizon. Now we should walk with our own map, not forgetting that our research sense is to improve the lives of people and contribute to better societies that are more inclusive and not at all violent.

References

Altman, D. (2008). Using participatory media to assess climate change impact on vulnerable communities. *Media Asia, 8*(2), 203–213.

Ballantyne, A. G. (2016). Climate change communication: What can we learn from communication theory? *Wiley Interdisciplinary Reviews: Climate Change, 7*(3), 329–344. https://doi.org/10.1002/wcc.392

Craig, R. T. (1999). Communication theory as a field. *Communication Theory, 9*(2), 119–161. https://doi.org/10.1111/j.1468-2885.1999.tb00355.x

Flecha, R. (2014, March 31). Cómo conseguir o aumentar el impacto de los proyectos y cómo liderar un proyecto de referencia [How to improve the social impact of the projects?]. Horizonte 2020 y Patrimonio Cultural: Investigación e Innovación, Madrid, Spain.

Flecha, R. (2015). *Successful educational actions for inclusion and social cohesion in Europe.* New York: Springer International Publishing.

Flecha, R., Soler-Gallart, M., & Sorde, T. (2015). Social impact: Europe must fund social sciences. *Nature, 528*(7581), 193. http://dx.doi.org/10.1038/528193d

Freimuth, V. S., & Quinn, S. C. (2004). The contributions of health communication to eliminating health disparities. *American Journal of Public Health, 94*(12), 2053–2055. https://doi.org/10.2105/AJPH.94.12.2053

Freire, P. (1970). *Pedagogy of the oppressed.* New York: Seabury Press.

Garde-Hansen, J., & Gorton, K. (2013). Social media, happiness, and virtual communities. In *Emotion online: Theorizing affect on the internet* (pp. 103–125). London, UK: Palgrave Macmillan. https://doi.org/10.1057/9781137312877_5

Hashim, F., Amir, Z., & Razak, N. A. (2011). Empowering rural women entrepreneurs with ICT skills: An impact study. In *Procedia-social and behavioral sciences* (Vol. 15, pp. 3369–3373). https://doi.org/10.1016/j.sbspro.2011.04.302

Heldman, A. B., Schindelar, J., & Weaver III, J. B. (2013). Social media engagement and public health communication: Implications for public health organizations being truly "Social". *Public Health Reviews*, *35*(1), 1–18. https://doi.org/10.1007/BF03391698

Jacobson, T. L. (2016). Amartya Sen's capabilities approach and communication for development and social change. *Journal of Communication*, *66*(5), 789–810. https://doi.org/10.1111/jcom.12252

Jensen, K. B. (2012). A handbook of media and communication research: Qualitative and quantitative methodologies. London: Routledge. https://doi.org/10.4324/9780203465103

Karlin, B., & Johnson, J. (2018). Measuring impact: The importance of evaluation for documentary film campaigns. *M/C Journal*, *14*(6), 6–9.

Kreps, G. L., & Neuhauser, L. (2013). Artificial intelligence and immediacy: Designing health communication to personally engage consumers and providers. *Patient Education and Counseling*, *92*(2), 205–210. https://doi.org/10.1016/j.pec.2013.04.014

Mirza, R. M., & Zaidi, S. (2015). Optimizing the relationship between healthcare professionals, patients and caregivers: Five conversations that can help improve health communication and care for elderly patients. *Gerontologist*, *55*(2), 669.

Parrott, R. (2004). Emphasizing "communication" in health communication. *Journal of Communication*, *54*(4), 751–787. https://doi.org/10.1093/joc/54.4.751

Ratzan, S. C. (2001). Health literacy: Communication for the public good. *Health Promotion International*, *16*(2), 207–214. https://doi.org/10.1093/heapro/16.2.207

Reale, E., Avramov, D., Canhial, K., Donovan, C., Flecha, R., Holm, P., . . . Van Horik, R. (2017, March). A review of literature on evaluating the scientific, social and political impact of social sciences and humanities research. *Research Evaluation*, 1–11. https://doi.org/10.1093/reseval/rvx025

Roberts, D. D., Morgan Roberts, L., O'Neill, R. M., & Blake-Beard, S. D. (2008). The invisible work of managing visibility for social change: Insights from the leadership of reverend Dr. Martin Luther King Jr. *Business & Society*, *47*(4), 425–456. https://doi.org/10.1177/0007650308323817

Seligman, M. E. P., Ernst, R. M., Gillham, J., Reivich, K., & Linkins, M. (2009). Positive education: Positive psychology and classroom interventions. *Oxford Review of Education*, *35*(3), 293–311. https://doi.org/10.1080/03054980902934563

Singh, S. (2017). Bridging the gender digital divide in developing countries. *Journal of Children and Media*, *11*(2), 245–247. https://doi.org/10.1080/17482798.2017.1305604

Socha, T. J., & Beck, G. A. (2015). Positive communication and human needs: A review and proposed organizing conceptual framework. *Review of Communication*, *15*(3), 173–199. https://doi.org/10.1080/15358593.2015.1080290

Soler-Gallart, M. (2017). *Achieving social impact: Sociology in the public sphere*. New York: Springer International Publishing.

Tulsky, J. A., Beach, M. C., Butow, P. N., Hickman, S. E., Mack, J. W., Morrison, R. S., . . . Pollak, K. I. (2017). A research agenda for communication between health care professionals and patients living with serious illness. *JAMA Internal Medicine*, *177*(9), 1361–1366. https://doi.org/10.1001/jamainternmed.2017.2005

Vidu, A., Valls, R., Puigvert, L., Melgar, P., & Joanpere, M. (2017). Second Order of Sexual Harassment-SOSH. *REMIE: Multidisciplinary Journal of Educational Reserarch*, *7*(1), 1–26. https://doi.org/10.17583/remie.2017.2505

Zanluca, C., & dos Santos, C. N. D. (2016). Zika virus: An overview. *Microbes and Infection*, *18*(5), 295–301. https://doi.org/10.1016/j.micinf.2016.03.003

3

WHAT CAN SCIENCE TELL US ABOUT HUMAN HAPPINESS (AND WHY AND HOW SHOULD WE DISSEMINATE IT)?

Gonzalo Hervás and Covadonga Chaves

Introduction

The science of happiness is a converging movement that brings together various scientific disciplines around a common goal: to better understand the underpinnings of human happiness and to provide ways of improving it. Positive psychology is one such discipline that stands out within this movement, yet we must not overlook the economists or sociologists whose contributions have deeply enriched our understanding and driven further scientific research into happiness.

The primary goal is scientific in nature, to investigate and to try to understand the topic under research as an end in itself, without ignoring that the science of well-being has always been about being useful to society. Similarly, the issues of personal well-being and happiness are so important to society at large. Even public policy is being shaped by the science of happiness, since it is becoming apparent that governments must not only look after economic indexes but also overall well-being of the population. There is clearly a need in our societies for a better understanding of happiness, in terms of the internal and external processes that can either nourish or dampen well-being. Informing the public about the science of happiness thus becomes a key task, albeit a sensitive one. Insights on well-being is so relevant to each individual's self-view, while it can be helpful, it can also produce critical misunderstandings. Hence, the aim of this chapter is to review the complex literature on well-being and then offer some recommendations on how to inform the public of the findings.

What Is Well-Being?

Happiness is probably the word most used by lay people for referring to emotional or psychological well-being. However, happiness is also a transient mood which tends to bias the meaning away from the deep and stable features that characterizes well-being (Vazquez & Hervas, 2012). Nevertheless, for the sake of simplicity we will use both terms interchangeably.

For years it was named "subjective well-being" which was conceived as a combination of both affective and cognitive ingredients (e.g., Diener, Scollon, & Lucas, 2003; Pavot & Diener, 1993). The cognitive component of subjective well-being referred to life satisfaction, and affective components included positive affect (experiencing pleasant emotions and moods) and low negative affect (experiencing unpleasant, distressing emotions and moods). High levels of subjective well-being do not imply the absence of negative emotions. Instead they are still there but less frequent and prominent than positive ones (Fredrickson, 2013).

Eudaimonic well-being approaches emphasize that it is crucial to include high functioning when assessing well-being, to get a more precise picture of the well-being of individuals (e.g., Hervas & Vazquez, 2013). However, to be able to assess how well-being emerges, it was necessary to define the core ingredients of well-being (i.e., the characteristics of a good life). Carol Ryff (1989) defined well-being as the consequence of high levels of autonomy, personal growth, self-acceptance, purpose in life, competence or environmental mastery, and positive relations with others. Other authors have emphasized that three of these areas (i.e., relations, autonomy, and competence) are more relevant for well-being than the rest (Deci & Ryan, 2000).

Martin Seligman (Seligman, 2002) argued that well-being is derived from experiencing positive emotions (the pleasant life), but also from experiencing a high level of engagement in satisfying activities (the engaged life) as well as experiencing a sense of connectedness to a greater whole (the meaningful life). Thus, a fulfilled life is one in which people may express and develop their maximum potentials leading to benefits, not only for themselves, but also for society at large (Waterman, 2008). More recently, the PERMA model expanded this approach to include five core elements of psychological well-being (i.e., Positive emotion, Engagement, Relationships, Meaning and purpose, and Accomplishment).

Obviously, overall well-being is influenced by multiple variables, both internal and external. These eudaimonic models try to differentiate which are key variables from those that act as moderators. For example, gratitude, emotional intelligence, or optimism are associated with well-being, but they can be considered contributors rather than key components.

The literature discussing the basis of well-being is extensive and reflects the inherent complexity of the subject. As a result, messages that reach us about happiness are confusing: some say that it is in our mind, in the temperament, or in the genes; others say that it is the enjoyment of the moment; and others argue that well-being heavily depends on the circumstances or even society. Although it is no easy task, we are going to review the literature on well-being as comprehensively and clearly as we can. At the same time, we will use the pattern typically seen in lay approaches to happiness.

Happiness Is in Our Mind

"It's all about attitude" or "happiness is in our mind" are common messages that we usually hear in our daily lives. Although these messages are not entirely false, they aim to point out that most vital circumstances do not seem to have a significant impact on levels of well-being. Furthermore, these assertions suggest that to become happier is easy, if you have the right attitude. Unfortunately, the real picture is not so clear.

Some well-established research has showed that some attitudes and traits are related to well-being. It cannot be denied that optimism is closely related to happiness, and even physical health, especially when facing adversity (Carver, Scheier, & Segerstrom, 2010). Additionally, optimism has been experimentally linked to a reduced experience of pain (Hanssen, Peters, Vlaeyen, Meevissen, & Vancleef, 2013). Another example is thankfulness. Gratitude arises as expressing appreciation for what one has, as opposed to an excessive emphasis on what one wants. Gratitude has been linked to positive outcomes, such as increased levels of positive affect, life satisfaction, optimism about the future, prosocial behaviors, and better health (Emmons & McCullough, 2003; Bono & McCullough, 2006). Moreover, a grateful attitude may help the individual find positive meaning in negative circumstances (Emmons & McCullough, 2003). Thus, this implies that it is easy to increase happiness by changing attitudes. While some research has showed that optimism, gratitude, as well as other traits and attitudes can be changed in the short-term through psychological programs, it is not so clear that such changes remain stable in the long-term (Boehm & Lyubomirsky, 2009).

Those who claim that happiness depends mostly on us often argue that there is evidence suggesting that demographic variables and general circumstances of life (economic situation, sex, educational level, etc.) do not explain a much of individual happiness (Sheldon & Lyubomirsky, 2006). Some authors have interpreted this to imply that external circumstances do not affect happiness levels so much and that we should not be too concerned about these. However, this is not accurate. When people face relevant adversities, for example, the loss of a loved one or not being able to get a job, a prolonged decrease in well-being is observed (e.g., Keyes et al., 2014). Low-income also seems to reduce happiness when it is severe or in the context of an economic crisis (Helliwell, Huang, & Wang, 2015). While it is true that people have an extraordinary capacity to adapt to negative life situations, this does not mean that circumstances do not matter. Resilience is a trait that is not spontaneous; it must be cultivated over time. Thus, recommending to people who are suffering to change their attitude can be ineffective in most cases, or even counterproductive in others.

At the same time, research suggests that changing one's life circumstances (e.g., marital status, career, location, and income) is not necessarily the only path to improving our well-being. Accumulated research convincingly suggests that generally a significant portion of happiness may be under people's control through the activities they prioritize and how they face situations in their lives (Sheldon & Lyubomirsky, 2006). Moreover, adopting the right attitude or approach can be of great benefit when facing adversity (e.g., optimism or emotional intelligence).

Beyond attitudes, there are several other factors that we should consider when defining determinants of happiness. For instance, twin, adoption, and family studies have found that well-being levels are significantly influenced by genetics (Bartels & Boomsma, 2009). Such evidence suggested that people's happiness levels are at least partly genetically explained. Recent research on epigenetics and gene-environment interactions has found that biology and environment continuously interact in a dynamic process to influence people's behavior (e.g., Plomin & Spinath, 2004). Thus, genetic predispositions are not deterministic. Set point can be substantively changed, which means that through particular vital changes a person could progressively increase their level of well-being.

One way through which our genes contribute to explain happiness is temperament. Behavioral genetics research suggests that individual differences in infant and child temperament are genetically influenced (Saudino, 2005). Numerous investigations in different countries of the world have shown that two features of the basic personality appear unequivocally associated with happiness and life satisfaction: extraversion and emotional stability (Morris, Burns, Periard, & Shoda, 2015). Extraversion is a feature characterized by the tendency to sociability and to engage in rewarding experiences. In fact, some authors argue that their sensitivity to experiences of enjoyment leads them to pay so much attention to the social world. Extraverted individuals are able to create positive and stimulating environments in which relationships are a source of habitual gratification. Moreover, they have greater social support, especially when facing adversities (Hervas, 2007). Even so, emotionally stable people tend to have moderate reactions to small and large events of life. If they experience negative emotions, these are less intense and less durable than those experienced by people with greater neuroticism. Stable people tend to better handle everyday difficulties, family problems, and failures. In addition, they have better self-esteem and a better ability to regulate their emotions. As cited above, other personality factors such as optimism are also related to happiness (Carver et al., 2010). In any case, it is worth mentioning that all people, introverts and extroverts, optimists or pessimists, might learn simple strategies (e.g., paying attention to positive experiences already available in their current daily life) so that their natural tendency does not diminish their chances of being happier.

In short, although individual differences in biology and life circumstances combine to explain part of the happiness variance, other elements such as attitudes, intentional activities and daily habits explain a large portion of individual differences in happiness (Lyubomirsky & Layous, 2013). Paths to greater happiness might be more complex than originally thought.

Happiness Is in the Moment

Many people spend their day-to-day life looking forward to an upcoming event or ruminating over one from the past. Such deeds lead us to lose the ability to be in the present and to fully enjoy life. Putting off our happiness for later may have a high cost for our well-being and mental health. Research on positive psychology has shown that appreciating and savoring small pleasures every day is one of the most powerful strategies to increase our happiness. For instance, as we have seen previously, there is a significant association between extraversion and happiness. But what exactly do extraverts do to be happier? Research has shown that the ability to enjoy small things is an essential path that makes extraverts happier than introverts. In a study in which the participants visualized a video that they had previously chosen, results showed that, when in a positive mood, extraverts had a greater preference for selecting positive videos than introverts (Hervas & López-Gómez, 2016). Thus, the ability to look for positive experiences as a priority and to enjoy them may be a significant route to happiness. And more importantly, this ability can be learned and incorporated into people's daily lives. Thus, savoring the present moment allows us to cultivate positive emotions and increase general life satisfaction.

Even though psychologists have studied emotions for over a century, research have focused mainly on negative emotions. Until recently, the study of positive emotions has been limited and scarce. Based on numerous studies, Barbara Fredrickson proposed the "Broaden and Build" theory (Fredrickson, 1998, 2001) that provides a useful theoretical framework to understand positive emotions. While negative emotions have been associated with survival and protection in response to a threatening situation, positive emotions have been related to the ability to explore the environment, to be open to new information, to create and build new resources. According to this theory, positive emotions broaden the scope of attention, enabling flexible thinking. This in turn facilitates the development of new skills, networks, and capacities that are essential to adaptively handle a stressful event (Fredrickson, Tugade, Waugh, & Larkin, 2003; Aspinwall, 2001). These personal resources include physical (e.g. healthy behaviors) (Cohen, Alper, Doyle, Treanor, & Turner, 2006), social (Kok et al., 2013), cognitive (Tugade & Fredrickson, 2002), and psychological resources (e.g., optimism, creativity; Scheier & Carver, 1993). In the long-term, people who experience more positive emotions are more satisfied with their lives, build more positive relationships with partners, get better jobs, or even have better health (see Lyubomirsky, King, & Diener, 2005). Therefore, even though positive emotions have been considered less relevant to human evolution, research has demonstrated that they may play an essential role in increasing or maintaining long-term well-being by channeling more effective coping resources (Tugade & Fredrickson, 2002).

There are several positive interventions that have already established their effectiveness in promoting positive emotions (Lyubomirsky & Layous, 2013). For instance, research has shown that learning to deliberately cultivate gratitude is an effective way to increase well-being (Emmons & McCullough, 2003).

Another effective way to cultivate positive emotions and savor the present is meditation. Meditation interventions such as mindfulness-based interventions have proven to be effective for increasing well-being and positive emotions (Rodríguez-Carvajal, García-Rubio, Paniagua, García-Diex, & Rivas, 2016). Mindfulness refers to the self-regulation of attention to one's experiences in the present moment with curiosity, openness, and acceptance (Bishop et al., 2004).

Research on mindfulness has shown that it is related to higher psychological well-being (Baer et al., 2008). Practicing mindfulness reduces anxiety and stress, decreases reactivity to emotional stimuli and improves emotional regulation by reducing over-involvement (rumination) or under-involvement (distraction) (Hervas, Cebolla, & Soler, 2016; Ortner, Kilner, & Zelazo, 2007). Moreover, some types of meditation, such as meditating on positive feelings toward self and others or compassion meditation, have been proven to reduce negative thoughts about oneself and strengthen social relationships (Fredrickson, Cohn, Coffey, Pek, & Finkel, 2008; Gilbert, 2009).

In short, research has defined an essential route to well-being. Paying attention to the present moment, savoring small daily pleasures, and cultivating an attitude of gratitude for the good things that happen in life is a significant pathway to happiness. And most importantly, these skills can be learned and developed intentionally.

Happiness Is in Society

One source of influence that it is usually underestimated is the role of society. By society, we mean the characteristics of the country as well as the city, and also includes the socioeconomic development and cultural features that can affect well-being. Some authors have labeled this component as social well-being (i.e., societal well-being), which derives from the perception that a country gives its citizens the opportunity to thrive, and this notion also includes other components such as the feelings of belonging to a community (Keyes, 1998).

Although the research in this area is mostly correlational, there are some relevant insights. For example, the differences in perceived freedom, equality, and corruption across countries may explain some of the differences in well-being (Veenhoven, 2004). Some of these factors are easily connected with personal well-being. For example, freedom in a society clearly promotes the individual's sense of autonomy. Similarly, there is also interesting research on economic factors. For example, we know that poverty as well as economic crises may severely affect well-being, both when analyzing countries and when exploring its effects on individuals within a given society (Helliwell et al., 2015). Inequality also seems to be negative, although there are some exceptions. In some countries, such as the United States, this relationship is reduced. Moreover, there is even some data showing that this relation can be reversed in some parts of China. The reason for this variable pattern is how individuals influenced by culture interpret inequality. In the US, most citizens believe they live in a mobile society, where inequality is interpreted as something that can be outwitted thanks to hard work. On the contrary, in Europe, which is perceived to be a steadier society, inequality is interpreted as something stable and unfair (Alesina, Di Tella, & MacCulloch, 2004). Other research has confirmed that inequality reduces well-being, not only because it produces poverty for some, but because it generates perceived unfairness and lack of trust for many others (Oishi, Kesebir, & Diener, 2011).

Environment issues also matter. There is an increasing consensus about the key role of green areas for citizens' well-being and health (e.g., Douglas, Lennon, & Scott, 2017). For example, a longitudinal study found that moving to greener urban areas was associated with sustained well-being improvements over the following three years (Alcock, White, Wheeler, Fleming, & Depledge, 2014).

Overall, distant societal factors seem to have a subtle yet significant influence on well-being, and it should not be underestimated.

Happiness Is in Living

Beyond basic traits and attitudes, eudaimonic well-being emerges from the quality of the structural elements of our lives: the quality and quantity of relationships, the quality and fit of our jobs, how we are engaged in our present and future, and more. Moreover, a good life comes from actions that are coherent with personal values that lead people to grow, and feel autonomous and competent.

The positive effect is very clear for relationships. Having a strong sense of relatedness is closely linked to well-being. Happy people report having more friends, having higher-quality relationships with others, and spending more time with others (Diener & Seligman, 2002; Lucas, Le, & Dyrenforth, 2008).

Similarly, developing a sense of meaning in life is associated with higher well-being (Steger, Frazier, Kaler, & Oishi, 2006). Although this is sometimes a matter of having an attitude that allows each individual to acknowledge their contributions, it also depends on whether the person finds an activity through expressing his or her values. Values-driven actions often imply a full commitment to something greater than oneself, which makes people feel alive and real (Ryan & Deci, 2001).

The key role of these issues explains why sometimes external circumstances are so disturbing. Losing a loved one as well as other life adversities commonly block some of the essential nutrients for well-being. For example, the experience of unemployment is usually associated with a restricted social network, a limited sense of competence and meaning of life, along with diminished autonomy and self-acceptance. Thus, a severe or chronic lack of satisfaction in these key themes may lead to psychological dysfunctions. For example, in a longitudinal study, people who scored low on psychological well-being (Ryff, 1989), as defined by nutrients, such as self-acceptance, autonomy, purpose in life, positive relationships with others, environmental mastery, and personal growth, were up to seven times more likely to experience significant symptoms of depression at the ten-year follow-up (Wood & Tarrier, 2010).

Overall, we should emphasize that beyond temperament, traits, and attitudes, the presence of psychological nutrients that allows us to fill our lives (i.e., eudaimonic well-being) are really crucial for understanding happiness. Although different unitary approaches about the nature of happiness are often underscored (e.g., it is in our mind, it is in the moment . . . etc.), we should conclude that happiness seems to be an outcome that relies on a variety of factors. Thus, any partial explanation will be misleading.

Communicating the Science of Well-Being

The science of well-being has given us a great deal of new insights and knowledge that we were not aware of. Most scientists and practitioners agree on the relevance of sharing useful information about well-being with the population at large, but there is also an increasing awareness that this is not as easy as expected. The transfer of knowledge from science to the general population can lead to iatrogenic effects (Grimshaw, Eccles, Lavis, Hill, & Squires, 2012). How should happiness research be effectively communicated? Can the way we inform spur a negative or unexpected effect? If so, how can we avoid this misinformation?

Below we provide some recommendations that may help with informing the population more effectively and accurately.

1. *Informing that well-being is a difficult issue has several advantages.* We may affirm that well-being is difficult in at least two senses: it is difficult to fully understand and it is difficult to build up. As stated earlier, individual happiness depends on many factors and how these are weighted can vary from person to person. As a result, what works for the average person, generally the target profile of most research, does not necessarily work for all other individuals. Therefore, general advice or guidelines have to be carefully offered. The idea that happiness is complex, and we are far from knowing everything about it, leaves room to expect some findings may

not apply to everyone to the same extent. Besides, when we recognize that being happy is not easy, at least for a significant amount of people, we avoid setting too high a standard for most people. As we reviewed, genetic factors and external circumstances can significantly reduce our capacity to improve well-being. The notion that happiness depends on oneself and that it is easy to attain may increase frustration especially in most vulnerable individuals, such as those who have to face more external or internal limitations (e.g., Gruber, Mauss, & Tamir, 2011).

2. *Being unhappy is not being a failure.* It is also important to explicitly address and normalize the notion that people may go through periods when they are unhappy. In fact, achieving a deeper and longer-lasting happiness sometimes involves putting in effort and taking on sacrifices that lead the person to be unhappy for a while. Besides, depending on the person and the situation, unhappiness may be unavoidable for months (i.e., as in the process of dealing with a serious illness of a loved one) or years (i.e., having a child with severe problems). Acceptance and change have to be balanced to approach happiness. For example, it is true that unhappiness may be the outcome of bad attitudes, lack of effort, or a psychological problem, and that addressing these factors may be the determinant for improving an individual's well-being. Only offering a balanced perspective that allows the person to be motivated to improve, without excessive urge or anxiety, will lead to better possible outcomes.

3. *Happiness is not the only motive.* Happiness is a key value for most people as demonstrated by ample evidence (e.g., Adler, Dolan, & Kavetsos, 2017). However, this does not mean that it is the only value, or even the primary value, for all people in all scenarios. It is obvious that a person can adopt many other values, such as justice, freedom, honesty, health, money, friendship, and family, among many others. However, in certain cases, circumstances can lead to the person sacrificing their own happiness to protect another value, which may occur depending on the person's hierarchy of values. For example, sometimes individuals make decisions at the expense of their well-being. The relative absence of other values in the public domain indirectly leads to putting all the focus on happiness. However, it all becomes clearer, if it is acknowledged that happiness does not have to be the *primus inter pares*, the highest value. Thus, it is useful to recognize that a variety of values drive us. Of these motives, the desire for happiness for oneself and happiness for loved ones may stand out in general, but not in specific situations.

Conclusion

Research on well-being has become a fruitful line of investigation over the last two decades. This process has evolved along with a growing interest among the general population who are keen to find out more on the nature of well-being. Unfortunately, it is not clear if the ideas that have taken root among readers and consumers of social media are really accurate or even beneficial. At any rate, the need for a deep understanding of well-being remains, and scientists should not miss this great opportunity for knowledge transfer with far-reaching potential implications.

References

Adler, M. D., Dolan, P., & Kavetsos, G. (2017). Would you choose to be happy? Tradeoffs between happiness and the other dimensions of life in a large population survey. *Journal of Economic Behavior & Organization, 139*, 60–73.

Alcock, I., White, M. P., Wheeler, B. W., Fleming, L. E., & Depledge, M. H. (2014). Longitudinal effects on mental health of moving to greener and less green urban areas. *Environmental Science & Technology, 48*(2), 1247–1255.

Alesina, A., Di Tella, R., & MacCulloch, R. (2004). Inequality and happiness: Are Europeans and Americans different? *Journal of Public Economics, 88*(9), 2009–2042.

Aspinwall, L. G. (2001). Dealing with adversity: Self-regulation, coping, adaptation, and health. In A. Tesser & N. Schwarz (Eds.), *Blackwell handbook of social psychology: Intraindividual processes* (pp. 591–614). Malden, MA: Blackwell Publishers.

Baer, R. A., Smith, G. T., Lykins, E., Button, D., Krietemeyer, J., Sauer, S., & Williams, J. M. G. (2008). Construct validity of the Five Facet Mindfulness Questionnaire in meditating and non-meditating samples. *Assessment, 15*, 329–342.

Bartels, M., & Boomsma, D. I. (2009). Born to be happy? The etiology of subjective well-being. *Behavior Genetics, 39*, 605.

Bishop, S. R., Lau, M., Shapiro, S., Carlson, L., Anderson, N. D., Carmody, J., Zindel V. Segal, Z. V., Abbey, S., Speca, M., Velting, D., & Devins, G. (2004). Mindfulness: A proposed operational definition. *Clinical Psychology: Science & Practice, 11*, 230–241.

Boehm, J. K., & Lyubomirsky, S. (2009). The promise of sustainable happiness. In C. R. Snyder & S. J. Lopez (Eds.), *The Oxford handbook of positive psychology* (pp. 667–677). Oxford, UK: Oxford University Press.

Bono, G., & McCullough, M. E. (2006). Positive responses to benefit and harm: Bringing forgiveness and gratitude into cognitive psychotherapy. *Journal of Cognitive Psychotherapy, 20*, 147–158.

Carver, C. S., Scheier, M. F., & Segerstrom, S. C. (2010). Optimism. *Clinical Psychology Review, 30*(7), 879–889.

Cohen, S., Alper, C. M., Doyle, W. J., Treanor, J. J., & Turner, R. B. (2006). Positive emotional style predicts resistance to illness after experimental exposure to rhinovirus or influenza A virus. *Psychosomatic Medicine, 68*, 809–815. Deci, E. L., & Ryan, R. M. (2000). The "what" and "why" of goal pursuits: Human needs and the self-determination of behavior. *Psychological Inquiry, 11*, 227–268.

Diener, E., Scollon, C., & Lucas, R. (2003). The evolving concept of subjective well-being. *Advances in Cell Aging and Gerontology, 15*, 187–219.

Diener, E., & Seligman, M. E. P. (2002). Very happy people. *Psychological Science, 13*, 81–84.

Douglas, O., Lennon, M., & Scott, M. (2017). Green space benefits for health and well-being: A life-course approach for urban planning, design and management. *Cities, 66*, 53–62.

Emmons, R. A., & McCullough, M. E. (2003). Counting blessings versus burdens: An experimental investigation of gratitude and subjective well-being in daily life. *Journal of Personality and Social Psychology, 84*, 377–389.

Fredrickson, B. L. (1998). What good are positive emotions? *Review of General Psychology, 2*, 300–319.

Fredrickson, B. L. (2001). The role of positive emotions in positive psychology: The broaden-and-build theory of positive emotions. *American Psychologist, 56*, 218–226.

Fredrickson, B. L. (2013). Updated thinking on positivity ratios. *American Psychologist, 68*, 814–822.

Fredrickson, B. L., Cohn, M. A., Coffey, K., Pek, J., & Finkel, S. M. (2008). Open hearts build lives: Positive emotions, induced through meditation, build consequential personal resources. *Journal of Personality and Social Psychology, 95*, 1045–1062.

Fredrickson, B. L., Tugade, M. M., Waugh, C. E., & Larkin, G. (2003). What good are positive emotions in crises? A prospective study of resilience and emotions following the terrorist attacks on the United States on September 11th, 2001. *Journal of Personality and Social Psychology, 84*, 365–376.

Gilbert, P. (2009). *The compassionate mind: A new approach to life's challenges.* London: Constable and Robinson.

Grimshaw, J.-M., Eccles, M. P., Lavis, J. N., Hill, S. J., & Squires, J. E. (2012). Knowledge translation of research findings. *Implementation Science, 7*, 50. https://doi.org/10.1186/1748-5908-7-50

Gruber, J., Mauss, I. B., & Tamir, M. (2011). A dark side of happiness? How, when, and why happiness is not always good. *Perspectives on Psychological Science, 6*, 222–233.

Hanssen, M. M., Peters, M. L., Vlaeyen, J. W., Meevissen, Y. M., & Vancleef, L. M. (2013). Optimism lowers pain: Evidence of the causal status and underlying mechanisms. *Pain, 154*, 53–58.

Helliwell, J. F., Huang, H., & Wang, S. (2015). The geography of world happiness. Chapter 2. In J. F. Helliwell, R. Layard, & J. Sachs (Eds.), *World happiness report 2015* (pp. 12–41). New York: Sustainable Development Research Network.

Hervas, G. (2007). La felicidad de las personas. In C. Vázquez & G. Hervás (Eds.), *El estudio científico del bienestar: Fundamentos de una Psicología Positiva.* Madrid: Alianza Editorial.

Hervas, G., Cebolla, A., & Soler, J. (2016). Intervenciones psicológicas basadas en mindfulness y sus beneficios: estado actual de la cuestión. *Clínica y Salud, 27*(3), 115–124.

Hervas, G., & López-Gómez, I. (2016). The power of extraverts: Testing positive and negative mood regulation. *Anales de Psicología/Annals of Psychology, 32*(3), 710–716.

Hervas, G., & Vazquez, C. (2013). Construction and validation of a measure of integrative well-being in seven languages: The Pemberton Happiness Index. *Health and Quality of Life Outcomes, 11*, 66.

Keyes, C. L. M. (1998). Social well-being. *Social Psychology Quarterly*, 121–140.

Keyes, K. M., Pratt, C., Galea, S., McLaughlin, K. A., Koenen, K. C., & Shear, M. K. (2014). The burden of loss: Unexpected death of a loved one and psychiatric disorders across the life course in a national study. *American Journal of Psychiatry*, *171*, 864–871.

Kok, B. E., Coffey, K. A., Cohn, M. A., Catalino L.I., Vacharkulksemsuk T., Algoe, S.B., Brantley, M., & Fredrickson, B.L. (2013). How positive emotions build physical health: Perceived positive social connections account for the upward spiral between positive emotions and vagal tone. *Psychological Science*, *24*, 1123–1132.

Lucas, R. E., Le, K., & Dyrenforth, P. S. (2008). Explaining the extraversion/positive affect relation: Sociability cannot account for extraverts' greater happiness. *Journal of Personality*, *76*, 385–414.

Lyubomirsky, S., King, L., & Diener, E. (2005). The benefits of frequent positive affect: Does happiness lead to success? *Psychological Bulletin*, *131*, 803–855.

Lyubomirsky, S., & Layous, K. (2013). How do simple positive activities increase well-being? *Current Directions in Psychological Science*, *22*, 57–62.

Morris, M. B., Burns, G. N., Periard, D. A., & Shoda, E. A. (2015). Extraversion: Emotional stability circumplex traits and subjective well-being. *Journal of Happiness Studies*, *16*(6), 1509–1523.

Oishi, S., Kesebir, S., & Diener, E. (2011). Income inequality and happiness. *Psychological Science*, *22*(9), 1095–1100.

Ortner, C. N. M., Kilner, S. J., & Zelazo, P. D. (2007). Mindfulness meditation and reduced emotional interference on a cognitive task. *Motivation and Emotion*, *31*(4), 271–283.

Pavot, W., & Diener, E. (1993). The affective and cognitive contest of self-reports measures of subjective well-being. *Social Indicators Research*, *28*, 1–20.

Plomin, R., & Spinath, F. M. (2004). Intelligence: Genetics, genes and genomics. *Journal of Personality and Social Psychology*, *86*, 112–129.

Rodríguez-Carvajal, R., García-Rubio, C., Paniagua, D., García-Diex, G., & Rivas, S. (2016). Mindfulness Integrative Model (MIM): Cultivating positive states of mind towards oneself and the others through mindfulness and self-compassion. *Anales de Psicología*, *32*, 749–760.

Ryan, R. M., & Deci, E. L. (2001). On happiness and human potentials: A review of research on hedonic and eudaimonic well-being. In S. Fiske (Ed.), *Annual review of psychology* (pp. 141–166). Palo Alto, CA: Annual Reviews, Inc.

Ryff, C. D. (1989). Happiness is everything, or is it? Explorations on the meaning of psychological well-being. *Journal of Personality and Social Psychology*, *57*, 1069–1081.

Saudino, K. J. (2005). Behavioral genetics and child temperament. *Journal of Developmental and Behavioral Pediatrics*, *26*(3), 214–223.

Scheier, M. F., & Carver, C. S. (1993). On the power of positive thinking: The benefits of being optimistic. *Current Directions in Psychological Science*, *2*, 26–30.

Seligman, M. (2002). *La auténtica felicidad*. Barcelona: Vergara.

Sheldon, K. M., & Lyubomirsky, S. (2006). How to increase and sustain positive emotion: The effects of expressing gratitude and visualizing best possible selves. *Journal of Positive Psychology*, *1*, 73–82.

Steger, M. F., Frazier, P., Kaler, M., & Oishi, S. (2006). The meaning in life questionnaire: Assessing the presence of and search for meaning in life. *Journal of Counseling Psychology*, *53*, 80–93.

Tugade, M. M., & Fredrickson, B. L. (2002). Positive emotions and emotional intelligence. In L. F. Barrett & P. Salovey (Eds.), *The wisdom in feeling* (pp. 319–340). New York: Guilford Press.

Vazquez, C., & Hervas, G. (2012). Addressing current challenges in cross-cultural measurement of well-being: The Pemberton Happiness Index. In A. Delle Fave & H. H. Koop (Eds.), *Anthology on cross-cultural advancements in positive psychology*. New York: Springer-Verlag.

Veenhoven, R. (2004). Happiness as an aim in public policy: The greatest happiness principle. In A. Linley & S. Joseph (Eds.), *Positive psychology in practice* (pp. 731–750). Hoboken, NJ: Wiley.

Waterman, A. S. (2008). Reconsidering happiness: A eudaimonist's perspective. *The Journal of Positive Psychology*, *3*, 234–252.

Wood, A. M., & Tarrier, N. (2010). Positive clinical psychology: A new vision and strategy for integrated research and practice. *Clinical Psychology Review*, *30*, 819–829.

PART I

Positive Interpersonal Communication

4

THE FUTURE OF POSITIVE INTERPERSONAL COMMUNICATION RESEARCH

Thomas J. Socha

This landmark volume stands as compelling evidence that adding the adjective "positive" to communication matters. This simple addition has not only stimulated new and important research but serves as a clarion call to communication scholars of all stripes to join the study communication's higher purposes. Following the lead of positive psychology (e.g., Seligman & Csikszentmihalyi, 2000; and see Socha, 2009), early efforts to understand positive interpersonal communication featured studies of aesthetic relating (Baxter, Norwood, & Nebel, 2012), synchrony (Kim, 2012), forgiveness (Kelley, 2012; Waldron & Kelley, 2008), and other similar topics considered to be "positive" (Socha & Pitts, 2012). Other efforts highlighted important connections between positive interpersonal communication, health, and wellness (Pitts & Socha, 2013), specifically links between positive interpersonal communication, stress management, cardiovascular benefits, and overall emotional well-being (Sullivan, 2013). Mirivel (2014) created a groundbreaking conceptual model of positive interpersonal communication featuring a set of message behaviors regarded typically to be positive: "greeting, asking, complimenting, disclosing, encouraging, listening, and inspiring" (p. 7). Finally, grounded in the psychology of needs-satisfaction (Sheldon, 2009) and contrasted with the darkside of interpersonal communication (Spitzberg & Cupach, 2007), Socha and Beck (2015) framed positive interpersonal communication as "message processes that facilitate human needs-satisfaction" (p. 188). According to Socha and Beck messages like compliments, encouragements, and similar others function as positive interpersonal communication when they seek to facilitate the satisfaction of human needs such as belongingness, love, esteem, self-actualization and more, whereas messages like insults, denigrations, and similar others function as darkside interpersonal communication when they seek to inhibit, frustrate, or deny fellow humans needs-satisfaction.

This chapter offers an added refinement to the evolving conceptual framing of positive interpersonal communication by arguing the merits of theorizing positive interpersonal communication (and for that matter all forms of positive communication) as a pattern of interpersonal communication patterns—a metapattern (Bateson, 1979; Volk, 1995). That is, it is useful theoretically to conceptualize the binaries of positive/negative and brightness/darkness (e.g., see Spitzberg & Cupach, 2007; Socha & Pitts, 2012) as patterns of interpersonal communication patterns—metapatterns. Both positive interpersonal communication and darkside interpersonal communication exist in everyday interpersonal discourse as patterns of interpersonal communication patterns. And potentially, any given interpersonal communication pattern can be framed, understood, and experienced at a meta-level as positive, dark, or in many shades of gray. In this chapter I will further explicate the notion of positive interpersonal communication as a metap-attern and will close by suggesting a few new pathways for the future of positive interpersonal communication research that includes urging interpersonal communication scholars to give greater research attention to studying positive interpersonal communication in the pursuit of "good" relationships (see Waldron & Kelley, 2015), higher purposes, and higher selves.

Positive Conceptual Ground

Positive Interpersonal Communication at Metapattern

In the prologue of *Metapatterns: Across Space, Time, and Mind,* Tyler Volk (1995), an NYU profes-sor of biology and environmental studies, suggested three ways to define the term "canoe." Let's follow Volk but instead examine an abbreviated chronology of past attempts to define positive interpersonal communication. According to Volk, one way to define positive interpersonal com-munication (and canoes) would be to *identify and describe its elements.* That is, we could pinpoint and agree on unique kinds of verbal messages, gestures, qualities of messages, and so on, that could distinguish "positive" interpersonal communication from darkside interpersonal communication as well as other shades-of-gray communicative forms.

Socha and Pitts (2012), for example, sought to do this by gathering a group of interpersonal communication scholars to describe and illuminate the qualities of topics that were defined a priori to be examples of "positive" interpersonal communication like humorous communication (Meyer, 2012), communication excellence (Mirivel, 2012), celebratory support (McCullough & Burleson, 2012), and more. This work drew attention to many kinds of communicative forms defined linguistically and a priori as "positive." However, drawing lines that neatly demarcate what is "positive" and what is "dark" is not easy or straightforward.

"Humor," for instance, in common vernacular is defined as a unique type of positive com-municative and humor abilities are a welcomed quality of communicators in personal and social relationships. Laughing and smiling are desirable behaviors and serve as indicators of marital satisfaction (Spanier, 1976). However, "making fun" (prosocial) and "making fun of" (antisocial) are different humorous processes that may or may not function as positive interpersonal com-munication by facilitating needs-satisfaction of physiological, belongingness, and leisure needs (Max-Neef, 1992). For example, "roasting," is a kind of ritualized making-fun-of that is intended to be interpreted as a kind of playful communication episode and its messages to be in-good-fun (prosocial and positive). However, roasting can also be interpreted as darkside interpersonal communication. For example, President Donald Trump did not see the humor in the roasting that was to take place at the annual 2017 White House Correspondents' Dinner (WHCD) and declined to be the guest of honor (the first US president since Ronald Regan to do so) (see Crouch, 2017; Ohlheiser & Yahr, 2017). The replacement guest of honor speaker, Hasan Minhaj, was asked (tongue-in-cheek) to not roast the president or his administration, but of course could not resist temptation (see Borchers, 2017). Whether "roasting" functions as positive interper-sonal communication, darkside interpersonal communication, or shades-of-gray interpersonal communication may not be easily or clearly determined, but is nonetheless consequential in the impression formation processes of others and relationships.

Another example of conceptual difficulties encountered in deciding a priori what is posi-tive and what is dark can be seen in the terms Mirivel (2014) selected for his model of positive talk—greeting, asking, complimenting, disclosing, encouraging, listening, and inspiring. Mirivel's model is groundbreaking, heuristic, conceptually sound, and a very useful instructional tool. However, like humor, sometimes, some of these positive message processes can also serve dark functions. That is, although "encouraging" is, by definition, positive it also depends on what is being encouraged. For example, a stalking victim may inadvertently communicate "encouragement" to a stalker by sharing even a causal "greeting" (e.g., see Spitzberg & Cupach, 2001). A more dramatic example is Seattle commuters stuck in morning traffic shouting "encouraging" messages of "Just do it!" to a woman who was about to jump off a bridge to her death (Restivo, 2017). In theory, any of Mirivel's messages may typically serve positive interpersonal communication functions if they are communicated as customarily intended. However, going forward, positive interpersonal communication researchers should also consider the power of the darkside to highjack even the most positive of messages for ill intent and dark (needs-inhibiting) purposes.

It is left to future positive interpersonal communication research to examine the qualities of patterns of interpersonal communication that communicators find to be "positive" and facilitate needs-satisfaction and uncover the rules and explanations shaping this form of discourse. That is, what is making a given message "positive?" Some messages at face may be widely understood, a priori, as "positive." However, they may also be high-jacked by the darkside. For example, "compliments" are discursively "positive." But compliments may be high-jacked to serve darkside communicative functions like when a manager of an accounting department says to an interviewee for an accounting job, "Nice _____!" If the manager uses the term "resume" after nice, the message is likely to be perceived and accepted as a situationally appropriate compliment (positive interpersonal communication). But, if instead the manager uses the term "legs" (or for that matter any body part) after the word "nice," although its form could still be interpreted linguistically as a "compliment," it is more likely that it will also be interpreted as situationally inappropriate and as function as sexual harassment. Further, how an accounting job interviewee chooses to respond to the accounting manager's "compliment" if the term legs was used, further illustrates the complexities of trying to positively manage encroaching darkside interpersonal communication episodes. For example, the interviewee may say: (a) "Thanks"; (b) "Thanks, your legs are nice too"; (c) "Excuse me, but that was inappropriate"; or (d) "Thank you, but this interview is over." Response (b) suggests that the "compliment" was also viewed as "flirting" and is being reciprocated; (c) and (d) interpret the "compliment" as dark; while (a) remains somewhat ambiguous insofar as it responds in a linguistically appropriate way by acknowledging it as a compliment but leaving vague whether it is seen as dark or not.

Research on positivity (e.g., Fredrickson, 2001, 2009) and marital communication (Gottman, 1993), show that darkside interpersonal messages exert considerable force on the perceptions and enactments of self as well as relationships on the order of at least three to one (i.e., according to Fredrickson, 2001, it takes at least three positive messages to balance the effects of one negative message). Thus, the power of the darkside must always be considered when studying that which is positive. Further, it remains an empirical question whether a three-to-one positive to negative ratio has found its way across communication contexts (groups, organizations, society).

Enactments of the term "positive," like all messages, create social realities that are co-constructed by communicators which in turn may or may not serve positive functions. It is up to interpersonal communication scholars to conduct ground-level research to understand the processes by which communicators are creating "positive" as well as "dark" worlds for themselves. Also, definitional research efforts are important to identifying initial sensitizing concepts for future study.

A second way Volk suggests to define positive interpersonal communication is to describe what positive interpersonal communication *does* or its functions. Socha and Beck (2015) took this approach when they theorized that positive interpersonal messages function as a means of needs-satisfaction. Although Maslow's (1943) hierarchy of needs is most famous, Socha and Beck also cited the work of Max-Neef (1992) who created an elaborate model of eight basic human needs (and associated qualities of being): (1) subsistence (e.g., physical, mental health), (2) protection (e.g., care, accountability), (3) affection (e.g., respect, sense of humor), (4) understanding (e.g., critical capacity, curiosity), (5) participation (e.g., adaptedness, dedication), (6) leisure (e.g., curiosity, tranquility), (7) creation (e.g., imagination, curiosity), and (8) identity (sense of belonging, self-esteem). Of special interest to interpersonal communication studies is that Max-Neef also associated "doing" qualities to each of these eight needs: (1) subsistence (e.g., feeding, resting, working), (2) protection (e.g., cooperating, planning, caring), (3) affection (e.g., sharing, love-making), (4) understanding (e.g., analyzing, investigating), (5) participation (e.g., affiliating, proposing, dissenting), (6) leisure (e.g., daydreaming, recalling, fantasizing), (7) creation (e.g., inventing, designing, composing), and (8) identity (e.g., integrating, understanding self, actualizing self). Some of these "doing" qualities are clearly communicative (e.g., sharing, proposing, dissenting), while all the rest in some way rely on communication.

With respect to the study of needs, it is assumed that: (a) needs are essential to human survival and quality of living, (b) having unmet needs is motivating or creates drive states, and (c) needs-satisfaction is "positive." Further, having lingering, unmet needs (deprivation) because of processes preventing needs-satisfaction is undesirable (or dark) as illustrated by Ted Robert Gurr's (1970) landmark book, *Why Men Rebel*, that argues the roots of human conflict and rebellion are planted in deprivation. Socha and Beck theorized connections between interpersonal communication and human needs-satisfaction by arguing that interpersonal communication which seeks to facilitate needs-satisfaction would be regarded as "positive" and that which seeks to inhibit needs-satisfaction would be regarded as darkside interpersonal communication. Socha and Beck also offered suggestions of specific communication processes that potentially can serve either positive or darkside interpersonal communication functions as related to levels of human needs, for example: communicating celebratory support vs. insulting can be related to esteem/respect/pride needs; affinity-seeking vs. bullying can be related to belongingness/participation/social support needs; and honesty vs. lying can be related to safety/security/protection needs.

A related-question about positive and darkside interpersonal communication and needs-satisfaction pertains to limits. How good (or bad) can interpersonal communication as well relationships get? Socha and Stoyneva (2014) pointed out that past empirical interpersonal communication research has focused on middling interpersonal outcomes described using anchor terms like "satisfying" and avoided studying communication that is "euphoric," "rapturous," or "organismic." They suggest that part of the explanation is that "satisfaction," like most psychosocial and communicative variables, is commonplace, whereas "ecstatic" is occasional, fleeting, and probably an unsustainable state over the long run. While they accept most of the logic of past choices to study satisfaction, they also counter that peak communication moments are incredibly motivating. People remember and cherish episodes of peak interpersonal communication and it may be these highly positive moments that potentially sustain relationships over long periods of time as well as define the bandwidths of how good relationships can get. For example, does the number of peak relational communication moments recalled in a relationship affect relational satisfaction and to what extent? Do people have sufficient interpersonal communication skills to enact peak episodes of interpersonal communication? More fundamentally, what do people expect from their interpersonal communication and are these expectancies too low or too high? We need to understand more about doing positive interpersonal communication and this leads us to Volk's (1995) final approach to defining positive interpersonal communication.

The third and final way to define positive interpersonal communication and what Volk (1995) uses to frame his book is to not comment directly about positive interpersonal communication but instead (following Volk's teacher Gregory Bateson) describe the patterns of *doing* positive interpersonal communication (or canoeing). Does engaging in episodes of communicating interpersonally accompany good or bad feelings? Does doing interpersonal communication feel inviting or off-putting? Peaceful or violent? Neighborly or alien? Does a given interpersonal communication episode feel like a gentle relational "nudge" or an abrupt relational "shove"?

Socha, Bernat, Harris, Hill, and Hurd (2016) conducted a pilot study to describe the autobiographical memories of doing episodes of peak communication at different points over the lifespan. Specifically, participants in the study were prompted with the following:

> Peak communication experiences are times when you felt that you fully got through to another person and another person fully got through to you. They are among the most positive communication encounters you have had, and they provide the highest levels of feelings of happiness. The study is being conducted so that we can learn more about peak communication experiences across the lifespan. You will be asked to recall these peak communication experiences, map them on a grid, and then will be asked to describe each of them.
>
> *(Socha et al., 2016, p. 9)*

Socha et al. (2016) found that most of the participants reported their first peak communication episode took place during the K–12 years with a well-known adult other (i.e., mother, mother's friend, or a teacher) or a same-age best friend. The topics of first recalled peak episodes included (in alphabetical order): a talk about the future, a talk about managing a significant life stressor (parental, divorce, spouse's funeral), learning about one's own past while reminiscing, or sharing funny stories or funny moments. Socha et al. also found that the terms used to define "peak" interpersonal communication episodes included a variety of communication purposes (in alphabetical order): acceptance, connectedness, encouragement, feeling heard, feeling special, love, inspiration, openness, relief, security, success, truthfulness, and validation. And, during peak communication episodes, participants reported to have experienced feeling (in alphabetical order): appreciated, cared for, challenged, connected, excited, happy, hopeful, inspired, joy, loved, pleased, positive, relieved, special, supported, transformed, and understood.

Socha et al.'s results suggest that future studies of doing peak interpersonal communication may find the following: (1) mothers and teachers may figure prominently in early peak interpersonal communication episodes; (2) special teachers and academic mentors may figure in later lifespan stages; (3) the numbers of "peak" interpersonal communication episodes experienced across the lifespan may vary from person to person, and (4) recollections of peak episodes are subject to distortion, revision, and memory decay. However, (5) memories of early peak episodes that are carried across lifespan stages into adulthood strongly influence the doing of positive interpersonal communication.

Summary

Positive interpersonal communication when conceptualized as a metapattern leads researchers to study: (a) the various kinds of interpersonal communication patterns that facilitate (or inhibit) human needs-satisfaction, (b) how these episodes are enacted and experienced, and (c) how darkside patterns may highjack positive interpersonal communication for dark purposes. This framing offers rich conceptual soil in which future interpersonal communication theory and research can grow. It assumes that positive interpersonal communication is a complex episodic process of co-construction where relational participants seek to use messages to facilitate (of inhibit) their own needs-satisfaction as well as their partners'. Or in other words, how do relational participants communicatively *invest* (or divest) in each other and in their relationship to their mutual benefit (or demise)? As an investment, positive interpersonal communication also seeks to strengthen individuals and relationships to increase resilience, so that inevitable future storms can be weathered (see Beck & Socha, 2015), whereas darkside interpersonal seeks to weaken individuals and relationships to increase vulnerability.

Positive Tiered Pathways

Thus far in this chapter, like Volk (1995), I have offered a kind of abbreviated travelogue about the metapattern of positive (darkside) interpersonal communication. To be sure, the editors of this landmark volume have assembled lots chapter that contain exciting new ideas and directions for positive communication in general as well as positive interpersonal communication. In the remainder of my allotted words, I would like to add to this positive chorus by pointing out a few future pathways that communication researchers might take toward increasing our understanding positive interpersonal communication that I will organize by using the Chinese pagoda.

In China, during the Song Dynasty (960–1279) for example, pagodas were seven-story structures with floors generally labeled as: (7) Buddha hall, (6) dharma hall, (5) monks' quarters, (4) depository, (3) gate, (2) pure land hall, and (1) toilet facilities (e.g., see Buswell & Lopez, 2013; Chen, 2002). The symbolic and spiritual (Buddhist) inspiration for the design of pagodas (and, by extension, society) is that higher levels serve higher purposes. That is, enlightenment is positioned at the top level of pagodas and caring for fundamental or basic needs resides closer to the pagoda's foundation. The organization of pagodas is like Maslow's and Max Neef's hierarchies of human values (discussed earlier) where self-actualization is found at the top of the hierarchy and physical needs at the foundation or base. Further, it is assumed that lower levels of needs (and pagodas) should be satisfied (reached) before proceeding to satisfy (or attempt to climb to) higher levels of needs or pagodas. I will invoke the organizing framework of the pagoda to briefly describe seven levels of positive interpersonal communication for researchers to consider for future study as we ascend to new heights of positive interpersonal communication theory and research.

Level 1: Positive Communibiology

According to McCroskey and Beatty (2000), "while nurture certainly has some effects (via cultural influences, formal education, experience, etc.), nature has set forth in one's genetic codes most of what one will become and do" (p. 2). While the term "most" in this statement is debated, few would disagree that biology is a fundamental aspect of being human and that biology can shape behavior. We all have physiological needs that must be met if we are to survive and these needs create drive states that send us in search of needs-satisfaction. Positive and darkside interpersonal communication can certainly play a role in facilitating and inhibiting humans' physiological needs. For example, we give advice to others (or lie) about where and how one's needs for food, clothing, and more can be met optimally. There are countless books, manuals, videos, and websites offering information and opinions, alongside advice from family, friends, and professionals to help us eat better, look better, have sex better, and more, as well as sell us creature comforts for better bathing, toileting, and more. Like all communication, patterns of communicating about our bodies and bodily habits can function positively or darkly, but are always consequential, especially for youth. According to WebMD (e.g., see *Help Teens Build a Healthy Body Image*, 2017), depression and eating disorders can arise from having a poor body image, which in turn is influenced by messages from significant others. Going forward, positive interpersonal communibiological studies are needed to examine the role of personality and temperament in positive communication outcomes. For example, studies of the big five personality factors (i.e., agreeableness, openness, extraversion, conscientiousness, and neuroticism, e.g., see Roccas, Sagiv, Schwartz, & Knafo, 2002, for a study of the big five related to human values) would shed light on the extent to which biology and genetics (nature) is shaping positive and dark interpersonal communication. For example, the personality trait of agreeableness and accompanying qualities like kindness, affection, and prosocial orientations would figure large in positive interpersonal communication development. That is, to what extent does exposure to positive interpersonal communication in early childhood shape to the development of positive interpersonal communication behaviors over the lifespan? Does biology offer an agreeableness set point that we must use communication to manage?

Level 2: Positive Interpersonal Communication Contexts and Settings

Approaching a pagoda, travelers encounter a vista that typically includes fountains, trees, and a view the pagoda in its entirety. During a trip to Xi'an China, as I approached the Big Goose Pagoda (built in the Tang Dynasty, 652; see Big Wild Goose Pagoda, 2017), I noticed an fountain as well as extensive landscaping. The elements of earth, water, nature, sky, and the pagoda's structure formed a gestalt that was both welcoming and inspiring but also intimidating as I neared the gate and anticipated entry. Contexts and settings are important elements in all forms of communication, but their impact on positive interpersonal communication may be under-appreciated or unnoticed by researchers and participants. Sometimes we work hard to stage places where we'd like certain kinds of communication episodes to take place (e.g., a bottle of wine, a flickering candle, and the sounds of Barry White might set the stage for romance). Future positive interpersonal communication studies should examine the "where" of positive interpersonal communication as well as the communication that occurs while anticipating a positive interpersonal communication episode; "We have been talking about the wedding for months and it is now here."

Level 3: Starting Positive Interpersonal Communication

In opening scenes of the American TV situation comedy *Cheers* (1982–1993; see Cheers, 2017), the character of Norm enters the bar as all of its patrons exclaim, "Norm!" This iconic greeting is a wonderful example of positive interpersonal communication that "welcomes" as a person transitions into a communication context. Norm is welcomed into the space with enthusiasm that echoes the lyrics of the show's theme song ". . . Where everybody knows your name and they're always glad you came" (see Portnoy, 2017). Mirivel's (2014) zeros-in on this idea when he featured "greeting" in his model of positive talk. For Mirivel, if positive interpersonal communication is to take place, it should start by a welcome and an invitation to join in the good times. Holding aside for a moment that greetings can be high-jacked by the darkside (discussed earlier), upon entering a pagoda (or *Cheers*), it is important to understand that positive interpersonal communication can lead to more positive interpersonal communication. For example, future research might ask about positive interpersonal communication and immediacy and other variables that than increase the potential for connectedness.

Level 4: Positive Public Interpersonal Communication

Upon entering the pagoda the discourse among strangers and new acquaintances will be shaped by positive social conventions such as politeness, civility, and more. This would include consideration terms of address (title plus last name, first name?), polite social rituals (May I/You may; Please/Thank you, etc.), prosocial topic engagement, positive management of disruptions, and so on. Prior to forming friendships, positive public interpersonal communication could function to satisfy human needs like participating (e.g., affiliating), leisure (e.g., recalling), and identity (e.g., integrating; Max-Neef, 1992). Future studies might ask how does positive public interpersonal communication facilitate participation, or increase participants' needs to affiliate, share memories, and begin to integrate? Before ascending to level five, participants need to be on solid footing with one another. Such footing is built by solidly positive communication rituals that lead to mutuality and good will.

Level 5: Positive Private Interpersonal Communication

Level five is where monks quarter, dwell, or live. It is here that daily private positive interpersonal communication habits become important for helping others and oneself to meet an ever-widening range of recurring needs such as subsistence, protection, affection, participation, leisure, and identity. Increased frequency of contact, potential for intimate contact, potential for self-disclosure, as well as potential for disruption and conflicts, accompanied by increases in vulnerability, and decreases privacy, all potentially risks needs-facilitation by having to rely on and trust others. Dwelling together places an increased emphasis on the need for private positive interpersonal communication habits. That is, day-to-day messages are repeated often including greetings, leave-taking, supporting, mood managing, and more. Due in part to their high frequency, positive private interpersonal communication patterns become regularized into routines and traditions that participants count on to support needs-satisfaction. Also, effective management of interpersonal disruptions is important given the high level of reliance on others in service of needs-satisfaction. Although there might be disagreements, conflicts, and hostilities, the process of human needs-satisfaction does not stop, but continues unabated and may intensify when relational systems are not adequately satisfying participants' needs. With so much going on in level five, it is easy to forget that there are two more floors above this level that not only will lead us to higher physical levels, but summon us to focus on our higher selves.

Level 6: Positive Interpersonal Communication Values and Education

The Dharma refers to a learning hall. It is on this level participants (and monks) are called to learn about each other, the world, and how to realize higher purposes (spiritual, intellectual, etc.). Communication education, like all learning, can take place in formal settings such as university classrooms. However, Socha and Yingling (2010) point out that as people engage in all forms of communication, participants are also learning informally about the process of communication. University communication curricula feature a wide array of theories and methods for communication students to learn and there is much written on instructional communication. What I want to add new at this level is that positive interpersonal communication researchers should consider researching "communication values," or what communicators value about communication itself (see Socha, 2012). A concern Socha (2012) expressed is the increase in valuing of communication expediency, or valuing communication that is quick, concise, and effortless (due in part to reliance on digital communication). There is nothing inherently wrong with expediency and the value may go well with digital communication. However, it clashes with slow, elaborate, effortful, long-form discourse necessary to sustain relationships or workout complex problems. To counter an overvaluing of communication expediency, Socha suggested that the value of communication mindfulness be considered. That is, we should learn to appreciate the details, subtleties, and beauty of longer, slower, more effortful forms of communication, and the many positive benefits these forms of discourse can offer. By learning about how we learn about communication across the lifespan, including what we value about communication itself, we can gain insights into ways to reach higher levels of needs-satisfaction like self- and relational-actualization.

Level 7: Positive Interpersonal Communication and the "Good" Relationship

At the top of pagodas and hierarchies-of-needs alike we summit to view vistas of our highest selves, transcendent relationships, just societies, utopias, and even heavens through philosophical, moral, spiritual, and religious lenses. At the summit of positive interpersonal communication, we hope to see and experience artistic, elegant, refined, and moral communicators; metapatterns of positive interpersonal communication that support self-actualization and relational transcendence; episodes of peak interpersonal communication, and more. Although this may sound like a big ol' pie-in-the-sky (or pig in a poke), Waldron and Kelley (2015) offer a preliminary guidebook to assist us to understand ". . . communication practices that make relationships good, in the moral sense of that word" (p. 1). They call on communication scholars to begin to connect communication ethics to interpersonal communication by developing to a moral vocabulary, a moral agenda, as well as new theories like Negotiated Morality Theory (Waldron & Kelley, 2008). In Waldron and Kelley's volume, Socha and Eller (2015) discuss the process of becoming moral communicators across the lifespan where communicators can learn to choose to engage in metapatterns of interpersonal communication that support human needs-satisfaction and prevent the darkside from spoiling the view at the top.

In conclusion, this chapter has argued that positive interpersonal communication is a metapattern that supports human needs-satisfaction and has suggested there are at least seven levels for interpersonal communication researchers to ascend that promise new vistas and prompt new questions for the continued advancement of positive interpersonal communication research.

References

Bateson, G. (1979). *Mind and nature: A necessary unity.* New York: Dutton.

Baxter, L. A., Norwood, K. M., & Nebel, S. (2012). Aesthetic relating. In T. J. Socha & M. J. Pitts (Eds.), *The positive side of interpersonal communication* (pp. 19–38). New York: Peter Lang.

Beck, G. A., & Socha, T. J. (Eds.). (2015). *Communicating hope and resilience across the lifespan.* New York: Peter Lang.

Big Wild Goose Pagoda in Xi'an of Shaanxi Province. (2017). Retrieved from www.china.org.cn/english/TR-e/43279.htm.

Borchers, C. (2017). Hasan Minhaj's Trump-bashing comedy routine at the White House correspondents' dinner, annotated. *The Washington Post.* Retrieved from www.washingtonpost.com/news/the-fix/wp/2017/04/30/hasan-minhajs-trump-bashing-comedy-routine-at-the-white-house-correspondents-dinner-annotated/?utm_term=.d4a4c091a040

Buswell, R., & Lopez, D. S. (2013). *Princeton dictionary of Buddhism.* Princeton, NJ: Princeton University Press.

Cheers. (2017). Retrieved from www.imdb.com/title/tt0083399/

Chen, J. (2002). An alternative view of the meditation tradition in China: Meditation in the life and works of Daoxuan (596–667). *T'oung Pao,* Second Series, *88*(4/5), 332–395.

Crouch, I. (2017, April 28). Why Donald Trump is skipping the White House correspondents' dinner. *The New Yorker.* Retrieved from www.newyorker.com/culture/cultural-comment/why-donald-trump-is-skipping-the-white-house-correspondents-dinner

Fredrickson, B. L. (2001). The role of positive emotions in positive psychology: The broaden and build theory of positive emotions. *American Psychologist, 56,* 218–226.

Fredrickson, B. L. (2009). *Positivity.* New York: Crown Business.

Gottman, J. M. (1993). *What predicts divorce.* New York: Psychology Press.

Gurr, T. R. (1970). *Why men rebel.* Princeton, NJ: Princeton University Press.

Kelley, D. L. (2012). Forgiveness as restoration: The search for well-being, reconciliation, and relational justice. In T. J. Socha & M. J. Pitts (Eds.), *The positive side of interpersonal communication* (pp. 193–210). New York: Peter Lang.

Kim, Y. Y. (2012). Bring in concert: An explication of synchrony in positive intercultural communication. In T. J. Socha & M. J. Pitts (Eds.), *The positive side of interpersonal communication* (pp. 39–58). New York: Peter Lang.

Maslow, A. (1943). A theory of human motivation. *Psychological Review, 50*(4), 370–396.

Max-Neef, M. (1992). Development and human needs. In P. Ekins & M. Max-Neef (Eds.), *Understanding wealth creation* (pp. 197–213). London: Routledge.

McCroskey, J. C., & Beatty, M. J. (2000). The communibiological perspective: Implications for communication in instruction. *Communication Education, 49,* 1–6.

McCullough, J. D., & Burleson, B. R. (2012). Celebratory support: Messages that enhance the effects of positive experience. In T. J. Socha & M. J. Pitts (Eds.), *The positive side of interpersonal communication* (pp. 229–247). New York: Peter Lang.

Meyer, J. C. (2012). Humor as personal relationship enhancer: Positivity for the long term. In T. J. Socha & M. J. Pitts (Eds.), *The positive side of interpersonal communication* (pp. 142–160). New York: Peter Lang.

Mirivel, J. C. (2012). Communication excellence: Embodying virtues in interpersonal communication. In T. J. Socha & M. J. Pitts (Eds.), *The positive side of interpersonal communication* (pp. 57–72). New York: Peter Lang.

Mirivel, J. C. (2014). *The art of positive communication: Theory and practice.* New York: Peter Lang.

Ohlheiser, A., & Yahr, E. (2017, April 29). A different sort of White House correspondents' dinner. *The Washington Post.* Retrieved from www.washingtonpost.com/news/reliable-source/wp/2017/04/29/a-different-sort-of-white-house-correspondents-dinner/?utm_term=.e68ab8255498

Pitts, M. J., & Socha, T. J. (Eds.). (2013). *Positive communication in health and wellness.* New York: Peter Lang.

Portnoy, G. (2017). *The Cheers story.* Retrieved from www.garyportnoy.com/cheersstory/

Restivo, J. (2017, August 30). Why bridge jumper was taunted. *ABC News.* Retrieved from http://abcnews.go.com/Health/story?id=117255&page=1

Roccas, S., Sagiv, L., Schwartz, S. H., & Knafo, A. (2002). The big five personality factors and personal values. *Personality and Social Psychology Bulletin, 28*(6), 789–801.

Seligman, M. E. P., & Csikszentmihalyi, M. (2000). Positive psychology: An introduction. *American Psychologist, 55,* 5–14.

Sheldon, K. (2009). Providing the scientific backbone for positive psychology: A multi-level conception of human thriving. *Psychological Topics, 18,* 267–284.

Socha, T. J. (2009). Family as agency of potential: Towards a positive ontology of family communication theory and research. In L. R. Frey & K. Cissna (Eds.), *The Routledge handbook of applied communication* (pp. 309–330). New York: Routledge.

Socha, T. J. (2012). In a southern minute: Messages, mindfulness, and pie. *Southern Communication Journal, 77,* 2–9.

Socha, T. J., & Beck, G. A. (2015). Positive communication and human needs: A review and proposed organizing conceptual framework. *Review of Communication, 15,* 173–199.

Socha, T. J., Bernat, S., Harris, S., Hill, B. J., & Hurd, V. (2016, April). *Peak interpersonal communication over the lifespan: Conceptualization and pilot study.* A paper presented at the annual meeting of the Southern States Communication Association, Austin, TX.

Socha, T. J., & Eller, A. (2015). *Parent/caregiver-child communication and moral development: Toward a conceptual foundation of an ecological model of lifespan communication and good relationships.* In V. R. Waldron & D. L. Kelley (Eds.). *Moral talk across the lifespan: Creating good relationships* (pp. 15–34). New York: Peter Lang.

Socha, T. J., & Pitts, M. J. (Eds.). (2012). *The positive side of interpersonal communication.* New York: Peter Lang.

Socha, T. J., & Stoyneva, I. (2014). Positive communication: Towards a new normal. In L. Turner & R. West (Eds.), *The Sage handbook of family communication* (Chapter 25). Thousand Oaks, CA: Sage Publications.

Socha, T. J., & Yingling, J. A. (2010). *Families communicating with children.* Cambridge, UK: Polity.

Spanier, G. B. (1976). Measuring dyadic adjustment: New scales for assessing the quality of marriage and similar dyads. *Journal of Marriage and Family, 38,* 15–28.

Spitzberg, B. H., & Cupach, W. R. (2001). Paradoxes of pursuit: Toward a relational model of stalking-related phenomena. In J. Davis (Ed.), *Stalking, stalkers and their victims: Prevention, intervention, and threat assessment* (pp. 97–136). Boca Raton, FL: CRC Press.

Spitzberg, B. H., & Cupach, W. R. (2007). *The dark side of interpersonal communication.* Mahwah, NJ: Lawrence Erlbaum Associates.

Sullivan, C. F. (2013). Positive relational communication: Impact on health. In M. J. Pitts & T. J. Socha (Eds.), *Positive communication in health and wellness* (pp. 29–42). New York: Peter Lang.

Volk. T. (1995). *Metapatterns: Across space, time, and mind.* New York: Columbia University Press.

Waldron, V., & Kelley, D. L. (2008). *Communicating forgiveness.* Thousand Oaks, CA: Sage Publications.

Waldron, V., & Kelley, D. L. (2015). *Moral talk across the lifespan: Creating good relationships.* New York: Peter Lang.

5

WHAT'S IN A SMILE?

Happiness and Communication From a Cultural Perspective

Jessie K. Finch and Celestino Fernández

Introduction

Cultural differences in communication are well documented in a variety of fields: psychology, sociology, and anthropology, for example. The acknowledgment that different social identities and groups will have different ways of speaking, behaving, and understanding is key to learning about cross-cultural exchange, especially around the topic of happiness. As sociologists, we know that context matters greatly in the daily lives of humans; social context establishes parameters and greatly influences our everyday actions, emotions, and quality of life, including how we communicate, our happiness, and our overall well-being. But how exactly does social context apply to the idea of happiness? Here, we examine how social factors including nationality, race/ethnicity, language, religion, gender, sexuality, age, ability, and socioeconomic status can influence verbal and nonverbal communications of happiness. We examine happiness as it is both understood hedonically (that is, subjective well-being and positive emotions) as well as eudaimonically (self-realization, psychological well-being) (Ryan & Deci, 2001), though most of the research relating to cross-cultural communication of happiness has emphasized the hedonic in investigating subjective well-being across cultures.

By examining several types of culturally specific communication styles, we summarize prior literature on what positive communication means in different social contexts. First, we investigate language differences and translation issues specifically related to the idea of happiness. Second, we look at nonverbal communication styles and positive communication, questioning common assumptions around things such smiling and laughter. Third, power distance and the role of inequality in certain cultural groups is assessed as it relates to cultural-specific communication issues. Finally, we evaluate how individualism versus collectivism influences cultural conceptions of happiness and in turn affects communication styles, including the role of listening and sharing. By examining these four areas of prior research on positive communication, we demonstrate the relevance of cultural differences in experiencing and communicating happiness.

Language Differences and Translation

When discussing happiness—even within one language—there is a spectrum of subtle differences from words that denote mere contentment and general well-being to more extreme words that highlight ecstasy, bliss, and jubilation. This also links back to hedonic versus eudaimonic conceptions—that is, life satisfaction versus personal fulfillment. There are cultural differences even within a language group that vary based on sociocultural differences such as nationality (one may offer a simple "Hi" in the United States compared to a jovial "Cheerio" in England), region ("Howdy"), race/ethnicity ("Yo"), and age ("Sup?").

Beyond differences within language, we can also see significant cross-cultural variation between languages. As Anna Wierzbicka, a Polish linguist asks, "if 14 percent of Germans declare themselves to be *sehr glücklich* whereas 31 percent of Americans declare themselves to be very happy, can these reports be meaningfully compared if *glücklich* does not mean the same thing as happy?" (2004, p. 35). Her work questions whether, and to what extent, national differences recorded in happiness levels can be trusted given potential translation issues as well as cultural differences in national expectations and "pressures" to report well-being (also see our later section on Individualism Versus Collectivism).

While some social scientists have noted this shortcoming (Myers & Diener, 1995; Layard, 2003), there is still much work to be done in better understanding and highlighting the cross-cultural linguistic differences of happiness. Lau, Cummins, and McPherson (2005) completed a study on the development of the Personal Well-being Index (PWI), which is intended for cross-cultural measurement of subjective well-being (SWB), or hedonic happiness. Their study found that across Hong Kong Chinese respondents and Australian respondents, the survey "demonstrated good psychometric performance in terms of its reliability, validity and sensitivity, which are comparable in both countries" (403). However, in looking to add a particular survey item called "satisfaction with own happiness" the Hong Kong population associated both the terms "satisfaction" and "happiness" as the same idea, leading to confusion in responding to the item. The authors suggest more locally contextualized translations for all surveys intended to compare cross-national populations.

Altrov (2013) suggests that recognizing emotion in the context of speech requires cultural context. Based on Russians trying to understand emotional context in Estonian, she finds that "to recognize vocal emotions expressed in another language it is necessary to live in the culture and communicate in its language" (159). At the minimum, deep cultural knowledge is necessary when translating survey instruments to assure common meaning across languages, cultures, and experiences.

Research by Coulmas (2008) documents how the Japanese language does not have exact equivalents for the English words "happy" and "happiness." He explores the meaning of several Japanese words (for example, *sachi*, *fuku*, and *kōfuku*) as they relate to these terms, noting that none of them are equivalent translations. For example, the word most commonly used to translate "happiness" is *shiawase* but Coulmas notes that this word most directly translates to "brining things together." Interestingly, the end result is that the word *happī* has been adopted into Japanese and is commonly heard in Japan when speakers are referring to "happy."

Given the innumerable words in a variety of languages for the deceptively complex concept of happiness, positive communication scholars must bear in mind both linguistic challenges within a language as well as, and particularly, between languages. Likewise, cultural differences, experiences, and contexts must be taken into account.

Nonverbal Communication

Beyond spoken and written language, there are numerous types of nonverbal communications that can signal happiness and they can significantly vary across cultures. While we may take for granted a laugh and a smile as direct communication of positive emotions, are these necessarily universal cues of positive communication? According to Elfenbein and Ambady (2003) "recent research has documented evidence for an in-group advantage, meaning that people are generally more accurate at judging emotions when the emotions are expressed by members of their own cultural group rather than by members of a different cultural group" (159). This has been specifically shown for facial expressions such as smiling. Recognition of happiness in nonverbal forms of communication also varies with one's level of cultural competency with a given group.

While some studies have shown the universality of recognizing facial expressions for several basic "near-universal" emotions (happiness, fear, disgust, anger, surprise, sadness), there are still important subtle cultural differences in each of these areas that allow for members of a cultural "in-group" to better distinguish happiness as demonstrated by facial expressions. Groups with closer-geographical proximity or more frequent cultural exchange do better at understanding the display rules of happiness (how people manage their emotions) as well as the decoding rules (acknowledgment of others' emotional displays) (Elfenbein & Ambady, 2003). This includes the smile, which is usually noted as a universal sign of happiness, though it may also have more nuanced meanings (e.g., a smug smirk or a sinister sneer).

Overall, psychologists have found that "happiness is the earliest and most accurately recognized emotion" in developing children (Vieillard & Guidetti, 2009, p. 79). In fact, children as young as two years old have been able to consistently identify happy faces. Some suggested reasons include the near-universality of the smile or the likelihood of children being greeted with happy faces and thus being able to recognize the only positive emotion of the near-universal emotions.

The smile can also be an indicator of "ideal affect match" or the concept that people have more positive relations with "those whose emotional expressions match how they ideally want to feel" (Park, Blevins, Knutson, & Tsai, 2017, p. 1083). This ideal affect match seems to predictably vary across cultures—even when race and gender are taken into account. In one study, Park et al. (2017) found that European-Americans were more likely to be generous with and trust those who are smiling at moderate and high intensity (meant to indicate excitement) while Koreans were more generous and trusting of those with no smile or a low-intensity smile, indicating calm. This finding suggests that people are more likely to trust and give to those who share culturally relevant emotional values and expressions.

Beyond facial expressions, other forms of nonverbal communication may also signal happiness differently across cultures. Paralinguistics are ways in which the voice is used other than speaking, such as tone, pitch, and sound cues. In studying these paralinguistic cues, laughter seems to be the most commonly associated cue with happiness. In Sauter, Eisner, Ekman, Scott, and Smith (2010) they explore the use of nonverbal emotional vocalizations for the near-universal emotions of anger, disgust, fear, joy, sadness, and surprise in both Western participants and those from secluded villages in Namibia that have not been culturally integrated. Laughter as a cue for amusement was "cross-culturally recognized as signaling joy" in both sets of participants (2010, p. 2411). This supports a "near-universal" acceptance of laughter as an international signifier, though the duration, tone, and pitch may vary with other social identities, such as gender and age. For example, a very early association for laughter comes from tickling between infants and parents.

Given the role of laughter across cultures and that laughter is catching (that is, when one person starts laughing, others frequently join in, even if they do not know what triggered the laughter in the initial person), it is no wonder that "laughter therapy" (also "humor therapy" and "laughter yoga") is now practiced in many countries, including, for example Brazil, England, India, and the United States, to help reduce stress and anxiety and promote overall health, wellness, and happiness. We know that laughing stimulates catecholamines, which in turn release endorphins, and endorphins help us feel relaxed and happy. The many psychological and physiological benefits of (both real and fake) laughter have been extensively documented (MacDonald, 2004).

Other nonverbal behaviors that can convey emotionality are posture, gesture, and body language. This area of communications study is known as kinesics and has been studied in relation to positive communication by a variety of fields, including neuropsychology, computer modeling, and robotics.

In studying affective posture recognition, animation engineers have worked on developing an avatars' body posture to inter-culturally signal specific types of emotionality. Using a generic, full-body, 3D avatar that was non-specific in its culture, gender, or race/ethnicity, researchers compared Japanese, Sri Lankan, and Caucasian Americans' interpretations of emotion from the given pictures of the avatar (Kleinsmith, De Silva, & Bianchi-Berthouze, 2006). Avatar body-models that had lowered heads and slouched posture were recognized as sad in all three cultures. Those with open arms, often raised above their heads, and a seeming saunter in their step (shown as one foot placed in front of another or slightly lifted) were all recognized as happy (Kleinsmith, 2006).

Other research has shown that gestures such as raised arms, a general lack of muscle tension, and leaning inwards can be recognized by adults with 90 percent accuracy to distinguish happiness (Boone & Cunningham, 1998). Indeed, these types of gestures are recognized in fields where the body is an instrument, such as dance. Shikanai, Sawada, and Ishii (2013) developed the Movements Impressions Emotions Model for dance and tested for the conveyance of three emotions through bodily movement: joy, anger, and sadness. In this study, they found that "movements in which the limbs use large amounts of space, turning, and jumping tend to have the greatest effects on the perception of joy" which support previous findings that suggest "expressions of happy feelings are characterized by high levels of energy, a large number of changes, skipping, jumping, and turning" (119). This dynamic demonstration of joy may be more attainable then through higher levels of physical ability to use one's body as a messenger of positivity.

Thus, if one wants to convey positive messages, it may be best do so with both language content that is culturally appropriate as well as recognizable nonverbal communicants of happiness: smiles, laughter, skipping, or, as numerous pop song videos would have us believe, throwing one's hands in the air and waving them around like one just does not care (one also can see clearly recognizable nonverbal communication of emotions in old silent films and by mimes throughout the world).

Power Distance and Inequality

Many cultural differences are based on assumptions of happiness and smiling in comparison to displays of dominance or aggression. This links together the idea that social and cultural position relative to others in a given social hierarchy or power structure may influence how one communicates, especially when and in what manner they are allowed to express happiness.

Hess, Adams, and Kleck (2005) suggest that the rules of facial expressions and happiness as related to power and inequality are different not just between cultures, but also within cultures and between social identities such as gender. She finds support for the stereotypes associated with gender and emotional displays. For example, her research supports the fact that in many Western societies, "anger displays are more appropriate for men and smiling is requisite for women" (Hess et al., 2005, p. 515). This implies men are rated as more dominant while women are rated as more affiliative. Men are expected to smile more frequently than women to be considered affiliative. Contrastingly, women have a more difficult time showing dominance given the masculine "morphological cues associated with perceived high dominance such as a square jaw, thick eyebrows, and receding hairlines" in comparison to women's more frequent "large eyes and narrow jaws [which] lead to perceptions of warmth, honesty, submissiveness, and incompetence" (534). These differences may be further complicated by issues of sexuality, in that non-heteronormative gender displays are often viewed differently.

In addition to these morphological cues, Keating (1981) found "a universal association between smiles and happiness" but in comparisons also found expressions of nonsmiling to be associated with dominance. For example, she also found that facial cues such as a lowered brow were associated with dominance, but in Westernized samples only.

Thus, beyond individual dominance, there is also much evidence to suggest that international differences in social and cultural equality would influence a culture's predisposition to positive communication. That is to say, in cultures where there is more equality, we might find more expression—verbal or nonverbal—of happiness through positive communication.

Other work has emphasized the cultural construction of happiness, especially in the European-American context (Kingfisher, 2013). This work questions the hegemonic nature of happiness as a Western construction and links it to forms of neoliberal governance. This may also manifest in other national- or cultural-level variables.

Throughout the world, racial/ethnic groups with less power and freedom generally tend to be less happy than the dominant racial/ethnic group. However, race/ethnicity and happiness are complicated issues. In particular, in the United States African Americans, Latinos, and indigenous communities tend to report being less happy than the dominant white population. For example, in a national survey, roughly 33 percent of whites stated that they were very happy compared to 28 percent of Hispanics (The Harris Poll #30, 2013). This is understandable in light of the fact that Latinos have been the targets of state and national anti-immigrant legislation (such as SB1070 in the state of Arizona) or ongoing discourse around building a wall on the US-Mexico border to keep out migrants.

Another study (Yap, Settles, & Pratt-Hyatt, 2011) found that among African Americans, the more participants identified with being black (or the more being black was an important part of their identity), the happier they were with life as a whole. This may indicate the positive embracement of one's racial/ethnic identity is key to well-being despite a socially subordinate position in a given racial hierarchy.

Stevenson and Wolfers (2009) found that happiness can be intersectional, affecting different racial groups by gender as well as other identity features. White women of all ages and incomes are substantially less happy today than in the 1970s, while black women have become much happier. In the 1970s white women were the happiest of any group. Stevenson and Wolfers call this "the paradox of declining female happiness" and attribute this problem to socioeconomic forces as well as changing social expectations put on women to now be both model mothers and wives as well as model workers (27).

Finally, as the saying goes, money has indeed been shown to buy happiness (at the minimum, it can by comfort). However, this monetary power differential has its limits as well. Kahneman and Deaton (2010) demonstrate that high income may increase one's overall life satisfaction (eudaimonic happiness) but not their emotional well-being (hedonic happiness). They found that emotional well-being, while associated with income fails to have an effect past an annual income of ~$75,000 in the United States. This demonstrates that one's happiness may be different based on one's socioeconomic status, at least between a threshold of being able to fully care for one's self and one's family. While this finding has not been explicitly replicated internationally, it seems likely that one's level of well-being will cease to increase with one's income past the point of basic necessities being met. Throughout the world, one can identify wealthy, powerful individuals who have "all the comforts of life" but are unhappy, indeed, some are quite miserable, as exemplified, for example, by some world leaders.

These international differences in socioeconomic status may also intersect with other cultural systems that convey power, such as religion. For example, Li & Bond (2010) found that secularism had a "small but statistically very significant" positive relationship to life satisfaction across four waves of the World Values Survey (1984–2004), which covers almost 100 countries and 90 percent of the world's population. However, this was moderated by the country's human development index, suggesting secularism may only increase well-being in more developed nations. This is likely linked to religious emphasis on tradition and conformity, which are also linked to power (Li & Bond, 2010).

As this section has shown, various power dynamics can influence one's happiness as well as how one is able to communicate that happiness. Any credible social science research should understand what power dynamics are at play in a situation to better contextualize the social relations—and as seen above, the search for understanding happiness is no different.

Individualism Versus Collectivism

A final area of exploration that links happiness and communication is the varying cultural predisposition of individualism versus collectivism in a given culture. This distinction is often highlighted at the national level where individualist countries are defined as those promoting independence and self-reliance (such as the United States, much of Continental Europe, Australia, etc.) while conversely, collectivist countries (such as many Asian and Scandinavian countries) highlight group cohesion, cooperation, and rights of the community over the individual. Much research has demonstrated that these are not necessarily mutually exclusive categories, but have nuances such as horizontal and vertical individualism and collectivism, which emphasize variation in power differences. These differences can vary based on demographic issues (race/ethnicity) as well as national level differences and can influence intercultural effectiveness in communication (Okoro, Cardon, Marshall, & Thomas, 2011).

These national level differences have been shown to affect reported well-being, such that "Anglo-American culture fosters and encourages cheerfulness [and] positive thinking" (Wierzbicka, 2004, p. 42) while other cultures may limit the public expression and reporting or expression of hedonic happiness. For example, Sheldon et al. (2017) suggest that Russians and Americans had similar levels of reported Subjective Well-Being, but the Russians were less likely to express or display their happiness, especially to strangers (as opposed to friends and family). This cultural difference highlights the potential for miscommunication based on external displays of happiness.

In our courses on happiness, numerous Asian students have commented on how smiling in public is much more prevalent in the United States than in their home countries. Indeed, these Asian students say that this is one of the cultural differences they immediately noticed when they moved to the United States. McDuff, Girard, and Kaliouby (2017) support this anecdotal evidence in their emphasis on cross-cultural differences in facial behavior. He argues that

> participants from more individualist cultures displayed more brow furrowing overall, whereas smiling depended on both culture and setting. Specifically, participants from more individualist countries were more expressive in the facility setting, while participants from more collectivist countries were more expressive in the home setting. Female participants displayed more smiling and less brow furrowing than male participants overall, with the latter difference being more pronounced in more individualist countries.
>
> *(p. 1)*

Other work by Walsh (1997) highlights the differences between communal broadcasting communication style of Aboriginal cultures in Australia compared to the dyadic nature of Western communication. These differences emphasize a Western individualist conversational habit of eye contact, turn-taking, and short messages compared to a more collectivists, listener-controlled, long-term conversational style used by Aboriginal cultures.

Anthropologist John Bodley (2013) proposes that countries that are organized in small units (one million or less) that allow more people to participate in the government are happier than those living in large nations with large governments. We also know that people living in democracies where they feel greater freedom are happier than those living under totalitarian governments where freedoms are often more restricted. Additionally, people living in countries with strong social safety nets (e.g., universal health care and free education, as is the case in Scandinavian countries) are happier than people living in countries with fewer such support systems (Helliwell, Layard, & Sachs, 2017).

Thus, this section shows that government and national culture provide a cultural lens through which happiness can be expressed and communicated. Those who communicate their well-being in one manner may not be understood by outsiders, or may not care to share that well-being with others from different cultures.

Conclusion

In summary, this chapter seeks to document how culture influences communications, particularly around happiness. While context and social groups can greatly influence how we experience and express happiness, including talking about it, it remains true that every human being has experienced happiness, even if only briefly and intermittently, during their life. Even under the most repressive social, political, religious, and economic environments, throughout the course of human history, people have found occasions for experiencing joy and reasons to celebrate. Such is the strength of the human spirit.

Although there are many cultural contexts and differences that influence happiness, and how we communicate it, smiling seems to be quite universal and genuinely communicates happiness, albeit with important nuances, across nations, cultures, genders, ages, class, etc. Likewise with laughter. One way of remaining upbeat, even under the most difficult and challenging circumstances, which all humans experience during their lifetimes, is to keep smiling: "Just keep smiling. Even when you're sad, keep smiling" (Weiner, 2008, p. 321). Likewise with laughter. Smiling and laughing during difficult situations does not mean that one should simply accept dire circumstances. Rather, it is a recognition of the healing power of smiles and laughter and the strength they give us to be able to carry on, to work against those problematic, repressive, and depressive circumstances in an effort to change them for the better. Such is the power of positive communication.

Both smiling and laughter have healthy physiological and psychological benefits, and both smiling and laughter are contagious. Thus, our smiles and laughter contribute not only to our well-being they do the same for the people around us, regardless of cultural or other social differences.

References

Altrov, R. (2013). Aspects of cultural communication in recognizing emotions. *Trames*, *17*(2), 159. doi:10.3176/tr.2013.2.04

Bodley, J. H. (2013). *The small nation solution: How the world's smallest nations can solve the world's biggest problems.* Lanham: Rowman and Littlefield.

Boone, R. T., & Cunningham, J. G. (1998). Children's decoding of emotion in expressive body movement: The development of cue attunement. *Developmental Psychology*, *34*(5), 1007–1016. doi:10.1037/001 2-1649.34.5.1007

Coulmas, F. (2008). *The quest for happiness in Japan* (DIJ Working Paper 2009/1). German Institute for Japanese Studies. http://tinyurl.com/Coulmas (last accessed 2018).

Elfenbein, H. A., & Ambady, N. (2003). Universals and cultural differences in recognizing emotions. *Current Directions in Psychological Science*, *12*(5), 159–164. doi:10.1111/1467-8721.01252

The Harris Poll #30. (2013). Are you happy? It may depend on age, race/ethnicity and other factors. Harris Insights & Analytics, Rochester, NY. Retrieved from www.theharrispoll.com/health-and-life/Are_You_Happy__It_May_Depend_on_Age__Race_Ethnicity_and_Other_Factors.html

Helliwell, J., Layard, R., & Sachs, J. (2017). *World happiness report 2017.* New York: Sustainable Development Solutions Network.

Hess, U., Adams, R., & Kleck, R. (2005). Who may frown and who should smile? Dominance, affiliation, and the display of happiness and anger. *Cognition & Emotion, 19*(4), 515–536. doi:10.1080/02699930441000364

Kahneman, D., & Deaton, A. (2010). High income improves evaluation of life but not emotional well-being. *Proceedings of the National Academy of Sciences of the United States of America, 107*(38), 16489–16493. doi:10.1073/pnas.1011492107

Keating, C. F. (1981). Culture and the perception of social dominance from facial expression. *Journal of Personality and Social Psychology, 40*(4), 615–626. doi:10.1037/0022-3514.40.4.615

Kingfisher, C. (2013). Happiness: Notes on history, culture and governance. *Health, Culture and Society, 5*(1), 67–82. doi:10.5195/hcs.2013.145

Kleinsmith, A., De Silva, P. R., & Bianchi-Berthouze, N. (2006). Cross-cultural differences in recognizing affect from body posture. *Interacting with Computers, 18*(6), 1371–1389. doi:10.1016/j.intcom.2006.04.003

Lau, A. L. D., Cummins, R. A., & McPherson, W. (2005). An investigation into the cross-cultural equivalence of the personal well-being index. *Social Indicators Research, 72*(3), 403–430. doi:10.1007/s11205-004-0561-z

Layard, R. (2003). Has social science a clue?: What is happiness? Are we getting happier? *Lionel Robbins Memorial Lectures,* London School of Economics, London, UK. http://eprints.lse.ac.uk/47425/1/__libfile_REPOSITORY_Content_Layard_Has%20social%20science%20a%20clue%20what%20is%20happiness_Has%20social%20science%20a%20clue%20what%20is%20happiness%20(LSE%20RO).pdf

Li, L. M. W., & Bond, M. H. (2010). Does individual secularism promote life satisfaction? The moderating role of societal development. *Social Indicators Research, 99*(3), 443–453. doi:10.1007/s11205-010-9591-x

MacDonald, C. M. (2004). A chuckle a day keeps the doctor away. *Journal of Psychosocial Nursing and Mental Health Services, 42*(3), 18–25.

McDuff, D., Girard, J. M., & Kaliouby, R. E. (2017). Large-scale observational evidence of cross-cultural differences in facial behavior. *Journal of Nonverbal Behavior, 41*(1), 1–19. doi:10.1007/s10919-016-0244-x

Myers, D. G., & Diener, E. (1995). Who is happy? *Psychological Science, 6*(1), 10–19. doi:10.1111/j.1467-9280.1995.tb00298.x

Okoro, E., Cardon, P. W., Marshall, B., & Thomas, O. (2011). Cross-cultural communication and dimensions: A hybrid analysis of horizontal and vertical individualist and collectivist tendencies among African American and European American management students. *Journal of Diversity Management (Online), 6*(3), 7–18.

Park, B., Blevins, E., Knutson, B., & Tsai, J. L. (2017). Neurocultural evidence that ideal affect match promotes giving. *Social Cognitive and Affective Neuroscience,* 1083–1096. doi:10.1093/scan/nsx047

Ryan, R. M., & Deci, E. L. (2001). On happiness and human potentials: A review of research on hedonic and eudaimonic well-being. *Annual Review of Psychology, 52*(1), 141–166. doi:10.1146/annurev.psych.52.1.141

Sauter, D. A., Eisner, F., Ekman, P., Scott, S. K., & Smith, E. E. (2010). Cross-cultural recognition of basic emotions through nonverbal emotional vocalizations. *Proceedings of the National Academy of Sciences of the United States of America, 107*(6), 2408–2412. doi:10.1073/pnas.0908239106

Sheldon, K. M., Titova, L., Gordeeva, T. O., Osin, E. N., Lyubomirsky, S., & Bogomaz, S. (2017). Russians inhibit the expression of happiness to strangers: Testing a display rule model. *Journal of Cross-Cultural Psychology, 48*(5), 718–733. doi:10.1177/0022022117699883

Shikanai, N., Sawada, M., & Ishii, M. (2013). Development of the movements impressions emotions model: Evaluation of movements and impressions related to the perception of emotions in dance. *Journal of Nonverbal Behavior, 37*(2), 107–121. doi:10.1007/s10919-013-0148-y

Stevenson, B., & Wolfers, J. (2009). *The paradox of declining female happiness.* Discussion Paper No. 4200. Institute for the Study of Labor, Bonn, Germany.

Vieillard, S., & Guidetti, M. (2009). Children's perception and understanding of (dis)similarities among dynamic bodily/facial expressions of happiness, pleasure, anger, and irritation. *Journal of Experimental Child Psychology, 102*(1), 78. doi:10.1016/j.jecp.2008.04.005

Walsh, M. (1997). *Cross cultural communication problems in Aboriginal Australia.* North Australia Research Unit (NARU). Retrieved from https://openresearch-repository.anu.edu.au/handle/1885/47329

Weiner, E. (2008). *The geography of bliss: One grump's search for the happiest places in the world.* New York: Hachette Book Group.

Wierzbicka, A. (2004). "Happiness" in cross-linguistic & cross-cultural perspective. *Daedalus, 133*(2), 34–43. doi:10.1162/001152604323049370

Yap, C. Y., Settles, I. H., & Pratt-Hyatt, J. S. (2011). Mediators of the relationship between racial identity and life satisfaction in a community sample of African American women and men. *Cultural Diversity and Ethnic Minority Psychology, 17*(1), 89–97.

6

ON THE NATURE OF PEAK COMMUNICATION

Communication Behaviors That Make a Difference on Well-Being and Happiness

Julien C. Mirivel

Introduction

In our interview with one of our participants, Kristen shared a moment with her father. The event took place on the same day she announced to her husband that she wanted to divorce. Driving through North Dakota, she met her father, a "stoic, hard core North Dakotan who doesn't talk," at her aunt's house. He sat next to her, not making direct eye contact. And as Kristen described the moment, her voice cracked for a second. He said: "I just want you to be happy." "That's all he said," she said in a whisper.

For Kristen, this moment exemplifies peak communication—a moment of human interaction that brought a great sense of fulfillment, happiness, and joy (see Gordon, 1985). It also illustrates that when it comes to human interaction, "there are no ordinary moments" (Millman, 2000, p. 138). Every moment of human communication is irreproducible and unique. And what people say and do—with words or deeds—can affect people in the present and in the future. This chapter explores the small, but concrete, behaviors that seem to create happiness and joy for people. In it, I pose the following questions: (a) What positive communication behaviors constitute peak communication? And (b) What are the short-term and long-term effects of peak communication moments on personal and relational happiness?

To answer these questions, I proceed as follows. First, I overview the literature on the study of positive communication. I describe its emergence in the field of communication and introduce a model of positive communication I developed (Mirivel, 2014). Then, I describe the project that is the basis for this chapter and our methodology. The heart of the paper reveals what speech acts tend to create peak moments of interpersonal communication. In the conclusion, I reflect on these findings and consider the practical and theoretical implications.

Review of Literature

In the field of communication studies, there is a growing movement that focuses on the nature and impact of positive communication (see Socha & Beck, 2015). This is, of course, exemplified by this volume. But there is an important history that got us to this point. In this section, I trace this history and introduce the key concepts that drive the chapter.

For decades, scholars in the field of communication have focused on the darkside (Cupach & Spitzberg, 2007). Researchers have studied people in conflict, the nature of hurtful messages, how revenge is experienced and enacted, and how aggression and violence occur in interpersonal communication (see respectively Ting-Toomey et al., 1991; Vangelisti, 2007; Yoshimura, 2007; Dailey, Lee, & Spitzberg, 2007; Morgan & Wilson, 2007). When the focus is not this explicit, the natural impulse has been to study the dilemmas or problems that people face in interaction (e.g., Tracy & Tracy, 1998). Even in most textbooks in the field, the focus is on what individuals or groups do not do well rather than what works. Today, however, there is a growing group of scholars who want to study what people do well in human interaction—on the great things that people are capable of doing rather than their shortcomings. It is scholarship designed to cultivate the best of human experience and improve communication *as a practice*.

The positive movement emerged in the field of psychology with the work of Seligman (2002). Seligman, for example, studied the nature of happiness and the virtues that exemplify human character and integrity. His work led to the development of several centers across disciplines that focus on the positive side. As just one example, the Ross School of Business at the University of Michigan created a *Center for Positive Organizations* that draws on Seligman's scholarship. In the field of communication, the positive movement is led by Tom Socha, Professor at Old Dominion University, who began with an article published in Frey and Cissna's (2009) *Routledge Handbook of Applied Communication Research*. The chapter, titled "Family as agency of potential," drew on Seligman's work and the other positive psychologists such as Mihalyi Csikszentmihalyi (1990) and made connections with research on family communication. That point of departure led to a theme on "Positive Communication" at the 2010 annual meeting of the Southern States Communication Association Conference. Today, there is an established agenda and framework for positive communication research and scholarship (for a review of this movement, see Socha & Beck, 2015).

In 2012, Socha and Pitts published the first volume on positive communication. The edited volume, titled "The Positive Side of Interpersonal Communication" united scholars to "articulate an initial framework for the study of interpersonal communication based on two key concepts drawn from positive psychology" (Socha & Beck, 2015, p. 6). Together, scholars explored the nature of virtues in human communication (Mirivel, 2012), the nature of intimacy and connection (Nussbaum, Miller-Day, & Fisher, 2012), and supportive communication (MacGeorge, Feng, Wildum, & Doherty, 2012). The edited volume and its chapters led the positive communication movement. It was followed in 2013 by another edited volume by Socha and Pitts (2013) titled "Positive communication in Health and Wellness." Overall, the book argued that positive communication, "as experienced in the contexts of relationships, groups, and organizations, is an essential part of good health and well-being" (Socha & Beck, 2015, p. 179). These volumes have accelerated the focus on positive communication.

In spite of these efforts, many questions remain unanswered. What is the nature of positive communication? What communication behaviors function positively in human interaction? What interpersonal communicative moments foster happiness and well-being? And what communicative actions embody the great virtues—compassion, courage, or justice? There are two concepts already existing in the field that can speak to those questions; the concepts of memorable messages and peak communication. Memorable messages are the first construct. Originally introduced by Knapp, Stohl, and Reardon (1981), memorable messages are "interpersonal messages reported to be remembered for a long time and to have a profound influence on a person's life" (p. 27). They capture short, meaningful phrases that are perceived to be influential. They can be inspiring. In their original article, for example, Knapp et al. (1981) quoted Carl Rogers's professor who said to him: "Don't be a damned ammunition wagon; be a rifle." But they can also be hurtful as in someone saying: "You will never amount to anything." With this concept, scholars studied a wide range of topics and contexts, including how parents teach the difference between what is right and what is wrong (Waldron, Kloeber, Goman, Piemonte, & Danaher, 2014), how mothers talk about relationships with their daughters (Kellas, 2010), or the nature of difficult conversations that take place between physicians and parents in intensive care (Brodsky et al., 2014). Memorable messages, in short, are impactful for recipients, but not necessarily positive or inspiring. They are simply examples of short phrases that people in everyday life can easily remember as having impacted them. Memorable messages are therefore different from our second concept: peak communication.

Peak communication, by definition, refers to "our 'greatest moments' in interpersonal communication, our moments of highest mutual understanding, happiness and fulfillment deriving from the process of communicating with other human beings" (Gordon, 1985, p. 824). Grounded in the work of the famous psychologist Abraham Maslow, peak communication is a form of peak experience. In the original work introducing the concept, Gordon found that most peak communicative moments were first described as moments involving "loving acceptance," "open-mindedness," and "spontaneity." Many participants, for example, rated the following statements to be very true: "I saw the beauty of the person I was communicating with, and the beauty of our communication itself, just as it was" or "I saw and heard without my own categories and labels and judgments getting in the way like they usually do." Gordon's research, however, was grounded in pre-developed statements about the nature of peak communication, not directly collecting narratives of peak communication. And more interestingly, the concept of peak communication has received little attention from scholars across the discipline. This chapters responds to these limitations and extends our understanding of peak communication.

With these concepts as a point of reference, I am asking: "What positive communication behaviors are constitutive of peak communication moments? Or said differently, what acts of communication are present when people experience happiness or joy or closeness?" To answer these questions, and the relationships between positive communication and peak communication, I draw on a model of positive communication that I developed (see Mirivel, 2014). The model is both descriptive and normative. As displayed in Figure 6.1, it features principles of human communication and speech acts that exemplify positive communication and it is designed to inspire everyday people to communicate more positively in personal and professional contexts. It is a model that is heuristic and theoretically grounded. Consider the proposal.

Positive communication refers to "any verbal and nonverbal behaviors that function positively in the course of human interaction" (p. 7). They are behaviors that researchers have shown to produce positive consequences or effects on the next turn of talk, the relationship, the context in which people operate, or the larger culture in which interactants are communicating. To draw on Pitts and Socha (2013), positive communication "includes all of the communicative processes and forms which we would be proud to model and teach to children" (p. 2012a, p. 324). The model, as shown in Figure 6.1, proposes six behaviors that exemplify the nature of positive communication: (a) greeting, (b) asking, (c) complimenting, (d) disclosing, (e) encouraging, and (f) listening. For each behavior in the model, there is a corresponding function, which is designed to promote a constitutive view of communication (see Craig, 2006). For example, the act of greeting serves the critical function of creating human contact and acknowledging that another person exists. Asking open-ended questions facilitates the process of discovery and changes the direction of interaction. Complimenting foregrounds a person's strengths and therefore affects a person's sense of self. Disclosing serves the primary function of deepening relationships and invites closeness and intimacy. Encouraging is an act of giving and provide social support. And listening, when it is practiced deeply, can transcend perceived differences. At the heart of the model is the idea that if a person chooses to practice positive communication, they are making the

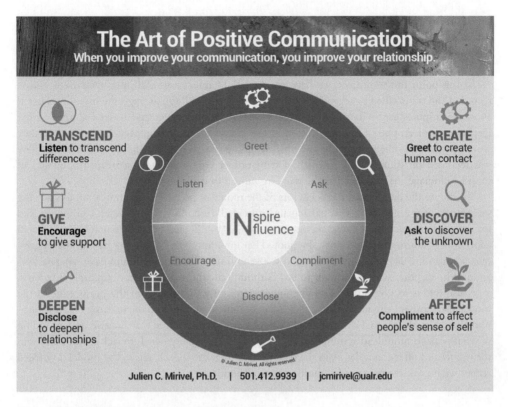

Figure 6.1 Mirivel's Model of Positive Communication

decision to inspire and influence others in a productive direction and helping to co-create better social words (for more information, see Mirivel, 2014, 2017; Mirivel & Fuller, 2017).

To summarize, this chapter explores what behaviors of positive communication create moments of happiness, joy, or mutual understanding. The simple objective is to identify what those behaviors might be and discover the ways in which a person could practice communication to make a difference on personal and social well-being. In the next section, I describe the methodology for this project.

Methodology

This chapter reflects the beginning phases of a larger project called *The UA Little Rock Peak Communication Project*. The project is directed by two major research questions:

RQ1: What positive communication behaviors constitute peak communication?
RQ2: What are the short-term and long-term effects of peak communication moments on personal and relational happiness?

To answer these questions, several graduate students and I are interviewing adults of all walks of life about their peak conversations. The interview is guided by a simple, semi-structured, interview schedule that asks participants to describe three instances of peak communication moments in their lives. For each peak communication moment, participants are asked to narrate the event, to describe what was said, to reflect on what they learned from the moment, and to think about the short and long-term effects of the interaction. In addition to collecting data about the nature of peak communication, the project is also creating meaningful moments of connection, recording stories that can be shared with others, and in some ways, providing an opportunity for participants to relive an experience that was good and positive for them.

At this point in the project, we have conducted 14 interviews. All interviews were video-recorded and transcribed to reproduce on paper what was said. On average, the interviews lasted about 25 minutes each. To recruit participants, a graduate student and I asked alumni of the Department of Applied Communication at the University of Arkansas at Little Rock if they would participate. Then, we used a snowball sampling system (Goodman, 1961). Each interview was recorded on campus and videotaped with proper equipment to maximize the quality of sound and image. After collecting the data, we moved toward the analysis.

To analyze the data, I used the behaviors of the model of positive communication to code the speech acts of the narratives that participants provided. In coding for messages, I simply looked for the general function of each message (e.g., Gee, 2014). So, for instance, when Kristen shared another peak communication story, she quoted her grandmother: "You don't have to marry any-one, you can live next door to the man you love and never marry them and have separate lives and just be together when you want to be." Although the message may serve multiple functions, a general one is to give advice and encourage autonomy. Viewed from the perspective of the model, this moment aligned with the speech act of "encouraging" and the research on social sup-port that grounds this part of the model. The objective is to provide a qualitative understanding of what peak communicative moments are about. In this chapter, then, I unpack each behavior in the model and offer examples from the data to show that the speech acts in the model do indeed reflect what peak communicative moments are all about.

Results

This section features some of the stories we collected to illustrate that positive communication behaviors cultivate experiences that produce happiness, joy, or mutual understanding. Our pre-liminary findings are that each behavior in the model of positive communication can contribute to personal and relational happiness and well-being.

In the first part of the model, I propose that greetings create human contact. We know from research in a variety of contexts, including education (Bernstein-Yamashiro, 2004), medicine (Makoul, Zick, & Green, 2007, p. 1174), the workplace (Waldvogel, 2007) and every day human interaction (Sacks, 1992), that greetings serve critical functions. They are used to acknowledge the presence of another person, initiates the interaction, cues the identity and relationship of participants, and often manage both relational and institutional goals. In this study, we also found that other-initiated greetings can produce peak communication and affect a person for the long-term. This is well-illustrated by Frankie's story.

In describing his third peak communication example, Frankie revealed some of the difficulties he had faced. "I was going through an emotional depression," he said, "I didn't want to wake up in the morning because I was stressed or overwhelmed." He added, "I was sleeping day after day and there is one person that just kind of flipped that." This is what happened:

> This person just approached me and said "how is your day going?" and I said "it's going well thank you for asking" and he's like, "no no, I mean, how are you doing?" I first thought he asked me how my day was going but he was really asking how I was personally doing. It caught me off guard and I said, "I'm doing well things are going great." That person just stopped and said, "I need you to go deeper because I know you are not doing ok."

The rest of the conversation is personal—with the person asking lots of questions and providing encouragement and Frankie feeling listened to and encouraged. In reflecting on the moment, Frankie said, "That moment pulled me out of where I was at and made me believe in myself."

One personal greeting is all it may take to affect another person positively and to impact them. This was certainly true for Frankie. Peak communicative moments, thus, can be created by the simple act of greeting which may pave the way for other important acts of human communication. One of the those is the use of questions.

In the same story, Frankie described how the other person directed the conversation with questions. He said, "I kept making it superficial and he just wanted to go deeper. He kept asking questions and saying I didn't have to respond but that he was there if I needed to talk." The model of positive communication proposes that questions can help people discover one another more deeply. Specifically, the model encourages the use of open-ended questions to liberate conversations. In this study, we are currently noting that, as illustrated in Frankie's story, asking questions also helps to create peak communication.

In one of our participants' story, for example, she described an encounter with a previous spouse. The moment was the last conversation she had with this person and it provided closure and relief. One of the key moments in the conversation involved the use of questions. She said, "we both talked about wanting the other to be happy." She quoted the moment: "Are you happy? I am happy. Are you happy? I am happy. Okay we are happy, we are good."

In another example, Sayra recounted an interaction between her and her daughter in which they celebrated one of her daughter's recital, for which unbeknownst to Sayra, she played the opening exercises. "I was proud and humbled," she said in the interview. In describing the moment, though, she zoomed in on her attempts to discover even more about what happened (since parents could not attend this church event). "I asked her," she explained, "'How did it feel?' and 'were you nervous?'" As she described it, she probed more and more about the events to share the moment with her daughter, asked about her experience, and ultimately learned to have more faith in her daughter's abilities.

Questions are at the heart of human interaction. The data show that asking questions can help to create peak communicative moments.

The third part of the model focuses on the speech act of complimenting. It proposes that complimenting is the communicative choice to affect others positively. This is grounded in the principle that communication is consequential and irreversible. By definition, complimenting is a "speech act which explicitly or implicitly attributes credit to someone other than the speaker" (Telaumbanua, 2012, p. 34). In our interviews, many stories of peak communication involved receiving compliments from others—often by parents, teachers, bosses, or mentors.

In one story, Alexandra reported on an email she received late in the night from her supervisor. This is what she said:

> My supervisor emailed me that night. It was pretty late, around midnight. The title of the email was "In case you didn't know." It was a three-paragraph long email discussing how she admired the way that I communicated in that moment because of the way I was offering advice [. . .] she said she admired the way I communicated and the confidence level I had. That made me cry because she is someone that I really admire.

Often, and as is displayed in Alexandra's story, a compliment can affect others positively. In many stories we collected thus far, it is the experience of being affirmed that matters most. Kerri, for instance, received a phone call from her best friend: "She just called me and said she was really proud of me [. . .] it was an affirmation that I made the right decision."

According to the model of positive communication, the most important lesson in the third part of the model is not complimenting *per se*; it is the realization that one's personal communication affects people. Our peak communication stories support this truth: that what is said and expressed matters.

In the fourth part of the model, I argue that disclosing deepens the relationships that we have with others. This claim is well supported by several key theories in the field, including Social Penetration Theory (Altman & Taylor, 1973), Relational Dialectics (Baxter & Montgomery, 1996), and Communication Boundary Management Theory (Petronio, 2002). I recognize, of course, that the process of revealing information is more complex than simply choosing to disclose—this is not a rule of law, but rather a guide for action. In the data, we found that the act of disclosing is the most dominant speech act in peak communication narratives. The decision to speak up and be vulnerable connects people more deeply.

In one story, a participant shared the first time he and his partner disclosed that they were in love. Caught in a small moment in the car, he made eye contact and said, "I think I am in love with you." Immediately, she responded: "I am in love with you too." Expressions of love or affection was a big focus, but often it was short news that made a difference. In another story, it was a graduate coordinator calling to say: "You've been accepted to graduate school." In another, it was a short email that confirmed a long-desired job. The point is that peak communicative moments are created by the willingness and courage to speak up, to reveal who we are and how we feel. And when people do that, they can create peak experiences.

The fifth part of the model draws on the vast literature on social support (see Burleson & MacGeorge, 2002). By definition, social support refers to "verbal and nonverbal communication between recipients and providers that reduces uncertainty about the situation, the self, the other, or the relationship and functions to enhance a perception of personal control in one's experience" (Albrecht & Adelman, 1987, p. 19). Based on the literature, there are multiple forms of social support, including instrumental support (sharing information), emotional support (reducing emotional distress), and esteem support (affecting another person's self-esteem). The model proposes that encouraging is one exemplifying form of social support in part because it moves a person toward their potential.

In the data, we found multiple examples of encouraging behaviors. My favorite story, though, was recounted by LaShonda. In her peak communication, she narrated an interaction with a college recruiter. To set it up, she talked about how she was just an "average kid with average grades in college" and had "never thought about going to college because we were so poor." In the story, the recruiter slowed down his speech and looked at LaShonda straight in the eyes and said: "you can be anything you want to be." LaShonda was, in fact, offered an athletic scholarship, attended college, and the recruiter kept in touch with her for the next two years. In the key conversation, as she was transferring to a better school, he said to her: "be confident, be strong, be resilient." Her voice slowed down at that point in her story and she added: "These words are my foundation, and I've built my life around them."

Receiving encouragements was at the heart of our participants' peak communicative experiences. Often, and as the act of encouraging is designed to do, it was simply a short message that pointed toward a person's future; "you should be a teacher," one of our participants recounted. The point is that any message that supports another person and provides a tangible act of giving matters in the realm of human connection.

The final behavior in the model of positive communication is listening. Here, I argue that listening deeply to another person can transcend human separateness. By its very nature, peak communicative experiences are memorable, connect people more deeply, and produce a state that positive psychologists refer to as flow (Csikszentmihalyi, 1990). During the experience, participants may be completely involved with one another, fully engaged, and immersed, and through that experience feel a deep sense of connection. One critical behavior in human interaction that sustains that kind of experience is the act of listening. As Bodie (2012) explained, "listening is *the* quintessential positive interpersonal communication behavior as it connotes an appreciation of and an interest in the other" (p. 109; emphasis in original).

Theoretically, deep listening involves a high degree of openness, empathy, a warm approach to others, and nonverbal cues that communicate investment and interest in the other. In one peak moment, Kristena described how she felt listened to and understood. "I had a conversation with my friend Melissa," she explained, "and it really resonated with me and made me feel really connected to her." In the interview, she did not describe what exactly was said or done, but she could describe the general experience and the topics being covered—the female body, self-acceptance, and self-love. "I felt happy," she said, "I felt like I wasn't alone." This conversation, she said, "helped to solidify who I was and it opened up our relationship."

The value of being listened to cannot underestimated. As one participant put it in a moment of gratitude, "I had someone that listened and generally cared." When people do that in human interaction, they can transcend their differences and create flow-like experiences.

In sum, the findings of this study show that the speech acts of greeting, asking, complimenting, disclosing, encouraging, and listening are constitutive of peak communicative experiences. With that in mind, let me consider the implications of this statement and conclude.

Conclusion

The UA Little Rock Peak Communication Project is designed to explore the nature of peak communication in people's lives. More importantly, it seeks to answer big, lifelong, questions about the nature of positive communication, the impact of such behaviors on individual and group happiness and well-being, and it will cultivate an appreciation of what human beings are capable of doing in the realm of human interaction. Overall, the project is posing two research questions: (a) What positive communication behaviors constitute peak communication? And (b) What are the short-term and long-term effects of peak communication moments on personal and relational happiness?

In this chapter, I answered the first question by applying a model of positive communication as a theoretical lens through which to examine the data. In examining the peak communication stories, I looked for the specific speech acts that participants reported and categorized the general function of the message, as a discourse analyst would do. Our preliminary findings support the model of positive communication: the behaviors of greeting, asking questions, complimenting, disclosing encouraging, and listening are all featured in our participants' peak communication narratives. More importantly, what the data are showing is that those behaviors are constitutive of peak experiences, and therefore can help to promote experiences in which participants feel joy, happiness, relief, and gratitude. In that sense, the data affirm the normative premise of the model—that practicing those behaviors can foster positive human emotions and relationships.

The findings should be taken with a grain of salt. These are preliminary findings designed to illustrate the functions of model in light of the narratives that we collected. More data will need to be collected to understand more fully the range of communication behaviors that foster peak communicative experiences. For example, I also found that parent-child interactions were particularly significant, but often did not illustrate any specific behaviors in the model. This is an area that needs to be further explored in part because peak communication moments might be less about what is said or done, and more about feeling connected to another person. Solving this puzzle and others is the quest of the UA Little Rock Peak Communication Project.

In the meantime, and for the purposes of this chapter and the handbook of which it is a part, I am proposing that practicing positive communication has the potential to create peak communicative experiences. Every person can make a difference in their lives and the lives of others by making simple communicative choices. When we greet others, we can create human contact and welcome connection. When we ask questions, we place ourselves in a mode of discovery. When we choose to compliment, we can affect another person's sense of self—who they are and who they become. When we have the courage to disclose personal information, we can deepen the relationships around us. When we choose to encourage others, we can use communication as a gift. And when we listen more deeply, we can transcend our perceived differences. And if we can all learn to make these small, but impactful, communicative choices, then I believe that we can realize the wisdom in Millman's (2000) novel, and transform any ordinary moment of human interaction into an extraordinary one.

References

Albrecht, T. L., & Adelman, M. B. (1987). *Communicating social support.* Thousand Oaks, CA: Sage Publications.

Altman, I., & Taylor, D. (1973). *Social penetration: The development of interpersonal relationships.* New York: Holt, Rinehart and Winston.

Baxter, L. A., & Montgomery, B. M. (1996). *Relating: Dialogues and dialectics.* New York: Guilford Press.

Bernstein-Yamashiro, B. (2004). Learning relationships: Teacher-student connections, learning, and identity in high school. *New Directions for Student Leadership*, (103), 55–70.

Bodie, G. D. (2012). listening as positive communication. In T. J. Socha & M. J. Pitts (Eds.). *The positive side of interpersonal communication* (pp. 109–126). New York: Peter Lang Publishing.

Brodsky, D., Lamiani, G., Andrade, O., Johnson, V. M., Luff, D., & Meyer, E. C. (2014). Memorable conversations in neonatal intensive care: A qualitative analysis of interprofessional provider perspectives. *Journal of Nursing Education and Practice, 4*(3), 38.

Burleson, B., & MacGeorge, E. (2002). Supportive communication. In M. K. Knapp & J. A. Daly (Eds.), *Handbook of interpersonal communication.* Thousand Oaks, CA: Sage Publications.

Craig, R. T. (2006). Communication as a practice. In G. J. Shepherd, J. St. John, & T. Striphas (Eds.), *Communication as . . .: Perspectives on theory* (pp. 38–47). Thousand Oaks, CA: Sage Publications.

Csikszentmihalyi, M. (1990). *Flow: The psychology of optimal experience.* New York: HarperCollins.

Cupach, W. R., & Spitzberg, B. H. (Eds.). (2007). *The dark side of interpersonal communication.* Mahwah, NJ: Lawrence Erlbaum Associates.

Dailey, R. M., Lee, C. M., & Spitzberg, B. H. (2007). Communicate aggression: Toward a more interactional view of psychological abuse. In W. R. Cupach & B. H. Spitzberg (Eds.), *The dark side of interpersonal communication* (pp. 297–326). Mahwah, NJ: Lawrence Erlbaum Associates.

Frey, L. R., & Cissna, K. N. (Eds.). (2009). *Routledge handbook of applied communication research.* New York: Routledge.

Gee, J. P. (2014). *An introduction to discourse analysis: Theory and method.* New York: Routledge.

Goodman, L. A. (1961). Snowball sampling. *The Annals of Mathematical Statistics*, 148–170.

Gordon, R. D. (1985). Dimensions of peak communication experiences: An exploratory study. *Psychological Reports, 57*(3), 824–826.

Kellas, J. K. (2010). Transmitting relational worldviews: The relationship between mother-daughter memorable messages and adult daughters' romantic relational schemata. *Communication Quarterly, 58*(4), 458–479.

Knapp, M. L., Stohl, C., & Reardon, K. K. (1981). "Memorable" messages. *Journal of Communication, 31*(4), 27–41.

MacGeorge, E., Feng, B., Wildum, K., & Doherty, E. (2012). Supportive communication: A positive response to negative life events. In T. Socha & M. Pitts (Eds.), *The positive side of interpersonal communication* (pp. 211–228). New York: Peter Lang.

Makoul, G., Zick, A., & Green, M. (2007). An evidence-based perspective on greetings in medical encounters. *Archives of Internal Medicine, 167*(11), 1172–1176.

Millman, D. (2000). *Way of the peaceful warrior: A book that changes lives.* Tiburon, CA: HJ Kramer Inc.

Mirivel, J. C. (2012). Communication excellence. In T. J. Socha & M. J. Pitts (Eds.), *The positive side of interpersonal communication* (pp. 57–72). New York: Peter Lang.

Mirivel, J. C. (2014). *The art of positive communication: Theory and practice.* New York, NY: Peter Lang Publishing.

Mirivel, J. C. (2017). *How communication scholars think and act: A lifespan perspective.* New York, NY: Peter Lang Publishing.

Mirivel, J. C., & Fuller, R. (2017). Relational talk at work. In B. Vine (Ed.) *The Routledge handbook of language in the workplace* (pp. 216–227). New York: Routledge.

Morgan, W., & Wilson, S. R. (2007). Explaining child abuse as a lack of safe ground. In W. R. Cupach & B. H. Spitzberg (Eds.), *The dark side of interpersonal communication* (pp. 327–362). Mahwah, NJ: Lawrence Erlbaum Associates.

Nussbaum, J. F., Miller-Day, M., & Fisher, C. L. (2012). "Holding each other all night long": Communicating intimacy in older adulthood. In T. J. Socha & M. J. Pitts (Eds.), *The positive side of interpersonal communication* (pp. 91–108). New York: Peter Lang.

Petronio, S. (2002). *Boundaries of privacy: Dialectics of disclosure.* Albany, NY: State University of New York Press.

Pitts, M. J., & Socha, T. J. (2013). *Positive communication in health and wellness.* New York, NY: Peter Lang Publishing.

Sacks, H. (1992). *Lectures on conversation.* Blackwell: Oxford.

Seligman, M. E. (2002). *Authentic happiness: Using the new positive psychology to realize your potential for lasting fulfillment.* New York: Free Press.

Socha, T. J., & Beck, G. A. (2015). Positive communication and human needs: A review and proposed organizing conceptual framework. *Review of Communication, 15*(3), 173–199.

Socha, T. J., & Pitts, M. J. (Eds.). (2012). *The positive side of interpersonal communication.* New York, NY: Peter Lang Publishing.

Telaumbanua, Y. (2012). Complimenting as a conversation opener: A strategy in teaching English speaking proficiency. *Journal Polingua, 1*(1), 32–38.

Ting-Toomey, S., Gao, G., Trubisky, P., Yang, Z., Soo Kim, H., Lin, S. L., & Nishida, T. (1991). Culture, face maintenance, and styles of handling interpersonal conflict: A study in five cultures. *International Journal of Conflict Management, 2*(4), 275–296.

Tracy, K., & Tracy, S. J. (1998). Rudeness at 911: Reconceptualizing face and face-attack. *Human Communication Research, 25*, 225–251.

Vangelisti, A. L. (2007). Communicating hurt. In W. R. Cupach & B. H. Spitzberg (Eds.), *The dark side of interpersonal communication* (pp. 121–142). Mahwah, NJ: Lawrence Erlbaum Associates.

Waldron, V. R., Kloeber, D., Goman, C., Piemonte, N., & Danaher, J. (2014). How parents communicate right and wrong: A study of memorable moral messages recalled by emerging adults. *Journal of Family Communication, 14*(4), 374–397.

Waldvogel, J. (2007). Greetings and closings in workplace email. *Journal of Computer-Mediated Communication, 12*(2), 456–477.

Yoshimura, S. (2007). The communication of revenge: On the viciousness, virtues, and vitality of vengeful behavior in interpersonal relationships. In W. R. Cupach & B. H. Spitzberg (Eds.), *The dark side of interpersonal communication* (pp. 277–296). Mahwah, NJ: Lawrence Erlbaum Associates.

7

PROSOCIAL RELATIONSHIP MAINTENANCE AND RESILIENCE/THRIVING

Nicole N. Zamanzadeh and Tamara D. Afifi

Prosocial Relationship Maintenance and Resilience/Thriving

Relational and family scholars spend most of their time studying problems. Of course, researchers study problems in relationships to prevent them from occurring. Because the bulk of the research is devoted to the stress and negative aspects of relationships. However, scholars know much more about relational deficits than resilience and thriving. The work on resilience is also atheoretical in nature, making it difficult for scholars, policy makers, and the lay public to articulate what it is and how to foster it. The research on resilience suggests that it is a complex phenomenon that is comprised of numerous factors (e.g., environment, socialization, personality, communication patterns). However, what is missing from this literature is a deeper understanding of how these factors are theoretically connected to each other. Additional research is necessary that can better delineate why it is that some relational partners and families are at risk when they experience something stressful and others are resilient and even thrive when confronted with the same stressful experience. In particular, researchers need to determine the role that positive communication patterns play in these processes.

Scholars are also unclear about whether resilience is a predictor, outcome, or process in relationships. We believe it functions in all of these ways, but it is primarily a process of calibration in relationships. Resilience is the ability to adapt positively when confronted with adversity or stress (Luther, 2003). But, this adaptation requires active participation of relational partners and family members. Relational partners (or family members) must continually gather feedback from each other about how they are managing their stress and adjust their relationship and communication patterns accordingly to help their relationship, and the individuals within it, adapt positively. This adaption process can translate to thriving, where individuals broaden their perspective, learn something positive, develop new coping skills, or expand their social relationships as a result of a stressful experience (Feeney & Collins, 2014). Because of the complexity of relationships, especially within families, it is often difficult to study resilience as a process. But, the research on relational resilience needs to better match the complexity of relationships as stress systems. We developed the Theory of Resilience and Relational Load (TRRL, Afifi, Merrill, & Davis, 2016) to address these limitations in the literature.

The TRRL emerged from a combination of previous literature and our own observations of couples and families' communication patterns over the past two decades. What was clear after observing numerous couples and family members interacting with each other in the laboratory and in their homes about a particular stressor (e.g., natural disaster, stress of a refugee camp, balancing work and family, chronic illness, daily stressors, financial uncertainty), is that they came to that interaction already resilient to a certain degree. Families could be characterized quite easily as "strong," "hardy," or "resilient" based upon their communication with each other. Strong families often used more humor, were emotionally supportive, engaged in positive reframing, problem solved, and used communal coping, among other communication patterns. In contrast, you would also see other family members blame each other for their stress, avoid talking about the topic, become defensive, and want to end the conversation out of frustration and anger. For instance, in a study on the Great Recession (Afifi et al., 2015), we found that unified/thriving couples uplifted each other and were unified in their fight against the recession, blamed external forces (e.g., the government, the Great Recession, banks) rather than each other, were responsive, and discussed how they had grown from their financial struggles. In sharp contrast, the at-risk couples were mismatched in their spending habits and management of money, spiraled very quickly into intractable conflict patterns, avoided talking about money, lacked empathy and active listening, and often blamed each other for their financial problems. Finally, pragmatic couples approached the conflict in a less emotional way, focusing on the practical aspects of the problem and trying to remedy it. But, what we often wanted to ask them was: How did you get here? What happened in your relationship history that created these patterns of communication? How did your communication with each other change after you left our study? As relational and family scholars who conduct observational research, we often study relationships in micro ways at one point in time during a single conversation. By doing this, however, we miss the rich history of communication patterns that characterize the process of resilience in these relationships. Communication patterns occur across time and shape the essence of resilience.

Overview of the Theory of Resilience and Relational Load (TRRL)

The theory of resilience and relational load (TRRL) was created to explain the interconnected nature of communication, psychology, environment, and biosocial stress responses in creating and preventing resilience in relationships. Building on the Theory of Emotional Capital (Feeney & Lemay, 2012; Gottman, 1999; Gottman, Driver, & Tabares, 2002), the TRRL assumes that when relational partners/family members maintain their relationships on a regular basis, they accumulate emotional capital or emotional reserves, which helps protect their relationships. This accumulated maintenance influences relational partners' appraisals of each other, the stressor, and their communication when they are stressed. The TRRL also argues that relational partners and family members who have more of a communal orientation toward stress, or who tend to view each other as a team in their approach to their stressors and life in general, are likely to invest in their relationships by maintaining them. When people have maintained their relationships, they tend to view each other in more benevolent ways, appraise relationally stressful situations from a broader mindset (see also Broaden and Build Theory; Fredrickson, 1998, 2001), and use communication patterns that protect their partner and the relationship. More secure appraisals and behaviors during stress are likely to foster resilience and possibly growth, minimize perceived and physiological stress, and promote health. Couples/family members who do not adequately maintain their relationship, and/or whose standards for relationship maintenance are unmet, are likely to engage in more threatening appraisals and conflict behaviors when they are stressed. Threatening appraisal and conflict patterns can be stressful and deplete a person's cognitive, emotional, and relational resources, especially if they occur frequently.

If the depletion occurs regularly over long periods of time, it can slowly wear away at the relationship, creating what is referred to in the TRRL as *relational load* or relational burnout. This, ultimately, can make relationships and the individuals within them more susceptible to poor mental, physical, and relational health. It can also make it more difficult for people to perceive each other from a communal orientation and invest in their relationships. To prevent relational load and provide opportunities to create resilience and possible thriving, relational partners must continually invest in their relationships by positively maintaining them. In the pages that follow, we briefly outline some key propositions of the TRRL and the assumptions that underlie them. We then discuss ways that it can and has already been tested to promote personal and relational health.

The TRRL applies a systems approach and a semi-evolutionary approach to relationships. This is best summarized by the analogy between the human body and relationships. Similar to how the human body responds automatically to its environment through feedback loops to regulate its self physiologically, relational partners must react to their environment and each other to regulate their relationship. If a body is malnourished, the entire bodily system suffers. If relationships are starved, the relational partners must feed it nutrients to sustain it and help it thrive. Unlike the body, however, whose stress responses automatically respond to fight against stress, relational partners must exert conscious effort to maintain their relationships. In TRRL, this regulation process is born from partners' physiological, emotional, cognitive, and behavioral responses to each other and their shared environment. In essence, it looks at individuals as embedded within larger relational and environmental stress infrastructures. The theory provides a tool for scholars to focus on resilient relationships through highlighting positive communication practices that promote resilience and thriving.

Assumptions of the TRRL

The TRRL has three main assumptions that underlie its claims about resilience in relationships. First, people have an underlying desire for validation and security in their relationships. As relational partners show appreciation and develop an attachment to one another, they build positive emotional reserves or a sense of appreciation and respect (Feeney & Lemay, 2012). However, people's expectations can vary in both the amount and the ways in which they give and receive validation (High & Steuber, 2014; Joseph, Afifi, & Denes, 2015; Priem & Solomon, 2015). These expectations can lead some people to need greater tokens of appreciation feel appreciated and secure. Although Attachment Theory (Bowlby, 1982) identified the human need for validation, the TRRL extends this work by providing an answer to how this need can be fulfilled and how it can help relational partners and families manage stress.

The second assumption is that stress is natural; it is neither good nor bad. The TRRL instead observes that people respond physiologically and psychologically when the brain senses an environmental challenge. The stress response is essential to people's ability to fight the stress they experience throughout their day. There are also cases where stress is beneficial, called eustress. The TRRL recognizes the potential benefit of challenges to relationships. Relational partners co-construct events as threats or opportunities through their communication with each other. Through positive communication strategies, relational partners can experience eustress, growth, and thriving.

Finally, the TRRL assumes that relationships have their own homeostasis. We do not refer to homeostasis as stability, but rather as people's preferred level of functioning (which could be chaos). Families, for example, have a preferences or norms for how their family members should behave. These norms are often revealed when they are broken. Similarly, families have preferred ways of communicating and managing their stress. They also have patterns of maintenance in their relationship that ebb and flow over the course of the relationship and events that transpire (e.g., birth of a child, marriage, new job, time of year). Sometimes the relational system can become dysregulated with chronic stress and the preferred homeostasis can be negatively affected. As a result, the family members need to continually calibrate or gather feedback from each other about their stress and how they are managing it to regulate their family functioning.

Central Elements of the TRRL

The TRRL includes ten propositions involving four central elements: relational maintenance, communal orientation, appraisals and communication, and relational load. In the rest of the chapter, we provide an overview of these central elements (see Afifi et al., 2016 for a more detailed explanation).

Relational Maintenance

Positive relational maintenance strategies contribute to emotional capital in close relationships. These relationship maintenance strategies are a central way people invest in their relationships, building positive emotional reserves over time. Expanding on the Theory of Emotional Capital (Feeney & Lemay, 2012), the TRRL identifies these investments as prosocial, strategic, and routine or habitual experiences, behaviors, and actions people use to maintain their relationships. Maintenance strategies vary and can include things like gifts or trips, showing affection, laughter, spending quality time together, "date nights," having dinner together, doing something for someone that shows gratitude and appreciation, making someone coffee each morning, saying "thank you," and various kinds of support.

Unlike the Theory of Emotional Capital (Feeney & Lemay, 2012), the TRRL focuses on stress management rather than "relational threats" (e.g., jealousy) to the relationship. In addition, the TRRL addresses the effects of other relational partners' investments as part of the relational system. Thus, investments in relationships involve one's own investments, one's relational partner's investments, and discrepancies between partners' investments. In terms of equitable relationships (e.g., marriage, friendship), however, the most important investment is likely what people receive out of that relationship or what people think their partner is investing in their relationship. Individuals are more likely to be affected by what their partner contributes to the relationship than what they are contributing to the relationship, even though both are important. For instance, Floyd (e.g., Floyd & Riforgiate, 2008) has found that receiving affection is a more powerful predictor of personal and relational health than giving affection. People also have individual expectations, ideals, or standards for relationships that each person brings to his/her relationships (Caughlin, 2003; Lemay & Venaglia, 2016). Romantic partners, for example, might experience discrepancies in their ideal use of or need for compliments, affection, and public displays of affection. Some might find public displays of affection important while others do not. Nevertheless, even though people differ in their standards for maintenance, they still likely experience the benefits of emotional capital the more that they maintain their relationship (or the sheer amount of maintenance experienced over time).

Communal Orientation

The TRRL is also unique in that it focuses on why couples and family members invest in their relationships in the first place. The second major tenant of TRRL argues that individuals are more likely to invest in their relationships when they have feelings of communal orientation. When people invest in their relationships, they are then also likely to feel more emotionally connected to each other and experience greater perceptions of communal orientation. *Communal orientation* is the degree that relational partners perceive each other as a cohesive unit or "team" in terms of their approach to stressors and life in general. It can develop from a sense of "we-ness," integration, and support such as communal coping (see also Reid, Dalton, Laderoute, Doell, & Nguyen, 2006). In essence, people need to know that their family member or partner is there for them in times of distress and that whatever they experience, they experience it together—as a team. Rooted in Attachment Theory (Bowlby, 1982), people need to know that they have someone they trust and can count on when times get difficult and that no matter what happens, that person always "has their back."

Communal orientation and relationship maintenance influence one another. For instance, when partners feel more unified or communally oriented toward each other, they are more likely to want to invest in their relationship, but if partners feel like they are not "on the same page" in their relationship (or communal orientation discrepancy), they would be less likely to want to invest in that relationship. Similarly, investments in the relationship can develop positive emotional reserves (i.e., validation, support, appreciation), which can contribute to communal orientation. For example, married couples who are communally oriented and therefore exhibit cognitive interdependence, such as thinking of each other's needs and viewing the partner as a team member, are more likely to feel motivated to engage in pro-relationship behavior and actions toward their partner (Agnew & Etcheverry, 2006; Finkel & Rusbult, 2008). In addition, exchanges of affection in grandchild-grandparent relationships have been found to promote greater feelings of family identity, as well as emotional closeness and relational resources for the grandchildren (Mansson, Floyd, & Soliz, 2017). Even though they do not have to be analyzed together in a single study or tested as bi-directional, maintenance strategies and communal orientation likely influence each other in close relationships.

Furthermore, communal orientation and accrued maintenance or investments affect relational partners' perceptions of stress. Both the *amount* of communal orientation and investments (i.e., positive emotional reserves) and the *discrepancies* in communal orientation and accrued maintenance affect perceptions and experiences of stressors. When relational partners, family members, and even whole families are unified in their approach to life and feel as if they can confront whatever comes their way together, when something stressful happens, they are less likely to see it as stressful. Likewise, when people invest in their relationships over time by maintaining them, they do not feel the stress as much as other people who do not take the time to maintain their relationship. The communal orientation and accrued maintenance build resilience so that when something stressful happens, relational partners know they are not alone in their fight against it. For example, Walsh, Neff, and Gleason (2017) studied the first three years of marriage in couples and found that when marital partners accumulated positive moments (emotional capital) over time with one another, they were less reactive on days when a partner behaved negatively. They also expressed more satisfaction in their relationship. This supported Feeney and Lemay's (2012) findings that accumulated positive feelings and experiences permits relationships to be less susceptible to threats and improves well-being. Yet, it is important to note that gaps in communal orientation can also exacerbate stress (Merill & Afifi, 2017). When couples are "not on the same page" about their relationship and do not feel unified, they will likely have more conflict and their conflict will be more stressful (Merrill & Afifi, 2017).

Security-Appraisals and Positive Communication Patterns

How people feel toward their partner and the extent to which they have maintained their relationship also affect how they appraise the stressor and communicate when they are stressed. The degree of unity (i.e., "weness") and emotional reserves obtained (i.e., accrued maintenance) can influence appraisals of threat and security in the relationship and the communication patterns in response to the stressor. When partners maintain their relationships over time, it builds a strong foundation and positive emotions. When something stressful happens, relational partners are then more likely to have benevolent feelings toward one another and communicate in ways that uplift and protect their partner and their relationship. For instance, Driver and Gottman (2004) found support that couples who continuously invested in their relationships over time used more positive conflict management during a conflict-inducing discussion. When people fail to take the time to adequately maintain their relationship, survival instincts set in and they are more likely to engage in "threat-based" communication patterns and appraisals. Their instinct is to protect the self rather than the partner when something stressful affects the relationship. Research shows that couples who are stressed and dissatisfied with their relationship tend to blame their partner during conflict discussions rather than blame themselves or their circumstances (Sillars, Roberts, Leonard, & Dun, 2000).

Moreover, security-appraisals and communication patterns prevent the depletion of emotional reserves when partners communicate about stressful issues. A recent investigation of the effects of supportive communication within marital couples and serious relationships facing involuntary unemployment revealed that communication of respect and harmony improved partner resilience and relational satisfaction (Beck, 2016). The opposite is true of threat appraisals and communication. TRRL contends that stress management affects self-control, which is a limited resource that dwindles when used repetitively (Baumeister, 2002). Self-control becomes depleted when conflict endures or when partners experience multiple rejections. This can lead to defensive and threat-based communication. However, supportive interactions bolster positive emotional reserves built via communication competence, affection, and other affirming behaviors. These acts of investment become buffers of stress. Fostering positive emotions allows relational systems to continue a positive feedback loop of resilience. People with more emotional reserves maintain their relationships with more security-based appraisals and communication patterns, which helps manage stress, improve personal and relational health, and foster resilience and the potential for thriving (see also Feeney & Collins, 2014). The opposite is true for those with fewer resources who engage in behaviors that continue to exacerbate their relational stress.

Relational Load

One of the other unique contributions of the TRRL is that it introduces a new concept called relational load. This idea is adapted from the notion of allostatic load, which is the "wear and tear" of chronic stress on the body's physiological stress response systems (McEwen, 1998). Over time, exposure to chronic stress can weaken the body's immune system, making it more susceptible to a host of diseases, including obesity, hypertension, coronary heart disease, diabetes, and premature aging (McEwen, 1998; McEwen & Stellar, 1993). Relational load is the wearing away of the relationship as a result of chronic relational stress and repeated depletion of one's emotional, psychological, and relational resources (Afifi et al., 2016). Relational load is similar to relational burnout, which could manifest itself in properties like relationship dissatisfaction, loneliness, depression, anxiety, negative moods, and thoughts of divorce.

Over time, the depletion of relational and emotional resources and increased stress creates relational load. When experiencing relational load, partners are less likely to put forth effort into maintaining their relationship. Though this has short-term consequences such as hurting relational partners' feelings, there are also long-term consequences for mental, physical, and relational health. Research shows that harmful conflict patterns and emotions (e.g., loneliness, depressive states) in romantic relationships and families put the people in these relationships at risk for weakened immune systems and greater propensity for disease (see Kiecolt-Glaser, Gouin, & Hantsoo, 2010). However, partners who engage in security-based appraisals and communication patterns facilitate resilience and better health. Simply put, people in satisfied relationships tend to have more positive communication patterns and are generally healthier—physically and relationally. However, the destructive impact of relational load can restrict opportunities for positive emotions and communication patterns, preventing resilience and thriving from occurring.

Relational partners can replenish their relationship or social system with maintenance strategies even during relational load. During stress, continuing to invest in a partner, building positive emotional reserves and engaging in secure appraisals and behaviors can foster resilience, as long as everyone in that relationship wants the relationship to work. By showing affection and appreciation, partners can provide each other a sense of safety and trust, slowing building greater feelings of communal orientation and a reserve of positive emotions and experiences to draw upon when they are stressed. This has been supported in a multitude of contexts (Feeney & Collins, 2014; Meneghel, Salanova, & Martinez, 2016; Walsh et al., 2017). For instance, imagine a parent who has experienced a great deal of conflict with their adolescent who has a chronic illness. The parent is constantly asking the child to take better care of his/her health, which the child views as controlling. The ensuing conflict has led to feelings of isolation, frustration, and anger in their relationship. The parent and the child might need to reinvest in their relationship by engaging in activities together that have nothing to do with the child's illness, focusing positive attention on each other. The child and parent might be consumed by the illness and the stressful communication patterns and emotions that it evokes. When they each feel validated and appreciated, it will allow them to have more positive emotions toward each other and have more productive conversations (e.g., collaboration, problem-solving, less blame) about the child's management of the illness. Slowly, if they maintain their relationship more effectively over time, it should build a stronger sense of communal orientation (with regard to their lives more broadly and the illness) and validation within their relationship and prompt them to communicate in more supportive and healthy ways.

Finally, the TRRL argues that because relational systems develop over time, maintenance behaviors and positive communication patterns can be learned and resilience can be fostered. Relationships are mechanisms that mature in response to new environmental demands and changing resources. Individuals need to repeatedly assess and adjust their relationships to keep them healthy and prevent relational load. This includes building strategies to improve communication patterns when stressed, build communal orientation, and routinely engaging in activities and behaviors that maintain the relationship. The benefits include building resilience, opportunities for thriving, and improved health.

Applications of the TRRL for Personal and Relational Health

There are numerous ways the TRRL could be applied to study and enhance positive psychological health. Even though the theory is new, Afifi and colleagues have already tested the theory in contexts of chronic illness, fast-paced families, long-term dating relationships, cancer, and marriage and voting patterns in the 2016 election. Initial tests of the TRRL have shown that increasing maintenance helps manage stress and promote communal orientation and thriving. For example, Afifi et al. (2017) found that couples who had a teen with type I diabetes who maintained their relationship had less conflict when talking about their child's diabetes, which reduced the couples' self-reported and physiological stress. Couples who were then randomly assigned to a two weeks intervention designed to increase their maintenance also reported more thriving, greater feelings of communal orientation, and less stress about their child's diabetes than the control. These effects were somewhat stronger for wives than husbands. Their children also reported less general life stress than the control group.

Afifi, Zamanzadeh, Harrison, and Acevedo Callejas (2017) also found in a study of fast-paced families of two parents and a teenager that family members who better maintained their relationships had less perceived stress over time, better physiological markers of stress, less conflict, and less loneliness. For wives, receiving greater maintenance from their husbands over the past month produced less conflict in their relationship, which, in turn, was associated with greater satisfaction balancing work and family. For husbands, their maintenance received from their wives predicted less conflict, but not greater satisfaction balancing work and family. As it is noted in the original TRRL, the theory should apply to both men and women, but there are likely gender differences that emerge with the theory because women have been socialized to be the "relationship maintenance experts" in their relationships and might also have higher standards for relationship maintenance in their close relationships.

In addition to supporting the theory, these initial results also suggest that interventions can be designed to help people maintain their relationships and subsequently improve their personal and relational health. A significant amount of work has also shown that interventions designed to increase the amount that people express affection and gratitude to close others enhances relationship quality, physiological stress responses, and mental health (e.g., Algoe, Gable, & Maisel, 2010; Floyd et al., 2009; Floyd & Riforgiate, 2008). For example, Floyd et al. (2009) randomly assigned married and cohabitating couples to an experimental condition where they asked them to kiss more than they normally do over a six weeks period. Compared to the control group, the couples in the experimental group had improvements in cholesterol, relationship satisfaction, and perceived stress over time. Researchers have found similar effects when couples are asked to show gratitude toward each other over an extended period of time (see Algoe et al., 2010). These types of interventions involve simple, free maintenance techniques that anyone can do and that can improve personal happiness and feelings about family members.

Technology can also be used as a tool to enhance relationship maintenance in couples and families. For example, virtual reality could help residents living in assisted living (AL) centers maintain their relationships with their adult children living at a distance and thrive in what otherwise might be a stressful and lonely period in their life. Many older adults who live in residential care facilities have been detached from their previous life and/or have physical challenges that limit their mobility. Virtual reality could allow residents to continue to travel with their family anywhere in the world, become immersed in family events and dinners, and be surrounded by a virtual world of family photos, providing important links between their past and entirely new frontiers. There are currently VR systems (see rendever.com) that allow multiple people's VR headsets to be synced so that they can experienced the same virtual worlds together from a distance. In general, scholars need to extend their notions of what constitutes relationship maintenance, which includes the use of multiple types of technology.

In sum, the TRRL suggests that relationship maintenance is a way that people can better manage the stress that affects their relationships and their psychological health. It offers one theoretical explanation as to why some relationships fare better than others when they are faced with adversity. The theory also provides avenues for interventions that can be designed to help relational partners and family members improve their relational and personal well-being.

References

Afifi, T. D., Davis, S., Merrill, A., Coveleski, S., Denes, A., & Afifi, W. (2015). In the wake of the Great Recession: Economic uncertainty, communication, and biological stress responses in families. *Human Communication Research*, *41*, 268–302. doi:10.1111/hcre.12048

Afifi, T. D., Granger, D., Ersig, A., Tsalikian, E., Davis, S., Shahnazi, A., Harrison, K., Acevedo Callejas, M., & Scranton, A. (2017). *Testing the Theory of Resilience and Relational Load (TRRL) in families with type I diabetes.* Manuscript submitted to publication.

Afifi, T. D., Merrill, A. F., & Davis, S. (2016). The theory of resilience and relational load. *Personal Relationships*, *23*(4), 663–683. https://doi.org/10.1111/pere.12159

Afifi, T. D., Zamanzadeh, N., Harrison, K., & Acevedo Callejas, M. (2017). *WIRED: The impact of technology use on biological stress (cortisol) and inflammation (interleukin IL-6) in fast paced families.* Manuscript submitted for publication.

Agnew, C. R., & Etcheverry, P. E. (2006). Cognitive interdependence: Considering self in relationship. In K. D. Vohs & E. J. Finkel (Eds.), *Self and relationships: Connecting intrapersonal and interpersonal processes* (pp. 274–293). New York, NY: Guilford Press.

Algoe, S., Gable, S., & Maisel, N. (2010). It's the little things: Everyday gratitude as a booster shot for romantic relationships. *Personal Relationships, 17*, 217–233.

Baumeister, R. F. (2002). Ego depletion and self-control failure: An energy model of the self's executive function. *Self and Identity, 1*, 129–136.

Beck, G. A. (2016) Surviving involuntary unemployment together: The role of resilience-promoting communication in familial and committed relationships, *Journal of Family Communication, 16*(4), 369–385. DOI: 10.1080/15267431.2016.1215315

Bowlby, J. (1982). Attachment theory and its therapeutic implications. *Adolescent Psychiatry, 6*, 5–33.

Caughlin, J. P. (2003). Family communication standards: What counts as excellent family communication and how are such standards associated with family satisfaction? *Human Communication Research, 29*, 5–40. doi:10.1093/hcr/29.1.5

Driver, J. L., & Gottman, J. M. (2004). Daily marital interactions and positive affect during marital conflict among newlywed couples. *Family Process, 43*, 301–314.

Feeney, B. C., & Collins, N. L. (2014). A new look at social support: A theoretical perspective on thriving through relationships. *Personality and Social Psychology Review, 47*, 1–35. https://doi.org/10.1177/1088868314544222

Feeney, B. C., & Lemay, E. P. (2012). Surviving relationship threats: The role of emotional capital. *Personality and Social Psychology Bulletin, 38*, 1004–1017. https://doi:10.1177/0146167212442971

Finkel, E. J., & Rusbult, C. E. (2008). Prorelationship motivation: An interdependence theory analysis of situations with conflicting interests. In J. Y. Shah, & W. L. Gardner (Eds.), *Handbook of motivation science* (pp. 547–560). New York: Guilford Press.

Floyd, K., Boren, J., Hannawa, A., Hesse, C., McEwan, B., & Veksler, A. (2009). Kissing in marital and cohabiting relationships: Effects on blood lipids, stress, and relationship satisfaction. *Western Journal of Communication, 73*, 113–133. doi:10.1080/10570310902856071

Floyd, K., & Riforgiate, S. (2008). Affectionate communication received from spouses predicts stress hormone levels in healthy adults. *Communication Monographs, 75*, 351–368. doi:10.1080/03637750802512371

Fredrickson, B. (1998). What good are positive emotions? *Review of General Psychology, 2*, 300–319.

Fredrickson, B. (2001). The role of positive emotions in positive psychology. *American Psychologist, 56*(3), 218–226.

Gottman, J. M. (1999). *The marriage clinic: A scientifically based marital therapy.* New York, NY: Norton.

Gottman, J. M., Driver, J., & Tabares, A. (2002). Building the sound marital house: An empirically derived couple therapy. In A. S. Gurman & N. S. Jacobson (Eds.), *Clinical handbook of couple therapy* (3rd ed., pp. 373–399). New York, NY: Guilford Press.

High, A., & Steuber, K. (2014). An examination of support (in)adequacy: Types, sources, and consequences of social support among infertile women. *Communication Monographs, 81*, 157–188. https://doi:10.1080/03637751.2013.878868

Joseph, A., Afifi, T. A., & Denes, A. (2015). Standards for support in romantic relationships: The short- and medium-term consequences of receiving (non)responsive support. *Communication Monographs, 83*, 163–193. https://doi.org/10.1080/03637751.2015.1068432

Kiecolt-Glaser, J., Gouin, J. P., & Hantsoo, L. (2010). Close relationships, inflammation, and health. *Neuroscience and Biobehavioral Reviews, 35*, 33–38. doi:10.1016/j.neubiorev.2009.09.003

Lemay, E. P., Jr., & Venaglia, R. B. (2016). Relationship expectations and relationship quality. *Review of General Psychology, 20*(1), 57.

Luther, S. S. (Ed.). (2003). *Resilience and vulnerability: Adaptation in the context of childhood adversities.* New York: Cambridge University Press.

Mansson, D. H., Floyd, K., & Soliz, J. (2017). Affectionate communication is associated with emotional and relational resources in the grandparent-grandchild relationship. *Journal of Intergenerational Relationships, 15*(2), 85–103. https://doi.org/10.1080/15350770.2017.1294007

McEwen, B. S. (1998). Protective and damaging effects of stress mediators. *New England Journal of Medicine, 338*, 171–179. doi:10.1016/S0079-6123(08)62128-7

McEwen, B. S., & Stellar, E. (1993). Stress and the individual: Mechanisms leading to disease. *Archives of Internal Medicine, 153*, 2093–2101.

Meneghel, I., Salanova, M., & Martinez, I. M. (2016). Feeling good makes us stronger: How team resilience mediates the effect of positive emotions on team performance. *Journal of Happiness Studies, 17*(1), 239–255. https://doi.org/10.1007/s10902-014-9592-6

Merrill, A. F., & Afifi, T. D. (2017). Couple identity gaps, the management of conflict, and biological and self-reported stress in romantic relationships. *Human Communication Research, 43*(3), 363–396.

Priem, J. S., & Solomon, D. H. (2015). Emotional support and physiological stress recovery: The role of support matching, adequacy, and invisibility. *Communication Monographs, 82*(1), 88–112. http://dx.doi.org/10.1080/03637751.2014.971416

Reid, D. W., Dalton, E. J., Laderoute, K., Doell, F. K., & Nguyen, T. (2006). Therapeutically induced changes in couple identity: The role of we-ness and interpersonal processing in relationship satisfaction. *Genetic, Social, and General Psychology Mono-Graphs, 132,* 241–284. doi:10.3200/MONO.132.3.241-288

Sillars, A., Roberts, L. J., Leonard, K. E., & Dun, T., (2000). Cognition during marital conflict: The relationship of thought and talk. *Journal of Social and Personal Relationships, 17,* 479–502. doi:10.1177/0265407500174002

Walsh, C. M., Neff, L. A., & Gleason, M. E. J. (2017). The role of emotional capital during the early years of marriage: Why everyday moments matter. *Journal of Family Psychology, 31*(4), 513–519. https://doi.org/10.1037/fam0000277

8

COMMUNICATION FOR A FLOURISHING AND THRIVING ROMANTIC RELATIONSHIP

Gary A. Beck and Joshua R. Pederson

Close partnerships are central to the human experience. People have an enduring need to be connected to others, as a way to give their lives meaning, experience life events, accomplish goals, and create a family legacy (Perlman & Vangelisti, 2006). Romantic relationships serve as the focal point for some of life's most meaningful experiences (e.g., love, partnership, even heartache), and as a platform to make life's dreams possible (Feeney & Collins, 2015a). Going it alone is certainly possible, but going with another that you like and understand is a social inclination with biological roots (e.g., *Need to belong theory*; Baumeister & Leary, 1995). In the interest of finding close partnerships that truly help us make the most of our lives, what allows those partnerships to be perceived as flourishing, or even thriving? Better yet, even if we happen to find a partner that enables the type of communication and understanding that promotes such desired qualities, how does one make it last, and last across one's lifespan?

Such questions fall under the purview of positive psychology (e.g., Csikszentmihalyi, 1990; Lyubormisky, Sheldon, & Schkade, 2005; Seligman, 2011), as well as research within allied disciplines including communication, family studies, and sociology. As a way to understand what goes right in life, as well as what contributes, exploring the positive opens up understandings of relationships beyond what more traditional social scientific work was previously positioned to explain (Shatte, Seligman, Gillham, & Reivich, 2005). Optimal relationship conditions, or even peak relational experiences (see Socha & Beck, 2015), explored here as flourishing and thriving, shift relationship goals from lay concerns like "How can we stay together?" and "How can we be happy?" to questions that address more advanced needs. The pursuit here is a more nuanced understanding of what making the absolute most of a partnership might entail (e.g., "How can we achieve and sustain life fulfillment through this relationship?"). From a research perspective, this means shifting focus from behaviors and processes that thwart relational satisfaction and commitment (e.g., Gottman, 1994) to exploring the processes of relating that lead to overflowing growth, joy, and deep gratification.

From a practical perspective, the more basic relational needs people feel (e.g., for companionship, security, acceptance, life partnership, love) have held across time, but the mediums used to address those needs have changed in recent times. Disruption of traditional dating paradigms (see Earhart Michel & Randick, 2014) has been a central feature of this change: The proliferation of online dating services (e.g., eHarmony, match.com) and SmartPhone applications (e.g., Tinder, Bumble) have expanded the relational landscape (see *Mixed-Media Relationships* (*MMRs*); Parks, 2017). Furthermore, communicating through devices has provided enriched channels for pursuing and maintaining partnerships and families (Bruess, 2015). Social norms have shifted to be more welcoming to casual sex (e.g., hookup culture, Earhart Michel & Randick, 2014), cohabitation, and just holding off on marriage (Ganong, Jamison, & Chapman, 2016), which can extend less committed and less obligated periods of romantic relationships.

Taken together, the characteristics of this relational era represent unique challenges for modern partnerships, and yet the pursuit of optimal relationship experiences persist. Flourishing and thriving romantic relationships are not just characterized by their use of positive communication and experience of positive emotion, but by deliberate efforts across the course of the relationship to a) accentuate positive experiences and b) effectively minimize and manage the impact of negative life circumstances. In this way, such romantic relationships are built not only for the good times, but set with a solid foundation for growth, unexpected challenges, and with a frame sturdy enough to last the test of time.

The purpose of this chapter is to review concepts related to the notions of flourishing and thriving in romantic relationships, discuss communication contributions, and provide practical guidance for pursuing such outcomes. To achieve this goal, the following chapter will first contextualize the exigency of flourishing and thriving as ideal states of relationships, review interdisciplinary conceptualizations, and then identify relevant communication contributions and manifestations. Finally, practical relational applications will be discussed.

Exigency for Optimal Relational States: Why Bother?

Why care about flourishing or thriving? Isn't it enough to just be committed to someone you love and want a good life? Shouldn't we just aim for happiness and let the rest sort itself out? Researchers like Seligman (2011) have identified that happiness is just one piece of the puzzle, falling a bit short in appreciation of the full range of personal (and relational) fulfillment. Acknowledging that relationships are complex experiences that unfold over their life and across each partner's lifespan, dogmatically pursuing any one fixed outcome potentially comes at the expense of others. For example, narrowly pursuing hedonistic forms of happiness may be better fits for early relationships, yet ever increasing intimacy prompts questions about commitment. Finally, life events prompt changes in one's affective state, like the honeymoon effect and subsequent drop in marital satisfaction following marriage and first born (i.e., *Emergent distress model*, see Caughlin & Huston, 2006). Other unexpected life challenges, such as chronic illness and financial strains, have the potential to challenge the "happily ever after" relationship myth. Therefore, when considering the reasons for pursuing flourishing and thriving, optimal relationship conditions, we must acknowledge the advantages, emerging challenges, and changing nature of romantic relationships.

First, close relationships are desired life circumstances that are universally regarding as an important aspect of life. Beyond one's family, romantic partners are sources of love, companionship, passion, and in many cases serve as a foundation for a new family unit. People often regard their partnership and the life they build together as important contributors to their identity, providing life with meaning, cohesion, and purpose (Aron & Aron, 1986). Biologically there is precedence for individuals to seek partners to bond with, raise children, and potentially develop a genetic legacy. Finally, relationships challenge us in ways that promote growth: The interdependent nature of relating creates incredible synergies and overlaps, but also highlights differences, which can lead to the type of turbulence that can help partnerships grow and transcend (Solomon, Knobloch, Theiss, & McLaren, 2016).

Second, close relationships present challenges, and are potentially fragile (Gottman, 1994). The divorce rate is Northern America is steady (between 40–50 percent), with cohabitation on the rise in the past decade (Ganong, Jamison, & Chapman, 2016). Casual relationship, via the popular "hook up culture" is increasingly popular among younger dater (Earhart Michel & Randick, 2014); This comes in concert with findings that suggest that emerging adults (ages 18–29) delay more "adult" decision-making for a variety of reasons, and move home with parents (which inhibits the financial need for coupling and finding a space together) (Arnett, 2004). With less taboo for divorce or even remaining committed, close committed relationships may be valued with less regard than in previous generations.

Finally, relationships invariably transform over time. Across one's lifespan, a partnership may go through phases or transitions as one ages, just as individuals do. Consider conventional terms for these relational periods: newlyweds, young parents, middle "sandwich" adults, older adults (e.g., nearing retirement), and elderly. Life phases present unique challenges (or crisis, see Erikson, 1963), and novel circumstances that provide both opportunities and challenges for romantic partnerships. Pursuing optimal relational states in mindful, comprehensive ways encourages a more multi-faceted approach to keeping one's relationship, further suggesting that the priorities of one phase may not be so compatible with the next (e.g., club-hopping in your early 20s may be less valuable or even counterproductive toward relationship functioning in your 50s). Different phases of life require different proverbial communication tools, and being prepared and even skilled with the right one when you need it can provide a robust approach to life's challenges.

If romantic relationships are sought after social situations, providing numerous physical and social benefits, keeping them stable and adaptive to challenges across time should be prioritized. Internal and external challenges to romantic relationships persist and place greater demands on producing and maintaining enduring partnerships. Clarifying how flourishing and thriving relational states persist over time may also help identify and enact "timeless communication practices" (Socha, 2014).

Flourishing and Thriving: Conceptualizations

The positive psychology movement provides an origin point for these concepts. With the founding of psychology, the three principle purposes of the discipline were to cure mental illness, nurture above-average talent, and promote satisfaction and fulfillment in all people (Shatte et al., 2005). Over the years, shaped by historical events and market forces, psychology stepped away from the third purpose. In Martin Seligman's 1998 American Psychological Association president's speech, he urged a return to attention on what makes life worth living, what helps people foster growth, and how people experience the best in life. As a response to this call, researchers in the 1990s and 2000s took up the call to "the pursuit of optimal life conditions and growth-fostering experiences." This calibration of the field's focus has led to estimated thousands of researchers (see Seligman, 2011) interested in concepts such as character strengths, virtues, optimism, confidence, grit, flow, resilience, positive relationships, and communication, among others.

Exploring the best aspects of life is clearly an interdisciplinary effort, with recent efforts in communication attempting to focus the efforts within the discipline (relevant here, see Socha & Pitts, 2012; Beck & Socha, 2015). Relevant to this volume, communication scholars have taken on these concepts through their own discipline's theorizing addressing relational topics like aesthetic relating (Baxter, Norwood, & Nebel, 2012), synchrony (Kim, 2012), and communicating intimacy in older adulthood (Nussbaum, Miller-Day, & Fisher, 2012). While such positive communication topics may have been explored in decades previous as disparate research agendas, an inclusive positive communication mosaic has emerged in published works and conference proceedings.

Included in this broader positive conceptual mosaic the current focus: Flourishing and thriving. These terms connote optimal personal and relationship states, both related in many academic portrayals to well-being. A very low resolution analogy could be farming: Flourishing represents a "bumper crop" or a crop that has exceeded all expectations; thriving, however, transcends just a crop surviving until the next season, but responding well to both challenges and fortuitous circumstances (season of exceptionally favorable weather). While there is some debate regarding the conceptual demarcation of the terms (see Seligman, 2011; Duan, Guan, & Gan, 2016), or situations when the terminology is rather casually used to describe the other, both represent an optimal sense of well-being, and in the case of this chapter, as experienced in romantic partnerships.

Flourishing

Flourishing brings to mind lush flora and fauna, an overabundance, or even an outpouring of positivity. The *Oxford English Dictionary* (2017), provides a consistent definition: "to grow or develop in a healthy or vigorous way, especially as the result of a particularly congenial environment." Martin Seligman (2011), in his book of the same name, suggests that flourishing is a product of the pursuit of well-being, a construct with contributions represented by the acronym PERMA: Positive emotions, engagement, relationships, meaning, and achievement. Summarizing here, the five qualify as sources of well-being due to an individual's capacity to a) choose them, b) pursue them for their own sake and c) be sufficiently distinct from each other. The five aspects of PERMA, when effectively combined in one's life, function to promote a sense of flourishing.

To characterize the construct in relevant populations, Huppert and So (2011) identified requisite primary indicators of flourishing, as well as secondary indicators that should be present to some degree. For an individual to be labeled as flourishing, she or he must core features of well-being: positive emotions, engagement, interest, meaning, and purpose. Additionally, they should possess three of the six additional features: self-esteem, optimism, resilience, vitality, self-determination, and positive relationships. Together, these indicators represent preconditions for individuals to flourish, and represent qualities that they would bring and enact within a romantic partnership.

Thriving

Conditions commonly thought of as "thriving" include circumstances where some social process has worked beyond expectation, or perhaps when risks were taken and paid off. In perhaps similar biological framing as the flourish definition, to thrive is to "(of a child, animal, or plant) grow or develop well or vigorously" (*Oxford English Dictionary*, 2017). Feeney and Collins (2015b) have provided a contextually appropriate approach to thriving in their research through a theoretical model called "thriving through relationships." Essentially, this model suggests that relational support is an important contributor to thriving, most notably occurring in circumstances of adversity and opportunity, and that support functions differently in the pursuit of thriving depending on the circumstance.

Feeney and Collins (2015b) represent thriving as an end-state composed of five components of well-being: 1) hedonic well-being, 2) eudemonic well-being, 3) psychological well-being, 4) social well-being, and 5) physical well-being. Important to a determination of "thriving" is the realization that this is an end-state that is a result of circumstances that promote these components. The romantic partner's communication plays an important role in contributing to these various forms of well-being, from day-to-day coordination of a shared lifestyle to more focused responses to negative events or opportunities to grow.

As such, thriving across one's lifespan can be an endless pursuit. Life circumstances and challenges change as work, family, and health fluctuate. Importantly some adversities and opportunities may be self-induced and anticipated (e.g., taking a risky promotion, adding another child to the family), or life imposed and seemingly random (e.g., a car accident, health diagnosis).

Resilience scholarship (Beck, 2016, 2017) suggests that couples accumulate a variety of assets and resources that help proactively prepare couples for challenging circumstances; This preparation then prompts more active and reactive responses to specific life or relational stressors.

Consolidating Perspectives

How does flourishing and thriving fit together within the context of romantic relationships? Beyond desired, optimal relational states, both concepts invoke hedonic and eudemonic well-being as an important contributor. Thus, feeling happy and fulfilled with deeper levels of meaning are important aspects to each relational state. Relationships and social-wellbeing seem to be linked, as does positive communication and emotional responses contributing to psychological well-being. There is enough reason to believe that aspects of each are sufficiently represented in the other, and perhaps there is a labeling conflict here over similar phenomena.

Taking an extended perspective however, romantic relationships involve time, and many are ideally pursued as a lifelong process and commitment. Considered this way, flourishing conveys a list of components for the best circumstances that promote the well-being (beyond just "happy" relating). Thus, happy, meaningful, and fulfilling relational experiences (i.e., flourishing well-being) require positive emotions, meaning beyond, positive social connections to others, and the achievement and celebration of victories in the process. While not entirely necessary, flourishing would seem to provide enough of a conceptual overlap that sufficient flourishing would promote thriving when opportunities arise.

Of course, exceptions persist. Major disruptions to the broader socioecological circumstances (Bronfenbrenner, 1979) would be extreme disruption. Additionally, flourishing so well may lead to an overconfidence that leads to blind spots or arrogance as issues arise (Gonzales, 2004). Finally, while likely less probable, the lack of flourishing may still present chance for thriving despite the circumstances given the opportunity strikes.

Importantly, both optimal relationship states each clearly benefit from communication's buffering or growth-fostering contributions. Communication choices in the general function of one's relationship can serve as an interpretive context (Weiss, 1980) as well as reliable, familiar interaction patterns (Beck, 2017) when confronted with novel circumstances (i.e., opportunity or adversity). The alternative would be attempting to invoke communication strategies that may be more complex than what the couple is used to or capable of coordinating. It follows that the simpler communication strategies (i.e., basic civility, coordination, helping each other, managing simple disagreements) may serve as reference points for more complex and ongoing social challenges.

Relational Communication: Manifestations and Contributions

While any number of communication messages, practices, or habits may contribute to a positive outcome in a relationship, which ones are most effective in promoting well-being? In what relational circumstances should positive communication make meaningful impacts on the capacity for relational flourishing or thriving? Rather than just review a wide range of communication that could be characterized as positive, we highlight relational messages below that would seem to address multiple criteria for optimal relational state outlined above. Thus, each of the following subsections features references the fit within the pursuit of well-being.

Kindness

Taking its root from "kin," as in family or in relation, communication that is kind attempts to promote the warmth, connection, and appreciation that represent the best of close family relationships. According to Seligman (2011), kindness serves as one of the biggest predictors of momentary well-being. Random acts of kindness are those positive gestures in which one doesn't expect something back in return, which communicate a genuine concern for the well-being others (Tolman, 2009). Examples could include holding a door, preparing a surprise, going out of one's way to assist, or demonstrate appreciation (e.g., writing a letter, giving a gift, sharing positive sentiments).

Affectionate Communication

Affection communication includes messages that express messages based on feeling of affection toward a target. Labeled the tripartite model of affectionate communication, Floyd and Morman (1998) identified three forms: verbal (e.g., "I love you."), direct nonverbal (e.g., hugging, kissing, touching), and indirect nonverbal (e.g., helping, lending care). While these seem part in parcel to a clichéd romantic relationship, enacting this form of communication has been shown to have numerous benefits: ability to handle stress (Floyd, 2006), general physical health benefits (e.g., hugs reducing blood pressure; Light, Grewen, & Amico, 2005), and higher levels of happiness, self-esteem, and overall mental health (Floyd, 2002). Such findings fall in line with *Tend-and-befriend theory* (Taylor et al., 2000), which promotes the exchange of feelings with loved ones as means to manage stress. Taking the time to show affection to one's partner would seem to have clear relevance to well-being, as well as promoting flourishing and thriving.

Relationship Maintenance

Representing a broader range of relational behaviors and communication, relationship mainte-nance seems to be an important contributor to the baseline expectations we would expect for romantic partnerships seeking to flourish or thrive. Poor maintenance would suggest a higher potential for anything to have challenges functioning in an optimal condition. Canary and Dainton (2006) view maintenance as the actions and activities engaged in by partners to sustain desired relational properties. Daiton (2003) further contends that maintenance occurs in four relevant contexts: a) the self, b) the relational system, c) the network (broader from the relational), and d) the culture (i.e., ideas, belief systems, rules, roles). Dindia (2003) identified five positive and proactive maintenance strategies within the relational context that have been broadly uti-lized: Positivity, Openness, Assurances, Social Networks, and Sharing tasks. Those five categories, in addition to further clarifications and extensions provide communication manifestations that strike parallel cords with the flourishing acronym PERMA and aspects of thriving theory. By extension, attempting to flourish without maintaining one's relationship seems neglectful and fallacious.

As a positive phenomenon that overlaps with flourishing and thriving, promoting resilience in relationships also finds overlaps with relationship maintenance. Afifi, Merrill, and Davis (2016), in their Theory of Resilience and Relational Load (see also in this book Zamanzadeh & Afifi, 2018), identify the couple's coordination and attending to maintenance behaviors as an important con-tributor to emotional reserves, which then enable more efficacious reactions to stress, setbacks, or challenges to the relationship.

Resilience Theory and Communication

Beyond Afifi et al. (2016)'s approach, resilience has seen a groundswell of attention in the communication field over the last decade (Buzzanell, 2010; Beck & Socha, 2015; Carr, 2015; Lucas & Buzzanell, 2012). These models position communication as an important contributor to discursively talking resilience into being (Buzzanell, 2010), promoting "a new normal" for the couple while back-grounding challenges and foregrounding what works (Lucas & Buzzanell, 2012). Beck (2016) posited a model of resilience-promoting communication, including sub-dimensions of communication characteristics in romantic relationships including *Tact, Respect/ Harmony, Partnership, Civility, Tension Release, and Restraint.* Such communication has potential to contribute positively when a challenge presents itself, but also contribute throughout the less problematic times to stabilize the relationship.

Forgiveness and Reflection

Given the ongoing and iterative nature of relationships across the lifespan, couples are provided with numerous opportunities to learn from each other, through novelty and familiarity, as well as great successes and mistakes. This process ensures that missteps are possible, warranting a priority on forgiving the trespasses of those closest to us, allowing for relationship negotiation, as well as healthy reflection process (Waldron & Kelley, 2008). It is this reflective process that across time potentially promotes as "steeling" and inoculation of further exposure to adversities (Rutter, 2007). This is an important part of seeing resilience as developed across time (Beck, 2017) and as a part of larger, lifespan developmental experience-gaining process (Kaplan, 2006).

Overall these communication manifestations represent relational communication behaviors that are function as a toolkit, either to be used spontaneously or in reaction to both positive and negative life events. Additional positive communication behaviors germane to relationships are explained further in Thomas J. Socha and Margaret Pitts' (2012) edited volume "The Positive Side of Interpersonal Communication." One note of caution is that these positive relational communication forms relate to "the goldilocks' principle," which suggests too much of a good thing is probably too much. For example, kindness unbound feels inauthentic or strategic, and excessive relationship maintenance behaviors can create an unhealthy imbalance in relationship function. This point emphasizes the importance of clarifying personal needs and expectations in a relationship early, as well as reassessing across the course of the relationship.

Embedding Communication in Flourishing/Thriving

The previous section highlighted important contributors to overall well-being, as experienced through flourishing and thriving. Across all of the contributors highlighted here, some notable patterns emerge as viable for practical implications. Notably, these communication practices, if proactively nurtured (Watzlawick. Weakland, & Fisch, 1974; Wilson & Gettings, 2012), can provide avenues to best take advantage of thriving opportunities. Further, general communication practices like kindness, affectionate communication, and relationship maintenance, can be iteratively tailored to better address the needs of one's partner over time, a natural process as one becomes more intimate and familiar with the other (Beck, 2017; Waldron, 2017). Finally, crucial or strategic moments will arise to maximally promote flourishing, and certainly crucial moments of challenge that dictate thriving outcomes. What follows are examples of two positive communication opportunities for both: finding play and pursuing virtues.

Play Opportunities and Episodes

The modern world is beset with "work": School can be seen as training for work, people work until they cannot work anymore, then they retire, sometimes taking temporary work or more manageable careers. Between work and taking care of family, when do adults find times for play? According to Baxter (1992), and extended by Aune and Wong (2012), adult play in personal relationships take the following forms: Idioms, role-play, teasing, physical play, games, gossiping, public performance, joking, intimate play, and nonverbal play. Aune and Wong (2012) also found that romantic partners tended to play more than friends, especially when it came to intimate play, as they likely spend more time with each other and tend to be closer. Play is shown to increase hedonic well-being, provide emotional release, and forge stronger connections, making it an ideal behavior if used in concert with other necessary life endeavors.

Pursuing and Embodying Virtues

The pursuit of the highest qualities of human existence, virtues, represents relational communication at its best. Virtues include compassion, generosity, prudence, justice, courage, and mercy (Comte-Sponville, 2001; Mirivel, 2012). Such guiding principles can serve as ethically consistent ways to pursue excellence in communication with our romantic partners and relating with others. Courage in the face of opportunity or adversity certainly connects with those capable of thriving, as well as practicing mercy and generosity when relational goals fall short. Additionally, compassion and understanding would seem to be universally applicable forms of communication excellence, useful throughout the course of one's romantic relationship.

Conclusion

Romantic partnerships face unique challenges in our modern era, yet there is still a desire for these meaningful relationships to become optimal experiences for our lives. Developing flourishing and thriving experiences as seen here is a product of communication practices tailored to the needs of one's partner, cast across time, iteratively developed and refined, while helping our partner strive toward new opportunities and face adversity. These are positive heights of the human experience that are only possible working together, communicating together.

References

Afifi, T. D., Merrill, A. F., & Davis, S. (2016). The theory of resilience and relational load. *Personal Relationships, 23*, 663–683. doi:10.1111/pere.12159

Arnett, J. J. (2004). *Emerging adulthood: The winding road from the late teens through the twenties.* New York: Oxford University Press.

Aron, A., & Aron, E. N. (1986). *Love and the expansion of self: Understanding attraction satisfaction.* New York: Hemisphere.

Aune, K. S., & Wong, N. C. H. (2012). Fun with friends, pranks with partners: How we play in our closest relationships. In T. J. Socha & M. J. Pitts (Eds.), *The positive side of interpersonal communication* (pp. 143–159). New York: Peter Lang.

Baumeister, R. F., & Leary, M. R. (1995). The need to belong: Desire for interpersonal attachments as a fundamental human motivation. *Psychological Bulletin, 117*(3), 497–529.

Baxter, L. A. (1992). Forms and functions of intimate play in personal relationships. *Human Communication Research, 18*, 336–363.

Baxter, L. A., Norwood, K. M., & Nebel, S. (2012). Aesthetic relating. In T. J. Socha & M. J. Pitts (Eds.), *The positive side of interpersonal communication* (pp. 19–38). New York: Peter Lang.

Beck, G. A. (2016). Surviving involuntary unemployment together: The role of resilience-promoting communication in familial and committed relationships. *Journal of Family Communication, 16*(4), 369–385.

Beck, G. A. (2017). Theorizing relational resilience at midlife. In V. Waldron (Ed.), *The middle years of marriage: Challenge, change, and growth* (pp. 143–164). New York: Peter Lang.

Beck, G. A., & Socha, T. J. (Eds.). (2015). *Communicating hope and resilience across the lifespan.* New York, NY: Peter Lang.

Bronfenbrenner, U. (1979). *The ecology of human development: Experiments by nature and design.* Cambridge, MA: Harvard University Press.

Bruess, C. J. (2015). *Family communication in the age of digital and social media.* New York: Peter Lang.

Buzzanell, P. M. (2010). Presidential address-resilience: Talking, resisting, and imagining, new normalcies into being. *Journal of Communication, 60*, 1–14. doi:10.1111/j.1460-2466.2009.01469.x

Canary, D. J., & Dainton, M. (2006). Maintaining relationships. In A. L. Vangelisti & D. Perlman (Eds.), *The Cambridge handbook of personal relationships* (pp. 727–744). New York: Cambridge University Press.

Carr, K. (2015). Communication and family resilience. In C. R. Berger & M. E. Roloff (Eds.), *International encyclopedia of interpersonal communication* (pp. 1–9). Hoboken, NJ: Wiley Blackwell. doi:10.1002/9781118540190

Caughlin, J. P., & Huston, T. L. (2006). The affective structure of marriage. In A. L. Vangelisti & D. Perlman (Eds.), *The Cambridge handbook of personal relationships* (pp. 131–156). New York: Cambridge University Press.

Comte-Sponville, A. (2001). *A small treatise on the great virtues: The uses of philosophy in everyday life.* New York: Metropolitan Books.

Csikszentmihalyi, M. (1990). *Flow: The psychology of optimal experience.* New York: Harper Perennial.

Daiton, M. (2003). Erecting a framework for understanding relational maintenance: An epilogue. In D. J. Canary & M. Dainton (Eds.), *Maintaining relationships through communication: Relational, contextual, and cultural variations* (pp. 299–321). Hillsdale, NJ: Lawrence Erlbaum Associates.

Dindia, K. (2003). Definitions and perspectives on relational maintenance communication. In D. J. Canary & M. Dainton (Eds.), *Maintaining relationships through communication: Relational contextual, and cultural variation* (pp. 1–30). Hillsdale, NJ: Lawrence Erlbaum Associates.

Duan, W., Guan, Y., & Gan, F. (2016). Brief inventory of thriving: A comprehensive measurement of well-being. *Chinese Sociological Dialogue, 1*(1), 15–31. doi:10.1177/2397200916665230

Earhart Michel, R., & Randick, N. M. (2014). Hook-up or healthy relationship? Counseling student part-nering through the college years. In S. Degges-White & C. Borzumato-Gainey (Eds.), *College student mental health counseling: A developmental approach* (pp. 113–131). New York: Springer International Publishing.

Erikson, E. H. (1963). *Childhood and society* (2nd ed.). New York, NY: Norton.

Feeney, B. C., & Collins, N. L. (2015a). A new look at social support: A theoretical perspective on thriving through relationship. *Personality and Social Psychology Review, 19*, 113–147.

Feeney, B. C., & Collins, N. L. (2015b). Thriving through relationships. *Current Opinion in Psychology, 1*, 22–28.

Flourish. (2017). Oxford English Dictionary. Retrieved September 15, 2017 from https://en.oxforddiction-aries.com/definition/flourish

Floyd, K. (2002). Human affection exchange: V. Attributes of the high affectionate. *Communication Quarterly, 50*, 135–152.

Floyd, K. (2006). Human affection exchange: XII. Affectionate communication is associated with diurnal variation in salivary free cortisol. *Western Journal of Communication, 70*, 47–63.

Floyd, K., & Morman, M. T. (1998). The measurement of affectionate communication. *Communication Quarterly, 46*, 144–162.

Ganong, L., Jamison, T., & Chapman, A. (2016). Assessing differences in intimate partner obligations based on relationship status, gender, and parental status. *Journal of Social and Personal Relationships, 33*(7), 867–891. http://dx.doi.org.proxy.lib.odu.edu/10.1177/0265407515605665

Gonzales, L. (2004). *Deep survival: Who lives, who dies, and why.* New York: W.W. Norton & Company.

Gottman, J. M. (1994). *What predicts divorce?* Hillsdale, NJ: Lawrence Erlbaum Associates.

Huppert, F. A., & So, T. T. C. (2011). Flourishing across Europe: Application of a new framework for defin-ing well-being. *Soc Indices Research, 110*(3), 837–861. doi:10.1007/s11205-011-9966-7

Kaplan, H. B. (2006). Understanding the concept of resilience. In S. Goldstein & R. B. Brooks (Eds.), *Handbook of resilience in children* (pp. 39–47). New York, NY: Springer.

Kim, Y. Y. (2012). Being in concert: An explication of synchrony in positive intercultural communication. In T. J. Socha & M. J. Pitts (Eds.), *The positive side of interpersonal communication* (pp. 39–56). New York: Peter Lang.

Light, K. C., Grewen, K. M., & Amico, J. A. (2005). More frequent partner hugs and higher oxytocin levels are linked to lower blood pressure and heart rate in premenopausal women. *Biological Psychology, 69*, 5–21.

Lucas, K., & Buzzanell, P. M. (2012). Memorable messages of hard times: Constructing short and long-term resiliencies through family communication. *Journal of Family Communication, 12*, 189–208. doi:10.1080/15267431.2012.687196

Lyubormisky, S., Sheldon, K. M., & Schkade, D. (2005). Pursuing happiness: The architecture of sustainable change. *Review of General Psychology, 9*, 111–113.

Mirivel, J. C. (2012). Communication excellence: Embodying virtues in interpersonal communication. In T. J. Socha & M. J. Pitts (Eds.), *The positive side of interpersonal communication* (pp. 57–72). New York: Peter Lang.

Nussbaum, J. F., Miller-Day, M., & Fisher, C. L. (2012). "Holding each other all night long": Communicating intimacy in older adulthood. In T. J. Socha & M. J. Pitts (Eds.), *The positive side of interpersonal communication* (pp. 91–108). New York: Peter Lang.

Parks, M. R. (2017). Embracing the challenges and opportunities of mixed-media relationships. *Human Communication Research*. Advance online publication. http://dx.doi.org.proxy.lib.odu.edu/10.1111/hcre.12125

Perlman, D., & Vangelisti, A. L. (2006). Personal relationships: An introduction. In A. L. Vangelisti & D. Perlman (Eds.), *The Cambridge handbook of personal relationships* (pp. 3–10). New York: Cambridge University Press.

Rutter, M. (2007). Resilience, competence, and coping. *Child Abuse & Neglect, 31*(3), 205–209.

Seligman, M. E. P. (2011). *Flourishing.* New York, NY: Free Press.

Shatte, A. J., Seligman, M. E. P., Gillham, J. E., & Reivich, K. (2005). The role of positive psychology in child, adolescent, and family development. In R. M. Lerner, F. Jacobs, & D. Werlieb (Eds.), *Applied developmental science: An advanced textbook* (pp. 61–80). Thousand Oaks, CA: Sage Publications.

Socha, T. J. (2014). Foreword. In J. F. Nussbaum (Ed.), *The Handbook of lifespan communication.* (pp. i–iii). New York, NY: Peter Lang.

Socha, T. J., & Beck, G. A. (2015). Positive interpersonal communication and human needs: A review and proposed organizing conceptual framework. *Review of Communication. 15*(3), 173–199 http://dx.doi.org/10.1080/15358593.2015.1080290

Socha, T. J., & Pitts, M. J. (Eds.). (2012). *The positive side of interpersonal communication.* New York, NY: Peter Lang.

Solomon, D. H., Knobloch, L. K., Theiss, J. A., & McLaren, R. (2016). Relational turbulence theory: Explaining variation in subjective experiences and communication within romantic relationships. *Human Communication Research, 42*(4), 507–532.

Taylor, S. E., Klein, L. C., Lewis, B. P., Gruenewald, T. L., Gurung, R. A. R., & Updegraff, J. A. (2000). Biobehavioral responses to stress in females: Tend-and-befriend, not fight-or-flight. *Psychological Review, 107*, 411–429.

Thrive. (2017). Oxford English Dictionary. Retrieved September 15, 2017 from https://en.oxforddictionaries.com/definition/thrive

Tolman, E. (2009). Creating opportunities for interaction and critical reflection in the interpersonal communication course: Completing random acts of kindness. *Communication Teacher, 23*, 132–136.

Waldron, V., & Kelley, D. (2008). *Communicating forgiveness.* Thousand Oaks, CA: Sage Publications.

Waldron. V. (2017). *The middle years of marriage: Challenge, change, and growth.* New York: Peter Lang.

Watzlawick, P., Weakland, J., & Fisch, R. (1974). *Change: Principles of problem formation and problem resolution.* New York, NY: W. W. Norton.

Weiss, R. L. (1980). Strategic behavioral marital therapy: Toward a model for assessment and intervention. In J. P. Vincent (Ed.), *Advances in family intervention, assessment, and theory* (Vol. 1, pp. 229–271). Greenwich, CT: JAI Press.

Wilson, S. R., & Gettings, P. (2012). Nurturing children as assets: A positive approach to preventing child maltreatment and promoting healthy youth development. In T. J. Socha & M. J. Pitts (Eds.), *The positive side of interpersonal communication* (pp. 277–296). New York, NY: Peter Lang.

Zamanzadeh, N. N., & Afifi, T. D. (2018). Prosocial relationship maintenance and resilience/thriving. In J. A. Muñiz-Velázquez & C. Pulido (Eds.). *The Routledge handbook of positive communication* (pp. 60–69). New York, NY: Routledge.

9

EXPLICATING POSITIVE COMMUNICATION WITHIN THEORIES OF FAMILY COMMUNICATION

Steven R. Wilson and Elizabeth A. Munz

Positive communication refers broadly to "message processes that promote hedonic and eudemonic happiness" as well as those that facilitate "individual, relational, and [collective] health and wellness" (Socha & Beck, 2015, p. 179). Although positive communication occurs in many contexts, families are an important domain in which to explicate the nature of positive communication. Defined as "a group of intimates who generate a sense of home and group identity and who experience a shared history and a shared future" (Koerner & Fitzpatrick, 2002, p. 714), family is the system in which most of us initially experience positive communication. Family ties typically are maintained across the lifespan, and families serve multiple critical functions for their members (e.g., belonging/identity, economic support, socialization, protection of vulnerable members; Patterson, 2002). Although "family" often associated is with idealized notions of acceptance and support (Caughlin, 2003), families are by no means inherently linked to positive communication. Families also are systems in which some members may experience abuse, marginalization, and estrangement (Scharp & Dorrance Hall, 2017).

Positive communication often is viewed in terms of the degree to which it helps satisfy basic human needs, though scholars vary in how they conceptualize and organize such needs (e.g., Jayawickreme, Forgeard, & Seligman, 2012; Socha & Beck, 2015). Building on this premise, we argue that positive communication can be fruitfully thought of as a "theoretical term"—that is, as a concept whose meaning depends, in part, on its horizontal linkage with other terms comprising specific theoretical frameworks (see Wilson & Sabee, 2003). Family communication theories themselves offer one resource for explicating positive communication; hence, comparing/contrasting multiple theories should offer important insights about both positive communication and families.

We explicate positive communication within three family communication theories: discourse-dependent families (Galvin, 2014), attachment theory (Bretherton, 1992), and family communication patterns (Koerner & Schrodt, 2014). Although by no means the only options, these frameworks have generated large bodies of scholarship, place communication at the center of family formation and functioning, and highlight family interaction across the life course. For each theory, we analyze key concepts and assumptions, basic human needs the theory highlights, message processes that the theory links to those needs, and insights revealed about positive communication (see Table 9.1). By analyzing how positive communication is—often implicitly—conceptualized within different theories, we hope to offer new insights about positive communication including

Table 9.1 Explicating Positive Communication within Three Theories of Family Communication

Theory	Key assumptions about families and communication	Needs highlighted by the theory	Message processes highlighted by the theory	Insights about positive communication and families
Discourse-Dependent Families (Galvin)	"Family" is created not just by blood or legal ties but also via discourse Families come in many forms (not just nuclear families)	Belonging/Shared Identity Communal Recognition/Acceptance Protection (from external disapproval)	Internal boundary management (naming, discussing, narrating, ritualizing) External boundary management (labeling, explaining, legitimizing, defending)	Positive family communication takes multiple, mundane forms (e.g., rituals) The need for/nature of positive communication depends on the interplay of families and larger communities
Attachment Theory (Bolwby, Ainsworth)	Humans have an innate need for attachment; infants who experience caregiver sensitivity develop secure working models; the attachment system is activated during stress; attachment continues across the lifespan	Security/safety Exploration Connection	Caregiver sensitivity Interpersonal behaviors associated with secure attachment in romantic relationships (e.g., conflict styles) Mentoring	Positive communication starts early, occurs across the lifespan Individuals differ in the extent to which they experience/exhibit positive communication Intergenerational transmission of positive communication
Family Communication Patterns Theory (Koerner, Fitzpatrick)	Families create a shared social reality via talk (conversation orientation) and/or by adhering to traditional structures (conformity orientation); four types; schemas	Understanding Participation Belonging to a collective Autonomy	Range of info processing and interpersonal variables (e.g., social support) that FCP studies explore – especially those linked to resilience	Positive communication not one size fits all (may vary by family type) Family formation = intercultural communication

the complex ways in which family interaction may facilitate and/or hinder family members' individual, relational, and collective happiness and well-being.

Galvin's Discourse-Dependent Families Perspective

Galvin's (2006, 2014) discourse-dependence perspective emphasizes that families are created not just through legal or biological ties, but also via discursive practices through which members create a shared family identity. Galvin begins by highlighting the increasing diversity of family forms in the US and many other places in the 21st century. In the US, trends such as people waiting later to marry, declines in marriage duration, increases in first births within cohabiting unions, and the legalization of same-sex marriage are making family forms more complex (see Galvin, 2006, 2014). Stepfamilies, single-parent families, families formed through visible (e.g., international, interracial) adoption, and families headed by gay/lesbian parents, among others, challenge the cultural assumption that families are composed of two hetero-sexual, married adults and their biological children.

Although discourse plays a role in creating a sense of shared identity in all families, it is especially important for diverse family forms:

> Family identity depends, in part, on members' communication with outsiders, as well as with each other, regarding their familial connection. Even though all families engage in some level of discourse-driven family identity building, less traditional forms are more discourse dependent, engaging in recurring discursive practices to manage and maintain identity.
>
> *(Galvin, 2006, p. 3)*

In situations such as when a mother of biological and internationally adopted children is asked "Are your daughters *real* sisters?" (Docan-Morgan, 2010), or a lesbian mother picking up her daughter from an after-school program is told "Oh, you're not the mom, I met her mom already" (Koenig Kellas & Suter, 2012), family members rely on discourse to define and justify their connection to outsiders as well as to each other.

According to Galvin (2006, 2014), discourse is used to construct both external and internal family boundaries. External boundary management "involves the use of discourse strategies to reinforce family identity when outsiders challenge that identity or the validity of a specific family relationship is misunderstood" (Galvin, 2014, p. 29). External strategies include: (a) *labeling*—creating titles to indicate the nature of a family connection (e.g., a stepdaughter introduces her stepfather as "my dad" as opposed to "my stepdad" or "my mom's husband"), (b) *explaining*—making a relationship understandable to others (e.g., "Michael is our cousin, but he's lived with us since we were little so we view him as our brother"), (c) *legitimizing*—appealing to a law or custom to claim a tie (e.g., "My parents adopted Reagan so she is my sister"), and (d) *defending*—actively justifying a relationship against attack (e.g., "of course they're real sisters, which you'd understand if you knew what family really meant"). Internal boundary management involves "ongoing communication practices designed to create [an] internal sense of family-ness" (Galvin, 2006, p. 11). Internal strategies include: (a) *naming*—creating labels for persons who are considered family but do not share blood or legal ties (e.g., calling a long-time family friend "Aunt Erma"), (b) *discussing*—talking about the ties that bind family members (e.g., parents talking with transracially adopted children about how they are family despite physical differences), (c) *narrating*—telling stories that affirm the family's identity (e.g., the story of how an adopted child entered the family), and (d) *ritualizing*—enacting traditions for particular occasions (e.g., members of a stepfamily all taking turns reading Else Minarik's "Birthday Soup" together on the occasion of each member's birthday).

The discourse-dependence framework has spurred a sizeable body of research exploring the discursive strategies enacted by adoptive families (e.g., Docan-Morgan, 2010, Suter, Reyes, & Ballard, 2011), foster families (e.g., Miller-Ott, 2017), families headed by gay/lesbian parents (e.g., Koenig Kellas & Suter, 2012), families of children with autism (e.g., Hays & Colaner, 2016), and voluntary kin (e.g., Braithwaite et al., 2010). Other research has explored associations between themes present in parents' stories about how foster children entered the family and those children's adjustment and relational closeness (Nelson & Horstman, 2017). Although discourse can enhance shared family identity, it also can deconstruct family ties (Galvin, 2014). Research has explored the discursive strategies that individuals who are estranged from or marginalized by their family of origin use to create/maintain distance, account for lack of contact, and establish family ties with others (Scharp & Dorrance Hall, 2017).

Galvin's (2014) framework highlights a number of basic human needs that animate family members (see Table 9.1). Members often want to feel part of a shared family identity, though this need for belonging can be complicated (e.g., when internationally adopted individuals discursively construct connections to both their adopted and birth families; Docan-Morgan, 2017). Members also want their family to be accepted as "legitimate" by others, and children may need protection from attacks by non-receptive outsiders (Suter et al., 2011). Discursive strategies function as positive communication when they fulfill human needs for belonging, legitimation, and protection. Enacting a discursive strategy, however, does not guarantee that it will function as positive communication; for example, external boundary management strategies used by parents in some cases affirm their adopted child's place in the family, but in other cases draw unwanted attention to the adoptee (Docan-Morgan, 2010). Positive communication requires adaptation and timing based on family members' preferences. In extreme cases, discourse that weakens family ties functions as positive communication by protecting individuals from ongoing pain (Scharp & Dorrance Hall, 2017).

Finally, Galvin's (2014) discourse-dependent family framework offers a number of important insights about positive communication. Positive communication occurs not just during consequential moments (e.g., support provided when a family member truly is in need), but also during mundane moments that enhance family connection (e.g., the ritual of reading a bedtime story together). Positive communication also must be tailored based on the needs of individual family members, but also based on how larger communities affirm/reject particular family forms.

Bowlby and Ainsworth's Attachment Theory

Attachment Theory (Bowlby, 1958) explains the impact of early caregiving experiences on children's social and personality development, Attachments are enduring emotional bonds. After observing children's responses to separation from or loss of a caregiver, Bowlby (1958) concluded that caregivers are not interchangeable and that the caregiver-child relationship is a necessity for a child's healthy growth and development.

Key components of Attachment Theory highlight a number of basic human needs starting with parent-child relationships and extending to other relationships throughout the lifespan (see Table 9.1). At the heart of attachment theory is the concept of security which is one of the basic human needs addressed by the theory. Attachment security is an individual's confidence in their attachment figure's responsiveness and availability (Ainsworth, Blehar, Waters, & Wall, 1978). In young children, secure attachment is exemplified by secure-based behavior, such as children's willingness to explore away from their caregivers but also the ways securely attached children seek out their caregivers in times of need or distress (Ainsworth et al., 1978). Secure-base behavior can also be found in adult attachment relationships, such as when adults who are stressed turn to romantic partners for comfort, safety, and protection (Fraley & Shaver, 2000).

Exploration is a second basic human need identified by attachment theory. Securely attached children utilize their caregiver as a secure-base from which to explore the world around them. For example, if a securely attached four-year-old became anxious while reading a book about going to kindergarten, the child would seek reassurance from their caregiver but then return to reading about what school will be like (Munz & Wilson, 2014). Attachment features in adult romantic relationships follow a specific sequencing with proximity-seeking behaviors emerging first (e.g., wanting to spend time with a romantic partner), followed by the safe haven phenomenon (e.g., an individual relying on a partner to calm them down when they are distressed) and ultimately secure-based behavior (e.g., exploring on their own but turning to their romantic partner in times of need) (Heffernan, Fraley, Vicary, & Brumbaugh, 2012).

The strongest predictor of secure attachment in infants and toddlers is caregiver sensitivity (De Wolff & van IJzendoorn, 1997). According to Ainsworth and colleagues (1978), sensitive caregiving is a prompt and appropriate response to an infant's signals coupled with meaningful and enjoyable interaction between attachment figures and children. Sensitive caregiving by an attachment figure fulfills an individual's need for connection with others (a third basic need highlighted by attachment theory). Conversely, caregiver insensitivity can take the form of detachment (e.g., missing cues that a child needs assistance) or intrusiveness (e.g., forcing a child to play with one toy when the child already is engaged with a different toy). Sensitive caregiving changes as children age because what is deemed "prompt and appropriate" will shift as children develop. Sources of stress and anxiety will change as children age but sensitive caregiving involves being responsive to needs for connection as they arise.

The mechanism through which children's early caregiving experiences shape their future relationships is known as the internal working model, or mental representations for expectations in relationships (Bowlby, 1988). Fivush (2006) summarizes Bowlby's assertions regarding internal working models by noting how the internal working model represents "the individual's experiences of early caregiving as generalized models of self, other, and the world" (p. 283). Within the realm of positive communication, individuals who are the beneficiaries of sensitive caregiving will come to view themselves as individuals worthy of those positive behaviors and will come to expect those behaviors from other significant individuals in their lives. Conversely, individuals who receive inconsistent caregiving behaviors or who do not have caregivers who respond promptly and appropriately to their needs may start to view themselves as unworthy of having their basic needs met and view others as untrustworthy.

Attachment Theory offers a number of important insights about positive communication. Secure attachment relationships benefit individuals because positive early caregiving experiences allow individuals to expect close relationships throughout their lifetime, or in positive communication terms, allow individuals to flourish (Seligman, 2011). Sensitive early caregiving promotes secure attachment, and through internal working models that security enables individuals to develop satisfying peer relationships in childhood (Sroufe, Carlson, & Shulman, 1993) as well as satisfying romantic relationships later in life. For example, participants report more relational satisfaction with partners who scored high in security and low in the insecure (i.e., dismissive and preoccupied) attachment styles (Guerrero, Farinelli, & McEwan, 2009).

Positive communication, in the form of sensitive caregiving, not only facilitates expectations for close current and future relationships, it also diminishes patterns of conflict avoidance, fearfulness, ambivalence, or dominance which can be present in individuals who do not have positive early caregiving experiences (LaValley & Guerrero, 2012). Fortunately, individuals can overcome the challenges of negative early caregiving experiences by forming attachment bonds with other significant others (e.g., romantic partners, extended family, mentors) who enable the individuals to trust in the availability and reliability of others and see themselves as people worthy of support. In other words, despite the pervasive impact of secure attachment on other relationships, internal working models can evolve when individuals form attachment bonds with other individuals in their lives. Early research on attachment theory focused almost exclusively on mothers as caregivers (e.g., Ainsworth, 1967) but research has expanded to fathers (e.g., Bureau et al., 2016), friends (e.g., Welch & Houser, 2010), and romantic partners (e.g., Heffernan et al., 2012; LaValley & Guerrero, 2012) suggesting a number of significant others may influence attachment security.

An additional insight from Attachment Theory suggests that the secure attachment that accompanies sensitive early caregiving facilitates the intergenerational transmission of positive communication (Verhage et al., 2016). A study looking at three generations determined this intergenerational transmission was particularly poignant for maternal lines with mothers' behaviors impacting their children's internal working models as well as their children's likelihood of exhibiting positive parenting behaviors with their own children (Cassibba, Coppola, Sette, Curci, & Costantini, 2016). Put differently, Attachment Theory highlights that positive communication has a historical dimension, as our experiences with it reflect not only our own early circumstances but those of our parents and other caregivers as well.

Koerner and Fitzpatrick's Family Communication Patterns Theory

Family communication patterns (FCP) theory (Koerner & Schrodt, 2014) argues that families achieve a shared social reality through a combination of two processes called conversation and conformity orientation. Crossing these two dimensions creates a communication-based typology that offers insights about individual and family well-being.

FCP theory originated in the work of McLeod and Chaffee (1972, 1973), who were interested in how families process media content. Drawing on Newcomb's (1953) theory of co-orientation, McLeod and Chafee argued that families need to achieve some degree of shared social reality (i.e., agreement and accuracy in understanding each other's views about an object that multiple family members orient toward) to function as a collective unit. They proposed families can achieve agreement about an object (e.g., a news story) in two distinct ways. First, families could openly discuss the nature of object and come to a shared understanding of how to conceptualize it (a process McLeod and Chaffee called concept-orientation). Second, members could come to agreement by adhering to one family member's (e.g., a parent's) view of the object, thereby prioritizing relationships between family members rather than attributes of the object itself (a process they called socio-orientation). FCP theory highlights how families help their members fulfill the basic human need for *understanding* the social world (e.g., what things mean, why things occur), while also modeling various ways of *participating* in the process of achieving a shared understanding (see Table 9.1). McLeod and Chafee showed that family members' interest in and susceptibility to specific media content (e.g., news, advertising) depends on how they employ these two processes (see Schrodt, Witt, & Messersmith, 2008).

Families co-orient to more than media stories; hence, Mary Anne Fitzpatrick and her colleagues (e.g., Koerner & Fitzpatrick, 2002) reconceptualized the two FCPs in terms of the communicative behaviors families employ to coordinate their views and actions in general. *Conversation orientation* is "the degree to which family communication creates a climate in which all family members are encouraged to participate in unrestrained interaction about a wide variety of topics" (Koerner & Fitzpatrick, 2004, p. 184). Families high in conversation orientation spend a lot of time talking and share their thoughts, feelings, and activities with each other freely; those lower in conversation orientation spend less time talking and view open communication as less central to family functioning. Conformity orientation is "the degree to which family communication stresses a climate of homogeneity of attitudes, values, and beliefs" (Koerner & Fitzpatrick, 2004, p. 184). Families high in conformity orientation stress harmony and interdependence among family members was well as obedience to parents; those lower in conformity orientation emphasize independence and are comfortable when family members hold diverse views.

Koerner and Fitzpatrick (2002) conceptualize the two FCPs as relationship-type schema, or knowledge and expectations that individuals hold about family relationships; such schema impact family members' routine and situation-specific communication. Because all families must achieve some level of co-orientation and the two FCPs represent ways of accomplishing this (i.e., discussing and defining issues together, adhering to traditional family structures and gender norms), Koerner and Schrodt (2014) argue that the two FPCs should exist in any culture. Having said this, the meaning of conversation and conformity orientation clearly are culturally grounded; for example, conformity orientation may have more positive connotations for US military families (where values such as self-sacrifice, prioritization of a common mission, and adherence to a chain of command may be internalized) than it does for much of the US civilian population (Wilson, Chernichky, Wilkum, & Owlett, 2014).

Koerner and Fitzpatrick (2004) also conceptualize the two FPCs as orthogonal; thus, crossing them creates four family types. *Consensual* families are high in both conversation and conformity orientation; parents in such families spend time explaining their ideas and values to their children but ultimately believe they should make final decisions. *Pluralistic* families are high in conversation and low in conformity orientation; hence, parents emphasize the open-exchange of ideas, evaluate arguments based on their merits, and encourage children to participate in decision-making. *Protective* families are low in conversation and high in conformity orientation; parents in such families believe they should make decisions for the family and see conflict as a threat to family harmony. *Laissez-faire* families are low on both conversation and conformity orientation; thus, parents do not feel the need to control decision-making but also display less interest in their children's ideas (Koerner & Schrodt, 2014).

FCP theory has generated a sizeable body of family communication research (see Koerner & Schrodt, 2014; Schrodt et al., 2008). FCPs have been linked to the degree to which parents and children manage conflict constructively, offer each other support, and express affection and conformation—all behaviors typically considered positive forms of communication (Socha & Beck, 2015). These behaviors mediate relationships between FCPs in one's family of origin and young adults' psychological (e.g., lack of depression) and social (e.g., closeness to friends and siblings) well-being (see Koerner & Schrodt, 2014). In general, conversational orientation is positively associated with psychological and relational well-being, whereas conformity orientation is either unrelated or negatively related (Schrodt et al., 2008), but there are exceptions. For example, conversation orientation benefits military youth when it makes them feel like other members of their family understand what it is like to have a parent deployed to a warzone; however, conversation orientation increases stress when it encourages at-home parents to disclose developmentally inappropriate information to their children (Chernichky-Karcher & Wilson, 2017). Likewise, conformity orientation can be positive when it creates a sense of belonging to a collective by encouraging family members to spend quality time exclusively with each other, but negative when parents engage in developmentally inappropriate control or discourage children from forming close relationships outside of the family (Hesse, Rauscher, Budesky, Goodman, & Couvrette, 2017).

FCP theory accentuates a number of basic human needs that motivate family members, including the desire to understand the social world, participate in family decision-making, and feel part of an important in-group while also creating relationships outside of the family. The theory also offers unique insights about positive communication (see Table 9.1). Koerner and Fitzpatrick (2004) assert that there is no one "best" family form; families can enhance individual and collective well-being through varying combinations of FCPs. As general family schemata, FCPs implicate a variety of positive forms of communication (e.g., support, constructive conflict management) that promote resilience when families face stressful events (Wilson et al., 2014). Finally, FCPs highlight how forming a new family, including negotiating a shared social reality about the nature of positive communication, can be akin to "intercultural" communication since partners may come from families of origin with quite different FCPs.

Conclusion

This chapter has explicated positive communication within three theories of family communication. Our primary point is that the meaning of positive communication depends, in part, on other theoretical terms to which it is linked (Wilson & Sabee, 2003), and hence different theories offer unique insights about positive communication (see Table 9.1). Treating positive communication as a theoretical term means that how it is conceptualized will vary to some extent across theoretical frameworks. Although treating positive communication as a theoretical term adds complexity to the process of explication, variations in theoretical emphasis also offer opportunities for gaining comparative insights about positive communication and families.

References

Ainsworth, M. D. (1967). *Infancy in Uganda: Infant care and the growth of love*. Baltimore: Johns Hopkins University Press.

Ainsworth, M. D., Blehar, M., Waters, E., & Wall, S. (1978). *Patterns of attachment*. Hillsdale, NJ: Lawrence Erlbaum Associates.

Bowlby, J. (1958). The nature of a child's tie to his mother. *International Journal of Psychoanalysis, 39*, 360–373.

Bowlby, J. (1988). *A secure base: Clinical applications of attachment theory*. London: Routledge.

Braithwaite, D. O., Bach, B. W., Baxter, L. A., DiVerniero, R., Hammonds, J. R., Hosek, A. M., . . . Wolf, B. M. (2010). Constructing family: A typology of voluntary kin. *Journal of Social and Personal Relationships, 27*, 388–407.

Bretherton, I. (1992). The origins of attachment theory: John Bowlby and Mary Ainsworth. *Developmental Psychology, 28*, 759–775. doi:10.1037/0012-1649.28.5.759

Bureau, J., Martin, J., Yurkowski, K., Schmiedel, S., Quan, J., Moss, E., . . . Pallanca, D. (2016). Correlates of child-father and child-mother attachment in the preschool years. *Attachment & Human Development, 19*, 1–21.

Cassibba, R., Coppola, G., Sette, G., Curci, A., & Costantini, A. (2016). The transmission of attachment across three generations: A study in adulthood. *Developmental Psychology, 53*, 396–405.

Caughlin, J. O. (2003). Family communication standards: What counts as excellent family communication and how are such standards associated with family satisfaction? *Human Communication Research, 29*, 5–40.

Chernichky-Karcher, S., & Wilson, S. R. (2017). Family communication patterns and adolescent experiences during parental military deployment and reunion: The role of inappropriate parental disclosures and perceived family understanding. *Communication Studies*. Published online ahead of print http://dx.doi.org/10.1080/10510974.2017.1318159

De Wolff, M. S., & van IJzendoorn, M. H. (1997). Sensitivity and attachment: A meta-analysis of parental antecedents of infant attachment. *Child Development, 68*, 571–591.

Docan-Morgan, S. (2010). Korean adoptees' retrospective reports of intrusive interactions: Exploring boundary management in adoptive families. *Journal of Family Communication, 10*, 137–157.

Docan-Morgan, S. (2017). Korean adoptees' discursive construction of birth family and adoptive family identity through names and labels. *Communication Quarterly*. Advance online publication.

Fivush, R. (2006). Scripting attachment: Generalized event representations and internal working models. *Attachment & Human Development, 8*, 283–289.

Fraley, R. C., & Shaver, P. R. (2000). Adult romantic attachment: Theoretical developments, emerging controversies, and unanswered questions. *Review of General Psychology, 4*, 132–154.

Galvin, K. M. (2006). Diversity's impact on defining the family: Discourse-dependence and identity. In L. H. Turner & R. West (Eds.), *The family communication sourcebook* (pp. 3–20). Thousand Oaks, CA: Sage Publications.

Galvin, K. M. (2014). Blood, law, and discourse: Constructing and managing family identity. In L. A. Baxter (Ed.), *Remaking "family" communicatively* (pp. 17–32). New York: Peter Lang.

Guerrero, L. K., Farinelli, L., & McEwan, B. (2009). Attachment and relational satisfaction: The mediating effect of emotional communication. *Communication Monographs, 76*, 487–514.

Hays, A., & Colaner, C. (2016). Discursively constructing a family identity after an autism diagnosis: Trials, tribulations, and triumphs. *Journal of Family Communication, 16*, 143–159.

Heffernan, M. E., Fraley, R. C., Vicary, A. M., & Brumbaugh, C. C. (2012). Attachment features and functions in adult romantic relationships. *Journal of Social and Personal Relationships, 29*, 671–693.

Hesse, C., Rauscher, E. A., Budesky Goodman, R., & Couvrette, M. A. (2017). Reconceptualizing the role of conformity orientation in family communication patterns theory. *Journal of Family Communication, 17*, 319–337.

Jayawickreme, E., Forgeard, M. J. C., & Seligman, M. E. P. (2012). The engine of well-being. *Review of General Psychology, 16*, 327–342.

Koenig Kellas, J., & Suter, E. A. (2012). Accounting for lesbian-headed families: Lesbian mothers' responses to discursive challenges. *Communication Monographs, 79*, 475–498.

Koerner, A. F., & Fitzpatrick, M. (2002). Toward a theory of family communication. *Communication Theory*, *12*, 70–91.

Koerner, A. F., & Fitzpatrick, M. A. (2004). Communication in intact families. In A. Vangelisti (Ed.), *Handbook of family communication* (pp. 177–214). Mahwah, NJ: Lawrence Erlbaum Associates.

Koerner, A. F., & Schrodt, P. (2014). An introduction to the special issue on Family communication patterns theory. *Journal of Family Communication*, *14*, 1–15.

LaValley, A. G., & Guerrero, L. K. (2012). Perceptions of conflict behavior and relational satisfaction in adult parent-child relationships: A dyadic analysis from an attachment perspective. *Communication Research*, *39*, 48–78.

McLeod, J. M., & Chaffee, S. H. (1972). The construction of social reality. In J. Tedeschi (Ed.), *The social influence process* (pp. 50–59). Chicago, IL: Aldine-Atherton.

McLeod, J. M., & Chaffee, S. H. (1973). Interpersonal approaches to communication research. *American Behavioral Scientist*, *16*, 469–499.

Miller-Ott, A. E. (2017). Developing and maintaining foster family identity through foster parents' identity work. *Journal of Family Communication*, *17*, 208–222.

Munz, E. A., & Wilson, S. R. (2014). Caregiver confirmation and children's attachment security during the transition to kindergarten. *Communication Research*, *44*, 668–690.

Nelson, L. R., & Horstman, H. K. (2017). Communicated meaning-making in foster families: Relationships between foster parents' entrance narratives and foster child well-being. *Communication Quarterly*, *65*, 144–166.

Newcomb, T. M. (1953). An approach to the study of communicative acts. *Psychological Review*, *60*, 393–404.

Patterson, J. M. (2002). Integrating family resilience and family stress theory. *Journal of Marriage and Family*, *64*, 349–360.

Scharp, K. M., & Dorrance Hall, E. (2017). Family marginalization, alienation, and estrangement: Questioning the nonvoluntary status of family relationships. *Annals of the International Communication Association*, *41*, 28–45.

Schrodt, P., Witt, P. L., & Messersmith, A. (2008). A meta-analytic review of family communication patterns and their association with information processing, behavioral, and psychosocial outcomes. *Communication Monographs*, *75*, 248–269.

Seligman, M. E. P. (2011). *Flourish*. New York, NY: The Free Press.

Socha, T. J., & Beck, G. A. (2015). Positive communication and human needs: A review and proposed conceptual organizing framework. *Review of Communication*, *15*, 173–199.

Sroufe, L. A., Carlson, E., & Shulman, S. (1993). Individuals in relationships: Development from infancy through adolescence. In D. C. Funder, R. D. Parke, C. Tomlinson-Keasey, & K. Widaman (Eds.), *Studying lives through time: Personality and development* (pp. 315–342). Washington, DC: American Psychological Association.

Suter, E. A., Reyes, K. L., & Ballard, R. L. (2011). Parental management of adoptive identities during challenging encounters: Adoptive parents as "protectors" and "educators". *Journal of Social and Personal Relationships*, *28*, 242–261.

Verhage, M. L., Schuengel, C., Madigan, S., Fearon, R. M. P., Ooosterman, M., Cassibba, R., . . . van IJzendoorn, M. H. (2016). Narrowing the transmission gap: A synthesis of three decades of research on intergenerational transmission of attachment. *Psychological Bulletin*, *142*, 337–366.

Welch, R. D., & Houser, M. E. (2010). Extending the four-category model of adult attachment: An interpersonal model of friendship attachment. *Journal of Social and Personal Relationships*, *27*, 351–366.

Wilson, S. R., Chernichky, K. M., Wilkum, K., & Owlett, J. S. (2014). Do family communication patterns buffer children from difficulties associated with a parent's military deployment? Examining deployed and at-home parts' perspectives. *Journal of Family Communication*, *14*, 32–52.

Wilson, S. R., & Sabee, C. M. (2003). Explicating communicative competence as a theoretical term. In J. O. Greene & B. R. Burleson (Eds.), *Handbook of communication and social interaction skills* (pp. 3–50). Hillsdale, NJ: Lawrence Erlbaum Associates.

10

SUPPORTIVE AND MINDFUL COMMUNICATION

Susanne M. Jones and Lucas J. Youngvorst

Supportive and Mindful Communication

Almost four decades of research confirm that people with fewer social support resources are between 1.5 and 3.0 times more likely to die from all causes compared to people with more robust social networks, even when controlling for self-reported and physiological markers of health risks (Berkman & Syme, 1979; Holt-Lunstad, Smith, & Layton, 2010). A 2010 meta-analysis showed that supportive relationships in particular benefit health on par with smoking cessation and reduced alcohol consumption (Holt-Lunstad et al., 2010). Not only does quality support allow people to cope more effectively with difficult emotions, but it also contributes to a relationship's emotional capital by allowing people to flourish in good *and* bad times (Feeney & Collins, 2015).

Emotional support is one particularly important type of social support because it facilitates the emotion regulation process (i.e., coping; Butler & Randall, 2013; Cutrona, 1990; Zaki & Williams, 2013). Emotional support is always enacted, which means that it is conveyed through verbal messages and in social interaction (Goldsmith, 2004; Jones & Bodie, 2014). Enacted emotional support must fulfill two functions: (a) to respond effectively to a distressed person and (b) to facilitate the alleviation of negative emotions experienced by that person (Jones & Bodie, 2014). Past research has identified several important factors, including mindfulness, that positively influence the accomplishment of these functions (Bodie & Burleson, 2008; Jones, Bodie, & Hughes, 2016; Stewart, Ahrens, & Gunthert, 2017). Mindfulness is defined as present-centered awareness and attention to internal and external experiences in a dispassionate, nonjudgmental way (Brown & Ryan, 2003). Although several studies have detected positive relationships between mindfulness, communication skills, and social support (Cacciatore & Flint, 2012; Jones et al., 2016), it is not well understood in what ways mindfulness influences enacted emotional support. We review work on both supportive communication and mindfulness, and point to crucial questions that require future research.

Supportive Communication

Enacted emotional support is frequently conceptualized as *person-centered* support. Person centeredness (PC) is an observable message property that expresses the extent to which the supportive listener communicates "affective, subjective, and relational aspects of [a] communication

89

context" (Burleson, 1987, p. 305, emphasis added by authors; for reviews see Jones & Bodie, 2014; Samter & MacGeorge, 2016). The hierarchical system used to code supportive messages for PC is organized into three major levels, each containing three sublevels (Applegate, 1980; Burleson, 1982, 1984; Samter & MacGeorge, 2016). Messages *low in person centeredness* (LPC) deny or minimize the feelings experienced and expressed by the upset person by condemning (level 1), challenging the legitimacy of (level 2), or ignoring (level 3) these feelings. *Moderate person-centered* (MPC) messages implicitly recognize the distressed person's emotional experiences by distracting attention away from the stressful event (level 4), acknowledging feelings without subsequently exploring why those feelings are felt (level 5), or offering non-feeling centered explanations for what happened (level 6). *High person-centered* (HPC) messages signal availability and compassion by explicitly acknowledging the distressed person's feelings (level 7), offering elaborated acknowledgments and explanations of those feelings (level 8), and/or helping the other see how expressed feelings fit a broader context (level 9).

More than four decades of research show that people regularly evaluate messages possessing HPC characteristics as more beneficial than either MPC or LPC messages (for a meta-analysis see High & Dillard, 2012). When testing for moderating influences (e.g., sex, cultural differences, cognitive complexity, attachment), linear trends for PC remain strong, even though slope coefficients decrease somewhat (Bodie & Burleson, 2008). The actual support people enact, however, rarely reflects PC levels higher than level six (Bodie, Jones, Youngvorst, Navarro, & Danielson, 2017; MacGeorge & Wilkum, 2012).

The vast majority of studies have used message-centered approaches to test how people evaluate and provide messages that vary in PC. Message-centered studies that examine PC evaluations ask people read and rate a set of hypothetical messages on various supportiveness dimensions (e.g., helpfulness; Goldsmith, McDermott, & Alexander, 2000). One hypothetical message reflects one PC level in the hierarchy. In message-production studies participants read a hypothetical stress scenario and write what they might say to the hypothetical person (e.g., friend, stranger) in the scenario. Written messages are then coded with the PC hierarchy by trained judges (e.g., MacGeorge & Wilkum, 2012). Both message-centered approaches continue to be used in computer-mediated contexts that focus on text-based exchanges (e.g., Rains, Brunner, Akers, Pavlich, & Tsetsi, 2016; Spottswood, Walther, Holmstrom, & Ellison, 2013), but allow us to draw only limited conclusions about real-life stressful events. Several research teams have therefore turned to supportive conversations as primary locations to examine PC support (Afifi, Afifi, Merrill, Denes, & Davis, 2013; High & Solomon, 2014; Jones & Wirtz, 2006; Priem & Solomon, 2015).

Conversational PC studies are usually conducted in the lab and involve a discloser discussing an upsetting event with a listener (e.g., stranger, friend) who enacts support. Conversations range from 5 to 20 minutes, and enacted support is either manipulated for PC (Jones & Guerrero, 2001; High & Solomon, 2014), general support (Afifi et al., 2013), or not at all (Priem & Solomon, 2015). Transcribed conversations are then rated for PC qualities (e.g., validates-invalidates) by trained judges (High & Solomon, 2016; Jones & Wirtz, 2006). Much like the message-centered approach, conversations rated higher on PC characteristics generate higher levels of emotional improvement than conversations rated lower on PC characteristics (using the three major PC levels as criteria). Conversations rated higher on PC also have durable positive effects three weeks after people have received this kind of support (High & Solomon, 2016), and encourage (*vs.* discourage) the exploration of thoughts and feelings which, in turn, influences emotion regulation (Jones & Wirtz, 2006). Last, conversations rated as possessing LPC characteristics can exacerbate the stress response and lead the support discloser to ruminate, which has deleterious effects for well-being and health (Afifi et al., 2013).

Supportive Conversations as Coping Sites

The primary goal of supportive conversations is to facilitate emotion regulation, which is commonly grounded in cognitive appraisal theory (CAT; Lazarus, 1991; Lazarus & Folkman, 1984). CAT is important for emotion regulation because a) the personal meaning analysis is based on only a small number of dimensions that determine harm, loss, or benefit, and b) just about any stimulus can produce just about any emotion. Appraisal dimensions are organized in two global stages: In the primary appraisal stage people assess a) whether and how the situation is important (motivational relevance); b) whether the situation is commensurate with personal goals (motivational congruence); and c) how much attention one gave this event. Secondary appraisals involve an assessment of a) responsibility; b) control; c) emotion-and problem-focused coping potentials; and d) whether the situation is likely to recur in the future (future expectancy; Ellsworth & Smith, 1988; Smith & Lazarus, 1993).

HPC and other high-quality forms of support putatively facilitate *cognitive reappraisal*, although this claim has not yet been rigorously tested with conversational data. Reappraisal is a benefit-finding strategy that reframes an initially upsetting event so as to alter one's emotional response to it (Shiota & Levenson, 2012). Marroquin (2011) theorized that reappraisals function as "affective repair mechanisms" that are triggered when people receive high-quality emotional support from their partner (p. 1280), which emphasizes the importance of supportive communication. Burleson and Goldsmith's (1998) theory of facilitated reappraisal conversations is the first theory that connects emotion regulation and enacted support. This framework maintains that reappraising difficult emotions is best accomplished by revisiting and re-evaluating thoughts and feelings of primary appraisals (i.e., motivational relevance, congruence, attention) and secondary appraisals (i.e., control, responsibility, coping potential, future expectancy) in talk.

Mindful Supportive Conversations

Powerful empirical evidence documents the personal benefits of mindfulness for a host of psychological, somatic, and stress-related illnesses (Eberth & Sedlmeier, 2012; Jones, 2015). Mindfulness enhances neural (Davidson et al., 2003), cognitive (Jha, Krompinger, & Baime, 2007) and affective functioning (McCarney, Schulz, & Grey, 2012), and positively affects relational satisfaction among couples (Barnes, Brown, Krusemark, Campbell, & Rogge, 2007; Carson, Carson, Gil, & Baucom, 2007). The interpersonal benefits of mindfulness are also emerging: Data show that mindfulness positively influences interpersonal communication skills (Jones et al., 2016; Jones & Hansen, 2015), interpersonal attunement (Parker, Nelson, Epel, & Siegel, 2015; Solano et al., 2012), prosocial orientations (Jones et al., 2016; Stewart et al., 2017; Youngvorst & Jones, in press), active-empathic listening (Jones et al., 2016), coping (Garland, Kiken, Faurot, Palsson, & Gaylord, 2016; Jones & Hansen, 2014), and interpersonal relational outcomes (Carson, Carson, Gil, & Baucom, 2006; Gambrel & Piercy, 2015; Lenger, Gordon, & Nguyen, 2017).

Mindfulness is a universal quality of consciousness. It is also metacognitive, which means that it focuses on higher-order cognitive processes (e.g., how we feel and how we plan behavior; Garland, Farb, Goldin, & Fredrickson, 2015). Mindfulness consists of five components—acting with awareness, observing, nonjudging, nonreacting, describing—that are not mutually exclusive and that interact with one another in meaningful ways (Baer, Smith, Hopkins, Krietemeyer, & Toney, 2006; for reviews see Brown, Creswell, & Ryan, 2015; Danielson & Jones, 2017). Central to mindfulness is *attention*, which is essential to all interpersonal communication processes (e.g., listening; Bodie, 2012). Bishop and colleagues (2004) propose that attention accomplishes two things: a) it encourages people to recognize their own affective state, and b) it orients people toward momentary contextual stimuli in a curious, open, and accepting way. Baer et al. (2008) further separates mindful attending into *mindful observing* of thoughts and feelings and *acting with awareness*. The latter factor includes attending to one's momentary activities. Acting with awareness is in direct opposition to acting mechanically or on auto-pilot (Baer, Smith, & Allen, 2004). Acting automatically serves adaptive functions (Sheeran, Gollwitzer, & Bargh, 2013), including physiological and sensory motor processes (e.g., digestion, proprioception). These are, however, not the processes that are targeted in mindfulness practice and two additional mindfulness facets, namely nonjudgment and nonreactivity, clarify this distinction.

Nonjudgment and *nonreactivity* of cognitive and emotional states stress the connection between mindfulness and emotion regulation. To accept momentary emotional states without judgment means to refrain from applying evaluative labels (e.g., good/bad, right/wrong; Baer et al., 2004) to these affective experiences, which is honed in mindfulness practice. Mindfulness practice encourages acceptance of difficult emotions, which ultimately leads to stress tolerance and resilience (Farb, Anderson, & Segal, 2012). A last mindfulness factor is mindful *describing*, or labeling one's thoughts and emotions (Baer et al., 2004; Segal, Williams, & Teasdale, 2013). This component is of particular interest to communication scholars because it is the only component that specifically addresses encoding thoughts and emotions. Mindful describing must not only include what is said, but also what is nonverbally expressed, because cues such as facial expression and gestures play crucial roles in the sense making process.

The Impact of Mindfulness on Providing Support

Providing high-quality support, such as HPC messages, requires skill and motivation. Whereas skill comes from communication practice, *an important motivational factor for enacting support is prosocial orientation*. Empathy and compassion are two prosocial orientations that have been reliably associated with social support (Collins, Jaremka & Kane, 2014; Crocker & Canevello, 2008; Devoldre, Davis, Verhofstadt, & Buysse, 2010). Empathy *means to* vicariously feel with a suffering person (Davis, 1994; Lamm, Batson, & Decety, 2007) is a fundamental human capacity anchored in evolution (Simpson & Beckes, 2010) that is crucial to socio-psychological functioning (Mikulincer & Shaver, 2005). Empathy has been strongly associated with prosocial *helping behaviors* (Eisenberg, 2000; Lebowitz & Dovidio, 2015; Stiff, Dillard, Somera, Kim, & Sleight, 1988), as well as PC (Youngvorst & Jones, in press). Because empathy is conceptualized as a vicarious affective response, it involves shared positive *and* negative emotions (Morelli, Lee, Arnn, & Zaki, 2015). Some *researchers view compassion as* involving positive emotions only (Klimecki, Leiberg, Lamm, & Singer, 2013), even though it, too, is conceptualized as *"the feeling that arises in witnessing another's suffering and that motivates a subsequent desire to help"* (Goetz, Keltner, & Simon-Thomas, 2010, p. 351).

Mindfulness is positively associated with prosocial orientations (Birnie, Speca, & Carlson, 2010; Dekeyser, Raes, Leijssen, Leysen, & Dewulf, 2008; Jones et al., 2016). Mindfulness facets such as nonreacting and nonjudging might be particularly important for prosocial orientations because these two capacities permit distance from difficult emotions, while at the same time attending to the suffering other. Some evidence also suggests that prosocial orientations can be enhanced with mindfulness practice (Fredrickson, Cohn, Coffey, Pek, & Finkel, 2008; Jazaieri et al., 2014; Jones, Youngvorst, & Danielson, 2017; Klimecki et al., 2013; Stewart et al., 2017). Jazaieri and colleagues (2014) found that relatively brief mindfulness interventions increased levels of compassion, and decreased levels of emotional worry and suppression. In a series of studies, Klimecki et al. (2013) also showed that mindfulness interventions can offset the negative effects of empathy (e.g., empathic fatigue) by enhancing levels of compassion, which seems to activate those brain regions that are associated with nurturing positive emotional experiences.

Jones et al. (2016) argued that due to its metacognitive quality, mindfulness indirectly affects enacted support, such as PC provision through cognitive-affective processes (e.g., prosocial motivations) and found some support for this claim. However, the claim has not been fully tested. Consequently, in what ways mindfulness directly influences enacted support, such as the provision of support that varies in PC (particularly in conversations) is not well understood and future research needs to examine the mechanisms that mediate the mindfulness-enacted support connection.

The Impact of Mindfulness on Coping

Per the facilitated reappraisal conversation framework proposed by Burleson and Goldsmith (1998), recipients ought to describe feelings so that the provider can effectively respond. Mindful describing allows the recipient to focus on external stimuli *in situ* and to visualize what happened. Visualization is an important tool in motivation, goal setting, and planning (Taylor, Pham, Rivkin, & Armor, 1998). In addition, being able to observe mindfully, yet not react to upsetting emotions, may make it easier for the recipient to appraise emotions.

People often become fused with emotions when they are stressed (Brown, Ryan, Creswell, & Niemiec, 2008; Herzberg et al., 2012). Fusion with negative emotions is unpleasant, and consequently, people often shy away from effectively processing events that caused these negative emotions. Garland et al. (2015) proposed Mindfulness-to-Meaning Theory (MMT) to explain the cognitive processes whereby mindfulness can cultivate decentering and thus improved coping. Decentering is a process whereby the person merely observes, yet does not react to or judge difficult emotional experiences (Hayes-Skelton & Graham, 2012). MMT proposes that the practice of mindfulness evokes a metacognitive state that suspends a person's momentary reaction to external stimuli via decentering which allows broadening of attention to contextual information and which may lead to positive reappraisals. One component of the MMT, the mindful reappraisal hypothesis, is particularly interesting because it proposes that mindfulness and reappraisal are reciprocally related: Recurrent engagement in the metacognitive state of decentering allows people to develop mindful dispositions which heighten the propensity to use positive reappraisals. Similarly, to the extent that they emerge from broadened attention and decentering, reappraisals can lead to greater mindfulness. Although much of this research is ongoing, Garland et al. (2016) recently tested the MMT by asking participants to complete a seven-week MBI and completing mindfulness and reappraisal measures immediately after each weekly meeting. Using longitudinal methods (i.e., latent growth curve modeling), the researchers found that increases in mindfulness in one week predicted increases in reappraisal in the next week. However, contrary to prediction, reappraisal did not lead to heighted mindfulness.

Conclusion

An important question that has guided research on enacted support concerns the factors that influence the supportive communication process and that allow a person to effectively cope with negative emotions. In this chapter, we proposed that mindfulness significantly influences enacted supportive messages that vary in person centeredness (PC), itself a message characteristic that signals a supporter's ability to emphasize with the recipient. Mindfulness is positively associated with prosocial orientations, which, in turn, influence enacted support, and also cultivate decentering in ways that foster improved emotional regulation and/or positive reappraisals. Much empirical work, however, remains to be done, and researchers are just now beginning to examine in what ways mindfulness influences interpersonal communication and particularly supportive communication.

While we have not differentiated mindful practices (i.e., what people do) from disposition (i.e., how people are), we want to close by noting that we propose that mindfulness can be practiced in social interaction. Mindfulness practiced with meditation emphasizes contemplative introspection in solitude, whereas mindfulness practiced in interaction emphasizes awareness of and attention to the moment-to-moment internal subjective sensations in context. This view apprehends mindfulness as an activity that is enacted in the presence of and with others (rather than in solitude), and connects mindfulness with interpersonal communication. In short, we become who we are in interaction and in relation to other people. In other words, the sites of mindfulness are our present "here and now" social interactions.

References

Afifi, T. D., Afifi, W. A., Merrill, A. F., Denes, A., & Davis, S. (2013). "You need to stop talking about this!": Verbal rumination and the costs of social support. *Human Communication Research, 39*(4), 395–421. doi:10.1111/hcre.12012

Applegate, J. L. (1980). Person-and position-centered teacher communication in a day care center: A case study triangulating interview and naturalistic methods. In N. K. Denzin (Ed.), *Studies in symbolic interaction* (Vol. 3, pp. 59–96). Greenwich, CT: JAI Press.

Baer, R. A., Smith, G. T., & Allen, B. J. (2004). Assessment of mindfulness by self-report: The Kentucky inventory of mindfulness skills. *Assessment, 11*, 191–206. doi:10.1177/1073191104268029

Baer, R. A., Smith, G. T., Hopkins, J., Krietemeyer, J., & Toney, L. (2006). Using self-report assessment methods to explore facets of mindfulness. *Assessment, 13*(1), 27–45. doi:10.1177/1073191105283504

Baer, R. A., Smith, G. T., Lykins, E., Button, D., Krietemeyer, J., Sauer, S., . . . Williams, J. (2008). Construct validity of the Five Facet Mindfulness Questionnaire in meditating and nonmeditating samples. *Assessment, 15*(3), 329–342. doi:10.1177/1073191107313003

Barnes, S., Brown, K. W., Krusemark, E., Campbell, W. K., & Rogge, R. D. (2007). The role of mindfulness in romantic relationship satisfaction and responses to relationship stress. *Journal of Marital and Family Therapy, 33*(4), 482–500. doi:10.1111/j.1752-0606.2007.00033.x

Berkman, L., & Syme, S. L. (1979). Social networks, host resistance, and mortality: A nine-year follow-up study of Alameda County residents. *American Journal of Epidemiology, 109*, 186–204. doi:10.1017/cbo9780511759048.005

Birnie, K., Speca, M., & Carlson, L. E. (2010). Exploring self-compassion and empathy in the context of Mindfulness-Based Stress Reduction (MBSR). *Stress and Health: Journal of the International Society for the Investigation of Stress, 26*(5), 359–371. doi:10.1002/smi.1305

Bishop, S. R., Lau, M., Shapiro, S., Carlson, L., Anderson, N. D., Carmody, J., . . . Devins, G. (2004). Mindfulness: A proposed operational definition. *Clinical Psychology: Science and Practice, 11*(3), 230–241. doi:10.1093/clipsy/bph077

Bodie, G. D. (2012). Listening as positive communication. In T. J. Socha & M. J. Pitts (Eds.), *The positive side of interpersonal communication* (pp. 109–125). New York: Peter Lang.

Bodie, G. D., & Burleson, B. R. (2008). Explaining variations in the effects of supportive messages: A dual-process framework. In C. S. Beck (Ed.), *Communication yearbook* (Vol. 32, pp. 355–398). New York: Routledge.

Bodie, G. D., Jones, S. M., Youngvorst, L., Navarro, M., & Danielson, C. (2017). *Mapping the terrain of person-centered conversations*. Manuscript submitted for publication.

Brown, K. W., Creswell, J. D., & Ryan, R. M. (2015). *Handbook of mindfulness: Theory, research, and practice.* New York, NY: Guilford Press.

Brown, K. W., Ryan, R. M., Creswell, J., & Niemiec, C. P. (2008). Beyond me: Mindful responses to social threat. In H. A. Wayment & J. J. Bauer (Eds.), *The quiet ego: Research and theory on the benefits of transcending egoistic self-interest* (pp. 75–84). Washington, DC: American Psychological Association.

Burleson, B. R. (1982). The development of comforting communication skills in childhood and adolescence. *Child Development, 53*(6), 1578–1588. doi:10.2307/1130086

Burleson, B. R. (1984). Age, social-cognitive development, and the use of comforting strategies. *Communication Monographs, 51*, 140–153. doi:10.1080/03637758409390190

Burleson, B. R. (1987). Cognitive complexity. In J. C. McCroskey & J. A. Daly (Eds.), *Personality and interpersonal communication* (pp. 305–349). Newbury Park, CA: Sage.

Burleson, B. R., & Goldsmith, D. J. (1998). How the comforting process works: Alleviating emotional distress through conversationally induced reappraisals. In P. A. Andersen & L. K. Guerrero (Eds.), *Communication and emotion* (pp. 246–275). Orlando, FL: Academic Press.

Brown, K. W., & Ryan, R. M. (2003). The benefits of being present: Mindfulness and its role in psychological well-being. *Journal of Personality and Social Psychology, 84*(4), 822–848. http://dx.doi.org/10.1037/0022-3514.84.4.822

Butler, E. A., & Randall, A. K. (2013). Emotional coregulation in close relationships. *Emotion Review, 5*(2), 202–210. doi:10.1177/1754073912451630

Cacciatore, J., & Flint, M. (2012). Attend: Toward a mindfulness-based bereavement care model. *Death Studies, 36*(1), 61–82.

Carson, J. W., Carson, K. M., Gil, K. M., & Baucom, D. H. (2006). Mindfulness-Based Relationship Enhancement (MBRE) in couples. In *Mindfulness-based treatment approaches: Clinician's guide to evidence base and applications* (pp. 309–331). San Diego, CA: Elsevier Academic Press.

Carson, J. W., Carson, K. M., Gil, K. M., & Baucom, D. H. (2007). Self-expansion as a mediator of relationship improvements in a mindfulness intervention. *Journal of Marital and Family Therapy, 33*(4), 517–528. doi:10.1111/j.1752-0606.2007.00035.x

Collins, N. L., Jaremka, L. M., & Kane, H. S. (2014). *Social support during a stressful task reduces cortisol reactivity, promotes emotional recovery, and builds caring relationships.* Unpublished manuscript, University of California Santa Barbara.

Crocker, J., & Canevello, A. (2008). Creating and undermining social support in communal relationships: the role of compassionate and self-image goals. *Journal of personality and social psychology, 95*(3), 555–75.

Cutrona, C. E. (1990). Stress and social support: In search of optimal matching. *Journal of Social and Clinical Psychology, 9*, 3–14. doi:10.1521/jscp.1990.9.1.3

Danielson, C., & Jones, S. M. (2017). The Five-Factor Mindfulness Questionnaire. In D. L. Worthington & G. D. Bodie (Eds.), *Sourcebook of listening research measures and methodology*. London, England: Wiley-Blackwell.

Davidson, R. J., Kabat-Zinn, J., Schumacher, J., Rosenkranz, M., Muller, D., Santorelli, S. F., . . . Sheridan, J. F. (2003). Alterations in brain and immune function produced by mindfulness meditation. *Psychosomatic Medicine, 65*(4), 564–570. doi:10.1097/00006842-200401000-00022

Davis, M. H. (1994). *Empathy: A social psychological perspective.* Boulder, CO: Westview.

Dekeyser, M., Raes, F., Leijssen, M., Leysen, S., & Dewulf, D. (2008). Mindfulness skills and interpersonal behavior. *Personality and Individual Differences, 44*(5), 1235–1245. doi:10.1016/j.paid.2007.11.018

Devoldre, I. Davis, M. H., Verhofstadt, L. L., & Buysse, A. (2010) Empathy and social support provision in couples: Social support and the need to study the underlying processes, *The Journal of Psychology, 144*(3), 259–284, doi: 10.1080/00223981003648294

Eberth, J., & Sedlmeier, P. (2012). The effects of mindfulness meditation: A meta-analysis. *Mindfulness, 3*(3), 174–189. doi:10.1007/s12671-012-0101-x

Eisenberg, N. (2000). Emotion, regulation, and moral development. *Annual Review of Psychology, 51*, 665–697. doi:10.1146/annurev.psych.51.1.665

Ellsworth, P. S., & Smith, C. A. (1988). From appraisal to emotion: Differences among unpleasant emotions. *Motivation and Emotion, 12*, 271–302. doi:10.1007/bf00993115

Farb, N. A., Anderson, A. K., & Segal, Z. V. (2012). The mindful brain and emotion regulation in mood disorders. *The Canadian Journal of Psychiatry/La Revue canadienne de psychiatrie, 57*(2), 70–77. doi:10.1177/070674371205700203

Feeney, B. C., & Collins, N. L. (2015). A new look at social support: A theoretical perspective on thriving through relationships. *Personality and Social Psychology Review, 19*(2), 113–147. doi:10.1177/1088868314544222

Fredrickson, B. L., Cohn, M. A., Coffey, K. A., Pek, J., & Finkel, S. M. (2008). Open hearts build lives: Positive emotions, induced through loving-kindness meditation, build consequential personal resources. *Journal of Personality and Social Psychology, 95*(5), 1045–1062. doi:10.1037/a0013262

Gambrel, L. E., & Piercy, F. P. (2015). Mindfulness-based relationship education for couples expecting their first child-part 1: A randomized mixed-methods program evaluation. *Journal of Marital and Family Therapy, 41*(1), 5–24. doi:10.1111/jmft.12066

Garland, E. L., Farb, N. A., Goldin, P. R., & Fredrickson, B. L. (2015). Mindfulness broadens awareness and builds eudaimonic meaning: A process model of mindful positive emotion regulation. *Psychological Inquiry, 26*, 293–314. doi:10.1080/1047840X.2015.1064294

Garland, E. L., Kiken, L. G., Faurot, K., Palsson, O., & Gaylord, S. A. (2016). Upward spirals of mindfulness and reappraisal: Testing the mindfulness-to-meaning theory with autoregressive latent trajectory modeling. *Cognitive Therapy and Research*, 1–12. doi:10.1007/s10608-016-9768-y

Goetz, J. L., Keltner, D., & Simon-Thomas, E. (2010). Compassion: An evolutionary analysis and empirical review. *Psychological Bulletin, 136*(3), 351–374. doi:10.1037/a0018807

Goldsmith, D. J. (2004). *Communicating social support.* Cambridge, UK: Cambridge University Press.

Goldsmith, D. J., McDermott, V. M., & Alexander, S. C. (2000). Helpful, supportive, and sensitive: Measuring the evaluation of enacted support in personal relationships. *Journal of Social & Personal Relationships, 17*, 369–391. doi:10.1177/0265407500173004

Hayes-Skelton, S., & Graham, J. (2012). Decentering as a common link among mindfulness, cognitive reappraisal, and social anxiety. *Behavioral and Cognitive Psychotherapy*, 1–12. doi:10.1017/s1352465812000902

Herzberg, K. N., Sheppard, S. C., Forsyth, J. P., Crede, M., Earleywine, M., & Eifert, G. H. (2012). The Believability of Anxious Feelings and Thoughts Questionnaire (BAFT): A psychometric evaluation of cognitive fusion in a nonclinical and highly anxious community sample. *Psychological Assessment, 24*(4), 877–891. doi:10.1037/a0027782

High, A. C., & Dillard, J. P. (2012). A review and meta-analysis of person-centered messages and social support outcomes. *Communication Studies, 63*, 99–118. doi:10.1080/10510974.2011.598208

High, A. C., & Solomon, D. H. (2014). Communication channel, sex, and the immediate and longitudinal outcomes of verbal person-centered support. *Communication Monographs, 81*(4), 439–468. doi:10.1080/03637751.2014.933245

High, A. C., & Solomon, D. H. (2016). Explaining the durable effects of verbal person-centered supportive communication: Indirect effects or invisible support? *Human Communication Research, 42*, 200–220. doi:10.1111/hcre.12077

Holt-Lunstad, J., Smith, T. B., & Layton, B. (2010). Social relationships and mortality: A meta-analysis. *PLoS Medicine, 7*, 1–20. doi:10.1371/journal.pmed.1000316

Jazaieri, H., McGonigal, K., Jinpa, T., Doty, J. R., Gross, J. J., & Goldin, P. R. (2014). A randomized controlled trial of compassion cultivation training: Effects of mindfulness, affect, and emotional regulation. *Motivation and Emotion, 38*(1), 23–35. doi:10.1007/s11031-013-9368-z

Jha, A. P., Krompinger, J., & Baime, M. J. (2007). Mindfulness training modifies subsystems of attention. *Cognitive, Affective, & Behavioral Neuroscience, 7*(2), 109–119. doi:10.3758/cabn.7.2.109

Jones, S. M. (2015). Mindfulness. In C. R. Berger & M. E. Roloff (Eds.), *International encyclopedia of interpersonal communication.* London, England: Wiley-Blackwell. doi:10.1002/9781118540190.wbeic264

Jones, S. M., & Bodie, G. D. (2014). Supportive communication. In C. R. Berger (Ed.), *Handbooks of communication science: Interpersonal communication* (Vol. 6, pp. 371–394). Berlin: De Gruyter Mouton.

Jones, S. M., Bodie, G. D., & Hughes, S. D. (2016). The impact of mindfulness on empathy, active listening, and perceived provisions of emotional support. *Communication Research* (February). doi:10.1177/0093650215626983

Jones, S. M., & Guerrero, L. K. (2001). The effects of nonverbal immediacy and verbal person centeredness in the emotional support process, *Human Communication Research, 27*(4), 567–596, https://doi.org/10.1111/j.1468-2958.2001.tb00793.x

Jones, S. M., & Hansen, W. (2015). The impact of mindfulness on supportive communication skills: Three exploratory studies. *Mindfulness, 6*(5), 1115–1128. doi:10.1007/s12671-014-0362-7

Jones, S. M., & Wirtz, J. G. (2006). How does the comforting process work? An empirical test of an appraisal-based model of comforting. *Human Communication Research, 32*(3), 217–243. doi:10.1111/j.1468-2958.2006.00274.x

Jones, S. M., Youngvorst, L., & Danielson, C. (2017). *Can meditation promote prosocial emotions and supportive communication?* University of Minnesota, Minneapolis, MN.

Klimecki, O. M., Leiberg, S., Lamm, C., & Singer, T. (2013). Functional neural plasticity and associated changes in positive affect after compassion training. *Cerebral Cortex, 23*(7), 1552–1561. doi:10.1093/cercor/bhs142

Lamm, C., Batson, C., & Decety, J. (2007). The neural substrate of human empathy: Effects of perspective-taking and cognitive appraisal. *Journal of Cognitive Neuroscience, 19*(1), 42–58. doi:10.1162/jocn.2007.19.1.42

Lazarus, R. S. (1991). *Emotion and adaptation.* New York: Oxford University Press.

Lazarus, R. S., & Folkman, S. (1984). *Stress, appraisal, and coping.* New York: Springer International Publishing.

Lebowitz, M. S., & Dovidio, J. F. (2015, February). Implications of emotion regulation strategies for empathic concern, social attitudes, and helping behavior. *Emotion*, (Pagination), No Pagination Specified. doi:10.1037/a0038820

Lenger, K. A., Gordon, C. L., & Nguyen, S. P. (2017). Intra-individual and cross-partner associations between the five facets of mindfulness and relationship satisfaction. *Mindfulness, 8*(1), 171–180. doi:10.1007/s12671-016-0590-0

MacGeorge, E. L., & Wilkum, K. (2012). Predicting comforting quality in the context of Miscarriage. *Communication Reports, 25*(2), 62–74. doi:10.1080/08934215.2012.719463

Marroquin, B. (2011). Interpersonal emotion regulation as a mechanism of social support in depression. *Clinical Psychology Review, 31*(8), 1276–1290. doi:10.1016/j.cpr.2011.09.005

McCarney, R., Schulz, J., & Grey, A. (2012). Effectiveness of mindfulness-based therapies in reducing symptoms of depression: A meta-analysis. *European Journal of Psychotherapy and Counselling, 14*(3), 279–299. doi:10.1080/13642537.2012.713186

Mikulincer, M., & Shaver, P. R. (2005). Attachment security, compassion, and altruism. *Current Directions in Psychological Science, 14*(1), 34–38. doi:10.1111/j.0963-7214.2005.00330.x

Morelli, S. A., Lee, I. A., Arnn, M. E., & Zaki, J. (2015). Emotional and instrumental support provision interact to predict well-being. *Emotion, 15*, 484–493. doi:10.1037/emo0000084

Parker, S. C., Nelson, B. W., Epel, E. S., & Siegel, D. J. (2015). The science of presence: A central mediator of the interpersonal benefits of mindfulness. In K. W. Brown, J. D. Creswell, & R. M. Ryan (Eds.), *Handbook of mindfulness: Theory and research* (pp. 225–244). New York: Guilford Press.

Priem, J. S., & Solomon, D. H. (2015). What is supportive about supportive conversation? Qualities of interaction that predict emotional and physiological outcomes. *Communication Research*, 1–31. doi:10.1177/0093650215595074

Rains, S. A., Brunner, S. R., Akers, C., Pavlich, C. A., & Tsetsi, E. (2016). The implications of Computer-Mediated Communication (CMC) for social support message processing and outcomes: When and why are the effects of support messages strengthened during CMC? *Human Communication Research, 42*(4), 553–576. doi:10.1111/hcre.12087

Samter, W., & MacGeorge, E. L. (2016). Coding comforting behavior for verbal person centeredness. In C. A. VanLear & D. J. Canary (Eds.), *Research interactive communication behavior: A sourcebook of methods and measures* (pp. 107–128). Thousand Oaks, CA: Sage Publications.

Segal, Z. V., Williams, J. M. G., & Teasdale, J. D. (2013). *Mindfulness-based cognitive therapy for depression* (2nd ed.). New York: Guilford.

Sheeran, P., Gollwitzer, P. M., & Bargh, J. A. (2013). Nonconscious processes and health. *Health Psychology, 32*(5), 460–473. doi:10.1037/a0029203

Shiota, M. N., & Levenson, R. W. (2012). Turn down the volume or change the channel? Emotional effects of detached versus positive reappraisal. *Journal of Personality and Social Psychology, 103*(3), 416–429. doi:10.1037/a0029208

Simpson, J. A., & Beckes, L. (2010). Evolutionary perspectives on prosocial behavior. In M. Mikulincer & P. Shaver (Eds.), *Prosocial motives, emotions, and behavior: The better angels of our nature* (pp. 35–53). Washington, DC: American Psychological Association.

Smith, C. A., & Lazarus, R. S. (1993). Appraisal components, core relational themes, and the emotions. *Cognition and Emotion, 7*(3/4), 233–269. doi:10.1080/02699939308409189

Solano, L., Nicolo, A. M., Di Trani, M., Bonadies, M., San Martini, P., Bonucci, C., . . . Tavazza, G. (2012). The marital love relationship: Construction and preliminary validation on 610 subjects of a psychoanalytically derived inventory. *Psychoanalytic Psychology, 29*(4), 408–428. doi:10.1037/a0030206

Spottswood, E. L., Walther, J. B., Holmstrom, A. J., & Ellison, N. B. (2013). Person-centered emotional support and gender attributes in computer mediated communication. *Human Communication Research, 39*, 295–316. doi:10.1111/hcre.12006

Stewart, K. I., Ahrens, A. H., & Gunthert, K. C. (2017). Relating to self and other: Mindfulness predicts compassionate and self-image goals. *Mindfulness*. Advance online publication. doi:10.1007/s12671-017-0760-8

Stiff, J., Dillard, J., Somera, L., Kim, H., & Sleight, C. (1988). Empathy, communication, and prosocial behavior. *Communication Monographs, 55*, 198–213. doi:10.1080/03637758809376166

Taylor, S. E., Pham, L. B., Rivkin, I. D., & Armor, D. A. (1998). Harnessing the imagination: Mental simulation, self-regulation, and coping. *American Psychologist, 53*(4), 429. doi:10.1037/0003-066x.53.4.429

Youngvorst, L. J., & Jones, S. M. (in press). The influence of cognitive complexity, empathy, and mindfulness on person-centered message evaluations. *Communication Quarterly*. Advance online publication. doi:10.1080/01463373.2017.1301508

Zaki, J., & Williams, C. (2013). Interpersonal emotion regulation. *Emotion, 13*, 803–810. doi:10.1037/a0033839

11

COMMUNICATION SAVORING AS POSITIVE INTERPERSONAL COMMUNICATION

Margaret Jane Pitts, Sara Kim, Holman Meyerhoffer, and Jian Jiao

Communication Savoring as Positive Interpersonal Communication

As a positive psychology construct, savoring refers to a person's capacity to recognize, appreciate, and elevate enjoyable life experiences, especially sensory experiences (Bryant & Veroff, 2007). Savoring also entails a social dimension wherein individuals enhance their pleasant experiences through interpersonal sharing. Recent research suggests that individuals can also savor communication directly. Pitts (2016) identified seven common interpersonal communication experiences that people savor: aesthetic communication, communication presence, nonverbal communication, recognition and acknowledgment, relational communication and disclosures, rare and novel communication moments, and implicitly shared communication. As such, savoring is one of many positive communication processes that serve to enhance, facilitate, and generate positive emotions and experiences (Pitts & Socha, 2013). Indeed, people may use communication savoring as one way to broaden and build upon positive communication resources and repertoires necessary for the development of quality of life and relational resilience (see Fredrickson, 2001).

This chapter centers on the notion of communication savoring as a deliberate, intentional process of mindfully attending to and deriving pleasure from verbal and nonverbal messages in current, remembered, or imagined interactions (Pitts, 2016). Although savoring is well established in the field of positive psychology, it is a relatively new construct in the field of interpersonal communication. Thus, our goal with this chapter is to highlight the social and communicative dimensions of savoring to extend its conceptual and practical reach into the domain of positive interpersonal communication. First, we present a brief overview of savoring as a positive psychology construct with a focus on the processes and outcomes of savoring. Next, we turn to the conditions that are necessary for savoring to occur and then to people's capacity for savoring. Before turning to the social dimensions of savoring, we briefly introduce strategies to stimulate or enhance savoring. The rest of the chapter focuses on communication savoring as a unique form of positive interpersonal communication and concludes with directions for further conceptual development inspired by Eastern cultural values of balance and harmony.

Savoring as a Positive Psychology Construct

In the late 1980s, savoring emerged as a positive cognitive construct that contributes to quality of life by allowing individuals to recognize pleasure in the moment and enhance it (Bryant &

Veroff, 1984). Bryant (1989) posited that if coping is a regulatory response to negative experience, savoring is the corresponding psychological construct regulating positive experience. Thus, savoring was adopted early into the positive psychology movement with its focus on the science of human flourishing and thriving (Gable & Haidt, 2005; Seligman, 2003; Seligman, & Csikszentmihalyi, 2000). In 2007, Bryant and Veroff proposed a theoretical model of savoring in their book *Savoring: A New Model of Positive Experience.*

Savoring is a form of emotional processing that allows individuals to enhance (or upregulate) the sensations of pleasure in daily life (Gentzler, Palmer, & Ramsey, 2015; Quoidbach, Dunn, Hansenne, & Bustin, 2015). The process of savoring involves first noticing a pleasant sensation and then attending to and amplifying one's enjoyment in reaction to that pleasant sensation (Bryant & Veroff, 2007). As such, savoring is a second-order phenomenon that involves not merely experiencing pleasure, but experiencing pleasure about that pleasure. Savoring can be triggered in response to external physical or sensory stimuli, such as enjoying the pleasurable experience of viewing a particularly vibrant sunset or eating a perfectly ripened fruit, or in response to internal reflections, such as enjoying the pleasant experience of recalling a treasured memory. Interpersonal communication may also serve as a cue to savor, a point we turn to later in the chapter.

Savoring positive experiences in the present moment increases a variety of positive outcomes (Giuliani, McRae, & Gross, 2008; Kurtz, 2008), such as positive affect (Jose, Lim, & Bryant, 2012; Quoidbach, Berry, Hansenne, & Mikolajczak, 2010), greater happiness, greater life satisfaction, decreased depression (Bryant, 2003; Hurley & Kwon, 2012; Smith & Hollinger-Smith, 2015), and enhanced flexibility (see Mikolajczak, 2009). Savoring increases both momentary happiness and global life satisfaction (Garland et al., 2017; Ng, 2012). Savoring is positively related to optimism, self-worth, affect intensity, and extraversion (Bryant, 2003; Feldman, Joorman, & Johnson, 2008), and is strongly associated with people we see as the wisest (Beaumont, 2011). In addition to generating and increasing positive outcomes, savoring can also buffer negative experiences, bolster resilience, and decrease and prohibit negative outcomes such as negative affect and depression (Hurley & Kwon, 2012).

Not only does savoring create opportunities to maintain or upregulate positive emotional responses to present circumstances (Bryant, 1989; Lindberg, 2004), savoring also allows individuals to transcend time by savoring the past through reminiscence and the future through anticipation (Bryant, 2003). As a positive reaction to positive events, savoring the current moment is a relatively short-lived response that involves cognitively or behaviorally attending to, intensifying, and prolonging the enjoyment derived from a current, ongoing positive circumstance. Savoring the current moment increases an individual's feelings of self-esteem, present happiness, and gratification while simultaneously lessening the negative impacts of strain and depression (Bryant, 2003). Savoring the past occurs when individuals generate positive feelings and emotions in the present through vivid recall of previous, favorable experiences (Quoidbach et al., 2010). When people luxuriate in reminiscence, they are savoring the past, a particularly effective strategy for up-regulating negative emotional states. Bryant, Morgan, and Perloff (1986) found that people were more likely to savor through reminiscence (60 percent) when they were feeling sad than when they were already feeling happy (10 percent). The amount of time spent reminiscing positively relates to self-reported happiness. Savoring the future arises when people anticipate or imagine positive future events to foster pleasure in the current moment (Quoidbach et al., 2010). Enjoying planning for a romantic honeymoon or envisioning a perfect performance are examples of anticipatory savoring. In general, people appear to be better able to savor the past through reminiscence than savoring the future though anticipation (Bryant, 2003; Quoidbach et al., 2010). However, savoring anticipated relational disclosures or interpersonal praise and recognition may be common forms of anticipatory savoring within the interpersonal context (Pitts, 2016).

Mindfulness and the Necessary Preconditions of Savoring

In their model of savoring, Bryant and Veroff (2007) identified three vital preconditions in order for savoring to occur: (1) being free from pressing needs, (2) being focused in the present moment, and (3) being aware of positive feelings as they occur. To expand on the first point, a person must be free of nagging distractions in the form of social or esteem needs. A mind focused on distractions fails to focus on anything else, including pleasure or enjoyment. For example, individuals focused on difficult tasks or complex performances are often too distracted to experience savoring until after the performance or the task is completed (Brown & Ryan, 2003; Schall, Goetz, Martiny, & Hall, 2017). Second, the individual must experience present awareness, or mindfulness. Mindfulness is "paying attention on purpose" (Paulson, Davidson, Jha, & Kabat-Zinn, 2013, p. 91) and requires noticing and attending to novel distinctions in everyday experiences in real time (Langer & Moldoveanu, 2000). Mindfulness promotes a "heightened state of involvement and wakefulness or being in the present" (Langer & Moldoveanu, 2000, p. 2), which can result in greater environmental and situational awareness, more open-minded attitudes toward new information, new ways of interpreting the world, and a greater ability to perspective-take. It is not, however, necessarily positive. It is merely the conscious act of focusing on each moment-to-moment experience as it arises (Brown & Ryan, 2003; Shapiro, Carlson, Astin, & Freedman, 2006). Thus, although mindfulness is a requirement for savoring, mindfulness itself is not savoring. Hurley and Kwon (2012) offer the following distinction:

Both mindfulness and savoring the moment focus on current experiences. However, one important distinction is that, in savoring the moment, attention is restricted to positive emotions, while in mindfulness the focus can be on any experience, emotion, or thought, be them positive, negative, or neutral. Also, the goal of savoring the moment is to enhance or prolong positive emotions, while in mindfulness the focus is on generally attending and experiencing and not on intensifying affect. (p. 580)

Finally, individuals must narrow the focus of their attention to the pleasant aspects of their present moment experience. If attention shifts to negative or neutral events, savoring cannot occur (Bryant, 1989). On the other hand, shifting attention *away* from negative or neutral events by directing focus toward the positive can initiate the savoring process (Garland et al., 2017).

State, Trait, and Capacity for Savoring

Savoring can be experienced as a subjective, transitory *state* and/or an individual *trait*, which varies from person to person (Bryant, 1989, 2001; Bryant & Veroff, 2007). Jose et al. (2012) distinguished trait savoring from momentary savoring, defining *trait savoring* as "a stable tendency in response to positive life events" and *momentary savoring* as a "transitory contextualized reaction that is used in a particular situation in response to a positive event" (pp. 177–178). For people who have a highly developed savoring trait, the three prerequisites of savoring are habituated and savoring is a common enjoyment. For others, any one of the three prerequisites, or all of them together, require more effort and savoring is rarer (Bryant, 1989, 2001; Bryant & Veroff, 2007) and experienced more as a transitory state (Jose et al., 2012).

Savoring capacity refers to individuals' personal beliefs about their ability to immerse in and prolong the enjoyment and pleasure derived from positive experiences (Bryant, 1989). Savoring capacity appears to be a relatively stable personality trait and a strong indicator of savoring potential (Bryant, 2003; Carl, Fairholme, Gallagher, Thompson-Hollands, & Barlow, 2014). For example, individuals who hold stronger beliefs regarding their capacity to savor positive experiences are more likely to upregulate their positive emotions utilizing multiple savoring strategies, while those who hold weaker beliefs tend to down-regulate their positive emotions (Bryant, 2003;

Jose et al., 2012). Esteem needs also predict savoring capacity with high self-esteem predicting a greater level of savoring capacity and low self-esteem leading to a tendency to dampen positive experiences (Bryant, 2003; Wood, Heimpel, & Michela, 2003). Moreover, both low self-esteem and neuroticism form barriers to savoring, while high self-esteem or an extroverted personality style promote savoring (Bryant, 2003; Ng, 2012; Ng & Diener, 2009). Capacity to savor is also influenced by current state. For example, savoring capacity is reduced by individual worries, tasks in progress, distracting thoughts, and beliefs concerning the value of pleasure (Schall et al., 2017).

Savoring Strategies

Although not everybody has trait-like capacity to savor, there are techniques for enhancing capacity to savor or brightening the experience of savoring. Bryant and Veroff (2007) organized savoring strategies into three distinct categories: nonverbal (behavioral) strategies, internal (cognitive) strategies, and interpersonal (sharing) strategies. Each category is comprised of several strategies (see also Quoidbach et al., 2010). *Behavioral strategies* include a range of nonverbal actions that convey positive feelings like laughing and smiling (Quoidbach et al., 2010). Noticing is another behavioral strategy that involves recognizing the focus of someone else's savoring and modeling after the savoring behavior (Bryant & Veroff, 2007).

There are several *(meta)cognitive strategies*. Metacognitively attending to the subtler features and affective responses to positive events offers both deeper and wider affective responses and appreciation for the savored moment (Garland, 2016). One strategy, memory building, involves actively anchoring all the details of delightful events or conversations in memory, so that the event can be recalled and savored in the present. Another strategy, daydreaming or fantasizing, involves vividly imagining a positive future event to generate pleasure in the present moment. A third strategy involves self-congratulation, or basking, wherein an individual upregulates emotions and emphasizes feelings of accomplishment and strengthens pride (Quoidbach et al., 2010). A fourth strategy, comparing, contrasts a current circumstance against an alternative circumstance or a current emotional state with the state of another, while absorption, a fifth strategy, is being fully immersed in present moment—an experience similar to *flow* (Csikszentmihalyi, 1997). Sixth, sensory-perceptual sharpening, or luxuriating, occurs when individuals deeply focus attention into one or more senses, while excluding or filtering out other potential foci. Luxuriating increases one's experience of physical pleasure (Quoidbach et al., 2010). Finally, temporal awareness is a strategy that individuals use to acknowledge the flux and fleeting nature of an experience to trigger the savoring response.

Interpersonal strategies are social/relational in nature and increase positive affect through implicit and explicit sharing. Sharing incorporates one's social network to upregulate a positive response through communicating good fortune or happy moments and is associated with higher levels of life satisfaction (Hurley & Kwon, 2012). Bryant and Veroff (2007) point out that communicating our savoring experiences while they are occurring can lead to a reciprocal or shared experience of savoring with our communication partners, which in turn creates further pleasant stimuli to prolong the payoff of savoring. The interpersonal strategies are an inherent aspect of the social dimension to savoring featured in this chapter.

The Social Dimension to Savoring

Savoring can be an individual, interior experience, but there is also a social dimension to savoring. Indeed, our ability to experience positive feelings at all is significantly associated with social factors (Lindberg, 2004). The social dimension appears to be twofold. First, the positive affect generated through intrapersonal (interior) savoring stimulates a desire to share that pleasure interpersonally. Sharing positive events results in positive affect above and beyond the initial experience (Langston, 1994). This occurs both verbally (talking about the experience) and non-verbally (laughing and smiling; Hurley & Kwon, 2012). Sharing good news with friends and family promotes health and well-being (Gable, Reis, Impett, & Asher, 2004); while communicating savoring enhances individual welfare and strengthens relational well-being (Borelli, Rasmussen, Burkhart, & Sbarra, 2015). Indeed, sharing positive affect is so powerful that simply imagining sharing the experience with someone results in enhanced enjoyment; as does savoring the pleasure of watching friends or family having fun (Bryant & Veroff, 2007).

Deriving pleasure from sharing savored experiences stimulates a process called capitalizing. Capitalizing refers to interpreting and responding to positive events *as positive* to augment the resulting positive affect through interpersonal means such as communicating with others and celebrating (Langston, 1994). People who capitalize their savoring through interpersonal sharing elevate their level of enjoyment beyond the initial pleasurable response and also experience increased relational satisfaction (Gable et al., 2004). Thus, the benefits of communicating positive experiences extend beyond the immediate interpersonal interaction to create "not only mutual enjoyment in the moment, but also enduring alliances, friendships or family bonds" (Fredrickson, 1998, p. 311). This includes bonds between strangers sharing the same pleasurable experience (Bryant & Veroff, 2007). Moreover, when relational partners receive communication about positive events enthusiastically, not only does it build relational closeness with that conversational partner, it also deepens trust and prosocial orientation across all relational types (Reis et al., 2010). It follows that sharing a savored moment is a relational investment that appears to pay immediate returns in positive affect (Langston, 1994) and may build reserves for the future (see Afifi, Merrill, & Davis, 2016). While the benefits of communicating savored moments can be a personal and relational boon, failure to capitalize on positive moments through interpersonal sharing can have compounding negative effects on relational success and satisfaction (Kashdan, Ferssizidis, Farmer, Adams, & McKnight, 2013).

Savoring Interpersonal Communication

Although savoring has not been centrally cast as a communication phenomenon, positive communication scholars will recognize the important role that communication plays in the process of savoring. For example, communication can serve as a cue to savor an experience. Hearing a person exclaim "wow, isn't this spectacular" may draw one's attention toward savoring an experience. We use communication to share a savored experience and as a strategy for enhancing an experience. We can also savor conversational exchanges and communication experiences where the pleasure of the interpersonal interaction itself is the object savored. To determine this, Pitts (2016) designed a phenomenological study that answered the questions: "Do people savor communication?" And if so, "what communication experiences do they savor and how do they experience them?" Pitts used an open-ended narrative solicitation questionnaire to ask 65 participants to tell a story in rich detail about a communication experience that they savored. The results of her study revealed that not only do people savor communication experiences, but that they can identify and recall them in vivid detail. From their narratives, Pitts used a constructivist grounded theory approach to develop a typology of communication savoring:

1. **Aesthetic Communication:** Savoring the beauty and playfulness of language as demonstrated in colorful language, strategic use of timing, surprising elements, and delight in the ability for language to "tickle" something deep inside.
2. **Communication Presence:** Savoring the experience of mutually and fully attending to a communicative moment, often resulting in the lack of awareness of time or of the presence of others.

3. **Nonverbal Communication:** Savoring meaningful messages that are conveyed through means other than talk, such as touch and eye gaze, as well as the surrounding environment, at times described as a sacred space or perfect setting.
4. **Recognition and Acknowledgment:** Savoring the experience of giving or receiving genuine praise or recognition.
5. **Relational Communication and Disclosures:** Savoring talk that moves a relationship toward greater intimacy or understanding.
6. **Rare and Novel Communication:** Savoring communication moments (especially face-to-face) that are rare, special, or novel.
7. **Implicitly Shared Communication:** Savoring the unspoken bond created through sharing an experience or witnessing an extraordinary event.

In alignment with Bryant and Veroff's (2007) model, participants in this study also gave evidence of past, present, and future savoring. For example, participants described anticipatory communication savoring in their expectations and desires to hear intimate disclosures from loved ones or words of praise from important others. They described present-focused communication as a deep sense of presence and mindfulness in the moment through (a) attending to the moment with purpose, (b) being absorbed in the moment, and (c) as an enhanced embodied experience (i.e., feeling overcome with joy or love). Participants also described savoring communication events that had already transpired, but bring pleasure in the present moment. Past-oriented communication savoring centered on retrospective accounts including (a) occasionally drifting to a memory of savored communication or (b) frequently and purposefully replaying savored interpersonal communication encounters as a form of upregulation to bring joy in a present moment. Study participants also reported feeling closer to family members and relational partners by recalling savored communication moments.

Communication savoring appears to be a meaningful interpersonal practice with potential for direct relational benefits. Participants vividly described previously savored communication experiences as a readily available source of pleasant emotions. Some participants' ability to recall and *re*-savor such vivid conversational moments resulted from their mindfulness during the initial encounter (Pitts, 2016). Thus, participants' detailed recollection of savored communication moments does more than make evident people's capacity and propensity to savor communication, but also suggests some individuals may be quite purposive and effective in their savoring attempts. Being able to bank positive communication moments through savoring may help develop resilience during difficult or turbulent moments by providing a ready resource from which to withdraw pleasant sensations. Savoring interpersonal communication, then, may be one communication practice that can uplift relational partners, as well as preserve, maintain, and enhance interpersonal relationships (see Afifi et al., 2016).

Future Directions: Pushing the Boundaries of Savoring

Enhancing the pleasurable aspects of interpersonal relationships and relational communication is only one function of savoring. Attending to and savoring the fuller range of affective experiences may contribute to personal and interpersonal well-being in good times, but also in times of stress. Within the field of positive psychology, and now communication, there have been significant efforts to conceptualize savoring and apply it to different social contexts. Yet, as a whole, the body of literature and applied research lacks a comprehensive cross-cultural understanding of savoring. Up to this point, our chapter has focused on the preconditions, processes, outcomes, and strategies for savoring as well as types of communication savoring. This discussion has been limited to Western (North American and European) cultural notions of positive affect, positive experience, and the management of positive emotions. The result is a limited perspective on life's enjoyments and precludes emotional balance by always shifting the bar toward the pleasant emotions but not taking into account potential also to savor life's meaningful moments that might be less pleasant but equally powerful and meaningful. Examining the differences between the Western and Eastern cultural perceptions of positive affect and bridging the two approaches is necessary to gain more holistic understanding of savoring and its potential within relational contexts.

Happiness and pleasure are perceived differently between Western and Eastern cultures. Psychologists in the West view happiness and positive emotions as basic elements of human functioning for both physical and mental health (Goldman, Kraemer, & Salovey, 1996; Salovey, Rothman, Detweiler, & Steward, 2000). In Western cultures, individuals may feel pressure to pursue, prolong, and amplify positive affect. On the other hand, in East Asian cultures, achieving emotional balance is more important than pure pleasantness (Frijda & Sundararajan, 2007). True happiness is experienced when there is moderation and balance between the positive and negative emotions. The coexistence and dialectical tension of feeling both emotions is desirable (Leu et al., 2010). Such perception of happiness originated from the prevailing philosophies in the East Asian culture including Buddhism, Daoism, and Confucianism (Bockover, 1995; Ivanhoe, 2001).

Buddhism discourages people from striving for pleasure and personal well-being because desire leads to eternal suffering (Leu et al., 2010). The Confucian tradition promotes harmony of social relationships and discourages autonomous pleasure that can destroy communal harmony (Uchida & Kitayama, 2009; Uchida, Norasakkunkit, & Kitayama, 2004). Daoism defines pleasant feelings as inherently tied to unpleasant feelings in a yin yang relationship creating expectations for the present situation to change and thus misery turns into happiness, and happiness turns into misery (Ji, Nisbett, & Su, 2001). Therefore, accepting contradiction by finding balance between the positive and the negative is encouraged (Peng & Nisbett, 1999) over maximizing positive and pleasant affect (Miyamoto & Ryff, 2011; Tsai, 2007).

We find the prospects of including Eastern philosophies on emotional balance and harmony a promising future direction for savoring research and application in relational contexts. The predominant body of savoring research has focused on practical cognitive and behavioral strategies to attend, amplify, and prolong positive feelings (Bryant & Veroff, 2007). Yet, according to the Chinese philosophy, as one example, savoring is a mental act or attitude of being sensitive to harmony of positive and negative feelings in their due degree and engaging in activities to search for harmony (Frijda & Sundararajan, 2007). The Chinese notion of savoring has a broader scope of what an individual may attend to and prolong. Individuals may prolong and stay within meaningful experiences that span both positive and negative emotional experiences. From this perspective, savoring involves self-reflexive awareness (Lambie & Marcel, 2002) where individuals focus their attention internally rather than to the external environment and engage in active meta-cognition about positive and negative emotional experiences. Thus, savoring does not have to focus solely on the pleasantness, but also on pain, sorrow, and loss (Frijda & Sundararajan, 2007). For example, individuals may grieve a loss, but may also simultaneously savor the feeling that life is meaningful and savor meaningful memories that arise within that grief. In other words, savoring can be bittersweet. Adopting this broader philosophy may promote a deeper sense of interconnectivity and meaning in response to all experiences, regardless of the pleasantness valence, and enhance relationships in good times and promote relational resilience in turbulent times.

Conclusion

Our goal with this chapter was to present a compelling case for the inclusion of savoring as a positive communication construct. Positive interpersonal communication is both an object of savoring and a means for enhancing positive affect and meaningful moments through savoring.

We turned first to the field of positive psychology to define the established parameters of savoring including the process, characteristics, and outcomes of savoring as well as techniques for enhancing savoring. Then we turned toward the social dimension of savoring noting its inherent connection to interpersonal communication. Communicating about savored moments either as they are occurring or through reminiscences enhances positive affect in the moment and strengthens relational bonds. Savoring promotes positive affect, psychological resilience, and well-being across the lifespan (see Bryant, Chadwick, & Kluwe, 2011; Smith & Hanni, 2017), and interpersonal savoring may promote relational resilience and relational satisfaction in the future (see Afifi et al., 2016; Borelli et al., 2015). Positive interpersonal communication is central to the pursuit and enactment of the life well lived (Nussbaum, 2007). We believe that savoring interpersonal communication may play an especially important role in the advancement of quality of life for individuals and relationships and therefore merits further scholarship. Moreover, broadening our conceptualization of savoring to include ideals of balance and harmony rooted in Eastern cultural philosophies is a promising future direction in this endeavor.

References

Afifi, T. D., Merrill, A. F., & Davis, S. (2016). The theory of resilience and relational load. *Personal Relationships, 23,* 663–683. doi:10.1111/pere.12159

Beaumont, S. L. (2011). Identity styles and wisdom during emerging adulthood: Relationships with mindfulness and savoring. *Identity, 11,* 155–180. doi:10.1080/15283488.2011.557298

Bockover, M. I. (1995). The concept of emotion revisited: A critical synthesis of Western and Confucian thought. In J. Marks & R. T. Ames (Eds.), *Emotions in East Asian thought: A dialogue in comparative philosophy* (pp. 161–180). Albany, NY: State University of New York Press.

Borelli, J. L., Rasmussen, H. F., Burkhart, M. L., & Sbarra, D. A. (2015). Relational savoring in long-distance romantic relationships. *Journal of Social and Personal Relationships, 32,* 1083–1108. doi:10.1177/0265407514558960

Brown, K. W., & Ryan, R. M. (2003). The benefits of being present: Mindfulness and its role in psychological well-being. *Journal of Personality and Social Psychology, 84,* 822–848. doi:10.1037/0022-3514.84.4.822

Bryant, F. B. (1989). A four-factor model of perceived control: Avoiding, coping, obtaining, and savoring. *Journal of Personality, 57,* 773–797. doi:10.1111/j.1467-6494.1989.tb00494.x

Bryant, F. B. (2001, October 6). *Capturing the joy of the moment: Savoring as a process in positive psychology.* Invited address presented at the 3rd annual meeting of the Positive Psychology Network, Washington, DC.

Bryant, F. B. (2003). Savoring Beliefs Inventory (SBI): A scale for measuring beliefs about savouring. *Journal of Mental Health, 12,* 175–196. doi:10.1080/0963823031000103489

Bryant, F. B., Chadwick, E. D., & Kluwe, K. (2011). Understanding the processes that regulate positive emotional experience: Unsolved problems and future directions for theory and research on savoring. *International Journal of Well-Being, 1,* 107–126. doi:10.5502/ijw.v1i1.18

Bryant, F. B., Morgan, L., & Perloff, L. S. (1986). *The role of reminiscence in everyday life.* Presented at the American Psychological Association Convention, Washington, DC.

Bryant, F. B., & Veroff, J. (1984). Dimensions of subjective mental health in American men and women. *Journal of Health and Social Behavior, 25,* 116–135. doi:10.2307/2136664

Bryant, F. B., & Veroff, J. (2007). *Savoring: A new model of positive experience.* Mahwah, NJ: Lawrence Erlbaum Associates.

Carl, J. R., Fairholme, C. P., Gallagher, M. W., Thompson-Hollands, J., & Barlow, D. H. (2014). The effects of anxiety and depressive symptoms on daily positive emotion regulation. *Journal of Psychopathology and Behavioral Assessment, 36,* 224–236. doi:10.1007/s10862-013-9387-9

Csikszentmihalyi, M. (1997). *Finding flow: The psychology of engagement with everyday life.* New York, NY: Basic Books.

Feldman, G. C., Joormann, J., & Johnson, S. L. (2008). Responses to positive affect: A self-report measure of rumination and dampening. *Cognitive Therapy and Research, 32,* 507–525. doi:10.1007/s10608-006-9083-0

Fredrickson, B. L. (1998). What good are positive emotions? *Review of General Psychology, 2,* 300. doi:10.1037/1089-2680.2.3.300

Fredrickson, B. L. (2001). The role of positive emotions in positive psychology: The broaden-and-build theory of positive emotions. *American Psychologist, 56*, 218–226. doi:10.1037/0003-066X.56.3.218

Frijda, N. H., & Sundararajan, L. (2007). Emotion refinement: A theory inspired by Chinese poetics. *Perspectives on Psychological Science, 2*, 227–241. doi:10.1111/j.1745-6916.2007.00042.x

Gable, S. L., & Haidt, J. (2005). What (and why) is positive psychology? *Review of General Psychology, 9*, 103–110. doi:10.1037/1089-2680.9.2.103

Gable, S. L., Reis, H. T., Impett, E. A., & Asher, E. R. (2004). What do you do when things go right? The intrapersonal and interpersonal benefits of sharing positive events. *Journal of Personality and Social Psychology, 87*, 228–245. doi:10.1037/0022-3514.87.2.228

Garland, E. L. (2016). Restructuring reward processing with Mindfulness-Oriented Recovery Enhancement: Novel therapeutic mechanisms to remediate hedonic dysregulation in addiction, stress, and pain. *Annals of the New York Academy of Sciences, 1373*, 25–37. doi:10.1111/nyas.13034

Garland, E. L., Thielking, P., Thomas, E. A., Coombs, M., White, S., Lombardi, J., & Beck, A. (2017). Linking dispositional mindfulness and positive psychological processes in cancer survivorship: A multivariate path analytic test of the mindfulness-to-meaning theory. *Psycho-Oncology, 26*, 686–692. doi:10.1002/pon.4065

Gentzler, A. L., Palmer, C. A., & Ramsey, M. A. (2015). Savoring with intent: Investigating types of and motives for responses to positive events. *Journal of Happiness Studies, 17*, 937–958. doi:10.1007/s10902-015-9625-9

Giuliani, N. R., McRae, K., & Gross, J. J. (2008). The up-and down-regulation of amusement: Experiential, behavioral, and autonomic consequences. *Emotion, 8*, 714–719. doi:10.1037/a0013236

Goldman, S. L., Kraemer, D. T., & Salovey, P. (1996). Beliefs about mood moderate the relationship of stress to illness and symptom reporting. *Journal of Psychosomatic Research, 41*, 115–128. doi:10.1016/0022-3999(96)00119-5

Hurley, D. B., & Kwon, P. (2012). Results of a study to increase savoring the moment: Differential impact on positive and negative outcomes. *Journal of Happiness Studies, 13*, 579–588. doi:10.1007/s10902-011-9280-8

Ivanhoe, P. J. (2001). *Readings in classical Chinese philosophy*. New York, NY: Seven Bridges Press.

Ji, L., Nisbett, R. E., & Su, Y. (2001). Culture, change, and prediction. *Psychological Science, 12*, 450–456. doi:10.1111/1467-9280.00384

Jose, P. E., Lim, B. T., & Bryant, F. B. (2012). Does savoring increase happiness? A daily diary study. *The Journal of Positive Psychology, 7*, 176–187. doi:10.1080/17439760.2012.671345

Kashdan, T. B., Ferssizidis, P., Farmer, A. S., Adams, L. M., & McKnight, P. E. (2013). Failure to capitalize on sharing good news with romantic partners: Exploring positivity deficits of socially anxious people with self-reports, partner-reports, and behavioral observations. *Behavior Research and Therapy, 51*, 656–668. doi:10.1016/j.brat.2013.04.006

Kurtz, J. L. (2008). Looking to the future to appreciate the present: The benefits of perceived temporal scarcity. *Psychological Science, 19*, 1238–1241. doi:10.1111/j.1467-9280.2008.02231.x

Lambie, J. A., & Marcel, A. J. (2002). Consciousness and the varieties of emotion experience: A theoretical framework. *Psychological Review, 109*, 219–259. doi:10.1037//0033-295X.109.2.219

Langer, E. J., & Moldoveanu, M. (2000). The construct of mindfulness. *Journal of Social Issues, 56*, 1–9. doi:10.1111/0022-4537.00148

Langston, C. A. (1994). Capitalizing on and coping with daily-life events: Expressive responses to positive events. *Journal of Personality and Social Psychology, 67*, 1112–1125. doi:10.1037/0022-3514.67.6.1112

Leu, J., Mesquita, B., Ellsworth, P. C., ZhiYong, Z., Huijuan, Y., Buchtel, E., . . . Masuda, T. (2010). Situational differences in dialectical emotions: Boundary conditions in a cultural comparison of North Americans and East Asians. *Cognition & Emotion, 24*, 419–435. doi:10.1080/02699930802650911

Lindberg, T. L. (2004). *Culture and savoring of positive experiences* (doctoral dissertation). University of British Columbia. Retrieved from https://open.library.ubc.ca/cIRcle/collections/ubctheses/831/items/1.0092290

Mikolajczak, M. (2009). La régulation des émotions négatives. In M. Mikolajczak, J. Quoidbach, I. Kotsou, & D. Nélis (Eds.), *Les Compétences Émotionnelles* (pp. 153–191). Paris: Dunod.

Miyamoto, Y., & Ryff, C. D. (2011). Cultural differences in the dialectical and non-dialectical emotional styles and their implications for health. *Cognition & Emotion, 25*, 22–39. doi:10.1080/02699931003612114

Ng, W. (2012). Neuroticism and well-being? Let's work on the positive rather than negative aspects. *The Journal of Positive Psychology, 7*, 416–426. doi:10.1080/17439760.2012.709270

Ng, W., & Diener, E. (2009). Feeling bad? The "power" of positive thinking may not apply to everyone. *Journal of Research in Personality, 43*, 455–463. doi:10.1016/j.jrp.2009.01.020

Nussbaum, J. F. (2007). Life span communication and quality of life: Presidential address. *Journal of Communication, 57*, 1–7. doi:10.1111/j.1460-2466.2006.00325.x

Paulson, S., Davidson, R., Jha, A., & Kabat-Zinn, J. (2013). Becoming conscious: The science of mindfulness. *Annals of the New York Academy of Sciences, 1303*, 87–104. doi:10.1111/nyas.12203

Peng, K., & Nisbett, R. E. (1999). Culture, dialectics, and reasoning about contradiction. *American Psychologist, 54*, 741–754. doi:10.1037/0003-066X.54.9.741

Pitts, M. J. (2016, June 22–25). *Communication savoring*. Presidential Address at the 15th International Conference on Language and Social Psychology held in Bangkok, Thailand.

Pitts, M. J., & Socha, T. (Eds.). (2013). *Positive communication in health and wellness*. New York, NY: Peter Lang Publishing.

Quoidbach, J., Berry, E. V., Hansenne, M., & Mikolajczak, M. (2010). Positive emotion regulation and well-being: Comparing the impact of eight savoring and dampening strategies. *Personality and Individual Differences, 49*, 368–373. doi:10.1016/j.paid.2010.03.048

Quoidbach, J., Dunn, E. W., Hansenne, M., & Bustin, G. (2015). The price of abundance: How a wealth of experiences impoverishes savoring. *Personality and Social Psychology Bulletin, 41*, 393–404. doi:10.1177/0146167214566189

Reis, H. T., Smith, S. M., Carmichael, C. L., Caprariello, P. A., Tsai, F., Rodrigues, A., & Maniaci, M. R. (2010). Are you happy for me? How sharing positive events with others provides personal and interpersonal benefits. *Journal of Personality and Social Psychology, 99*, 311–329. doi:10.1037/a0018344

Salovey, P., Rothman, A. J., Detweiler, J. B., & Steward, W. T. (2000). Emotional states and physical health. *American Psychologist, 55*, 110–121. doi:10.1037//0003-066X.55.1.110

Schall, M., Goetz, T., Martiny, S. E., & Hall, N. C. (2017). It ain't over 'til it's over: The effect of task completion on the savoring of success. *Motivation and Emotion, 41*, 38–50. doi:10.1007/s11031-016-9591-5

Seligman, M. E. P. (2003). Foreword: The past and future of positive psychology. In C. L. M. Keyes & J. Haidt (Eds.), *Flourishing: Positive psychology and the life well-lived* (pp. xi–xx). Washington, DC: American Psychological Association.

Seligman, M. E. P., & Csikszentmihalyi, M. (2000). Positive psychology: An introduction. *American Psychologist, 55*, 5–14. doi:10.1037/0003-066X.55.1.5

Shapiro, S. L., Carlson, L. E., Astin, J. A., & Freedman, B. (2006). Mechanisms of mindfulness. *Journal of Clinical Psychology, 62*, 373–386. doi:10.1002/jclp.20237

Smith, J. L., & Hanni, A. A. (2017). Effects of a savoring intervention on resilience and well-being of older adults. *Journal of Applied Gerontology*. Online first. doi:10.1177/0733464817693375

Smith, J. L., & Hollinger-Smith, L. (2015). Savoring, resilience, and psychological well-being in older adults. *Aging and Mental Health, 19*, 192–200. doi:10.1080/13607863.2014.986647

Tsai, J. (2007). Ideal affect: Cultural causes and behavioral consequences. *Perspectives on Psychological Science, 2*, 242–259. doi:10.1111/j.1745-6916.2007.00043.x

Uchida, Y., & Kitayama, S. (2009). Happiness and unhappiness in East and West: Themes and variations. *Emotion, 9*, 441–456. doi:10.1037/a0015634

Uchida, Y., Norasakkunkit, V., & Kitayama, S. (2004). Cultural constructions of happiness: Theory and empirical evidence. *Journal of Happiness Studies, 5*, 223–239. doi:10.1007/s10902-004-8785-9

Wood, J. V., Heimpel, S. A., & Michela, J. L. (2003). Savoring versus dampening: Self-esteem differences in regulating positive affect. *Journal of Personality and Social Psychology, 83*, 566–580. doi:10.1037/0022-3514.85.3.566

PART II

Happiness and Media

12

POSITIVE MEDIA PSYCHOLOGY

Emerging Scholarship and a Roadmap for Emerging Technologies

Mary Beth Oliver and Arthur A. Raney

Scholarship in media psychology has often examined the variety of harms that media consumption can have on individuals and society, including increased aggression, stereotyping, health problems, and misplaced values, such as materialism. We recognize the importance of examining these negative effects, as doing so may provide a means by which we may work toward reducing (or at least drawing attention to) the deleterious outcomes that can be associated with media use. At the same time, however, we also applaud a growing body of scholarship that recognizes the positive sides of media consumption, including the use of media for purposes of enhancing feelings of purpose and meaningfulness; for creating a greater recognition of connectedness with others; for heightening compassion for individuals who may be oppressed or stigmatized; and for increasing motivations for altruism or social good.

We are heartened by this direction of research, as it suggests that there is an untapped resource that may be harnessed for bringing about our better selves. Further, the exploding number of emerging technologies in our contemporary media landscape implies that potential positive media influences can be realized through a variety of venues, including more traditional forms of media (e.g., film, television) as well as more recent media technologies (e.g., mobile communication). Our overarching goal in this chapter is to examine research on positive media across a diversity of media platforms. We begin our chapter by overviewing the foundational assumptions driving scholarship in positive media psychology. We then turn to how research has examined positive outcomes associated traditional forms of media, and last, how emerging media technologies may be utilized for purposes of enhancing well-being and social good.

Growing Research in Positive Media Psychology

Foundational research on individuals' uses of media have frequently highlighted the importance of pleasure or positive affect to individuals' media experiences. For example, scholarship from a uses and gratifications perspective typically finds that leisure or "passing the time" is one of the most important motivations that people report for consuming television (Rubin, 2008). Likewise, research on media entertainment has frequently implied that enjoyment or pleasure is the primary affective experience sought by viewers, with enjoyment largely defined in terms of portrayals of heroic characters prevailing and villains succumbing to their "just" desserts (Zillmann, 1988; Zillmann & Bryant, 1994).

Perhaps because foundational research seems (at first glance) to assume hedonic motivations and experiences, it is not surprising that numerous scholars have puzzled over the seeming paradox of the "enjoyment of sad films" (Oliver, 1993; Zillmann, 1998). More recently, however, scholars have shifted their focus from the issue of *sad* media to, instead, media that may be *meaningful*. In so doing, scholars have borrowed from ancient writings (Aristotle, 1961) to differentiate hedonic (e.g. pleasurable) experiences from eudaimonic (e.g., meaningful) experiences (Oliver & Bartsch, 2010; Oliver & Raney, 2011). In brief, this line of research argues that although much of the landscape of media content (and particularly entertainment content) is aimed at eliciting pleasure from consumers, a notable type of content is aimed at providing viewers with meaningful, touching, and moving experiences. Likewise, scholars have very recently noted that in some instances, media portrayals of inspiring displays of love and kindness may elicit self-transcendent experiences characterized by feelings of awe, elevation, and inspiration; a heightened sense of connection with others, nature, and the universe; and with a heightened motivation for greater altruism and performing acts of social good (Oliver et al., in press). With this background in mind, then, we now turn our attention to the contexts in which "positive media psychology" has been studied thus far.

Positive Media Psychology and Traditional Media Formats

Although media technologies are evolving at a dizzying pace, more "traditional" forms of media continue hold a large share of individuals' total media diets. Further, some forms of traditional media seem to be particularly adept at telling in-depth stories pertaining to weighty and meaningful questions such as the human condition or purpose in life. In this section we overview positive media research that has examined more traditional media with a longer history—media that have understandably received the preponderance of research attention.

Literature/Written Texts

Aside from stories told orally or performed live, literature or written texts (broadly defined) are our oldest form of "media" communication. Literature or narratives allow us to not only learn *about* characters, but to get inside a character's head, to hear their thoughts, and to become intimate with their motivations. In short, literature seems to provide an ideal platform for grappling with meaningful and profound questions concerning human tragedy, beauty, and purpose in life.

Within the social science community, perhaps one of the most studied concepts regarding experiences of reading is *transportation* or *engagement*. In brief, this concept refers to the idea that when involved in a narrative, individuals' attention is focused almost entirely within the story world, and less so on their immediate physical surroundings (Busselle & Bilandzic, 2008; Green, 2004; Green & Brock, 2000). In essence, we become "lost" in the story. Although the concept of transportation is not meant to imply positive effects necessarily, scholars have entertained numerous favorable outcomes associated with heightened levels of engagement. For example, Green (2004) wrote that individuals generally appreciation the experience of transportation, as it allows them to experience a wide array of emotions and experiences, including even negative experiences. Likewise, a substantial amount of research has also shown that transportation into a narrative featuring prosocial lessons is more likely to be accepted by audiences who are engaged with the story and are therefore less likely to counter argue persuasive messages (Slater & Rouner, 2002).

Because consuming narratives in book-length form may span across hours, days, or even weeks, it stands to reason that engagement with this form of media may be particularly influential. At the same time, however, the logistics involved in testing such long-term involvement via social scientific means are particularly challenging and, by definition, time intensive. With this in mind, it is understandable that many studies of meaningful media have examined electronic or digital media formats that can be consumed in a single setting.

Film

Of all mediums, movies or cinematic media has arguably received the largest amount of research attention among social scientists studying meaningful media. This focus likely reflects the idea that some types of films seem to be specifically designed to help viewers grapple with meaningfulness, including sad films, dramas, tragedies, and additional genres that focus on questions regarding the human spirit.

Many of the measures initially developed to assess motivations for consuming meaningful media and responses reflecting appreciation (e.g., moved, tender) were developed in the context of cinematic portrayals (Oliver & Bartsch, 2010; Oliver & Raney, 2011). In many instances, these studies have asked viewers to recall their responses to and report their memories of both the content and of their reactions to the content. For example, Oliver and Hartmann (2010) asked viewers to name a meaningful (or a pleasurable) film and to indicate both the types of values the film portrayed, as well as their emotional reactions at the time of viewing. These authors found that many meaningful film experiences reflected the concept of elevation—the feeling of inspiration in response to seeing others perform extraordinary acts of moral beauty (e.g., compassion, kindness; Haidt, 2003). Additional research using archival, content-analytic approaches showed that these types of portrayals seem to be particularly valued by viewers, as movies featuring emotional and even "dark" content were particularly likely to receive both critical acclaim (e.g., cinematic awards) and favorable audience ratings (e.g., ratings on Rotten Tomatoes; Oliver, Ash, Woolley, Shade, & Kim, 2014).

In addition to examining the characteristics of content and audience response, a growing body of work is now beginning to study the positive outcomes associated with viewing moving, meaningful, and sometimes even tragic cinematic offerings. As with many studies of elevating content, research reports that viewing inspiring films appears to heighten prosocial motivations to do good for others or to be a better person (Oliver, Hartmann, & Woolley, 2012). In addition, experimental work also suggests that films can heighten positive outcomes such as increasing feelings of gratitude (Knobloch-Westerwick, Gong, Hagner, & Kerbeykian, 2013), helping viewers grapple with fears of death (Hofer, 2013), and providing a means by which viewers can cope with trauma and stress in their own lives (Khoo & Oliver, 2013).

Television

Although scholars have arguable attended most to film when studying meaningful and positive entertainment, television remains the leisure activity of choice. According to US Bureau of Labor statistics, in 2016 American adults reported spending more than half (53.2 percent) of their leisure time watching television (U.S. Bureau of Labor, 2017).

The breadth of television content—genres, narrative formats, specialized networks, the sheer volume of programs—would seemingly make the medium ideal for the pursuit of meaning and purpose in life. The same could be said of the periodic and serial nature of typical programming, which (at least theoretically) promotes ritualistic viewing, long-term, intense identification with characters, and extended storylines that explore the depths of personal and family relations, love, tragedy, suffering, aging, success, failure, birth, death, and countless related existential questions. Data from a few of our own US-based studies support these claims. In one nationally representative survey, 80.2 percent of American adults reported having been previously touched, moved, or inspired by television; drama (30.9 percent) was the genre of programming most often cited as the source of this inspiration, followed by documentaries, Christian/spiritual shows, and reality programs.

Nevertheless, despite the general information about the genres of programming that are more likely to inspire, little is known about the specific portrayals and narrative forms of television that might foster meaningfulness. Our own work has focused on known elicitors of self-transcendent emotions found in television and on YouTube reported to be inspirational or tagged as such. In both projects, characters demonstrating behaviors and motivations associated with hope (e.g., someone overcoming a struggle) and an appreciation of beauty and excellence (e.g., beautiful of nature and vastness, displays of kindness) were by far the most plentiful—suggesting that themes related to and portrayals of hope and moral beauty may play key roles in meaningful and inspiring televisual content (Dale, Raney, Janicke, Sanders, & Oliver, 2017)

As with films, a few laboratory studies have emerged in recent years specifically examining the effects of viewing meaningful television content on emotional reactions and behavioral intentions and actions, though most have relied on short-form narratives as stimulus materials. For instance, Prestin (2013) found that YouTube videos depicting underdog characters struggling to achieve their goals despite unfavorable odds generated hopeful emotional responses among viewers in both the short- and the long-term (up to three days past exposure). Likewise, viewing a short clip of the *Oprah Winfrey* show was shown to elicit elevation among viewers, who in turn were significantly more likely to volunteer assistance to others afterward than nonviewers (Schnall, Roper, & Fessler, 2010).

To sum, it is clear that people can and do find meaning and inspiration from television programming and television-like videos. Portrayals of hope and moral beauty, at least according to initial studies, seem to be quite prevalent in that content. Moreover, the extent to which exposure to that content can promote self-transcendent emotions such as elevation and hope, and the potential benefits to psychological well-being, human flourishing, and social connectedness are encouraging.

Games

Similar to many forms of entertainment, video games in particular seem to be associated with unpalatable content and/or outcomes such as violence, mindlessness, or stereotyping. Further, gaming is frequently characterized as "low brow" entertainment (Ebert, 2010), and, as such, not frequently featuring the types of themes identified thus far as consequential to meaningful media experiences (e.g., hope, displays of transcendence, altruism). However, the landscape of games has undoubtedly matured to include not only stereotypical shooting games, but also serious games that grapple with "weighty" issues such as illness, death, sorrow, and the vastness of the universe.

Emerging scholarship on gaming suggests that, similar to other forms of media, game play has the ability to arouse deep feelings of appreciation and insight. Perhaps not surprisingly, one study of gaming found that strong narratives or storylines were the best predictor of gamers' appreciation (more so than controllers, for example) (Oliver et al., 2015). This finding may imply that gaming is not really different from traditional forms of entertainment (e.g., film) in the ways that it may arouse feelings of meaningfulness. Yet we believe that additional work needs to be conducted on gaming affordances that may uniquely predict eudaimonic and self-transcendent media experiences. For example, Elson, Breuer, Ivory, and Quandt (2014) argued that researchers would be well advised to consider the *context* of gaming, as factors such as co-playing may be consequential to meaningful experiences.

Summary

Traditional forms of media provide viewers with a wide array of opportunity for positive and meaningful experiences. Such experiences frequently involve stories—narratives about compassion, generosity, or even tragedy. Yet scholarship on gaming illustrates that as media formats evolve and change, so do the means by which media may inspire or elevate its viewers/users. With this in mind, we now turn to the second part of our chapter pertaining to emerging technologies.

The Potential for Realizing the Positive in Emerging Technologies

Were we to have written this chapter even 20 years ago, we likely would have a difficult time envisioning the media landscape as we know it today. It might have seemed unlikely, if not impossible, that people would carry their media with them wherever they went, that individuals would invest incredible amounts of time corresponding about and sharing personal information in quasi-public settings as a form of leisure, that media depictions could be made so life-like as to mirror reality, or that the words "reader" or "viewer" would become somewhat obsolete in a time when individuals are also the *creators* of content rather than just the receivers. With this backdrop in mind, we end our chapter by considering the possible unique ways that newer technologies can be used and harnessed to enhance social good.

Mobile Communication

In many respects, it may not seem surprising that recent estimates of individuals' daily media use exceed 10 hours per day (Lynch, 2016). The advent of mobile communication means that we not only have media at our side during most of the day, but that for many people, the mobile phone is kept by the bedside and is utilized from the first waking moments. The prevalence and salience of mobile technologies has a resulted in a large variety of cautionary essays and studies outlining the multitude of its potential harms, including the disruption of interpersonal communication, the shortening of attention spans, and the necessity of being "permanently online," among many others (see, for example, Vorderer, Krömer, & Schneider, 2016).

While we acknowledge the potential harms that mobile technologies may invite, we also believe that there are a multitude of avenues where they may provide meaningful and positive experiences and outcomes. For example, numerous scholars have written about the important role that cell phones play in fighting political oppression (e.g., Al-Jenaibi, 2014). Likewise, recent events regarding police shootings suggest that the availability of digital recordings in mobile devices may serve to make vivid and salient social problems that may have otherwise gone unreported (e.g., Taibbi, 2015).

With regard to more individual level effects, research in health communication provides evidence that readily available apps encourage a variety of healthy behaviors, including increased exercise, practicing mindfulness, and the cessation of unhealthy behaviors such as smoking (Payne, Lister, West, & Bernhardt, 2015). The ease of using mobile technologies, as well as the format of messages that they typically employ, also makes them ideally suited for many social networking sites, including those that employ images as texts (e.g., Instagram), as well as those that employ brief texts (e.g., Twitter). Although a host of studies have reported deleterious effects of social networking sites including outcomes such as bullying and envy (Livingstone & Brake, 2010; Tandoc, Ferrucci, & Duffy, 2015), we also note that such sites offer opportunities for social support, for sharing of inspiring media content, and for nurturing social relationships. The extent to which these positive outcomes offset the possible harmful effects of mobile technologies on interpersonal interaction represents an important area of investigation for those interested in the overall impact of technological changes on well-being.

Virtual Reality

Virtual reality (VR) offers another avenue for future meaningful media research. As a technology, VR is a simulated environment created through the combination of software, stereoscopic display, stereo sound, motion tracking, and (at times) other sensory inputs. As an experience, VR is an immersive and interactive computer-generated, three-dimensional environment that, to our senses (primarily sight and sound), appears real. Applications of VR technology have been and are continuing to be developed for a number of purposes, including health care, business, scientific visualization, fashion, construction, and, of course, entertainment. VR holds great promise for meaningful and self-transcendent entertainment experiences because of two primary features. First, the environments created through VR can be incredibly intricate, complex, and vast. As such, VR may offer new (e.g., Icelandic lava fields, Taipei's Shilin Night Market) or otherwise impossible (e.g., 16th-century Spanish galleon at sea on a starry night, Martian moonscapes) opportunities for individuals to experience the self-transcendent emotion of awe, which is conceptualized as a reaction to perceptually vast stimuli which exceeds our ordinary frames of reference, level of experience, or cognitive schemas (Keltner & Haidt, 2003; see also Chirico, Yaden, Riva, & Gaggioli, 2016). Second, the immersive and interactive nature of simulated VR environments promotes the feeling of presence, or the psychological state in which our perception fails to accurately acknowledge the role of the technology in a particular experience, resulting in a sense of "being there" socially, spatially, and sensorially. Thus, VR has the potential for people to explore situations in which they, for instance, can see the world through the eyes of an elderly person, which may lead to a reduction in age-based stereotyping (Yee & Bailenson, 2006), or in which they can participate in a simulation of Milgram's famous experiments on authoritarianism, which may be an eye-opening experience of a different sort (Slater et al., 2006). The introduction of Sony PlayStation VR in late 2016 and the continued development of other (relatively) affordable, consumer-grade virtual reality systems (e.g., Oculus Rift, HTC Vive) will likely usher in a new era in media entertainment, some of which will undoubtedly deliver meaningful and contemplative experiences to users. Media psychologists will be tasked with exploring the impact of these experiences on well-being, social connectedness, human flourishing.

User-Generated Content

Just as emerging technologies have changed the way that media content is delivered, so, too, has it changed the way that media content is created. No longer are individuals only the recipients of information, but now they are major *sources* or *creators* of media content as well. Not only do individuals post and share information on platforms such as blogs and social media as discussed previously, but they now are creators of sometimes elaborate videos and narratives uploaded onto streaming sites such as YouTube and Snapchat. Indeed, recent research suggests that teens more closely identify with YouTube creators than they do with traditional celebrities from television, film, or sports (O'Neil-Hart & Blumenstein, 2016).

The implications of traditional versus user-generated media for purposes of well-being and social good are only beginning to be considered by media researchers. However, we believe that this is a fruitful direction of scholarship for several reasons. First, we note that unlike more traditional types of entertainment such as television or news that employ writers and producers creating content for the specific purpose of revenue generation, individuals who become creators on platforms such as YouTube may have broader or alternative motivations such as self-disclosure or personal engagement. As a result, YouTube may represent a venue where more intimate and deeply emotional issues can be exchanged and considered.

Second, from a "media effects" perspective, user-generated experiences may represent a completely new type of "effect"—one that arises not from the consumption of media content, but rather from the act of creating media content. Our initial work on the creation of inspiring content, be it via video editing or photography, suggests that feelings of elevation are enhanced when individuals engage in the act of creation rather than in only consumption. Consequently, we believe that future scholarship may benefit from examining how the creative process afforded by emerging technologies can provide further avenues for social good.

Finally, we note that user-generated media not only provide a unique opportunity for the creation of content, but also for the *collaborative* creation of content. For example, the nonprofit organization *Playing for Change* posts numerous videos from musicians from around the world coming together virtually to sing about social justice and moral beauty. Although the musicians are geographically dispersed, their common efforts and collaborative harmonies not only inspire and illustrate shared efforts for social good, but they also highlight the common humanity that exists throughout a diversity of contexts and cultures.

Summary and Outlook

The association of media with harmful outcomes has a long history in media psychology. Yet the opportunities for media to help us see our better sides is evident in a diversity of formats. In our chapter, we have treated these technologies as discrete experiences, yet we also believe that their similarities highlight the importance of our use of media in all of its forms to help us recognize our common humanities and our deep longings for meaning and purpose. As technologies continue to evolve, it is our hope that the use of media for social good, as well as our careful study of these meaningful experiences, will also continue keep pace with these deeply gratifying and elevating experiences.

References

Al-Jenaibi, B. (2014). The nature of Arab public discourse: Social media and the "Arab Spring". *Journal of Applied Journalism & Media Studies, 3*(2), 241–260. http://doi.org/10.1386/ajms.3.2.241_1

Aristotle. (trans. 1961). *Poetics* (S. H. Butcher, Trans.). New York: Hill and Wang.

Busselle, R., & Bilandzic, H. (2008). Fictionality and perceived realism in experiencing stories: A model of narrative comprehension and engagement. *Communication Theory, 18*, 255–280. doi:10.1111/j.1468-2885.2008.00322.x

Chirico, A., Yaden, D. B., Riva, G., & Gaggioli, A. (2016). The potential of virtual reality for the investigation of awe. *Frontiers in Psychology, 7*, 1766. Retrieved from http://journal.frontiersin.org/article/10.3389/fpsyg.2016.01766/full doi:10.3389/fpsyg.2016.01766

Dale, K. R., Raney, A. A., Janicke, S. H., Sanders, M. S., & Oliver, M. B. (2017). YouTube for good: A content analysis and examination of elicitors of self-transcendent media. *Journal of Communication.* Advance online publication. doi:10.1111/jcom.12333

Ebert, R. (2010, April 16). Video games can never be art. *Chicago Sun Times.* Retrieved from http://blogs.suntimes.com/ebert/2010/04/video_games_can_never_be_art.html

Elson, M., Breuer, J., Ivory, J. D., & Quandt, T. (2014). More than stories with buttons: Narrative, mechanics, and context as determinants of player experience in digital games. *Journal of Communication, 64*(3), 521–542. doi:10.1111/jcom.12096

Green, M. C. (2004). Transportation into narrative worlds: The role of prior knowledge and perceived realism. *Discourse Processes, 38*(2), 247–266. doi:10.1207/s15326950dp3802_5

Green, M. C., & Brock, T. C. (2000). The role of transportation in the persuasiveness of public narratives. *Journal of Personality and Social Psychology, 79*(5), 701–721. doi:10.1037//0022-3514.79.5.701

Haidt, J. (2003). Elevation and the positive psychology of morality. In C. L. M. Keyes & J. Haidt (Eds.), *Flourishing: Positive psychology and the life well-lived* (pp. 275–289). Washington, DC: American Psychological Association.

Hofer, M. (2013). Appreciation and enjoyment of meaningful entertainment: The role of mortality salience and search for meaning in life. *Journal of Media Psychology: Theories, Methods, and Applications, 25*(3), 109. doi:10.1027/1864-1105/a000089

Keltner, D., & Haidt, J. (2003). Approaching awe, a moral, spiritual, and aesthetic emotion. *Cognition & Emotion, 17*(2), 297–314. doi:10.1080/02699930302297

Khoo, G. S., & Oliver, M. B. (2013). The therapeutic effects of narrative cinema through clarification: Reexamining catharsis. *Scientific Study of Literature, 3*(2), 266–293. doi:10.1075/ssol.3.2.06kho

Knobloch-Westerwick, S., Gong, Y., Hagner, H., & Kerbeykian, L. (2013). Tragedy viewers count their blessings: Feeling low on fiction leads to feeling high on life. *Communication Research, 40*(6), 747–766. doi:10.1177/0093650212437758

Livingstone, S., & Brake, D. R. (2010). On the rapid rise of social networking sites: New findings and policy implications. *Children & Society, 24*(1), 75–83. doi:10.1111/j.1099-0860.2009.00243.x

Lynch, J. (2016, June 27). U.S. adults consume an entire hour more of media per day than they did just last year. *Adweek*. Retrieved from www.adweek.com/tv-video/us-adults-consume-entire-hour-more-media-day-they-did-just-last-year-172218/

Oliver, M. B. (1993). Exploring the paradox of the enjoyment of sad films. *Human Communication Research, 19*(3), 315–342. doi:10.1111/j.1468-2958.1993.tb00304.x

Oliver, M. B., Ash, E., Woolley, J. K., Shade, D. D., & Kim, K. (2014). Entertainment we watch, and entertainment we appreciate: Patterns of motion picture consumption and acclaim over three decades. *Mass Communication & Society, 17*, 853–873. doi:10.1080/15205436.2013.872277

Oliver, M. B., & Bartsch, A. (2010). Appreciation as audience response: Exploring entertainment gratifications beyond hedonism. *Human Communication Research, 36*(1), 53–81. doi:10.1111/j.1468-2958.1993.tb00304.x

Oliver, M. B., Bowman, N. D., Woolley, J., Rogers, R., Sherrick, B. I., & Chung, M.-Y. (2015). Video games as meaningful entertainment experiences. *Psychology of Popular Media Culture, 5*(4), 390–405. doi:10.1037/ppm0000066

Oliver, M. B., & Hartmann, T. (2010). Exploring the role of meaningful experiences in users' appreciation of "good movies". *Projections: The Journal of Movies and Mind, 4*(2), 128–150. doi:10.3167/proj.2010.040208

Oliver, M. B., Hartmann, T., & Woolley, J. K. (2012). Elevation in response to entertainment portrayals of moral virtue. *Human Communication Research, 38*, 360–378. doi:10.1111/j.1468-2958.2012.01427.x

Oliver, M. B., & Raney, A. A. (2011). Entertainment as pleasurable and meaningful: Identifying hedonic and eudaimonic motivations for entertainment consumption. *Journal of Communication, 61*, 984–1004. doi:10.1111/j.1460-2466.2011.01585.x

Oliver, M. B., Raney, A. A., Slater, M. D., Appel, M., Hartmann, T., Bartsch, A., et al. (in press). Self-transcendent media experiences: Taking meaningful media to a higher level. *Journal of Communication*.

O'Neil-Hart, C., & Blumenstein, H. (2016). *Why YouTube stars are more influential than traditional celebrities*. Retrieved from www.thinkwithgoogle.com/consumer-insights/youtube-stars-influence/

Payne, H. E., Lister, C., West, J. H., & Bernhardt, J. M. (2015). Behavioral functionality of mobile apps in health interventions: A systematic review of the literature. *JMIR Mhealth Uhealth, 3*(1), e20. doi:10.2196/mhealth.3335

Prestin, A. (2013). The pursuit of hopefulness: Operationalizing hope in entertainment media narratives. *Media Psychology, 16*(3), 318–346. doi:10.1080/15213269.2013.773494

Rubin, A. M. (2008). Uses-and-gratifications perspective on media effects. In J. Bryant & M. B. Oliver (Eds.), *Media effects: Advances in theory and research* (3rd ed., pp. 165–184). New York: Routledge.

Schnall, S., Roper, J., & Fessler, D. M. T. (2010). Elevation leads to altruistic behavior. *Psychological Science, 21*(3), 315–320. doi:10.1177/0956797609359882

Slater, M. D., Antley, A., Davison, A., Swapp, D., Guger, C., Barker, C., Pistrang, N., & Sanchez-Vives, M. V. (2006). A virtual reprise of the Stanley Milgram obedience experiments. *PLoS One, 1*(1), e39. doi:10.1371/journal.pone.0000039

Slater, M. D., & Rouner, D. (2002). Entertainment; education and elaboration likelihood: Understanding the processing of narrative persuasion. *Communication Theory, 12*, 173–191. doi:10.1111/j.1468-2885.2002.tb00265.x

Taibbi, M. (2015, April 9). Are cell phones changing the narrative on police shootings? *Rolling Stone*. Retrieved from www.rollingstone.com/politics/news/are-cell-phones-changing-the-narrative-on-police-shootings-20150409

Tandoc, E. C., Ferrucci, P., & Duffy, M. (2015). Facebook use, envy, and depression among college students: Is Facebooking depressing? *Computers in Human Behavior, 43*, 139–146. doi:10.1016/j.chb.2014.10.053

U.S. Bureau of Labor. (2017). *American time use survey summary*. Retrieved from www.bls.gov/news.release/atus.nr0.htm

Vorderer, P., Krömer, N., & Schneider, F. M. (2016). Permanently online-Permanently connected: Explorations into university students' use of social media and mobile smart devices. *Computers in Human Behavior, 63*, 694–703. http://doi.org/10.1016/j.chb.2016.05.085

Yee, N., & Bailenson, J.N. (2006). Walk a mile in digital shoes: The impact of embodied perspective-taking on the reduction of negative stereotyping in immersive virtual environments. *Proceedings of PRESENCE 2006: The 9th Annual International Workshop on Presence*. August 24–26, Cleveland, Ohio, USA.

Zillmann, D. (1988). Mood management: Using entertainment to full advantage. In L. Donohew, H. E. Sypher, & E. T. Higgins (Eds.), *Communication, social cognition, and affect* (pp. 147–171). Hillsdale, NJ: Lawrence Erlbaum Associates.

Zillmann, D. (1998). Does tragic drama have redeeming value? *Siegener Periodikum für Internationale Literaturwissenschaft, 16*, 1–11.

Zillmann, D., & Bryant, J. (1994). Entertainment as media effect. In J. Bryant & D. Zillmann (Eds.), *Media effects: Advances in theory and research* (pp. 437–461). Hillsdale, NJ: Lawrence Erlbaum Associates.

13

ON BEING HAPPY THROUGH ENTERTAINMENT

Hedonic and Non-Hedonic Entertainment Experiences

Matthias Hofer and Diana Rieger

Introduction

If someone would ask a random person on the street what is most important to him or her in life, some might answer "being rich" or "being famous," others would consider being healthy to be the most desirable state. However, more than a few of them would probably answer "being happy is most important to me."

But what exactly does it mean to "be happy"? Feeling good instead of feeling bad most likely comes to mind, or being satisfied with one's life (Kahneman, Diener, & Schwarz, 2003). However, this *hedonic* notion has been extended by a so-called *eudaimonic* perspective. Having its roots in ancient Greece and being an ethical principle about the good life, the notion of eudaimonic well-being has been adopted by scholars of positive psychology (Waterman, 1993; Ryff, 1989; Ryff & Singer, 2006). According to this view, happiness can be regarded as positive psychological functioning according to one's standards, norms, and values. It entails having a certain purpose in life, being able to grow personally in an autonomous and competent manner, accepting oneself, and having positive relations with others.

These two forms of happiness (hedonic and non-hedonic/eudaimonic) can be pursued (at least in the short-term) using different kinds of media, as media are most readily available to most people. People can have a good time by watching a comedy or playing a video game. They may even find a higher sense of meaning and self-acceptance during watching a drama movie. Not surprisingly, both the hedonic and the eudaimonic perspective have been adopted by entertainment scholars. More precisely, the hedonic and the eudaimonic view have been used to explain both motivations for using media and the resulting experiences. We start with a discussion of the hedonic perspective on entertainment experiences.

Hedonic Approaches

Perhaps the most prominent theoretical explanation for why people turn to one or the other form of entertainment has been proposed by Dolf Zillmann. According to his *Mood Management Theory* (MMT; Knobloch-Westerwick, 2006; Zillmann, 1988a, 1988b) the media user is conceived as an individual striving to diminish (the intensity of) bad moods and prolong and/or intensify good moods. The motives for selection of certain media stimuli are associated with the regulation of unwanted circumstances, namely negative mood with too high or too low-intensity (i.e., being stressed out or being bored). Notably, Zillmann (1988b) emphasized that individuals are not necessarily "cognizant of the reasons for their choices" (p. 329). He argues that "the comprehension of motivational circumstances is not necessary [italics in original] for the formation of mood-specific preferences" (p. 329). Thus, most of the time media selection happens on an unconscious level.

Zillmann and his colleagues identified four characteristics of media messages to have the potential to impact viewers' moods: (1) The *excitatory potential* is likely to go along with an increase in viewers' sympathetic arousal. (2) Bad moods are especially well impaired by media messages with a high *absorption potential* because such messages use up cognitive capacity that would be used to process or rehearse the aspects of negative moods. However, the absorption potential of a message may be considerably reduced by (3) the *semantic affinity* between a viewer's preexisting mood and the message. Finally, of utmost importance in terms of a viewer's mood is (4) the *hedonic valence* of a message, as pleasant messages are most likely to uplift a person in a bad mood. For instance, MMT would argue that bored and under-aroused individuals would favor exciting over calm and soothing content, which has a certain semantic affinity to their boredom.

In terms of the experience during or after exposure to media entertainment, most scholars use the term *enjoyment* (Bosshart & Macconi, 1998; Vorderer, Klimmt, & Ritterfeld, 2004). In their model of media entertainment Vorderer and colleagues (2004) regard enjoyment as the core of media entertainment. According to Bosshart and Macconi (1998) enjoyment is characterized by relaxation, diversion, fun, and joy. Finally, Tamborini et al. (2010) conceptualize enjoyment as the result of fast and intuitive reasoning which occurs through the satisfaction of one or more intrinsic needs. For instance, romantic comedies might satisfy the need for relatedness and the need for humor. Following the work of Zillmann (1988a, 1988b) Vorderer (2011) has a similar view and claims that enjoyment results from the satisfaction of the need for pleasure and the need for comprehension.

Affective Disposition Theory (ADT, Zillmann, 1994) explains how enjoyment emerges as a function of the viewer's disposition toward the protagonists and the outcome of the story. ADT was first developed to explain the effects of humor on audiences, but it is also applicable to sports or drama (Raney, 2006). According to ADT audience members first morally assess the actions of the protagonist and either disapprove or approve of them. If the viewer approves of the actions, he or she starts liking the character; in the case of disapproval of his or her deeds, the character is most probably disliked. Enjoyment emerges if liked characters experience positive outcomes and if disliked characters experience negative outcomes. Therefore, if liked characters experience negative outcomes, as it is often the case in sad films, tearjerkers or tragedies, enjoyment is most unlikely to emerge. And yet, such media content seems to be both selected and enjoyed by its audiences.

The Sad Film Paradox

The fact that (1) individuals seem to select entertainment that elicit rather sad and somber moods and (2) they seem to experience enjoyment while watching such entertainment offerings is referred to as *sad film paradox* (Oliver, 1993; Hofer, 2017; Hofer & Wirth, 2012). This paradox has a *motivational* and an *experiential* component. Whereas the former component deals with the question of why people select sad films and tragedies, the latter is concerned with the question of how viewers can enjoy watching sad films. Scholars have offered several theoretical explanations for both components of the paradox.

To solve the motivational component, personality-based explanations have been proposed. For instance, it has been suggested that people with higher levels of sensation seeking are more likely to watch sad movies because they enjoy the possibly intense negative arousal (Zuckerman, 2006). Another explanation for the selection of tearjerkers, which is not based on personality, is the opportunity for downward social comparison (Mares & Cantor, 1992). In other words, viewers are motivated to watch other people suffer because they can compare the tragic fate of these characters with their own situation, which is often much better. Thus, people select sad films because they expect to be given the opportunities to compare themselves favorably with others. Another explanation for the motivational component of the sad film paradox is that sad films are selected because they provide viewers with the opportunity to experience empathy (Mills, 1993).

In terms of the experiential component the concept of *meta-emotions* (Bartsch, Vorderer, Mangold, & Viehoff, 2008; Hofer & Wirth, 2012; Oliver, 1993) was used to explain the paradoxical situation of the concurrence of deep sadness and enjoyment. Meta-emotions are emotions that arise from appraising one's own emotions. For instance, a person can be sad about his or her schadenfreude. Using a deeply sad story, Hofer and Wirth (2012) could show that if people appraise their sadness as being compatible with moral values and norms, the sadness' negative valence was transformed into a positive meta-emotion (i.e., enjoyment). This process in which a negative emotion is transformed into a positively valenced meta-emotion is called *valence transformation* (Schramm & Wirth, 2010). Insofar, enjoyment can be regarded as the positive experience of one's emotions during watching a sad film or a tragedy.

Non-Hedonic/Eudaimonic Approaches

It seems that the sad film paradox can be solved quite elegantly. The theoretical claims are well supported by empirical data. However, maybe sad movies or tearjerkers should not only be characterized in terms of their sad and tragic nature, but in terms of their *meaningfulness* (Oliver & Bartsch, 2011). That is, films like *Schindler's List* or *Hotel Ruanda* are not only tragic, but can provoke audiences to contemplate life's meaning or human connections. Although the terms meaning and meaningfulness are still lacking a comprehensive definition (Leontiev, 2013), one could start with a definition of the term *meaning*. Park and Folkman (1997) define meaning as "*personal significance* [italics in original]" (p. 115). Applied to media messages, one could argue that, to be meaningful, these messages have to have a certain personal significance for their viewers. Meaningful entertainment can provide viewers with a deeper insight into their own lives or in life itself, human values and virtues, and human relationships. Exploring the audience's understanding of what constitutes a movie's meaningfulness Oliver and Hartmann (2010) found that films are perceived as meaningful if they address the fact that human life is limited or the value of virtue and human connections. In addition, emotional reactions to meaningful entertainment are characterized by the co-occurrence of positive and negative affect. Such co-occurrence is often referred to as *mixed emotions* (e.g., Ersner-Hershfield, Mikels, Sullivan, & Carstensen, 2008). Participants also described meaningful portrayals as those that depict moral virtues such as care, courage, persistence, and love (Bartsch & Oliver, 2016).

The motives driving reception of these forms of entertainment should accordingly go beyond a purely hedonic pursuit of pleasure (Oliver, 1993; Oliver & Raney, 2011). In the light of such considerations, Oliver and Raney (2011) introduced the notion of eudaimonic motivations for entertainment consumption. Eudaimonic motivations go along with a need for greater introspection, the seeking of insight, and the motivation to contemplate life's profundities. In a similar vein, Lozano Delmar, Sánchez-Martín, and Muñiz-Velázquez (2016) developed a scale to capture eudaimonic motivations of fans and non-fans, the *Eudaimonic Spectator Questionnaire* (ESQ). The scale measures eudaimonic motivations on two dimensions: (1) cognitive-intellectual growth and (2) social-emotional growth (see Lozano Delmar, & Sánchez-Martín, 2018).

In terms non-hedonic or eudaimonic experiences during and after media use, Oliver and Bartsch (2010) introduced the concept of *appreciation*. Appreciation is defined as "the perception of deeper meaning, the feeling of being moved, and the motivation to elaborate on thoughts and feelings inspired by the experience" (Oliver & Bartsch, 2010, p. 76). Appreciation may inspire questions on a deeper meaning of life or existential thoughts and feelings (Oliver & Bartsch, 2010). Media usage characterized by appreciation leads to multi-layered, even bipolar feelings (positive and negative), such as the state of feeling moved, inspired, touched, melancholy, or stricken at the same time. Such feelings are referred to as *tender affective states* (Oliver, 2008), *meaningful affect* (Oliver, Hartmann, & Woolley, 2012), *mixed emotions* (Ersner-Hershfield et al., 2008), or poignancy (Slater, Oliver, & Appel, 2016). Finally, based on research by Ryff (1989) and Waterman (1993) Wirth, Hofer, and Schramm (2012) conceive eudaimonic entertainment experiences as a multidimensional concept consisting of a feeling of (1) relatedness, (2) activation of central values, (3) autonomy, (4) competence, and (5) self-acceptance and purpose in life.

Theoretical Explanations

The emergence of hedonic and non-hedonic entertainment experiences is conceptualized differently by two research approaches both of which are based on dual-process models (Evans & Stanovich, 2013). The first approach describes entertainment in terms of a hierarchy of needs (Vorderer, 2011). That is, as mentioned above, hedonic entertainment experiences result from the satisfaction of lower-order needs (i.e., the need for pleasure and the need for comprehension), whereas non-hedonic entertainment experiences are based on higher-order needs. More precisely, based on *self-determination theory* (Ryan & Deci, 2000) it is assumed that the satisfaction of the needs for autonomy, competence, and relatedness lead to appreciation.

The second explanation is very similar to the first one. However, it is not based on a hierarchy of needs (Lewis, Tamborini, & Weber, 2014). It distinguishes enjoyment and appreciation by two types of processing. As mentioned above, enjoyment is conceived as a quick and intuitive response that occurs when one or more intrinsic needs are satisfied. By contrast, appreciation is a slower and more deliberate response that occurs when there is a conflict between different needs. This conflict requires audience members to respond more slowly to accept and appraise this conflict between needs. For instance, Walter White, the protagonist of the series *Breaking Bad*, repeatedly violates moral norms and breaks the law by cooking meth. On the other hand, he always is keen to protect his family. As a result, viewers of the series are constantly confronted with conflicting needs. This conflict, in turn, requires more intense cognitive processing than when there are no conflicting needs (Lewis et al., 2014).

Antecedents of Hedonic and Eudaimonic Entertainment Experiences

In the section on hedonic entertainment we have discussed antecedents of this type of experiences and motivations. Message-related variables, such as the arousal potential or the hedonic valence of the message in combination with the user's mood have been found to influence the hedonically driven selection of messages. According to ADT, the disposition toward the media character in combination with the plot's resolution affect the hedonic experience.

Scholars have also addressed the question of what drives eudaimonic entertainment experiences. Unlike, hedonic entertainment experiences, eudaimonic entertainment experiences do not seem to depend on whether a movie has a happy or a sad ending (Wirth et al., 2012). As Oliver and Bartsch (2011) pointed out, it is rather a film's meaningfulness that affects non-hedonic entertainment experiences.

Another important antecedent of eudaimonic entertainment experiences can be found in the realm of *Terror Management Theory* (TMT, Pyszczynski, Greenberg, & Solomon, 1997). The general hypothesis states that once people are reminded of their own death (i.e., mortality salience) they appreciate a meaningful movie to a higher extent than if they have not been reminded of their mortality (Hofer, 2013; Klimmt, 2011; Rieger et al., 2015; Rieger & Hofer, 2017). The rationale behind this argument is that mortality salience leads to a paralyzing terror that has to be coped with. Typically, research has shown three different so-called *anxiety buffers*: (1) adherence to cultural worldviews, (2) enhancement of one's self-esteem, and (3) maintenance of or engagement in close relationships (Burke, Martens, & Faucher, 2010). In the context of communication science, research shows that meaningful movies can help viewers cope with their mortality (Hofer, 2013; Rieger et al., 2015)—especially when films combine depictions of the meaning of life with a message about life's strength (i.e., when the protagonist survives a serious illness; Rieger & Hofer, 2017). Likewise, contemplating a tragedy after watching it could increase entertainment experiences, in particular for those who had recently experienced a personal hardship in their life (Khoo, 2016).

Chronological age (or more precisely: perceived lifetime left) has been found to be another antecedent of both non-hedonic entertainment motivations and experiences (Bartsch, 2012a; Hofer, Allemand, & Martin, 2014). Applying socio-emotional selectivity theory, it has been argued that people with a limited perceived lifetime (i.e., older people or people with a terminal illness) are in greater need of meaningful experiences and, as a result, experience higher levels of eudaimonic entertainment during watching a meaningful film.

Effects of Hedonic and Non-Hedonic Entertainment Experiences

Both hedonic and eudaimonic entertainment experiences are linked to different outcomes, such as information processing, well-being (both hedonic and eudaimonic), or morality (Bartsch, Kalch, & Oliver, 2014; Bartsch & Schneider, 2014; Oliver et al., 2012; Roth, Weinmann, Schneider, Hopp, & Vorderer, 2014).

Only recently, studies have examined the effect of hedonic and eudaimonic entertainment experiences on information processing. For instance, Bartsch and Schneider (2014) found that eudaimonic entertainment experiences (in their case: the feeling of being moved, negative and mixed affect, and arousal) stimulate systematic processing. Similarly, Bartsch and colleagues (2014) found that eudaimonic entertainment experiences (assessed in the same way as Bartsch & Schneider, 2014) can lead to self-reflective thoughts. In a similar vein, Lewis et al. (2014) found appreciation to go along deeper information processing. This finding was supported by Roth, Weinmann, Schneider, Hopp, Bindl, & Vorderer (2017). In an earlier study, Roth et al. (2014) found appreciation to be positively related to a feeling of being informed by a political talk show.

In terms of well-being, studies show that both the satisfaction of intrinsic needs and inner growth and the meaning of life are connected to psychological health and well-being (Reis, Sheldon, Gable, Roscoe, & Ryan, 2000; Ryan, Bernstein, & Brown, 2010; Ryan & Deci, 2001). As inner growth and meaning in life are regarded as facets of eudaimonic entertainment (Wirth et al., 2012), it is plausible that this form of entertainment experience can have a positive effect on viewers' eudaimonic well-being. Rieger, Reinecke, Frischlich, and Bente (2014) showed that both eudaimonic and hedonic entertainment experiences can contribute to well-being. More precisely, they found that eudaimonic entertainment facilitated mastery experiences, which in turn increased vitality. However, vitality was also influenced by feelings of detachment and relaxation, which were affected by hedonic entertainment experiences. Applying these results to the work context, Janicke, Rieger, Reinecke, and Connor (2017) could replicate the former model and demonstrate that during work, short meaningful YouTube videos increased vitality through enhanced mastery experiences. Additionally, well-being for workers was amplified through an effect of YouTube videos on relaxation, which in turn could increase work satisfaction.

However, there are still open questions when it comes to the effects of hedonic and non-hedonic entertainment experiences on well-being. For instance, it is unclear whether eudaimonic and hedonic entertainment experiences also lead to different effects of media reception beyond the mere reception experience. Although it has been postulated that both forms of entertainment can contribute to increased well-being in the short-term, this long-term influence has not yet been tested empirically.

Other effects of eudaimonic entertainment experience can be found in the realm of morality. Certain features of meaningful entertainment become important, namely the portrayal of moral virtue. Oliver and colleagues (2012) demonstrated that such portrayals can increase motivations to do something good for other people or being a better person. Portrayals of moral virtue can even have an effect on actual behavior: Slater and colleagues (2016) found that brief eudaimonic video clips fortified people's willingness to delay rewards due to experiencing poignancy (a mixed emotional response). Similarly, participants in a study by Schnall, Roper, and Fessler (2010) were more likely to help a fellow student after having watched a portrayal of moral virtue than after watching a control film.

Conclusion and Outlook

This brief description of research on entertainment experiences provides evidence for the existence of at least two different motivations (Lozano Delmar et al., 2016), modes or processes (Lewis et al., 2014; Vorderer, 2011), and experiences (Oliver & Bartsch, 2011; Wirth et al., 2012): Hedonic and non-hedonic experiences resulting from entertainment fare were found to be associated with positive effects on its viewers, such as enhanced well-being, coping strategies, moral motivations, and prosocial behavior.

While hedonic entertainment experiences are well-defined and understood as one dimension in the context of experiencing positive affect, fun, and enjoyment, eudaimonic or non-hedonic entertainment experiences still lack a thorough definition. To advance our understanding of meaningful entertainment and the resulting eudaimonic entertainment experiences, we have to work toward a more precise definition of meaningfulness. As outlined in the definition of meaning by Park and Folkman (1997), meaning has an idiosyncratic component and is nurtured by personal relevance and further unfolds over time (Leontiev, 2013).

The common denominator in the definition of meaningful entertainment seems to be the potential to elicit mixed affect, but falls short in explaining the other non-affective processes associated with eudaimonic experiences. For instance, not much is known about whether motivational outcomes differ between hedonic and eudaimonic entertainment experiences. Is there a hierarchy of need satisfaction in the sense that lower-order needs are better tackled by hedonic entertainment whereas higher-order needs are more successfully addressed by non-hedonic forms (see also Bartsch, 2012b)? Research on the first- and the third-person effect in response to both entertainment forms at least suggest an expectancy-based distinction (Hofer, 2015). In an attempt to explain different layers within the definition and the effects of meaningful media, Oliver and colleagues (in press) recently proposed meaningful entertainment to serve the higher cause of self-transcendence (as taken from moral psychology; see e.g., Haidt, 2003).

In the context of motivational mechanisms, research on meaningful entertainment has largely overlooked the social component (but see Lozano Delmar et al., 2016): Social needs and their thwarting, such as the feeling of being isolated and ostracized, were found to shape our contact with media (for an overview, see Vorderer & Schneider, 2017). The satisfaction of such social needs, in turn, was associated with an enhanced social well-being (Gallagher, Lopez, & Preacher, 2009). Computer games (in particular multi-player games) were found to satisfy the need for relatedness (Tamborini et al., 2011). Although new interactive media (such as social media) can serve needs of relatedness (Reinecke, Vorderer, & Knop, 2014) and enhance well-being (Rieger,

Hefner, & Vorderer, 2017), research so far has not addressed the specific component of meaning-fulness in social media.

The current chapter as well as the potential avenues for future research, however, point toward the possibility of entertainment fare to contribute to our happiness; be it through experiencing pleasure, or through the (cognitive and emotional) engagement with challenges, questions of the human condition, moral beauty, and potentially even self-transcendence.

References

Bartsch, A. (2012a). As time goes by: What changes and what remains the same in entertainment experience over the life span? *Journal of Communication, 62*, 588–608. https://doi.org/10.1111/j.1460-2466.2012.01657.x

Bartsch, A. (2012b). Emotional gratification in entertainment experience: Why viewers of movies and television series find it rewarding to experience emotions. *Media Psychology, 15*, 267–302. https://doi.org/10.1080/15213269.2012.693811

Bartsch, A., Kalch, A., & Oliver, M. B. (2014). Moved to think: The role of emotional media experiences in stimulating reflective thoughts. *Journal of Media Psychology: Theories, Methods, and Applications, 26*, 125–140. https://doi.org/10.1027/1864-1105/a000118

Bartsch, A., & Oliver, M. B. (2016). Appreciation of meaningfull entertainment experiences and eudaimonic well-being. In L. Reinecke & M. B. Oliver (Eds.), *The Routledge handbook of media use and well-being: International perspectives on theory and research on positive media effects* (pp. 80–92). Abingdon, UK: Routledge.

Bartsch, A., & Schneider, F. M. (2014). Entertainment and politics revisited: How non-escapist forms of entertainment can stimulate political interest and information seeking. *Journal of Communication, 64*, 369–396. https://doi.org/10.1111/jcom.12095

Bartsch, A., Vorderer, P., Mangold, R., & Viehoff, R. (2008). Appraisal of emotions in media use: Toward a process model of meta-emotions and emotion regulation. *Media Psychology, 11*, 7–27. https://doi.org/10.1080/15213260701813447

Bosshart, L., & Macconi, I. (1998). Defining "entertainment". *Communication Research Trends, 18*, 3–6.

Burke, B. L., Martens, A., & Faucher, E. H. (2010). Two decades of terror management theory: A meta-analysis of mortality salience research. *Personality and Social Psychology Review, 14*, 155–195. https://doi.org/10.1177/1088868309352321

Ersner-Hershfield, H., Mikels, J. A., Sullivan, S. J., & Carstensen, L. L. (2008). Poignancy: Mixed emotional experience in the face of meaningful endings. *Journal of Personality and Social Psychology, 54*, 158–167. https://doi.org/10.1037/0022-3514.94.1.158

Evans, J. S. B. T., & Stanovich, K. E. (2013). Dual-process theories of higher cognition: Advancing the debate. *Perspectives on Psychological Science, 8*, 223–241. https://doi.org/10.1177/1745691612460685

Gallagher, M. W., Lopez, S. J., & Preacher, K. J. (2009). The hierarchical structure of well-being. *Journal of Personality, 77*, 1025–1050. https://doi.org/ 10.1111/j.1467-6494.2009.00573.x

Haidt, J. (2003). The moral emotions. In R. J. Davidson, K. R. Scherer, & H. H. Goldsmith (Eds.), *Handbook of affective sciences* (pp. 852–870). Oxford: Oxford University Press.

Hofer, M. (2015). Effects of light-hearted and serious entertainment on enjoyment of the first and third person. *Journal of Media Psychology, 27*, 1–7. https://doi.org/10.1027/1864-1105/a000150

Hofer, M. (2017). Responses to sad media/tragedy. In P. Rössler, C. A. Hoffner, & L. van Zoonen (Eds.), *The international encyclopedia of media effects* (pp. 1731–1743). Hoboken, NJ: John Wiley and Sons, Inc.

Hofer, M., Allemand, M., & Martin, M. (2014). Age differences in nonhedonic entertainment experiences. *Journal of Communication, 64*, 61–81. https://doi.org/10.1111/jcom.12074

Hofer, M., & Wirth, W. (2012). It's right to be sad: The role of meta-appraisals in the sad-film paradox – A multiple mediator model. *Journal of Media Psychology, 24*(2), 43–54. doi:10.1027/1864-1105/a000061Hofer, M. (2013). Appreciation and enjoyment of meaningful entertainment. *Journal of Media Psychology: Theories, Methods, and Applications, 25*, 109–117. https://doi.org/10.1027/1864-1105/a000089

Janicke, S. H., Rieger, D., Reinecke, L., & Connor, W. (2017). Watching online videos at work: The role of positive and meaningful affect for recovery experiences and well-being at the workplace. *Mass Communication & Society, 21*(3), 345–367. https://doi.org/10.1080/15205436.2017.1381264

Kahneman, D., Diener, E., & Schwarz, N. (2003). *Well-being: The foundations of hedonic psychology: Health San Francisco.* New York, NY: Russell Sage Foundation.

Khoo, G. S. (2016). Contemplating tragedy raises gratifications and fosters self-acceptance. *Human Communication Research, 42*, 269–291. https://doi.org/10.1111/hcre.12074

Klimmt, C. (2011). Media psychology and complex modes of entertainment experiences. *Journal of Media Psychology: Theories, Methods, and Applications, 23*, 34–38. https://doi.org/10.1027/1864-1105/a000030

Knobloch-Westerwick, S. (2006). Mood management: Theory, evidence, and advancements. In J. Bryant & P. Vorderer (Eds.), *Psychology of entertainment* (pp. 239–254). Mahwah, NJ: Erlbaum Associates.

Leontiev, D. A. (2013). Personal meaning: A challenge for psychology. *The Journal of Positive Psychology, 8*, 459–470. doi:10.1080/17439760.2013.830767

Lewis, R. J., Tamborini, R., & Weber, R. (2014). Testing a Dual-Process Model of Media Enjoyment and Appreciation. *Journal of Communication, 64*(3), 397–416, https://doi.org/10.1111/jcom.12101

Lozano Delmar, J., & Sánchez-Martín, M. (2018). Eudaimonic flourishing in media consumption: Love, know and experience as a fan. In J. A. Muñiz-Velázquez & C. Pulido (Eds.), *The Routledge handbook of positive communication* (pp. 129–136). New York, NY: Routledge.

Lozano Delmar, J., Sánchez-Martín, M., & Muñiz-Velázquez, J. A. (2016). To be a fan is to be happier: Using the eudaimonic spectator questionnaire to measure eudaimonic motivations in Spanish fans. *Journal of Happiness Studies, 25*, 123. https://doi.org/10.1007/s10902-016-9819-9

Mares, M.-L., & Cantor, J. (1992). Elderly viewers' responses to televised portrayals of old age: Empathy and mood management vs. social comparison. *Communication Research, 19*, 459–478. https://doi.org/10.1177/009365092019004004

Mills, J. (1993). The appeal of tragedy: An attitude interpretation. *Basic and Applied Social Psychology, 14*, 255–271. https://doi.org/10.1207/s15324834basp1403_1

Oliver, M. B. (1993). Exploring the paradox of the enjoyment of sad films. *Human Communication Research, 19*, 315–342.

Oliver, M. B. (2008). Tender affective states as predictors of entertainment preference. *Journal of Communication, 58*, 40–61. https://doi.org/10.1111/j.1460-2466.2007.00373.x

Oliver, M. B., & Bartsch, A. (2010). Appreciation as audience response: Exploring entertainment gratifications beyond hedonism. *Human Communication Research, 36*, 53–81. https://doi.org/10.1111/j.1468-2958.2009.01368.x

Oliver, M. B., & Bartsch, A. (2011). Appreciation of entertainment. *Journal of Media Psychology: Theories, Methods, and Applications, 23*, 29–33. https://doi.org/10.1027/1864-1105/a000029

Oliver, M. B., & Hartmann, T. (2010). Exploring the role of meaningful experiences in users' appreciation of "good movies". *Projections: The Journal of Movies and Mind, 4*, 128–150. https://doi.org/10.3167/proj.2010.040208

Oliver, M. B., Hartmann, T., & Woolley, J. K. (2012). Elevation in response to entertainment portrayals of moral virtue. *Human Communication Research, 38*, 360–378. https://doi.org/10.1111/j.1468-2958.2012.01427.x

Oliver, M. B., & Raney, A. A. (2011). Entertainment as pleasurable and meaningful: Identifying hedonic and eudaimonic motivations for entertainment consumption. *Journal of Communication, 61*, 984–1004. https://doi.org/10.1111/j.1460-2466.2011.01585.x

Oliver, M. B., Raney, A. A., Slater, M. D., Appel, M., Hartmann, T., Bartsch, A. . . . Das, E. (in press). Self-transcendent media experiences: Taking meaningful media to a higher level. *Journal of Communication.*

Park, C. L., & Folkman, S. (1997). Meaning in the context of stress and coping. *Review of General Psychology, 1*, 115–144. doi:10.1037/1089-2680.1.2.115

Pyszczynski, T., Greenberg, J., & Solomon, S. (1997). Why do we need what we need? A terror management perspective on the roots of human social motivation. *Psychological Inquiry, 8*, 1–20.

Raney, A. A. (2006). The psychology of disposition-based theories of media enjoyment. In J. Bryant (Ed.), *Psychology of entertainment* (pp. 137–150). Mahwah, NJ: Erlbaum Associates.

Reinecke, L., Vorderer, P., & Knop, K. (2014). Entertainment 2.0? The role of intrinsic and extrinsic need satisfaction for the enjoyment of facebook use. *Journal of Communication, 64*, 417–438. https://doi.org/10.1111/jcom.12099

Reis, H. T., Sheldon, K. M., Gable, S. L., Roscoe, J., & Ryan, R. M. (2000). Daily well-being: The role of autonomy, competence, and relatedness. *Personality and Social Psychology Bulletin, 26*, 419–443.

Rieger, D., Frischlich, L., Högden, F., Kauf, R., Schramm, K., & Tappe, E. (2015). Appreciation in the face of death: Meaningful films buffer against death-related anxiety. *Journal of Communication, 65*, 351–372. https://doi.org/10.1111/jcom.12152

Rieger, D., Hefner, D., & Vorderer, P. (2017). Mobile recovery? The impact of smartphone use on recovery experiences in waiting situations. *Mobile Media & Communication, 5*, 161–177. https://doi.org/10.1177/2050157917691556

Rieger, D., & Hofer, M. (2017). How movies can ease the fear of death: The survival or death of the protagonists in meaningful movies. *Mass Communication and Society, 18,* 1–24. https://doi.org/10.1080/15 205436.2017.1300666

Rieger, D., Reinecke, L., Frischlich, L., & Bente, G. (2014). Media entertainment and well-being-linking hedonic and eudaimonic entertainment experience to media-induced recovery and vitality. *Journal of Communication, 64,* 456–478. https://doi.org/10.1111/jcom.12097

Roth, F. S., Weinmann, C., Schneider, F. M., Hopp, F. R., & Vorderer, P. (2014). Seriously entertained: Antecedents and consequences of hedonic and eudaimonic entertainment experiences with political talk shows on TV. *Mass Communication & Society,*(3), 379–399. http://dx.doi.org/10.1080/15205436.201 4.891135

Roth, F. S., Weinmann, C., Schneider, F. M., Hopp, F. R., Bindl, M. J., & Vorderer, P. (2017). Curving entertainment: The curvilinear relationship between hedonic and eudaimonic entertainment experiences while watching a political talk show and its implications for information processing. *Psychology of Popular Media Culture.* Advance online publication. https://doi.org/10.1037/ppm0000147

Ryan, R. M., Bernstein, J. H., & Brown, K. W. (2010). Weekends, work, and well-being: Psychological need satisfactions and day of the week effects on mood, vitality, and physical symptoms. *Journal of Social Clinical Psychology, 29,* 95–122.

Ryan, R. M., & Deci, E. L. (2000). Self-determination theory and the facilitation of intrinsic motivation, social development, and well-being. *American Psychologist, 55,* 68–78. https://doi.org/10.1037// 0003-066X.55.1.68

Ryan, R. M., & Deci, E. (2001). On happiness and human potentials: A review of research on hedonic and eudaimonic well-being. *Annual Review of Psychology, 52,* 141–166.

Ryff, C. D. (1989). Happiness is everything, or is it? Explorations on the meaning of psychological well-being. *Journal of Personality and Social Psychology, 57*(6), 1069–1081. http://dx.doi.org/10.1037/002 2-3514.57.6.1069

Ryff, C. D., & Singer, B. H. (2006). Best news yet on the six-factor model of well-being. *Social Science Research, 35,* 1103–1119. https://doi.org/10.1016/j.ssresearch.2006.01.002

Schnall, S., Roper, J., & Fessler, D. M. (2010). Elevation leads to altruistic behavior. *Psychological Science, 21,* 315–320. https://doi.org/10.1177/0956797609359882

Schramm, H., & Wirth, W. (2010). Exploring the paradox of sad-film enjoyment: The role of multiple appraisals and meta-appraisals. *Poetics, 38,* 319–335. https://doi.org/10.1016/j.poetic.2010.03.002

Slater, M. D., Oliver, M. B., & Appel, M. (2016). Poignancy and mediated wisdom of experience: Narrative impacts on willingness to accept delayed rewards. *Communication Research,* 1–22. https://doi. org/10.1177/0093650215623838

Tamborini, R., Bowman, N. D., Eden, A., Grizzard, M., & Organ, A. (2010). Defining media enjoyment as the satisfaction of intrinsic needs. *Journal of Communication, 60,* 758–777. https://doi. org/10.1111/j.1460-2466.2010.01513.x

Tamborini, R., Grizzard, M., David Bowman, N., Reinecke, L., Lewis, R. J., & Eden, A. (2011). Media enjoyment as need satisfaction: The contribution of hedonic and nonhedonic needs. *Journal of Communication, 61,* 1025–1042. https://doi.org/10.1111/j.1460-2466.2011.01593.x

Vorderer, P. (2011). What's next? Remarks on the current vitalization of entertainment theory. *Journal of Media Psychology, 23,* 60–63. https://doi.org/10.1027/1864-1105/a000034

Vorderer, P., Klimmt, C., & Ritterfeld, U. (2004). Enjoyment: At the heart of media entertainment. *Communication Theory, 14,* 388–408. https://doi.org/10.1111/j.1468-2885.2004.tb00321.x

Vorderer, P., & Schneider, F. M. (2017). Social media and ostracism. In K. D. Williams & S. A. Nida (Eds.), *Ostracism, exclusion, and rejection* (pp. 240–257). New York, NY: Psychology Press.

Waterman, A. S. (1993). Two conceptions of happiness: Contrasts of personal expressiveness (eudaimonia) and hedonic enjoyment. *Journal of Personality and Social Psychology, 64,* 678–691. https://doi.org/10.10 37//0022-3514.64.4.678

Wirth, W., Hofer, M., & Schramm, H. (2012). Beyond pleasure: Exploring the eudaimonic entertainment experience. *Human Communication Research, 38,* 406–428. https://doi.org/10.1111/j.1468-2958.2012.01434.x

Zillmann, D. (1988a). Mood management: Using entertainment to full advantage. In L. Donohew, H. E. Sypher, & E. T. Higgins (Eds.), *Communication, social cognition, and affect* (Vol. 31, pp. 147–171). Hillsdale, NJ: Erlbaum.

Zillmann, D. (1988b). Mood management through communication choices. *American Behavioral Scientist, 31,* 327–340. https://doi.org/10.1177/000276488031003005

Zillmann, D. (1994). Mechanism of emotional involvement with drama. *Poetics, 23,* 33–51.

Zuckerman, M. (2006). Sensation seeking in entertainment. In J. Bryant (Ed.), *Psychology of entertainment* (pp. 367–387). Mahwah, NJ: Erlbaum Associates.

14

EUDAIMONIC FLOURISHING IN MEDIA CONSUMPTION

Love, Know, and Experience as a Fan

Javier Lozano Delmar and Milagrosa Sánchez-Martín

Fans, Identity, and Happiness

The aim of this chapter is to approach the consumption of fictional products in cinema and television from positive psychology and eudaimonic happiness perspectives. As established by fandom scholars in several seminal works (Abercrombie & Longhurst, 1998; Fiske, 1992; Gray, Harrington, & Sandvoss, 2007; Hellekson & Busse, 2014; Hills, 2002; Jenkins, 1992; Lewis, 1992; Sandvoss, 2005), media fans live a full consumption of their favorite audiovisual content. According to Duffett (2013), "Media fandom is the recognition of a positive, personal, relatively deep, emotional connection with a mediated element of popular culture" (p. 2). Fans are spectators who create a deep emotional and cognitive bond with the product. Rejecting negative stereotypes, Jenkins (1992) thinks of fans as active producers, manipulators of meanings, and active audiences:

> [The] ability to transform personal reaction into social interaction, spectatorial culture into participatory culture, is one of the central characteristics of fandom. One becomes a "fan" not by being a regular spectator of a particular program but by translating that viewing into some kind of cultural activity, by sharing feelings and thoughts about program content with friends, by joining a "community" of other fans who share common interests.
>
> *(Jenkins, 2006, p. 41)*

Grandío-Pérez (2016) considers the emotions of fans to be one of the circumstances that best explain the phenomenon of television series fandom. For the author, a television series' reception by fans has implicit rational and cognitive as well as emotional aspects:

> The series are able to offer stories full of values and sensations that forge the individual and also collective identity as group consciousness, an identifying characteristic of fan phenomena. We cannot ignore the social aspect of constructing meaning through the community in which a shared symbolic space is built.
>
> *(p. 22)*

Scolari (2016), speaking of degrees of fan participation in transmedia storytelling, clarifies that not all receivers are fans or prosumers:

> We can imagine a pyramid where, at the base, there are the receivers that limit their enjoyment of a media product. At the level immediately above would be the first fans, or recipients who consume various media of that narrative world and, as appropriate, participate in social networks to discuss what happens in story. At the top of the pyramid would be the "hardcore" group of fans, collectors who try to make their whole world a narrative world. Finally, at the tip of the pyramid would be the prosumers, the fans that generate new content. They are few but fundamental for the renewal and expansion of the narrative world.
>
> *(Grandío-Pérez, 2016, p. 134)*

This coincides with what other authors have already noted (Bourdaa & Lozano Delmar, 2016; Grandío-Pérez, 2016; Jenkins, 2014; Zubernis & Larsen, 2012). In this way, fan identity should not be linked only to receivers that are involved in the creation of content but rather, the spectrum should be extended to other activities that also involve participation, searching for information or interaction.

In a qualitative study about fans of the *Game of Thrones* series (HBO, 2011) in France and in Spain (Lozano Delmar & Bourdaa, 2015), five of the most common reasons for why respondents considered themselves *Game of Thrones* fans were established: (1) Their devotion to the show and (2) their experience of it as something that goes beyond the simple act of reception, (3) the urgency of watching every episode, (4) the fact that they collect memorabilia from the show, and (5) the fact they are already a fan of the universe via the books.

The conclusions obtained, subsequently validated in another qualitative study about fan identity as authors and marketers (Bourdaa & Lozano Delmar, 2016), are interesting because they link the identity of the fan to the act of viewing and acting within a community (modes of consumption, immersive reception, experiencing, and collecting) rather than creation or content production, coinciding in part with what has been proposed by Scolari (in Grandío-Pérez, 2016) and Zubernis and Larsen (2012), among others. In this way, the focus would be on those spectators who love the film/TV show; experience it in a deeper and more emotional way; have a knowledge of the universe, stories, and characters; collect a great deal of material related to it; and, finally, view it in a compulsive and addictive way. These items defining what a fan is also coincide, in part, with those suggested in the recent study by Grandío-Pérez (2016):

> The fan of a series fulfills four premises with both individual and social implications: 1) high consumption of the series, 2) high degree of gratification, 3) great emotional and cognitive connection and involvement with the world or universe of that series, and 4) a social desire to live and share that cultural experience collectively.
>
> *(p. 26)*

However, the academic debate does not seem to agree on the definition of what a fan is and is not. Hills (2002) poses a methodological problem and notes that "the ethnographic process of 'asking the audience,' although useful in many cases, constitutes a potentially reductive approach" (p. 38). Paul Booth, in an interview with Grandío, states that fandom is simultaneously more than just a single identity and more than just a single behavior (2016). Duffett (2013, p. 154) indicates that "any attempt to understand the reasons for each individual's emergence as a fan, and the exact way in which it happened, presents a minefield of research problems for interested scholars."

With this work, we try to move away from the debate over fan identity. The main objective is not to define the fan but rather, to identify a series of common elements that serve as a starting point to analyze the cultivation of cognitive-intellectual growth and social-emotional growth in media spectators. Although many of the studies reviewed above involve deep engagement by the spectator and a cognitive and emotional involvement of the fan with the media object of consumption, few studies regarding fandom have been developed from the field of positive psychology.

One of the few exceptions is a recent study published in *Psychology of Popular Media Culture* (Tsay-Vogel & Sanders, 2017), where it is stated that media consumption by fans involves not only hedonic but also eudaimonic motivations. As we can see in other chapters of this book (Rieger & Hofer, 2018) research has shown that eudaimonic and hedonic entertainment experiences are the result of two different processes: one slow and deliberate (eudaimonic), and the other automatic, fast, and intuitive (hedonic), associated to the concept of *enjoyment*. Eudaimonia motivations connect to "meaningful" experiences, or reflection and understanding of oneself and the world (Oliver & Bartsch, 2010; Oliver, Hartmann, & Woolley, 2012). In their work, Tsay-Vogel and Sanders (2017) state that "eudaimonically driven individuals are perhaps interested in more cognitively involved media experiences that enhance psychological well-being (i.e., the search for meaning in life), rather than media offerings which solely provide excitement, delight, and escapism" (p. 34). Therefore, one of the hypotheses of that study was "that individuals with stronger eudaimonic motivations are more likely to exhibit stronger levels of fandom" (p. 34).

The connection of this eudaimonic catalyst to the study of the consumption of audiovisual fiction by fans was also the subject of another study focused on the Spanish context, which serves as a starting point to this work (Lozano Delmar, Sánchez-Martín, & Muñiz-Velázquez, 2018). Here, the eudaimonic motivations of the Spanish fan audience were compared with those of non-fans. For this purpose, the *Eudaimonic Spectator Questionnaire* was designed and validated. This questionnaire allowed the observation of two factors of eudaimonic motivations (the cultivation of cognitive-intellectual growth and social-emotional growth) among the Spanish spectators who considered themselves fans. Similar to the results obtained in the previous work (Tsay-Vogel & Sanders, 2017), it is shown that those spectators who connect and relate in a more active, participatory, and passionate way with movies and television series are simultaneously developing a series of strengths and virtues of human flourishing (Peterson & Seligman, 2004).

Analyzing the Elements of Being a Fan

This study is based on the data from a questionnaire administered to 1003 Spanish subjects who fulfilled the criterion of habitually consuming movies and television series. The items used for this work are part of a more extensive study in which several constructs related to the reception of audiovisual fictions by Spanish spectators are assessed, which collected data from a consumer panel that was administered online in 2015. Characteristics of the entire sample are available in Lozano Delmar, Sánchez-Martín, and Plaza (2015).

As has already been noted, the aim of this work is to link a series of common patterns or elements of the fan spectator with human flourishing in media consumption. To this end, the mentioned *Eudaimonic Spectator Questionnaire* was used to explore the eudaimonic motivations associated with the consumption of audiovisual fiction. The questionnaire consists of 4 items that make up the Cognitive-Intellectual Growth (CIG) dimension and another 5 items that correspond to Socio-Emotional Growth (SEG), as shown in Table 14.1.

In addition to the questionnaire, five keywords and five items obtained in the study on the common characteristics of *Game of Thrones* fans (Lozano Delmar & Bourdaa, 2015) were used, as summarized in Table 14.2. The participants responded by stating their degree of agreement or disagreement with each of the items.

Table 14.1 Items of the *Eudaimonic Spectator Questionnaire*

CIG (Cognitive-Intellectual Growth)	SEG (Social-Emotional Growth)
I1. I like films and TV series that teach me new things	I5. I like encouraging a group of friends or acquaintances to construct activities or create material around the film or TV series
I2. I like films and TV series that make me think and reflect	I6. I enjoy myself more when we view in a group and we form a community that analyzes and discusses the film or TV series
I3. I like films and TV series that are original, inventive, and pose new ways of telling a story	I7. I like thinking about a film or TV series as if it were an adventure
I4. I like films and TV series that arouse my curiosity and challenge me to go on exploring and getting to know the story	I8. I like feeling close and belonging to a group of people who like the same film or TV series
	I9. My favorite films and TV series are those with complex plots that require more active participation

Table 14.2 Fan Identity Items

Game of Thrones Fans (Lozano Delmar & Bourdaa, 2015)	Keywords	Fan Identity Items
Devotion to the show: plot, character, and production values.	PLEASURE	I consider myself a fan of well-made and well-developed movies or TV series with interesting characters and plots that are worth my time.
Experience of the TV show as something that goes beyond the simple act of reception.	EXPERIENCE	I consider myself a fan when I get involved in the experience of the movie or TV series, looking for additional information on the Internet, participating and generating content on social networks.
The urgency of watching every episode.	VIEWING	I consider myself a fan when my consumption of a movie or television series is repetitive and constant, almost addictive.
Collection of memorabilia.	COLLECTING	I consider myself a fan when I collect material related to the movie or television series.
Fan of the universe via the books.	KNOWING	I consider myself a fan when I enjoy exploring and knowing about all the products related to the story (sequels, books, comics . . .).

After analyzing the means, it is observed, on a general level, that the elements that contribute the most to fan identity are, first, those who consider themselves a fan when films or television series are well-made and developed with characters and interesting plots that are worth their time ($M = 5.78$, $SD = 1.50$). Next are those who consider themselves fans when their consumption of a movie or TV series is repetitive and constant, almost addictive ($M = 4.57$, $SD = 1.97$), those who explore and know all the products related to the story, such as sequels, books, or comics, for example ($M = 4.31$, $SD = 1.93$), those who get involved in the experience of the film or television series, look for additional information on the Internet, participate and generate content on social networks ($M = 4.11$; $SD = 1.92$), and, finally, those who collect material related to the film or television series ($M = 3.71$, $SD = 2.06$).

Table 14.3 Correlation between fan characteristics and eudaimonic motivation dimensions

		1. Films and series well-made	*2. Collect related material*	*3. Involved in experience*	*4. Explore related products*	*5. Repetitive consumption*
CIG	r (p)	.555 (.000)	.157 (.000)	.247 (.000)	.289 (.000)	.233 (.000)
SEG	r (p)	.175 (.000)	.415 (.000)	.501 (.000)	.452 (.000)	.293 (.000)

Table 14.4 Association of eudaimonic growth factors with fan identity

CIG (Cognitive-intellectual growth)	PLEASURE	I consider myself a fan of well-made and well-developed movies or TV series with interesting characters and plots that are worth my time.
SEG (Social-emotional growth)	EXPERIENCE	I consider myself a fan when I get involved in the experience of the movie or TV series, looking for additional information on the Internet, participating and generating content on social networks.
	KNOWING	I consider myself a fan when I enjoy exploring and knowing about all the products related to the story (sequels, books, comics . . .).
	COLLECTING	I consider myself a fan when I collect material related to the movie or television series.

Pearson's correlations have been used to explore the level of association shown by the characteristics of the fans with the eudaimonic motivations of the spectators of audiovisual fiction. As seen in Table 14.3, the five analyzed characteristics of the fans correlate significantly and positively with the two dimensions of eudaimonic motivation, cognitive-intellectual growth (CIG) and socio-emotional growth (SEG); that is, the more the spectator agrees with the fan identity item to which they are responding, the higher the level of CIG and SEG. In Table 14.3, we can see which elements of the fan identity correlate more with each of the dimensions of eudaimonic motivation.

The association between CIG and the taste for well-crafted fiction clearly stands out (r = .555), as do the associations between SEG and the involvement in experience (r = .501), exploring of related products (r = .452) and collecting related material (r = .415). Therefore, the more in agreement the spectators are in linking fan identity with well-made and well-developed films or TV series (Pleasure), the higher the cognitive-intellectual growth score. Likewise, the more they agree on linking the fan identity with Collecting, Experience, or Knowing, the more the values increase with regard to social-emotional growth (see Table 14.4).

Increasing the level of specificity, we wanted to check which items (see Table 14.1) of cognitive-intellectual growth and socio-emotional growth are more closely related to fan identity. As seen in the correlation values in Table 14.5, the element of fan identity that is most associated with all the items of the CIG dimension is Pleasure. The other elements of fan identity are also associated with the CIG items, but to a much lesser extent than Pleasure. Furthermore, the CIG item with which Pleasure is most strongly associated is "I like films and TV series that are original, inventive and pose new ways of telling a story" (r = .501).

On the other hand, in Table 14.6, we observe through the values of the correlation that the elements of fan identity that best relate to the SEG items are those related to Experience, Knowing, and Collecting. In this sense, the item with the highest correlation is "I like thinking about a film or TV series as if it were an adventure," which is positively related to the fan characteristic of

Table 14.5 Correlation between fan characteristics and elements of cognitive-intellectual growth

	Items	1. PLEA-SURE	2. COL-LECTING	3. EXPE-RIENCE	4. KNOW-ING	5. VIEW-ING
CIG r (p)	1. I like films and TV series that teach me new things	.484 (.000)	.129 (.000)	.197 (.000)	.252 (.000)	.216 (.000)
	2. I like films and TV series that make me think and reflect	.472 (.000)	.104 (.001)	.169 (.000)	.181 (.000)	.171 (.000)
	3. I like films and TV series that are original, inventive, and pose new ways of telling a story	.501 (.000)	.093 (.003)	.187 (.000)	.191 (.000)	.175 (.000)
	4. I like films and TV series that arouse my curiosity and challenge me to go on exploring and getting to know the story	.437 (.000)	.198 (.000)	.276 (.000)	.340 (.000)	.227 (.000)

Table 14.6 Correlation between fan characteristics and elements of socio-emotional growth

	Items	1. PLEA-SURE	2. COL-LECTING	3. EXPERI-ENCE	4. KNOW-ING	5. IEWING
SEG r (p)	5. I like encouraging a group of friends or acquaintances to con-struct activities or create mate-rial around the film or TV series	.008 (.805)	.334 (.000)	.387 (.000)	.350 (.000)	.195 (.000)
	6. I enjoy myself more when we view in a group and we form a community that analyzes and discusses the film or TV series	.176 (.000)	.307 (.000)	.379 (.000)	.313 (.000)	.196 (.000)
	7. I like thinking about a film or TV series as if it were an adventure	.203 (.000)	.317 (.000)	.383 (.000)	.396 (.000)	.292 (.000)
	8. I like feeling close and belong-ing to a group of people who like the same film or TV series	.212 (.000)	.309 (.000)	.380 (.000)	.325 (.000)	.285 (.000)
	9. My favorite films and TV series are those with complex plots that require more active participation	.080 (.011)	.316 (.000)	.387 (.000)	.344 (.000)	.155 (.000)

Experience. The fan identity item Pleasure (films and series well-done) has a weaker correlation with respect to the rest of the items, which may be because it correlates strongly with the CIG. Finally, it is interesting to note how the item Viewing (being considered a fan when consumption of movies or television series is repetitive and constant, almost addictive) is associated in a very similar way with both dimensions of eudaimonic motivation, as seen in Tables 14.5 and 14.6.

Becoming a Happy Fan

According to the data obtained, the five items proposed to define fan identity correlate posi-tively with the items that measure eudaimonic motivations. In other words, it makes sense to speak of eudaimonic growth and to link it to fan identity actions: Pleasure, Viewing, Knowing,

Experience, and Collecting. This finding expands and reinforces the results obtained in previous research, demonstrating that active audiences or fans develop a series of skills or abilities that connect the consumption of audiovisual fiction products with eudaimonic growth.

For Spanish spectators, the most important factor for identifying as a fan is related to the item Pleasure, which identifies those spectators who especially value well-made and developed films and TV series with characters and interesting stories that are worth their time. With regard to eudaimonic growth, this item correlates positively and strongly with cognitive-intellectual growth (CIG), so it is reasonable the items that define CIG are explored more in depth (see Table 14.1). The elements of CIG are related to the strengths of Creativity, Curiosity, Judgment, Love of Learning, and Perspective, all linked to the virtue of Wisdom proposed by Peterson and Seligman (2004).

Simply valuing and appreciating the audiovisual product (Pleasure) does not appear to be one of the determining factors in socio-emotional growth (SEG), which is mainly linked to Experience (which also correlates strongly with CIG) and Knowing. In summary, those spectators who associate their fan identity with experience and knowledge develop eudaimonic growth linked to socio-emotional aspects that refer directly to strengths such as Bravery and Persistence, are associated with the virtue of Courage, Love, and Social Intelligence, linked to the virtue of Humanity, or Teamwork, and are associated with the virtue of Justice (Peterson & Seligman, 2004). The SEG item most associated with items of fan identity is "viewing it as if it were an adventure," allowing the spectator to explore, experience, and know the world of the story and its characters.

Although Collecting correlates positively with both components (CIG and SEG), it is more closely linked to SEG, although to a lesser extent than Experience and Knowing. This does not mean that Collecting is not a determining factor in defining fans, but it has lower values than the other items in terms of eudaimonic growth. Similarly, viewing has lower correlations than the other items in both components of eudaimonic growth.

In short, taking all these findings into account, it can be said that eudaimonic growth takes place, especially when the fan identifies with and is associated with the characteristics of Pleasure, Experience, and Knowing. This is very interesting because it highlights the role of fans who not only consume the fictional content but, above all, become active participants in the fictional universe. This role is vital, for example, in transmedia storytelling or in the development of complex stories told through several films or television products that require the effort and participation of their audience to understand the entire universe.

Ultimately, it can be concluded that when the spectator identifies himself or herself as a fan, he or she does so with a highly active sense of discovery, turning the viewing into a cognitive-intellectual and socio-emotional "meaningful" adventure that makes him or her grow eudaimonically. In other words, being a fan and developing fan spectator activities allows strengths to be trained that lead to human flourishing.

References

Abercrombie, N., & Longhurst, B. (1998). *Audiences: A sociological theory of performance and imagination.* London: Sage Publications.

Bourdaa, M., & Lozano Delmar, J. (2016). Contemporary participative TV audiences: Identity, authorship and advertising practices between fandom. *Participations: Journal of Audience and Reception Studies, 13*(2), 2–13.

Duffett, M. (2013). *Understanding fandom: An introduction to the study of media fan culture.* New York, [etc.]: Bloomsbury Academic.

Fiske, J. (1992). The cultural economy of fandom. In L. A. Lewis (Ed.), *The adoring audience: Fan culture and popular media* (pp. 30–49). London and New York: Routledge.

Grandío-Pérez, M. D. M. (2016). *Adictos a las series: 50 años de lecciones de los fans.* Barcelona: UOC.

Gray, J., Harrington, C. L., & Sandvoss, C. (2007). *Fandom: Identities and communities in a mediated world.* New York and London: New York University Press.

Hellekson, K., & Busse, K. (2014). *The fan fiction studies reader.* Iowa City, IA: University of Iowa.

Hills, M. (2002). *Fan cultures.* London: Routledge.

Jenkins, H. (1992). *Textual poachers: Television fans & participatory culture.* New York, NY: Routledge.

Jenkins, H. (2006). *Fans, bloggers, and gamers: Exploring participatory culture.* New York: New York University Press.

Jenkins, H. (2014, November 19). *Where fandom studies came from: An interview with Kristina Busse and Karen Hellekson (part two)* [Web log post]. Retrieved from http://henryjenkins.org/2014/11/where-fandom-studies-came-from-an-interview-with-kristina-busse-and-karen-helleckson-part-two.html

Lewis, L. A. (1992). *The adoring audience: Fan culture and popular media.* London and New York: Routledge.

Lozano Delmar, J., & Bourdaa, M. (2015). Case study of French and Spanish fan reception of Game of Thrones. *Transformative Works and Cultures, 19.* http://dx.doi.org/10.3983/twc.2015.0608

Lozano Delmar, J., Sánchez-Martín, M., & Muñiz-Velázquez, J. A. (2018). To be a fan is to be happier: Using the eudaimonic spectator questionnaire to measure eudaimonic motivations in Spanish fans. *Journal of Happiness Studies, 19*(1), 257–276. doi:10.1007/s10902-016-9819-9

Lozano Delmar, J., Sánchez-Martín, M., & Plaza, J. F. (2015). Portrait Robot d'un fan Espagnol. Analyse sociodémographique et habitudes de consommation chez le fan de films et de séries télé en Espagne. *Revue française des sciences de l'information et de la communication, 7.* Retrieved from http://rfsic.revues.org/1692

Oliver, M. B., & Bartsch, A. (2010). Appreciation as audience response: Exploring entertainment gratifications beyond hedonism. *Human Communication Research, 36*(1), 53–81. doi:10.1111/j.1468-2958.2009.01368.x

Oliver, M. B., Hartmann, T., & Woolley, J. K. (2012). Elevation in response to entertainment portrayals of moral virtue. *Human Communication Research, 38*(3), 360–378.

Peterson, C., & Seligman, M. E. P. (2004). *Character strengths and virtues.* New York: Oxford University Press.

Rieger, D., & Hofer, M. (2018). On being happy while consuming entertainment: Hedonic and non-hedonic modes of entertainment experiences. In J. A. Muñiz-Velázquez & C. Pulido (Eds.), *The Routledge handbook of positive communication* (pp. 120–128). New York: Routledge.

Sandvoss, C. (2005). *Fans: The mirror of consumption.* Cambridge: Polity Press.

Scolari, C. (2016). Alfabetismo transmedia. Estrategias de aprendizaje informal y competencias mediáticas en la nueva ecología de la comunicación. *Telos, 103,* 13–23.

Tsay-Vogel, M., & Sanders, M. S. (2017). Fandom and the search for meaning: Examining communal involvement with popular media beyond pleasure. *Psychology of Popular Media Culture.* Advance online publication. http://dx.doi.org/10.1037/ppm0000085

Zubernis, L., & Larsen, K. (2012). *Fandom at the crossroads: Celebration, shame and fan/producer relationships.* Newcastle upon Tyne: Cambridge Scholars.

15

MEDIA, WELL-BEING, AND HEALTH DURING CHILDHOOD AND ADOLESCENCE

Margarida Gaspar de Matos, Cátia Branquinho, and Tania Gaspar

Introduction

The aim of this chapter is to understand the use of screen time in children and adolescents and its impact on the various dimensions of the perception of well-being and quality of life, considering gender and age. The importance of screen time on the healthy development of children and adolescents will be highlighted, and will be pointed out appropriate educational and health-promoting strategies for developing personal and social competences to deal with information and communication technologies as a tool to promote well-being and perceived quality of life.

Subjective perception of well-being is considered an important aspect of health promotion (Detmar et al., 2006; Ravens-Sieberer et al., 2001). Besides individual factors, the social system, institutions, culture, national policies, and the characteristics of the ecological and geographical ethos where individuals live have to be considered (Mendoza & Sagrera, 1990).

Leisure time has been pointed out as an important variable in health promotion and a key factor in the quality of life and health of children and adolescents because of their voluntary and joyful nature (Gaspar et al., 2012; Matos, 2015; Matos & Sampaio, 2009). One of the most frequent behaviors in the occupation of leisure time is the time spent with the media, watching television or using other equipment such as video, video games, and the Internet, especially since there are now broadly available integrated mobile devices (Boniel-Nissim et al., 2015; Matos & Ferreira, 2013). Some studies suggest that, on average, children spend between three and five hours a day using these instruments (Kennedy, Strzempko, Danford, & Kools, 2002), which is more than leisure time in physical activities (Roberts, Foehr, & Rideout, 2006) and which is associated with a higher probability of adopting risk behaviors such as drug, alcohol, and tobacco use and violent behaviors (Scheidt, Overpeck, Wyatt, & Aszmann, 2000). Accordingly to Mérelle and colleagues (2017), a problematic video-gaming use is intensely associated with conduct problems, hyperactivity, and sedentary behavior. Sedentary behavior is also correlated with social media use in boys and girls, low fitness in girls (Sandercock, Alibrahim, & Bellamy, 2016), poor sleep quality, low self-esteem, and higher levels of anxiety and depression (Woods & Scott, 2016). However, some research show benefits both in terms of cognitions (Linebarger & Walker, 2005) and behaviors, such as increased empathy and acceptance of diversity through modeling of social behavior (Hogan & Strasburger, 2008). Other research surfaced less positive effects on health/well-being, such as aggressive and violent behavior, sexual risk behavior, substance use and abuse, eating disorders, low physical activity, and low self-esteem (Strasburger et al., 2010). According to Anderson (2002), the healthy effects of television can be improved, and the harmful effects mitigated by the presence of an adult moderator. When integrated mobile devices became available, at least in some countries, there was a decrease in TV popularity an in computer use: adolescents tend to use smartphones where they seem to be permanently "on" (Boniel-Nissim et al., 2015; Matos & Ferreira, 2013; Matos & Sampaio, 2009; Matos, Simões, Camacho, Reis, & Aventura Social, 2015), and some recent studies actually try to understand where begin the Internet abuse or PIU (Problematic Internet Use) and what is indeed an addiction (Gamito et al., 2016; Matos, 2015).

Media can have an impact on children' and adolescents' quality of life perception, and should raise the concern of health professionals, education technicians, and parents (Strasburger, Wilson, & Jordan, 2009; Trallero, 2010). The media, in recent times, hinders family dialogue, and become the main source of information for adolescents in almost all subjects that concern them (Strasburger et al., 2010). Beyond youth cultures, this type of information can determine approaches and attitudes, such as the weight they attach to many health risk behaviors and how should relate to each other (Firminger, 2006). The inevitable access of young people to "new" technologies and the change in the amount of time where adolescents are involved in screen activity, can bring new challenges that must be addressed: (a) the increase of risk behaviors associated with "screen use," namely substance use and violence, social withdrawal; (b) sleep deprivation and energetic drinks intake (Matos, Paiva, Costa, Gaspar, & Galvão, 2016; Paiva, Gaspar, & Matos, 2016); (c) "screen" abuse and Problematic Internet Use (PIU) which are linked with physical and psychological consequences (Paiva et al., 2016); (d) the impact on the adolescent brain development of this screen time (and the "new" media), so often combined with multiple tasks (Small & Vorgan, 2008).

The impact of the screen increases significantly with the presence of television and the computer in the adolescent's bedroom, fostering their progressive autonomy from their parents, greater peer engagement, increased risk behaviors, and solitary life (Jordan et al., 2010). There is a lower participation rate in activities such as reading and active leisure (Strasburger et al., 2009), and fewer hours of sleep (Paiva et al., 2016; Jordan et al., 2010). Today's teenagers have unprecedented access to "new" media and use them in expected and unexpected way, they are creative in the use of "new" technologies, and this creativity can raise the anguish of parents, teachers, and health care providers (Christakis, 2009). In adolescents aged 11 to 19, the lowest school performance increases proportionately to the number of daily hours before the screen, especially if movies, games, and surfing on the Internet are not appropriate (Sharif & Sargent, 2006). Adolescents are increasingly involved in multiple simultaneous tasks with the media (Rideout, 2010), but it is unclear whether they mitigate the effects of media or whether they affect cognitive processing. Some neuro-scientists are beginning to worry about the impact of all these new technologies on adolescent brain development (Small & Vorgan, 2008). Adolescents use screen time a lot, both in terms of games and in terms of computer use, although they spend more time listening to music (Roberts, Henriksen, & Foehr, 2004). Adolescents who spend more time on screen are more likely to have an association with low self-esteem, worse perception of health status, higher prevalence of smoking, more somatic symptoms, use of alcohol and illicit substances, poorer quality of life and relationships less time investing in social interactions, solving personal problems or testing the limits of one's own cognitive and physical abilities (Iannotti, Kogan, Janssen, & Boyce, 2009). Screen time can influence energy balance by shifting physical activity, increasing caloric intake or reduced metabolic rate, and increasing the odds of obesity (Boone, Gordon-Larsen, Adair, & Popkin, 2007). It is a general objective of this study to characterize and understand the time that children and adolescents spend with screen activities, and the relation of this behavior to their perception of quality of life. In the present chapter, we will present the results of a study by Gaspar, Matos, Ribeiro, and Leal (2006), within a broader study of the KIDSCREEN Group Europe (2006). The screen activities used were the time spent with television and videos, *Play-Station*, computer, and Internet/chats. Age and gender were also considered. Understanding how the children and adolescents use their leisure, especially in front of the screen, can help parents, educators, and health professionals in the adoption of strategies and lines of action that enhance the adolescent's personal resources attenuate possible risk behaviors, improve the quality of offers and contexts, and promote a healthier development.

Method

Participants

The sample consists of 3.195 students, 50.8 percent are female. With a mean age of 11.81 and between the ages of 10 and 16, 41.10 percent are between 10, 11 years old, and 58.9 percent between 12 and 16 years old. The vast majority of the participants are Portuguese nationals (90.2 percent), and 3.1 percent are nationals of an African Country of Portuguese Official Language. Regarding socioeconomic status (SES), 38.8 percent had a mean SES/high and 62.2 percent had SES.

The sample consisted of children and adolescents of the fifth and seventh grades of the regular public education of the five education regions of mainland Portugal and their respective parents. Questionnaires were sent to 112 schools, including 199 classrooms: 98 grades from the fifth grade and 101 grades from the seventh grade. Questionnaires were sent to 3.958 students and received 3.195 (81 percent). The distribution was representative for each of the five continental Portuguese geographical regions.

Instruments

Quality of Life related to Health (KIDSCREEN-52©) is a cross-cultural European instrument that measures the quality of life in children and adolescents. KIDSCREEN-52© is a generic instrument that can be used for measurement, monitoring, and evaluation. It is a self-completion questionnaire, applicable in children and adolescents between eight and 18 years old and their parents, in the field of health and chronic disease. The application time is 10 to 15 minutes (Gaspar & Matos, 2011; Ravens-Sieberer et al., 2001; KIDSCREEN Group Europe, 2006). There are 10 dimensions of the KIDSCREEN instrument, which describe health-related quality of life (HRQoL): (1) Health and Physical Activity; (2) Feelings; (3); State of Global Humor; (4) Self-perception (about oneself); (5) Autonomy/Leisure; (6) Family; (7) Money matters; (8) Friends (interpersonal relationships of social support); (9) School Environment and Learning; and (10) Bullying (Gaspar et al., 2006; Gaspar, Matos, Ribeiro, Leal, & Ferreira, 2009).

The questions used to assess the screen time of children and adolescents were taken from the instrument of the study Health Behavior in School-Aged Children (Currie, Samdal, Boyce, & Smith, 2001; Matos et al., 2015). The main objectives of this study are to initiate and maintain national and international research on health, health behaviors, and their contexts in children and adolescents; contribute theoretically and methodologically, and to increase knowledge in this area; monitor and compare health and health behaviors at national and international levels; and promote and support health promotion in these age groups through national and international action networks. The study aims to identify and characterize the health behaviors of children and adolescents, in a random sample and representative of the sixth, eighth, and tenth grades. The questionnaire addresses issues related to the contexts and actors with which children and adolescents move, namely physical activity and leisure, food and hygiene, substance use, body image, physical and psychological symptoms, sexual behavior, future expectations, family relationship, peer group relationship, school involvement, and community involvement.

In the present study, four questions were used: "In your Leisure, how many hours a day do you do the following activity: watch television/videos or DVD; play *PlayStation*; play on the computer and go to the Internet and chats."

Procedure

The application was carried out within the Social Adventure team with the same protocol and procedure used in the international study Health Behavior School Aged-Children, to a random national sample representative of the fifth and seventh years of schooling (Currie et al., 2001; Matos et al., 2015). This study has the collaboration and authorization of the Ministry of Education, the Ethics Committee of the São João Oporto Hospital, and the Data Protection Commission.

All schools were contacted by telephone to confirm their willingness to participate in the investigation. An envelope was sent requesting the participation of randomly selected classes, containing a letter of instruction addressed to the teacher to be read aloud, before filling out the questionnaire, 25 questionnaires to be completed by the students and 25 questionnaires to be completed by the respective parents. Parental and pupils' consent was obtained. The questionnaires (parents/children) were numbered and paired to remain anonymous. In the present work, only pupils' data will be analyzed.

The data was analyzed with the SPSS software. Several levels of analysis were performed, univariate descriptive analysis and bivariate analysis.

Results

The results are presented in relation to the percentages of time students spend with each of the screen activities (Tables 15.1 to 15.4). Gender and age differences are illustrated (Tables 15.5 to 15.6). Finally, the relationship between each of the screen activities and their impact on the dimensions of quality of life in Tables 15.7 to 15.11 is portrayed.

Table 15.1 During leisure time, how many hours a day do you watch TV/video?

Hours a day watching TV/Video	N	%
No	181	5.9
Up to 2h a day	2065	67.7
3 or more hour a day	804	26.4

Table 15.2 During leisure time, how many hours a day do you play with *Playstation?*

Hours a day playing Playstation	N	%
No	1498	49.8
Up to 2h a day	1085	36.1
3 or more hour a day	426	14.2

Table 15.3 During leisure time, how many hours a day do you use a computer?

Hours a day using computer	N	%
No	879	29.1
Up to 2h a day	1651	54.7
3 or more hour a day	487	16.1

Table 15.4 During leisure time, how many hours a day do you use Internet/chats?

Hours a day using Internet/Chats	N	%
No	1503	50.5
Up to 2h a day	1090	36.6
3 or more hour a day	382	12.8

Table 15.5 Gender differences regarding screen time

Screen time	Boys		Girls		F
	X	SD	X	SD	
TV/videos	2.20	0.52	2.21	0.54	n.s.
Playstation	**1.93**	0.74	1.37	0.56	542.81***
Computer	**1.95**	0.69	1.80	0.62	40.07***
Internet/Chats	**1.69**	0.71	1.56	0.68	27.74***

Note: n.s.= non-significant; ***p≤.001

Table 15.6 Age differences regarding screen time

Screen Time	10–11 years old		12 or more years		F
	X	SD	X	SD	
TV/videos	2.12	0.51	**2.27**	0.53	59.78***
Playstation	1.64	0.70	1.65	0.72	n.s.
Computers	1.82	0.64	**1.91**	0.67	12.23***
Internet/Chats	1.53	0.68	**1.69**	0.71	35.91***

Note: n.s.= non-significant; ***p≤.001

Table 15.7 Watching TV/Video and Dimensions of Kidscreen 52-HRQL

Watching TV/Video and Dimensions of Kidscreen 52—HRQL	No		Up to 2 hours/day		3 or more hours a day		F
	X	SD	X	SD	X	SD	
Health and physical activity	69.65	20.22	71.96	17.00	71.52	18.34	n.s.
Feelings	77.32	20.72	**80.70**	16.21	79.26	17.45	4.63**
Humor	74.67	19.32	**77.99**	18.57	74.31	20.40	11.31***
About yourself	73.03	20.21	**74.49**	17.95	71.43	18.32	8.01***
Leisure	74.80	25.16	76.55	20.43	76.25	20.93	n.s.
Family	75.63	24.61	**81.09**	18.84	78.84	20.88	8.47***
Friends	73.74	24.03	77.02	19.44	77.63	19.23	n.s.
School and learning	66.57	25.00	**71.45**	19.02	66.05	20.66	23.14***
Money matters	66.76	32.00	74.50	26.50	**75.80**	26.44	8.05***
Bullying	75.52	25.73	**80.51**	21.45	79.50	22.56	4.37**

Note: n.s.= non-significant; ***p≤.001;**p≤.01

Table 15.8 Playing *Playstation* and Dimensions of Kidscreen 52-HRQL

Playing Playstation and Dimensions of Kidscreen 52—HRQL	No		Up to 2 hours/day		3 or more hours a day		F
	X	SD	X	SD	X	SD	
Health and physical activity	68.81	17.70	73.58	17.06	**76.67**	17.06	42.68★★★
Feelings	78.65	17.37	81.57	15.82	**81.85**	16.94	11.82★★★
Humor	75.46	19.33	**78.30**	18.71	77.96	19.60	7.38★★★
About yourself	71.24	18.85	75.71	17.20	**76.63**	17.12	25.37★★★
Leisure	74.14	21.60	77.87	19.73	**80.70**	20.25	20.14★★★
Family	77.80	20.89	**82.82**	18.08	81.76	19.41	21.47★★★
Friends	75.44	20.20	78.27	19.28	**79.55**	18.34	10.13★★★
School and learning	69.88	19.46	**71.14**	19.56	65.38	22.20	12.64★★★
Money matters	71.33	28.00	**78.00**	24.82	77.08	26.30	21.28★★★
Bullying	78.53	22.79	**81.94**	20.28	81.57	22.77	8.45★★★

Note: ★★★p≤.001

Table 15.9 Computer use and Dimensions of Kidscreen 52-HRQL

Computer use and Dimensions of Kidscreen 52—HRQL	No		Up to 2 hours/day		3 or more hours a day		F
	X	SD	X	SD	X	SD	
Health and physical activity	69.15	18.10	72.07	17.20	**75.16**	17.38	18.42★★★
Feelings	79.07	17.06	**80.94**	16.05	79.91	18.49	3.60★★
Humor	76.12	19.35	**77.76**	18.66	75.19	20.54	4.11★★
About yourself	72.80	19.03	**74.49**	17.54	72.25	19.04	4.02 ★★
Leisure	74.96	21.98	77.06	19.92	**77.32**	21.47	3.28★★
Family	77.23	20.96	**81.96**	18.26	79.73	22.05	16.16★★★
Friends	74.25	21.17	78.18	18.66	**78.59**	19.26	12.77★★★
School and learning	68.89	20.80	**71.30**	18.94	66.80	21.63	10.77★★★
Money matters	67.83	29.01	76.79	25.35	**78.80**	25.37	39.21★★★
Bullying	78.53	23.14	**80.88**	20.95	80.08	23.43	3.23★★

Note: ★★★ p ≤.001;★★ p≤.01

Boys most often refer to screen activities. There are some statistically significant differences between boys and girls and between age groups.

Regarding the differences in TV/video viewing, playing *PlayStation*, using computers, Internet use/chats, and Health-Related Quality of Life Dimensions, there are different statistically significant differences, according to different dimensions of Health-related with Quality of life.

Table 15.11 systematizes and points out a screen time pattern in the various dimensions of the perception of quality of life.

It is verified that students who report developing screen activities up to two hours daily perceive the perception of a more positive quality of life in the dimensions "State of Humor"; "Family"; School and learning; and Bullying. In relation to the dimensions, "Health and physical

Table 15.10 *Internet/chats* use and Dimensions of Kidscreen 52—HRQL

Internet/Chats use and Dimensions of Kidscreen 52—HRQL	No		Up to 2 hours/day		3 or more hours a day		F
	X	SD	X	SD	X	SD	
Health and physical activity	69.45	17.72	73.77	16.83	**74.16**	17.71	23.22***
Feelings	79.75	16.92	80.56	16.27	80.37	18.46	n.s.
Humor	76.65	19.51	77.45	18.53	75.47	20.80	n.s.
About yourself	73.37	18.89	74.35	17.42	72.26	18.52	n.s.
Leisure	75.16	21.43	77.22	19.95	**79.02**	21.05	6.29**
Family	79.28	20.11	**81.32**	18.82	79.99	21.54	3.26**
Friends	74.73	20.94	78.71	17.81	**81.22**	18.11	22.34***
School and learning	**70.32**	20.17	70.09	19.08	66.16	21.91	6.68***
Money matters	70.44	28.30	77.83	25.15	**80.82**	23.48	35.79***
Bullying	79.08	22.30	81.17	21.32	**81.29**	22.19	3.44**

Note: n.s.= non-significant; *** p ≤.001;** p≤.01

Table 15.11 Screen Time and Dimensions of Kidscreen 52—HRQL

Screen Time and Dimensions of Kidscreen 52—HRQL	TV/Videos	Playstation	Computer	Internet/chats
Health and physical activity	—	3 + hours	3 + hours	3 + hours
Feelings	Up to 2 hours	3 + hours	Up to 2 hours	—
Humor	Up to 2 hours	Up to 2 hours /	Up to 2 hours	—
About yourself	Up to 2 hours	3 + hours	Up to 2 hours	—
Leisure	—	3 + hours	3 + hours	3 + hours
Family	Up to 2 hours	Up to 2 hours	Up to 2 hours	Up to 2 hours
Friends	—	3 + hours	3 + hours	3 + hours
School and learning	Up to 2 hours	Up to 2 hours	Up to 2 hours	No
Money matters	3 + hours	Up to 2 hours	3 + hours	3 + hours
Bullying	Up to 2 hours /	Up to 2 hours	Up to 2 hours /	3 + hours

activity"; "Leisure"; "Friends"; and "Money matters" are students who report developing screen activities three or more hours a day who have a more positive perception of quality of life.

Discussion

Screen activities have a privileged place in the choices of leisure activities for children and adolescents. The Education Committee of the American Academy of Pediatrics (2010) recommends that infants and children under the age of two years not be exposed to the screen and that children and adolescents, to ensure healthy development, do not have screen time higher than the average of two hours per day. Although the recommendation does not specify an optimum gradation of time according to concrete age groups, or make a distinction between days of the workweek and the days of the weekend, it establishes a reference of the desirable.

The results of this study show that a minority of children and adolescents surpasses the reference of the two hours daily screen, with the exception of watching television/video that about a quarter spends three or more hours a day with these activities. These results are in line with the analysis by Roberts et al. (2006) that adolescents tend to have more time in front of the screen than in any other activity, except for sleep. There are gender and age differences in the time spent on screen activities. Boys refer more time performing screen activities than girls (PlayStation, computer, and Internet/chats). There are no gender differences in watching television/video. Roberts and colleagues, in 2004, had found similar results. In any case, it seems that watching television will be a more passive time occupation than playing or using the computer. That is, the female screen time seems to have more passive contours than the male gender. There are the oldest students (12 years old or more) that most refer to screen activities (television and/or videos, use of the computer and Internet/chats). The number of screen hours increases progressively between the 10- and 16-year-old or more. On the one hand, this may mean the extraordinary attractive power of "old" and "new" media (Strasburger et al., 2009).

On the other hand, as Trallero (2010) points out, he may say of the increasing influence of the screen on the conception of the world, life, and reality although with age it tends to increase the critical sense and decrease the receptivity. Given the literature that emphasizes the negative consequences of screen time in terms of health/well-being, it can be a matter of public health and citizenship, as increases in screen time may help to ferment and enhance risk behaviors of various kinds: deregulated feeding, violence, substance use, obesity, unprotected sexual activity, and others (Strasburger, Jordan, & Donnerstein, 2010). An impact and a relationship between the dimensions of perception of quality of life and screen time were identified. This relationship has some specificities for each of the different types of screen activities. The results reveal that, in general, students who do not report developing screen activities have a less positive perception of quality of life. In general, students who spend up to two hours a day on screen activities have a more positive perception of quality of life, except for the use of Internet/chats where students spend more time (three hours or more a day) who has a perception of their most positive quality of life. As Roberts and colleagues (2006) point out, screen offers are extensive and varied and even foster emotional satisfaction and well-being.

The literature documents numerous studies where we observe the negative effects, at the cognitive level, of too much screen time (Jordan et al., 2010; Rideout, 2010; Strasburger et al., 2009). At the same time, although with fewer studies, the literature reveals that certain screen offers show benefits in both cognitions, behaviors, and quality of life (Linebarger & Walker, 2005). Therefore, questions of creativity to occupy leisure not around the screen. Parents, youth and sports associations, organizations of all kinds, communities, schools, municipalities, and soci-ocultural animators have a huge challenge here to make the leisure time for teenagers healthier a source of greater satisfaction.

The time spent with "new" technologies, such as watching television, computer use, and Internet access, has been increasing in recent years, especially in the adolescent age group, more than in any other age group. An interesting conclusion of the present study was that the total non-use of screen time activity is indeed a risk factor, undermining the perception of positive quality of life. These results and current literature suggest that screen time activities can be a protective factor and a factor of socio-cognitive development and well-being, if screen time is not excessive; especially that it does not prevent the performance of other activities of screen, occupation, and other forms of social interaction and parental supervision.

Leisure and Active Citizenship With and Beyond Media: The Dream Teens Project

A key aspect of a Positive Youth Development framework is that all young people should be involved in maintaining or developing healthy behaviors, and to help finding solutions for problems if properly heard and if they become more active and participative in their life contexts and society. This includes with property this issue of the use and abuse of technologies of information and communication.

The *Dream Teens* project mission (Matos, 2015; Matos & Simões, 2016) was to ensure a nation-wide opportunity for youth to be included and empowered as agents of change, to have their voices heard, and at the same time to participate and engage as partners in decision-making about issues that affect their lives and communities.

Young people used media to learn and to interact: they interacted via *Facebook* and were called to react and debate the topics of interest regularly posted by the senior staff team. Dissemination was also made available through media, social media, a web page (www.dreamteens. aventurasocial.com), and three web-blogs (http://dreamteens2014-2015.blogspot.pt/; http:// dreamteensaventurasocial.blogspot.pt; http://dreamteensaventurasocial.blogs.sapo.pt). The Dream Teens project was, thus, grounded in a positive and proactive view of promotional interventions with young people and moreover media were used to promote social development and development, that is as an asset, a positive resource. Media come to stay and its development presents borders hard to define: they are useful to learn, to leisure time, to socialize, but they also have pitfalls, and perverse side effects. Media was essential in the developing of the Dream Teens network, for good.

It is thus also possible to use media for health promotion, for increasing family and community togetherness and strategies to increase the good use and limit the problems urge. Screen time activities can be a protective factor and a factor of socio-cognitive development and well-being; especially that it does not prevent other leisure or work activities.

Definitively young people have a specific place in human development, and the political and professional understanding of this fact will not only allow young people to have a voice, abut also will allow professionals to provide better health and educational services.

References

American Academy of Paediatrics: Committee on Public Education. (2010). Media education. *Pediatrics, 126*(5), 1012–1017. Retrieved September 15, 2011 from http://pediatrics.aappublications.org/content/126/5/1012.full.pdf+html. doi:10.1542/peds.2010-1636

Anderson, C. (2002). The effects of media violence on society. *Science, 295,* 2377–2389. doi:10.1126/science.1070765

Boniel-Nissim, M., Lenzi, M., Zsizos, E., Matos, M. G., Gommans, R., Harel-Fisch, Y., . . . Van der Sluijs, W. (2015). International trends in Electronic Media Communication (EMC) among 11- to 15-year-olds in 30 countries from 2002 to 2010: Association with ease of communication with friends of the opposite sex. *European Journal of Public Health, 25*(2), 41–45. doi:10.1093/eurpub/ckv025

Boone, J., Gordon-Larsen, P., Adair, L., & Popkin, B. (2007). Screen time and physical activity during adolescence: Longitudinal effects on obesity in young adulthood. *International Journal of Behavioral Nutrition and Physical Activity, 4*(26), 1–10. Retrieved September 27, 2011 from www.ijbnpa.org/content/4/1/26. doi:10.1186/1479-5868-4-26

Christakis, D. (2009). The effects of infant media usage: What do we know and what should we learn? *Acta Paediatrica, 98*(1), 8–16. doi:10.1111/j.1651-2227.2008.01027.x

Currie, C., Samdal, O., Boyce, W., & Smith, R. (2001). *HBSC, and WHO cross national study: Research protocol for the 2001/2002 survey.* Copenhagen: WHO.

Detmar, S., Bruil, J., Ravens-Sieberer, U., Gosch, A., Bisegger, C., & the European KIDSCREEN Group (2006). The use of focus group in the development of the KIDSCREEN HRQL questionnaire. *Quality of Life Research, 1*(5), 1345–1353. doi:10.1007/s11136-006-0022-z

Firminger, K. B. (2006). Is he boyfriend material? Representation of males in teenage girl's magazines. *Men and Masculinities, 8,* 298–308. doi:10.1177/1097184X05282074

Gamito, P. S., Morais, D. G., Oliveira, J. G., Brito, R., Rosa, P. J., & Matos, M. G. (2016). Frequency is not enough: Patterns of use associated with risk of Internet addiction in Portuguese adolescents. *Computers in Human Behavior, 58,* 471–479. doi:10.1016/j.chb.2016.01.013

Gaspar, T., & Matos, M. G. (2011). Self-regulation and eating behaviour in Portuguese children and adolescents: Concept mapping methodology. *Journal of Child and Adolescent Psychology, 4,* 73–94.

Gaspar, T., Matos, M., Ribeiro, J., & Leal, I. (2006). Qualidade de vida e bem-estar em crianças e adolescentes. *Revista Brasileira de Terapias Cognitivas, 2*(2), 47–60. ISSN: 1982-3746.

Gaspar, T., Matos, M. G., Ribeiro, J. L., Leal, I., Erhart, M., & Ravens-Sieberer, U. (2012). Health-related quality of life in children and adolescents: Subjective well-being. *Spanish Journal of Psychology, 15*(1), 177–186. doi:10.5209/rev_SJOP.2012.v15.n1.37306

Gaspar, T., Matos, M. G., Ribeiro, J., Leal, I., & Ferreira, A. (2009). Health-related quality of life in children and adolescents and associated factors. *Journal of Cognitive and Behavioral Psychotherapies, 9*(1), 33–48. ISSN: 1584-7101.

Hogan, M. J., & Strasburger, V. C. (2008). Media and prosocial behavior in children and adolescents. In L. Nucci & D. Narvaez (Eds.), *Handbook of moral and character education* (pp. 537–553). Mahwah, NJ: Lawrence Erlbaum Associates.

Iannotti, R., Kogan, M., Janssen, I., & Boyce, W. (2009). Patterns of adolescent physical activity, screen-based media use and positive and negative health indicators in the U.S. and Canada. *Journal of Adolescent Health, 44*(5), 493–499. doi:10.1016/j.jadohealth.2008.10.142

Jordan, A., Bleakley, A., Manganello, J., Hennessy, M., Stevens, R., & Fishbein, M. (2010). The role of television access in viewing time of U.S. adolescents. *Journal of Children and Media, 4*(4), 355–370. doi:10.1080/17482798.2010.510004

Kennedy, C., Strzempko, F., Danford, C., & Kools, S. (2002). Children's perceptions of TV and health behavior effects. *Journal Nursing Scholarship, 34*(3), 289–294. doi:10.1111/j.1547-5069.2002.00289.x

KIDSCREEN Group Europe. (2006). *The KIDSCREEN questionnaires: Quality of life questionnaires for children and adolescents.* Hamburg, Germany: Pabst Science Publishers.

Linebarger, D. H., & Walker, D. (2005). Infants' and toddlers' television viewing and language outcomes. *American Behavioral Scientist, 48*(5), 624–645. doi:10.1177/0002764204271505

Matos, M. G. (Coord.). (2015). *Dream teens: Adolescents in safe navigation through unknown waters.* Lisboa: Coisas de Ler. ISBN: 978-989-8659-54-5.

Matos, M. G., & Ferreira, M. (2013). *Nascidos Digitais* [Born digital]. Lisboa: Coisas de Ler. ISBN: 978-989-8659-09-5.

Matos, M. G., Paiva, T., Costa, D., Gaspar, T., & Galvão, D. (2016). Caffeine, sleep duration and adolescents' perception of health related quality of life. *British Journal of Education, Society & Behavioral Science, 16*(2), 1–9. doi:10.9734/BJESBS/2016/23894

Matos, M. G., & Sampaio, D. (Coord.). (2009). *Jovens com saúde: diálogos com uma geração [Healthy young people: Dialogue with a generation].* Lisboa: Texto Editores, Lda. ISBN: 978-972-4740-28-7.

Matos, M. G., & Simões, C. (2016). From positive youth development to youth's engagement: The dream teens. *The International Journal of Emotional Education, 8*(1), 4–18.

Matos, M. G., Simões, C., Camacho, I., Reis, M., & Aventura Social (2015). *A saúde dos adolescentes portugueses em tempos de recessão [The health of adolescents in times of recession].* Lisboa: FMH/ULisboa. ISBN: 978-989-9834-61-3.

Mendoza, R., & Sagrera, M. (1990). *Los escolares y la Salud—avance de los resultados del segundo estudio español sobre conductas de los escolares relacionadas com a Salud.* Madrid: Plan Regional sobre Drogas—Ministerio de Educacion e Cultura.

Mérelle, S. Y. M., Kleiboer, A. M., Schotanus, M., Cluitmans, T. L. M., Waardenburg, C. M., Kramer, D., . . . Rooji, A. J. (2017). Which health-related problems are associated with problematic video-gaming or social media use in adolescents? A large-scale cross-sectional study. *Clinical Neuropsychiatry, 14*(1), 11–18. ISSN: 1724-4935.

Paiva, T., Gaspar, T., & Matos, M. G. (2016). Mutual relations between sleep deprivation sleep stealers and risk behaviors in adolescents. *Sleep Science, 9*(1), 7–13. doi:10.1016/j.slsci.2016.02.176

Ravens-Sieberer, U., Gosch, A., Abel, T., Auquier, P., Bellach, B., Bruil, J., . . . European KIDSCREEN Group. (2001). Quality of life in children and adolescents: A European public health perspective. *Preventivmed, 46*(5), 294–302.

Rideout, V. (2010). *Generation M2: Media in the lives of 8 to 18-year-olds.* Menlo Park, CA: Kaiser Family Foundation.

Roberts, D. F., Foehr, U., & Rideout, V. (2006). *Generation M: Media in the lives of 8–18 year olds.* Menlo Park, CA: Kaiser Family Foundation.

Roberts, D. F., Henriksen, L., & Foehr, U. G. (2004). Adolescent and media. In R. Lerner & L. Steinberg (Eds.), *Handbook of adolescent psychology* (pp. 85–125). Hoboken, NJ: Wiley. ISBN: 978-0-471-69044-3.

Sandercock, G. R., Alibrahim, M., & Bellamy, M. (2016). Media device ownership and media use: Associations with sedentary time, physical activity and fitness in English youth. *Preventive Medicine Reports, 4,* 162–168. doi:10.1016/j.pmedr.2016.05.013

Scheidt, P., Overpeck, M., Wyatt, W., & Aszmann, A. (2000). Adolescents' general health and well-being. In C. Currie, K. Hurrelmann, W. Settertobulte, R. Smith, & J. Todd (Eds.), *Health and health behavior among young people.* Copenhagen: HEPCA series. World Health Organization.

Sharif, I., & Sargent, J. (2006). Association between television, movie, and video game exposure and school performance. *Pediatrics, 118*(4), 1061–1070. doi:10.1542/peds.2005-2854

Small, G., & Vorgan, G. (2008). *iBrain: Surviving the technology alteration of the modern mind.* New York, NY: HarperCollins Publishers.

Strasburger, V. C., Jordan, A. B., & Donnerstein, E. (2010). Health effects of media on children and adolescents. *Pediatrics, 12*(4), 756–767. Retrieved September 5, 2011 from http://pediatrics.aappublications.org/content/125/4/756.full.html. doi:10.1542/peds.2009-2563

Strasburger, V. C., Wilson, B. J., & Jordan, A. B. (2009). *Children, adolescents, and the media* (2nd ed.). Thousand Oaks, CA: Sage Publications. ISBN: 1412944678.

Trallero, J. (2010). *El Adolescente en su Mundo. Riesgos, problemas y trastornos.* Madrid: Ediciones Pirámide. ISBN: 978-843-6823-67-7.

Woods, H. C., & Scott, H. (2016). #Sleepyteens: Social media use in adolescence is associated with poor sleep quality, anxiety, depression and low self-esteem. *Journal of Adolescence, 51,* 41–49. doi:10.1016/j.adolescence.2016.05.008

PART III

Happiness, Advertising, and Marketing Communication

16

POSITIVE MARKETING, VIRTUE, AND HAPPINESS

Dawn Lerman and Santiago Mejia

An aim of marketing, both as a discipline and a practice, is to make people happy (Bagozzi & Nataraajan, 2000). Marketers' intentions are captured in Coca-Cola's tagline "Open happiness," Nesquik's "You cannot buy happiness, but you can drink it!" campaign, and Zappos' focus on "delivering happiness." A key word search on "marketing and happiness" in the scholarly business literature yields 5,980+ results and happiness has been an increasingly popular topic in marketing courses and course materials. One popular textbook, for example, is entitled *Consumer Behavior: Human Pursuit of Happiness in the World of Goods*, and Bishop's University in Canada has offered an entire course on happiness marketing (Wang, 2013).

Despite this noble aim, marketing is often blamed for causing individual and societal discontent. Concerns about the perception, if not also the reality, of marketing's ill effects has spawned a variety of academic marketing movements focused on individual and societal well-being as well as new industry practices and standards around social responsibility. This chapter reviews the relationship between marketing and well-being with a particular focus on happiness. It identifies where marketing has been successful in bringing happiness to individuals and society and where and why it has fallen short, and lays out what can be done to improve marketing's performance in this regard. The chapter also explains how a positive marketing approach can help the field achieve its happiness aims.

Marketing and (Un)Happiness

The marketing concept, which serves as the basis for modern marketing, claims that a marketer's job is to develop a thorough understanding of human needs and then design products and brands—along with comprehensive marketing programs around those products and brands—to fulfill those needs. Key among these needs is happiness needs (Lyubomirsky, 2008). Research shows that happiness is distinct from, though in some instances related to, the five human needs captured by Maslow's well-known Hierarchy of Needs and referenced in nearly every basic marketing textbook: basic, or sustenance needs; safety and protection needs; social needs; ego needs; and self-actualization needs. When defined as life satisfaction, happiness can result from fulfillment of the needs described by Maslow (Tay & Diener, 2011), but attainment of happiness as an affective, ephemeral state of pleasure can also be a motivator in its own right (cf. Lyubomirsky, Tkach, & DiMatteo, 2006).

Research shows that consumers not only tend to make purchase decisions based on their beliefs about what will bring them happiness (Mogilner Aaker, & Kamvar., 2012) but that consumption can indeed bring consumers happiness. Research has uncovered, for example, the positive impact of experiences (e.g., spas, concerts, movies, and vacations) on happiness (see, for example, Bhattacharjee & Mogilner, 2014; Caprariello & Reis, 2013; Gilovich, Kumar, & Jampol, 2015) and the role of technical (i.e., what is delivered) and functional (i.e., how it is delivered) service quality in increasing happiness (De Keyser & Lariviere, 2014). Consumption of particular brands can also bring happiness. For example, the Center for Positive Marketing's annual survey of consumers shows that among big brands, Facebook, Walmart, and Google are some of the most successful in fulfilling their customers' happiness needs (V-Positive Report, 2017).

At the same time, research suggests a relationship between consumption and unhappiness. While consumers may make a purchase on the promise (tacit or explicit) that a branded product will contribute to their happiness, the purchase and/or usage of the product may not actually contribute to happiness (e.g., Desmeules, 2002; Hsee & Hastie, 2006). It is also possible that any derived happiness may be short-lived, particularly if the product or brand is intended to make consumers feel good in the moment.

Hedonic happiness, or feeling good in the moment, is the kind of happiness that consumers may have in mind when making many purchase decisions. Many marketers strive to focus on hedonic happiness when serving customers (e.g., Coca-Cola's "Open Happiness" or McDonald's Happy Meal). Since these kinds of positive emotions are transient, people tend to engage in additional consumption (including, for example, repeat purchase of a Coca-Cola soft drink or McDonald's Happy Meal) in an attempt to regain and sustain positive feelings. What is more, pleasurable short-term experiences tend to become normalized in the long-term; as you repeatedly seek the pleasure produced by a particular experience, the satisfaction you get from it tends to decrease. Researchers refer to this phenomenon as the hedonic treadmill (Brickman & Campbell, 1971).

In contrast, eudaimonic happiness corresponds to the kind of happiness that arises from living a full and meaningful life, also referred to as a flourishing life. Eudaimonic happiness is associated with long-term well-being and cannot be achieved via consumption alone. Research reveals that the kind of consumption that brings happiness now—hedonic happiness—does not necessarily bring eudaimonic happiness. For example, as pointed out earlier, a strong body of research suggests that people should purchase and engage in experiences to increase happiness and that these experiences will bring more happiness than that brought about from material goods. Sääksjärvi, Hellén, and Desmet (2016) found, however, that engaging in experiences is much more effective in increasing short-term happiness than long-term happiness. According to their research, experiences can positively impact long-term happiness but only when they are paired with a material object associated with that experience (e.g., not only listening to your favorite music but owning the boxed set of this music).

Finally, the plethora of human needs and the variety of products, services, or experiences that may contribute to their fulfillment make it difficult to isolate the impact of any one particular product, service, or experience on long-term happiness. According to the humanistic model of management, flourishing and well-being are not the result of the fulfillment of any one particular need but rather the result of the fulfillment of needs across four need categories or drives—the drive to acquire, the drive to defend, the drive to bond, and the drive to comprehend (Pirson, 2017). Attaining a flourishing life requires a "balance" in these four drives (Pirson, 2017, p. 73), which is unlikely to be achieved through the purchase or consumption of one product, service, or experience. What is more, and as scholars in moral philosophy have argued, our needs do not stand in isolation. They often complement one another in such a way that their contribution is not aggregative but holistic (Kristjánsson, 2013). Their specific contribution to a person's life can only be properly be assessed in the context of how each of them contribute to a person's overall flourishing.

From this perspective, and as difficult as it may be, marketers must seek to understand the effects of consumption on eudaimonic happiness and overall well-being. Using this understanding to inform marketing practice will help ensure that marketing can fulfill its true aim.

Historical Background

As a function, marketing has existed as long as trade (Bartels, 1976). While the language of marketing has since evolved and the tools available to marketers have expanded exponentially, Bartels (1976) argues that societal benefits have always been at the core of marketing practice:

> Marketing must be regarded not merely as a business practice, but as a social institution. Marketing is essentially a means of meeting and satisfying certain needs of people. It is a highly developed and refined system of thought and practice characteristic of a period in the development of a market economy. A latent presumption in the practice of marketing has been that marketing gives to society more than society gives to it. The fact is that marketing is but one of several means of accomplishing a social objective.
>
> *(p. 1)*

Fast forward just a few decades and this view of marketing sounds like idealism. While Bartels (1976) describes marketing as a system based on reciprocity and exchange, critics of marketing would describe it as anything but. Lerman (2016) reports on the growing imbalance that is seen in commercial exchange as favoring marketers and hurting both individuals and society. As she points out, the criticism comes in many forms—boycotts, legislation, negative press, cultural critiques—and from many camps, including marketers themselves. Furthering the critique, only 35 percent of marketers surveyed for an Adobe-commissioned study deem their profession valuable (Parekh, 2012).

Criticism of marketing is certainly not new as made clear by Stoeckl and Luedicke (2015) in their review of 60 years of marketing criticism from academics, activists, and the media. Yet, it does appear that the criticism has grown in recent years. There are likely many reasons for this, including increasing commercialization as well as new modes of communication and technologies that have made people increasingly reliant on marketers while they have also made them more savvy consumers. It is also the case that people who have not studied or worked in marketing likely think of marketing as advertising or sales, the two components of marketing that are most visible to them and where, perhaps, it is more common to encounter questionable practices. Some of these criticisms, therefore, arise from lack of a comprehensive understanding of the marketing function or its role—actual and potential—in helping individuals, families, and society flourish.

In a broad sense, consumers see the value potential in marketing when they turn to marketers to solve their problems, from mundane decisions such as what to eat for dinner to complex matters such as how to care for an aging parent. However, this value potential is not what comes to mind when they think about marketing. Kachersky and Lerman (2013) found that people view marketing as primarily serving business needs rather than the needs of ordinary people and that when they do consider marketing in terms of its effect on ordinary people, they view it as a nuisance.

Toward a More Positive Marketing

How can marketing fulfill—and be recognized for fulfilling—its intended contribution to society and the people it serves? This and similar questions have spawned a variety of new movements wherein consumer and marketing researchers are focusing their academic research on individual and societal well-being. It includes, for example, a group of scholars in the Macromarketing Society who investigate the interaction among markets, marketing, and society, as well as the Transformative Consumer Research (TCR) movement, which seeks to use consumer research to address consumer well-being. To the extent to which the fruits of this research can ultimately provide guidance as to how best to procure the social conditions where individual human beings can flourish, this research dovetails nicely with research on eudaimonistic happiness. Similarly, on the corporate side, marketers have dramatically increased their focus on sustainability and corporate social responsibility with the intention to facilitate the flourishing of individuals through social improvements. Bridging the academic and corporate approach is among the central aims of positive marketing which, according to Mittelstaedt, Kilbourne, and Shultz (2015) "can play an important role in marketing strategy formulation and in advising the objectives of organizations wishing to make positive change in society" (p. 2515).

In "recognizing that there is room to improve the actions of marketplace participants" (Mittelstaedt et al., 2015, p. 2513), positive marketing offers an approach that can help disentangle the effects of marketing on (un)happiness and help ensure that marketers deliver on eudaimonistic happiness. Positive marketing has been defined as "marketing in its ideal form, in which parties— individual customers, marketers, and society as a whole-exchange value such that individually and collectively they are better off than they were prior to exchange" (www.CenterforPositiveMarketing.org). This holistic focus on individuals, marketers, and society distinguishes positive marketing from other prosocial marketing concepts such as cause marketing, green marketing, and social marketing, each of which typically create value for a more limited set of stakeholders (Gopaldas, 2015).

Green marketing and social marketing primarily aim at providing societal value and may or may not yield value for the firm or the individual customer. In practicing green marketing, a firm would seek to create environmental value (McDaniel & Rylander, 1993) as Unilever has in its efforts to reduce greenhouse emissions. While much needed and certainly noble, such efforts may or may not be valued by consumers depending on the consumer's own needs and values (e.g., Barbarossa & De Pelsmacker, 2016) and could result in greater costs for the firm.

Cause marketing, which links consumer purchases to corporate philanthropy (Varadarajan & Menon, 1988) aims at providing individual customer and firm value but not necessarily societal value. Cause marketing has been criticized as "post-hoc compensation" (Gopaldas, 2015, p. 2) for society's ills since it intends to deliver value through peripheral donations (e.g., Porter & Kramer, 2006) rather than by addressing societal issues head-on. Gopaldas (2015) contrasts this "give back" approach to corporate responsibility with the "give forward" approach of building societal value into a firm's marketplace offerings from the outset as in positive marketing (Gopaldas, 2015).

Positive marketing does not redefine marketing but rather offers a frame through which to view marketing in general. The American Marketing Association defines marketing as follows:

> Marketing is the activity, set of institutions, and processes for creating, communicating, delivering, and exchanging offerings that have value for customers, clients, partners, and society at large.
> *(Retrieved at www.ama.org/AboutAMA/Pages/Definition-of-Marketing.aspx)*

Positive marketing shifts the focus to the latter part of the definition and recognizes the interdependency of the parties mentioned therein. That is, in the course of a single market-based exchange, positive marketing delivers value to customer(s), firm, and society at large. As we suggested, positive marketing should be seen as an essential part of an organization's business model in that the value to all parties is achieved "via core services" (Gopaldas, 2015, p. 2) as opposed to via add-ons.

Gopaldas (2015) offers Amazon's Frustration Free Packaging as an example of a marketplace offering that simultaneously delivers value to customers, the firm, and society. Frustration Free Packaging was born out of Amazon's decision to exchange heat-sealed, difficult to open clam-shell packaging for many of its consumer packed goods for easy-to-open, minimalist packaging that doubles as a shipping container. For customers, this packaging solves a legitimate issue by enabling them to open packages without box-cutters, knives, or scissors. It delivers value to the firm through cost reduction but also in the goodwill that it generated among customers; Amazon observed a 73 percent reduction in negative feedback on "Frustration Free" packaged products compared to their standard-packaged counterparts. For society at large, the minimalist, eco-friendly materials mean less depletion of finite natural resources used in the production and delivery of packages.

Beyond Amazon, Gopaldas (2015) identifies 15 instances of positive marketing across indus-tries as diverse as fashion, health and beauty, flooring, and energy, thereby showing the widespread applicability of a positive marketing frame. Nonetheless, examples of positive marketing remain hard to find. Moreover, many companies that can be lauded for doing good in certain areas can be criticized for other practices (e.g., Walmart has brought everyday necessities to individuals who otherwise lacked access but is widely criticized for its labor practices) (Lerman & Kachersky, 2012). Such companies can be viewed as fostering the happiness of some stakeholders at the cost of the happiness of others.

What, then, is required for positive marketing to thrive? A review of both the marketplace and the academic literature suggests that for positive marketing to thrive we must, at a minimum, come to rely on a broader array of metrics to assess marketing success; uncover the long-term impact of immediate need satisfaction and the holistic way in which our different needs contrib-ute to our flourishing; and seek to develop a positive marketing culture.

Reliance on a Broader Array of Metrics to Assess Marketing Success

Marketers rely heavily on metrics to evaluate and track marketing performance. Common met-rics include, among other things, the number of unique clicks on a web-based advertisement (click-through rate), the consumer's ability to recall the names of brands they saw advertised on television (aided and unaided recall), the likelihood that a customer will recommend a particular brand to a friend (Net Promoter), and the economic value that a customer will bring to your business over his or her lifetime (Customer Lifetime Value, or CLV). Such metrics have been critical for legitimizing marketing expenditures as well as the role of marketing within the organ-ization (Petersen et al., 2009). To refute skepticism of marketing "as a questionable cost rather than worthy investment" (Kumar & Shah, 2011), Kumar and Shah (2009) designed a study to show that certain types of marketing efforts can indeed create shareholder value and affect stock prices, and that they can do so in a predictable way. Based on a field experiment with two For-tune 1000 firms, they found that Customer Lifetime Value (CLV)—the discounted net present value of expected cash flows from a customer or, more simply, the expected profitability from a customer—can reliably predict the market capitalization of the firm. They also showed that mar-keting strategies directed at increasing an individual's CLV can both increase the firm's stock price and beat market expectations. As a result CLV, along with a wide array of other commonly used marketing metrics, have come to play an important role in capturing marketing's value to firm.

While metrics that capture individual consumer and societal value are less commonly used, there are a handful available to marketers for tracking how their activities contribute to improving people's lives. Examples include the Dow Jones Sustainability Index, Havas Group's Meaningful Brand Index, and the Center for Positive Marketing's Consumer Value Index. The Consumer Value Index, for example, tracks movements in consumer value as indicated by

V-Positive, a measure of the positive impact that marketing and specific brands have on people's lives (V-Positive Report, 2017). V-Positive considers the need levels of individuals across seven life dimensions and the degree to which specific brands, and marketing in general, help satisfy those needs. These seven life dimensions are based on an augmented version of Maslow's Hierarchy of Needs. Havas Group takes a similar approach in that it bases its Meaningful Brand Index on a range of dimensions including social, emotional, financial, physical, community, government, natural, and environmental (Yonavjak & Galizia, 2013).

Incorporating these kinds of metrics would help companies track their progress in contributing to individual and societal well-being. What is more, there is evidence that to the degree that firms seek to improve their performance on these metrics, they would also be helping their bottom line. Researchers at the Center for Positive Marketing, for example, report consistently robust correlations between the V-Positive scores of individual brands and their financial values as reported in Interbrand's Best Global Brands study and Millward Brown's BrandZ study. Similarly, Havas Group reports on its website (www.meaningful-brands.com/en) that "Meaningful Brands have outperformed the stock market by a staggering 206 percent over a ten-year period between 2006 and 2016."

Greater Focus on the Long-Term Impact of Immediate Need Satisfaction

Positive marketing requires that we understand the long-term impact of immediate need satisfaction and that we recognize that well-being requires the holistic satisfaction of a diversity of needs. A health-related example makes this all too clear. Smoking a cigarette may, in the present, bring a smoker pleasure (hedonistic happiness needs), help her fit into the bar scene (social needs), and satisfy a physical addiction to nicotine (basic needs). However, the negative long-term impact of smoking is clear; smoking tends to cause lung cancer, emphysema, and a variety of other diseases and ailments. Many products and services designed to meet immediate needs may not contribute positively to long-term well-being. How do we weigh the trade-offs that are involved in such cases? For marketers to understand how to strike a balance, they need a full understanding of the diverse ways in which the fulfillment of our needs contributes to flourishing. Consumer research has only started to ask and investigate such questions.

Encouraging individuals to make consumption choices consistent with long-term well-being can be challenging, even when the trade-offs are known. Consumers do not always make choices in their best self-interest and this can lead to lackluster performance for companies on a mission to do the right thing. Consider, for example, the case of PepsiCo as it embraced a new mission to invest in what it called "good for you" brands, designed to be more nutritious and contain far less sugar and salt than the brands that originally built the company. While these efforts have since paid off for the company, PepsiCo and its CEO came under intense fire on Wall Street in 2012 for the negative effects that they had had on firm performance up to that point (Esterl, 2012). This suggests that in addition to seeking to understand the long-term impact of various types of immediate need satisfaction, marketers may need to transform consumer choices so as to help them select goods and services that contribute to their eudaimonistic happiness. For example, Bublitz and Peracchio (2015) show that businesses which produce healthy foods have achieved success with marketing campaigns that adapt and mimic the promotional efforts of hedonic foods (e.g., junk food that is pleasurable and fun to eat), campaigns that also promote healthier eating habits.

Development of a Positive Marketing Culture

Positive marketers are committed, as a matter of principle, to the view that firms should attempt to foster human flourishing and, consequently, that they should attempt to be socially responsible:

"pre-requisites for a positive marketing culture include a desire to fulfill human needs and a passion for alleviating societal problems" (Gopaldas, 2015, p. 2450). Gopaldas (2015) claims that fostering a positive marketing culture cannot happen without prosocial actors within the firm, most particularly in leadership positions. Fostering such a culture also requires marketers with a deep understanding of people and their needs, both short and long-term, and the impact of various types of consumption on overall well-being.

This kind of approach puts human flourishing at its center. This has led some positive marketers to be somewhat pessimistic about the ability of firms to pursue initiatives that address societal problems (Lerman & Shefrin, 2015). For example, Gopaldas (2015) argues that social interests tend to remain an afterthought and that as a result, positive marketing depends on the work of individuals bound by a prosocial responsibility and not of corporate entities that have a legal mandate to generate profits for investors. This is a call to marketing education to incorporate a humanistic approach grounded in social science (see Lerman, 2016) and a call to those existing prosocial actors within firms to seek out and hire individuals with this background.

An alternative view posits that the alleged "either/or" between producing profits for shareholders and promoting the well-being and flourishing of all the stakeholders is a false dichotomy. A growing body of research has shown that, at least in countries with a good rule of law and a free press, pursuing socially responsible endeavors and generating profits tend to go hand in hand in the long-term. We saw earlier, for example, that delivering value to consumers and society benefits firms financially. In addition, it has been shown that investing in employee well-being increases firm performance (Edmans, 2012) and that superior performance on corporate social responsibility strategies leads to better access to finance (Cheng, Ioannou, & Serafeim, 2014).

Some of these benefits may arise from the good reputation that is built by adhering to a socially responsible orientation. Various studies have shown that such a reputation pays off in lower costs, higher sales, better customer loyalty, an ability to charge higher prices, and better capacity to attract and retain workers (www.ethicalsystems.org/content/ethics-pays). This suggests that fostering human flourishing by incorporating social responsibility directly into the business model need not be done at the expense of profit. Rather, it can enhance profit. Thus, the kind of enlightened leaders that positive marketing extols can be ones for whom their prosocial orientation also makes good financial sense.

Beyond teaching, the university and its faculty play a role in pushing marketing's purpose and responsibility through research. In one study, Kachersky, Lerman, and Flicker (2013) found that over the course of one year, researchers whose articles were published in three of the four American Marketing Association's academic journals disproportionately reported on the implications of their research results for firms. By identifying and reporting on the implications for individual consumers and society as well as firms, researchers can help empower marketers to make a more positive impact in their customer's lives and in the larger world.

Conclusion

The many individuals whose lives are made more comfortable by a range of widely available products and services, especially in advanced economies, suggest that marketing can and does make positive contributions. At the same time, marketing as both a discipline and a practice has far from fulfilled its true aim. Approaching marketing theory and practice with a positive marketing frame will help ensure that marketing provides the kind of value for individuals, firms, and society that fosters overall well-being and happiness. This reframing requires expansion of the metrics that firms use to assess their performance, research designed to generate new knowledge about the impact of marketing activities on individuals and society, and a commitment within academia and industry to foster a positive marketing culture. The groundwork has been laid, but much work remains to be done.

References

Bagozzi, R. P., & Nataraajan, R. (2000). The year 2000: Looking forward. *Psychology & Marketing*, 17(1), 1–11. doi:10.1002/(SICI)1520-6793(200001)17:1<1::AID-MAR1>3.0.CO;2-Y

Barbarossa, C., & De Pelsmacker, P. (2016). Positive and negative antecedents of purchasing eco-friendly products: A comparison between green and non-green consumers. *Journal of Business Ethics*, 134, 229–247. doi:10.1007/s10551-014-2425-z

Bartels, R. (1976). *The history of marketing thought.* Bournemouth: Grid Publishing.

Bhattacharjee, A., & Mogilner, C. (2014). Happiness from ordinary and extraordinary experience. *Journal of Consumer Research*, 41(June), 1–17. doi:10.1086/674724

Brickman, P., & Campbell, D. T. (1971). Hedonic relativism and planning the good society. In M. H. Appley (Ed.), *Adaptation level theory: A symposium* (pp. 287–302). New York: Academic Press.

Bublitz, M. G., & Peracchio, L. A. (2015). Applying industry practices to promote healthy foods: An exploration of positive marketing outcomes. *Journal of Business Research*, 68(12), 2484–2493. doi:10.1016/j.jbusres.2015.06.035

Caprariello, P. A., & Reis, H. T. (2013). To do, to have, or to share? Valuing experiences over material possessions depends on the involvement of others. *Journal of Personality and Social Psychology*, 104(2), 199–215. doi:10.1037/a0030953

Cheng, B., Ioannou, I., & Serafeim, G. (2014). Corporate social responsibility and access to finance. *Strategic Management Journal*, 35(1), 1–23.

De Keyser, A., & Lariviere, B. (2014). How technical and functional service quality drive consumer happiness: Moderating influences of channel usage. *Journal of Service Management*, 25(1), 30–48. doi:10.1108/JOSM-04-2013-0109

Desmeules, R. (2002). The impact of variety on consumer happiness: Marketing and the tyranny of freedom. *Academy of Marketing Science Review*, 12, 1–18.

Edmans, E. (2012). The link between job satisfaction and firm value, with implications for corporate social responsibility. *Academy of Management Journal*, 26(4), 1–19.

Esterl, M. (2012, January 13). PepsiCo board stands by Nooyi: Shareholders grouse but company unlikely to break up. *Wall Street Journal*, B1.

Gilovich, T., Kumar, A., & Jampol, L. (2015). A wonderful life: Experiential consumption and the pursuit of happiness. *Journal of Consumer Psychology*, 25(1), 152–165. doi:10.1016/j.jcps.2014.08.004

Gopaldas, A. (2015). Creating firm, customer and societal value. *Journal of Business Research*, 68(12), 2446–2451. doi:10.1016/j.jbusres.2015.06.031

Hsee, C. K., & Hastie, R. (2006). Decision and experience: Why don't we choose what makes us happy? *Trends in Cognitive Science*, 10(1), 31–37. doi:10.1016/j.tics.2005.11.007

Kachersky, L., & Lerman, D. (2013). Bridging marketing's intentions and consumer perceptions. *Journal of Consumer Marketing*, 30, 544–552. doi:10.1108/JCM-06-2013-0624

Kachersky, L., Lerman, D., & Flicker, M. (2013). Imbalanced implications in marketing research. Proceedings from the 2nd Annual Conference for Positive Marketing, New York, NY.

Kristjánsson, K. (2013). *Virtues and vices in positive psychology: A philosophical critique.* New York: Cambridge University Press.

Kumar, V., & Shah, D. (2009). Expanding the role of marketing: From customer equity to market capitalization. *Journal of Marketing*, 73(6), 119–136. doi:10.1509/jmkg.73.6.119.

Kumar, V., & Shah, D. (2011, June 22). Can marketing lift stock prices? *MIT Sloan Management Review.* Retrieved from http://sloanreview.mit.edu/article/can-marketing-lift-stock-prices/

Lerman, D. (2016). Reflections on refocusing business education: A human-centered approach. In T. de Waal Malefyt & R. J. Morais (Eds.), *Ethics in the anthropology of business: Explorations in theory, practice and pedagogy.* New York: Routledge.

Lerman, D., & Kachersky, L. (2012, May 2). Walmart's (in)action in Mexico hurts everyday Americans. *Huffington Post.* Retrieved from www.huffingtonpost.com/dawn-lerman/walmarts-inaction-in-mexi_b_1471583.html

Lerman, D., & Shefrin, H., (2015). Positive marketing: Introduction to the special section, *Journal of Business Research*, 68(12), 2443–2445, https://EconPapers.repec.org/RePEc:eee:jbrese:v:68:y:2015:i:12:p:2443-2445.

Lyubomirsky, S. (2008). *The how of happiness: A scientific approach to getting the life you want*. New York, NY: Penguin Press.

Lyubomirsky, S., Tkach, C., & DiMatteo, M. R. (2006). What are the differences between happiness and self-esteem. *Social Indicators Research, 78*(3), 363–404. doi:10.1007/s11205-005-0213-y

McDaniel, S. W., & Rylander, D. H. (1993). Strategic green marketing. *Journal of Consumer Marketing, 10*(3), 4–10. doi:10.1108/07363769310041929

Mittelstaedt, J. D., Kilbourne, W. E., & Shultz, II, C. J. (2015). Macromarketing approaches to thought development in positive marketing: Two perspectives on a research agenda for positive marketing scholars. *Journal of Business Research, 68*(12), 2513–2516. doi:10.1016/j.jbusres.2015.06.038

Mogilner, C., Aaker, J., & Kamvar, S. (2012). How happiness affects choice. *Journal of Consumer Research, 39*(2), 429–443. doi:10.1086/663774

Parekh, R. (2012, October 24). Marketers rate below politicians, bankers on respectability scale. *Advertising Age*. Retrieved from http://adage.com/article/news/marketers-rate-politicians-bankers-respectability/237937/

Petersen, J. A., McAlister, L., Reibstein, D. J., Winer, R. S., Kumar, V., & Atkinson, G. (2009). Choosing the right metrics to maximize profitability and shareholder value. *Journal of Retailing, 85*(1), 95–111. doi:10.1016/j.jretai.2008.11.004

Pirson, M. (2017). *Humanistic management: Protecting dignity and promoting well-being*. New York, NY: Cambridge University Press.

Porter, M. E., & Kramer, M. R. (2006). The link between competitive advantage and corporate social responsibility. *Harvard Business Review, 84*(12), 78–92.

Sääksjärvi, M., Hellén, K., & Desmet, P. (2016). The effects of the experience recommendation on short and long-term happiness. *Marketing Letters, 27*(4), 675–686. doi:10.1007/s11002-015-9382-x

Stoeckl, V. E., & Luedicke, M. K. (2015). Doing well while doing good? An integrative review of marketing criticism and response. *Journal of Business Research, 68*(12), 2452–2463. doi:10.1016/j.jbusres.2015.06.032

Tay, L., & Diener, E. (2011). Needs and subjective well-being around the world. *Journal of Personality and Social Psychology, 101*(2), 354. doi:10.1037/a0023779

Varadarajan, P. R., & Menon, A. (1988). Cause-related marketing: A coalignment of marketing strategy and corporate philanthropy. *Journal of Marketing, 52*(3), 58–74. doi:10.2307/1251450

V-Positive Report. (2017). *Center for positive marketing*. Retrieved from www.centerforpositivemarketing.org/about-c1et

Wang, Y. (2013). *Happiness Marketing course syllabus*. Retrieved July 3, 2017 from www3.ubishops.ca/fileadmin/bishops_documents/course_outlines/2013/fall/wsb/BMK355-Fall- 2013-Wang.pdf

Yonavjak, L., & Galizia, M. (2013, October 8). What is a "meaningful" brand? Retrieved from https://cbeyale.wordpress.com/2013/10/08/what-is-a-meaningful-brand/

17

ADVERTISING AND AUTHENTIC HAPPINESS

Can They Be Good Friends?

José Antonio Muñiz-Velázquez and Juan F. Plaza

Introduction: Advertising, Happiness, and Unhappiness

In the advertising industry, no one wants anyone to be happy since happy people do not consume. This idea is what the French publicist Beigbeder asserted (2002) in his incendiary autobiographical novel. Beyond this literary anecdote, the truth is that the relationship between advertising, happiness, and well-being has long been controversial (O'Guinn, Allen, & Semenik, 2007). From the beginning, modern advertising has based its foundations on the proposal of an implicit sale, an underlying promise that will always be the same. This is the promise of nothing other than happiness that is attainable through the consumption of the products that it advertises. Therefore, advertising is called "the happiness factory," but it is a factory of false and superficial happiness (Eguizábal, 2007) and is always related to a product.

However, by promising such happiness based on consumption, what advertising communication truly spreads are unhappiness, dissatisfaction, and unease. By appearing to be a continuous source of desirable objects, what is actually conveyed is a feeling of something desired yet missing, which leads to a particular emptiness that, in the long-term, could be associated with a generalized discontent with life. Advertising needs to demonstrate a problem or deficiency to be able to offer a solution later, i.e., the products. Thus, advertising could lead us to a chronic state of dissatisfaction, which is antagonistic to the state of fullness, which supports happiness (Csikszentmihalyi, 2008).

Accordingly, except for a few cases in which advertising has been defended (Cohan, 2001), most approaches and analyses have related commercial advertising to unease and unhappiness rather than to well-being or happiness (André, 2004) from different perspectives: advertising and subjective social comparisons as well as creating psychological unrest (Richins, 1995); advertising and anxiety created by status (Botton, 2004); advertising, family, and social conflict (Buijzen & Valkenburg, 2003); advertising and more serious psychopathological disorders, such as eating disorders (Termini, Roberto, & Hostetter, 2011), among many others (Sarason & Sarason, 1984).

It is not easy to associate advertising with happiness, whether hedonia or eudaimonia. At a hedonic level of human happiness (see Hervás & Chaves, 2018), for example, the distance between our subjective well-being and commercial advertising can be significant in several ways. For instance, consider the mental timeframe in which individuals usually move. If we assume that thinking systematically (only) in the future implies certain damage to psychological well-being, it is easy to realize that advertising can harm us in this regard. The advertising mechanism of generating desires in consumers and maintaining a continuous state of desire may interfere with their perception of life satisfaction.

Moreover, excessive satisfaction from hedonistic desires and pleasure associated with advertised products or brands cannot be a good friend who makes one happy. It is true that hedonism is not completely antagonistic to our well-being. Veenhoven (2003, p. 437), who defines hedonism as "a way of life in which pleasure plays an important role," says that there is an inverted U relationship between the two variables. That is, hedonism and hedonic happiness are positively correlated to some extent, but when hedonism crosses a certain threshold, it begins to become negatively correlated. Accordingly, Irvine (2008) says that we spend our lives attempting to achieve the objects of our desires, and he is convinced that if we had what we wanted, we would find this ever-present happiness. However, when we get what we want, we discover that this act only offers transient happiness.

On the other hand, from the eudaimonic point of view, the question is even more critical. From Aristotle's time, individual happiness has not been understood without considering collective happiness, so it will be linked inexorably to ethics (Camps, 2013). Thus, it appears difficult to find a reconciliation between happiness and a discourse such as advertising, which has traditionally glorified the individual and the satisfaction of his desires above all other considerations, accordingly nurturing his narcissism. Additionally, Rifkin (2010) says that narcissism became the preferred ammunition for the advertising industry, in which it appeared to be feedback for personal insecurities and the need to be accepted. Certainly, this way of life, depending on others' opinions, appears to be highly correlated with unhappiness and dissatisfaction with life in general (Lyubomirsky, 2008).

At this point, if commercial advertising creates, provokes, or arouses desires and pushes us into immediate fulfillment, we could only relate this to hedonism, narcissism, and individualism. Therefore, would it be possible to reconcile advertising and real well-being? Is there any further scope for consideration in which advertising could have positive effects on people's happiness—happiness that is not spurious but authentic in current scientific terms? This does not appear easy, but it is certainly not impossible.

Reconciling Contemporary Advertising and (Authentic) Happiness

According to the previously described scenario, studies on the psychological effects of advertising, as in other areas of mass communication research, have traditionally been between positions that minimized such effects and those that maximized them from a negative and adverse point of view but never from a positive perspective. It was normal to hear that advertising has been negatively influencing behaviors and ways of being and thinking negatively (González Martín, 1991). Instead, we argue that it is also possible that certain forms of behavior, being or thinking generated by advertising can also be positive. Is it possible for commercial advertising to have psychological effects related to positive growth? Could it teach us values and therefore help us to build our happiness not just in hedonic terms but also in a eudaimonic dimension?

An association between advertising and hedonia appears simpler since some advertisements promote positive emotions, at least in the short-term. For example, when using humor or aesthetics, the message itself provides hedonic or subjective well-being, enjoyment, etc. However, if we focus on the level of human thriving in eudaimonic terms, growing evidence of this connection also appears. This can be observed not only in consumption sectors or industries that are closer to one another, for example, but this presence of values and virtues in the clearly commercial advertising discourses has been increasing over the last several years.

We have had to waiting to observe advertising campaigns that are putting their focus on human values with notable frequency (Chang, 2006; Romero & Sánchez, 2012). Somehow, it appears that many other advertisers and agencies have picked up the gauntlet that Ogilvy &

Mather threw down with its *The big ideaL™*, a strategic vision that builds brand communication in association with an ideal or a social cause, in the first decade of the current century. One agency that has also taken this path is Leo Burnett. With its *Humantype* framework, they want to "return marketing to that nobler thing" (Bernardin & Tutssel, 2010, p. 14), for which it is essential to understand what it means really to be human—a person—beyond a consumer.

Along the same lines, the international movement for constructing a model and guidelines for positive marketing, in which positive advertising should be included, is paradigmatic. This movement is supported by different initiatives around the world, as we read in the previous chapter by Lerman and Mejia (2018). Following these authors, the ultimate goal of marketing, and therefore of commercial communication and advertising, should be to contribute to the real well-being of the consumer and society.

The same notion in different words can be found in the model of *goodvertising* by Kolster (2012); *goodvertising* is a neologism that simply means to do good through advertising that is intended as a real benefit for the individual, society, and the planet. Along these line, for example, *femvertising* and other growing and current advertising trends can be included. We can summarize the essence of this trend as advertising that empowers women in one sense or another. Zayer, Coleman, and Rodriguez Orjuela (2018) illustrate this in this book in greater depth.

However, to approach to all these recent positive tendencies in a more inclusive way, especially if we consider the eudaimonic dimension of human well-being, we can use the classic model of six virtues and 24 character strengths by Peterson and Seligman (2004), which we can see in Table 17.1. This table is a model used in recent positive psychological research that analyzes the underlying positive values in a commercial message or campaign.

Table 17.1 The 24 character strengths

Set of six virtues and twenty-four character strengths

Virtue 1: Wisdom and knowledge: Cognitive strengths that entail the acquisition and use of knowledge.
1. **Creativity:** thinking of novel and productive ways to perform tasks.
2. **Curiosity**: taking an interest in the entirety of an ongoing experience.
3. **Judgment**: thoroughly considering matters and examining them from all sides.
4. **Love of learning:** mastering new skills, topics, and bodies of knowledge.
5. **Perspective:** being able to provide wise counsel to others.

Virtue 2: Courage: Emotional strengths that involve the exercise of will to accomplish goals in the face of opposition, external or internal.
6. **Honesty:** speaking the truth and presenting oneself in a genuine way.
7. **Bravery**: not shrinking from threats, challenges, difficulty, or pain.
8. **Persistence**: finishing what one starts.
9. **Zest:** Approaching life with excitement and energy; not doing things halfway or halfheartedly; living life as an adventure; feeling alive and activated.

Virtue 3: Humanity: Interpersonal strengths that involve "tending and befriending" others.
10. **Kindness:** doing favors and good deeds for others.
11. **Love:** valuing close relations with others.
12. **Social intelligence:** being aware of the motives and feelings of oneself and others.

Virtue 4: Justice: Civic strengths that underlie healthy community life.
13. **Fairness:** treating all people the same according to notions of fairness and justice.
14. **Leadership:** organizing group activities and ensuring that they happen.
15. **Teamwork:** working well as a member of a group or team.

Table 17.1 Continued

Set of six virtues and twenty-four character strengths

Virtue 5: Temperance: Strengths that protect against excess.

16. **Forgiveness:** forgiving those who have done wrong.
17. **Modesty:** letting one's accomplishments speak for themselves.
18. **Prudence:** being careful about one's choices; not saying or doing anything that might be regretted later.
19. **Self-regulation or self-control:** regulating what one feels and does.

Virtue 6: Transcendence: Strengths that forge connections to the larger universe and provide meaning.

20. **Appreciation of beauty and excellence**: noticing and appreciating beauty, excellence, and/or skilled performance in all domains of life.
21. **Gratitude:** being aware of and thankful for good things that happen; taking time to express thanks.
22. **Hope and optimism:** expecting the best and working to achieve it; believing that a good future is something that can be manifested.
23. **Humor:** liking to laugh and joke; making others smile.
24. **Spirituality, religiousness, faith, purpose:** having coherent beliefs about the higher purpose and meaning of the universe; having beliefs about the meaning of life that shape conduct and provide comfort.

(Source: Parki, Peterson, & Seligman, 2006)

Advertising and Character Strengths

In line with the observation of values in advertising from a broader perspective, Pollay (1986) elaborated upon his classic "distorted mirror theory," in which he extracted a set of quasi-universal values present in advertising. Indeed, 11 of the 42 values noted by the author would be close to some of Peterson & Seligman's character strengths, such as morality, humility, modesty, plainness, security, nurturance, family, community, health, neatness, and succor.

Along these lines, Castelló Martínez, Ramos Soler, and del Pino Romero (2013) studied the positive values that advertising discourse started to construct in the last years. After an advertising campaign sampling in Spanish media, they conclude that, unlike the self-centeredness, utilitarianism, and materialism that prevailed in the advertising discourse from better times before the recent economic crisis, current discourses begin to focus on people and social and altruistic responsibility.

Davis and Brotherton (2013) related current advertising to human thriving in their analysis. They focus on analyzing how the appeal of human thriving is being used by advertising professionals, albeit in an incipient way. However, their study is based only on three case studies; recognizing its limitations, the authors appeal to the scientific community "to recognize the popularity and usefulness of the human thriving appeal and to begin to study it in greater depth" (Davis & Brotherton, 2013, p. 92).

It appears that commercial advertising campaigns can also convey examples and models of virtuous behavior and eudaimonic values with or without the agency or advertiser's clear intention and apart from specific marketing goals. Furthermore, both marketing goals and eudaimonic values can be good friends, as we observed in a recent study. To understand the extent to which successful advertising campaigns had messages associated with eudaimonic values, we put the focus on winning campaigns in the EFI Prizes awarded by the Advertisers Association in Spain from 2009 to 2014 (Muñiz-Velázquez, Lozano-Delmar, & Plaza, 2014).

Four previously trained observers independently oversaw, quantified, and coded the presence or absence of Peterson & Seligman's character strengths. The presence of some specific examples was accepted if the discourse of the campaign, according to observers, attempted to encourage behaviors conducive to the cultivation of that strength in the receiver implicitly or explicitly. They found that while 33 percent of winning campaigns had associated their brands or products with at least one character strength in 2009, in 2013, this percentage increases to 75 percent. This appears to be a lasting trend.

In the 2017 Super Bowl, most commercials had associated positive values closely to eudaimonic values. We examined the more successful commercials in this event based on the Super Bowl Ad Review prepared by the Kellogg Business School at Northwestern University (Muñiz-Velázquez, 2017).

We can even find a relationship between advertising and one of the more remote a priori character strengths with regard to commercial communication: spirituality, a key factor in a several aspects of happiness (Van Dierendock, 2012). In this sense, it is worth mentioning the research done by Marmor-Lavie and her colleagues. With their Spirituality in Advertising Framework (SAF), they analyzed a good set of advertising discourses and found that they were imbued with core spiritual ideas—research that we can see also in this book (see Marmor-Lavie, 2018).

Thus, we are gradually legitimized to speak of a "eudaimonic ROI" as a return on advertising investment in terms of psychological well-being on the public that is independent of the advertiser marketing goals. Furthermore, we propose that this alleged "eudaimonic ROI" would be good for advertising and marketing objectives; that is, eudaimonic advertising could also be effective advertising.

Conclusion and Final Questions

Divesting happiness of scientific disregard has been a lengthy battle given the scorn and pejorative aspects with which a large number of contemporary intellectuals and scientists have associated it. *Denial* of a possible existence of full happiness in *this* life has been denied to people from the Middle Ages until the end of the 20th century (Bok, 2010). Russell (1971) issued a warning about our fate of eternal unhappiness, which has been imposed on humanity in literary, philosophical, or artistic scopes. We find that Schopenhauer affirmed that even happiness is always negative, being limited only to the termination of pain. We can also examine psychoanalysis, such the "Freudian scientific myth" according to Onfray (2011, p. 165), which is one of the main agents of the limited and limiting Western conception of happiness, which, by contrast, appears to be a great ally, not only of the consumption socioeconomic system but also of hyper utilitarianism (Rifkin, 2010). If full happiness is impossible to achieve in this life, at least we have consumption.

Fortunately, over the last two decades, several modern branches of science have been rejecting these ideas without denying its complexity. Mainly due to positive psychology, human happiness is its own scientific topic. When we talk about happiness today, we know we are talking about hedonia or subjective well-being as well as eudaimonia, which is wider than a hedonic step (Huta, 2016) that is translated to psychological well-being and the fulfillment of life through virtue. Moreover, several authors add a third dimension, social well-being, in a triadic and more holistic conception of happiness (Keyes, 2002; Hervás & Vázquez, 2013) to human flourishing (Seligman, 2011).

It is reasonable to question whether this new positive outlook can be extrapolated to other scientific and professional areas, such as the field in which we are interested: advertising communication. It is time to inquire whether it is possible to have another relationship between this integral and scientifically supported notion of happiness and a new advertising paradigm.

This paper intends to show that a type of "eudaimonic advertising" is a reality today, a reality that has been arising since the last decade, even between successful campaigns. Therefore, the critical views described at the beginning of this chapter may be incorrect, outdated, or at least incomplete.

Future studies should delve into the relationship between certain types of character strengths and advertisers, specific business sectors, products, etc. Likewise, it would also be interesting to conduct a longitudinal observation to establish whether this trend signifies a profound change to "eudaimonic advertising" or if it is just a passing tendency. It would also be interesting to observe not only advertising messages but also their effects on the individual psyche. Beyond the "goodness" of the ad content, can advertising facilitate subjective and psychological well-being? Another interesting debate questions whether these possible "eudaimonic campaigns" might even have certain adverse effects. For example, could they arouse negative emotions in the audience by exposing their own lack of eudaimonia?

There are many ways to proceed. In the aforementioned positive psychology, a field that assesses what makes life worth living, Seligman and Csikszentmihalyi (2000) state that reconciliation between commercial advertising and hedonic and eudaimonic happiness finally appear possible. Thus, it is not only ethically desirable but also possible to construct a marketing campaign that sells products, services, and brands while "selling" sincere, transparent, and mature well-being—happiness that obviously does not deny consumption but also does not rely on it, less so on consumerism.

Post (2005) asserted that practicing virtue and being good to oneself and others is beneficial, especially for the people who practice this behavior. At this point, we believe that this is true not only for individuals but also for brands and advertising. Positive advertising is good for marketing communication effectiveness in addition to being good for recipients, their well-being, and society as a whole.

References

André, C. (2004). *El placer de vivir: Psicología de la Felicidad*. Barcelona: Kairós.

Beigbeder, F. (2002). *13,99 Euros*. Barcelona: Anagrama.

Bernardin, T., & Tutssel, M. (2010). *Humankind*. New York, NY: PowerHouse Books.

Bok, S. (2010). *Exploring happiness: From Aristotle to brain science*. New Haven, CT: Yale University Press.

Botton, A. (2004). *Ansiedad por el estatus*. Madrid: Taurus.

Buijzen, M., & Valkenburg, P. M. (2003). The effects of television advertising on materialism, parent-child conflict, and unhappiness: A review of research. *Journal of Applied Developmental Psychology, 24*(4), 437–456. https://doi.org/10.1016/S0193-3973(03)00072-8

Camps, V. (2013). *Breve historia de la ética*. Barcelona: RBA.

Castelló Martínez, A., Ramos Soler, I., & del Pino Romero, C. (2013). El discurso publicitario en la crisis económica: nuevos valores y redes sociales. *Historia y Comunicación Social, 18*, 657–672.

Chang, C. C. (2006). Beating the news blues: Mood repair through exposure to advertising. *Journal of Communication, 56*(1), 198–217. doi:10.1111/j.1460-2466.2006.00010.x

Cohan, J. A. (2001). Towards a new paradigm in the ethics of women's advertising. *Journal of Business Ethics, 33*(4), 323–337. https://doi.org/10.1023/A:1011862332426

Csikszentmihalyi, M. (2008). *Fluir*. Barcelona: Random House Mondadori.

Davis, C., & Brotherton, T. (2013). Human flourishing theory in advertising: Case studies. *Journal of Marketing Development and Competitiveness, 7*(2), 83–94.

Eguizábal, R. (2007). *Teoría de la publicidad*. Madrid: Cátedra.

González Martín, J. A. (1991). La comunicación publicitaria. In J. A. González Martín, S. Zunzunegui, & R. Oleaga (Eds.), *La publicidad, desde el consumidor* (pp. 13–57). Elorrio: Eroski.

Hervás, G., & Chaves, C. (2018). What can science can tell us about human happiness (and why and how should we disseminate it)? In J. A. Muñiz-Velázquez & C. Pulido (Eds.), *The Routledge Handbook of Positive Communication* (pp. 20–28). New York, NY: Routledge.

Hervás, G., & Vázquez, C. (2013). Construction and validation of a measure of integrative well-being in seven languages: The Pemberton Happiness Index. *Health and Quality of Life Outcomes, 11*, 66. https://doi.org/10.1186/1477-7525-11-66

Huta, V. (2016). An overview of hedonic and eudaimonic well-being concepts. In L. Reinecke & M. B. Oliver (Eds.). *Handbook of media use and well-being* (pp. 14–33). New York, NY: Routledge.

Irvine, W. B. (2008). *Sobre el deseo. Por qué queremos lo que queremos.* Barcelona: Paidós.

Keyes, C. L. M. (2002). The mental health continuum: From languishing to flourishing in life. *Journal of Health Social Behaviour, 43*, 207–222.

Kolster (2012). *Goodvertising: Creative advertising that cares by Thomas Kolster.* New York: Thames & Hudson Inc.

Lerman, D., & Mejia, S. (2018). Positive marketing, virtue and happiness. In J. A. Muñiz-Velázquez & C. Pulido (Eds.), *The Routledge Handbook of Positive Communication* (pp. 151–159). New York, NY: Routledge.

Lyubomirsky, S. (2008). *The how of happiness: A scientific approach to getting the life you want.* New York, NY: Penguin Press.

Marmor-Lavie, G (2018). Spirituality and advertising. In J. A. Muñiz-Velázquez, & C. Pulido (Eds.), *The Routledge Handbook of Positive Communication* (pp. 213–222). New York: Routledge.

Muñiz-Velázquez, J. A. (2017). Cinco grandes lecciones publicitarias. *Harvard Deusto Marketing y Ventas, 146*, 50–56.

Muñiz-Velázquez, J. A., Lozano-Delmar, J., & Plaza, J. F. (2014). *Advertising effectiveness and eudaimonic happiness can be good friends.* Paper presented at the Positive Marketing Conference, New York, NY: Fordham University.

O'Guinn, T. C., Allen, C. T., & Semenik, R. J. (2007). *Publicidad y comunicación integral de marca.* México, DF: Thomson.

Onfray, M. (2011). *Freud. El crepúsculo de un ídolo.* Madrid: Taurus.

Parki, N., Peterson, C., & Seligman, M. E. P. (2006). Character strengths in fifty-four nations and the fifty US states. *The Journal of Positive Psychology, 1*(3), 118–129.

Peterson, C., & Seligman, M. E. P. (2004). *Character strengths and virtues: A handbook and classification.* Oxford: Oxford University Press.

Pollay, R. W. (1986). The distorted mirror: Reflections on the unintended consequences of advertising. *Journal of Marketing, 50*, 15–36.

Post, S. (2005). Altruism, happiness, and health: It's good to be good: International. *Journal of Behavioral Medicine, 12*(2), 66–77. doi:10.1207/s15327558ijbm1202_4

Richins, M. L. (1995). Social comparasion, advertising and consumer discontent. *American Behavioral Scientist, 38*, 593–607.

Rifkin, J. (2010). *The empathic civilization: The race to global consciousness in a world in crisis.* New York City: Jeremy P. Tarcher Inc.

Romero, M., & Sánchez, M. (2012). Análisis del uso del impacto emocional y la felicidad como recursos publicitarios en tiempos de crisis. In *II Congreso Publiradio.* Barcelona: Universidad Autónoma de Barcelona.

Russell, B. (1971). *The conquest of happiness.* New York, NY: Liberight.

Sarason, I. G., & Sarason, B. R. (1984). *Abnormal psychology: The problem of maladaptive behavior.* Englewood Cliffs, NJ: Prentice-Hall, Inc.

Seligman, M. E. P. (2011). *Flourish: A visionary new understanding of happiness and well-being.* New York, NY: The Free Press.

Seligman, M. E. P., & Csikszentmihalyi, M. (2000). Positive psychology: An introduction. *American Psychologist, 55*, 5–14.

Termini, R. B., Roberto, T. A., & Hostetter, S. G. (2011). Food advertising and childhood obesity: A call to action for proactive solutions. *Minnesota Journal of Law, Science & Technology, 12*(2), 619–651.

Van Dierendock, D. (2012). Spirituality as an essential determinant for the good life, its importance relative to self-determinant psychological needs. *Journal of Happiness Studies, 13*, 685–700. https://doi.org/10.1007/s10902-011-9286-2

Veenhoven, R. (2003). Hedonism and happiness. *Journal of Happiness Studies, 4*, 437–457. https://doi.org/10.1023/B:JOHS.0000005719.56211.fd

Zayer, L., Coleman, C. A., & Rodriguez Orjuela, J. L. (2018). Femvertising discourses and online consumer engagement: A case analysis of under Armour's #IWillWhatIWant brand campaign. In J. A. Muñiz-Velázquez & C. Pulido (Eds.), *The Routledge Handbook of Positive Communication* (pp. 203–212). New York, NY: Routledge.

18

BRAND ENGAGEMENT AND POSITIVE ADVERTISING

David Alameda and Irene Martín

Introduction

This chapter explores how a positive advertising approach and managing brands with a conscience generate greater engagement with the consumer. The focus in recent years has been on how brands are using their marketing and advertising strategies to develop positive messages where the brand reaches out to consumers according to their interests and lifestyles. Different researchers have started to concentrate on achieving happiness in the consumer. The emphasis has therefore been on adding the happiness concept to the brands (Mogilner & Aaker, 2009), which implies developing marketing strategies where happiness is the focal point. Brands, products, and services use happiness as the main purchasing advantage, whether implicitly or explicitly, to move and touch the heart of consumers, become involved in their life expectations or values connected with the idea of being happy. However, the same type of happiness is not used in the current strategies of the brands. On the one hand, a series of advertising pitches that follow the paradigm of hedonistic happiness can be seen. In other words, they are advertising strategies where choosing the product or services increases the happiness of the consumer. Yet, on the other hand, there is currently another way of addressing happiness in advertising and involves using brand pitches that transmit positive values in line with the paradigm of eudaimonic happiness. In this case, "positive advertising" is used, which focuses on values such as well-being in society, safety, calmness, sharing with others, opportunities, and character strengths. Thus, brands are like people, with their own identity and conscience, far removed from the individual sphere focused on hedonism and on success that advertising strategies promoted in the past.

Hedonia, Eudaimonia, and Their Link to the Brands

The search for happiness is consistently present in the human being. Positive psychology studies it, and its relationship with creativity, flow, resilience, optimism, human, emotional intelligence, and the rest of the components of well-being. In this sense, can brands in the current context contribute to the (real) happiness of consumers? If we strive to build our brands, products or services on some of the above concepts, we will perhaps be nearer to achieving our consumers not only displaying their conviction, but also their preference and affection. The brands that manage to trigger feelings of well-being seem to fill emotional spaces and possibly change the way of seeing the world. That is where the connection, the engagement, between people and brands lie, in the capacity to recover those states of feeling positive, absent, or lost in modern society.

Therefore, companies must focus not only on establishing the very characteristics of their products, but also on recognizing the needs, desires, and interests that drive people to prefer them, the purchasing decision process of consumers and the fundamental reasons for their decisions (Pike, Bianchi, Kerr, & Patti, 2010).

As we can read in other chapters of this volume, the majority of researchers agree that the contents of well-being fall under two higher-order umbrellas, hedonia and Eudaimonia, and that it is important to assess concepts from both umbrellas (Ryan & Deci, 2001). As Huta (2017) points out, hedonic contents imply pleasure, enjoyment, satisfaction and comfort, painlessness, and ease. These variables are associated with certain mind-sets, including a balance between focusing on the self, the present moment and the tangible, and a focus on taking and consuming what one needs and wants. On the other hand, Huta and Waterman (2014) found contents that appeared in the majority of or all eudaimonic-related definitions: meaning, value, relevancy in a broader context, personal growth, self-fulfilment, maturity and excellence, ethics, quality and authenticity, autonomy, and integration. These variables are associated with certain mind-sets, including a balance of focusing on the self and on others, a balance between focusing on the present and the future, a tendency to be guided by abstract and big picture concepts, and a focus on cultivating and building what one values and envisages.

However, if we want to discover how the brands think to respond to those contents linked to happiness and to well-being, we have to think about how people consume and the variability in that consumer response. The most important changes in the brand landscape have been the outcome of the changes in the consumers, in their motivations and needs. There is currently a different type of need, that of the people who use the brands to express themselves and reinforce their personality, by embracing the essence of the brand and becoming in tune with the community of people that the brand itself has generated.

People, as consumers, look for products and brands whose cultural meanings match what we aspire to be and therefore they combine hedonic and eudaimonic variables. The purchase criteria depend on consumer behavior, determined by a set of acts that comprise the personal identity. This identity, determined by external influences such as society, competitors' brands, etc., will mature (with their maturity being taken to mean their self-fulfilment) and, we can thus conclude, become more human.

The *How Brands Influence People's Happiness* report (La Despensa, 2017), directly relating to hedonic contents, highlights a recent change in the behavior of Spaniards with the arrival of micro-happiness: everyday small things are those that bring most happiness. Emotional aspects continue to be better positioned than the functional aspects. The study reveals a different happiness concept, much realer and more present in everyday life, known as micro-happiness. This consists of the sum of small moments based on the "here and now" and challenges that are achievable in the short-medium term; namely, dreams in the framework of the possible. In other words, we can directly link it to hedonia, but not that alone. That "here and now" is seen as being too fleeting for a consumer who strives further and whose aspiration includes a huge desire for self-fulfilment with deeper needs associated to eudaimonism. The latter is deemed by brands to be more sustainable in the long-term. Therefore, both contents are considered to be necessary and complementary to achieve that well-being sought by the individuals and to which the brands are faced with the challenge of contributing.

Therefore, the brands must construct a well-defined specific personality, while they combine the whole communication strategy around human values that are integral to their identity and essence with contents that not only speak of micro-happiness—hedonic contents—but also eudaimonic ones. The key is to place the people as the main characters of the narratives and position the brand as an active partner of that relationship, listening, and understanding, if it wants to remain a leader in a changing environment (De Salas, 2016, p. 174).

Positive Marketing

The current economic context, where many of the values and principles of the consumer economy as they have been understood since the 1960s are being questioned, means that other realms that bring companies closer to the consumer should be explored. The globalization of the markets, the communication technologies and their ensuing glut of information, the lack of trust in the institutions, and the empowerment of the consumer are some of these new realms that are already situated in the so-called post-truth society. Furthermore, the corporate marketing communications with their potential audiences are not only faced with those generated by the other competitors of their sector, as was the case in the former product-focused paradigm, but also with all the other stimuli to which potential consumers may turn their attention (attention economy in the words of Goldhaber, 2006).

Precisely, it is not sustainable to continue communicating a product level and in terms of supply and demand in this context of lack of attention and glut of information and where there has been a shift in the trust shown toward the companies. The goal is no longer merely to satisfy a consumer with a quality product, but it is also to associate it with positive thoughts and moods to meet a higher and universal need, happiness. Accordingly, positive marketing seeks to achieve a connection between the happiness of the customer and the brand of the company. The time when marketing strategies focused on the virtues of the product has passed, and we are now witnessing a new marketing concept where powerful brands that provide the consumer with value are needed to generate relevancy on the market. If the previous marketing was to do with products, marketing today is related with the experiences that it provides to the consumer. Furthermore, those experiences are better remembered and, therefore, with a possibility for brand affiliation if based on the emotional. This emotional branding (Gobé, 2005) aspires to generate relevant and unique brand experiences in the consumer. Human brands and those that awaken greater feeling in people will be those that generate greater emotional links with consumers, those that go beyond rational arguments or showcasing the virtues of the product (De Salas, 2016, p. 169). Happiness among the positive emotions is essential in consumer behavior (Bagozzi, Gopinath, & Nyer, 1999). Bettingen and Luedicke (2009) also argue that happiness may result from consumer experiences with the brands. Based on the premise that brands may affect happiness, brands that can be expected to make customers happy will have a competitive edge that may lead to brand preference, brand loyalty, and ultimately, brand capital.

The positive marketing is based on the new paradigm of the happiness economy that links the term happiness with the Aristotelian concept of eudaimonism, with well-being or the good life in contrast to hedonism. The happiness economy derives from the well-being economy, a branch of the economy developed in Europe and the United States from the second half of the 20th century and that seeks in a humanist resurgence to find the link between the economy and the well-being of people. Specifically, the happiness economy seeks to explain the relationship existing between happiness and the economy, and to use subjective measures of satisfaction with life as a reflection of utility.

The studies conducted so far within the happiness economy have shown a very limited relationship between the level of income or possessions and happiness. This is known as the noted Easterlin Paradox (1974), which has been corroborated years later (Layard, 2005). Those findings coincide to a great extent with the happiness definition proposed by Seligman (2011), where he links it to well-being and proposes a model that allows that happiness to be achieved. This model, known by the acronym PERMA, comprises five aspects of human life: positive emotion, engagement, relationship, meaning, and accomplishment. In turn, Dolad, Peasgood, and White (2008, p. 97) consider that the generic influences of happiness (using measures of satisfaction) include "income, personal characteristics, socially developed characteristics, how respondents spend their time, attitudes and beliefs toward self/others/life, relationships, and the wider economic, social and political environment." However, as Bettingen and Luedicke (2009, p. 310) point out, much recent research coincides that happiness depends on personal characteristics and life circumstances.

In this regard, marketing needs to reach out to the assumptions of the happiness economy, as its brands, products, and messages need to connect with the consumers who are shifting to becoming beings driven by the search for their well-being and their happiness. Based on this trend, a new customer-company relationship paradigm has emerged underpinned by the following principles (EOI, 2015):

- Happiness is reached thanks to perception of coincidence between what companies do with the values of the customer.
- A happy customer gives more importance to their relationship with the brand and not so much to the product purchased.
- Making what is expected to coincide with what the company gives or does is a way of obtaining happy customers.
- Satisfaction-based marketing has customers, while the organizations seeking happiness have opinion leaders, loyal and lucrative brand fans.
- Marketing that reduces relations to merely commercial interactions only achieves satisfied but not happy customers, who are obtained by observing the individual and their environment and bringing the brand in line with their way of life, concerns, and values. However, authors such as Hanson and Arjoon (2010) have researched the topic and discovered that are six marketing activities or stimuli that help to determine the happiness of the consumer: sales and discounts, special offers, more reasonable or low prices, gifts, excellent quality service, and the first-rate quality of the products. As we can see, the elements identified with the happiness generation continue to be closely linked to the components of the traditional marketing mix or 4 Ps.

In this new model, the company finds that it has to change its mindset to adopt new attitudes that make it relevant for its audience. What were previously communication plans can be called cooperation plans in the best of hypotheses: cooperation with the public in the search for meaning (Cavallo, 2015, p. 17).

From this approach, the brands that most contribute are those that are created and managed to benefit not only the organization itself, but also society and its set of stakeholders (Ind & Horlings, 2016; Gopaldas, 2015). This same meaning can be found in the very definition of the positive marketing concept of Fordham University (2011): "Positive marketing is marketing in its ideal form in which parties—individual customers, marketers, and society as a whole-exchange value such that individually and collectively they are better off than they were prior to exchange." They are the so-called brands with a conscience that have a clear purpose and shared beliefs that imply that they transcend the mere business objectives to achieve a positive impact on society and on the different communities where the company operates. Furthermore, conscious brands are open, transparent, and held to account. The true premise of long-lasting and great success lies in the capacity of the company to create happiness and prosperity for the greatest possible number of customers and stakeholders (Cavallo, 2015, p. 74).

This consideration is also made by Solana (2010) when stating that, in the past, brands merely talked, but now, brands are invited to strike up conversations, to listen, to act, to relate to people in social spaces, to define ways of behaviour, attitudes and ethical standards. Brands have begun to need to be aware of themselves. They are no longer just about communication.

(p. 252)

In this line, authors such as Malone and Fiske (2013) have called them human brands. That means brands that inspire greatest trust, integrity, and transparency, between other virtues. So, we are therefore witnessing the shift from storytelling to storydoing. It is no longer about acting in real time, but the brand actions must focus on helping them to be more transparent and embark on recovering the trust that consumers have lost of late. Those premises lay the foundations to construct the relationship with new consumers where concepts such as the collaborative or social economy are becoming increasingly more important. Brands need to define a value proposal that is adapted to a constantly changing society where its citizens have raised the bar and are calling to evolve toward a more transformational economic model. Our main objective today is to live, feel, and experience the brand, its values, and its stories in all the interactions with the brand. The art of storytelling has begun face risks that were previously unknown. It is no longer a point of differentiation and we have to evolve toward storydoing: moving from telling to doing (Montague, 2013).

According to Cavallo (2015), marketing needs to be focused on this search for happiness for companies to fulfill their function of contributing to the development of the collective that it serves:

A brand can only prosper and fulfil its role if it contributes to the happiness of a group of people, however small or large. Therefore, discovering what makes a person happy is the essential basis for a brand to be able to contribute to the harmonious development of the (local or global) collective that it serves.

(p. 63)

It can therefore be seen that brands are developing positive marketing strategies, in other words, where the brand is located at the level of consumer proximity and according to their interests. Gone are the narratives focused on the products and their utilitarian and tangible characteristics to make way for advertising that achieves connections that create a feeling of which one is the trusted brand, which one deserves to be chosen by the values that it generates in the public. (López, 2007, p. 38)

Brands, products, and services offer well-being as the main competitive edge, thus becoming involved in the life expectations of the consumers or of the context. In fact, Gopaldas (2015, p. 2451) links positive marketing to the activities of the companies and we can call it positive provided that those activities contribute to innovation, serve the different stakeholders, enable the companies to take part in the political and cultural debate and can address the structural roots of the social problems. Statman (2010) defines positive marketing as "being about creating positive effect for the combination of utilitarian, value expressive, and emotional benefits." To which Lerman and Shefrin (2015, p. 2444) add that this practice includes activities to address external effects of the companies such as environmental considerations and shared consumption, or which the economists call a public good.

From Advertising Happiness to Positive Advertising

Advertising Happiness

There is the idea in the consumer culture that products are a means to be happy; satisfaction in life is not achieved by religious contemplation or social interaction or simply with life, but rather by owning and exchanging goods. This idea is supported by Belk and Pollay (1985, p. 394) in their definition of materialism: "*the tendency to view worldly possessions as important sources of satisfaction in life.*" That is, materialism can influence the satisfaction of the consumer with their standard of living. Lipovetsky (2010) believes that the post-modernist era has ended and we have embarked on what he calls the "hyper-modern time," which in turn is based on "hyper-consumerism," a situation that is associated with the relentless search for well-being to a great extent. Or as Cavallo claims (2015, p. 59) "*it is clear that prosperity and happiness in our culture are two closely related categories.*"

In this regard, Richins (1987) considers different studies that show the direct relationship between advertising with happy consumers and owning products. In other words, according to those studies, consumers exposed to this type of advertising value material possessions more highly than those less exposed to this type of advertising.

Precisely, advertising happiness has existed ever since advertising became mass in nature and we began to see adverts with smiling people, happy to purchase that product or service being offered (Pellicer, 2013, p. 14). This happiness concept started implicitly in the adverts, in other words, first by creating dissatisfaction, as, as Eguizabal (2009) pointed out, the creation process of this advertising happiness would be:

> the starting point for the advertising mechanism to work would have to be a certain degree of dissatisfaction of the individuals. Its first goal is therefore to produce in the consumer a certain discontent, a disappointment with their life, their belongings, their physique or their relations, etc. Once that awareness had been created, the solution is shown to be easy, because there is always the message that comes to relieve us, to console us, to provide us with the way to free us from that problem. Advertising worries about you. It is there to help you with your shortcomings, to guide you in your behavior, to indicate what is correct and incorrect, so that, in a nutshell, you do not need to think too much.
>
> *(p. 21)*

Thus, advertising becomes that guarantee that allows the person to be what they were not, which allowed them to be what they want to be and, furthermore, very easily. This resource in happiness advertising as a main selling point is therefore justified because happiness is what every human being wants. It all comes down to whether or not one is happy, because that happiness includes the other things in life (Pellicer, 2013, p. 16). If marketing initially extolled those functional attributes of the products, modern marketing is based on intangible values and on self-fulfillment and social needs and including what many consider to be the most important: the relentless pursuit of happiness. Brands, today, use the strategy of promising happiness through well-being, to place their products and services in the day-to-day life of people (Chicaiza, 2012, p. 42).

This happiness concept is handled in advertising in two main ways. On the one hand, we find examples of the explicit use of happiness, in other words, discussing it directly. In this first option, there are increasingly more brands that dare to mention happiness explicitly in their adverts, which then become standards of that well-known emotion. As Spence (2014, p. 164) recognizes, some campaigns exemplifying this would be that of "*Happiness is . . . Hunday,*" that of the perfumes of the Clinique brand with the "*Happy, Clinique Happy*" slogan and a woman who looks to be happy or that of the Kraft brand with "*Have a happy sandwich.*" Another of the clear examples of this strategy is the Coca-Cola brand, which may be the one that has best exploited and embraced the happiness concept, not only by mentioning and showing happiness directly in its adverts, but also by creating a Happiness Institute. Adverts such as that of the "*Happiness*

Table 18.1 Analyzed Campaigns

Campaign	You are here to be happy
Brand	Coca-Cola Spain
Agency	McCann Erickson
Positioning values	proximity, optimism, overcoming, enjoying life, happiness
Url	www.youtube.com/watch?v=tzc3FFJDKU8
Campaign	Happiness is your progress
Brand	Coca-Cola Spain
Agency	Mc Cann Lima
Positioning values	progress, improvement, possibilities, smile, happiness
Url	www.youtube.com/watch?v=tzc3FFJDKU8
Campaign	For a happier head
Brand	H&S
Agency	Saatchi & Saatchi
Positioning values	feeling good, beauty, recognition, success
Url	www.youtube.com/watch?v=pJ9myJudELs
Campaign	Happy tummies, Activia people
Brand	Danone (Activia)
Agency	Vinizius Young Rubicam
Positioning values	feeling good, nutrition, looking after yourself, being happy
Url	www.youtube.com/watch?v=ENb29YNvhSI

Factory" or slogans such as *"You are here to be happy"* or *"Serving up happiness since 1886"* are just some of the many examples that can be found for this brand.

Other examples can be seen with brands such as Bavaria and its *slogan "Happiness does not last forever,"* with H&S and its *"For a happier head"* or with Danone with its campaign with different celebrity opinion leaders *"Happy tummies, Activia people."*

Yet, on the other hand, there is the association of the indirect happiness concept by means of associating values and attributes leading to happiness. It is also achieved by means of smiles and happiness gestures where selecting that product or service advertised offers happiness to the consumer. Spence (2014, p. 165) points out, among others, values and attributes such as friendship, truth, romance, gracefulness, elegance, caring, freedom, independence, beauty, and love are typically associated to the brands. He cites as some examples of those values: "friendship with bourbon in the Jim Bean ad: *real friends, real bourbon*; truth with the Calvin Klein perfume *Truth*; amazing grace with a woman's watch in an ad by Pulsar; romance with the perfume *Romance* by Ralph Lauren; elegance with a watch in ad by Longines; carefree with a brand name for tampons; a declaration of independence with the perfume *Tommy Girl*; and, not least, lovable with *Lovable*, a brand of women´s lingerie." In the words of the author, "the association of consumer products with the concept and image of happiness are designed to create in consumers the same pro-attitude or predisposition toward the products advertised as people have toward their happiness and its contributing associated values" (2014, p. 166).

That is the common and traditional perspective in the advertising narratives and which seeks to generate a positive association being well-being and product consumption, to thus possess or yearn for what we desire. It is a superficial happiness concept linked to success, hedonism, or the tangible. One example of this is the Fanta campaign with its slogan *"Have a Fanta"* envisages having fun to be happy as the main goal in life. The pride of belonging is represented by means

Table 18.2 Analyzed Campaigns

Campaign	Have a Fanta
Brand	Fanta
Agency	McCann Erickson
Positioning values	fun, happiness, lack of rules
Url	www.youtube.com/watch?v=wBChXbUionc
Campaign	Have a Fanta
Brand	Fanta
Agency	McCann Erickson
Positioning values	fun, happiness, lack of rules
Url	www.youtube.com/watch?v=wBChXbUionc
Campaign	Proud to belong to the Mutua
Brand	Mutua Madrileña
Agency	Comunica + A
Positioning values	happiness, reassurance, safety, peace of mind, pride, joy
Url	www.youtube.com/watch?v=bXs4Lp729To
Campaign	Pay with lovin'
Brand	McDonald's
Agency	Leo Burnett
Positioning values	sharing, emotions, joy, love
Url	www.youtube.com/watch?v=SFxzDwjsj-A
Campaign	Win a life
Brand	ONCE
Agency	desire, opportunities, freedom, dreams, excitement, plenitude
Positioning values	sharing, emotions, joy, love
Url	www.youtube.com/watch?v=SFxzDwjsj-A

of the happiness felt by the users who belong to the Mutua, the value of friendship is exemplified in the McDonald's campaign and all the opportunities that the ONCE lottery offers us to be happy can be seen in the *"Win a life"* campaign. Desiring something, being happy or being satisfied do not mean the same thing from the philosophical point of view, but marketing, from that perspective, has turned it into something similar.

Positive Advertising

However, as we have already discussed, this advertising happiness comes up against a more recent happiness concept, given the need for a new relational paradigm between the brands and the individuals, related to positive marketing and brands with a conscience, that seek to contribute to the well-being of the consumer and which include several key *insights* that come from the happiness economy. Some examples are the Campofrío strategies (*"Everyone's CV"*), that of Dove (*"You are more beautiful than you think"*), that of Aquarius (*"A place of called world"*), or that of Volkswagen (*"The sunny side of life"*).

Apart from showcasing products and services, the role of advertising has shifted to injecting a moment of well-being in society, turning brands into givers. Peace, tranquility, reasons to continue, sharing with others, opportunities, personal strengths as basic aspects of well-being, the

Table 18.3 Analyzed Campaigns

Campaign	Everyone's CV
Brand	Coca-Cola Spain
Agency	McCann Erickson
Positioning values	solidarity, sharing, teamwork, bravery, progress
Url	www.youtube.com/watch?v=Jz9ZfU_Zlt0
Campaign	Citizens of a place called world
Brand	Aquarius
Agency	SCPF
Positioning values	sharing, union, opportunities, union, companionship, joy
Url	www.youtube.com/watch?v=hoAJ_gAMQlk

positive contribution to the social environment, etc., are some of the levers fostered by the brands. These are part of the individual sphere in relation to other people and not so much of the individual sphere focused on hedonism and the success that advertising fostered in previous decades. If the value of well-being was more associated to individual prosperity in the previous paradigm, the well-being is more social and collective in this model. Here is where the connection, "the engagement" between people and brands lies. In the capacity of recovering those states of feeling positive, absent, or lost in modern society. They are brands that allow us to recover those spaces of emotions, which give people the opportunity to feel more real or genuine, to return to their natural state. The effort, joy, trust, sharing, optimism, being forward looking, capacity to love and be loved, generosity, sense of humor, etc., are the new positioning stances of the brands and some are very closely related to the 24 character strengths of the human being of Peterson and Seligman (2004), as you can also see more carefully in Muñiz-Velázquez and Plaza (2018).

Conclusions

In marketing literature, the term *happiness* is used associated to concepts such as subjective well-being, satisfaction with life, utility, and prosperity (Easterlin, 2003; Mogilner, Aaker, & Kamvar, 2012; Nicolao, Irwin & Goodman, 2009). Yet apart from those terms that are more closely related to old marketing practices that focus on the utility of consumers and their hedonism, a whole trend of researches and practices related to positive marketing have emerged and whose benchmark is the happiness economy. We are facing a type of happiness more in line with eudaimonism and which is reflected in those business and marketing strategies, in general, that seek to develop positive values such as well-being in society, safety, sharing with others, personal opportunities, and character.

The great challenge for companies is to raise the degree of humanization to create mature, responsible brands that are committed to their consumers and society overall to work with them to construct brands capable of experiencing happiness not only through the hedonic, but also the eudaimonic pathway, which is more sustainable in the long-term as that implies not only the here and now happiness, but also a full life. Ultimately, we are witnessing a new value-oriented marketing, with a main goal of making the world a better place (Kotler, Kartajaya, & Setiawan, 2010).

References

Bagozzi, R., Gopinath, M., & Nyer, P. (1999). The role of emotions in marketing. *Journal of the Academy of Marketing Science, 27*(2), 184–206.

Belk, R. W., & Pollay, R. W. (1985). Materialism and magazine advertising during the twentieth century. *Advances in Consumer Research, 12,* 394–398.

Bettingen, J. F., & Luedicke, M. K. (2009). Can brands make us happy? A research framework for the study of brands and their effects on happiness. In A. L. McGill & Sh. Shavitt (Eds.), *Advances in consumer research* (pp. 308–318). Duluth, MN: Association for Consumer Research.

Cavallo, G. (2015). *El marketing de la felicidad.* Madrid: Códice.

Chicaiza, T. (2012). Vendiendo felicidad: el nuevo paradigma de las marcas. *Retos, 3,* 37–52.

De Salas, N. (2016). *Brand soul. Del corazón de las personas, al alma de las marcas.* Madrid: LID Editorial Empresarial.

Dolan, P., Peasgood, T., & White, M. (2008). Do we really know makes us happy? A review of the economic literature on the factors associated with subjective well-being. *Journal of Economic Psychology, 29*(1), 94–122.

Easterlin, R. A. (1974). Does economic growth improve the human lot? Some emipirical evidence. In P. A. David & N. W. Reder (Eds.), *Nations and households in economic growth: Essays in honor of Moses Abramowitx* (pp. 89–125). New York, NY: Academic Press.

Easterlin, R. A. (2003). Explaining happiness. *Proceedings of the National Academy of Sciences, 100*(19), 11176–11183.

Eguizabal, R. (2009). *Industrias de la conciencia: una historia social de la publicidad en España (1975–2009).* Barcelona: Península.

EOI. (2015). *Economía de la felicidad. Sectores de la nueva economía 20+20.* Madrid: EOI (ESCUELA DE ORGANIZACIÓN INDUSTRIAL). Retrieved from www.eoi.es/es/savia/publicaciones/21111/sectores-de-la-nueva-economia-2020-economia-de-la-felicidad

Gobé, M. (2005). *Branding emocional. El nuevo paradigma para conectar las marcas emocionalmente con las personas.* Barcelona: Paidós.

Goldhaber, M. H. (2006). The value of openness in an attention economy. *First Monday, 11*(6).

Gopaldas, A. (2015). Creating firm, customer, and societal value: Toward a theory of positive marketing. *Journal of Business Research, 68,* 2446–2451.

Hanson, D. S., & Arjoon, S. (2010). Marketing for happiness. *Advances in Management, 3,* 7–14.

Huta, V. (2017). An overview of hedonic and eudaimonic well-being concepts. In L. Reinecke & M. B. Oliver (Eds.), *Handbook of media use and well-being: International perspectives on theory and research on positive media effects* (pp. 14–33). New York, NY: Routledge.

Huta, V., & Waterman, A. S. (2014). Eudaimonia and its distinction from hedonia: Developing a classification and terminology for understanding conceptual and operational definitions. *Journal of Happiness Studies, 15,* 1425–1456.

Ind, N., & Horlings, S. (2016). *Brands with a conscience.* London: Kogan Page.

Kotler, P., Kartajaya, H., & Setiawan, I. (2010). *Marketing 3.0: From products to customers to the human spirit.* Hoboken: John Wiley and Sons, Inc.

La Despensa. (2017). *Cómo las marcas influyen en la felicidad de las personas.* Madrid. Retrieved from www.ladespensa.es.

Layard, R. (2005). *Happiness: Lessons from a new science.* London: Penguin.

Lerman, D., & Shefrin, H. (2015). Positive marketing: Introduction to the special section. *Journal of Business Research, 68*(12), 2503–2512.

Lipovetsky, G. (2010). *La felicidad paradójica* (3ª ed.). Madrid: Anagrama.

López, B. (2007). *Publicidad emocional.* Madrid: ESIC.

Malone, C., & Fiske, S. (2013). *The human brand: How we relate to people, products and companies.* San Francisco, CA: Jossey-Bass Publishers.

Mogilner, C., & Aaker, J. (2009). The Time vs. Money effect: Shifting product attitudes and decision through personal connection. *Journal of Consumer Reseach, 36*(2), 277–291.

Mogilner, C., Aaker, J., & Kamvar, S. D. (2012). How happiness affects choice. *Journal of Consumer Research, 36*(2), 188–198.

Montague, T. (2013). *True story: How to combine story and action to transform your business.* Boston, MA: Harvard Business Review Press.

Muñiz-Velázquez, J. A., & Plaza, J. F. (2018). Advertising and authentic happiness: Can they be good friends? In J. A. Muñiz-Velázquez & C. Pulido (Eds.), *The Routledge Handbook of Positive Communication* (pp. xx–xx). New York, NY: Routledge.

Nicolao, L., Irwin, J. R., & Goodman, J. K. (2009). Happiness for sale: Do experiential purchases make consumers happier than material purchases? *Journal of Consumer Research, 36*(2), 188–198.

Pellicer, M. T. (2013). La promesa de la felicidad en los mensajes de la publicidad comercial. *Pensar la Publicidad*, 7(1), 13–23.

Peterson, Ch., & Seligman, M. (2004). *Character strengths and virtues: A handbook and classification.* New York, NY: Oxford University Press.

Pike, S., Bianchi, C., Kerr, G., & Patti, C. (2010). Consumer-based brand equity for Australia as a long-haul tourism destination in an emerging market. *International Marketing Review, 27*(4), 434–449.

Richins, M. L. (1987). Media, materialism, and human happiness. *Advances in Consumer Research, 14*, 352–356.

Ryan, R. M., & Deci, E. L. (2001). On happiness and human potentials: A review of research on hedonic and eudaimonic well-being. *Annual Review of Psychology, 52*, 141–166.

Seligman, M. (2011). *Flourish: A visionary new understanding of happiness and well-being.* New York, NY: The Free Press.

Solana, D. (2010). *Postpublicidad.* Barcelona: Arts Gràfiques.

Spence, E. (2014). The advertising of happiness and the branding of values. In M. Boylan (Ed.), *Business ethics* (pp. 163–176). West Sussex: Wiley Blackwell.

Statman, M. (2010). *What investors really want: Know what drives investor behavior and make smarter financial decisions.* New York, NY: McGraw-Hill.

19

USING ETHNOGRAPHIC INSIGHTS TO FOSTER POSITIVE VALUE EXCHANGE BETWEEN CONSUMERS AND CORPORATIONS

A Case Study With FedEx

Timothy de Waal Malefyt

This chapter explores the ways in which qualitative ethnographic research can reveal the positive aspects of consumer relationships with products, brands, and services that might otherwise be overlooked in other types of research. Since insights are said to arrive from a "viewpoint of difference" (Bateson, 1972), this research suggests ethnography works best when using an "emic" and "etic" model that compares and contrasts insider and outsider viewpoints (Arnould & Wallendorf, 1994; Pike, 1967). The positive value discovered through emic insights from ethnographic research has strong implications for the way corporations market to and develop a range of products, service, and advertising for consumers.

Here we are going to present a study in which insights gained from ethnographic research with small business managers about their use of overnight shipping services (FedEx) helped generate new strategic ideas for a shipping company. As such, positive valuations of consumer relationships with brands and services that offer an "insider view" are more likely to produce positive messages that are meaningful to those consumers than messages that assume an incorrect stance and are less relevant to consumers.

Methodology

The author was employed as a corporate anthropologist for over 15 years, where he led an in-house ethnographic insight group for an advertising agency. The project on researching small business managers was initiated in 2009 by the ad agency's client, FedEx, which approached the author and his team to gain a deeper understanding of the small business mindset. FedEx reportedly had an image problem with small business managers. Although their research showed the brand was the preferred shipping carrier for many big businesses, perceptions among smaller businesses lagged behind its main competitor, UPS. This research set out to visit small business managers to ascertain the meaning of running a small business, understand the issues they faced, explore brand identities of FedEx and competitors, and investigate ways FedEx could add value.

Fifteen ethnographic interviews with small business managers were conducted in the markets of San Diego, Raleigh-Durham and Chicago. These markets were chosen for indexing high as rising metro areas for small business growth. Respondents were selected for the project through the use of a marketing recruiter. Criteria for selecting respondents were based on their direct involvement as key shipping decision-makers (small business managers) who owned and managed or directly managed a small business, and were split among male and female managed, and blue and white-collar businesses. The small businesses, themselves, ranged in size from five to 150 employees. The types of small businesses interviewed were:

*   **1–5 employees:** A candy store; Security video surveillance; Camera Brokers (buy/sell new and used cameras); Office Systems (computer service and repair); Court-legal reporting
*   **6–25 employees:** Lock and key repair; Auto body repair; Fishing rod manufacturing; Insurance sales; Attorneys at law firm; Coffee distributors.
*   **26–75 employees:** Office services (healthcare billing); Travel agency; Manufacturing representatives; Industrial shows and exhibits.

Interviews were conducted on the site of each business operation, and held during regular hours to get a sense of business dynamics and social interactions. Each interview lasted for three hours. The interview included a tour of the operation and a sit-down discussion with the key decision maker (manager) of shipping services. Key research issues directed from the FedEx client were to gain a deeper understanding of the small business person; understand what's unique to his or her lifestyle and mindset; discover how FedEx was a lifestyle brand through exploring the small business person's interests and behaviors as well as uncovering the values and attitudes toward work, family, and life in general. The ethnographic research hoped to uncover what customer needs FedEx currently fulfilled and what gaps existed.

Theoretical Approach

A fundamental assumption that drives qualitative analysis is that symbolic and socially constructed meanings are inherent to human life (Arnould & Thompson, 2005). Qualitative research importantly accesses symbolic and socially constructed meanings through an in-depth investigation of the categories and relationships that consumers themselves create. The range of qualitative methods such as cultural analysis or market-oriented ethnography (Arnould & Wallendorf, 1994; Belk, Sherry, & Wallendorf, 1988a, 1988b, 2003; Malefyt, 2009; McCracken, 1988; Olsen, 1995, 2009; Ritson & Elliott, 1999; Sherry, 1983, 1987, 1990; Sherry & Kozinets, 2001; Sunderland & Denny, 2007), semiotic analysis (Cefkin, 2009) hermeneutic and existential-phenomenology (Thompson, Locander, & Pollio, 1989, 1990, 1994) inform detailed representations of the consumer's lived experience and relationships they develop with brands and services.

Of these methods, the ethnographic interview is one of the most important research tools for discovering insights into a brand's social use, contextual relevance, and symbolic meaning in a consumer's life. Market-oriented ethnography is particularly useful as a "systematic process" for conducting consumer research (Arnould & Wallendorf, 1994, p. 484). Ethnography has revealed the positive relations and unspoken truths between consumers and commodities in a range of naturalistic settings, such as flea markets, swap meets, or a person's private collections (Belk et al., 1988a, 1988b; Sherry, 1990). This positions ethnographic research apart in design and goals from those of quantitative approaches.

On the one hand, quantitative research is designed to isolate and define a consumer category as precisely as possible (McCracken, 1988). Quantitative research thus excels at determining the nature of relationships between and across precise categories. It often employs large samples of respondents to deliver on this goal, which allows researchers to compare and contrast one consumer category with other categories.

Qualitative research, on the other hand, is used to investigate the very nature and depth of a consumer category itself, where the socially constructed category is the object of inquiry (Arnould & Wallendorf, 1994; Fournier, 1998; McCracken, 1988; Sunderland & Denny, 2007). This requires more research time and smaller samples. Direct observations and interviews in specific contexts allow for symbolic and practice analysis to access respondents lived experiences with brands and services. As such, ethnographic analysis reveals the cognitive world and situated practices of individuals.

In the specific contexts of small business operations, we used ethnography to ascertain the lived categories and logic by which individuals see the world and operate in their daily routines. This methodology allowed us to discover the behavioral dynamics and situated practices that relate to brand usage and attendant meaning. Such approaches are vital to understanding "insider" and "outsider" issues that differentiate consumer understandings, and can lead to positive value exchange, which can ultimately enhance the overall relationship between corporation and individual. Positive value exchange is defined here as marketing in its ideal form, in which all parties—individual customers, marketers, and society as a whole-exchange value such that individually and collectively they are "better off" than they were prior to the exchange (Centerforpositivemarketing.org).

Beyond merely data collecting, ethnography seeks to make manifest the implicit behaviors and practices that constitute cultural experience. The patterns exposed in contextual research are cultural and experiential rather than cognitive (Arnould & Wallendorf, 1994, p. 485). In this way, ethnography shows the relevance of contextual experience (emic) that is "experience near" and how it compares with external (etic) or "experience distant" approaches that corporations may utilize (Geertz, 1983). Specifically, an emic approach to consumer analysis is culturally determined, and is applied to one culture or community at a time. It is therefore relative, such that elements are responsive to their own internal logic within that system. In contrast, an etic approach to consumer analysis is comparative, using criteria that are external to the system. The criteria are absolute so that elements of one system may be compared and contrasted to another system (Pike, 1967, p. 37; see also Arnould & Wallendorf, 1994; Arnould & Price, 2006).

Two theories of contextual analysis helped our investigation of emic and etic categories. First, implicit and explicit in consumers' conversations about shipping brands were the relationships they valued with suppliers, work colleagues, and shipping carriers. Relationships are importantly expressed as key to small business owner's needs and perceptions of success. Fournier's relationship theory (1998) is therefore useful to parse out and prioritize the various needs and motivations that drive small business relationships. Second, in our conversations with small business managers, specific terms, phrases, and figures of speech helped to identify the internal logic and motivations that were unique to perceptions of running and operating a small business. Insights were therefore gleaned from listening for the disjuncture between what consumers idealized in relation to a particular shipping service, and their actual experience with a shipping service. Thus, metaphoric analysis and concepts of consumer-brand relationships were applied to unpack the meaning of running a small business and various interactions encountered with shipping services.

Relationship Theory

The great value that small business managers' place on maintaining and fostering relationships with suppliers, vendors, and service providers became evident immediately in discussions about running a business. Fournier's Relationship Theory (1998) is particularly useful in the analysis of consumer-brand relationships through four dimensions of relationships that consumers may encounter with brands. By understanding the depth of relationship qualities, researchers can determine the positive value and interactive potential between an individual and brands, such as among shipping service providers. Malefyt has likewise shown that a focus on positive relationships in advertising can also foster positive bonds between consumers (Malefyt, 2015). First, consumer-brand relationships are mutually beneficial when they involve reflexive or reciprocal exchange between active partners. Brands are animated, active, and contributing "partners" in the relationship (Aaker, 1997; Holt, 2004; Olsen, 1995). Second, relationships must also show purposeful engagement that is meaningful to both partners at its core. Other research concurs that brand meaning shapes the significance of the relationship a person or people have with an object, and adds structure to their lives (Belk, 1988; Csikszentmihalyi & Rochberg-Halton, 1981; Douglas & Isherwood, 1979; McCracken, 1988; Wallendorf & Arnould, 1991). Third, consumer-brand relationships must encourage exchange across several dimensions of experience, providing a range of benefits over various uses and in different contexts (Arnould & Thompson, 2005; Lindstrom, 2010; Pine & Gilmore, 1999; Schmitt, 1999). Fourth, relationships are most meaningful when they maintain their value over time, that is, they adapt to change across life circumstances (Appadurai, 1986; Holt, 2004; Kopytoff, 1986).

Discussions with small business managers revealed a range of relationship associations they had with various shipping carriers. Some carriers demonstrated more of the qualities valued in relationships with small business managers than did other carriers, thereby instilling a greater emotional connection with managers than other shipping services. In fact, research revealed how important relationship concepts were with brands, such that the shipping carrier represented the brand identity and served as the "face of the brand" in consumer comments. This aspect becomes more evident in the metaphors that small business consumers expressed in their relationship with shipping services.

Metaphoric Language of Relationships

Metaphors are recognized as a powerful means for understanding consumer perspectives on social meaning (Belk, Ger, & Askegaard, 2003; Glucksberg, 2003; Lakoff & Johnson, 1980; McQuarrie & Mick, 2003; McQuarrie & Phillips, 2005; Thompson, Pollio, & Locander, 1994). Metaphor is not just a linguistic phenomenon; it is a cognitive structure that mediates interactions in the consumers' world (Johnson, 1995; Lakoff & Johnson, 1980). Most of our conceptual thinking is metaphorical in nature; it structures how we perceive, how we think, and what we do (Lakoff & Johnson, 1980, p. 4). Analysis of consumer expressive language can reveal how metaphors structure categories of cognition and help orient consumer relationships in their social lives (Johnson, 1995, p. 157). Moreover, in a business setting where small business managers conduct daily work and depend on other vendors, suppliers, and shippers for service, metaphors extend their sense of selves and the value of possessions and identities in their workplace to others in meaningful terms (Tian & Belk, 2005).

Small Business Sense of Self

Our research revealed that small business managers used expressive language and particular uses of metaphor to suggest a different orientation in their view of work. For many respondents, running or working in a small business was a natural progression in their lives. Many had worked for large corporations but felt it was not for them. Large corporations were negatively described as places of "back stabbing" and unfriendly "competitive behavior." Most felt they were "under appreciated" for their hard work. As one respondent commented, "In a large company, they can't even spell your name on your paycheck."

But it wasn't only the negatives of large business that motivated them as small business managers. Many felt inspired to start their own company, "Being Captains of their own ship," even knowing the risks involved. It was their dream of fulfilling the American spirit of entrepreneurship.

This research discovered three beliefs that formed the basis of their dream. First, small business managers believed that they would have independence and "the ability to control their own destiny." They mentioned the sense of control and independence in "not having to work for anyone else," and "getting tired of jumping through someone else's hoops, so now they control the shots." Second, they expressed a desire in having the freedom to "run the business the way they wanted." This sense of freedom was played out in their vision of operating a small business and in doing what they felt "was right." They mentioned that they had a vision about how they wanted things run, and running a business was an expression of this freedom. In this regard, their sense of self was strongly connected to the success of their business. Third, their dream was about being involved in all they did. This meant being fully engaged in all that goes on. Since it was "their" operation, they felt no shame in doing all that needed to be done, from making coffee and buying office supply equipment, to arranging meetings and presentations to clients. Full buy-in meant everyone was responsible for everything, and also that everyone was more or less on the same level playing field. This was seen positively, compared to the rank and hierarchy of large corporations.

Reality of Running a Small Business

While all small business managers we spoke to were pleased with their decision and most would never go back to a large corporation, the reality of running a business did challenge many of their previously held idealistic expectations. It meant working long hours with unstable financial rewards. As one respondent said, "You work harder, longer, without making the money."

The high degree of personal involvement also meant assuming a greater sense of responsibility when things went wrong. In a small business, many felt there was more at stake personally as well as professionally. Sometimes they felt overwhelmed, and felt that they had no one or nowhere to turn to for help, that you "go it alone."

Another problem of running a small business that managers confronted was finding loyal employees. Managers mentioned the difficulties of hiring the right people: "I went in very naïve about it. I thought everyone was like in my previous job. I wined and dined my employees, then I found out that people were dishonest."

Tensions Between Idealized Beliefs and Reality

The gap between idealized beliefs in starting a small business and the actual experience of running a business left respondents in a position with certain tensions. There was a need to justify their course of action and resolve the tension. Their justifications focused on themselves and their personal satisfaction, as well as the economic order of their success.

Respondents spoke of the personal satisfaction of watching their small business grow and thrive, about being recognized in their community for their capabilities, and of feeling a sense of connection with other small businesses. They evaluated success and personal satisfaction relative to their connection with other people, "I measure success by how long I've kept a client. *Your* name is out there, and those people you do business with will never forget you. If you don't have that, how can you have success?" This sense of personal connection with others like them, outweighed the negatives of feeling tied down, committed to their work, working long hard hours, and having labor difficulties. Their pride of personal satisfaction and their need for recognition became an internal mantra they said to themselves. This meant they appreciated others who identified with what it was like to run and operate a small business.

$$\text{Dream/Idealized self} \longleftrightarrow \text{Reality}$$
$$\text{(reason for starting a small business)} \qquad \text{(actual experience)}$$

The tension between the idealized self and the reality of running a small business also manifests in the metaphors that small business managers used to describe themselves and what they do. Three metaphors were most significant: "Captain of your own ship," "Wearing many hats," and "Going the extra mile."

Each figure of speech reflected the idealized joys and real pressures of operating a small business. For instance, the ideal sense of self one gains from "being captain of your own ship" offers a greater chance to shine, and personally take the credit one deserves. As a respondent said, "It's great to be recognized for your efforts." Aligned with this ideal was taking pride in what one does, "I can feel good about what I do, helping others." This led to a sense of ownership for many, "You know it's from your efforts," "It's you who's made a difference."

Another ideal frequently referenced by respondents was the total involvement required with every aspect of running the business. Being involved in every aspect of work was expressed in the metaphor "wearing many hats." Total involvement was expressed in comments such as, "everybody has to play their part," and that employees "interchange jobs with others" providing a greater sense of responsibility and seeing projects through from start to finish. Employees said this helped them feel committed, expressing a passion for what they did, where "every detail matters." "You have to enjoy what you do or you'll be miserable," said one manager, "Even if I didn't need the money, I'd probably do it anyway."

Still another ideal that attracted them to small business was the sense of personal commitment required. This was expressed in the metaphor, "going the extra mile." What is expected from one's own involvement and from other vendors meant doing more than was required. This is strongly linked to relationships that are symbolic of "partnerships" (Fournier, 1998), which extend over time and across circumstances. More critically, this ideal reflects perceptions on how a small business should run. Their belief in the value of investing in others is reflected in statements such as, "It's about trust, caring and support in others" and that relationships are "a real piece of life." For small business managers customer service is everything. They expressed joy and pride in "going the extra mile" for their customers where everyone counted, from employees, clients, suppliers, to service people and shipping carriers.

Nevertheless, the ideals of running a small business were tempered by the reality of life, which involved several factors. For one, the greater risk in their work generated a higher level of uncertainty. "You never know if your next paycheck is on time," said one respondent. This led to a sense of vulnerability, followed by the metaphor, "No one to back you up." Countering feelings of independence revealed an actual dependency on others to make things run smoothly, as well as counting on others to function on a daily basis, "You can't go it alone in a small business."

The reality of total involvement in small business meant that many respondents found they traded in a 9-to-5 job at a bigger corporation for a 24/7 lifestyle. Often we heard respondents discuss how they "can't let it go," meaning that work-life involves extra effort, such as stopping by weekends to check-up on an upcoming project, or that they might call in the office at night to see if there were problems that needed their assistance. One respondent said, "This is not a job you leave at the end of the day." Rather, work in small business requires a level of personal commitment and the ability to adapt to multiple roles. Some of the roles described were: "Mr. fix-it," "the intellectual analyzer," "the friendly public and social self," and "the listening ear." These roles, described in metaphoric language, expressed the perceived time and attention required to carry a project through.

As a consequence, when employees become fully involved in their work, personal life tends to blur with work-life. Family time blended with work time and employees found relations with friends in similar entrepreneurial tracks. They shared similar values and could more easily relate to similar others, such as juggling schedules to make it work. Work thus became integral to concepts of self-identity. An added benefit was the feeling of a mutual support structure, "We bounce ideas off each other." As such, personal hobbies often coincided with business interests, "I'm in the fishing business (manufacturer of fishing rods) and I fish for fun." A more fully involved sense-of-self meant they were more likely to take the good and the bad personally. "It's all on your shoulders," where the "successes are great, but the failures more painful."

Resolving the Tension

Small business people bridge the ideal versus reality tension by projecting a *greater emphasis* on personal relations in all they do. They operate by a key metaphor in their extended but dependent relationships in business. Tension is resolved through the feeling of "family" that many managers project on their employees and toward other vendors with which they do business. As one respondent said, "It's about the relationships and the camaraderie. It's a smaller setting and you all pull together. We're all working, doing our thing." When they can, some managers hire other family members as trustworthy employees, "I can depend on my sisters." Other times, they cannot physically hire family members so they extend the same familial feelings and treat employees as personal extensions of themselves. Another respondent said, "I treat my employees as I would want to be treated. I consider them my children." Since employees work together in close quarters and assume many roles, they know each other personally and feel a type of *fictive kinship* toward one another. In the metaphor of extended "family" they placed greater value on exchanges of service and friendship, where everyone appears to be helping each other out. The sense of friendly, co-operative personal relations of "helping hands," plays to this ideal, that others are there when you need them. This also reduces apparent formality in relations, as all greetings and personal acknowledgments tend to exist on a first name basis.

As Fournier (1998) states of consumer-brand relationships, metaphors that express the value of *partnership* in relationships can extend to other brands such as shipping services. Active partners in the relationship show "purposeful engagement" that is meaningful to both partners, so that small business managers encourage familial exchange across several dimensions of experience over time. Beyond just delivering packages on time, some shippers such as UPS carriers more regularly "extended a helping hand" by moving boxes or helped pick up supplies in the back of the store and consequently became more meaningful to small business managers in relationships. This is reflected below in managers' concepts of brand identity. Moreover, the personal attention of getting to know one's family, such as a shipping carrier bringing in pictures of his family to share with managers, provided a personal context for emotional "familial" exchange beyond business relations. In terms of consumer-brand relationships these expressions of stated and implied dependence on another, reveal relationships that maintain their value over time and adapt to change across life circumstances (Fournier, 1998).

Brand Identities as Extended Relations

From a consumer perspective, all shipping companies had positive and negative images that reflected the value of relationships. FedEx and UPS shared the strongest impressions because they were most active and visible in their relations to small business managers, while Airborne and US

Postal Service (USPS) shared the weakest impressions. Stories of great service drove loyal relations and exemplary behavior, such as a carrier going out of his way, led customer loyalty. But small business managers also spoke of problems as if personally let down or betrayed. These impressions reflected the small business managers' deep sense of personal relationship with each vendor, and specifically with shipping carriers. Brand image thus is reflective of positive or negative brand experiences that can be transposed and analyzed as extensions of relationships.

FedEx Brand Image

When discussing brand associations of FedEx with consumers, the brand's positive associations related to its role of delivering goods on time. FedEx was first and foremost referred to as the shipping company that was fast and reliable. Most positive associations linked the company to sending packages dependably. Consumers affirmed this in comments such as, "By 10 AM tomorrow means what they say," and "I never had a problem with a package getting lost." These associations also led to comments of the consumer-brand relationship as "Trustworthy," "A leader," "The premiere shipping company," "A top carrier." Other positive associations described the brand as a premium service in how it confers "extra importance" to the package sent to a client. "Using FedEx says to my clients that I think they are important to me," and that "it's the service I use for my high-end clients."

This positive aura in the relationship also reflected well on the sender. One manager stated, "Customers would lose confidence in me if the package I sent them got lost or was late." And related to this was the brand's omnipresence, "I see FedEx trucks everywhere." FedEx as a brand humanized (Holt, 2004) in these relationships also embodied perceptions of care. This was perceived in ways that FedEx treats its employees, "FedEx carriers are non-union labor, so their employees are happier," and also of care given to packages, "The packages arrive in better shape," "I like the tracking with FedEx packages. It shows they care."

Nevertheless, a range of negative associations with the FedEx brand also revolved around service relationships. For one, small business managers perceived FedEx as "too corporate," and modeled on serving the needs of big business and large corporations first, and "not concerned about small business." Another consumer commented, "FedEx is not hungry enough for my business." Along these lines, FedEx is perceived as more expensive, "FedEx users don't care about the price. I do!" As such, FedEx was perceived to lack the flexibility that is required in a familial or partnership relationship for working with small business.

By extension, many small business managers felt FedEx was governed by corporate mandates. It was a brand that kept to efficiency over human interests. One consumer responded, "They are governed by rules, their rules. You work by their rules." Another commented, "Their drivers are always in a hurry," and "Their employees are running like mad dogs, which means the company is either a slave driver or not well organized." As one respondent spoke of her re0lationship with FedEx, "They don't have time for me, I'm not important enough." And exemplifying a formal, distant relationship with consumers, another manager commented, "They are the coldest people in the entire world. You say hello and they don't even say hello back."

Other shipping carriers also held positive and negative perceptions by small business managers. The brand UPS was esteemed in its relationship with managers as friendly and neighborly. Friendliness was a key relationship term used to describe the UPS carrier. As one respondent mentioned, "I always see them around." And the UPS brand was described relationally as "for normal, everyday persons like me," in which the small business owner can more easily associate as a partner or neighbor. Another respondent described the brand as "a staple of America, like McDonald's and GE." The UPS brand was also perceived as omnipresent, "everywhere you look." Yet, this also reflected on the brand's negative side, such as "sloppy, uncaring in what they do," and a less reliable service. Moreover, UPS was held as less responsible for its errors. If a package and contents were damaged from their conveyer belt, the perception was that carriers were quick to say, "it wasn't our fault."

The US Postal Service received the greatest share of negative comments. From a positive relationship perspective, it was thought of as convenient and very accessible, especially when the mail person picks up packages. The USPS was also perceived as cost effective for non-sensitive items shipped and very American for supporting US workers. However, the service was felt to be highly bureaucratic, "a zillion government forms," and associated not with business interests, but rather a government entity that can't compete with private companies. Furthermore, its service was described as mediocre. Some respondents commented on mail carriers as not caring in what they do, and that they were "less reliable." Others encountered problems with letters getting lost, cumbersome forms to fill out, and a lack of customer service, "Someone is always going on a break at the window." Delivery people were viewed as less friendly than FedEx or UPS, with carriers disgruntled. As one person commented, "Things in life didn't work out for them, so they became a postman."

Both Airborne and DHL received fewer comments, overall. Airborne was generally perceived as an upscale service "used by doctors and lawyers," and more economical than FedEx. But Airborne was not as familiar as a service provider, and thus minimized in the relationship context. As a brand, it suffered from a lack of visibility. DHL was thought of as more international, as a global carrier. But the negative for DHL was that it was not any more impressive than other carriers, "not worth going out of way to use them."

Discussion

The way in which small business managers expressed their close relationships with shipping brands has strong implications for the value of using ethnography to unearth insights in research. Through in-depth interviews and direct observations, we were able to access small businesses lifestyles and worldviews from an insider (emic) perspective, and understand the meaning of relationships in language and practice. Within managers' close-knit sense of "family," shipping plays a major role in terms of dependency on exchanges to support relationships. Managers' ongoing relations of exchange with shippers thus can be shown to exemplify an ancient form of extending and maintaining social bonds.

Shipping relations can be understood as a modern-day system of gift exchange. According to this theory (Mauss, 1990), the spirit of the giver resides in the gift or in the accouterments of the gift, such as the shipping package. Reciprocity in exchange systems means that the object given and received is not inactive; rather, it possesses some "essence" of the giver, it possesses "a soul" (Mauss, 1990, p. 10). To offer a gift to another person is to make a present of some part of oneself. Concomitantly, to accept a gift from another person is to accept some part of his or her spiritual essence or soul. Invested with life, the object often possesses some aspect of the giver's individuality. To refuse to reciprocate would cause social disaster. In the case of business relations, reciprocity is the foundation of all economically oriented transactional societies.

In other studies of gift exchange, gifts are total social phenomena (Mauss, 1990; Durkheim, 2008). In theory, exchanges are voluntary; but in reality, gifts are given and reciprocated obligatorily. FedEx and other shippers become part of the gift exchange system and enter into obligation to reciprocate. Gift exchange for small business means persons in the system of operations enter into an economic system of transactions. "Total service" means the entire small business transacts on behalf of the sender and receiver. This establishes the obligation to reciprocate.

Systems of exchange not only create bonds of reciprocity, but also maintain and continue relations between "partners" (Fournier, 1998) based on commitment and obligation between parties. The physical exchange of letters and packages tap into a form of exchange commitment that, in ancient times, cemented relationships between clan members, family, and outsiders. Shipping can be understood as a modern-day version of extending such bonds of reciprocity, where the shipping brands play a vital role. The fleeting exchange of words and promises in relations between customers, clients, and business partners over the phone, in person or by email, are transformed into a formal tangible exchange of official documents, contracts, and signed commitments through shipping carriers. Promises become concrete. This also has the effect of making far-off relationships close and essential, and especially for small business managers, the transactions become more meaningful through real time, face-to-face relations with the shipping carriers themselves, from whom the "gifts" are delivered.

The shipping exchange system extends into the heart of small business relations. First, the importance of shipping content demands an immediate response. This became evident in consumer comments, such as "IBM can wait a few days for shipments. I need my computer parts immediately or I lose my customers." As such, the daily and weekly deliveries and pick-ups of shipping overnight letters and packages allow small businesses to operate on "just-in-time inventory." They often operate with limited storage capacity for overstocked goods and a minimum of warehousing to store items. This means that small business managers depend on immediate exchange to create ongoing transactions as a business and personal lifeblood.

Second, the small business manager is shown to care almost obsessively for his or her customer with whom he or she has the exchange. Managers frequently fret about "going the extra mile" for their customer, reaffirming the notion that relationships with clients and customers are at the heart of shipping exchanges. As one manager exclaimed, "We are dealing with personalities, not packages." So, extending courtesies, offering friendliness, exchanging jokes, and congratulations on behalf of the shipping carrier eases anxiety over relations and overall concern for the other party in governing the exchange system. Personal touches that "lent an extra hand" were evidence of "care" on part of the shipping carriers themselves that went above and beyond regular delivery service. Extra service, such as the carrier personally bringing packages inside the office instead of leaving them in the hallway, or dropping off packages around back where employees were working instead of the front door, or yielding an extra day for check receipt payments instead of demanding them immediately, were esteemed dimensions of "partnership" relations.

Sending and Receiving Dynamics

We can now better understand the cultural dynamics of shipping services for small businesses and the value of exchange from an emic viewpoint. From a small business perspective, shipping is of course explicitly valued for its functional efficiency. This view corresponds with a corporation's etic (outside) view. But beyond expected service of all shipping brands, small business managers also implicitly expected "reciprocal exchange" to foster and build symbolic relationships that operate on personal transactions, an emic view. The symbolic *and* functional meanings of shipping exchange are therefore not equally weighed in the mind of the small business customer. Shipping exchanges are compartmentalized into different sending and receiving interchanges, and each exchange holds particular meaning in maintaining bonds of reciprocity due to different emotional states of giving and receiving in the consumers' mindset.

Sending packages and letters creates a momentary imbalance in the relationship exchange. It symbolically fosters a temporary separation, until the other side of the exchange receives the gift and is obliged to reciprocate. Sending imparts a feeling of "departure," which requires a more cognitive, rational, and dedicated thought process to the action. There are more variables to deal with; a greater variety of shipping choices to consider such as, type of service used (ground, air); shipping company; cost; drop off location. There are also other options to weight, "For every

Table 19.1 Shipping Exchange Summary

Sending Separation	Receiving Reconnection
"Departure"	"Arrival"
• Evokes rational choices	• Evokes emotional reactions
• Consumer behavior involved in making functional decisions regarding variables	• Consumer behavior involved in symbolic variables
• Carriers	• Face-to-face contact
• Methods	• Familiarity
• Costs	• Conversations
• Different drop-off locations	• Excitement and anticipation (what's inside?)
• Different people	• Reestablishes tangible flow of goods and reconnects relations
• Momentarily separates flow of goods and relations	

piece of paper that goes out, I have to figure out who's the best carrier, their availability, how much I want to spend." Thus, sending is the point of entry for the shipping category. Small business managers expect that all shipping companies will do a good job getting a package there on time. The notion of sending also reverts back to receiving, mentally converting sending into receiving by thinking about receiving on the other end. "After I send a letter I make a follow-up call. Not to see if it got there or not, but as good business practice to say hello to my new clients."

But whereas sending is about *departure*, receiving is about the physical *arrival* from the other. Receiving packages, letters, and documents fosters a physical *reconnection* or reunion with far-off relationships. "Getting" a letter or package is a more emotional process since it is physically gratifying. It engages a tangible and visceral experience that involves anticipation, excitement, and the unexpected in what may or what one hopes will arrive. As one small business manager exclaimed, "it's like getting a present at Christmas. It might be Grandma's check for my birthday." The impression is that what is important arrives by shipping. "You get fun stuff by FedEx and bad stuff, such as bills, by mail." Receiving was also expressed as "reconnection with a far-off client." Package arrival meant that the small business relation kept going. Arrival of a carrier with a letter became a more charged moment, the "face" of a client appearing. "When I get FedEx I know it's my Miami shipment." Receiving or "getting" then becomes the emotionally charged, human touch point of shipping exchanges, so that the relationship of gift exchange with the carrier reflects the image of the company.

Conclusion

This study presented a case study on developing customer service for a client, and offered suggestions on how marketers can utilize the emic model to uncover consumer insights in ethnographic research. Such use of insights provides corporations a better chance of fostering positive value relations with its customers by better understanding their needs from an insider point of view.

In our investigation of small business managers' use of shipping services, clear emic categories emerged regarding the positive value of relationships in exchange, and managers' motivations for one brand preference over another. One service, UPS, stood out as more in-tune with small business operations and attendant needs of fostering emotional connection and relationships than other shipping brands. The UPS carriers knew small business managers by name and tended to help out more extending personal services. Research revealed that the FedEx brand, while perceived as efficient, was not delivering positive value in terms of developing personal relationships and enhancing symbolic exchange with small business managers on a face-to-face basis. When it came to discussing the value of shipping services, small business managers felt FedEx delivered packages on time, but was oriented toward a big business model of efficiency. This became evident in metaphoric language consumers used. Managers mentioned that FedEx did not extend "helping hands," nor did it "wear many hats" as did other shipping services such as UPS.

Another emic insight on small business relations revealed the value managers placed on *receiving* letters and packages over *sending* them. "Receiving" is a tangible value in relations of exchange, and lies at the heart of the entire relationship experience. It stands for a metonym in action (Lakoff & Johnson, 1980). Receiving is symbolic of personal relationships and represents values central to running a small business: face-to-face relations, familiarity, care, trust, and physical exchange. This also means that the delivery occasion is "bigger" than just receiving. Informally, delivery is an occasion when small business customers chat with their carrier, while formally the customer may also learn about products, services, company policies and so forth. This was expressed in comments, such as "If I trust my driver, everybody behind him would be trustworthy." In other words, receiving as an exchange dynamic is an unmet opportunity for a brand to acknowledge small business practices of relationships. Small business managers, when dividing shipping dynamics between sending and receiving, stated that for sending urgent letters, FedEx was preferred, but for receiving letters and everyday shipping needs, UPS was the preferred brand because they understood the needs of small business. This emphasized the importance of personal face-to-face relations, demonstrated how friendliness drives positive brand image and impacts loyalty, and that customer satisfaction and loyalty can spread via word of mouth. The results of the study led FedEx to revise its service for small businesses by instigating a "purple promise," which better catered to the actual work conditions of small businesses and helped to make the FedEx brand less intimidating and more accessible.

Brand communications for FedEx were subsequently developed to resonate more strongly with the target audience. Since small business managers' concepts of success were based on self-worth, personal pride as managers from hard work and perseverance was emphasized in communication. Messaging rewarded the small business entrepreneurial efforts toward the achieving the American dream. A final dimension of communication portrayed employees as a natural part of the small business network of relations. Personal service is the "reason for being" of small business and also the chief source of satisfaction for the owner and employee in the form of accolades from customers. Communications that recognized the contribution of personal service and relations of exchange came from an emic understanding in ethnographic research, and helped the company succeed among this target.

In sum, this research helped identify the importance of engaged relationships between small business managers and their shipping carrier. An emic approach to market research recognized "partnering" in the world of small business managers. Notions of reciprocal relations (Mauss, 1990) and partnerships (Fournier, 1998) that promoted a sense of cooperation and helpfulness were central to the small business value system and generating positive value exchange. The small business mindset sought engaged personal interaction, which translated into better service and ultimately of perceptions of success for their business. Other studies are needed to further point out the value of ethnographic research in identifying consumer needs and creating positive value exchange between consumers and marketers. Marketing, in this way, can contribute to building positive brand associations and to enhancing mutual understandings that can benefit all parties involved.

References

Aaker, J. (1997, August). Dimensions of brand personality. *Journal of Marketing Research, 34*, 347–357.
Appadurai, A. (Ed.). (1986). *The social life of things: Commodities in cultural perspective.* Cambridge, MA: Cambridge University Press.

Arnould, E., & Price, L. (2006, September). Market-oriented ethnography revisited. *Journal of Advertising Research, 46,* 251–262.

Arnould, E., & Thompson, C. J. (2005, March). Consumer Culture Theory (CCT): Twenty years of research. *Journal of Consumer Research, 31,* 868–882.

Arnould, E., & Wallendorf, M. (1994). Market oriented ethnography. *Journal of Consumer Research, 31,* 484–504.

Bateson, G. (1972). *Steps to an ecology of mind.* New York, NY: Ballantine.

Belk, R. (1988). Possessions and the extended self. *Journal of Consumer Research, 15*(2), 139–168.

Belk, R., Ger, G., & Askegaard, S. (2003, September). The fire of desire: A multisited inquiry into consumer passion. *Journal of Consumer Research, 30,* 326–351.

Belk, R., Sherry, J. F., Jr., & Wallendorf, M. (1988a, March). A naturalistic inquiry into buyer and seller behavior at a swap meet. *Journal of Consumer Research, 14,* 449–470.

Belk, R., Wallendorf, M., Sherry, J., Holbrook, M., & Roberts, S. (1988b). Collectors and collecting. In M. J. Jouston (Ed.), *Advances in consumer research* (pp. 548–553). Provo, UT: Association for Consumer Research.

Cefkin, M. (Ed.). (2009). *Ethnography and the corporate encounter: Reflections on research in and of corporations.* New York, NY: Berghahn Books.

CenterforpositiveMarketing.org. Retrieved February 13, 2014 from www.google.com/search?q=centerfor postivemarketing.org&ie=utf-8&oe=utf-8&aq=t&rls=org.mozilla:en-US:official&client=firefox-a

Csikszentmihalyi, M., & Rochberg-Halton, E. (1981). *The meaning of things: Domestic symbols and the self.* Cambridge, MA: Cambridge University Press.

Douglas, M., & Isherwood, B. (1979). *The world of goods: Towards an anthropology of consumption.* London: Routledge.

Durkheim, E. (2008/1912). *The elementary forms of the religious life.* Oxford: Oxford University Press.

Fournier, S. (1998). Consumers and their brands: Developing relationship theory in consumer research. *Journal of Consumer Research, 24*(4), 343–353.

Geertz, C. (1983). *Local knowledge: Further essays in interpretive anthropology.* New York, NY: Basic Books.

Glucksberg, S. (2003). The psycholinguistics of metaphor. *Trends in Cognitive Science, 7,* 92–96.

Holt, D. (2004). *How brands become icons: The principles of cultural branding.* Boston, MA: Harvard Business School Press.

Johnson, M. (1995) Introduction: Why metaphor matters to philosophy. *Metaphor and Symbolic Activity, 10*(3), 157–162, DOI: 10.1207/s15327868ms1003_1

Kopytoff, I. (1986). The cultural biography of things: Commoditization as process. In A. Appadurai (Ed.), *The social life of things: Commodities in cultural perspective* (pp. 64–91). Cambridge, MA: Cambridge University Press.

Lakoff, G., & Johnson, M. (1980). *Metaphors we live by.* Chicago: University of Chicago Press.

Lindstrom, M. (2010). *Brand sense: Sensory secrets behind the stuff we buy.* New York, NY: The Free Press.

Malefyt, T. de W. (2009). Understanding the rise of consumer ethnography: Branding techno-methodologies in the new economy. *American Anthropologist, 111*(2), 201–210.

Malefyt, T. de W. (2015). Relationship advertising: How advertising can enhance social bonds. *Journal of Business Research,* (68), 2494–2502.

Mauss, M. (1990). *The gift* (W. D. Halls, Trans.). New York, NY: Norton.

McCracken, G. (1988). *The long interview.* London: Sage Publications.

McQuarrie, E. F., & Mick, D. G. (2003). Visual and verbal rhetorical figures under directed processing versus incidental exposure to advertising. *Journal of Consumer Research, 29*(4), 579–587.

McQuarrie, E. F., & Phillips, B. (2005). Indirect persuasion in advertising: How consumers process metaphors presented in pictures and words. *Journal of Advertising, 34,* 7–20.

Olsen, B. (1995). Brand loyalty and consumption patterns: The lineage factor. In J. F. Sherry (Ed.), *Contemporary marketing and consumer behavior* (pp. 245–281). Thousand Oaks, CA: Sage Publications.

Olsen, B. (2009). Rethinking marketing's evolutionary paradigm and advertisers' role as cultural intermediary. In J. F. Sherry, Jr. & E. Fischer (Eds.), *Explorations in consumer culture theory* (pp. 57–82). New York, NY: Routledge.

Pike, K. (1967). *Language in relation to a unified theory of the structure of human behavior.* The Hague: Mouton de Gruyter.

Pine, J. B., & Gilmore, J. H. (1999). *The experience economy.* Boston, MA: Harvard Business School Press.

Ritson, M., & Elliott, R. (1999, December). The social uses of advertising: An ethnographic study of adolescent advertising audiences. *Journal of Consumer Research, 26,* 260–277.

Schmitt, B. (1999). *Experiential marketing: How to get customers to sense, feel, think, act, relate to your company and brands*. New York, NY: The Free Press.

Sherry, J. F., Jr. (1983, September). Gift giving in anthropological perspective. *Journal of Consumer Research, 10*, 157–168.

Sherry, J. F., Jr. (1987). Advertising as a cultural system. In J. Umiker-Sebeok (Ed.), *Marketing and semiotics, new directions in the study of signs for sale* (pp. 441–461). New York, NY: Mouton de Gruyter.

Sherry, J. F., Jr. (1990, June). A sociocultural analysis of a Midwestern American flea market. *Journal of Consumer Research, 17*, 13–30.

Sherry, J. F., Jr., & Kozinets, R. V. (2001). Qualitative inquiry in marketing and consumer research. In D. Iacobucci (Ed.), *Kellogg on marketing* (pp. 165–194). New York, NY: Wiley and Sons.

Sunderland, P., & Denny, R. (2007). *Doing anthropology in consumer research*. Walnut Creek, CA: Left Coast Press.

Thompson, C. J., Locander, W. B., & Pollio, H. R. (1989, September). Putting consumer experience back into consumer research: The philosophy and method of existential-phenomenology. *Journal of Consumer Research, 16*, 133–146.

Thompson, C. J., Locander, W. B., & Pollio, H. R. (1990, December). The lived meaning of free choice: An existential-phenomenological description of everyday consumer experiences of contemporary married women. *Journal of Consumer Research, 17*, 346–361.

Thompson, C. J., Pollio, H. R., & Locander, W. B. (1994). The spoken and the unspoken: A hermeneutic approach to understanding the cultural viewpoints that underlie consumers' expressed meanings. *Journal of Consumer Research, 21*(3), 432–452.

Tian, K., & Belk, R. (2005). Extended self and possessions in the workplace. *Journal of Consumer Research, 32*(2), 297–310.

Wallendorf, M., & Arnould, E. (1991). We gather together: Consumption rituals of Thanksgiving Day. *Journal of Consumer Research, 18*(1), 13–31.

20

BRANDING AND THE HAPPINESS FORMULA

*Belén Gutiérrez-Villar, Pilar Castro-González, Rosa Melero-Bolaños,
and Mariano Carbonero-Ruz*

Introduction

At present, everything related to people's happiness and well-being is of interest. Until a few years ago, we did not worry about knowing so-called "happiness" because our main motivation was survival. However, as a result of the increase in life expectancy, happiness has become an end in itself and an object of study (Punset, 2005). The end of World War II also brought with it the concern of leaders for the happiness and well-being of the inhabitants of their countries. Little by little, this issue has ceased to be only a First World matter and has extended to developing countries, which are increasingly committed to increasing quality of life. An example of this phenomenon is the increase in the importance of indexes such as the Gross National Happiness (GNH), an index whose implementation was pioneered in Bhutan already in the 1970s, promoted by its leaders with the aim of forgetting the country's image regarding high levels of poverty and child mortality that it had until some decades ago.

On the other hand, the search for happiness has also become a matter of importance for brands. If until recently the important thing was to sell, then presently, the really important thing is to reach the customer and to create an emotional relationship with him or her. The concern of brands to associate with values that impact consumer happiness in a positive manner is increasingly common because it same customer demands the contribution of intangible values beyond the pure material product. Additionally, because consumers are in a central position in all of this (Gobé, 2005), brands are tending to follow this current with the objective of satisfying them.

Our objective is to evaluate the relationship between the level of people's happiness and the sense of well-being that brands provide. This idea is not new; there are some studies, although not very numerous or very conclusive, that point to the existence of a positive relationship between the two facts.

To that end, we analyze the measurement of happiness using two indexes: the Happy Planet Index (HPI) and the World Happiness Report (WHR). Regarding the degree of well-being that brands provide to the subjects, we use the index elaborated by the Havas Group, using data from 2017.

Happiness, Rankings, and Branding

The word *happiness* is used with different meanings; thus, we can say that there is no single or globally accepted definition. Following Harris (2007), happiness has two very different meanings: a) a sense of pleasure, joy, or satisfaction, and b) a rich, full, and meaningful life. It is not the purpose of this work to define happiness, but it is necessary to clarify that in its broadest sense, it is a catch-all for terms such as "well-being" and "quality of life," although they are not all synonymous (Veenhoven, 2009).

In the last decade, the concept of happiness has enjoyed great resonance among researchers in many disciplines (see Hervás & Chaves, 2018). In this sense, enormous progress has been made, from positive psychology, in themes such as the study of the causes of happiness (Diener & Seligman, 2002) and in the demonstration of the importance of happiness for the human being, in the sense of the contribution of subjective well-being to health and longevity (Diener & Chan, 2011).

Undoubtedly, in the national and supranational spheres, the concern for happiness is beginning to be raised by politicians from numerous nations, enrolled in a race to show the world that their countries occupy privileged places in some of the happiness rankings that are periodically published. For example, there is the unusual case of the kingdom of Bhutan, which has made happiness a real "country brand" and which, with its GNH calculation, as an alternative to gross domestic product (GDP), not only has achieved being known and located on the map but also has generated an interesting proposal that seems to serve as a model for other nations; if the initiatives thrive, in the near future, it will be possible to count on a GNH indicator that can be standardized to other countries and other non-Bhutanese citizens.

Even large corporations and their global brands are not unfamiliar with this situation, frequently associating their brand names with attributes such as subjective well-being or happiness, such that we can say that there is a battle for the minds of consumers attempting to position themselves and be loved and valued by individuals across the planet as vehicles to achieve subjective and collective well-being. In this sense, we can consult articles that study so-called "advertising happiness" (Villalba, 2012; Pellicer, 2013) and whose thesis is summarized in that happiness is the goal and necessity of all human beings and that, at present, it is the best advertising, being the association—explicit or implicit—of brand happiness with strategic success. However, consumers do not always value brands equally, and it is difficult to differentiate them, as demonstrated by Schultz, Block, and Viswanathan (2014) in their study of "no brand preference."

Thus, we briefly analyze, first, the happiness rankings and second, the premises and advances in marketing and branding that have served the object of study developed in this research.

Happiness and Well-Being: Measurement and Rankings

The word *happiness* is used with different meanings; thus, we can say that there is no single or globally accepted definition. It is not the purpose of this work to define happiness, but it is necessary to clarify that in its broadest sense, it is a catch-all for terms such as "well-being" or "quality of life," although they are not all synonymous (Veenhoven, 2009).

We argue in this work for the term *well-being*, understanding it as a construct composed of several measurable, real elements, each contributing to well-being but none of them defining well-being by itself (Seligman, 2011). Thus, well-being is typically understood as an abstract construct with subjective connotations but correlated with objective economic factors.

Compound indicators are a valuable tool for measuring a complex phenomenon. At present, we have almost unlimited mechanisms to measure what we like. However, measuring a phenomenon alone is not enough for decision-making; an evaluation process is required. To evaluate is to appreciate the value of something (a nation, a phenomenon, a characteristic, or a brand). For example, there is evaluation when we say that a process is inefficient, after having measured the performance through indicators and having compared the result with a previously established criterion or having compared it with other values obtained, for example, in other countries, through rankings.

Thus, rankings sort based on an indicator that condenses heterogeneous information about the characteristics and/or results of the objects studied (in our study, countries and brands). Rankings simplify complexity but with the advantages and disadvantages of aggregating variables into a single result: they facilitate their valuation for individuals or work for organizations that do not have the time or the training to analyze the performance achieved in depth, but they hide differential features of the studied objects that may be relevant for understanding the differences or similarities between them.

To return to the principle of this section, the rankings that are subsequently reviewed contribute to playing with ambiguity, recognizing even in its methodologies the non-equivalence between the terms well-being and happiness; however, they may be used synonymously, not as a result of methodological confusion but, rather, as an outcome of searching for a more "salable" result by explicitly bearing "happiness" in their title or simply as a consequence of meeting the resolution of the General Assembly of the United Nations (2011), which urges the nations of the world to measure the happiness of their peoples to ultimately serve as a guide for their policies.

If the desire is to increase the happiness of a greater number of people, then it is necessary to measure it, and it is here that multiple methodologies have been made available to governments and citizens in general, which at the collective level add variables to obtain indexes by country. The methodologies of two indexes, the basis of our research, the WHR and the HPI, are summarized below.

The World Happiness Report (WHR) arises from the United Nations and, in particular, the noted resolution of the General Assembly of the UN. Independent experts led by John F. Helliwell of the Vancouver School of Economics, Richard Layard, the director of the Well-Being Program at the Center for Economic Performance at the London School of Economics, and Jeffrey D. Sachs, the director of the Earth Institute of Columbia University, created the WHR. The index provided by this report measures the added subjective well-being; that is, the well-being of society is viewed as the sum total of the subjective happiness of the people who live in it. It combines six factors that can explain the trends of happiness: real GDP per capita, the hope of leading a healthy life, social support (having someone to count on), perceived freedom in making life decisions, the perception of corruption, and generosity. To date, there have been three published reports (2012, 2015, 2017), in the last of which the number of countries analyzed is 155.

The Happy Planet Index (HPI) is another of the best-known indexes worldwide. It is produced by the independent British organization the New Economics Foundation. In this case, the index is a measure of efficiency, and countries are classified by relating the happy life that they produce to the environmental resources that they consume. Thus, the HPI creates a measure of subjective life satisfaction (subjective well-being) and life expectancy at birth; these two measures are multiplied to obtain the numerator of a fraction whose denominator is the ecological footprint. The ecological footprint is a measure of the number of hectares of average (global) fertile land needed to support the level of consumption of the state in question.

Branding and Happiness: The Possible Influence of Positive Emotions on the Value of Brands

Moods, such as subjective well-being, can have an influence on the cognitive processes of individuals and can condition the decisions that they make. In fact, the literature shows that being in a positive mood affects cognition, making people able, for example, to be more prone to abstract thinking rather than focusing on immediate and near-immediate concerns (Labroo & Patrick, 2009) or making people be more creative in solving problems (Isen, 1999). The sense of happiness also seems to directly influence the manner in which people decide (for example, decision-making is faster; Isen & Means, 1983) and the choices that they make. Thus, there is evidence that in the presence of a positive mood, less risky options tend to be chosen (Isen & Patrick, 1983), the level of skepticism decreases (Forgas & East, 2008), and the choice of more *prosocial* alternatives increases (Fishbach & Labroo, 2007).

In the field of marketing, it is increasingly important to study brands and their associations as a key element in the differentiation of companies and, among other aspects, the influence that they can exert on consumer behavior. Companies are increasingly involved in brand management as one of their main assets, and there is increasing research that seeks to understand how individuals behave toward brands and how they can influence their behavior. Thus, according to Keller (1993, 1998), brand value is the differential effect of brand awareness on the consumer response to a company's marketing actions: value is positive (negative) if the response at the level of perceptions, preferences, or behavior is more (less) favorable than it would be if the product were sold under another name or without a brand. At this point, it is interesting to provide some evidence of how the association with happiness can increase the value of brands:

- The consultant Milward Brown (creator of the BRANZ ranking) conducted an analysis of 6,065 brands between 2001 and 2003 and concluded that the most powerful brands had a greater connection with emotions of a positive nature.
- In another study, Mogilner, Aaker, and Kamvar (2012) selected the main brands in the Interbrand ranking, distinguishing between those that provide "ordinary" and "extraordinary" experiences, to subsequently associate them with the happiness that the brand provides to the respondents and their feeling of personal connection with the brand; they concluded that the brands that are most associated with happiness are those that provide extraordinary experiences.

However, it is undoubtedly the study by the Havas Group called Meaningful Brands, the most recognized in the field at hand, that concerns us, given that it is the first *framework of global analysis* that connects brands and well-being (Havas Group, 2017). In general, from the beginning of the study, a low valuation of brands and their contribution to consumer well-being is observed. All of this leads to the fact that at the global level, consumers declare that they would not mind if 74 percent of all brands disappeared.

Since its inception in 2007, the Meaningful Brands Index (MBI) has evolved from a study more focused on the sustainability of brands, that is, whether they contributed to a greater or lesser extent to sustainability from the environmental, ecological perspective, etc., to an index more concerned with knowing the influence of brands on the well-being and quality of life of people in 33 markets. The index, which is published biannually, is calculated as the sum of the performance of the brand in society (brand performance) and the performance measures or key performance indicators (KPIs) of the brands analyzed, of which there were 1,500 worldwide in the 2017 study.

In its most recent version (field work June–July 2016), the MBI explores the functional, collective, and personal benefits that brands bring and how they tangibly improve people's lives. Specifically, the dimensions that contain each of the benefits analyzed by the index are the following:

- Collective benefits or the role that brands play in society: the government and ethics, the environment, the community, the workplace, and the economy.
- Personal benefits or how brands tangibly improve people's lives: physical, organizational, financial, intellectual, social, emotional, and natural attributes.
- Functional or market benefits such as: quality, category leader, safety and responsibility, co-interaction, delivery, fair prices, innovation, and labeling.

In short, the MBI measures the benefits, in terms of quality, that the brands analyzed contribute to the well-being of the people interviewed, 375,000 globally (Havas Group, 2017), with the subjective component and consumer perception that this entails.

Analysis and Results

Once we have described the three indexes that we address in this chapter, we focus on the analysis of the results.

HPI, WHR, and the Unified Index

Globally, there is no single method of measuring happiness; in the data analysis, we have attempted to verify how the differences in the concept between the two indicators (WHR and HPI) lead to differences in the evaluation of happiness, also attempting to find geographical patterns (if any) for these differences. The fact that the HPI focuses on environmental aspects and the WHR much more on socioeconomic well-being makes it reasonable to expect that the former will reach higher values in better conserved areas and the latter in more developed areas.

To attempt to cushion the discrepancies between these indexes, we constructed a compromise index between the two in which they were combined. Previously, we unified the list of countries, given that they are not the same countries considered in each of the indexes. The WHR 2017 contains information for 155 countries, the HPI 2016 for 140, and the unified list for 134, i.e., virtually all countries.

To compare the indexes expressed in different scales (the HPI varies between 12 and 45, the WHR varies between 3 and 8, and both values are rounded), we resort to index ranking; that is, the important thing is not so much the value (or differences between values) but rather, the order of the countries in each list.

This led us to two lists, numbered from 1 to 134, in which the smallest values corresponded to the least happy and the highest values corresponded to the happiest countries.

If the indexes were measured equally, then the resulting score in each list for a given country would be the same, such that if we represented both scores on a pair of axes, then we would obtain a diagonal straight line.

The following graph, in which RWHR and RHPI indicate the ranges in each index, shows that the situation is far from that which was assumed and that the representation is not at all similar to the expected diagonal. That is, if both indexes coincided, then the countries would be located along the diagonal of Figure 20.1.

How do the differences between indexes occur? To answer this question, we have simplified the classification, dividing each into four practically equal parts: the 34 least happy countries of each have been labeled as 1, the next 34 as 2, the next 34 as 3 and, finally, the 32 happiest of each list as 4.

Table 20.1 shows the distribution of the 134 countries among the 16 possible combinations of both lists: from 1 in the WHR ranking with a value of 1 in the HPI to 4 in both:

As we can observe, only 62 countries (sum of the diagonal: 16,13,16, and 17), slightly less than 46.3 percent, coincide in the same segment: not only are there differences in the classification according to both rankings, but in many cases, the classifications are also substantially different,

Table 20.1 Simplified classification; number of countries in each category.

		RWHR			
		1	2	3	4
RHPI	1	16	8	9	①
	2	12	13	4	5
	3	3	6	16	9
	4	③	7	5	17

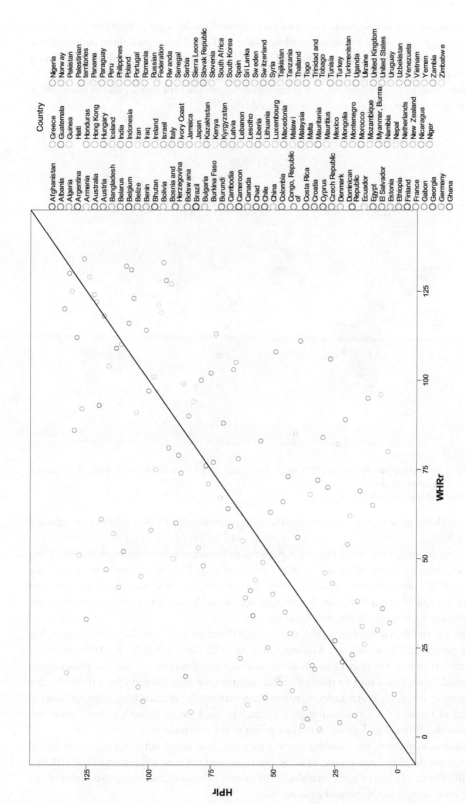

Figure 20.1 Re-scaled WHR and HPI indexes
(Source: prepared from the HPI 2016 and the WHR 2017)

Country

Afghanistan	Greece
Albania	Guatemala
Algeria	Guinea
Argentina	Haiti
Armenia	Honduras
Australia	Hong Kong
Austria	Hungary
Bangladesh	Iceland
Belarus	India
Belgium	Indonesia
Belize	Iran
Benin	Iraq
Bhutan	Ireland
Bolivia	Israel
Bosnia and Herzegovina	Italy
Botswana	Ivory Coast
Brazil	Jamaica
Bulgaria	Japan
Burkina Faso	Kazakhstan
Burundi	Kenya
Cambodia	Kyrgyzstan
Cameroon	Latvia
Canada	Lebanon
Chad	Lesotho
Chile	Liberia
China	Lithuania
Colombia	Luxembourg
Congo, Republic of	Macedonia
Costa Rica	Malawi
Croatia	Malaysia
Cyprus	Malta
Czech Republic	Mauritania
Denmark	Mauritius
Dominican Republic	Mexico
Ecuador	Mongolia
Egypt	Montenegro
El Salvador	Morocco
Estonia	Mozambique
Ethiopia	Myanmar, Burma
Finland	Namibia
France	Nepal
Gabon	Netherlands
Georgia	New Zealand
Germany	Nicaragua
Ghana	Niger
Nigeria	Sierra Leone
Norway	Slovak Republic
Pakistan	Slovenia
Palestinian territories	South Africa
Panama	South Korea
Paraguay	Spain
Peru	Sri Lanka
Philippines	Sweden
Poland	Switzerland
Portugal	Syria
Romania	Tajikistan
Russian Federation	Tanzania
Senegal	Thailand
Serbia	Togo
	Trinidad and Tobago
	Tunisia
	Turkey
	Turkmenistan
	Uganda
	Ukraine
	United Kingdom
	United States
	Uruguay
	Uzbekistan
	Venezuela
	Vietnam
	Yemen
	Zambia
	Zimbabwe

with four countries in the opposite extremes: one country (see light grey circle) with a score of four according to the WHR but one according to the HPI (Sri Lanka), and three countries (see black circle) are in the first column of the WHR but in the fourth row of the HPI (the United States, Trinidad and Tobago, and Luxembourg).

The following map shows the four areas corresponding to the HPI index, colored from lowest to highest intensity according to the four indicated levels:

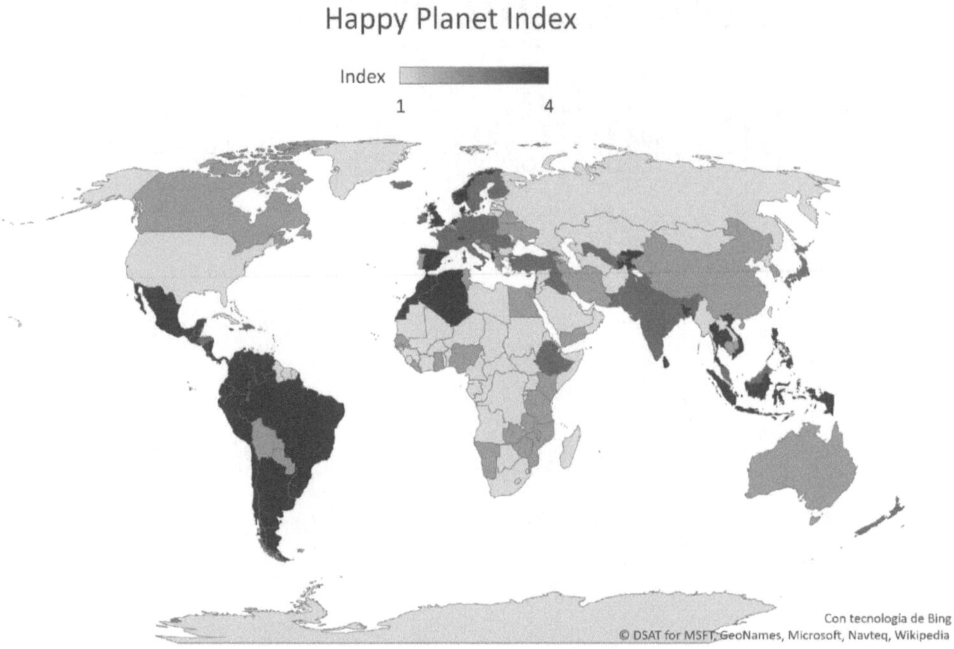

Happy Planet Index

Figure 20.2 Areas corresponding to the HPI index: four areas from lowest to highest happiness, according to color intensity
(Source: prepared from the HPI 2016).

Similarly, with the same scaling of intensities, the value according to WHR would be that reflected in Figure 20.3.

There are not only similarities but also substantial differences because although the HPI gives the highest score to almost all countries in South America and much of Southeast Asia, to the detriment of African countries and some European countries and the United States, the tables are turned in the case of the WHR, which scores European and South American countries higher, to the detriment, above all, of the African continent.

Except for the four countries noted above, the differences in the ranking are extreme, but they are geographically significant. Unfortunately, in both cases, sub-Saharan Africa occupies the unhappiest area of the planet from both the environmental and socioeconomic perspectives.

As noted above, to attempt to reconcile both measures, we have constructed a unified index (global index) based on both indexes; it has been statistically obtained by factorial analysis (extracted variance = 74.6 percent) applied to the classified values of both indexes (to avoid, once again, the differences derived from their different measurement scales).

In addition, to quantify the contribution of each of the two initial indexes, a regression model has been constructed to estimate the value of the combined index as a function of the HPI and the WHR. The coefficient of both variables in the model is the same, indicating that both indexes have the same weight in the unified construction.

World Happiness Report

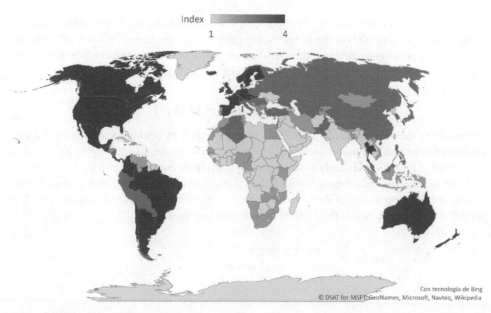

Figure 20.3 Areas corresponding to the WHR index: four areas from lowest to highest happiness, according to color intensity
(Source: prepared by WHR 2017).

The countries were classified again according to the indicator, the global index, in four sections, and the resulting map is as follows:

Global Index

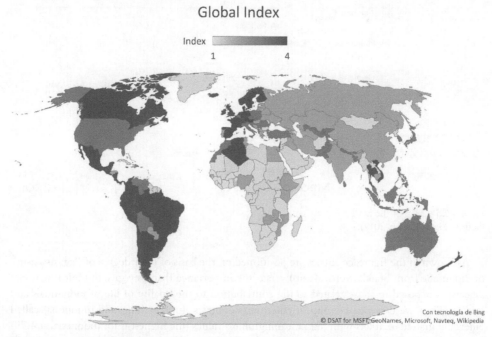

Figure 20.4 Unified global index: four areas from lowest to highest happiness, according to color intensity
(Source: prepared from the HPI 2017).

As expected, the new index combines the "extreme" characters of the two previous classifications.

In view of the results shown by the figures, we can conclude that there are countries that are considered happy regardless of the index used. Similarly, there are areas of countries that do not improve their position regardless of the measurement index. On the other hand, Western Europe and the US have some positional differences depending on the index.

Brands and Well-Being: MBI (*)

According to the data provided by the Havas Group through its headquarters in Spain, the perception of value that consumers have in relation to brands continues to decline globally (less than 27 percent of brands significantly contribute to improving our quality of life).

If we focus on the relationship between the value of the meaningfulness index (vertical axis) and the relative importance of the benefits analyzed by the index (horizontal axis), then we find the following map on which the 33 countries analyzed are positioned:

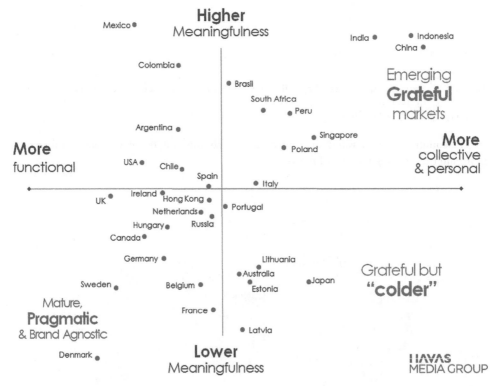

Figure 20.5 Map of the MBI
(Source: Havas Group, 2017).

As shown in the figure, countries are positioned on the basis of their degree of "agnosticism" or distancing from brands (vertical axis) versus the importance that they give to their functional aspects, as opposed to those related to the contribution to the quality of life of individuals and society. Thus, we can find a group of emerging countries (India, China, and Indonesia) called emerging grateful markets with high meaningfulness values (the highest is for Indonesia, at 4.79) in addition to a high intensity of personal and collectivist aspects (greater than 64 percent in all three cases). In contrast, we find a group of older European countries (Sweden, France, Belgium, and Germany) that are pragmatic and very agnostic about the contribution of brands, headed by Denmark, which has meaningfulness values close to 3.15 percent and an intensity of 54 percent. Additionally, we can find another group of countries, called grateful but "colder," such as Japan and Latvia, with more extreme values, and Estonia, Lithuania, and Australia, with very similar values (59 percent and 3.62 in the case of Lithuania, which is the country that obtains the highest scores of the three countries).

Conclusions

The main conclusion that we reach after the development of this chapter is that there is no single method of measuring happiness. In fact, we have focused on only three indexes of the many that are published annually: the HPI, the WHP, and the MBI.

In attempting to relate the HPI and the WHP, we observed that only 62 countries were in the same segment. In some cases, the ranking positions were diametrically opposite. From both an environmental (HPI) and socioeconomic (WHP) perspective, sub-Saharan Africa occupies the unhappiest area in the world.

Constructing a unified index to attempt to reconcile the two previous indexes, we conclude that there are countries that are happy regardless of the index, others that do not improve their position, and some such as the US and some Western European countries that vary their position based on the index used.

In relation to the MBI, emerging countries are those that most believe in the value of brands and in their role in contributing to happiness, compared to countries that are considered more developed, which are on the opposite end.

In line with the objectives of the chapter and after evaluating the relationship between the level of people's happiness and the sense of well-being that brands provide, we can conclude that companies have a long way to go to provide values that contribute to people's well-being. There-fore, it is the task of brands to improve their contribution of benefits, mainly personal, to build a relationship with consumers that conveys positive values through relevant content to contribute to this growing demand for brand involvement in the well-being of society.

Some future lines of research could focus on detecting which strategies make brands contrib-ute the most to collective well-being so that they can serve as a reference to other brands, among whose lines are the contribution to the well-being of theirs consumers and the construction of a long-term relationship. Similarly, we consider that it would be interesting to perform future estimates of the global index proposed in this chapter and to compare whether governments are investing in policies that improve the well-being of their countries, as proposed by the resolution of the General Assembly of the UN.

Acknowledgments

We would like to thank the Havas Group and, specifically, Dionisia Mata Prado, Insights-Analytics Area Director, Meaningful Brands Director Spain, for providing the latest data from the Mean-ingful Brands 2017 study, which have been of great help for the elaboration of this chapter.

References

Diener, E., & Chan, M. Y. (2011). Happy people live longer: Subjective well-being contributes to health and longevity. *Applied Psychology: Health and Well-Being, 3*(1), 1–43.
Diener, E., & Seligman, M. E. (2002). Very happy people. *Psychological Science, 13*(1), 81–84.

Fishbach, A., & Labroo, A. A. (2007). Be better or be merry: How mood affects self-control. *Journal of Personality and Social Psychology, 93*(2), 158.

Forgas, J. P., & East, R. (2008). On being happy and gullible: Mood effects on skepticism and the detection of deception. *Journal of Experimental Social Psychology, 44*(5), 1362–1367.

Gobé, M. (2005). *Branding emocional. El nuevo paradigma para conectar las marcas. Barcelona.* Barcelona: DIVINE EGG.

Harris, R. (2007). *The happiness trap: Stop struggling, start living.* London: Little, Brown Book Group.

Havas Group (2017). *Meaningful Brands®.* Retrieved from https://havasmedia.com/meaningful-brands-reap-greater-financial-rewards/

Helliwell, J., Layard, R., & Sachs, J. (2012). *World happiness report 2012.* New York, NY: Sustainable Development Solutions Network.

Helliwell, J., Layard, R., & Sachs, J. (2015). *World happiness report 2015.* New York, NY: Sustainable Development Solutions Network.

Helliwell, J., Layard, R., & Sachs, J. (2017). *World happiness report 2017.* New York, NY: Sustainable Development Solutions Network.

Hervás, G., & Chaves, C. (2018). What can science can tell us about human happiness (and why and how should we disseminate it)? In J. A. Muñiz-Velázquez & C. Pulido (Eds.), *The Routledge handbook of positive communication* (pp. 20–28). New York, NY: Routledge.

Isen, A. M. (1999). On the relationship between affect and creative problem solving: Affect, creative experience, and psychological adjustment, 3, 17. In S. W. Russ (Ed.), *Affect, creative experience and psychological adjustment* (pp. 3–18). Philadelphia: Brunner and Mazel.

Isen, A. M., & Means, B. (1983). The influence of positive affect on decision-making strategy. *Social Cognition, 2*(1), 18–31.

Isen, A. M., & Patrick, R. (1983). The effect of positive feelings on risk taking: When the chips are down. *Organizational Behavior and Human Performance, 31*(2), 194–202.

Karen Jeffrey, K., Wheatley, H., & Abdallah, S. (2016). *Happy Planet Index report: A global index of sustainable well-being.* Retrieved from https://static1.squarespace.com/static/5735c421e321402778ee0ce9/t/57e0052d440243730fdf03f3/1474299185121/Briefing+paper+-+HPI+2016.pdf

Keller, K. L. (1993). Conceptualizing, measuring and managing customer-based brand equity. *The Journal of Marketing, 57*(1), 1–22.

Keller, K. L. (1998). *Strategic brand management: Building, measuring, and managing brand equity.* NJ, USA: Prentice-Hall, Inc.

Labroo, A. A., & Patrick, V. M. (2009). Providing a moment of respite: Why a positive mood helps seeing the big picture. *Journal of Consumer Research, 35*(5), 800–809.

Mogilner, C., Aaker, J., & Kamvar, S. D. (2012). How happiness affects choice. *Journal of Consumer Research, 39*(2), 429–443.

Pellicer, M. T. (2013). La promesa de felicidad en los mensajes de la publicidad comercial. *Pensar la Publicidad, 7*(1), 13–23.

Punset, E. (2005). *El viaje a la felicidad. Las nuevas claves científicas.* Barcelona: Destino.

Schultz, D. E., Block, M. P., & Viswanathan, V. (2014). Brand preference being challenged. *Journal of Brand Management, 21*(5), 408–428.

Seligman, M. (2011). *La vida que florece.* Barcelona: Ediciones B.

United Nations. (2011). *Resolution 65/309 Happiness: Towards a holistic approach to development.* Retrieved from undocs.org/A/65/309

Veenhoven, R. (2009). Measures of gross national happiness. *Psychosocial Intervention, 18*(3), 279–299.

Villalba, T. C. (2012). Selling happiness: The new paradigm of brands. *Retos, 2*(3), 38–51.

21

FEMVERTISING DISCOURSES AND ONLINE CONSUMER ENGAGEMENT

A Case Analysis of Under Armour's #IWillWhatIWant Brand Campaign

Linda Tuncay Zayer, Catherine A. Coleman, and Jose Luis Rodriguez Orjuela

As Don Draper, advertising's fictional, quintessential poster boy of Madison Avenue explains, "Advertising is based on one thing: happiness. And you know what happiness is? Happiness is the smell of a new car. It's freedom from fear. It's a billboard on the side of a road that screams with reassurance that whatever you're doing is OK. You are OK." This notion that advertising promises to relieve universal social anxieties, such as the search for happiness, through a consumption ethic is echoed by scholars such as Jhally (2002), who argues that advertising's fundamental job as a discursive form is to tell "a story about human happiness. That's how it sells. That's how it does its job. It sells products by convincing people that their happiness is connected to buying products. And particularly to buying *this* product" (see also Jhally, 1990; Miller, 2015). Much criticism of marketing and advertising has focused on the claims, as O'Shaughnessy and O'Shaughnessy (2002, p. 524) describe, "that today's consumer society is hedonistic, due largely to modern day marketing practices." Further, "'consumerism' and 'hedonism' are part of a rhetoric of reproval and reprobation, suggesting that selfish, irresponsible pleasure-seeking has come to dominate life" (p. 528).

However, O'Shaughnessy and O'Shaughnessy (2002) suggest these critiques to be exaggerated at best, pointing to the complex ways in which consumers engage with advertising content and make decisions, and to complexities and nuances of human happiness beyond self-interested pleasures. These nuances are further supported by scholarship on hedonic (broadly associated with personal pleasures and enjoyments) and eudaimonic (broadly associated with concepts such as meaning, self-actualization, and authenticity) well-being (Huta, 2017). In this chapter, we examine a contemporary example of a purportedly positive and empowering brand campaign, which draws from a discourse of self-actualization, meaning, and excellence often associated with eudaimonic well-being. More specifically, we explore the pro-woman empowerment discourse in Under Armour Women's "I Will What I Want" campaign by examining trade press and brand-generated content as well as online consumer engagement with the campaign to consider how consumers respond to the idea that the brand promotes positive messages for women through its female empowerment narratives.

Prior Literature on Gender, Well-Being, and Happiness

While primarily agreeing that advertising is an important platform for inquiry, scholars have long debated advertising's role in society, whether it reflects or constructs social realities (Grow & Wolburg, 2006), and its relationship to well-being and happiness from a variety of macro-social (e.g., Galbraith, 1998; Pollay, 1986; Holbrook, 1987) and micro-psychological (e.g., Vargas & Yoon, 2006) vantage points. Some have voiced concerns over mechanisms of contemporary life, including media myths and representations broadly and advertising specifically, that embed unending consumption—of material goods and of symbolic meaning for identity work—in the pursuit of happiness (e.g., O'Shaughnessy & O'Shaughnessy, 2002; Giddens, 1991; Schudson, 1984; Miller, 2015).

Further, as Miller (2015) argues, the pursuits of happiness as represented in consumer culture, including advertising, are distinctly gendered. That is, what is deemed acceptable to pursue, how it is pursued, and in what context it may be pursued, as presented through the discourses of advertising and marketing, are different for men and women in consequential ways. For example, scholars have examined gender stereotypes in advertising and their relationship with cultural values, gendered implications of social comparison and positive or negative self-evaluation, body image, and eating disorders that affect women's and men's abilities to pursue and achieve happiness (e.g., Grabe, Ward, & Hyde, 2008; Wolf, 1991; Wood, 1989; Harper & Tiggemann, 2008; Zayer & Otnes, 2012).

These gendered differences in advertising texts have been a point of critique for more than 50 years by feminist scholars and cultural theorists. Concerns about the negative impact on women (and more recently on men) of gender-based portrayals include subordinating and demeaning stereotypes, which often tie women's happiness with the ability to conform to certain ideals of beauty and to limited social roles, and misvalued consumption-based solutions to systemic social and political inequalities (e.g., Wolf, 1991). Various 20th-century examples exist of advertisers' attempts to address these critiques (e.g., Grow, 2008; Lambiase, Bronstein, & Coleman, forthcoming). Goldman, Heath, and Smith (1991) point to the ways in which advertisers responded to the feminist movement of the 1970s through market-motivated commodity feminism, or re-appropriation of the female body as a site of power, while at the same time commodifying the self. However, the past decade in particular has witnessed an increased responsiveness by marketers to gender critiques in the form of variously termed "go-girl marketing," "empowerment marketing," or "femvertising," a term coined in 2014 by SheKnows Media (Stampler, 2014) to identify campaigns that contain messages of female empowerment. Dove's Real Beauty campaign is generally credited with breaking boundaries through a "'dawning realisation' of the female consumer" (Davidson, 2015) that ushered in a wave of femvertising, subsequently picked up by brands such as Google, Chevrolet, Always, Pantene, and Under Armour.

Many, in particular in popular press, have lauded these campaigns for their progressive stances on gender and their potential to promote positive change. Based on a SheKnows Media report (2014), these are important issues for female consumers: more than 90 percent of women believe stereotyping of women as sex symbols in advertising is harmful and that advertising directly impacts girls' self-esteem, and a majority of women surveyed (81 percent) also believe that pro-female ads are important for younger generations to see. Importantly, according to the survey, they believe advertisers should be held responsible for promoting positive messages to women (71 percent; SheKnows Living editors, 2014). Many of these campaigns are clearly drawing from a long history of feminist activism. However, marketing, advertising, and feminism have a complicated history (Maclaran, 2012), with prior scholarship arguing that consumer culture is "anti-feminist," and with contemporary advertisers hesitant to claim feminist lineage. Critics argue that brands are co-opting and simultaneously marginalizing or dismissing (Myers, 2013, p. 198), through empowerment marketing and femvertising, the long history of feminist work and activism that has fought for positive change. McRobbie (2009, p. 158), for example, has argued that the "pro-capitalist femininity-focused repertoire . . . plays directly into the hands of corporate consumer culture eager to tap into this market on the basis of young women's rising incomes." Others have suggested, however, that the potential of these campaigns, in the context of contemporary commodity culture, is more complex. For example, Johnston and Taylor (2008) point to the potentially transformative messages of Dove's Campaign for Real Beauty in disrupting gender norms and expanding definitions of female beauty, but ultimately, they argue, the empowerment of "feminist consumerism" still hinges on an ideological system that legitimizes and reproduces gendered beauty-focused consumption practices.

Context: Under Armour Women's #IWILLWHATIWANT Campaign

Prior and continued scholarship using discursive analyses and critical and cultural approaches to corporate messaging provide important insights into what types of messages are produced, legitimized, and reproduced, and what messages of empowerment are offered in consumer culture. It is also important to understand how consumers engage with these messages. Consumer online engagement is particularly important in this context, given that the digital revolution and women's use of social media has "created a seismic shift in the industry's approach to marketing" and has been a critical impetus for brands' female empowerment messages (Davidson, 2015). The Under Armour "I Will What I Want" campaign was seen as a "major marketing shift" (Feldman, 2014) for the athletic wear brand, which traditionally marketed to men through messages of power, will, and performance, by centering on the idea of female empowerment and employing a range of strong female endorsers, including skier Lindsey Vonn, supermodel Gisele Bündchen, ballerina Misty Copeland, and tennis player Sloane Stevens. The campaign consisted of television spots on ESPN, E!, MTV and ABC, digital advertising efforts on *Glamour, Mode, People, Refinery29, Us Weekly, Well + Good*, among others, utilization of a social media hashtag, as well as the creation of a fitness focused app. Within the first six months of the campaign, by January 2015, sales of Under Armour Women reportedly increased by 28 percent (Tour, 2015). Due to the success of the campaign, Under Armour was named *Ad Age*'s Marketer of the Year for 2014 (Schultz, 2014). Their branding efforts were also widely discussed in the popular press as one example of the trend of "femvertising," or "advertising that employs pro-female talent, messages and imagery to empower women and girls" (Castillo, 2014).

As we note through this chapter, Under Armour's focus in the "I Will What I Want" campaign is on female perseverance, empowerment, and self-actualization. At the same time, we are mindful of scholars such as Miller (2015), who suggest that happiness offered by advertising is illusory insofar as it both implies a consumption ethic while masking mechanisms (i.e., wealth) required to achieve it, and feminist scholars such as McRobbie (2008; 2009), who are concerned about the ways in which the post-feminist, neoliberal appropriation of terms such as empowerment and choice may actually serve to de-emphasize critical analysis of systemic sexism for which institutions such as advertising have long been under scrutiny. Indeed, having attended the announcement event of Under Armour Women and the subsequent "I Will What I Want" campaign, *Sneaker Report* editor Calvy Click (2014) notes, "Listening to Under Armour's founder speak yesterday, it is apparent that the company craves a different customer. #IWILLWHATIWANT is in an effort to inspire women to *shop*, which has been no easy feat for their competitors."

Within the broader context of these debates around femvertising, we utilize the case of Under Armour to investigate: 1) How did the Under Armour brand draw from gender discourses surrounding its global branding campaign targeting women? 2) What are consumers' responses to a so-called "femvertising" campaign as enacted on social media?

Method

We examine these questions using a case study method exploring this campaign at the height of its launch and by analyzing social media responses online. First, following research by Parmentier and Fischer (2014) on the dynamics behind brand audiences, we engaged in the netnographic analysis of multiple sources of data, including press releases, trade, and popular press articles from *Advertising Age* and *Adweek* for a period of one year surrounding the launch, as well as components of the brand campaign. As Parmentier and Fischer (2014, p. 1238) state, "The wider contexts in which brands come into existence contain many cultural narratives . . ." Thus, we attempted to gain a thorough understanding of not only the discourses utilized within the content of the campaign but also the cultural narratives put forth by Under Armour corporate executives (through press releases, media interviews, corporate website, social media) as well as by trade press.

To examine consumer responses, we engaged in data mining, collecting approximately 8,000 tweets from Twitter by both verified and general twitter users using the campaign hashtag #IWILLWHATIWANT from June 2014 to December 2016. The data was initially collected using web-scraping techniques to capture historical data from twitter that was later analyzed using R, an open-source data analytics package. Data preparation began by collecting historical tweets using the hashtag #IWILLWHATIWANT using python, javascript, and XML techniques that allow for capture of historical data from the twitter website in raw format. The data was then transformed to rows and columns (csv file) format for text cleaning, segmentation, and analysis using R. A string matching technique was used to divide the tweets by their different components and users. Components became the columns containing the information extracted from the raw data. Main components of tweets were identified as follows: 1) Profile picture-avatar, 2) Account verification, 3) Twitter @username, 4) Twitter account full name, 5) Tweet time stamp/date, 6) Tweet text, 7) Links, 8) Hashtags, 9) Tweet actions (favorite, retweets, replies).

Data Analysis

To explore the cultural discourses surrounding the launch of the "I Will What I Want" campaign, members of the research team engaged in a hermeneutic analysis of the text to uncover themes. Because the textual data was pulled using search terms for both "I will what I want" as well as "Under Armour," some articles were not relevant to the campaign analysis itself, and were excluded from the analysis. From the remaining articles, researchers discussed the themes that emerged from the textual data and converged on interpretation.

To examine the 8,000 tweets, text mining and analytics techniques were used. More specifically, researchers used frequency analysis, a text analysis technique commonly used to find patterns in text, to identify themes within the data. The dataset was split between verified Twitter users (N = 193), who are often public figures and more likely to be influencers, and non-verified Twitter users (N = 3586). Further, graphs displaying word associations and cluster dendograms were also generated to seek out additional patterns.

Findings

Discourse Analysis

Changemaking

Analysis of the trade press and press releases surrounding the first year of the launch reveals that the campaign, as well its agency Droga5, are often positioned as *changemakers*. In a press release from Under Armour, CEO Kevin Plank describes the campaign, saying, "Today, Under Armour inspires the next generation of athletes to unleash their inner resolve and our I WILL trademark confirms our promise to continuously redefine the future of performance through innovation that will help give athletes an edge." Often touted as breaking new ground, being innovative, and challenging norms, the trade conversation around the campaign is also filled with rhetoric that largely praises both the brand and the agency. For example, in an *Adweek* article on female leadership in the industry and the pay gap, Under Armour, along with brands such as Always, are couched as producing "conversation-changing work" (Kaplan, 2015). An article in *Advertising Age* proclaiming Under Armour as "Marketer of the Year" discusses the "groundbreaking women's campaign" and further positions the brand as somewhat of an underdog utilizing a "a take-no-prisoners approach embodied by Mr. Plank, a feisty former University of Maryland football player . . . whose goal is to topple Nike and become the world's top retail sports brand" (Schultz, 2014). Others industry insiders call out specific elements of the campaign, such as an Under Armour website which drew in real time consumer feedback with regard to model and Under Armour spokesperson, Gisele Bündchen—describing it as "digitally innovative" (Nudd, 2015). In *Advertising Age*, McCarthy (2014) calls the campaign, ". . . a smart way for UA to stand out."

Celebrating

The most salient theme that emerged from the analysis is the notion of *celebrating women*—a discourse supported by both the press and the Under Armour executives. This theme largely embodies a celebration of women, a "women-festo" and of inclusive empowerment. In a press release from Under Armour on July 31, 2014, spokesperson Misty Copeland states, "I am excited to be part of the new Under Armour Women's campaign and to be able to inspire women as they find the will to pave their own way, just as I have in my own career. I am honored to be a part of a brand that recognizes the power of hard work and dedication over fate and luck. That kind of inner strength is what keeps me going." Indeed, Copeland is a centerpiece in the launch of the campaign—a spot that features her dancing in a studio with a voiceover reading a rejection letter; however, the spot ends with her dancing on a stage and defiantly looking into the camera as it fades to the I Will What I Want tagline. Interestingly, when notions of gender and feminism are posed to Under Armour leadership by the press, executives are careful to tread lightly, taking full advantage of the positivity related to awareness of gender equality issues, but failing to claim alignment with a feminist discourse. For instance, in an article on female leadership in boardrooms, CEO Kevin Plank is quoted as stating, "We learned some incredibly hard lessons. We learned nine men sitting around a table cannot do products for women. The first shipment never went out to retailers. We buried it" (Diaz & Zmuda, 2014). However, at the same time, Under Armour executives call the campaign strategy a "woman-a-festo" (Schultz, 2014) and as exemplifying "girl power" (Zmuda & Diaz, 2014). One of the key players behind the campaign, Leanne Fremar, senior vice president and creative director for Under Armour Women, says, "The goal was to celebrate women who had the physical and mental strength to tune out the external pressures and turn inward and chart their own course" (Schultz, 2014). Moreover, Under Armour explicitly distances themselves from an association with feminism. In a separate article, Fremar is quoted as stating, "the generations that really paved the way for feminism and the women that are living in the bliss and freedom that feminism provided" is "very interesting, but maybe not a brand conversation" (Zmuda & Diaz, 2014). In a similar vein, Heidi Sandreuter, vice president, women's marketing, agrees, "We think women are already empowered. They don't need a pat on the back. We want to celebrate women living their lives on their own terms" (Zmuda & Diaz, 2014). Executive VP and creative director at Leo Burnett (and creator of the Always brand's Like A Girl campaign) provides one explanation in an *Advertising Age* article discussing the recent "femvertising" trend: "I don't think anybody wants to talk about feminism anymore. It's one of the most misunderstood and controversial words out there. [But] if you talk about it as 'girl power,' that's purely positive. At its heart it's not that different from feminism, but it is a fresh new way to think about it" (Zmuda & Diaz, 2014). With an understanding of the macro discourses surrounding the campaign as a celebration of women and one that exemplifies innovation and change, we now turn to insights from our quantitative analysis of social media responses on Twitter.

Frequency Analysis

All Users

Frequency analysis is commonly used to find patterns in the rhetoric of the document text— in this case the collected tweets about the campaign—and reveals themes in the social media responses, both by verified users and by general users. From the frequency analysis of the hashtags of all user types (verified and non-verified), the most frequently used hashtags alongside #IWILL-WHATIWANT were largely fitness related (#sweataday, #fitness, #yoga #fitfam, #sweatpink, #toneitup, etc.). This reveals the wide range of Under Armour's marketing initiatives at this time related to its core business, including its #SweatADay Instagram challenge led by Shauna Harrison, and its relationships with other spokespersons such as yoga enthusiast Kathryn Budig. However, two of the most frequently used hashtags were #mistycopeland and #ballet, demonstrating the prominence of the Misty Copeland ad. Of note are also hashtags such #inspiration and #girlpower which signal the positivity of the campaign and its connections to the empowerment of "girls" (yet little to no association with feminism or gender equality). Connections between #IWILLWHATIWANT and other campaigns are also made—both within Under Armour, such as former branding campaigns #protectthishouse and subsequent campaigns #ruleyourself—as well as unrelated brands, such as Procter & Gamble's Always brand, which launched a "femvertising" message around the same time with the #likeagirl campaign, as well as #nikeplus (Nike being a direct competitor of Under Armour). From the frequency analysis of the mentions by all user types, we can see the emergence of conversations surrounding Misty Copeland once again. Despite the use of many high-profile spokespersons, relative unknown Misty Copeland (@mistyonpointe) is the most frequently mentioned and appears to be the driver of social media engagement online. Other common mentions include female public figures related to the campaign, including Shauna Harrison (@shauna_harrison), Gisele Bündchen (@giseleofficial), Lindsey Vonn (@lindseyvonn) as well as the advertising agency that developed the campaign Droga5 (@droga5). An analysis of the words most frequently associated with the hashtag #IWILL-WHATIWANT reveals that a majority of the words convey positive sentiments. In addition to "will," "new," "day," "campaign," "women," "can," "just," "want," "today" (likely describing the campaign), "misty," and "copeland" are among the most frequently used terms. Most interestingly, the data reveals other frequent words are "love," "thanks," "great," "story," "like," "good," "inspiring," "amazing," "awesome," "beautiful," "excited," "strong," and "happy."

Verified Users

For further insights, we examined the most used hashtags by verified users, which we posited may be influencers in the conversation surrounding the campaign. Besides the expected #underarmour, #iwill, the analysis reveals hashtags such as #aimtrue—mentioning the yoga and recipe book by UA spokesperson Kathryn Budig and #indycar, referring to UA spokesperson Indy Car Series driver Pippa Mann, as well as #uarun. There are also frequent hashtags which illustrate positive messaging, such as #staytrue, #mondaymotivation, #eraselldoubt, #earnyourarmour, #blessed, and #badass to a lesser extent. From the frequency analysis of mentions by verified users, it is clear that the Under Armour Women's account and female public figures associated with the campaign are the most mentioned—led by @mistyonpointe, and followed by @lindeseyvonn and @giseleofficial. From the frequency analysis of the verified users' tweets, we can again uncover the words most often associated with the hashtag by verified users. These include terms such as "thanks," "will," "day," "great," "workout," "women," "support," "new," "day," and "campaign" "movement." Once again, positive sentiments also emerge, including words such as "love," "great," "awesome," and "happy."

Word Associations

Utilizing graphical representations of the data, we examined illustrations of the association of the words most commonly used in the tweets we collected. Because Misty Copeland emerged as a main driver of the #IWILLWHATIWANT campaign, we examined the words most commonly associated with "Copeland," revealing terms such as "starring" and "fame" (also linked to "inspiring"), "stunning," "jaw" (connected to "dropping" ie. jaw-dropping), and "professional." Emergence of other connected words such as "atypical," "unlikely," "disruptive," and "stereotype" signals the "disruptive choice" phrase used by Under Armour executives to describe its selection of Copeland as a spokesperson. Looking at a similar graphical representation for the word "women," we again found a range of positive words including "powerful," "great," "coolest," "love," "empowering," "motivating," "positive," "excellent," "amazing," "inspiring," and "stereotypes."

Discussion and Implications

From our qualitative and quantitative analysis, we can see the overarching discourses surrounding the campaign of celebrating women largely matched the responses on social media—both from verified Twitter users (perhaps influencers) and general Twitter users (consumers). That is, the intended message was received overwhelmingly in a positive manner by consumers as they often found the campaign inspirational and expressed a range of emotions such as happiness and love. In other words, Under Armour's #IWILLWHATIWANT campaign served as a form of positive communication in consumer's lives, with positively oriented messages from the brand and from consumers capturing elements of both hedonic and eudaimonic experiences, as outlined by Huta (2017). For example, the changemaking narrative surrounding the brand serves as a proxy for both hedonic experiences such as positive affect (as evidenced in words like happy) and eudaimonic experiences such as elevation (as evidenced in words such as inspiring, empowering, amazing, support) and accomplishment (motivating, strong) as expressed by Twitter users. Engagement was particularly driven by the story behind the Misty Copeland video (viewed 6 million times in a little over a month alone, McCarthy, 2014), which exemplified a sense of empowerment. The choice of Copeland as a spokesperson is particularly interesting as, although she is touted as "disruptive choice" by Sandreuter, Under Armour's vice president, women's marketing (McCarthy, 2014), the firm appears to have largely sought to avoid any overt political statements. Copeland was only the third African-American woman soloist in the more than seven-decade history of the American Ballet Theater (Newman, 2014). Moreover, ballet is typically not perceived as a sport and ballerinas are not traditionally seen as athletes. However, while the brand attempted to engage in marketing with a purpose, they avoided any high profile political conversations.

The brand was particularly careful to avoid associating itself as a feminist campaign, although many of its messages aligned with feminist discourses. Rather, the brand couched itself in a particular kind of discourse—some calling it "soft feminism." As David Rodgers, professor from Columbia Business School, notes in Zmuda and Diaz (2014), "It's not really about pursuing feminism through government action or legislation. There's this idea of 'Let's pursue feminist goals,' beginning internally rather than externally." The notion of individual focused pursuit of social change is particularly striking given feminism's long political history, driven by communities of women. However, feminism and marketing have had a complicated history (Maclaran, 2012) and past scholars have noted that consumer culture is "anti-feminist"; that is, "taking feminism into account" while simultaneously "dismissing it" (Myers, 2013, p. 198).

The emergence of social media, as Kozinets (2010, p. 39) has pointed out, has altered the manner in which people seek to change the world and how they serve as social agents of change. With only 26 percent of Americans considering themselves feminists according to a 2016 You-Gov poll (less than one-third of women and less than one-fifth of men), Under Armour may have had their pulse on the cultural conversations of gender in the US And while possibly a strategically wise move to encourage female empowerment while avoiding the feminist label, what does this signal for the broader discourse of feminism? The wave of femvertising has only served to intensify since the launch of #IWILLWHATIWANT, with recent campaigns by Audi, H&M, Brawny, and even Barbie all attempting to capitalize on the femvertising trend. And consumers are responding—a 2014 SheKnows survey found that over half of women bought a product because of the way the brand portrayed women. While consumers may respond positively to such branding efforts on an individual level, what does the co-optation of feminism mean for society more broadly? Moreover, what are the connections between these discourses, gender relations and individual well-being and happiness? Future research should explore the trend of femvertising in more depth and how femvertising discourses fit in with larger conversations surrounding the politics of gender and feminism in society. Indeed, as Peterson and Seligman (2004) highlight, there are three areas of focus for positive psychology—subjective experiences, individual traits, and the study of institutions that shapes these two elements. By understanding the institutions of advertising and how they shape gender and political discourse, we may further uncover its connections to individual well-being and happiness within the context of broader gender relations.

References

Castillo, M. (2014). *These stats prove femvertising works.* Retrieved from www.adweek.com/news/technology/these-stats-prove-femvertising-works-160704

Click, C. (2014). *Under armour women launches their largest campaign to date with #I Will What I Want.* Retrieved from http://sneakerreport.com/news/under-armour-women-launches-their-largest-campaign-to-date-with-iwillwhatiwant/

Davison, L. (2015). Femvertising: Advertisers cash in on #feminism. *The Telegraph.* Retrieved from https://www.telegraph.co.uk/women/womens-life/11312629/Femvertising-Advertisers-cash-in-on-feminism.html

Diaz, A., & Zmuda, N. (2014). *Less talk, more woman at the top.* Retrieved from http://adage.com/article/agency-news/talk-women-top/294782/

Feldman, J. (2014). Misty Copeland's under Armour Ad is like nothing you've seen. *Life.* Retrieved from https://www.huffpost.com/entry/under-armour-misty-copeland_n_5638927

Galbraith, J. K. (1998). *The affluent society* (40th Anniversary ed.). New York, NY: Houghton Mifflin Company.

Giddens, A. (1991). *Modernity and self-identity. Self and society in the late modern age.* Stanford: Stanford University Press.

Goldman, R., Heath, D., & Smith, S. L. (1991). Commodity feminism. *Critical Studies in Mass Communication, 8,* 333–351. doi:10.1080/15295039109366801

Grabe, S., Ward, L. M., & Hyde, J. S. (2008). The role of the media in body image concerns among women: A meta-analysis of experimental and correlational studies. *Psychological Bulletin, 134*(3), 460–476. doi:10.1037/0033-2909.134.3.460

Grow, J. (2008). The gender of branding: Early Nike women's advertising as a feminist antenarrative. *Women's Studies in Communication, 31*(3), 312–343. doi:10.1080/07491409.2008.10162545

Grow, J. W., & Wolburg, J. (2006). Selling truth: How Nike's advertising to women claimed a contested reality. *Advertising & Society Review, 7*(2), 55–79.

Harper, B., & Tiggemann, M. (2008). The effect of thin ideal media images on women's self-objectification, mood, and body image. *Sex Roles, 58,* 649–657. doi:10.1007/s11199-007–9379-x

Holbrook, M. (1987). Mirror, mirror, on the wall, what's unfair in the reflections on advertising? *Journal of Marketing, 51*(3), 95–103. doi:10.2307/1251650

Huta, V. (2017). An overview of hedonic and eudaimonic well-being concepts. In L. Reinecke & M. B. Oliver (Eds.), *Handbook of media use and well-being.* New York, NY: Routledge.

Jhally, S. (1990). *The codes of advertising: Fetishism and the political economy of meaning in the consumer society.* New York, NY: Routledge.

Jhally, S., & O'Barr, W. M. (2002). Interview with Sut Jhally. *Advertising & Society Review, 3*(2). Project MUSE. doi:10.1353/asr.2002.0005

Johnston, J., & Taylor, J. (2008). Feminist consumerism and fat activists: A comparative study of grassroots activism and the dove real beauty campaign. *Signs, 33*(4), 941–966. doi:10.1086/528849

Kaplan, K. (2015). *Women need to get into corporate boardrooms to close the gender pay gap.* Retrieved from www.adweek.com/brand-marketing/women-need-get-corporate-boardrooms-close-gender-pay-gap-163897/

Kozinets, R. (2010). *Netnography: Doing ethnographic research online.* London: Sage Publications.

Lambiase, J., Bronstein, C., & Coleman, C. A. (forthcoming). Women vs. Brands: Sexist advertising and gender stereotypes motivate trans-generational feminist critique. In P. J. Kreshel & K. Golombisky (Eds.), *Feminists, feminism and advertising: Some restrictions apply.* Lanham, MD: Lexington Books.

Maclaran, P. (2012). Marketing and feminism in historic perspective. *Journal of Historical Research in Feminism, 4*(3), 462–469. doi:10.1108/17557501211252998

McCarthy, M. (2014). *Ad of the day: Under Armour presents Gisele Bündchen like you've never seen her.* Retrieved from www.adweek.com/brand-marketing/ad-day-under-armour-presents-gisele-b-ndchen-youve-never-seen-her-159871/

McRobbie, A. (2008). Young women and consumer culture: An intervention. *Cultural Studies, 22*(5), 531–550. doi:10.1080/09502380802245803

McRobbie, A. (2009). *The aftermath of feminism: Gender, culture and social change.* Los Angeles: Sage Publications.

Miller, C. (2015). Finding the golden egg: Illusions of happiness in an age of consumer capitalism. In L. Hockley & N. Fadina (Eds.), *The happiness illusion: How the media sold us a fairytale* (pp. 89–106). New York, NY: Routledge.

Myers, K. (2013). Anti-feminist messages in American television programming for young girls. *Journal of Gender Studies, 22*(2), 192–205. doi:10.1080/09589236.2012.714074

Newman, A. A. (2014). *Under Armour heads off the sidelines for a campaign aimed at women.* Retrieved from www.nytimes.com/2014/07/31/business/media/under-armour-heads-off-the-sidelines-for-a-campaign-aimed-at-women.html?mcubz=0&_r=0

Nudd, T. (2015). *Droga5's Gisele campaign for under armour scores the cyber grand prix at cannes.* Retrieved from www.adweek.com/brand-marketing/droga5s-gisele-campaign-under-armour-scores-cyber-grand-prix-cannes-165541/

O'Shaughnessy, J., & O'Shaughnessy, N. J. (2002). Marketing, the consumer society and hedonism. *European Journal of Marketing, 36*(⅚), 524–547. doi:10.1108/03090560210422871

Parmentier, M. A., & Fischer, E. (2014, February). Things fall apart: The dynamics of brand audience dissipation. *Journal of Consumer Research, 41,* 1228–1251. doi:10.1086/678907

Peterson, C., & Seligman, M. (2004). *Character strengths and virtues: A handbook and classification.* New York, NY: Oxford University Press.

Pollay, R. W. (1986). The distorted mirror: Reflections on the unintended consequences of advertising. *Journal of Marketing, 50*(2), 18–36. doi:10.2307/1251597

Schudson, M. (1984). *Advertising, the Uneasy Persuasion.* New York: Basic Books.

Schultz, E. J. (2014). *Ad Age's 2014 marketer of the year: Under Armour.* Retrieved from http://adage.com/article/news/marketer-year-armour/296088/

SheKnows unveils results of its Fem-vertising survey. (2014). Retrieved from www.sheknows.com/living/articles/1056821/sheknows-unveils-results-of-its-fem-vertising-survey-infographic

Stampler, L. (2014). Here's how women respond to all those 'female empowerment' Ads. *Times.* Retrieved from http://time.com/3502904/heres-how-women-respond-to-all-those-female-empowerment-ads/

Tour, M. (2015). *Droga5 is no. 6 on ad age's 2015 agency a-list.* Retrieved from http://adage.com/article/special-report-agency-alist-2015/droga5-6-ad-age-s-2015-agency-a-list/296713/

Vargas, P. T., & Yoon, S. (2006). On the psychology of materialism: Wanting things, having things, and being happy. *Advertising & Society Review, 7*(1). Project MUSE. doi:10.1353/asr.2006.0022

Wolf, N. (1991). *The beauty myth: How images of beauty are used against women.* New York, NY: Morrow.

Wood, J. V. (1989, September). Theory and research concerning social comparison of personal attributes. *Psychological Bulletin, 106,* 231–248. doi:10.1037/0033-2909.106.2.231

Zayer, L. T., & Otnes, C. C. (2012). Climbing the ladder or chasing a dream: Men's responses to idealized portrayals of masculinity in advertising. In C. C. Otnes & L. T. Zayer (Eds.), *Gender, culture, and consumer behavior* (pp. 87–110). New York, NY: Routledge.

Zmuda, N., & Diaz, A. (2014). *Marketers go soft on feminism: Female empowerment is the hot trend as brands from Pantene to Verizon pitch girl power: But are these ads culture-changing or simply "pinkwashing?".* Retrieved from http://adage.com/article/cmo-strategy/marketers-soft-feminism/294740/

22

SPIRITUALITY AND ADVERTISING

Galit Marmor-Lavie

Introduction

Happiness in advertising is commonly used in the restricted form of hedonism (Campbell, 1987; Pollay & Mittal, 1993). Hedonism is a sense of pleasure that usually involves the following mind-sets: "a focus on the self, the present moment, and the tangible, and a focus on taking and consuming what one needs and wants" (Huta, 2017, p. 15). With the spirit of hedonism in the mind of the adviser, no wonder that over the years, ads were filled with sex, status, and egotistic needs. As a result, scholars have accused advertising in nurturing a distorted sense of self and egotistic tendencies among consumers (Kilbourne, 1999; Muñiz-Velazquez, Lozano-Delmar, & Plaza, 2014; Pollay, 1986; Potter, 1954). Moreover, academics such as Potter, Galbraith, Williams, and Schudson suggested that advertising "eroded personal character, destabilized cultural norms, rewrote value systems, promoted individualism—and conformity" (Restad, 2014, p. 775). Based on that knowledge, it seems rather unlikely to combine between advertising and concepts such as spirituality and eudaimonic happiness that in contrast to hedonism emphasize deep authenticity and higher purpose. However, current trends in global consciousness and advertising practice point toward that new direction precisely (Albion, 2006; Kofman, 2006; Marmor-Lavie, Stout, & Lee, 2009; Marmor-Lavie & Stout, 2016; Rinallo, Scott, & Maclaran, 2012; Turak, 2010; Zohar & Marshall, 2004). Advertising in its essence isn't bad, it is simply a tool, a powerful tool, in the hands of human beings. As with any powerful position in life (i.e. a teacher, a parent, a manager, etc.), the choice of how to use that power is in the hands of the person who holds it. Abraham Maslow elaborates on this point: "in the hands of a mature, healthy human being . . . power . . . is a great blessing. But in the hands of the immature, vicious, or emotionally sick, power is a horrible danger" (Maslow, 2000, p. 146). The same goes for advertising, if the people in the industry choose to operate from a place of positive consciousness, the possibilities of combining constructs such as eudaimonic happiness and spirituality are plentiful. However, if they choose to act from a place of egocentric, profit-only narrowness, the destructive dimension of advertising, as we have witnessed thus far, will continue.

This book sets forward the eudaimonic happiness paradigm and offers it as an overarching platform or an alternative to the existing reality of hedonism in communication. Specifically, this chapter focuses on the concept of spirituality in the field of advertising. Eudaimonic happiness and spirituality have a lot in common. As with eudaimonia, spirituality is also connected to the notions of meaning, personal growth, excellence, and authenticity (Huta & Waterman, 2014).

Moreover, spirituality is often mentioned in discussions about eudaimonic experience and elevation (Huta, 2017; Piedmont, 1999), eudaimonic functioning (Huta, 2017; Emmons, 2003), and as a character strength in the positive psychology literature (Peterson & Seligman, 2004). Veronika Huta (2017) mentions how important it is to balance between eudaimonia and hedonia, due to their potential dark sides. She recommends that eudaimonia will rein hedonia. The advantage of spirituality, if used correctly and with consciousness, is indeed the ability to balance between these two processes well.

This chapter begins with a review of the emerging literature of spirituality and advertising. Then, it offers a conceptual fusion and understanding between the worlds of spirituality and advertising, and finally discusses ethics and future direction in the field.

Literature Review

One of the basic assumptions of the study of spirituality and advertising is that although religion and spirituality are overlapping concepts, they are not the same. Religion put more emphasis on sectarian and distinct organized groups that are usually affiliated with structure, the external, a set of beliefs and dogma. Spirituality, on the other hand, is more individualistic, not limited to a certain group, internal, fluid, inclusive, less structured, and eclectic (Allport, 1976; Fowler, 1981; Fromm, 1967; Rinallo et al., 2012; Saucier & Skrzypinska, 2006; Zinnbauer et al., 1997). The study of spirituality in advertising is a rather new approach in the field and focuses on spirituality as "a conscious path, a practice toward fulfillment that emphasizes unity (both internally and externally), interconnectedness, and human growth. It is the seed, the innate common human desire, and thus goes deeper and beyond religion" (Marmor-Lavie & Stout, 2016, p. 171). Past explorations focused solely on religion in advertising and point out to three different research branches (Knauss, 2016):

1. advertising as religion,
2. religious content in advertising, and
3. advertising used by religious communities.

The first research branch argues that advertising functions as a religion or holds various religious dimensions (Jhally, 1989; Sheffield, 2006; Sullivan, 2010). The second branch probes religious content in advertising and mostly examine the description and effectiveness of religious imagery, symbols, and motifs in ads (Barnes, 2000; Maddock & Fulton, 1996; Maguire & Weatherby, 1998; Mallia, 2009; Moore, 2005). In the third research branch, studies discuss the somewhat unsettling combination between advertising and religious bodies such as churches and religious organizations and how they use advertising to promote their own agendas (Abelman & Hoover, 1990; Broyles, 2000; Einstein, 2008; Engel, 1993). Beyond those three research branches, the literature offers a fourth direction that takes a very critical-ethical approach toward advertising and religion. According to this line of research, advertising in its essence erodes spiritual and social values and thus cannot be combined with religious or spiritual ideas. Attempt to combine between the two is for the sole purpose of manipulating consumers to buy more products (Hoffman & Hoffman, 2006; Pollay, 1986; Potter, 1954).

Recently, scholars have suggested to shift the focus from religion to spirituality in the field of advertising (Marmor-Lavie et al., 2009; Marmor-Lavie & Stout, 2016). The following reasons were discussed:

1. The increase of global interest in the idea of spirituality that is not religion (Couchman, 2005; Smith, 2003). Accounts especially refer to the generation of millennials (born between

1980–2000) who specifically tends toward spirituality, meaning, the inward, and nonmaterialistic approaches (Faw, 2014). Therefore, advertising should be aware and adapt to the voices of the 21st century.

2. The general need to explore the real essence of spirituality in relation to the world of consumption, advertising, and branding. Understanding the relationships between the company, the advertiser, and the consumer, from a deeper-global spiritual perspective, is crucial in an era that emphasizes the connection with the consumer. It is also the time to go further and beyond the mere investigation of religious imagery in ads (Marmor-Lavie et al., 2009; Marmor-Lavie & Stout, 2016). After all, the investigation of spirituality (which is global and holistic) rather than religion (which is sectarian and specific) is much more suitable in the context of advertising.

3. The urge to further explore the topic of matter and consciousness (see previous work: Csikszentmihalyi & Rochberg-Halton, 1982; Hirschman, 1985; James, 1902) and to harness it to the study of advertising.

4. Advertising has always centered the notion of meaning and meaning making (McCracken, 1986). The same goes for spirituality and the individual focus of the meaning of life (Frankl, 1984; Jung, 1933). Accordingly, there is a lot of room for cooperation.

5. Finally, advertising suffers from a bad reputation among the public due to the reasons that were discussed in the beginning of the chapter. The study of spirituality in advertising could provide a positive opportunity to shift the consciousness and ignite authenticity in the world of advertising and its affiliates (Marmor-Lavie et al., 2009; Marmor-Lavie & Stout, 2016; Muñiz-Velazquez et al., 2014).

The emerging field of spirituality and advertising has taken a few steps thus far. The first step focused on the definition of spirituality and the creation of a theoretical framework, suitable for the study of advertising. Marmor-Lavie et al. (2009) have created the Spirituality in Advertising Framework (SAF) which currently consists of 17 spiritual core ideas (Marmor-Lavie & Stout, 2016). They define spirituality based on the following five principles: spirituality goes beyond religion; it is practiced in our day-to-day lives; helps us to reach our highest potential; provides us with tools to disentangle suffering; and keeps pushing us toward questions about the meaning of life. The 17 spiritual core ideas of the SAF are as follows: the action component, the big picture, letting go, more than instant gratification, constant examination of life, unity of all humankind (or interconnectedness), integration with others, long-term journey, ritualism, self-actualization, anything is possible, live in the present, sharing, take responsibility, gratitude, transformation, suffering, and sharing (Marmor-Lavie et al., 2009; Marmor-Lavie & Stout, 2016). The SAF was formed based on a unique combination of an extensive literature review and the viewing of plenty of ads. Since not enough studies have yet used or implemented the SAF, it is still in the process of adaptation and refinement. Knauss (2016) claims that broad definitions of religion include spirituality and thus there is no need to distinct between these two concepts. Therefore, she criticizes Marmor-Lavie et al. (2009) for trying to do so with their emerging framework.

Nonetheless, additional steps were taken in the field. In the second step, researchers examined the advertising message and whether or not it consists of SAF spiritual core ideas. Specific television ads were examined in a systematic qualitative methodology, identifying SAF spiritual core ideas in ads (Marmor-Lavie et al., 2009; Marmor-Lavie & Stout, 2016). It was found that the various layers of the advertising message, including images, music, words, and metaphors were imbued with SAF spiritual core ideas. For example, a Louis Vuitton commercial puts forward existential questions about the meaning of life; a JCPenney commercial emphasizes the concept of gratitude with their slogan of "Every Day Matters"; and a Bank of America commercial discusses the concept of thinking big and the manifestation of dreams into a reality. Is this enough though to declare that spirituality resides in advertising? Hardly not, it just means that advertisers use spiritual undertones in ads. At this point, the intention of the advertiser or the reaction of the consumer is not clear yet. In fact, studies point out it might very well be a manipulative technique by the advertiser to breakthrough the clutter (Hoffman & Hoffman, 2006). This leads to the third step in the field—the examination of consumers' responses to spiritual messages in advertising. Marmor-Lavie and Stout (2016) interviewed consumers about spiritually dense commercials. The results indicate that consumers demand extra authenticity when spirituality is being used in the context of advertising. Consumers would like to see real spiritual intentions and actions throughout the business process for them to truly connect with the brand and the advertising message. Finally, the last advancements in the field are moving toward the companies, their use of spirituality and the connection to the advertising spiritual message. This research is still in the works.

The Fusion Between Spirituality and Advertising

A survey by the American Association of Advertising Agencies reports on a great mistrust toward advertising among the public: Virtually no one in the survey said the ad industry acts with integrity; it was ranked at the bottom of the list of other industries, including financial institutions, the legal profession, the pharmaceutical industry, and the newspaper industry (Morrison, 2015).

This is hardly surprising considering the reasons provided by scholars at the beginning of this chapter and the focus of advertising on hedonism. Consumers understand that advertising is an industry that is meant to break promises. No, you are not going to become happier, healthier, wealthier, or more beautiful just because an ad says so. Why then did advertising become a force that is associated with an illusion and deception? In the era of mass production and industrial society, consumers lost direct connection with the actual product. In the past, a person went to the market; got to know the owner; was able to feel the product; smell and hear the story behind it first handedly. The owners were actually giving a part of themselves, through their product, to the consumers (Jhally, 1989, p. 219). In our time, space was created between consumers and business owners/companies. Big corporations have emerged and brought with it the necessity of factories, technicality, formalism, isolation, and a sense of coldness, in which the meaning and its context were pulled away from the product (Jhally, 1989). Not surprisingly the need for the function of advertising has emerged. Advertising brings back the meaning into an empty space whereas connection between products and consumers is plausible again (e.g. Jhally, 1989; Kleine, Kleine, & Kernan, 1993). As the liaison unit between companies and consumers in our society, advertising provides meaning about products, the world and how we fit in it (Aaker, 1996; McCracken, 1986).

However, as a powerful tool in our culture we must ask ourselves: does advertising fulfill its intended purpose? Does advertising bring the product to the consumer in its entirety and purity? Unfortunately, in most cases the answer is no, and thus advertising is perceived as the promoter of an illusionary reality that manipulates consumers' minds (plays on desires and wants) to buy things they don't really need (see Restad, 2014). The responsibility of what became out of advertising is certainly not on the advertiser alone. The environment and the market in which we live in today puts a lot of pressure on all its players, including consumers, to choose a path of illusion and deception. As Nobel Prize winners Akerlof and Shiller describe so vividly: "the competitive pressures for businessmen to practice deception and manipulation in free markets lead us to buy, and to pay too much for products that we do not need; to work at jobs that give us little sense of purpose; and to wonder why our lives have gone amiss" (Akerlof & Shiller, 2015, p. VII).

However, this cycle of illusion is breakable, should advertisers choose a path of a changed consciousness. The study of spirituality and advertising opens up a new framework and opportunity

Table 22.1 The Process of a Changed Consciousness in Advertising.

Phases of Changed Consciousness	Application to Advertising
Desire (Seed)	The authentic *Middle Place*
Thought (Cognition)	Promoting authentic desires in the *circle of pressure*
Intention (Emotion)	Higher purpose and the injection of care
Words	Translation of desires into big ideas and investment in authentic relationships
Action (Behavior)	Consciousness into action (the campaign, agency culture and relationships)

to restore, heal, and reconstruct the relationship between advertising and the public. Paradoxically, there is an extensive research on persuasion and attitude change related to advertising (Hovland, Janis, & Kelley, 1953; Lavidge & Steiner, 1961; Pollay & Mittal, 1993). It is time to harness these building blocks of knowledge to make a real shift of consciousness in advertising. Table 22.1 offers a structure of the various phases needed to begin a process of a changed consciousness in advertising.

> **Desire**: an authentic change of consciousness begins at the seed level, at the source of whereas every advertising action begins—the advertiser's true desire. Advertisers constantly discuss the concept of desire (Restad, 2014) and the need to ignite and satisfy a deprivation felt by the consumer (Kotler, 1991), via a tangible product. The motivation behind this, centers the basic desire of the advertiser to "sell-or else" (David Ogilvy). In spirituality, the concept of desire is related to a longing for a long-lasting, internal and intangible fulfilment (Allport, 1976; Fromm, 1967; James, 1902). The idea of spirituality in advertising is to merge between these two desires. To transform the relationship between advertisers and consumers, we must look at the relationship from a higher place. Indeed, the function of advertising is selling. However it is still a very limited way to perceive the exchange between the company-advertiser-consumer triad, as previously discussed. In fact, the company is providing energy, through its product, to the consumer who desires it. The advertiser's job is to mediate, translate, adapt, or facilitate the flow of energy from the company to the consumer in its most authentic way. Even if advertising is being paid by the company, it must not ignore its natural and original existence as the *middle place* between companies and consumers.

Thus, the initial desire must shift from a selfish, "bottom line only" consciousness to a desire based on a balanced force of sharing and authenticity between companies and consumers. Meaning, advertisers should practice advertising as a unique force that is emotionally neutral, and thus serves as a place to pause, process, and reflect the meaning and purpose of the transaction to all sides involved. It is the *middle place* where you pause (halting the automatic cycle of selling and shopping), inject consciousness (asking why and what is the purpose of the company, the product, the purchase, the selling, etc., and add value (adding value/reason to customers and companies alike about the purchase; the traditional role of marketing and advertising, according to the literature (Kotler, 1991)). Consequently, the basic seed desire of the advertiser should be: "to serve as the most authentic *middle place* between companies and consumers." Other mini-seed desires could be: "helping consumers to connect with products they truly need and desire" or "helping companies to connect with their true and authentic consumers" or "helping both companies and consumers to connect with their true desires and not their illusions."

Thought (Cognition): in the process of translating the aforementioned desires into a reality, we next tackle the thought process of the advertiser. Research establishes that advertisers have the power to set and create an environment, a mood, a state of mind or an atmosphere (Batra & Stayman, 1990). For example, we are all familiar with the increased "shopping desire atmosphere," created by the advertiser during the holiday season or special occasions such as "Father's Day" or "Mother's Day." Through the creation of an environment, advertisers are literally creating a *circle of pressure* that influences consumers' desires. This point of power is precisely where advertisers should shift their consciousness from implanting false desires to implanting authentic desires. For example, advertisers should ask themselves: "what are the type of desires we choose to enhance in the *circle of pressure?*" "Are these authentic desires?" "Do these desires represent authentically the product and the consumers that are using it?" "Do these desires promote growth or an illusion?"

Intention (Emotion): the next step would be to inject emotion and passion toward the process of changing the advertiser's consciousness. Through an educational procedure inside the agencies, advertisers will need to learn more about the bigger picture and the higher purpose of their job, including the power of advertising and the social/spiritual responsibility that comes with it. Consequently, with the new meaning, advertisers will become more passionate and motivated to make a real difference in the lives of companies and consumers. Ultimately, advertisers should envelop the process of production and consumption with great care, passion, and respect, while understanding and honoring their job as the *middle place*, which carries energy from companies to consumers.

Words: after reshaping the desires and intention of the advertiser, comes the phase of the "words" which brings us closer to manifestation. At this stage, advertisers use their words, strategy, and talents in two main levels: 1) to translate the initial desires to big ideas and organizing ideas that would most authentically represent a product and its consumer in a campaign, and 2) to promote their job as the *middle place* between companies and consumers. Meaning, re-educating and confronting companies (if need be) about the true essence of the advertiser's job, which is being a mediator who truly cares about consumers and the company's authenticity. Evidently, this time, the words of the advertiser will also be used to re-build authentic relationships with both companies and consumers.

Action (Behavior): on one level, the actual advertising campaign, created by the advertiser, is the "action" level. Indeed, advertisers should use their entire creative toolbox to manifest and promote the new consciousness of the advertiser, its authentic desires, and emphasis on growth instead of an illusion. On another level, action would also mean training and manifesting the new consciousness inside the agencies while creating an entire different culture. Finally, the last level includes maintaining healthy relationships between the advertiser and both companies and consumers. To keep the middle place consciousness, advertisers should strive to deeply understand each side's position through research and first-hand experience, yet remain distant enough to fulfil their purpose as mediators.

Looking Forward

The opportunity to inject a different type of consciousness (such as spirituality and eudaimonic happiness) into the field of advertising is timely. Yet, we must pause and warn the industry to make a wise use of the knowledge. Both companies and advertisers should go through training for the right implementation of spirituality in their organizations. If spirituality will be used as a manipulation tool in the hands of advertisers and companies, ramifications could be dangerous for all sides involved. Consumers will feel betrayed, companies could lose their reputation and purpose, and advertisers will lose once again their value, trust, and reputation.

For example, the recent scandals of Volkswagen's emissions testing and Wells Fargo's fake bank accounts showed how manipulation backlashes. Both companies manipulated the public and as a result suffered from a tremendous financial and reputational loss (Corkery, 2016; Hotten, 2015). Their initial and wrongful desire was to "sell or else," as the following quote implies about VW: "VW has had a major push to sell diesel cars in the US, backed by a huge marketing campaign trumpeting its cars' low emissions," (Hotten, 2015, p. 1) which turned out to be a blunt lie. The problem was the narrow-selfish initial desire of the companies that lost their authenticity. Advertisers, with the *middle place* consciousness should always strive to push companies toward their unique place of authenticity.

Future research and practice in the field of spirituality and advertising should follow the structure provided in Table 22.1. Following and experimenting with the various phases of changed consciousness in advertising, could push toward new and creative directions in which companies, advertisers, and consumers relate to each other. Next, these new forms of relationships should be tested and checked for their restoration of trust.

References

Aaker, D. A. (1996). *Building strong brands.* New York, NY: The Free Press.

Abelman, R., & Hoover, S. M. (Eds.). (1990). *Religious television: Controversies and conclusions.* Norwood, NJ: Ablex Press.

Akerlof, G., & Shiller, R. (2015). *Phishing for phools: The economics of manipulation & deception.* Princeton, NJ and Oxford: Princeton University Press.

Albion, M. (2006). *True to yourself.* San Francisco, CA: Berrett-Koehler Publishers, Inc.

Allport, G. W. (1976). *The individual and his religion.* New York, NY: Macmillan Publishing Company.

Barnes, B. E. (2000). *Un-holy war? Does religious-themed advertising work: And should it?* Paper presented at the American Academy of Advertising Conference, Newport, Rhode Island.

Batra, R., & Stayman, D. M. (1990, September). The role of mood in advertising effectiveness. *Journal of Consumer Research, 17,* 203–214.

Broyles, S. J. (2000). *Beyond the church page: Religious institutions say "Amen" to advertising.* Paper presented at the American Academy of Advertising Conference, Newport, Rhode Island.

Campbell, C. (1987). *The romantic ethic and the spirit of modern consumerism.* Oxford: Blackwell Publishers.

Corkery, M. (2016, October 14). Wells Fargo says customers shied away after scandal. *The New York Times.*

Couchman, D. (2005). Understanding the times. *Evangel, 23*(2), 47–52.

Csikszentmihalyi, M., & Rochberg-Halton, E. (1982). *The meaning of things: Domestic symbols and the self.* Cambridge, MA: Cambridge University Press.

Einstein, M. (2008). *Brands of faith: Marketing religion in a commercial age.* New York, NY: Routledge.

Emmons, R. A. (2003). *The psychology of ultimate concerns: Motivation and spirituality in personality.* New York, NY: Guilford Press.

Engel, J. F. (1993). Will the great commission become the great ad campaign. *Christianity Today,* 26–28.

Faw, L. (2014, November 7). Millennials misperceived as self-entitled-value experiences over materialism. *WWW.MEDIAPOST.COM.* Retrieved from www.mediapost.com/publications/article/237862/millennials-misperceived-as-self-entitled-value-e.html

Fowler, J. W. (1981). *Stages of faith: The psychology of human development and the quest for meaning.* New York, NY: HarperCollins Publishers.

Frankl, V. E. (1984). *Man's search for meaning.* Boston, MA: Beacon Press.

Fromm, E. (1967). *Psychoanalysis and religion.* New York, NY: Bantam Books.

Hirschman, E. C. (1985, September). Primitive aspects of consumption in modern American society. *Journal of Consumer Research, 12,* 142–154.

Hoffman, E., & Hoffman, C. (2006). *Staying focused in the age of distraction: How mindfulness, prayer & meditation can help you pay attention to what really matters.* Oakland, CA: New Harbinger.

Hotten, R. (2015, December 10). Volkswagen: The scandal explained. *BBC News.*

Hovland, C. I., Janis, I. L., & Kelley, H. H. (1953). *Communications and persuasion: Psychological studies in opinion change.* New Haven, CT: Yale University Press.

Huta, V. (2017). An overview of hedonic and eudaimonic well-being concepts. In L. Reinecke & M. B. Oliver (Eds.), *The Routledge Handbook of Media Use and Well-being* (pp. 14–33). New York: Routledge.

Huta, V., & Waterman, A. S. (2014). Eudaimonia and its distinction from hedonia: Developing a classification and terminology for understanding conceptual and operational definitions. *Journal of Happiness Studies, 15,* 1425–1456.

James, W. (1902). *The varieties of religious experience: A study in human nature.* Cambridge, MA: The Riverside Press.

Jhally, S. (1989). Advertising as religion: The dialectic of technology and magic. In I. Angus & S. Jhally (Eds.), *Cultural politics in contemporary America* (pp. 217–229). London: Routledge.

Jung, C. G. (1933). *Modern man in search of a soul.* New York, NY: Harcourt Brace Jovanovich, Publishers.

Kilbourne, J. (1999). *Can't buy my love: How advertising changes the way we think and feel.* New York, NY: Touchstone.

Kleine, R. E., Kleine, S. S., & Kernan, J. B. (1993). Mundane consumption and the self: A social-identity perspective. *Journal of Consumer Psychology, 2*(3), 209–235.

Knauss, S. (2016). "Get to know the unknown": Understanding religion and advertising. *Journal of Media and Religion, 15*(2), 100–112.

Kofman, F. (2006). *Conscious business.* Boulder, CO: Sounds True.

Kotler, P. (1991). *Marketing management: Analysis, planning, implementation, & control* (7th ed.). Englewood Cliffs, NJ: Prentice-Hall, Inc.

Lavidge, R. J., & Steiner, G. A. (1961). A model for predictive measurements of advertising effectiveness. *Journal of Marketing, 25*(6), 59–62.

Maddock, R. C., & Fulton, R. L. (1996). *Marketing to the mind: Right brain strategies for advertising and marketing.* Westport, CT: Quorum Books.

Maguire, B., & Weatherby, G. A. (1998). The secularization of religion and television commercials. *Sociology of Religion, 59*(2), 171–178.

Mallia, K. L. (2009). From the sacred to the profane: A critical analysis of the changing nature of religious imagery in advertising. *Journal of Media and Religion, 6*(3), 172–190.

Marmor-Lavie, G., & Stout, P. A. (2016). Consumers' insights about spirituality in advertising. *Journal of Media and Religion, 15*(4), 169–185.

Marmor-Lavie, G., Stout, P. A., & Lee, W.-N. (2009). Spirituality in advertising: A new theoretical approach. *Journal of Media and Religion, 8*(1), 1–23.

Maslow, A. (2000). *The Maslow business reader.* New York, NY: Wiley and Sons.

McCracken, G. (1986). Culture and consumption: A theoretical account of the structure and movement of the cultural meaning of consumer goods. *Journal of Consumer Research, 13*(1), 71–84.

Moore, R. C. (2005). Spirituality that sells: Religious imagery in magazine advertising. *Advertising & Society Review.* Retrieved from http://muse.jhu.edu.ezproxy.lib.utexas.edu/journals/advertising_and_society_review/v006/6.1moore.html

Morrison, M. (2015, April 24). No one trusts advertising or media (except fox news). *Advertising Age.*

Muñiz-Velazquez, J. A., Lozano-Delmar, J., & Plaza, J. F. (2014). *Advertising effectiveness and eudaimonic happiness can be good friends.* Paper presented at the Positive Marketing Conference, New York.

Peterson, C., & Seligman, M. E. P. (2004). *Character strengths and virtues: A handbook and classification.* New York, NY: Oxford University Press and Washington, DC: American Psychological Association.

Piedmont, R. L. (1999). Does spirituality represent the sixth factor of personality? Spiritual transcendence and the five-factor model. *Journal of Personality, 67,* 985–1013.

Pollay, R. W. (1986, April). The distorted mirror: Reflections on the unintended consequences of advertising. *Journal of Marketing, 50,* 18–36.

Pollay, R. W., & Mittal, B. (1993). Here's the factors, determinants and segments in consumer criticism of advertising. *Journal of Marketing, 57*(3), 67–89.

Potter, D. M. (1954). *People of plenty: Economic abundance and the American character.* Chicago: University of Chicago Press.

Restad, P. (2014). The third sex: Historians, consumer society, and the idea of the American consumer. *Journal of Social History, 47*(3), 769–786.

Rinallo, D., Scott, L., & Maclaran, P. (2012). *Consumption and spirituality.* New York, NY: Routledge.

Saucier, G., & Skrzypinska, K. (2006). Spiritual but not religious? Evidence for two independent dispositions. *Journal of Personality, 74*(5), 1257–1292.

Sheffield, T. (2006). *The religious dimensions of advertising.* New York, NY: Palgrave Macmillan.

Smith, J. W. (2003, January/February). Marketing that's good for the soul. *Marketing Management, 12,* 52.

Sullivan, P. A. (2010). Theology in "contact with its own times": Advertising and evangelization. *New Blackfriars*, *92*(1040), 443–463.

Turak, A. (2010). What bolsters the bottom line? Selfless marketing. *Advertising Age*. Retrieved from http://adage.com/cmostrategy/article?article_id=146581

Zinnbauer, B. J., Pargament, K. I., Cole, B., Rye, M. S., Butter, E. M., Belavich, T. G., . . . Kadar, J. L. (1997). Religion and spirituality: Unfuzzying the fuzzy. *Journal for the Scientific Study of Religion*, *36*(4), 549–564.

Zohar, D., & Marshall, I. (2004). *Spiritual capital: Wealth we can live by*. London: Bloomsbury Publishing Plc.

PART IV

New Public Relations for a New Economy

23

CORPORATIONS FOR A NEW ECONOMY OF HAPPINESS

Luis Rivas and Elias Soukiazis

Introduction

In 1776, Adam Smith wrote his *magnum opus, An Inquiry into the Nature and Causes of the Wealth of Nations,* a fundamental work in classical economics which has had, and still has, a huge impact on the vast majority of modern societies. Since then, economists the world over have capriciously interpreted and adapted the Scottish economist and moral philosopher's work to a culture in which households and businesses alike make decisions based on their particular interests. Therefore, a fundamental, and at times practically unique, objective was imposed at the time: to increase the production of goods and services. Only 17 years earlier, Smith had written, *The Theory of Moral Sentiments,* a book that would be doomed to oblivion. In this work, he considers generosity, humanity, kindness, compassion, sympathy, mutual friendship, and esteem, while also referring to resentment, revenge, virtue, admiration, corruption, and justice and their fundamental role in society and the economy.

Thus, throughout the Industrial Revolution, the main objective was to generate the greatest amount of goods and services per worker. This would condition the lives of people who would see how their day-to-day existence was subject to the rhythm of the economy. Topics and issues relating to development, the environment, solidarity, cooperation, altruism, personal satisfaction, and happiness were neglected. The marginalist debate revolved around the principles of profit maximization/cost minimization (entrepreneur) and utility (consumer). Bentham, the founder of British utilitarianism, referred to happiness more or less as a situation in which there was no pain. Furthermore, Nietzsche claimed that man was not conceived for happiness. The adoption of the liberal approach would give priority to freedom over happiness. Together, they laid the foundations of the economic system that would condition future generations for whom, it would seem, economics, and happiness were markedly incompatible.

The first part of the 20th century was marked by a successive chain of major events (WWI, the Great Crash, WWII) which would leave little room for the development of the branch of economic science known as the Economy of Happiness. Economists were busy coming up with explanations and solutions for historical, military, and economic cycles, devoting much of their efforts and talents to preparing for, or resolving, conflicts. It would be necessary to wait until the second half of the century, with the outbreak of the 1973 oil crisis, to witness the birth of an important current relating to the Economy of Happiness from both an academic (economics, psychology, and sociology) and political perspective. At the time, people across the world gradually became aware of the two elements making up the definition of economic science (scarce resources vs. unlimited needs) and to discuss economic development, income distribution and poverty, cooperation, and the sustainability of the planet (1972: The Club of Rome, *The Limits to Growth*). Despite this new approach, the world's most developed societies continued to pivot around private consumption that would reach 60 percent of the GDP. Now, in the 21st century, economies still apply the same productive-capitalist paradigm—albeit to different populations, resources, needs, and problems—that was used 250 years ago. However, in many developed societies personal satisfaction or happiness has remained constant over the last decades, while per capita income has increased substantially. A representative example of this paradox is Singapore: according to a Gallup World Poll life satisfaction data, despite being the country with the highest per capita income in the world, the Singaporeans' satisfaction with life is one of the lowest, below that of citizens of countries like Haiti, Afghanistan, Iraq, and Syria. In contrast, eight out of 10 of the countries where the level of satisfaction is the highest are Latin American and do not figure among the 50 with the highest per capita income in the world.

Theoretical, Social, and Political Framework

Theoretical

In the late 1980s, HM Jigme Singye Wangchuck, the fourth King of Bhutan, enunciated the principles of the philosophy of Gross National Happiness (GNH) as the main guiding force of his country (Ura & Galay, 2004). For centuries, happiness has been a central theme of philosophy. Sociologists (Veenhoven, 1993, 1999, 2000; Lindenberg, 1986) and political scientists (Inglehart, 1990; Lane, 2000) have also made important contributions to the issue. For many years, the empirical study of happiness has been the province of psychology (Argyle, 1987; Michalos, 1991; Diener, 1984; Myers, 1993; Ryan & Deci, 2001; Nettle, 2005). Only recently has psychological research been linked to economics. The early contribution of Richard Easterlin (1974) was noted by many economics scholars, but it found few supporters at the time. General interest among economists in the measurement and determinants of reported subjective well-being was aroused by a 1993 symposium in London, the proceedings of which were published later in *The Economic Journal* (Frank, 1997; Ng, 1997; Oswald, 1997). Although they have focused on mental processes, psychologists have made major contributions to how economic factors (particularly income) affect subjective well-being (see, e.g. Diener & Biswas-Diener, 2002). In 2002, the Sveriges Riksbank Prize in Economic Sciences in Memory of Alfred Nobel was awarded to two psychologists: Daniel Kahneman and Vernon L. Smith. Also noteworthy is the contribution of George Akerlof (2009), Economics Nobel Prize laureate in 2001, who, with Robert Shiller, co-authored the book, *Animal Spirits: How Human Psychology Drives the Economy*. Moreover, the new and important branch of the economy known as neuro-economics has made significant strides thanks to authors such as Singer and Fehr (2005).

Happiness, as an object of study, is gaining ground in economics (e.g. Frey & Stutzer, 2000). Reviews of this research literature have been published by Argyle (1987) and Diener (2000). Economists are particularly interested in the economic determinants of happiness and their consequences for economic policy, but their research goes well beyond that. Examples include studies that have attempted to determine the relationship between happiness and unemployment (Di Tella, MacCulloch, & Oswald, 2003; Clark, Diener, Georgellis, & Lucas, 2008; Falk & Knell, 2004; Ruhm, 2000; Clark, Georgellis, & Sanfey, 2001; Lucas, Clark, Georgellis, & Diener, 2004), happiness and inflation (Shiller, 1997; Wolfers, 2003; Fischer, 1981; Lucas, 1981; Drifill, Mizon, & Ulph, 1990), and inequality and life satisfaction (Deaton, 2005; Alesina & Glaeser, 2004; Alesina & La Ferrara, 2005; Tanzi & Schuknecht, 2000; Di Tella & MacCulloch, 1996), and to quantify happiness (Kahneman et al., 2004; Kahneman & Krueger, 2006). Finally, it is important to highlight the work of the Noble Prize-winning economist Jean Tirole, embodied in his latest book, *Economics for the Common Good*.

In contrast with other areas of the social sciences, disciplines are integrated to such an extent in current happiness research that it is impossible to identify whether a particular contribution is from an economist, psychologist, sociologist, or political scientist. This is highly significant, above all in view of the increasingly greater differentiation between economics and the other social sciences. Lane (2000), Frey and Stutzer (2002a), and Nettle (2005) have already written books on the subject, while Ng (1997), Diener, Suh, Lucas, and Smith (1999), Easterlin (2004), Frey and Stutzer (2002b, 2004a, 2004b, 2005a, 2005b), Diener and Seligman (2004), and Di Tella and MacCulloch (2006) have published survey papers. The literature also includes useful collections of papers (e.g. Easterlin, 2004) and important monographs focusing on various aspects of economic happiness research (e.g. Graham & Pettinato, 2002a; van Praag & Ferrer-i-Carbonell, 2004; Layard, 2005; Bruni & Porta, 2005). Last, studies are being published in many different journals and there is also a specialized *Journal of Happiness Studies*.

Social and Political

From a social and political perspective, happiness economics has become increasingly important due to greater private demand (households and companies) and the consequent reaction of governments. States have thus established political goals, which have not been taken into account until only recently, as new challenges of our times: participatory democracy, quality of institutions, justice, community, social empathy, culture, environment, leisure, job quality, social inclusion, equity, mental health, peace, etc. And not only of our times: Aristotle expounded the concept of "eudaimonia"—happiness as human flourishing and purpose to life—rather than the modern hedonistic concept. The most famous statement of the 1776 Declaration of Independence of the United States of America is that which asserted certain basis rights for every man, including life, liberty, and the pursuit of happiness.

In 1930, John Maynard Keynes talked about the "art of life" and, in 1968, Robert Kennedy delivered a speech at the University of Kansas: "We cannot measure national spirit by the Dow Jones average, nor national achievement by the gross domestic product." In 1972, as has already been noted, the then king of Bhutan HM Jigme Singye Wangchuck, coined the novel term "Gross National Happiness" which regarded mental health, harmony with nature, and culture, among other factors, as priority objectives for the collective well-being of the Bhutanese. In 2006, following the coup d'état, the Thai government created a personal well-being index, promising the Thai people not only to protect their personal wealth, but also their happiness.

In 2010, British Prime Minister David Cameron urged economists and citizens to stop using GDP as an indicator of growth, at the expense of General Well-Being (GWB), and to give greater priority to personal well-being over the material kind. In 2012, the General Assembly of the United Nations, in its resolution 66/281 of 12 July, proclaimed 20 March the International Day of Happiness, thus recognizing the relevance of happiness and well-being as universal goals and aspirations in the lives of human beings worldwide and the importance of their recognition in public policy objectives.

In the USA, that same year, Vermont lawmakers passed a bill for the gradual replacement of GDP as an indicator of well-being by an alternative index called the Genuine Progress Indicator (GPI), taking into account concepts such as welfare, equity, and efficiency. And, in 2013, the Venezuelan government, for its part, created a Ministry of Supreme Happiness.

All this has coincided with the emergence of economic indicators that attempt to classify the different economies of the planet in terms of life satisfaction and the immaterial or spiritual well-being of its citizens. These indicators, which consider variables such as the environment or ecological footprint, leisure time, life expectancy, education, culture, compassion, and solidarity, include the following: the UN World Happiness Report (WHR) and Human Development Index (HDI); the New Economic Foundation's Happy Planet Index (HPI); Redefining Progress' Genuine Progress Indicator (GPI); the Satisfaction with Life Index (SLI), created by Adrian G. White at the University of Leicester; and the Canadian Index of Well-being (CIW), developed by the Canadian government in 2011, the same year in which the OECD launched its Better Life Index (BLI). Yet another example is the World Happiness Report (WHR), launched in 2012 by John F. Helliwell, Richard Layard, and Jeffrey Sachs at New York University, or the World Database of Happiness (WDH), created by Erasmus University Rotterdam.

Paradigm Shift in Industrial Organizations

According to Otto Scharmer (2018), senior lecturer at the Massachusetts Institute of Technology (MIT), there are eight ways of shifting outdated capitalism into a 21st century economy that creates well-being for all. The institutional innovations that could update the economic system by shifting the economic logic from ego- to eco-system awareness are as follows:

1. Nature: instead of considering raw materials as a gift of nature which can be purchased, used and discarded, the natural world should be treated as an eco-system that must be cultivated.
2. Entrepreneurship: the concept of work should be perceived not only as a job, but also as a passion-driven personal project.
3. Money: instead of being extractive, capital must serve social interests, reinforcing rather than damaging the real economy.
4. Technology: everyone should be encouraged to be creators and inventors, rather than passive consumers of technology.
5. Leadership: instead of individual superegos, there is a need to co-sense and co-shape the future on a whole-system level.
6. Consumption: there needs to be a shift from consumerism and production or GDP to collaborative consumption, using indicators such as GNH and the GPI.
7. Governance: the three older mechanisms (hierarchies, markets, and special interest groups) should be complemented by a fourth, involving actions based on shared awareness and thinking outside the box.
8. Property: an effort must be made to move beyond the old forms of private and public ownership by creating a third type: commons-based ownership that does more to safeguard the interests of future generations.

Healthier and Happier Workers: The Impact of Happiness on Workers' Productivity

Nowadays, the mainstream approach tries to explain labor productivity levels by considering employee happiness or personal satisfaction levels. The findings to date suggest that there are elements, such as identification with the company, pride of belonging, family reconciliation or work-life balance, good internal organization, adequate incentives, confidence, camaraderie, justice, credibility, respect, recognition, and cooperation, among others, which have a positive impact on workforce productivity and, therefore, on its performance, results and, finally, the sustainability of the project and the pursuit of excellence (Amabile, Barsade, Mueller, & Staw, 2005; Argyle, 1989; Benabou & Tirole, 2002; Boehm & Lyubomirsky, 2008; Compte & Postlewaite, 2004; Freeman, 1978; Hermalin & Isen, 2008; Isen, Daubman, & Nowicki, 1987; Wright & Staw, 1998).

Great Place to Work is an organization that analyzes aspects of work climate, working conditions, and business culture to create a ranking of the best companies to work for. This analysis takes into account the following aspects to classify companies according to their workers' satisfaction: credibility, respect, impartiality, camaraderie, and pride. Moreover, many companies have already introduced a post called chief happiness officer (CHO), whose job it is "to create motivational initiatives and team-building dynamics to promote happiness and job satisfaction." Some examples in this respect include Jenn Lim (Delivering Happiness, an offshoot of Zappos), Chade-Meng Tan (Google, actual title: Jolly Good Fellow), Alexander Kjerulf (Woo-Hoo, a Denmark-based consulting company), and Christine Jutard (Kiabi, a French clothing company). To these must be added Ronald McDonald, who in 2003 became perhaps the first CHO in the USA.

Another real example, Johnson & Johnson set itself the goal of helping its workers give up smoking (resulting in a reduction of two-thirds over the past 15 years), while simultaneously implementing other welfare programmes. These measures have allowed the company to save US $250 million in health costs; that is to say, every dollar spent on these programmes between 2002 and 2008 has brought a return of US $2.71. In addition, its employees are more productive and work absenteeism has decreased.

Beyond Trade-Offs: Fair-Trade, Shared Value, and Profitable Non-Profits

In economic science, over the past few centuries, it has been assumed that a trade-off takes place between business and social benefits. Namely, it is a zero-sum game in which any increase in social benefits causes a reduction in business profits. In neoclassical thinking, any requirement for social improvement (safety at work, hiring disabled people, etc.) entails a restriction for the company in question, in the form of higher costs resulting in a loss of profits. According to the prevailing conception, this dilemma is overcome and both society and companies benefit from one another's good results. They are not considered rivals, but participants and partners in the same economic "game."

Recent studies of Ivory Coast cocoa farmers claim that while fair-trade can increase local farmers' incomes by 10–20 percent, shared value investments can do so by 300 percent. Although the initial investment is important, the return of this type of initiative is much higher than the profitability of older ideas, although still valid as the aforementioned fair-trade.

There is sometimes a thin line between for-profit and nonprofit organizations. New types of hybrid companies are emerging rapidly. For example, WaterHealth International, a high-growth, for-profit company, uses innovative water purification techniques to distribute clean water at a minimal cost to more than one million people in rural India, Ghana, and the Philippines. Its investors include not only the Acumen Fund, offering new approaches to social impact investing, and the International Finance Corporation of the World Bank Group, but also Dow Venture Capital—an investment arm of the Dow Chemical Company. Revolution Food, a newly created US venture capital firm, delivers fresh, healthy meals daily to 60,000 students, with far higher profit margins than its traditional competitors. Waste Concern, another nonprofit hybrid company that started out in Bangladesh 15 years ago, is capable of transforming 700 tons of rubbish a day, collected from poorer neighborhoods, into organic fertilizers, thus increasing harvests and reducing CO_2 emissions. Working with capital from the Lions Club and the United Nations Development Fund, the company improves citizens' health, while obtaining substantial profits from the sale of fertilizers and coal credits.

The nonprofit sector has grown significantly over the last 10 years, both in size and financially. Between 2005 and 2015, the number of nonprofit companies increased by 25 percent, from 1,259,764 to 1,574,674. This sector's growth rate has exceeded both those of the private and public sectors. Employing 10 percent of the workforce and representing 9 percent of the total salaries paid, in 2015 its contribution to the GDP, in relative terms, was 5.4 percent.

Reconsidering Products and Markets: Low-Income Consumers

Intel and IBM are devising ways to control digital intelligence to save energy. Wells Fargo has developed a line of products and tools that help clients to manage their budgets and credit, or to pay their debts. With sales of its Ecoimagination products reaching US $18 billion in 2009, GE predicts that the growth of these revenues will double that of its other revenue sources over the next five years. The social benefits of providing low-income consumers with appropriate products and services can be profound, while the benefits to businesses can be substantial. For example, the sale of low-cost mobile phones that provide banking and financial services are helping lower-income citizens to save money safely and, at the same time, transforming the ability of small farmers to produce and sell their crops. In Kenya, the banking services provided by Vodafone's M-Pesa succeeded in registering 10 million users in three years; the fund currently manages accounts for people representing 11 percent of the country's GDP.

In India, Thomson Reuters has developed a special service for farmers and ranchers with annual revenues of US $2,000. For a fee of $5 per quarter, it provides meteorological and crop-related information, as well as agricultural advice. Around two million farmers are already benefitting from this service and some research studies estimate that it has helped to increase their income by around 60 percent. In this regard, it is also worth mentioning the microcredit model designed for low-income earners in Bangladesh by social entrepreneur and Nobel Peace Prize-winner Muhammad Yunus.

Business and the Environment: Circular Economy

The over-packaging of many products, together with the greenhouse gasses this produces, is costly for both the environment and companies as a whole. Walmart, for example, was able to deal with both problems by reducing its packaging and redefining the routes its lorries used to cut 160 million kilometers in 2009, saving US $200 million even when transporting more goods. Coca-Cola reduced its worldwide water consumption by 9 percent between 2004 and 2012. Dow Chemical was able to reduce water consumption by 10 billion gallons (enough water to supply 40,000 people in the US during a year). A very similar water-saving strategy was implemented by the Indian company Jain Irrigation, a leading manufacturer worldwide of comprehensive irrigation systems for water-saving and conservation, allowing it to increase its income by 41 percent over the last five years.

In Spain, a clear example of environmental and economic profitability is the company Grupo Matarromera, dedicated to the production of wine and olive oil, among other products, and winner of the 2014 Expansion Prize for the Best Sustainable SME (circular economy).

Peer-to-Peer Rental: Booming Economy Sharing

Another clear example of the paradigm shift in the processes and conception of the economy itself has taken place in a context of crisis especially in the USA, with the companies making up the so-called "Sharing Economy." These companies play a role as intermediaries and are engaged in bringing people or consumers into contact to exchange services or goods with one another. In this way, any family that needs a car, a surfboard, or a home can exchange their goods temporarily with other people for those they need or simply rent them for hours or days. The idea of sharing has thus mutated from a local to a global concept thanks to the Internet and information technologies. Pending consistent legislation (local licenses, rates, taxation, etc.), these companies, which are here to stay, have been expanding exponentially over the past few years and now form part of our daily economy. Some examples are Airbnb, RelayRides, Blablacar, and Respiro Car Sharing.

Crowdfunding: Technology and Thousands of Wills at the Service of Innovative Projects

The processes of crowdfunding are not new. They are to be found in the "micro" strategy developed by the mobile app business model, among others, which has changed the software distribution model: instead of a few consumers paying high prices to cover production costs, a large number of them pay a very small amount to defray them jointly. Thus, crowdfunding has developed as an innovative tool in the initial processes not only of start-ups, but also of cultural products, charities, and even social events. The process uses online platforms as necessary catalysts. In recent years, Kickstarter, GrowVC, Verkami, and Lánzanos, to name but a few, have become pacesetters in this activity in which more or less anonymous Internet users fund proposals with financial contributions that vary in size.

But in exchange for what? Generally speaking, crowdfunding systems are based on a rewards programme in which, in exchange for their contributions, backers are compensated with something of much lesser value, such as a T-shirt, a badge, a party invitation, priority when receiving cultural content, dinner with a film star, or even a hug or the heartfelt thanks of those requesting the funding. However, and here is the secret of its success, in reality the reward lies in the emotional involvement generated by feeling "part of" something; in the thrill of becoming an active, constituent, and decisive element in the launching of a project for very little money. This is still the case even with the certainty of knowing that there are no shareholder's rights over the result, but rather a kind of moral paternity that provides a proportionally higher emotional return on investment than even traditional sponsorship. Crowdfunding also has certain collateral advantages for the beneficiary, since backers become, in turn, advertising vehicles and prescribers, since it is easy to understand the pride with which they will then endorse the product or activity in which they are involved.

Ethical Products: Socially Responsible Banking

Finally, a good example of the paradigm shift is found in the banking sector. New business initiatives have emerged that are similar in appearance to traditional banks, but with totally different content, objectives, operative guidelines, and structure. Like their traditional counterparts, these banks in the ethical banking sector also have creditors, debtors, bank accounts, financing, and profits. However, that is where the similarities end: financing is restricted to supporting small entrepreneurs and charity, development, or environmentally sustainable projects, which bring a positive return for society at large and are always subject to the approval of all the shareholders who are also the savers. Good examples of these innovative banks are Triodos, Fiare, and Coop57.

References

Akerlof, G. A., & Shiller, R. J. (2009). *Animal spirits: How human psychology drives the economy, and why it matters for global capitalism.* Princeton, NJ: Princeton University Press.

Alesina, A., & Eliana La Ferrara. (2005). Preferences for redistribution in the land of opportunities. *Journal of Public Economics, 89*(5–6), 897–931.

Alesina, A., & Glaeser, E. (2004). *Fighting poverty in the US and Europe: A world of difference.* Oxford: Oxford University Press.

Amabile, T. M., Barsade, S. G., Mueller, J. S., & Staw, B. M. (2005). Affect and creativity at work. *Administrative Science Quarterly, 50*, 367–403.

Argyle, M. (1987). *The psychology of happiness.* London: Methuen.

Argyle, M. (1989). Do happy workers work harder? The effect of job satisfaction on job performance. In R. Veenhoven (Ed.), *How harmful is happiness? Consequences of enjoying life or not.* The Netherlands: Universitaire Pers Rotterdam.

Benabou, R., & Tirole, J. (2002). Self-confidence and personal motivation. *Quarterly Journal of Economics, 117*, 871–915.

Boehm, J. K., & Lyubomirsky, S. (2008). Does happiness promote career success? *Journal of Career Assessment, 16*, 101–116.

Bruni, L., & Porta, P. (2005). *Economics and happiness: Framing the analysis.* Oxford: Oxford University Press.

Bruni, L., & Porta, P. (2008). *Handbook on the Economics of Happiness.* Cheltenham: Edward Elgar Publishing.

Clark, A., Georgellis, Y., & Sanfey, P. (2001). Scarring: The psychological impact of past unemployment. *Economica, 68*(270), 221–241.

Clark, A. E., Diener, E., Georgellis, Y., & Lucas, R. E. (2008). Lags and leads in life satisfaction: A test of the baseline hypothesis. *The Economic Journal, 118*, 222–243. doi:10.1111/j.1468-0297.2008.02150.x

Compte, O., & Postlewaite, A. (2004). Confidence-enhanced performance. *American Economic Review, 94*, 1536–1557.

Deaton, A. (2005). Measuring poverty in a growing world. *Review of Economics and Statistics, 87*, 1–19.

Diener, E. (1984). Subjective well-being. *Psychological Bulletin, 95*(3), 542–575.

Diener, E. (2000). Subjective well-being: The science of happiness and a proposal for a national index. *American Psychologist, 55*(1), 34–43.

Diener, E., & Biswas-Diener, R. (2002). Will money increase subjective well-being? *Social Indicators Research, 57*, 119–169.

Diener, E., & Seligman, M. (2004). Beyond money: Toward an economy of well-being. *Psychological Science in the Public Interest, 5*, 1–31.

Diener, E., Suh, E., Lucas, R., & Smith, H. (1999). Subjective well-being: Three decades of progress. *Psychological Bulletin, 125*(2), 276–303.

Di Tella, R., & MacCulloch, R. (1996). *An empirical study of unemployment benefit preferences.* Economic Series Working Paper 99179. Department of Economics, Oxford: Oxford University Press.

Di Tella, R., & MacCulloch, R. (2006). Some uses of happiness data in economics. *Journal of Economic Perspectives, 20*, 25–46.

Di Tella, R., MacCulloch, R., & Oswald, A. (2003). The macroeconomics of happiness. *Review of Economics and Statistics, 85*(4), 809–827.

Driffill, J., Mizon, G. E., & Ulph, A., (1990). Costs of inflation. In B. M. Friedman & F. H. Hahn (Ed.), *Handbook of monetary economics* (pp. 1013–1066). Amsterdam: Elsevier.

Easterlin, R. (1974). Does economic growth improve the human lot? Some empirical evidence. In P. A. David & M. W. Reder (Eds.), *Nations and households in economic growth: Essays in honor of Moses Abramovitz.* New York, NY: Academic Press.

Easterlin, R. (2004). Explaining happiness. *Proceedings of the National Academy of Sciences, 100*, 1176–1183.

Falk, A., & Knell, M. (2004). Choosing the Joneses: Endogenous goals and reference standards. *Scandinavian Journal of Economics, 106*(3), 417–435.

Fischer, S. (1981). Towards an understanding of the costs of inflation: II. *Carnegie-Rochester Conference Series on Public Policy, 15*, 5–41.

Frank, R. (1997). The frame of reference as a public good. *Economic Journal, 107*(445), 1832–1847.

Freeman, R. B. (1978). Job satisfaction as an economic variable. *American Economic Review, 68*, 135–141.

Frey, B., & Stutzer, A. (2000). Happiness, economy and institutions. *Economic Journal, 110*(446), 918–938.

Frey, B., & Stutzer, A. (2002a). *Happiness and economics: How the economy and institutions affect well-being.* Princeton, NJ: Princeton University Press.

Frey, B., & Stutzer, A. (2002b). What can economists learn from happiness research? *Journal of Economic Literature, 40*(2), 402–435.

Frey, B., & Stutzer, A. (2004a). *Economic consequences of mispredicting utility.* Working Paper 218. IEW (Institute for Empirical Research in Economics), University of Zurich.

Frey, B., & Stutzer, A. (2004b). Reported subjective well-being: A challenge for economic theory and economic policy. *Schmollers Jahrbuch, 124*, 191–231.

Frey, B., & Stutzer, A. (2005a). Testing theories of happiness. In L. Bruni & P. Porta (Eds.), *Economics and happiness: Framing the analysis.* Oxford: Oxford University Press.

Frey, B., & Stutzer, A. (2005b). Happiness research: State and prospects. *Review of Social Economy, 62*, 207–228.

Graham, C., & Pettinato, S. (2002a). *Happiness and hardship: Opportunity and insecurity in new market economies.* Washington, D.C.: Brookings Institution Press.

Hermalin, B. E., & Isen, A. M. (2008). A model of the effect of affect on economic decision-making. *Quantitative Marketing and Economics, 6,* 17–40.

Inglehart, R. (1990). *Culture shift in advanced industrial society.* Princeton, NJ: Princeton University Press.

Isen, A. M., Daubman, K. A., & Nowicki, G. P. (1987). Positive affect facilitates creative problem-solving. *Journal of Personality and Social Psychology, 52,* 1122–1131.

Kahneman, D., & Krueger, A. B. (2006). Developments in the measurement of subjective well-being. *Journal of Economic Perspectives, 20*(1), 3–24.

Kahneman, D., Krueger, A. B., Schkade, D. A., Schwarz, N., & Stone, A. A. (2004). A Survey method for characterizing daily life experience: The day reconstruction method. *Science, 306*(5702), 1776–1780.

Lane, R. (2000). *The loss of happiness in market economies.* New Haven, CT: Yale University Press.

Layard, R. (2005). *Happiness: Lessons from a new science.* London: Penguin.

Lindenberg, S. (1986). The paradox of privatization in consumption. In A. Diekmann & P. Mitter (Eds.), *Paradoxical effects of social behavior.* Heidelberg: Physica.

Lucas, R., Jr. (1981). Discussion of Stanley Fischer, towards an understanding of the costs of inflation: II. *Carnegie-Rochester Conference Series on Public Choice, 15,* 43–52.

Lucas, R., Clark, A., Georgellis, Y., & Diener, E. (2004). Unemployment alters the set-point for life satisfaction. *Psychological Science, 15,* 8–13.

Michalos, A. (1991). *Global report on student well-being, volume 1: Life satisfaction and happiness.* New York: Springer.

Myers, D. (1993). *The pursuit of happiness: Who is happy and why?* New York: Avon.

Nettle, D. (2005). *Happiness: The science behind your smile.* Oxford: Oxford University Press.

Ng, Y. (1997). A case for happiness, cardinalism, and interpersonal comparability. *Economic Journal, 107*(445), 1848–1858.

Oswald, A. J. (1997). Happiness and economic performance. *Economic Journal, 107,* 1815–1831.

Ruhm, C. (2000). Are recessions good for your health? *Quarterly Journal of Economics, 115*(2), 617–650.

Ryan, R., & Deci, E. (2001). On happiness and human potentials: A review of research on hedonic and eudaimonic well-being. *Annual Review of Psychology, 52.*

Scharmer, O. (2018). *The essentials of theory u: core principles and applications.* San Francisco, CA; Berrett-Koehler Publishers.

Shiller, R. (1997). Why do people dislike inflation? In C. Romer & D. Romer (Eds.), *Reducing inflation: Motivation and strategy.* Chicago: University of Chicago Press.

Singer, T., & Fehr, E. (2005). The neuroeconomics of mind reading and empathy. *American Economic Review, 95*(2), 340–345.

Tanzi, V., & Schuknecht, L. (2000). *Public spending in the 20th century.* Cambridge, MA: Cambridge University Press.

Ura, K., & Galay, K. (2004). *Gross national happiness and development.* Thimphu: Centre for Bhutan Studies.

Van Praag, B., & Ferrer-i-Carbonell, A. (2004). *Happiness quantified: A satisfaction calculus approach.* Oxford: Oxford University Press.

Veenhoven, R. (1993). *Happiness in nations: Subjective appreciation of life in 56 nations 1946–1992.* Rotterdam: Erasmus University Press.

Veenhoven, R. (1999). Quality-of-life in individualistic society: A comparison in 43 nations in the early 1990s. *Social Indicators Research, 48*(2), 159–188.

Veenhoven, R. (2000). Freedom and happiness: A comparative study in 46 nations in the early 1990s. In E. Diener & E. Suh (Eds.), *Culture and subjective well-being* (pp. 257–288). Cambridge, MA: MIT Press.

Wolfers, J. (2003). Is business cycle volatility costly? Evidence from surveys of subjective well-being. *International Finance, 6,* 1–31.

Wright, T. A., & Staw, B. A. (1998). Affect and favorable work outcomes: Two longitudinal tests of the happy-productive worker thesis. *Journal of Organizational Behavior, 20,* 1–23.

24

RETHINKING INTERNAL COMMUNICATION

Building Purpose-Driven Organizations

Ángel Alloza Losana and Clara Fontán Gallardo

Introduction

The environment in which enterprises operate is fraught with emergent challenges: new competitors reinventing traditional business models; changing demographic, regulatory, and socio-political conditions; new modes of work; and an ongoing paradigm shift in how individuals communicate with one another and engage more actively with organizations. Evolution in the face of these new realities is required if companies want to be relevant in a context where competition is no longer focused only on financial variables.

Nowadays, over 50 percent of the total value of an organization lies in its intangible assets, in contrast with past decades (IIRC, 2013; Brand Finance, 2017). In some cases, it is estimated that over half the value of the global market cap is determined by the value of intangible assets (Figure 24.1). Many academic studies have shown the growing importance of intangible assets and resources in value creation (Hall, 1992; Deephouse, 1997; Fombrun, 1996; Jo Hatch & Shultz, 2010; Cees van Riel, 2012; Carreras et al., 2013; Argenti, 2012). We are also seeing that companies no longer compete for financial variables. Instead they are more concerned with earning the respect, admiration, empathy, and support of those whom are crucial for their survival: their stakeholders, i.e. employees, customers, investors, and society in general.

In this new reputation economy, no company can succeed in the market if its interests are not aligned with the needs of its internal and external stakeholders (Van Riel, 2012, p. 13).

The key to success lies in the recognition of our stakeholders. For this reason, it is crucial to know and adequately meet their expectations to gain their respect, empathy, and support. Studies show that the management of intangible assets is the only proven way to guarantee the sustainability of a business project over time. This is, qualitative variables related to the experience and perception of different stakeholders: customers, employees, investors, and society as a whole. Among all intangible assets, corporate reputation has sparked off the most interest and attention over the past years, due to its contribution to generate corporate value.

To build a solid reputation able to last over time, it is important to be consistent and coherent between what you say and what you do or, in other words, between the expectations generated and the experiences actually delivered through all touchpoints. Recognition of stakeholders can be achieved thanks to a collection of three elements: the user's direct experience when acquiring a product or service; the corporate discourse of the company itself and the discourse shared regarding the positive or negative experience delivered by the company offering that product or service.

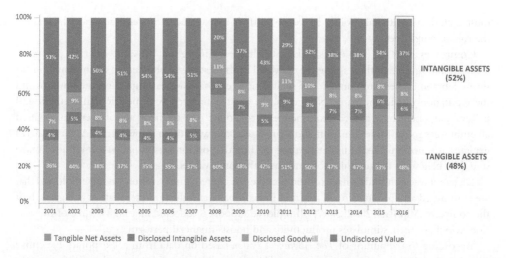

Figure 24.1 Value of intangible assets as a proportion of total enterprise value
(source: 2017 Brand Finance Global Intangible Tracker, GIT™)

Figure 24.2 The Reputation-building Process
(source: Corporate Excellence & Estudio de Comunicación, 2016).

The Role of Employees: Key in All Value Creation Processes

To achieve excellence, companies should lead by the recognition of their stakeholders and include improvement plans based on the expectations and demands of different groups of interest. This new way of doing business is expected to revolutionize organizational management, as companies that are put under the scrutiny of their stakeholders over time and consider essential areas of management in a holistic way are inevitably closer to achieving corporate excellence (Alloza, 2015).

These days, sources of differentiation are no longer based on the product, which can be easily copied, but on who you are, what you're like, and why you choose to do things the way you do. That's why companies give so much importance to brand and corporate reputation. In this new context, known as a "reputation economy" or an "intangible assets economy"—term coined in 2011 at the *XV International Conference on Corporate Reputation, Brand, Identity and Competitiveness* hosted by Reputation Institute in New Orleans (USA)—employees play a key role. Companies have traditionally been managed solely taking into account value creation for shareholders. Now, however, they are beginning to understand that to guarantee their long-term sustainability, they must include a multi-stakeholder approach in their management model, with special focus on the role of employees.

Companies now see employees as key stakeholders throughout all value creation processes. They are responsible of the experience delivered to the rest of stakeholders in all the touchpoints where a brand comes into contact, and their actions can have a great impact on the business and the reputation of the company. Nowadays, the areas connected with people management and cultural alignment have gained prominence in corporate management, and it is crucial to align all employees in the same direction and share a purpose with them. However, as Argenti (2012) explains, it is not only about understanding the brand's positioning and *raison d'être*, but to make sure they believe in the organization and share the same values.

Different research studies have proven that there is a direct link between having employees that are committed and proud to form a part of the company and the good reputation and growth of the company (Van Riel, 2012, p. 17): "Employee support is reflected in a high degree of motivation, which, in turn, stimulates productivity and boosts financial performance."

According to the author of *The Alignment Factor*, based on data from a Corporate Executive Board study, a 10 percent increase in internal alignment leads to a 6 percent increase in employee motivation which, in turn, improves the general performance of a company by 2 percent. An increase of 10 percent of this type also reduces the risk of employees leaving a company by 9 percent (Figure 24.3). All experts agree that employee commitment reduces rotation, increases profits, brings about greater annual growth, and improves productivity.

There is empirical evidence showing that companies where employees are happy and committed with the business project in which they work, perform better. In fact, according to Van Riel (2012, p. 73), "from 1999 to 2008, the group formed by Fortune's 100 Best Companies to Work For had an annual profitability of 4.1 percent higher than the rest of companies." So much so that that the concept of companies encouraging happy work environments is gaining interest and there is now a greater focus on companies that (Delivering Happiness, 2013):

- Are more innovative (Harvard Business Review).
- Have higher rates of productivity (Hay Group).
- Have increased sales (Shawn Achor).
- Have higher profitability rates (Gallup).
- Have less risks and operating incidents (Babcock Marine Clyde).
- Have less rotation rates (Gallup).
- Have less absenteeism rates or sick leaves (Forbes).
- Have lower levels of exhaustion or fatigue (HBR).

It is not easy to create aligned behaviors amongst employees. However, once that challenge has been successfully met, company performance is vastly improved. Cees van Riel (2012, p. 114) says that the journey to internal alignment is founded on three essential pillars:

- Information. Companies should communicate the company's global strategy to its employees and explain its impact on everyday activities, their professional career and the future of the organization.
- Motivation. Companies should promote programs to motivate employees, stressing individual opportunities and giving meaning to employee contribution as an essential part of the corporate project.
- Development. Companies need to assist the development of their employees' capabilities and skills through training and development programs.

The company's commitment
The company complies with customer & stakeholders commitments
Exemplary behavior of the company
Good performance in the local communities in whick the company operates

Communication
Information
Feedback channels

Work conditions
Good conditions
Perception of the desire to improve and trust in the fulfillment of commitments

Reputation according to the employee
Perception about the reputation of the company by employees

Social usefulness
Prescriptions emanated from the culture and social environment of the company

Perceived usefulness
Perception that my company's reputation is good for me

Personal norm
Personal conviction about my behavior in the promotion of the reputation of my company

Figure 24.3 Elements of the Employee and Reputation Model
(source: Corporate Excellence & Estudio de Comunicación, 2016).

As we have already seen, different researches show that many employees are willing to defend and promote positive behaviors toward their organizations if they identify with the values and beliefs that the entity represents. In this sense, one of the main challenges ahead is to be able to find those employees that are engaged and identify themselves with the business project and to turn them into internal influencers and ambassadors of the organization in the external field. Much has been already written about internal and employee branding, and we will be seeing lots of progress in this area in the following years.

We agree that employees need to be seen as the main ambassadors of a brand and one of the most trusted social actors, but how can we activate their engagement and advocacy? According to the results of the *Modelo Empleados y Reputación* (Employee and Reputation Model), the levers that need to be activated to increase employees' responsibility toward corporate reputation are related to four operable factors (the company's commitment, reputation according to the employee, communication, and work conditions), two driving elements (social usefulness and perceived usefulness), and a focal element (personal norm) that becomes the facilitator to foster the intention of "promoting corporate reputation." The weight of these factors and how they affect the expected behavior, together with the assessment of them, depend on the reality of the organization where the model is applied, which allows companies to design unique action plans.

Building Purpose-Driven Organizations

However, under my point of view, the key to truly create aligned behaviors among employees is to actively include them in the process of defining values and purpose. It is essential that all employees in a company can, through internal consultancy, express their personal values, the values they see in the corporate culture and the organization itself and the values that they would like to form a part of the future culture. Employees will only engage if they feel that they are a part of the process. In this sense, and from the point of view of internal communication management, it is essential to promote an open dialogue at all levels, develop participatory mechanisms, and encourage a climate of trust where all employees can freely express themselves.

Employees play a fundamental role in the definition of corporate character, because their behavior represents the company's *raison d'être*. All experts agree that employees have become the main voices of the organization compared to other stakeholders (Van Riel, 2012, p. 14): "Employees are the authentic brand ambassadors, as they can better understand the very character of the company, its reason for existing."

Internationally, companies that are more advanced in this sense are those which have implemented the new communication model promoted by Arthur W. Page Society, the premier professional association for senior corporate communications executives in the United States. The *Building Beliefs Model* is motivating 25 of the Fortune 50 companies in the United States (Archer Daniels Midland, AT&T, Best Buy, Cardinal Health, Chevron, Dow Chemical, ExxonMobil, Ford, General Electric, General Motors, The Home Depot, IBM, JPMorgan Chase, Kraft Foods, Kroger, Lockheed Martin, Marathon Oil, Pfizer, Sears, United Health Care Group, UPS, Verizon, Walgreens, WellPoint, and so on) to promote processes to redefine, activate, and align their corporate character with the needs and expectations of their stakeholders. In Spain, companies such as BBVA, Banco Santander, CaixaBank, DKV Seguros Médicos, Gas Natural Fenosa, MAPFRE, Repsol, and Telefónica, among others, are also engaged in alignment processes relating to their purpose, vision, and corporate values.

Defining and implementing a single unique character is essential. Such is the conclusion of an analysis developed by Jim Stengel (2011) on more than 50,000 brands from all global industries (Figure 24.5). Research shows that the common attribute of the 50 companies that have grown the most over the past decade is that they have defined and redefined their identity and undertaken internal alignment processes relating to their corporate purpose. Corporate character

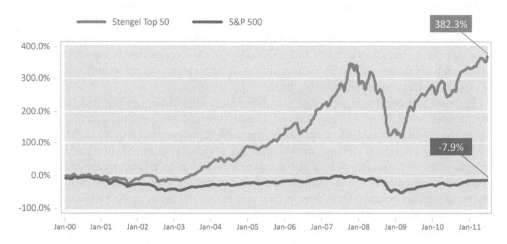

Figure 24.4 World's 50 fastest growing brands
(source: Stengel, 2011).

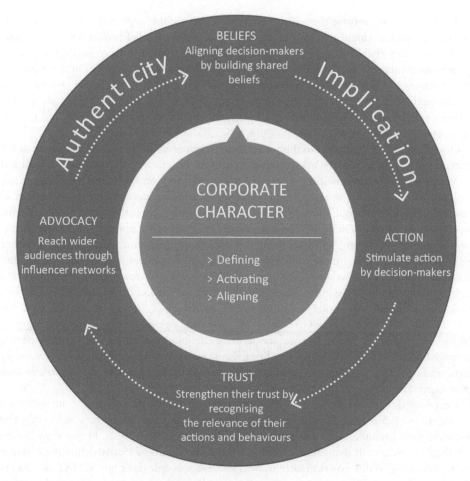

Figure 24.5 New communication model: Building beliefs
(source: Corporate Excellence, 2013; adaptation of Arthur W. Page Society, 2012).

includes the company's vision and purpose, but it also takes into account its values, philosophy, and culture; all the attributes which make it unique and enable a context of shared beliefs with its stakeholders (Jo Hatch & Shultz, 2010; Argenti, 2012; Alloza, 2015).

As Argenti explains in *Corporate Communication*, the elements that help create a single unique identity are:

1. An aspirational corporate vision.
2. Good brand positioning.
3. Being able to express corporate culture in all areas in a consistent and coherent way.

Employee behavior is an expression of the corporate culture, the principles of the organization. It is employees whom have a direct impact on the values of stakeholders and this consequently generates favorable attitudes which, in turn, influence values pertaining to investment, procurement, recommendations, and performance. As Argenti says (2012), it's not just about employees understanding the brand's positioning and the *raison d'être* of the company, but also about them believing in the company and sharing the values of the organization. To achieve this, companies must involve them in a shared dream. Hence the importance of the new communication model, which upholds the importance of a shared belief system with the various stakeholders that enables commitment and identification with company ideals and, consequently, invites stakeholders, starting with employees, to express their interests in the organization and actively advocate its products and services. It is therefore important to communicate and disseminate information on a large scale-, from employees up—so that information flows between employees and clients, clients, and potential clients, and potential clients and the rest of society as a whole.

One of the main peculiarities of this model is that it places employees at the very center of the strategy and considers them the main spokespeople of the organization as they generate trust and credibility with other stakeholders. Currently, third-party opinion has a greater influence than what the company is able to say through its corporate communication channels or through its managers. Employees (people like you and me) are, along with experts, the ones who generate the most trust according to Edelman Trust Barometer (2017). Keeping in mind this reality, organizations need to be able to implement integral communication systems with a greater influence on those actors who enjoy more credibility. Working with employees is strategically important, as it will always be easier to strengthen bonds with those who are closer. Thus, communication with employees is one of the most challenging and vital tasks for an organization. Cees Van Riel, professor at Rotterdam School, Erasmus University, claims (2012) that its success will be determined by the ability of companies to create a discourse that inspires all communication programs, both internally and externally. The best way to make employees feel more closely connected is to generate honest and authentic stories that bring them closer to the organization. A powerful story and a unified culture start from the inside and is extrapolated to the rest of the key stakeholders of an organization.

Corporate discourse describes the organization's essence, underlines its unique attributes and highlights core ideas that must be stressed in all communication. To boost action, corporate discourse must be authentic, trustworthy, and emotional (Van Riel, 2012). In this sense, Simon Sinek (2013) points out that the key to success for companies is to clearly define the reason it exists. According to this expert in international leadership, people don't buy WHAT you do but WHY you do it. Only by defining a shared goal and giving meaning to what we do can we inspire others to act:

> The biggest leaders are able to inspire people and make them act. Those who are able to inspire others, give people a purpose, the feeling of belonging to something that has little to do with any external incentive or any profit that can be obtained.
>
> *(Sinek, 2013, p. 21)*

Sinek explains that most organizations base their communication on what they do, i.e. their products, characteristics, and benefits, but these factors don't create a call to action and they don't enable people to connect. The theory of the golden circle explains why people choose to engage and follow certain movements, organizations, and individuals over others and how certain organizations and leaders know how to stand out by building their positioning around their "why."

To be able to stand out is a challenge during a long period of time, as it is to seed loyalty only based on [factors like] price, quality, or services (Sinek, 2013, p. 72). According to Sinek, this theory offers a way of communicating that is completely aligned with the way people make decisions: when companies communicate from their "why," from the raison d'être of the company, they are talking from inside to outside, straight to people's limbic brain, which is responsible for feelings, human behavior and decision-making. Sinek says that leading companies stand out because "their message begins with 'why,' a purpose, cause or belief that has nothing

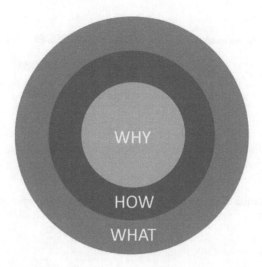

Figure 24.6 Golden Circle Model
(source: Sinek, 2013, p. 61).

to do with what they do. What they do—the products that they make, from computers to small electronics—no longer serves as the reason to buy" (Sinek, 2013, p. 66).

According to Sinek, companies need to clearly define their corporate character, goal, mission, and vision and boost an inside-out system of shared beliefs and values if they want to create projects with which they can engage. Organizations and leaders such as Steve Jobs, the Wright brothers, Martin Luther King, Howard Schultz, Walt Disney and Harley Davidson have managed to stand out over time because they have a very well-defined "why," that's to say, their raison d'être is clear. They have formulated visions and identities anchored in universal values so that their stakeholders can easily identify with them and be open to purchasing their products. This also helps attract talent and investment and aids the obtaining and maintenance of operating licenses. Some examples of these visions and characters based on big ideals can be found in the Stengel Top 50 companies (2011), which also correspond to those companies which have grown the most over the last decade.

In *Grow: How Ideals Power Growth and Profit at the World's Greatest Companies*, Stengel explains five key points to define a great ideal:

1. Deliver an experience of happiness to people: encourage them and make them feel at home.
2. Connect people with the outer world: make them feel part of something bigger and greater.
3. Explore new horizons with them: take them out, and discover yet unknown paths.
4. Develop confidence and stamina: help them explore their inner strength and build confidence.
5. Generate a positive influence on society: help them challenge the status quo and embrace change.

Rethinking Internal Communication

This is the transformational change that's needed in companies, they must clearly define their purpose. It has to be simple but powerful, and above all, it must summarize why the company exists and why it does what it does. A specific example in this sense, with good results, can be found with KPMG, which redefined its purpose to promote greater internal engagement and

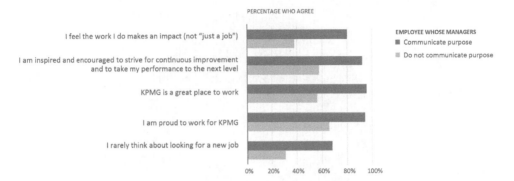

Figure 24.7 Communicating the purpose or raison d'être of the company raises employee engagement— KMPG case
(source: KPMG).

reinforce their system of shared beliefs. From an extensive analysis on the surveys conducted, KPMG formulated a new positioning: "Inspire Confidence. Empower Change." But they didn't stop there, once they had their purpose defined, they launched an internal campaign to motivate a stronger emotional connection with the project. The goal was to make all employees live up to that purpose throughout their daily routines. They focused on the experience. All employees had the opportunity to discuss how they lived by the principle of "Inspire Confidence. Empower Change." They recorded videos and made digital posters—that went viral inside the company—where employees were always the main actors. The results of the study revealed that 90 percent of staff admitted to feeling proud of being a part of the team. After one year, 89 percent of employees said that KPMG was a good place to work. That helped the company position itself as the best company to work within its category in the ranking Best Place to Work. At the same time, 76 percent of employees claimed to have a special sense of purpose and that it wasn't just a job for them. This example shows the importance of defining a purpose in both a powerful and simple way, which can be shared by everyone and means something to everyone involved (Figure 24.7).

As demonstrated in the previous case, once the character has been defined, the next step is to activate said character so that it can be translated into competitive advantages, which cannot be copied and generate value for the organization. Making people believe in your project is a very complex challenge, but it is also a very powerful tool. Nobody will be able to stop a group of people motivated by truth and the knowledge that they know why they do what they do. Identity is activated through corporate values and the behavior of employees on a daily basis. Consequently, there is a clear opportunity to stand out by behaving well internally. It is important to consider that if culture determines how a company behaves, its behavior reflects how that company really thinks. Organizations and their brands can learn a lot about how they grow and project their values and raison d'être and how they boost and promote the development of who makes it possible, i.e. their own employees. To create spaces where people can grow and develop by themselves and in harmony with shared values and goals is the big challenge that will make a difference between companies.

Over the past years, internal communication is gaining much more importance as a lever to promote corporate purpose and help align all employees around a common code of values and principles. The line between internal and external communication is more and more blurred and employees are now considered key communication agents in the company. Thus, regarding the new internal communication, the following premises should be taken into account:

1.   For employees, defending the company's reputation is directly linked to the defense of their own professionality, so they usually help promote it in a positive way, as it benefits both parts. That is why it is so important to strengthen their engagement and motivate positive behaviours and authentic advocacy.

2.   Reputation must be integrated in the internal communication agenda. Employees have to know how their actions impact the reputation of the company they work for. When companies clearly communicate their unique values and the behaviours associated to them, it is easier to create a shared "social norm" that puts "social pressure" and influence the final behavior of stakeholders. From the point of view of internal communication, it is not only about eplaining the organization's values, principles and purpose, but about creating a dialogue internally to discuss these values that make a company unique, the behaviours connected to them and the actual performance achieved.

3.   Employees demand their companies to act responsibly, coherently, and consistently. Companies need to openly provide information that is authentic and trustworthy so that their employees feel that the organization is living up to the committements made with all its stakeholders.

What Makes a Company a Great Place to Work

According to the report *How's life? 2015*, developed by the Organization for Economic Cooperation and Development (OECD), there are some shared benchmarks which establish the general welfare of citizens and constitute the Better Life Index, enabling the measurement of the welfare of member states according to 11 variables with a direct impact on this issue: citizen engagement, social relationships, level of income, property, environmental quality, work-life balance, security, education, personal satisfaction, and health. Among the different criteria that directly impact on happiness or personal welfare in the 2015 issue, education, personal satisfaction, and health stood the most.

The report notes that the welfare of citizens is determined by life satisfaction, which relates to feelings and experiences. With these data in mind, only those companies able to give meaning to the lives of those that make the company possible—employees—will succeed. Thus, companies must "make them tick," in the words of Margarita Álvarez, chief marketing and communication officer at Adecco Group and precursor of the Coca-Cola Happiness Institute in Spain. Experts claim that happiness is 50 percent genetic predisposition, 10 percent context, and 40 percent individual personally. This last figure gives much consideration to emotional intelligence and to people's control of their own motivation capacity. It also provides great opportunities to promote happiness at work by encouraging positive emotional states, based on the idea that emotions are contagious and favorable environments have a direct impact on productivity and performance.

This matters so much that one of the seven key dimensions that form the global reputation of a company—according to RepTrak Pulse model of the Reputation Institute—is directly linked with the workplace and the way employees are treated. In other words, together with "Products/Services," "Financial Performance," "Innovation," "Leadership," "Citizenship," "Ethics," and "Governance," "Workplace" is one of the attributes with a direct impact on stakeholder attitudes—favorable or adverse—toward a company. In particular, according to Weber Shandwick, what employees think and say about their organization has an impact of approximately 42 percent on the global reputation of said company. That's why corporate leaders give so much importance to encouraging a good working environment so that employees are empowered and feel they are part of something with meaning. This link between reputation and happiness can also be observed in the findings of the last study on country reputation, *Country RepTrak 2015* and the *World Happiness Report 2015*. The analysis of findings offered by both studies reveals that the happiest nations are also the ones with the best reputations.

The results of the Havas Media (2017) global survey on meaningful brands are also remarkable. It collected the views of 300,000 participants in 31 countries regarding 1,500 brands and showed that people care about the fact that companies contribute to improving the quality of life and collective well-being (75 percent). The study also shows that only 40 percent of participants consider that companies are working hard to improve the quality of life and collective well-being (table 1), so, one year more, it demonstrates that most of us would not care if 74 percent of brands disappeared.

It is therefore necessary to introduce a new way of leading in organizations that is able to look beyond profits or financial loss and take into account the implications of their actions with a much broader perspective. It is important to include non-financial indicators in scorecards to complement traditional financial indicators. By non-financial indicators we mean indicators to measure corporate reputation, brand strength, customer satisfaction, probability of recommendation, and also, employee commitment. All these data show that companies with a high rate of employee commitment deliver a more positive performance. This indicator should be included in organization scorecards to allow a multi-stakeholder approached focused on the long-term in and on decision-making processes. If traditional financial indicators show how you earned money in the past, non-financial indicators offer relevant data about the future of the company. This integral and holistic approach has begun to appear in other areas of society. An example of this can be seen in the case of Bhutan's initiative to boost its Gross National Happiness Index and assess the life quality of countries in a more comprehensive way than the GDP, which until now was the main indicator for development. Or the Social Progress Index recently created by Scott Stern from MIT and The Social Progress Imperative which measures a country's performance in different social and environmental spheres, enabling an integral framework for measuring social progress.

Conclusion

Companies must undergo a significant transformation and start placing employees at the center of all decision-making processes. They need to understand the strategic importance of ensuring that everyone working in a company pulls in the same direction. To do so, it is essential to develop a bottom-up and open communication system and promote an inclusive corporate culture where employees are taken into account. We are talking about a new kind of leadership, where hierarchy and vertical structures lose ground to cross-cutting work teams characterized by fluent, open, and transparent interaction, between members of the same team but also with the company as a whole.

Zappos, a North American online shoe shop, is a good example of this model. The company, which has over 1,500 employees and over $1 billion in annual sales, has demonstrated that promoting happiness and well-being in the workplace has a direct impact on outcome. Its "Delivering Happiness" Model has become such a success that it will be a turning point in the journey to an excellent management in organizations. Zappos has recently launched a new work model, which removes middle-ranking positions and regroups all employees into multi-disciplinary work teams that work on a project basis and are able to set their roles and goals. This is one of the elements valued by millennials, those born between 1980 and 1990 who, according to Forbes, will account for 75 percent of working professionals by 2025. However, it is not something tightest in stone that society is taking on, but a new attitude that needs to be assumed. Knowing what new generations value, expect, and demand is critical from a corporate perspective to attract and retain talent. Young professionals put greater priority on balancing family and working life, having a healthy lifestyle and working in a creative and innovative environment rather than focusing on the formal aspects of salary and professional career. Above all, they want to make the world a better place and give their job a meaning. Trends expected for the coming years include:

- Companies need to understand the strategic role of their employees and place them at the center, where customers are.
- New employees require companies to get involved in their teams' well-being and respond to their needs.
- An internal culture is highly regarded when it promotes open dialogue, active listening and immediate feedback.
- Companies are also rewarded when they work on a goal-driven basis and empower their employees to organize their time and develop flexible working policies.
- Employees engage with a project and commit to it when, in return, the company offers proximity, personalization, and confidence.

In this regard, some authors and experts claim that the chief transformation officer, chief cultural officer, or chief internal communication officer—function is what matters, not the name—will play a fundamental role in the transformational change that all companies urgently need to undertake if they want to meet all the upcoming challenges. This role should be responsible for leading this new corporate discourse and translating it into actions by considering all stakeholders and more specifically, all employees. The real issue goes beyond giving a title to this position. What really matters is that companies must include this role in their teams to offer a new approach in corporate management and implement a broader multi-stakeholder vision, enabling better decision-making.

References

Alloza, A. (2015). Aproximación a la reputación y a la responsabilidad corporativa. In J. Benavides & A. Monfort (Eds.), *Comunicación y Empresa Responsable*. Barañáin (Navarra): EUNSA.

Argenti, P. A. (2012). *Corporate communication* (6th ed.). New York: McGraw-Hill.

Arthur W. Page Society. (2012). *Building belief: A new model for activating corporate character & authentic advocacy*. Retrieved from https://page.org/thought-leadership/building-belief

Brand Finance. (2017). *Global intangible financial tracker 2017*. Retrieved from http://brandfinance.com/knowledge-centre/reports/global-intangible-finance-tracker-gift-2017/

Carreras, E., Alloza, A., & Carreras, A. (2013). *Corporate reputation*. Corporate Excellence Library. Madrid: LID Editorial Empresarial.

Corporate Excellence. (2013). *Nuevo Modelo de Comunicación: construir creencias compartidas*. Retrieved from http://blog.corporateexcellence.org/el-nuevo-modelo-de-comunicacion

Corporate Excellence & Alcor (hoy Estudio de Comunicación). (2016). *El impacto de los profesionales en el fomento de la reputación: ¿Cómo medirlo y cómo activarlo?* Retrieved from http://www.corporateexcellence.org/index.php/

Deephouse, D. L. (1997). The effect of financial and media reputations on performance. *Corporate Reputation Review, 1*, 68–71.

Edelman. (2017). *Edelman trust barometer 2017*. Retrieved from https://www.edelman.com/trust2017/

Fombrun, C. (1996) *Reputation: Realizing value from the corporate image*. Boston, MA: Harvard Business School.

Hall, R. (1992), The strategic analysis of intangible resources. *Strategic Management Journal, 13*, 135–144. doi:10.1002/smj.4250130205

Havas Media. (2017). *Meaningful brands*. Retrieved from https://www.meaningful-brands.com/en

Hsieh, T. (2013). *Delivering Happiness. ¿Cómo hacer felices a tus empleados y duplicar tus beneficios?* Barcelona: Profit.

IIRC (2013). *Business and Investors explore the sustainability perspective of integrated reporting.* London: International Integrated Reporting Council.

Jo Hatch, M., & Schultz, M. (2010). *Esencia de marca.* Madrid: LID Editorial Empresarial.

Sinek, S. (2013). *La clave es el porqué.* Barcelona: Península.

Stengel, J. (2011). *Grow: How ideals power growth and profit at the world's greatest companies.* New York: Crown Business.

Van Riel, C. B. M. (2012). *Alinear para ganar.* Madrid: LID Editorial Empresarial.

25

AUTHENTIC COMMUNICATION AND SUBJECTIVE WELL-BEING

The Case of a Nonprofit Public Service Organization

Antonio Ariza-Montes, Antonio L. Leal-Rodríguez,
Horacio Molina-Sánchez, and Jesús Ramírez-Sobrino

Introduction

Plenty of studies are currently pointing that the ultimate goal in a person's lifetime should never be just surviving and facing adversities, but flourishing and growing (Park, Peterson, & Sun, 2013). All human being deserves to live a happy, healthy, and complete life. Enjoying a good life is something achievable for most people, but often it requires from hard work and the application of the adequate strategies. In this vein, the field of positive psychology has been offering interesting contributions aimed at enabling the understanding of the concepts of happiness and well-being and the discovery of its main drivers.

The employees' subjective well-being (SWB) has become an interesting issue for firms, since several studies reveal that those employees with higher SWB are more productive (e.g. Baker, Cahalin, Gerst, & Burr, 2005). However, this topic has been scarcely examined within nonprofit public service organizations. Moreover, the role exerted by the employees' authentic communication remains unknown. And all this despite the fact that scholars like Fusco, O'Riordan, and Palmer (2015) have argued that authenticity stands as a key factor while enhancing communication and sharing knowledge, that may lead to the attainment of competitive advantages and superior performance.

In the last years, the term "authenticity" has ignited plenty of discussion at the academic level and for practitioners and an emergent body of research stresses the importance of being authentic for human functioning (Boucher, 2011; Grandey, Foo, Groth, & Goodwin, 2012). Authentic individuals are those people who project open-mindedness, self-awareness, understanding, acceptance, and confidence. They attain their personal and professional goals by remaining stuck to their own beliefs, principles, and ideas, and by inspiring and involving others. This leads them to adopt basic communication styles which enable them to reach their goals, as well as to help others to encounter theirs.

The most successful individuals prosper by developing their own potential, not by attempting to replicate others' behaviors or styles. Being authentic encompasses being your best version of yourself, namely being trustful, warm, open, and human. Authenticity creates a climate of trust because it promises others the freedom to act without a need to build protective walls. Being and behaving in an authentic manner contributes to generate a positive atmosphere that might lead in turn to the establishment of empathy and affinity, while it builds relationships and fosters communication. The actions of authentic people tend to be in line with their words. Individuals that act coherently with themselves feel more comfortable and do not lose energy in pretending to be someone else (Van den Bosch & Taris, 2014a). Therefore, it is widely assumed that authentic people are inclined to behave, communicate, and interrelate better with others, thus attaining higher degrees of happiness and well-being.

However, while authenticity might be widely considered very positive for the person's development and satisfaction, it may also contain a negative side (Dewett, 2015). The empirical results linking authenticity and well-being are still scarce and often inconclusive. Thus, with the aim of shedding light upon this issue we attempt to explore in depth the link between authenticity and subjective well-being adopting the tridimensional framework of a person developed by Wood, Linley, Maltby, Baliousis, and Joseph (2008). Consequently, the main purpose of this study is to explore the relationship between authenticity and subjective well-being within a scarcely explored context, which is the one shaped by a public service institution. To this aim, we focus on a large international organization with a strong presence in the south of Spain and the Canary Islands. The labor accomplished by this nonprofit organization is mainly grounded in the education segment (pre-university education) and in the social work sector, which is mainly shaped by residences for elder people, orphanages, and social dining rooms.

This study aims to cover the research gap that exists as for the relationship between authenticity and subjective well-being within the scarcely researched context of employees belonging to a public service organization. To this aim, this chapter continues as follows: in section 2, we present a review of the most relevant literature and posit our research model and hypotheses. Section 3 describes the methodology we followed in this study. Section 4 presents the main results obtained from the empirical assessment of the hypothesized links. In section 5, we discuss the most critical empirical results. The chapter ends with the main implications, limitations, and suggestions for future lines of research.

The Link Between Authenticity and Subjective Well-Being

The deep social and economic changes originated lately are generating a social complexity that has boosted the appearing and prominence of new agents that act in the market, complementing the traditional offer of private or public services (Anshell & Gash, 2008). Precisely, this work is grounded upon one of these new civil organizations that belong to the Third Sector and that have emerged in recent years of crisis favored, or rather forced by "State deregulation" and the dismantling of certain public services. The purpose of the Third Sector's organizations roots on the articulation of a set of social initiatives aimed at promoting certain rights, satisfying certain needs, and the correction of potential errors or shortcomings made by the public administration or the market. Therefore, nonprofit public service organizations perform nowadays significant contributions to the welfare state in sectors of activity as critical as are education, health care, social services, arts, culture, etc. (Ariza-Montes & Lucia-Casademunt, 2013).

Despite its importance, these organizations have been scarcely assessed from the organizational perspective. However, a key element of its long-term survival roots in knowing how do their members actually feel. Precisely this work hypothesizes that an authentic communication contributes to improve the level of subjective well-being of the individuals that shape these organizations.

As posited by Grandey et al. (2012), in the last years there is a growing body of research that stresses the importance of being authentic. This circumstance is mainly due to the impulse of positive psychology, discipline that, in the search to cultivate the best part of individuals for themselves and for society, revived the interest in the study of authenticity (Seligman &

Csikszentmihalyi, 2000). The interest about the assessment of authenticity at the workplace context is linked to the rising of the authentic leadership concept, referred to those organization's members who are fully aware of their beliefs and values, which make them act coherently with it, as well as transparently toward other people (Carvalho de et al., 2015). In this sense, transparency in communications stands as a central issue. Likewise, Rafferty and Griffin (2004) concluded that more authentic leaders transmit better a firm's mission and vision, inspire more when they communicate, are more intellectually stimulating, are more supportive with the rest of the firm's members and publicly disclose the level of performance. In sum, these leaders are more effective at communicating a clear, inspiring, and unifying strategy and future direction, namely the organization's purpose.

In general, Harter (2002) defines authenticity as the individual's capacity to act in accordance with him/herself. Being authentic is important because it generates positive effects between the employees, who enjoy more and find their work more meaningful (Reich, Kessel, & Bernieri, 2013; Ménard & Brunet, 2011). This contributes in turn to generate healthier organizations and social environments (Carvalho de et al., 2015). On the contrary, the lack of authenticity produces anxiety and psychopathologies among the individuals, who have to develop forced or unnatural behaviors.

This work adopts as framework the model proposed by Wood et al. (2008). These authors consider that the authentic behavior encompasses three dimensions: a) self-alienation, understood as the extent to which an individual experiences a certain level of incongruence between his/her awareness and the real experience (in the workplace, this would correspond to the subjective experience of not knowing very well who is one at work); b) authentic life, which implies being faithful to one's self in most of the occasions, living and acting in accordance with his/her own values and beliefs; c) external influence acceptance, which refers to the extent to which the influence of other people is accepted, while one is forced to comply with others' expectatives. Following Wood et al. (2008), an adequate combination of high authentic life and reduced levels of self-alienation and external influence acceptance may lead to the optimal level of authenticity.

Although authenticity has been central to psychological theories regarding people's ability to achieve their full potential, to reach a high authentically standard is a utopia. Human beings, as social ones, are partially influenced by the close environment and consequently they will decrease the authentically as opportunism or self-alienation will rise. In nonprofit organizations with strong ideological component settings, opportunistic workers could take non-authentic behaviors, seeking labor advantages such as a better career development.

Logically, individual well-being—in the workplace or in any other sphere of their life—will be harmed when individuals turn out to be forced to show behaviors contradictory with their own feelings and conducts, and lead them in turn to renounce to be themselves. Similarly, Sheldon, Ryan, Rawsthorne, and Ilardi (1997) point out that individuals who experience their behavior as a true expression of their own self in different contexts generally attain superior levels of health and well-being.

Authors like Huta and Ryan (2010) posit that well-being is a multidimensional concept that integrates aspects of the eudemonic and hedonic views. This research adopts the integrative conception proposed by Diener et al. (2010), who consider that subjective well-being is a second-order construct shaped by three dimensions—two dimensions linked to the hedonic perspective (life satisfaction and the presence of positive and negative feelings) and a third dimension rooted in both perspectives, flourishing, which describes the individual's subjective perception in critical areas of human activity that comprise from positive relations, to competency and self-esteem feelings, as well as life meaning and purpose—. Following Cortina and Berenzon (2013) flourishing is a mental health state featured by high levels of subjective, psychological, and social well-being, linked to a high proportion of positive affectivity. Prior studies such as the one developed by Bono, Davies, and Rasch (2012) have related flourishing at work with prosperity, happiness, engagement, self-motivation, success, and learning at work.

The interest in the study of the connection between authentic communication and well-being has recently been intensified with the advent of Positive Psychology. The link between Authenticity and well-being is certainly intuitive given that, as indicated by Sheldon et al. (1997), well-being depends to a big extent on the extent to which people behaves authentically under different circumstances with distinct people. For instance, a study by Mazutis and Slawinski (2008) revealed that highly authentic working environments derive in an organizational culture characterized by dialogue and transparency, as well as by organizational learning. Authenticity generates well-being, since it provides individuals with a clear and consistent sense of themselves. On the contrary, when individuals are forced to act against their values and deepest aspirations, this normally results in disorientation and dissatisfaction.

Several studies have found significant evidence of the relationship between authenticity, and certain measures of well-being are the following: (i) Goldman and Kernis (2002) link authenticity with self-esteem and subjective well-being; (ii) Neff and Harter (2002) relate authenticity to self-esteem and depression); (iii) Lopez and Rice (2006) assess the impact of authenticity on individuals' levels of depression, self-esteem, anxiety, and life satisfaction; (iv) Wood et al. (2008) link authenticity to subjective well-being and stress reduction; and (v) Boyraz, Waits, and Felix (2014) relate authenticity to life satisfaction.

Nevertheless, none of the mentioned studies was carried out at the business context. Landing in the workplace scenario, Ménard and Brunet (2011) observed that authentic communication increases subjective well-being in a sample shaped by executives, although this relationship turned out to be partially mediated by the meaning that work possess for these individuals. Besides, a study carried out in the health care sector by Grandey et al. (2012), revealed that Authenticity reduces strain, at the same time that cushioned the emotional exhaustion inherent to this profession. Similarly, the research conducted by Van den Bosch and Taris (2014a) revealed that authenticity (specially the self-alienation dimension) explained a substantial amount of the variance in the prediction of well-being within a broad sample of German workers.

On the basis of the postulated above, we hypothesize: *H1: Authenticity is positively related to subjective well-being in the context of nonprofit public service organizations.*

Methodology

The empirical part of this research encompassed the design and elaboration of an ad hoc questionnaire that was administered to all the employees belonging to the organization (N = 1753 employees) through the application of Google Forms. The field work was carried out between April and May 2016, receiving a total of 793 questionnaires. However, 46 questionnaires have been rejected, since they presented some sections uncompleted, resulting in a final sample of n = 747 valid questionnaires, which represents a 42,6 percent response rate.

This study relies on the use of previously tested and validated scales to measure the different constructs. On one hand, to measure authenticity we apply the Individual Authenticity Measure at Work scale developed by Van den Bosch and Taris (2014a), and an adaptation to the working environment of the authenticity scale developed by Wood et al. (2008). On the other hand, to measure subjective well-being we use the multidimensional scale posited by Diener et al. (2010), which comprises: a) the Satisfaction With Life Scale (SWLS), b) the Scale of Positive and Negative Experience (SPANE), and c) the Flourishing Scale (FS).

This work aims to show that a more authentic communication significantly determines the level subjective well-being of the employees shaping a nonprofit public service organization. For this purpose, we use a student's t distribution, with 95 percent confidence interval (CI), to contrast the possible mean difference between employees who present high authenticity levels (authenticity scores above the median) and those who are confined to hide part of their authentic feelings (authenticity scores below the median). Data are expressed as mean and standard deviation, considering significant values of $p < 0.05$.

Results

As it was previously mentioned, the total sample was segmented into two subsamples: individuals scoring a low level of authenticity (comprising values between 1 and 4, using the median as a cut-off point) and individuals scoring a high level of authenticity (involving values of 4 and 5 points). Bearing in mind these criteria, it should be stressed that most of the surveyed are women (82.1 percent of the total sample; 82.6 percent among the surveyed with low authenticity and 81.7 percent among the surveyed with high authenticity). The average age is 43.13 years (SD=9.79) (43.08 and 43.05 years, respectively) and an average seniority of 13.17 years (SD=9.67) (13.36 and 13.10, respectively). 73.8 percent of the surveyed declares having accomplished University studies, 16 percent have finished secondary studies and the remaining 10.2 percent only possess primary education (65.4 percent, 21.9 percent and 12.7 percent among the individuals with low authenticity; 80.3 percent, 11.4 percent and 8.3 percent among the individuals with high authenticity). Furthermore, 72.7 percent of the surveyed affirms to live in couple (72.5 percent and 72.9 percent, respectively).

With regard to the sector of activity, 63.4 percent of the surveyed work in education, while the remaining 36.6 percent work in the social sector. Among the employees that present lower authenticity, 43.4 percent work in the social sector, while 56.6 percent work in education. These ratios are 31.3 percent and 68.7 percent, respectively among the employees with high authenticity.

Finally, 8 percent of the surveyed occupy executive positions in contrast to 92 percent who are employees. These ratios are reduced to 5.8 percent among the individuals who present a low level of authenticity and escalate to 9.7 percent among those who denote a high degree of authenticity.

With regard to the central variables in this study, Table 25.1 presents the main descriptive statistics, the Cronbach alpha for each analyzed construct, and the bivariate correlations between the main research variables. As it can be observed, the surveyed show elevated levels of authenticity (especially in the authentic living dimension: 4.21 over a maximum of 5). At the same time, these subjects denote a high level of subjective well-being in all its dimensions (flourishing: 4.43; satisfaction with life: 3.89; and positive-negative feelings balance: 2.17). Table 25.1 also reveals that the main variables are significantly related between each other, which is consistent with the most relevant research theories mentioned above.

Table 25.1 Descriptive statistics, Cronbach's alpha and inter-correlations for the study variables.

Variable	Mean	SD	Cronbach's alpha	1	2	3	4	5	6
1. Self-alienation	4.16	0.938	0.737	1					
2. Authentic living	4.21	0.692	0.743	0.212**	1				
3. External influences	3.65	1.010	0.790	0.439**	0.127**	1			
4. Life satisfaction	3.89	0.792	0.876	0.153**	0.393**	0.141**	1		
5. Feelings (+/-)	2.17	1.191	0.904	0.241**	0.239**	0.206**	0.491**	1	
6. Flourishing	4.43	0.713	0.907	0.266**	0.646**	0.087*	0.440**	0.347**	1

$*p < 0.05; **p < 0.01; ***p < 0.001$

Table 25.2 Means and standard deviations of all variables for high authenticity versus low authenticity.

Value	High authenticity		Low authenticity		Sig.(*)
	M	SD	M	SD	
SWB					
Life satisfaction	4.068	0.678	3.701	0.834	0.000
Feelings (+/-)	2.451	1.029	1.861	1.249	0.000
Flourishing	4.621	0.435	4.274	0.775	0.000

* Significant difference at a 95 percent confidence interval.

Finally, Table 25.2 presents the means contrast between the two groups under study. As it can be observed, employees who are more authentic in the work environment have higher levels of flourishing (4.621 versus 4.274), life satisfaction (4.068 versus 3.701) and positive-negative feelings balance (2.451 versus 1.861). These differences are statistically significant at a 95 percent confidence level. Thus, it is possible to affirm that authentic communication constitutes an element related to the biggest or least grade of well-being of the personnel working at nonprofit organizations.

Discussion

The ties between being oneself and well-being shapes a very recent research topic (Mengers, 2014). Given the large number of hours that currently are passed in the workplace is very important to understand the impact that has on the personnel to experience authenticity in the work environment. Prior investigations have revealed that the most authentic individuals, those that remain faithful to their own being, show major well-being levels (i.e., Ménard & Brunet, 2011; Grandey et al., 2012; Van den Bosch & Taris, 2014a). Nevertheless, there exists a noteworthy research gap in the context of nonprofit public service organizations. This gap is especially worrying in this type of organizations, since the possibility that its members express themselves with comfort, without obstacles, and act this way in congruity with its beliefs and personal experiences, it turns out to be critical for the development of feelings of belonging, a basic factor as for the survival of nonprofit organizations. It should not be forgotten that many of the people who choose to work in nonprofit organizations belonging to the third sector do so because they are attracted by certain ideological issues (mission, values, service vocation, etc.).

In return, on many occasions, this sector offers working conditions more precarious than market. On this issue, Bacchiega and Borzaga (2003) sustain that these organizations only attract those employees that are not mainly motivated by economic remuneration (extrinsic compensation). Precisely, among the conditions of intrinsic nature that this sector might provide there can be stressed without doubt the effective management of emotions at work, and in relation to this aspect, a fundamental element of effective communication is the ability to express themselves frankly and openly, in short, the possibility of being authentic at the workplace.

The idea underlying this chapter is that there is a positive relationship between authenticity and subjective well-being. Both the descriptive analysis and the statistical mean differences analysis realized in the present investigation reveal that the most authentic individuals, those that are transparent and say what they think without mufflers and hypocrisy, show a major level of subjective well-being in its three dimensions. The most authentic people are more transparent in their interpersonal relationships, resulting in improved organizational communication, a climate that emphasizes information dissemination and the role of organizations' stakeholders in identifying organizational needs (Cotterrell, 2000). Coherently with what Hannah, Avolio, and Walumbwa (2011) posit, more authentic leaders communicate more clearly and this fact could influence the context in matters that support employees' moral courage.

Consequently, the main contribution of this study deals with revealing that the three-dimensional model of authenticity stands as a key predictor of subjective well-being in the workplace within the particular and scarcely explored context of nonprofit public service organizations. The main practical implication that derives from this research is that nonprofit organizations should build a climate distinguished by smooth and transparent communication flows, which may enable the flow of relevant and substantial information in a free and effective way. This strategy should rest in encouraging the ascending (bottom-up) communication and the participation of all the members of the organization. Only this way, through the coordination effort of communication professionals, organizational leaders, and human resources managers there will be achieved this ambience of authenticity that redounds to the employees' well-being at the individual level and, hence, to the progress of organizational efficacy.

References

Anshell, C., & Gash, A. (2008). Collaborative governance in theory and practice. *Journal of Public Administration Research and Theory, 18*(4), 543–571.

Ariza-Montes, A., & Lucia-Casademunt, A. M. (2013). La implicación emocional en asalariados del sector no lucrativo. *Revista de Fomento Social, 68*, 71–90.

Bacchiega, A., & Borzaga, C. (2003). The economics of the third sector: Toward a more comprehensive approach. In H. K. Anheier & A. Ben-Ner (Eds.), *The study of the nonprofit enterprise: Theories and approaches* (pp. 27–48). Dordrecht, The Netherlands: Kluwer, Academic and Plenum.

Baker, L. A., Cahalin, L. P., Gerst, K., & Burr, J. A. (2005). Productive activities and subjective well-being among older adults: The influence of number of activities and time commitment. *Social Indicators Research, 73*(3), 431–458.

Bono, J. E., Davies, S. E., & Rasch, R. L. (2012). Some traits associated with flourishing at work. In K. Cameron & G. M. Spreitzer (Eds.), *The Oxford handbook of positive organizational scholarship* (pp. 125–137). New York, NY: Oxford University Press.

Boucher, H. C. (2011). The dialectical self-concept II: Cross-role and within-role consistency, well-being, self-certainty, and authenticity. *Journal of Cross-Cultural Psychology, 42*, 1251–1271.

Boyraz, G., Waits, J. B., & Felix, V. A. (2014). Authenticity, life satisfaction, and distress: A longitudinal analysis. *Journal of Counseling Psychology, 61*(3), 498–505.

Carvalho de, R. S., Ferreira, M. C., Valentini, F., & Van den Bosch, R. (2015). Construct validity evidence for the individual Authenticity Measure at Work in Brazilian samples. *Revista de Psicología del Trabajo y de las Organizaciones, 31*(2), 109–118.

Cortina, L. G., & Berenzon, S. (2013). Traducción al español y propiedades psicométricas del instrumento Positivity Self Test. *Psicología Iberoamericana, 21*(1), 53–64.

Cotterrell, R. (2000). Transparency, mass media, ideology and community. *Cultural Values, 3*, 414–426.

Dewett, T. (2015). La autenticidad tiene un lado negativo. *Revista Vinculando.* Retrieved from http://vinculando.org/psicologia_psicoterapia/lado-negativo-de-la-autenticidad.html

Diener, E., Wirtz, D., Tov, W., Kim-Prieto, C., Dong-won, C., Oishi, S., & Biswas-Diener, R. (2010). New well-being measures: Short scales to assess flourishing and positive and negative feelings. *Social Indicator Research, 97*, 143–156.

Fusco, T., O'Riordan, S., & Palmer, S. (2015). Authentic Leaders are . . . Conscious, competent, confident, and congruent: A grounded theory of group coaching and authentic leadership development. *International Coaching Psychology Review, 10*(2), 131–148.

Goldman, B. M., & Kernis, M. H. (2002). The role of authenticity in healthy psychological functioning and subjective well-being. *Annals of the American Psychotherapy Association, 5*, 18–20.

Grandey, A., Foo, S. C., Groth, M., & Goodwin, R. E. (2012). Free to be you and me: A climate of authenticity alleviates burnout from emotional labor. *Journal of Occupational Health Psychology, 17*, 1–14.

Hannah, S. T., Avolio, B. J., & Walumbwa, F. O. (2011). Relationships between authentic leadership, moral courage, and ethical and pro-social behaviors. *Business Ethics Quarterly, 21*, 555–578.

Harter, S. (2002). Authenticity. In C. R. Snyder & S. J. Lopez (Eds.), *Handbook of positive psychology* (pp. 382–394). Oxford: Oxford University Press.

Huta, V., & Ryan, R. M. (2010). Pursuing pleasure or virtue: The differential and overlapping well-being benefits of hedonic and eudaimonic motives. *Journal of Happiness Studies, 11*(6), 735–762.

Lopez, F. G., & Rice, K. G. (2006). Preliminary development and validation of a measure of relationship authenticity. *Journal of Counseling Psychology, 53,* 362–371.

Mazutis, D., & Slawinski, N. (2008). Leading organizational learning through authentic dialogue. *Management Learning, 39,* 437–456.

Ménard, J., & Brunet, L. (2011). Authenticity and well-being in the workplace: A mediation model. *Journal of Managerial Psychology, 26,* 331–346.

Mengers, A. A. (2014). *The benefits of being yourself: An examination of authenticity, uniqueness, and well-being.* Capstone Projects, 63. Philadelphia: University of Pennsylvania. http://repository.upenn.edu/mapp_capstone/63

Neff, K. D., & Harter, S. (2002). The authenticity of conflict resolutions among adult couples: Does women's other-oriented behavior reflect their true selves? *Sex Roles, 47,* 403–417.

Park, N., Peterson, C., & Sun, J. K. (2013). La psicología positiva: investigación y aplicaciones. *Terapia psicológica, 31*(1), 11–19.

Rafferty, A. E., & Griffin, M. A. (2004). Dimensions of transformational leadership: Conceptual and empirical extensions. *Leadership Quarterly, 15,* 329–354.

Reich, W. A., Kessel, E. M., & Bernieri, F. J. (2013). Life satisfaction and the self: Structure, content, and function. *Journal of Happiness Studies, 14,* 293–308.

Seligman, M. E. P., & Csikszentmihalyi, M. (2000). Positive psychology: An introduction. *American Psychologist, 55*(1), 5–14.

Sheldon, K. M., Ryan, R. M., Rawsthorne, L. J., & Ilardi, B. (1997). Trait self and true self: Cross-role variation in the Big-Five personality traits and its relations with psychological authenticity and subjective well-being. *Journal of Personality and Social Psychology, 73,* 1380–1393.

Van den Bosch, R., & Taris, T. W. (2014a). Authenticity at work: Development and validation of an individual authenticity measure at work. *Journal of Happiness Studies, 15*(1), 1–18.

Wood, A. M., Linley, P. A., Maltby, J., Baliousis, M., & Joseph, S. (2008). The authentic personality: A theoretical and empirical conceptualization and the development of the authenticity scale. *Journal of Counseling Psychology, 55,* 385–399.

26

SOCIALLY RESPONSIBLE CONSUMPTION AND HAPPINESS

Rafael Araque-Padilla, María José Montero-Simó,
and José Javier Pérez-Barea

Introduction

The pursuit of happiness has consequences for both individuals and society. We find that if happiness is related to consumption, then on the one hand, higher levels of consumption are not associated with higher levels of happiness. On the other hand, thoughtless consumerism has environmental consequences that can be troubling, ranging from the promotion of unfair social conditions to causing serious environmental deterioration.

As a result, it would seem appropriate to rethink the relationship between consumption and happiness. This article advocates a model of responsible consumption that is not based on over-consumption or overexploitation and takes social and environmental consequences into account to produce higher levels of individual and social well-being. In short, this consumption model would be socially aware and committed to what some authors have termed "sustainable happiness" (O´Brien, 2005).

For the last few decades, the concept of "Socially Responsible Consumption" has attracted scholarly attention as an object of study. What, however, is meant by socially responsible consumption? How has it evolved? How is it measured? These are some of the issues addressed in this chapter.

Toward Sustainable Happiness Through a New Way of Understanding the Consumer

Our economic system currently promotes excessive consumption that is focused on the here and now and has been gradually becoming more rooted in the consumer society in which we are immersed. Economics seems to be identified with simple unlimited growth or pure increases in material well-being, reducing the human being to a potential consumer. Our society encourages a lifestyle where success is conferred by possession and status symbols. It speaks of a consumer society, which is not synonymous with a society in which everyone consumes (something clearly needed to survive) but is instead a society in which people consume superfluous items that are not necessary. This consumption legitimizes politics and economics. Consumption is in the marrow of our societies. In this consumption, "we live, we move and we are" (Cortina, 2004).

The relationship between consumption and happiness has been controversial and frequently studied. Apart from a minimum to ensure our basic needs, do higher levels of consumption create greater happiness? Are more consumerist societies happier societies? There is much scientific evidence on this point that says no. DeLeire and Kalil (2010), based on the Health and Retirement Study (HRS) in the US, underline that "material goods cannot buy happiness." In other words, spending a lot of money to buy material goods does not seem to be very effective at increasing the happiness of consumers (Borrero, 2010). Other studies suggest that the happiest people save more, spend less, and have a lower marginal propensity to consume (Guven, 2009—DNB Household Survey from the Netherlands and the German Socio-Economic Panel).

The experiential and subjective character often associated with the idea of happiness introduces more complexity to the relationship with consumers whenever that personality appears as an influential factor. According to Brown and Kasser (2005), people more attuned to extrinsic values (social recognition, financial success, popularity, image, etc.) have lower levels of subjective well-being than those who are more attuned to intrinsic values (personal development, acceptance, human relations, physical well-being. involvement in the community, etc.). Individuals with intrinsic values, in other words, tend to be less materialistic and more inclined to have greater social and environmental commitments.

Extant research and exploratory analyses suggest that people could improve their happiness-to-consumption efficiency through activities that let them achieve a sense of mastery and belonging and by engaging in experiential and social consumption (Borrero, 2010).

As a result, it seems that the quest for a consumption that is more liberating, fairer, and more accountable to the community is not only *not* contradictory to happiness and subjective well-being, but it in fact helps achieve higher levels of happiness, both individually and collectively. As suggested by Vittersø (2016), we know more about the good life, which puts us in a position to build a society that can support and provide opportunities to help all citizens achieve it. In this sense, O'Brien (2016) suggested the "Sustainable Happiness" concept, defined as "happiness that contributes to individual, community, or global well-being without exploiting other people, the environment, or future generations" (n. p.).

Achieving this sustainable happiness leads us to, among other things, rethink our way of understanding the consumer. In fact, this is the approach that has come to make up "socially responsible consumption," a concept that was created decades ago but has witness a resurgence in recent years.

Socially Responsible Consumption

The enhancement of the social and environmental considerations of the consumer reflects a new way of understanding consumption that can give different meaning to the action of consumption and how one feels that different values, acts, and effects interact with one another. Although it is still a minority, particularly from the choice of products based on the value for money, social, and environmental issues arising from the acquisition of products and services are taken into account more often in the behaviors of people purchasing and consuming goods. This is beginning to become relevant via a new mode of consumption: so-called socially responsible consumption (from here on out "SRC").

Authors usually place the beginning of the conceptualization of SRC with the work of Webster (1975), which created a scale to study *"socially conscious consumption."* Its definition of the socially conscious consumer was a basic reference for all subsequent literature that emerged around the concept of SRC. According to Webster (1975, p. 188), this consumer "(. . .) considers the public consequences that may arise from their private consumption, or tries to use their purchasing power to promote social change."

The conceptual domain of SRC has undergone an evolution (see Figure 26.1) that has produced extensions, restrictions, and new focuses. This has given rise to several scales of measurement that have made impacts in this area of knowledge.

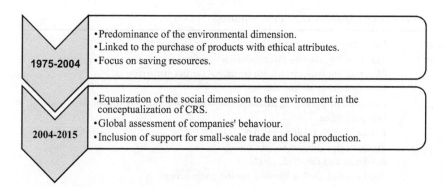

Figure 26.1 Evolution of the concept of SRC over time.

It should be noted that studies conducted since the mid–1970s to the mid-2000s were domi-nated by a concept of SRC associated with i) environmental issues through the purchase of prod-ucts with positive environmental impacts and ii) reductions in consumption (saving resources).

Subsequently, the content of the SRC concept began to include purchase choices based on ethical behaviors of enterprises and introduced more forcefully a social dimension that, although it was present in the first definitions of the concept, was ignored in the metric used. More recently, researchers began to include as manifestations of an SRC ethical concerns that had to do with characteristics of enterprises, such as their geographical origin or its size.

The different scales used by the authors to measure SRC (Table 26.1) encompass a wide vari-ety of consumer behaviors (Table 26.2).

In an attempt to go beyond the dichotomy between social and environmental behavior, in this chapter, we classify behaviors by four criteria that respond to different patterns of responsible consumption choices:

1. ethical attributes of products (social/environmental impacts)
2. (un)ethical behaviour of the companies that manufacture the products
3. features (size and geographic origin) of the businesses
4. consumption philosophies.

Table 26.1 SRC measurement scales.

Authors	Year	Scale
BACKGROUND		
Harris	1957	Social Attitude Scale (SAS)
Berkowitz and Daniels	1964	Social Responsibility Scale (SRC)
Kinnear et to the.	1974	Social Responsibility Scale Revised (SRC)
SOCIALLY RESPONSIBLE CONSUMPTION SCALES		
Webster	1975	Socially Conscious Consumer Index (SCCI)
Antil and Bennett	1979	Socially Responsible Consumption Behavior Scale (SRCB)
Roberts	1995	Socially Responsible Consumer Behavior Scale (SRCB)
LeCompte and Roberts	2006	Socially Responsible Consumption Scale (SRC)
Webb, Mohr, and Harris	2008	Socially Responsible Purchase and Disposal Scale (SRPD)
Sudbury-Riley and Kohlbacher	2016	Ethically Minded consumer Behavior (EMCB)

Table 26.2 Choices of socially responsible consumption patterns

Ethical product attributes	Not using scarce natural resources from raw materials
	Materials/ingredients that produce less pollution
	Materials/ingredients that are beneficial for the environment
	Recycled materials/ingredients
	Eco-friendly packaging (reusable, materials that produce less pollution)
	Less packaging
	Reusable or recyclable products
	Products that support social causes
	Solidarity and fair-trade products
	Products that are less harmful for the environment
Ethical company behavior	More environmentally friendly manufacturing processes
	Ethical management of human resources (decent working conditions, no child labor, respect for employees, hiring disabled employees, not discriminating against minorities, lack of labor disputes)
	Ethical communication (not using misleading advertising, respecting women, telling the truth)
	Philanthropy
	Socially responsible companies
Company features	Supporting small businesses against larger ones
	Supporting local production
	Supporting companies according to geographical proximity
Consumption philosophies	Recycling
	Composting
	Reusing products
	Reducing consumption
	Using recyclable packaging
	Substituting behaviors that are more respectful to the environment for those that are less (e.g., using public transportation instead of one's own vehicle)

Considering these different patterns of consumption leads us to think that far from there being only one way to understand SRC, it is possible for socially responsible consumer behavior to manifest itself in many different ways depending on one's beliefs or perceptions about the right way to exercise his or her ethical commitments.

Therefore, responsible consumers do not have to manifest their commitment into concrete actions that move together in the field of five established domains. This means accepting that they can give inconsistent purchase choices in terms of the responsibility assumed in the various manifestations of CRS.

This assumption has been explored in the work of Pérez-Barea, Montero-Simó, and Araque-Padilla (2015), which supports the idea that related but independent SRC dimensions exist. Although it is still necessary to continue providing evidence, the results seem to indicate that consumers do not feel that there is only one way to express responsibility when they consume. This could be a reflection of the ambiguity of the concept itself or of the difficulties behaving in ways that are compatible with one another, even if they are also contradictory.

All this could be expressions of what it is like to be a consumer in the postmodern era, where individuals without a single, coherent, and self-centred set of preferences can respond to multiple representations of themselves in their relationship with social reality.

Socially Responsible Consumer Profiles

Many studies on SRC are primarily interested in defining and knowing more about the ethics and feelings of responsibility of consumers. In other words, who seeks sustainable happiness through their consumption choices? The answer is not simple. It is very difficult to understand what underpins certain models of consumption because it is difficult to model issues such as motivation, attitudes, cultural influences, interests, and sociodemographic characteristics, which are often interlinked with one another. In fact, this constraint has been problematic since the beginning of research into SRC, resulting in numerous controversies and often providing contradictory evidence.

The first investigations about socially responsible individuals attempted to study and build different profiles of consumers (Gough, McClosky, & Meehl, 1952; Harris, 1957; Berkowitz & Lutterman, 1968; Anderson & Cunningham, 1972) by using variables such as age, sex, social class, education level, the type of residence or political allegiance. However, the evidence shows not only differences in predictive ability among these studies but also discrepancies about this relationship.

From the demographic point of view, the main variables discussed in the literature were age, sex, income, education level and place of residence. For age, the general belief is that environmental and responsible consumption behavior increases with age. In the case of green consumption, positive relationships with age were found in Balderjahn (1988), Scott and Willits (1994), Straughan and Roberts (1999), Gilg, Barr, and Ford (2005), and Binninger and Robert (2008). In the case of SRC, positive relationships with age were also found in Durif et al. (2011). Although less common, some authors have found a negative relationship between age and both green consumption and CRS (Sarmaniotis & Tilikidou, 1998), while others have found no significant relationship (Antil, 1984; Shrum, McCarty, & Lowrey, 1995; Zhao, Gao, Wu, Wang, & Zhu, 2014).

When sex is analyzed as a predictor for both green consumption and SRC, most evidence in the literature shows us no significant relationship (Webster, 1975; Antil, 1984; Sarmaniotis & Tilikidou, 1998; Straughan & Robert, 1999; Gilg et al., 2005; Zhao et al., 2014). More discrepancies are observed with income level in regard to predicting responsible consumption.

This variable is interesting because this type of consumption usually entails higher prices (Nielsen Report, 2012), which sometimes produces a kind of consumer heroism appeal for those with limited resources. However, the evidence about this is contradictory. There are studies that demonstrate the absence of a significant relationship (Webster, 1975; Antil, 1984; Balderjahn, 1988; Shrum et al., 1995; Sarmaniotis & Tilikidou, 1998; Straughan & Roberts, 1999; Zhao et al., 2014), while others show a positive one (Scott & Willits, 1994) Sarmaniotis & Tilikidou, 1998; Gilg et al., 2005), and still others show a negative one (Roberts & Jones, 2001).

Another common independent variable is the level of education. General appreciation is the conscious and responsible consumption related to an increased formation of consumers. Although the literature seems to support this hypothesis (Webster, 1975) Balderjahn, 1988; Scott & Willits, 1994), some scholars also found no relationship (Antil, 1984; Shrum et al., 1995) or a negative relationship. (Straughan & Roberts, 1999). Sarmaniotis and Tilikidou (1998), though, found a positive relationship with green consumption and no relationship with SRC. Individual occupation does not appear to be a good predictor variable either with SRC (Sarmaniotis & Tilikidou, 1998) or for the more specific case of green consumption (Balderjahn, 1988; Zhao et al., 2014).

It is very complex to establish demographic profiles of socially responsible consumers because there is no consensus on the evidence that has heretofore been uncovered. However, there seem to be certain psychographic variables that establish significant relationships with SRC or some of its manifestations despite the difficulty posed by measuring them.

This is the case for political orientation. Although authors such as Scott and Willits (1994) found no significant relationships with this variable, later studies have found a relation between socially responsible consumers and liberal ideology (Straughan & Roberts, 1999; Roberts & Jones, 2001; Gilg et al., 2005). We have also found significant evidence of the predictive capacity of altruism (Straughan & Roberts, 1999; Chia-Ju, 2013). Another common variable in the literature that has been shown to be relevant is perceived consumer effectiveness (PCE). Numerous studies have corroborated this positive relationship with SRC and green consumption (Webster, 1975; Antil, 1984; Straughan & Roberts, 1999; Webb et al., 2008; Chia-Ju, 2013; Zhao et al., 2014).

Knowledge about environmental issues has also been of interest as a predictor, in particular with explaining green consumption (Schlegelmilch, Bohlen, & Diamantopoulos, 1996; Zhao et al., 2014). From the pioneering work of Berkowitz and Lutterman (1968) on social responsibility and individual personalities, some authors have tried to use this feature to define the profile of socially responsible consumers. This is the case in the works of Webster (1975), Antil (1984), and Sarmaniotis and Tilikidou (1998), who found a positive and significant relationship. Another variable that has been studied is the collectivism/activism of individuals. Although we found a positive and significant relationship in some older studies (Webster, 1975; Schlegelmilch et al., 1996), this relationship has not been corroborated in recent studies (Webb et al., 2008; Chia-Ju, 2013).

There is no doubt that one of the psychographic variables that has greater relevance in predicting consumer behavior is attitude (Stern & Oskamp, 1987). Different attitudes can have both positive and negative influences on an individual's behavior. In the case of SRC, the study of attitudes has traditionally been focused on the green or ecological consumers (Dueñas Ocampo et al., 2013). Defined as those individuals who display an attitude of environmental concern when purchasing products or services (Elkington & Hailes, 1989), this categorization dominated discussion during the onset of this branch of study. In the literature review, one of the attitudes most frequently used to explain the specific consumption behavior of green purchasing was environmental concern (Weigel & Weigel, 1978; Scott & Willits, 1994; Shrum et al., 1995; Schlegelmilch et al., 1996; Roberts & Bacon, 1997; Mainieri, Barnett, Valdero, Unipan, & Oskamp, 1997; Straughan & Roberts, 1999; Bamberg, 2003; Fraj & Martinez, 2006; Do Paço et al., 2015; Zhao et al., 2014).

In short, is there a defined profile of a socially responsible consumer? In light of the studies we have analyzed, we can conclude that it is possible to establish some psychographic traits but not specific sociodemographic profiles. This makes it difficult to establish responsible consumer segments but also opens up the possibility that this type of consumption could eventually find its way to all segments of the population.

Conclusions and Research Horizons

Pursing sustainable happiness is not possible without changing our patterns of consumption toward more socially responsible behaviors, as different authors have proposed. As a result, our goal in this chapter of defining what is meant by that kind of consumption as well as which variables promote it is far from trivial.

It is possible that there might not be just one type of responsible consumer but rather many types. In spite of studies on SRC becoming more relevant within the consumer behavior literature, it is still a topic that needs to be better understood. In this regard, the concept of SRC is something that still needs further study, both in regard to the practices that define it and its possible evolution over time. Future research should continue to define scales and compare the results they obtain with extant ones.

Comparing samples between different cultures should also be studied to develop comparative studies on this type of consumption. Furthermore, one could also investigate the relation with other demographic variables to establish typologies of socially responsible consumers. It would be necessary to foment it toward the pursuit of a sustainable happiness so necessary in our present society.

As a result, it would also be very useful to determine which factors inhibit or facilitate socially responsible consumer behavior. What leads conscious consumers to adopt more responsible consumer behavior? How much does culture influence this and why? Is information a key aspect in making responsible buying decisions? If so, what role can new technologies have? How can strategies such as the use of sustainable stamps be facilitators for SRC? More research and new evidence is necessary to design policies that promote more engaged consumers. It is not only important to create awareness but also to provide the means for these behaviors to materialize. This is just one of the concerns of social marketing, an area that could be key for working with all these issues. In addition, we should also consider what causes certain social campaigns promoting SRC to fail? Do these campaigns address all SRC domains? How? Why do they focus on certain domains and not others? How much influence do consumerist ideologies have on SRC?

Of particular interest is the impact of certain sociocultural trends such as new social movements about avoiding waste and pursuing sustainability. We can ask ourselves about the extent to which movements such as collaborative systems, platforms for sale between individuals, and organic gardens generate greater awareness in the population.

One key point of studies on shopping behavior is the existence of a gap between intentions and actual behavior, and in this sense the SRC could be mixed with considerations of social desirability. Despite all the progress that has been made in the design of theoretical models (mainly in the field of psychology), this is still a controversial issue. Above all, we have to address the thorny issue of measuring the actual behavior of consumers. All this opens a necessary body of research to continue investigating knowledge about SRC. New methodologies need to also be explored.

Finally, we need greater insight into the psychology of responsible consumers. To what extent does SRC respond to a real concern for the consequences of consumption, to a search for sustainable happiness, or to a desire to be cool? How much does it respond to a search for one's own personal image or group self-affirmation as well of the construction of a personality or the pursuit of a more hedonistic type of happiness?

If we look at the world as a whole, happiness is not a trait that characterizes our societies en masse. The vast majority of people do not see their right to life as being fulfilled, and many others do not find happiness through consumerism. Happy consumption should be fair, global, and sustainable consumption; a type of consumption such that everyone can consume in that way. Investigating which features are part of that kind of consumption is still a relevant, and dare we say urgent, issue.

References

Anderson, W. T., & Cunningham, W. H. (1972). The socially conscious consumer. *Journal of Marketing, 36*(1), 23–31.

Antil, J. H. (1984). Socially responsible consumers: Profile and implications for public policy. *Journal of Macromarketing, 4*(2), 18–39.

Antil, J. H., & Bennett, P. D. (1979). Construction and validation of a scale to measure socially responsible consumption behavior. In K. E. Henion, II & T. C. Kinnear (Eds.), *The conserver society* (pp. 51–68). Chicago: American Marketing Association.

Balderjahn, I. (1988). Personality variables and environmental attitudes as predictors of ecologically responsible consumption patterns. *Journal of Business Research, 17,* 51–56.

Bamberg, S. (2003). How does environmental concern influence specific environmentally related behaviors? A new answer to an old question. *Journal of Environmental Psychology, 23,* 21–32. http://dx.doi.org/10.1016/S0272-4944(02)00078-6

Berkowitz, L., & Daniels, L. R. (1964). Affecting the salience of the social responsibility norm: Effects of past help on the response to dependency relationships. *The Journal of Abnormal and Social Psychology, 68*(3), 275–281.

Berkowitz, L., & Lutterman, K. G. (1968). The traditional socially responsible personality. *Public Opinion Quarterly, 32*(2), 169–185.

Binninger, A. S., & Robert, I. (2008). Consommation et développement durable: vers une segmentation des sensibilités et des comportements. *La Revue des Sciences de Gestion, Direction et Gestion, 229*, 51–59.

Borrero, S. (2010). The happiness-to-consumption ratio: An alternative approach in the quest for happiness. *Estudios Gerenciales, 26*(115), 15–35.

Brown, K. W., & Kasser, T. (2005). Are psychological and ecological well-being compatible? The role of values, mindfulness, and lifestyle. *Social Indicators Research, 74*, 349–368.

Chia-Ju, Lu. (2013). *An empirical study on the antecedents of socially responsible consumption behavior.* Seventh International Conference on Complex, Intelligent, and Software Intensive Systems (CISIS), Taichung, Taiwan: Browse Conference Publications.

Cortina, A. (2004). *Por una ética del consumo.* Madrid: Taurus.

DeLeire, T., & Kalil, A. (2010). Does consumption buy happiness? Evidence from the United States. *International Review of Economics, 57*(2), 163–176.

Do Paço, A., Ferreira, J. M., Raposo, M., Rodrigues, R. G., & Dinis, A. (2015). Entrepreneurial intentions: Is education enough? *Journal of International Entrepreneurship and Management Journal, 11*(1), 57–75.

Dueñas Ocampo, S., Perdomo-Ortiz, J., & Villa Castano, L. E. (2013). El concepto de consumo socialmente responsable y su medición. Una revisión de la literatura. *Estudios Gerenciales, 30*, 287–300.

Durif, F., Boivin, C., Rajaobelina, L., & Lecompte, A. (2011). Socially responsible consumers: Profile and implications for marketing strategy. *International Review of Business Research Paper, 7*(6), 215–224.

Elkington, J., & Hailes, J. (1989). *The green consumer guide: From shampoo to champagne: High-street shopping for a better environment.* London: Penguin.

Fraj, E., & Martinez, E. (2006). Environmental values and lifestyles as determining factors of ecological consumer behavior: An empirical analysis. *Journal of Consumer Marketing, 23*(3), 133–144.

Gilg, A., Barr, S., & Ford, N. (2005). Green consumption or sustainable lifestyles? Identifying the sustainable consumer. *Futures, 37*(6), 481–504. ISSN 0016–3287.

Gough, H. G., McClosky, H., & Meehl, P. E. (1952). A personality scale for social responsibility. *The Journal of Abnormal and Social Psychology, 47*(1), 73–80. Guven, C. (2009). Reversing the question: Does happiness affect consumption and savings behavior? *SOEPpapers on Multidisciplinary Panel Data Research* 219, Berlin, The German Socio-Economic Panel (SOEP).

Harris, D. B. (1957). A scale for measuring attitudes of social responsibility in children. *The Journal of Abnormal and Social Psychology, 55*(3), 322–326.

Kinnear, T. C., & Taylor, J. R., & Ahmed, S. A. (1974). Ecologically concerned consumers: Who are they? *Journal of Marketing, 38*(2), 20–24.

Lecompte, A. F., & Roberts, J. A. (2006). Developing a measure of socially responsible consumption in France. *Marketing Management Journal, 16*(2), 50–60.

Mainieri, T., Barnett, E. G., Valdero, T. R., Unipan, J. B., & Oskamp, S. (1997). Green buying: The influence of environmental concern on consumer behavior. *Journal of Social Psychology, 137*(2), 189–204.

Nielsen Report. (2012). *The global, socially-conscious consumer.* New York: The Nielsen Company.

O'Brien, C. (2005). *Planning for sustainable happiness: Harmonizing our internal and external landscapes.* Paper prepared for the 2nd International Conference on Gross National Happiness, Nova Scotia, Canada.

O'Brien, C. (2016). *Education for sustainable happiness and well-being.* Abingdon, UK: Routledge.

Pérez-Barea, J. J., Montero-Simó, M. J., & Araque-Padilla, R. (2015). Measurement of socially responsible consumption: Lecompte's scale Spanish version validation. *International Review on Public and Nonprofit Marketing, 12*, 37–61. https://doi.org/10.1007/s12208-014-0123-2

Roberts, J. A. (1995). Profiling levels of socially responsible consumer behavior: A cluster analytic approach and its implications for marketing. *Journal of Marketing Theory and Practice, 3*(4), 97–117.

Roberts, J. A., & Bacon, D. R. (1997). Exploring the subtle relationships between environmental concern and ecologically conscious consumer behavior. *Journal of Business Research, 40*, 79–89.

Roberts, J. A., & Jones, E. (2001). Money attitudes, credit card use, and compulsive buying among American college students. *Journal of Consumer Affairs, 35*(2), 213–240.

Sarmaniotis, C., & Tilikidou, I. (1998). *Dimensions of the ecological consumer behaviour: A research study in the area of Thessaloniki.* Applied Research Review. Piraeus: TEI.

Schlegelmilch, B. B., Bohlen, G. M., & Diamantopoulos, A. (1996). The link between green purchasing decisions and measures of environmental consciousness. *European Journal of Marketing, 30*(5), 35–55.

Scott, D., & Willits, F. K. (1994). Environmental attitudes and behaviour: A Pennsylvania Survey. *Environment and Behaviour, 26*(2), 239–260.

Shrum, L. J., McCarty, J. A., & Lowrey, T. M. (1995). Buyer Characteristics of the Green Consumer and Their Implications for Advertising Strategy. *Journal of Advertising, 24*(2), 71–90.

Stern, P. C., & Oskamp, S. (1987). Managing scarce environmental resources. In D. Stokols & I. Altman (Eds.), *Handbook of environmental psychology* (pp. 1043–1088). New York: John Wiley.

Straughan, R. D., & Roberts, J. A. (1999). Environmental segmentation alternatives: A look at green consumer behavior in the new millennium. *Journal of Consumer Marketing, 16*(6), 558–575. https://doi.org/10.1108/07363769910297506

Sudbury-Riley, L., & Kohlbacher, F. (2016). Ethically minded consumer behavior: Scale review, development, and validation. *Journal of Business Research, 69*(8), 2697–2710.

Vittersø, J. (2016). *Handbook of eudaimonic well-being.* Cham, Switzerland: Springer International Publishing.

Webb, D. J., Mohr, L. A., & Harris, K. E. (2008). A re-examination of socially responsible consumption and its measurement. *Journal of Business Research, 61*(2), 91–98.

Webster, F. E., Jr. (1975). Determining the characteristics of the socially conscious consumer. *Journal of Consumer Research, 2*(3), 188–196.

Weigel, R., & Weigel, J. (1978). Environmental concern: The development of a measure. *Environment and Behavior, 10*, 3–15.

Zhao, H., Gao, Q., Wu, Y.-p., Wang, Y., & Zhu, X.-d. (2014). *What affects green consumer behavior in China?* A case study from Qingdao. *Journal of Cleaner Production, 63*, 143–151.

PART V

Happiness and Positive Digital Technologies

27

POSITIVE TECHNOLOGY

From Communication to Positive Experience

Giuseppe Riva, Silvia Serino, Alice Chirico, and Andrea Gaggioli

Introduction

More and more of our communicative experience depend on some kind of interactive device or digital service (Haddon, 2016). Furthermore, the use of information and communication technologies (ICTs) is not limited to the long hours that we spend at the office. Our free time, too, has been increasingly colonized by technology-mediated experiences delivered through smartphones, tablets, and other personal wearable devices (Hamilton, 2016; Murray, 2015).

However, understanding the full extent of this new trends and its implication for our well-being, requires an interdisciplinary approach that integrates the scientific principles of positive psychology into the design of e-experiences that foster positive change (Heeks, 2010; Ihm & Hsieh, 2015).

A possible path toward this goal is outlined by an emerging research area in Psychology and Communication Studies: *Positive Technology* (Botella et al., 2012; Gaggioli, 2015; Gaggioli & Riva, 2014; Riva, Baños, Botella, Mantovani, & Gaggioli, 2016; Riva, Baños, Botella, Wiederhold, & Gaggioli, 2012; Riva et al., 2015; Riva, Villani, et al., 2016).

Positive Technology is an emergent field within human computer interaction that seeks to understand how interactive technologies can be used in evidence-based well-being interventions (Villani, Cipresso, Gaggioli, & Riva, 2016). It's focus of analysis is twofold: at the theoretical level, positive technology aims to develop conceptual frameworks and models for understanding how computers can be effectively used to help individuals achieve greater well-being. At the methodological and applied level, positive technology is concerned with the design, development, and validation of digital experiences that promote positive change through pleasure, flow, meaning, competence, and positive relationships. The chapter will introduce the concept of positive technology presenting different practical examples of the concept.

Positive Technology: A Definition

The recent discoveries of cognitive sciences and the emergence of the field of positive psychology (Seligman, 2002; Seligman & Csikszentmihalyi, 2000) suggest the possibility of a new research paradigm—*positive technology*—whose main objective is to use technology to manipulate and enhance the features of our personal experience, by manipulating presence and social presence, for increasing wellness, and generating strength and resilience in individuals, organizations, and society (B.K. Wiederhold & Riva, 2012).

This concept has some similarities with the concept of *Positive Computing* (Calvo & Peters, 2012, 2014): "The research and development of technology to support well-being and human potential" (p. 2). In particular positive technology shares with it the methodological approach to the technology design for well-being (Calvo & Peters, 2014): the identification of key factors from existing theories of well-being and their use for prevent detriments of well-being (prevention), actively integrated promotional design (action), and the development of technologies aimed specifically at promoting well-being (creation).

The main difference, however, is in the focus: Calvo and Peters focus their analysis on the concept of well-being, while positive technology focuses its analysis on the concept of personal experience.

What Is Behind This Difference?

The Merriam Webster Dictionary defines experience both as "a) the fact or state of having been affected by or gained knowledge through direct observation or participation" (personal experience), and "b) direct observation of or participation in events as a basis of knowledge" (subjective experience). In other words, we both shape and are shaped by experience (Riva, 2012a): we can intentionally control the contents of our experience (subjective experience), but at the same time it defines our future emotions and intentions (personal experience).

The difference between the two sides of experience also suggests that, independently from the subjectivity of any individual, it is possible to alter the features of our experience from outside. In other words, personal experience becomes the dependent variable that may be manipulated through the use of communicative technologies and studied by external researchers. In particular cognitive and positive psychology identified three determinants of personal experience that can be manipulated through ICTs (see Table 27.1 and the next section for a more detailed description): *emotional quality, engagement/actualization and connectedness* (Inghilleri, Riva, & Riva, 2015).

These three variables can also be used to classify the possible applications of positive technologies (Botella et al., 2012; B. K. Wiederhold, Riva, & Graffigna, 2013):

- *Hedonic (emotional quality)*: technologies used to induce positive and pleasant experiences. Examples of hedonic technologies are the ones used to regulate and control emotions. Our team developed different immersive (computer-based) and non-immersive (smartphone and tablet-based) experiences to improve emotional control in untrained individuals (Carissoli, Villani, & Riva, 2015; Grassi, Gaggioli, & Riva, 2011; Manzoni et al., 2006, 2009; Preziosa, Grassi, Gaggioli, & Riva, 2009; Raspelli et al., 2011). The feeling of presence and the immersive visual cue provided by virtual reality (VR) are known to facilitate relaxation, reduce stress, and improve positive emotional states (Serino et al., 2014; Villani, Lucchetta, Preziosa, & Riva, 2006; Villani, Preziosa, Riva, & Riva, 2006; Villani, Riva, & Riva, 2007). When aimed at relaxation, VR lends is also associated with biofeedback training (Cipresso et al., 2012; Riva, 2009). Biofeedback is a coaching and training technique that helps people learn how to change their physiological response patterns to improve their mental and emotional functioning (Repetto et al., 2009). The person is connected to psychophysiological biosensors and uses the information provided as feedback to increase awareness or consciousness of the changes in the functioning of the body/mind (Gaggioli, Cipresso, et al., 2014; Riva, Algeri, et al., 2010).
- *Eudaimonic (engagement/actualization)*: technologies used to support individuals in reaching engaging and self-actualizing experiences. The theory of Flow (optimal experience), developed by Positive Psychology pioneer Mihaly Csíkszentmihályi (1990), provides a

useful framework for addressing this challenge. Flow is a positive and complex state of consciousness that is present when individuals act with total involvement. The basic feature of this experience is the perceived balance between high environmental opportunities for action (challenges) and adequate personal resources in facing them (skills). Among the different types of interactive technologies investigated so far, immersive systems (VR and Augmented Reality—AR) are considered the most capable of supporting the emergence of this experience (Gaggioli, Bassi, & Delle Fave, 2003; Riva, Castelnuovo, & Mantovani, 2006; Riva, Raspelli, et al., 2010). In particular, using VR, is possible to develop transformative experiences (Gaggioli, 2015; Riva, Baños, et al., 2016; Riva, Villani, et al., 2016) that provide knowledge that is epistemically inaccessible to the individual until he or she has that experience, while at the same time transforming the individual's worldview. An example of this approach is a recent study by Chirico and colleagues showing that the use of immersive VR videos could enhance one of the drivers of transformative change, that is, the complex emotion of awe (A. Chirico et al., 2017). Awe entails both a perception of something grand and the urge to incorporate such new stimulus into our pre-existing mental frames. Since the stimulus is too much astonishing and intense, we are forced to accommodate our mental frames in line with it, and not vice versa. Authors showed that immersive 360° videos could enhance the intensity of this emotional state even in the lab, if compared to a conventional emotion-induction technique. Participants reported highest levels of awe in the immersive VR condition. Moreover, this study confirmed and expands findings from a previous research about the psychophysiological profile of this emotion (A. Chirico, Cipresso, & Gaggioli, 2016; Shiota, Neufeld, Yeung, Moser, & Perea, 2011). Awe resulted as an emotion characterized by a sympathetic withdrawal as well as by a great parasympathetic activation. Since awe is conceived as a driver of transformative change, it is surprising to note that transformation entails a moment of psycho-physio-behavioral *freezing* (or immobilization) and not a general system's activation. Indeed, reproducing this state in the lab has always been a huge challenge for researcher, a bigger one for people interested in applying it in real life. Virtual reality has resulted as effective in modeling people' experience even at this deeper level. However, the long-term impact of this manipulation is still to be tested yet.

- *Social/Interpersonal (connectedness)*: technologies used to support and improve social integration and/or connectedness between individuals, groups, and organizations. An interesting example of this approach is the use of technologies to improve inter-generational reminiscence (Gaggioli, Morganti, et al., 2014). Inter-generational reminiscence offers the potential for reducing existing barriers between generations by transmitting the heritage of folk traditions and by triggering the interest of younger people concerning their roots (Webster & McCall, 1999). To facilitate this process Gaggioli and colleagues used an interesting approach: a) the elderly narrated their life experiences they liked most or that they found more meaningful to share with their young audience; b) during storytelling, children were encouraged to express their interest toward specific aspects of the reminiscence and ask questions; c) the older adults were asked to collect material (photographs, letters, newspaper articles, etc.) that could help them document the aspects of their memories selected by the young audience; d) to allow further discussion and sharing, older and younger participants reported the content of the most interesting reminiscences in a website, by integrating texts with multimedia objects. Different examples of collected reminiscences are available on the project's website Nostalgia Bits (http://nobits.it/).
- Another example is the use of social media to support education (Greenhow & Lewin, 2016; Selwyn & Stirling, 2016). Greenhow and Lewin, using two different studies—one in US and one in Europe—demonstrated how students using social media are able to harness the power

of the network and seek relevant expertise (Greenhow & Lewin, 2016). More they demonstrated an improved self-determination (in terms of learning purpose) and self-direction (in terms of learning process)

Designing e-Experiences for Personal Transformation

In the previous sections, we have proposed positive technology as a conceptual framework for the design of interactive e-experiences that promote empowerment and positive change. Specifically, we identified three key experiential variables—Emotional Quality (affect regulation); Engagement/Actualization (presence and flow); Connectedness (collective intentions and networked flow)—that can be controlled and assessed to guide the design and development of positive technologies. Herein, we will describe a series of design suggestions for the development of positive communication tools and e-experiences supporting positive psychological change (Gaggioli, Chirico, Triberti, & Riva, 2016; Gaggioli, Riva, Peters, & Calvo, 2017). In Table 27.1 we examine the key factors influencing them, the theories that can explain their behavior and some strategies allowing their manipulation.

The different examples discussed before show that technology can be used to manipulate the features of an experience in three separate but related ways (Figure 27.1):

- *By structuring it* using a goal, rules and a feedback system (McGonigal, 2011): The goal provides subjects with a sense of purpose focusing attention and orienting his/her participation in the experience. The rules, by removing or limiting the obvious ways of getting to the goal, push subjects to see the experience in a different way. The feedback system tells players how close they are to achieving the goal and provides motivation to keep trying.
- *By augmenting it* to achieve multimodal and mixed experiences. Technology allows multisensory experiences in which content and its interaction is offered through more than one of the senses. It is even possible to use technology to overlay virtual objects onto real scenes
  (Chicchi Giglioli, Pallavicini, Pedroli, Serino, & Riva, 2015; Pallavicini et al., 2016; Rosenblum, 2000).

- *By replacing it* with a synthetic one. Using VR it is possible to simulate physical presence in a synthetic world that reacts to the action of the subject as if he/she was really there. Moreover, the replacement possibilities offered by VR has given a novel context for the experimental induction of the illusory ownership over an artificial body (i.e., a virtual avatar) as a method for altering the bodily experience
  (Riva, 2016a; Riva, Serino, Di Lernia, Pavone, & Dakanalis, 2017; Serino & Dakanalis, 2016).

However, as we have argued elsewhere (Gaggioli, 2016; Riva, Baños, et al., 2016), the potential of positive technology may go beyond the level of personal change, achieving *personal transformation*. Within the field of psychology, personal change is regarded as continuous and linear process, which requires different stages (Adele M. Hayes, Laurenceau, Feldman, Strauss, & Cardaciotto, 2007; A.M. Hayes & Yasinski, 2015; Prochaska & DiClemente, 1982).

Still, personal change does not always occur in a gradual manner. As noted by Miller and C'de Baca (Miller & C'de Baca, 2001), individuals may have "transformative experiences" able to produce a deep and enduring restructuration of one or more personal dimension. However, not all personal changes occur in a linear or gradual manner. According to Mezirow's Transformative Learning Theory (22, 23), these experiences can be triggered by a "disorienting dilemma"

Table 27.1 Personal Experience factors manipulated by positive technology

Determinants of Personal Experience	Key Factors	Literature & Theory	Strategies (Augmentation, Structuration, and Replacement)
Emotional Quality (Hedonic Level)	**Positive Emotions**	*Building & Broadening Effect* (Fredrickson); *Writing Therapy* (Pennebaker) *Hedonic Psychology* (Kahneman);	Writing Therapy; Exposure Therapy and Relaxation; Savoring; Positive ruminating; Reframing Compassion & meditation.
	Mindfulness	*Mindfulness based Stress Reduction* (Kabat Zinn);	Mindfulness meditation; MBSR strategies; MBCT strategies.
	Resilience	*Psychology of resilience* (Seligman, Keyes); *Building & Broadening Effect* (Fredrickson).	Positive psychology interventions; SuperBetter.
Engagement & Actualization (Eudaimonic Level)	**Engagement & Presence**	*Flow Theory* (Csikszentmihalyi). *Presence* (Riva & Waterworth) *Patient Engagement* (Graffigna, Barello & Riva)	Challenge and Skills; Intrinsic and extrinsic rewards;
	Self-Efficacy & Motivation	*Self-Efficacy* (Bandura) *Transtheoretical Model of change* (Prochaska & DiClemente) *Self-determination Theory* (Ryan & Deci);	Life summary; Online CBT study; Technology-Mediated Reflection.
Connectedness (Social/Interpersonal level)	**Networked Flow**	*Networked Flow* (Gaggioli & Riva) *Psychological Selection* (Delle Fave, Inghilleri, Massimini)	Presence and Social Presence Transformation of Flow
	Gratitude	*Psychology of Gratitude* (Emmons & McCullough).	Gratitude visit; Gratitude journal.
	Empathy	*Emotional Intelligence* (Salovey & Mayer; Goleman); *Affective and Cognitive empathy* (Gerdes et al; Singer); *Compassion Focused Therapy* (Paul Gilbert).	Role playing; Perspective taking; Emotion recognition training.
	Altruism	*Empathy Altruism* (Bateson).	Prosocial games; Role playing helping behavior.

(adapted from Inghilleri et al., 2015)

usually related to a life crisis or major life transition (e.g., death, illness, separation, or divorce), which forces individuals to critically examine and eventually revise their core assumptions and beliefs. The outcome of a transformative experience is a significant and permanent change in the expectations—mindsets, perspectives, and habits of mind—through which we filter and make sense of the world.

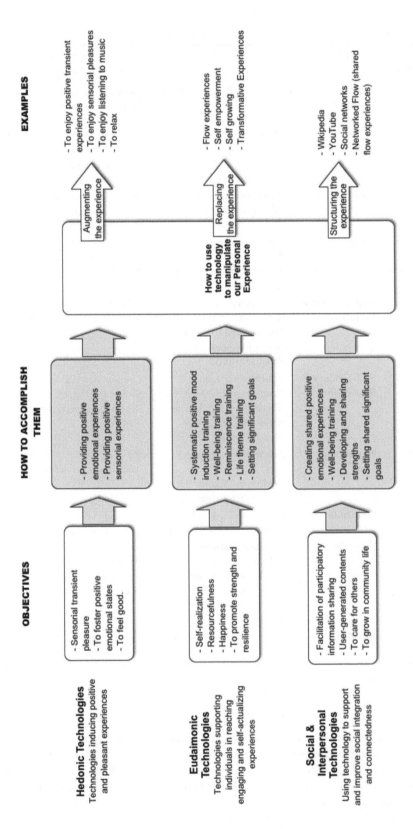

Figure 27.1 The design of positive technology (adapted from Inghilleri et al., 2015).

Riva et al. (Riva, Baños, et al., 2016), have identified three critical steps in this process:

1. The emergence of transformative experiences, which confronts the individual with a "disorienting dilemma" or psychological conflict (e.g., a perceived distance between self and reality);
2. An intense focus on the particular instance or experience creating the conflict: by exploring this experience as thoroughly as possible, the individual can relive and identify all of the significant elements associated with it (e.g., conceptual, behavioral, emotional, and motivational) facilitating their reorganization;
3. The belief of personal efficacy: individuals have to believe that they have the power to effect changes through their actions. Without it there, they are not willing to act, or to keep on acting in the face of problems and difficulties.

Thus, personal transformation requires the active engagement of the individual in the generation of new meanings as well as the perception that the experience being lived is self-relevant (Gaggioli, 2016). We have suggested that next-generation of virtual and augmented reality systems may provide new tools to design synthetic experiences that can be used to invite, elicit or facilitate positive personal transformation, through the (controlled) alteration of sensorial, perceptual, cognitive, and affective processes. The main opportunity offered by VR as a transformative medium lies in its unique capability of simulating a "possible self," by generating an artificial sense of embodiment, or the subjective experience of using and having a body (Riva, 2016b). Thanks to this feature, VR can also be used to allow the user to vividly experience the sensations of another person and feel as if they have merged with that person (Ahn, Le, & Bailenson, 2013). We have identified two broad types of *experiential affordances* that can be integrated in a simulated experience to leverage its transformative potential (Gaggioli, 2016): (i) *emotional affordances*; (ii) *epistemic affordances*.

Emotional affordances are perceptual cues that are aimed to elicit a deep emotional involvement in the user, i.e. by inducing exceptional appraisals of admiration, wonder, elevation, awe, etc. Emotional affordances are designed to re-create the basic "aesthetic dimension" of a transformative experience, which otherwise would be very difficult to encounter/reproduce in real-world contexts. For example, using VR it is possible to re-create the feeling of vastness that astronauts perceive during space flight—the so-called "overview effect" (A. Chirico, Yaden, Riva, & Gaggioli, 2016).

Epistemic affordances are cognitive cues that are meant to provide the participant with the opportunity to integrate/build new knowledge structures. These are, in essence, structured narratives conceived to trigger reflection and transformative insights. Epistemic affordances might be either represented by explicit messages or be conveyed through implicit or evocative contents, that is, symbolic-metaphoric situations (i.e. one bright and one dark path leading from a crossroads). From this perspective, epistemic affordances are meant to create open-ended "experiments of the self," for example, simulated dilemmatic situations that situate the participants in disorientation and puzzlement, which are also turning points out of which new insights for personal change may arise (Gaggioli, 2016).

Conclusions

In this chapter we introduced and described the *positive technology* research field—the scientific and applied approach to the use of technology for improving the quality of our personal experience—as a way of framing a suitable object of study in the field of positive communication (Graffigna, Barello, Wiederhold, Bosio, & Riva, 2013; Riva, 2012b; Riva, Bannños, Botella, Wiederhold, & Gaggioli, 2012; B.K. Wiederhold & Riva, 2012).

First, we have classified positive technologies according to their effects on these three features of personal experience:

- *Hedonic:* technologies used to induce positive and pleasant experiences.
- *Eudaimonic:* technologies used to support individuals in reaching engaging and self-actualizing experiences.
- *Social/Interpersonal:* technologies used to support and improve the connectedness between individuals, groups, and organizations.

Additionally, for each level we have identified critical variables—affect regulation for the Hedonic, flow and presence for the eudaimonic; social presence, collective intentions and networked flow for the Social/Interpersonal—that can be manipulated and controlled (Table 27.1) to guide the design and development of positive technologies.

Finally, the different examples show that technology can be used to manipulate the features of an experience in three separate but related ways (Figure 27.1):

- *By structuring it* using a goal, rules and a feedback system.
- *By augmenting it* to achieve multimodal and mixed experiences.
- *By replacing it* with a synthetic one.

Despite the complexity of experience, new technologies can really augment human ability to grasp all relevant aspects of it jointly or separately, to pursue a greater human's well-being and foster general human progress.

References

Ahn, S. J., Le, A. M. T., & Bailenson, J. N. (2013). The effect of embodied experiences on self-other merging, attitude, and helping behavior. *Media Psychology, 16*(1), 7–38.

Botella, C., Riva, G., Gaggioli, A., Wiederhold, B. K., Alcaniz, M., & Banos, R. M. (2012). The present and future of positive technologies. *Cyberpsychology, Behavior and Social Networking, 15*(2), 78–84. doi:10.1089/cyber.2011.0140

Calvo, R. A., & Peters, D. (2012). Positive computing: Technology for a wiser world. *ACM Interactions, 19*(2), 28–31.

Calvo, R. A., & Peters, D. (2014). *Positive computing: Technology for well-being and human potential.* Cambridge, MA: MIT Press.

Carissoli, C., Villani, D., & Riva, G. (2015). Does a meditation protocol supported by a mobile application help people reduce stress? Suggestions from a controlled pragmatic trial. *Cyberpsychology, Behavior, and Social Networking, 18*(1), 46–53. doi:10.1089/cyber.2014.0062

Chicchi Giglioli, I. A., Pallavicini, F., Pedroli, E., Serino, S., & Riva, G. (2015). Augmented reality: A brand new challenge for the assessment and treatment of psychological disorders. *Computational and Mathematical Methods in Medicine,* (862942), 1–13.

Chirico, A., Cipresso, P., & Gaggioli, A. (2016). Psychophysiological correlate of compex spherical awe stimuli. *Neuropsychological Trends,* November, 79–80.

Chirico, A., Cipresso, P., Yaden, D. B., Biassoni, F., Riva, G., & Gaggioli, A. (2017). Effectiveness of immersive videos in inducing awe: An experimental study. *Scientific Reports, 7*(1), 1218. doi:10.1038/s41598-017-01242-0

Chirico, A., Yaden, D. B., Riva, G., & Gaggioli, A. (2016). The potential of virtual reality for the investigation of awe. *Frontiers in Psychology.* doi:10.3389/fpsyg.2016.01766

Cipresso, P., Gaggioli, A., Serino, S., Raspelli, S., Vigna, C., Pallavicini, F., & Riva, G. (2012). Inter-reality in the evaluation and treatment of psychological stress disorders: The Interstress Project. *Studies in Health Technology and Informatics, 181,* 8–11.

Csíkszentmihályi, M. (1990). *Flow: The psychology of optimal experience.* New York: HarperCollins.

Gaggioli, A. (2015). Transformative experience design. In A. Gaggioli, A. Ferscha, G. Riva, S. Dunne, & I. Viaud-Delmon (Eds.), *Human computer confluence: Transforming human experience through symbiotic technologies* (pp. 97–121). Warsaw: De Gruyter Open.

Gaggioli, A. (2016). Transformative experience design. In A. Gaggioli, F. A., G. Riva, S. Dunne, & I. Viaud-Delmon (Eds.), *Human computer confluence: Transforming human experience through symbiotic technologies* (pp. 97–121). Warsaw: De Gruyter Open.

Gaggioli, A., Bassi, M., & Delle Fave, A. (2003). Quality of experience in virtual environments. In G. Riva, W. A. I. Jsselsteijn, & F. Davide (Eds.), *Being there: Concepts, effects and measurement of user presence in synthetic environment* (pp. 121–135). Amsterdam: Ios Press. Retrieved from www.emergingcommunication.com/volume5.html

Gaggioli, A., Chirico, A., Triberti, S., & Riva, G. (2016). Transformative interactions: Designing positive technologies to foster self-transcendence and meaning. *Annual Review of CyberTherapy and Telemedicine, 14*, 169–173.

Gaggioli, A., Cipresso, P., Serino, S., Campanaro, D. M., Pallavicini, F., Wiederhold, B. K., & Riva, G. (2014). Positive technology: A free mobile platform for the self-management of psychological stress. *Studies in Health Technology and Informatics, 199*, 25–29.

Gaggioli, A., Morganti, L., Bonfiglio, S., Scaratti, C., Cipresso, P., Serino, S., & Riva, G. (2014). Intergenerational group reminiscence: A potentially effective intervention to enhance elderly psychosocial well-being and to improve children's perception of aging. *Educational Gerontology, 40*(7), 486–498. doi:10.10 80/03601277.2013.844042

Gaggioli, A., & Riva, G. (2014). Psychological treatments: Smart tools boost mental-health care. *Nature, 512*(7512), 28. doi:10.1038/512028b

Gaggioli, A., Riva, G., Peters, D., & Calvo, R. A. (2017). Chapter 18: Positive technology, computing, and design: Shaping a future in which technology promotes psychological well-being. In M. Jeon (Ed.), *Emotions and affect in human factors and human-computer interaction* (pp. 477–502). London: Elsevier.

Graffigna, G., Barello, S., Wiederhold, B. K., Bosio, A. C., & Riva, G. (2013). Positive technology as a driver for health engagement. *Studies in Health Technology and Informatics, 191*, 9–17.

Grassi, A., Gaggioli, A., & Riva, G. (2011). New technologies to manage exam anxiety. *Studies in Health Technology and Informatics, 167*, 57–62.

Greenhow, C., & Lewin, C. (2016). Social media and education: Reconceptualizing the boundaries of formal and informal learning. *Learning, Media and Technology, 41*(1), 6–30.

Haddon, L. (2016). *The social dynamics of information and communication technology.* New York: Routledge.

Hamilton, N. F. (2016). Love and relationships online. In I. Connolly, M. Palmer, H. Barton, & G. Kirwan (Eds.), *An introduction to cyberpsychology* (pp. 71–85). New York: Routledge.

Hayes, A. M., Laurenceau, J.-P., Feldman, G., Strauss, J. L., & Cardaciotto, L. (2007). Change is not always linear: The study of nonlinear and discontinuous patterns of change in psychotherapy. *Clinical Psychology Review, 27*(6), 715–723. doi:10.1016/j.cpr.2007.01.008

Hayes, A. M., & Yasinski, C. (2015). Pattern destabilization and emotional processing in cognitive therapy for personality disorders. *Frontiers in Psychology, 6*(107).

Heeks, R. (2010). Do information and communication technologies (ICTs) contribute to development? *Journal of International Development, 22*(5), 625–640.

Ihm, J., & Hsieh, Y. P. (2015). The implications of information and communication technology use for the social well-being of older adults. *Information, Communication & Society, 18*(10), 1123–1138.

Inghilleri, P., Riva, G., & Riva, E. (Eds.). (2015). *Enabling positive change: Flow and complexity in daily experience.* Berlin: De Gruyter Open. Retrieved from www.degruyter.com/view/product/449663

Manzoni, G. M., Cesa, G. L., Villani, D., Castelnuovo, G., Molinari, E., & Riva, G. (2006). VR-enhanced treatment of anxiety in obese subjects: A follow-up study on trait-anxiety, psychological symptornatology, and generalized self-efficacy. *Cyberpsychology & Behavior, 9*(6), 699–700.

Manzoni, G. M., Pagnini, F., Gorini, A., Preziosa, A., Castelnuovo, G., Molinari, E., & Riva, G. (2009). Can relaxation training reduce emotional eating in women with obesity? An exploratory study with 3 months of follow-up. *Journal of American Dietetic Association, 109*(8), 1427–1432. doi:S0002-8223(09)00626-9 [pii]10.1016/j.jada.2009.05.004

McGonigal, J. (2011). *Reality is broken: Why games make us better and how they can change the world.* New York: The Penguin Press.

Miller, W. R., & C'de Baca, J. (2001). *Quantum change: When epiphanies and sudden insights transform ordinary lives.* New York: Guilford Press.

Murray, D. C. (2015). Notes to self: The visual culture of selfies in the age of social media. *Consumption Markets & Culture, 18*(6), 490–516.

Pallavicini, F., Serino, S., Cipresso, P., Pedroli, E., Chicchi Giglioli, I. A., Chirico, A., Manzoni, G. M., Castelnuovo, G., Molinari E., & Riva, G. (2016). *Testing augmented reality for cue exposure in obese patients: An exploratory study*. Cyberpsychology, Behavior & Social Networking, Insert final Volume and Pages.

Preziosa, A., Grassi, A., Gaggioli, A., & Riva, G. (2009). Therapeutic applications of the mobile phone. *British Journal of Guidance & Counselling, 37*(3), 313–325. doi:10.1080/03069880902957031

Prochaska, J. O., & DiClemente, C. C. (1982). Transtheoretical therapy: Toward a more integrative model of change. *Psychotherapy: Theory, Research & Practice, 19*, 276–288.

Raspelli, S., Pallavicini, F., Grassi, A., Cipresso, P., Balgera, A., Meazzi, D., . . . Riva, G. (2011). Validation of a narrative as an emotional-induction technique through different non-invasive psychophysiological monitoring devices: Preliminary results. *Journal of Cybertherapy and Rehabilitation, 4*(2), 261.

Repetto, C., Gorini, A., Vigna, C., Algeri, D., Pallavicini, F., & Riva, G. (2009). The use of biofeedback in clinical virtual reality: The INTREPID project. *Journal of Visualized Experiments*, (33). doi:1554 [pii]10.3791/1554

Riva, G. (2009). Virtual reality: An experiential tool for clinical psychology. *British Journal of Guidance & Counselling, 37*(3), 337–345. doi:10.1080/03069880902957056

Riva, G. (2012a). Personal experience in positive psychology may offer a new focus for a growing discipline. *American Psychologist, 67*(7), 574–575.

Riva, G. (2012b). What is positive technology and its impact on cyber psychology. *Studies in Health Technology and Informatics, 181*, 37–41.

Riva, G. (2016a). Embodied medicine: What human-computer confluence can offer to health care. In A. Gaggioli, A. Ferscha, G. Riva, S. Dunne, & I. Viaud-Delmon (Eds.), *Human computer confluence: Transforming human experience through symbiotic technologies* (pp. 55–79). Warsaw: De Gruyter Open.

Riva, G. (2016b). Embodied medicine: What human-computer confluence can offer to health care. In A. Gaggioli, F. A., G. Riva, S. Dunne, & I. Viaud-Delmon (Eds.), *Human computer confluence: Transforming human experience through symbiotic technologies*. Warsaw: De Gruyter Open.

Riva, G., Algeri, D., Pallavicini, F., Repetto, C., Gorini, A., & Gaggioli, A. (2010). The use of advanced technologies in the treatment of psychological stress. *Journal of CyberTherapy & Rehabilitation, 2*(2), 169–171.

Riva, G., Baños, R. M., Botella, C., Mantovani, F., & Gaggioli, A. (2016). Transforming experience: The potential of augmented reality and virtual reality for enhancing personal and clinical change. *Frontiers in Psychiatry, 7*(164). doi:10.3389/fpsyt.2016.00164

Riva, G., Baños, R. M., Botella, C., Wiederhold, B. K., & Gaggioli, A. (2012). Positive technology: Using interactive technologies to promote positive functioning. *Cyberpsychology, Behavior and Social Networking, 15*(2), 69–77. doi:10.1089/cyber.2011.0139

Riva, G., Botella, C., Baños, R., Mantovani, F., García-Palacios, A., Quero, S., . . . Gaggioli, A. (2015). Presence-inducing media for mental health applications. In M. Lombard, F. Biocca, J. Freeman, W. I. Jsselsteijn, & R. J. Schaevitz (Eds.), *Immersed in media* (pp. 283–332). New York: Springer International Publishing.

Riva, G., Castelnuovo, G., & Mantovani, F. (2006). Transformation of flow in rehabilitation: The role of advanced communication technologies. *Behavior Research Methods, 38*(2), 237–244.

Riva, G., Raspelli, S., Algeri, D., Pallavicini, F., Gorini, A., Wiederhold, B. K., & Gaggioli, A. (2010). Inter-reality in practice: Bridging virtual and real worlds in the treatment of posttraumatic stress disorders. *Cyberpsychology, Behavior, and Social Networking, 13*(1), 55–65. doi:10.1089/cyber.2009.0320 [pii]

Riva, G., Serino, S., Di Lernia, D., Pavone, E. F., & Dakanalis, A. (2017). Embodied medicine: Mens sana in corpore virtuale sano. *Frontiers in Human Neuroscience, 11*(120). doi:10.3389/fnhum.2017.00120

Riva, G., Villani, D., Cipresso, P., Repetto, C., Triberti, S., Di Lernia, D., . . . Gaggioli, A. (2016). Positive and transformative technologies for active ageing. *Studies in Health Technology and Informatics, 220*, 308–315.

Rosenblum, L. (2000). Virtual and augmented reality 2020. *Ieee Computer Graphics and Applications, 20*(1), 38–39.

Seligman, M. E. P. (2002). *Authentic happiness: Using the new positive psychology to realize your potential for lasting fulfillment*. New York: Free Press.

Seligman, M. E. P., & Csikszentmihalyi, M. (2000). Positive psychology. *American Psychologist, 55*, 5–14.

Selwyn, N., & Stirling, E. (2016). Social media and education . . . now the dust has settled. *Learning, Media and Technology, 41*(1), 1–5.

Serino, S., & Dakanalis, A. (2016). Bodily illusions and weight-related disorders: Clinical insights from experimental research. *Annals of Physical and Rehabilitation Medicine*. doi:10.1016/j.rehab.2016.10.002

Serino, S., Triberti, S., Villani, D., Cipresso, P., Gaggioli, A., & Riva, G. (2014). Toward a validation of cyber-interventions for stress disorders based on stress inoculation training: A systematic review. *Virtual Reality, 18*(1), 73–87. doi:10.1007/S10055-013-0237-6

Shiota, M. N., Neufeld, S. L., Yeung, W. H., Moser, S. E., & Perea, E. F. (2011). Feeling good: Autonomic nervous system responding in five positive emotions. *Emotion, 11*(6), 1368.

Villani, D., Cipresso, P., Gaggioli, A., & Riva, G. (Eds.). (2016). *Integrating technology in positive psychology practice.* Hershey, PA: IGI-Global.

Villani, D., Lucchetta, M., Preziosa, A., & Riva, G. (2006). Narrative versus environment: The role of media content in emotional induction. *Cyberpsychology & Behavior, 9*(6), 724–725.

Villani, D., Preziosa, A., Riva, F., & Riva, G. (2006). Presence enhances relaxation: A preliminary controlled study. *Cyberpsychology & Behavior, 9*(6), 723–724.

Villani, D., Riva, F., & Riva, G. (2007). New technologies for relaxation: The role of presence. *International Journal of Stress Management, 14*(3), 260–274.

Webster, J. D., & McCall, M. E. (1999). Reminiscence functions across adulthood: A replication and extension. *Journal of Adult Development, 6*(1), 73–85. doi:10.1023/A:1021628525902

Wiederhold, B. K., & Riva, G. (2012). Positive technology supports shift to preventive, integrative health. *Cyberpsychology, Behavior and Social Networking, 15*(2), 67–68. doi:10.1089/cyber.2011.1533

Wiederhold, B. K., Riva, G., & Graffigna, G. (2013). Ensuring the best care for our increasing aging population: Health engagement and positive technology can help patients achieve a more active role in future healthcare. *Cyberpsychology, Behavior, and Social Networking, 16*(6), 411–412. doi:10.1089/cyber.2013.1520

28

YOUTH PROSUMERS AND CHARACTER STRENGTHS

Paula Herrero-Diz, Marina Ramos-Serrano, and Ashley Woodfall

Introduction

Current paradigms relating to young people's participation online break with preconceptions of the individualistic materialist. These new paradigms are recasting young people as digital content creators—prosumers—who are motivated by a sense of justice and solidarity which they share, from their ideologies, tastes, appearances, values, sexual options, and hobbies to their identities (Reig, 2013). Despite the media's insistence on portraying younger people as isolated and individualistic members of a "me" generation, what can be observed on the Internet is the emergence of a younger generation who are concerned about the issues that surround them. What can be seen as a "we" generation, as opposed to a "me" generation, foregrounds authenticity and assumes the responsibility of transforming reality, as well as claiming ownership of certain aspects of their immediate environment (*Íbidem*, 2013, p. 69).

According to a study from the Pew Research Center's *Internet & American Life Project* (2014), Internet users are "better people" in terms of universal values. Mihailidis (2014) refers to "the good citizenship" of individuals who promote good-heartedness and use the power of social media to advocate for causes that improve people's lives. Video sharing site YouTube has become the preferred medium for self-projection and presentation, particularly for the youngest—who according to Ofcom's *Children and Parents: Media Use and Attitudes Report* (2016), find inspiration through engaging with content, and each other, through the platform. Other studies have tended to show that peer-to-peer video websites contribute to an improvement in moral and psychological development by raising awareness and providing models of moral values and behaviors (Koh, 2014).

The production of online video blogging content has brought to the fore active and influential "YouTube stars" or "common gurus" (Golovinski, 2011, p. 65). Normally, these creators specialize in certain topics and their popularity is measured through the number of followers and subscribers to their channel, the number of views, the comments they receive, and the number of times their content is reposted and shared through other social networks—plus, of course, the number of positive ratings their content receives. Children and adolescents are important participants in this commenting, re-posting, and posting, as they construct their technological identities through the production and sharing of videos (Lange, 2014): these young people are the new "televised media prosumers" (Aguaded & Urbano-Cayuela, 2014, p. 137). Their media productions are successful not only because of the immediacy and accessibility of "participatory" production tools (Jenkins, 2006), but also because of the immediacy of the sharing and comment culture fostered by YouTube and similar platforms.

YouTubers with the largest audiences tend to be those who manage to interact with visitors and establish relationships with them through dialogue (Strangelove, 2010). Young YouTube users are readily sharing their *inspirational* content, and when they do, they are able to transmit emotions and "powerful memes" across distance (Rodríguez, 2013, p. 61) in ways that are not possible on other, less open, platforms. Significantly, the use of YouTube combined with other social media networks can also be said to have a positive effect on the content creators themselves (Hutter, Wood & Turner, 2013).

This chapter is a review of the ways in which social media networks, especially YouTube, can act as a vehicle for the transmission of happiness in terms of eudaimonia—well-being and flourishing—and how they might contribute to young people's personal growth and to the development of their human capacities.

Digital Identity: From the "Me" Generation to the "We" Generation

We, as human beings, have the ability to construct and reconstruct our identities—according to Bauer (2016, pp. 162–167) constantly and throughout our lifetimes "cultivating a good life story"—and we do this in relation to our experiences, histories, personalities, and other subjective and objective elements, including the cultural narratives that come from literature, cinema, politics, or the consumption of other mainstream media messages and products. This ability to transform our "me" makes us, argues Bauer, potential owners of "a good life story," or put in another way, "a story of a good life," which apart from configuring our identity, also favors our growth in terms of the development of eudaimonia.

If we think about youth (a period in which there are constantly changing reference models for behavior, exposure to insecurities, to the influence of peers and superficial, ephemeral, and contradictory messages) the construction of the self becomes deeply complex. We need to account for the ways in which the personality, identity work, and relationships of young people can now be rehearsed and developed across virtual spaces, and how young people experience these spaces in hyperconnected ways. Far from considering hyperconnectivity to be something to be anxious about, because it has the potential to promote isolated, "me generation," individualistic people, it could be argued that the sociability of young people on social media platforms and online in general, presents an opportunity for forming "better identities" in relation to "universal values" such as empathy, solidarity, or a sense of justice—that is to say, a "we generation" (Reig & Vilches, 2013, pp. 68–69). We tend to find however a more apocalyptic vision of new communication technologies and of young people (Navarrete, 2017) at play, especially when it relates to the Internet and social media networks; with a negative stance often fed by a hyperbolic sensationalist news media.

Facing these positions and given the potential of the technologies, many researchers are advocating for media literacy education that can empower young people. Ito (2008) recognizes the potential in young people when she highlights "super adolescents" and others note the elevating of young people's nature from the tenderest years; "babies with superpowers" (Reig & Vilches, 2013, p. 69). Barbalho (2014, p. 83) simply defends the "young creative type" and the "young communicator" who can achieve whatever they want through the Internet. Mihailidis (2014) proposes the figure of "good citizenship" to describe the efficient use of social media on the part of young people, in particular foregrounding the potential for activism. Here the "good citizen" is an effective creator and communicator, who can combine political participation with participation in and through the media, and it is precisely the media that has facilitated their participation and has reinforced a sense of civic responsibility—with new opportunities to connect with other individuals who might share similar concerns.

Technology on its own is of course not enough to promote civic participation. Access to the creative participatory tool and the affordances of social media is potentially significant and powerful (Reig & Vilches, 2013, p. 70; Mihailidis, 2014), but this should be balanced with an emphasis on values in education—and noting the increasingly earlier exposure to the Internet, with this education beginning at younger ages—and in line with the idea that the consequences of social media use can be positive. In other words, (media literacy) education is more important than ever when young people can learn to construct and manage their personalities and digital identities within the multiple new environments they find themselves operating across.

This is especially significant when young people are reaffirming their "real world" existence through social media, as Rodríguez (2013, pp. 41–53) suggests: "The social interactions that we engage in online everyday [. . .] elevate our oxytocin levels [. . .]. We react to electronic rejection the same as we would to rejection in real life [. . .]. Each time we receive a 'like' or someone ticks a publication we've uploaded with a heart, we feel an addictive pat on the back, that we belong and that we are recognized." Ultimately, sharing what we know, talking to other people, looking for new sensations and finding people to connect with, is an innate human desire, whether that be online or in real life.

Emotions Through the Screen: Happiness on YouTube Is Contagious

The Internet is a propitious place for finding happiness, because it not only permits the empowerment of users, but it also favors social relationships and exchange between individuals, and here Hongladarom (2007) considers the affordances of interactive technology for promoting happiness, whilst drawing on Aristotelian spirituality and well-being in eudaimonic terms. Hongladarom considers the importance of the participatory Internet to the establishment of social connections because happiness can be reached in this environment only when individuals feel they belong to a group and if the information they share is done in an open and transparent manner: it's not about mere isolated individuals who surf the Internet only for the sake of consuming.

Other studies in relation to the Internet and social networks point to the possibility that happiness like other emotions, can be transmitted from one user to the next by simply being connected through a channel that allows them to interact. We can find an explanation in the work of Fowler and Christakis (2008, p. 17). They believe that just as there are other phenomena that spread across social networks, the same ought to be true with happiness, and they centered their research to find out whether or not happiness is a networked phenomenon. To make this determination, they started from the premise that if happiness spreads within at least three degrees of separation (from friends to friends or between family and acquaintances) as occurs with other social behaviors—like smoking—where people imitate each other, in social networks here geographical and personal barriers are diluted, it should also be possible for a person's health and well-being to be affected by others, because people take on the emotional states that they observe in others. Despite not being able to find the causes for the transmission of happiness, they did manage to conclude that there were psychoneuroimmunological mechanisms that supported the fact that interacting with other happy people has beneficial health effects.

Kramer, Guilloory, and Hancocck (2014) in their research in to emotional contagion through social networks conducted a "massive-scale" study through Facebook (2012) in which they analyzed the effects that reading negative or positive posts through their news feeds had on user's emotional states. The results showed that emotional states can be transferred to others through social networks like Facebook—and this process could be argued therefore to be something that can readily occur across other social media platforms as like YouTube, where audiovisual content predominates and the interface also encourages conversation (Duncum, 2013). Here it is worth noting the words of YouTube user NenoBrasil (cited in Kellner & Kim, 2010, p. 17) who argues that relationships will never be the same again post the rise of YouTube, because "it is a tool that allows us to meet people all around the world to share our thought, problems, happiness, beliefs and everything." Additionally, Bloom and Johnston (2013, p. 118) highlight how YouTube favors greater self-reflection and awareness between individuals because of its asynchronous nature, that is, by the mere fact that the users can play a channel's video content over and over again.

Youth Prosumer: YouTubers' Character Strengths

On YouTube we can find young people who may help support Reig and Vilches's (2013) optimism for the Internet's capacity not only for sociability but also for the defense of causes that people consider just. We can also find example that support of Bauer's (2016) position on how to "cultivate a good life story." This is the case of the activist and 2014 Nobel Peace Prize-winner Malala Yousafzai, who after suffering an attack from the Taliban that almost killed her, decided to dedicate her life to improving the lives of the children of the world, and articulated her cause through social media. And then there is Jazz Jennings, a transgender teen who uses her channel to lead campaigns to raise awareness to combat discrimination against transgender people like herself. And a significant case in relation to this chapter, is the young YouTuber Robby Novak, also known as "the kid president," who, through his channel, transmits messages that promote happiness, advocates for individual potential, the power to change things and leading a full life.

At the age of nine, in 2012, Robby uploaded his first video, introducing himself as a candidate for the president of the United States. Today his words of encouragement and his ability to generate an online conversation captivate a growing audience—as of 2017 he has around 2 million subscribers and more than 6 million views and hundreds of thousands of followers on Twitter, Instagram, and Facebook.

In 2013, the mainstream media CNN has invited Robby to tell his story on news and entertainment shows, presenting the young man as "the inspiration of the nation." On the Internet he has become significant enough to warrant an entry in the online zeitgeist *knowyourmeme.com* website, and the website portal of TedxTalk features several of his motivational videos from talks across the United States. It has been argued that this is precisely part of his success; that he uses social media as a tool or a resource to construct and share positive emotions which can be beneficial to others (Vella-Brodrick, 2016, p. 396). In *Watching YouTube. Extraordinary Videos by Ordinary People*, Strangelove (2010) explores the ways in which everyday representational practices are being reshaped by cameras in the hands of ordinary people. Here we find the reason for Robby Novak's popularity; he is a content creator who specializes in a topic that combines snippets of his ordinary daily life with sketches, in a style which is known as "speaker."

What is extraordinary about this case is the motivation that is behind the creation of the content—that is to explicitly make other people happy. Robby suffers from the congenital disease osteogenesis imperfecta which leads to bone degeneration, but it hasn't stopped him from making himself "president" of a nation (on YouTube) or from transmitting a message of optimism to society. As he declared in one of his videos, his effort resides in developing an online formula for making other people laugh which at the same time serves as an antidote to the disease he's suffering from. Peterson and Seligman's (2004) theory on the cognitive strength of individuals, assures that this occurs. One of the theories argues precisely that when content creators use information and a sense of humor for improving the lives of others, it captivates the audience, just as this young man has done. But a priori, one also observes many of the other strengths among the 24 proposed by these authors, such as leadership, because the videos encourage YouTube viewers to do things, to change the world, to transcend themselves in life. The videos offer motivation for filling life with meaning and for appreciating beauty. They encourage appreciating the extraordinary and the simplest essence of things; or awe and fascination for the ordinary and for learning new things; and even valor, bravery, and hope because Novak turns his illness into a virtue and a life lesson for wisdom and especially, as a reflection of gratitude, because the young man invites his followers to be grateful for what they receive.

Equally, Novak is an example of how to transmit happiness in hedonic terms as well as eudaimonic ones, because the YouTuber defends not only the value of the material things that we have the luck to enjoy, but he also defends that each individual is a unique being, incredible, and without limitless potential, for which individuals should be grateful and simply happy.

On the other hand, his ability to transmit emotions stands out through the videos that he produces; they make you laugh, they make you cry, they even make you jump for joy or out of surprise. In addition to the verbal communication—the content and the depth of his messages—he is characterized by having a very expressive face that reinforces his dialogue. Despite there being quite a lot of study on the subject, it is difficult to control the ten thousand combinations of facial movements a person can make (Ekman & Rosenberg, 1997). In any case, facial expression usually holds affective or emotional meaning (Ekman, Sorenson, & Friesen, 1969; Ekman & Cordano, 2011). In addition to what the face exteriorizes in a video format, the mood equally influences the emotional contagion between individuals. Studies such as the one carried out by Lewinski (2015, p. 241) start from the premise of the theories cited before, precisely demonstrate the importance of emotions—particularly those transmitted by facial expressions—to explain the popularity of a YouTube video (number of views). Among these, the affiliative emotions—happiness and sadness—generate greater empathy from observers, even though this also occurs with expressions that are non-emotional such as surprise.

Conclusions

Our goal throughout this chapter has been to contribute to other studies on positive communication by providing more recent theories which attempt to eliminate some of the prejudices about online user conduct, specifically that of younger people. Contrary to the more apocalyptic views about the way young people use the Internet and social media, the truth is that the contents they create and share also allow us to confirm that authentic participation in the online conversation can help young people to reinforce their strengths as human beings and benefit the common good.

For one thing, we can expand the concept of the social media network to that of the idea of a network of people thanks to cybernetic emotions, as defended by Kramer et al. (2014). The fact that people also express their emotions and feelings online demystifies that as users they distinguish between real life and virtual life (or second life) in their behavior. This, in turn, explains the awareness that being natural and expressing yourself spontaneously, have larger positive effects; in other words, it is more beneficial to be yourself online. This is why it is increasingly common for individuals to take charge of what they project about themselves online, and to control the creation of their own digital identities. Additionally, young people improve their identities insofar as they construct them in a social space, as we have seen throughout different theories, because in this space they share universal values related to the common good (Reig & Vilches, 2013).

In this sense, perhaps there should be a more profound analysis of how constant interaction with a community of followers impacts the personality of young content creators. Although a high level of interaction is useful as a way of gaging whether or not content is adjusted to the demands of the public, it is true that this could also affect the personality of the creator. The obsession with being popular or obtaining more followers and likes is also a reality that affects not only young people's use of social media but might affect their personalities as well. To this point, we must also consider the impact of a post's popularity—be it an image, a video, or a text (Sherman, Hernández, Greenfield, & Dapretto, 2016). Young people are attracted to posts that are popular with their peers, which demonstrates the power of contagion and the influence of peers at a stage of development where young people are forging their personalities.

In the same way that there are online haters (those who promote hate speech), gamers (those who focus their online activity on the game), and influencers (those who set trends in relation to consumption), the Internet has given rise to a new user profile: the good citizen (Mihailidis, 2014). The good citizen is a user who creates positive content for the benefit of others in a common environment of interests. Therefore, we can say that social media also presents a space and the potential opportunity to be a good citizen, because it allows us to construct a "story of a good life" or a "good life story" over and over again, as Bauer (2016) points out.

All the same, this phenomenon is occurring regardless of the age of the individuals. There are numerous cases of young people who are creating digital content that impacts their peers because the material deals with issues that concern them. This also breaks with stereotypes of a self-absorbed, superficial generation that uses technology for consumer purposes, and recasts it as a generation of transformative, active, and responsible users. The examples mentioned above, such as that of Malala or Jazz Jennings, are just a small sample of a generation of younger people who are taking advantage of the power of the Internet to demonstrate that "being good" online has positive effects. On the one hand, we have confirmed that interactions in social media spaces favor a sense of belonging which is very important at the stage of development where young people's personalities are being formed.

On the other hand, they achieve a sense of personal well-being insofar as their participation is recognized by others through likes, shared content, or favorable comments, as in the case of the YouTuber Robby Novak. This in turn means that the Internet is also a place where, just as some find love, others experience feelings and emotions that reinforce other human qualities and strengths. To this regard it would be interesting to administer the Peterson and Seligman (2004) scale based on Novak, for studying the relationship between online activity and eudaimonic happiness, and to obtain a sample of the group who follow the social media accounts, because as Vella-Brodrick (2016) explains, the success of social media networks is precisely the possibility they offer for sharing emotions, which would explain the popularity of Robby, as well as the loyalty of those who consume his messages.

Additionally, we can find a relationship between emotions and messages going viral; we see that users share content in a massive way when something is offered in return, and a discourse conveying values, or appealing to emotions—which may range from joy to tears—will more likely be disseminated. Beyond whether or not a user finds particular content more or less satisfying, the reason messages get shared is because of affiliative emotional reasons—happiness or sadness.

This is an example of the mirror effect that experts talk about, which occurs in the same way on screen as it does face to face. In the specific case of YouTube, we point to an emotional narrative reaching its maximum expression through the video blogging network because of the video's transmission capacity, as we have seen with the paradigms of Lewinski (2015) and Strangelove (2010). Through its blog Creator Academy, the platform itself offers four lessons to "unleash the power of narrative appealing to the hearts and minds of viewers." Although they recognize that "there is no formula that determines which keys to press to provoke emotions," through the blog they admit that a good story, an adequate approach, precise words, an appropriate creative treatment and if necessary, the right music to go along with the story, can provoke reactions in the audience such as laughing or crying, and perhaps most importantly, can motivate the audience to act. These guidelines seem to coincide with Peterson and Seligman's (2004) description of individual cognitive strengths, and taking advantage of using information and emotions to improve the lives of others.

All this is evident in the cases outlined here, but this community of digital creators, on You-Tube and on many other social networks, is growing. Every day more people are consciously or unconsciously pursuing an increase in their own happiness as well as that of their followers, through the generation of a new narrative that is emotional and positive. This narrative may contribute to making the Internet a virtual space where experiencing and diffusing a kind of well-being that could be best described as eudaimonic.

References

Aguaded, J. I., & Urbano-Cayuela, R. (2014). Nuevo modelo de enseñanza europeo a través del prosumidor infantil televisivo. *Comunicación y Hombre, 10,* 131–142.

Barbalho, A. (2014). *La creación está en el aire: juventudes, política, cultura y comunicación.* Barcelona: UOC.

Bauer, J. J. (2016). Eudaimonic growth: The development of the goods in personhood (or: Cultivating a good life story). In J. Vittersø (Ed.), *Handbook of eudaimonic well-being* (pp. 147–174). Switzerland: Springer International Publishing.

Bloom, K., & Johnston, K. M. (2013). Digging into YouTube videos: Using media literacy and participatory culture to promote cross-cultural understanding. *Journal of Media Literacy Education, 2*(2), 3.

Duncum, P. (2013). Creativity as conversation in the interactive audience culture of YouTube. *Visual Inquiry, 2*(2), 115–125.

Ekman, P., & Cordano, D. (2011). What is meant by calling emotions basic? *Emotion Review, 3*(4), 364–370. doi:10.1177/1754073911410740

Ekman, P., & Rosenberg, E. L. (1997). *What the face reveals: Basic and applied studies of spontaneous expression using the Facial Action Coding System (FACS).* Oxford, USA: Oxford University Press.

Ekman, P., Sorenson, E. R., & Friesen, W. V. (1969). Pan-cultural elements in facial displays of emotion. *Science, 164*(3875), 86–88.

Fowler, J. H., & Christakis, N. A. (2008). Dynamic spread of happiness in a large social network: Longitudinal analysis over 20 years in the Framingham Heart Study. *British Medical Journal, 337,* 1–9. doi:10.1136/bmj.a2338

Golovinski, M. S. (2011). *Event 3.0: How generation Y & Z are re-shaping the events industry.* Retrieved from Lulu.com

Hongladarom, S. (2007). Web 2.0: Toward happiness and empowerment through interactive technology. In *Conf. on Gross National Happiness* (Bangkok, Nov 26–28).

Hutter, R., Wood, C., & Turner, R. N. (2013). Individuation moderates impressions of conflicting categories for slower processors. *Social Psychology, 44,* 239–247. DOI: 10.1027/1864-9335/a000108

Ito, M. (2008). Education vs. entertainment: A cultural history of children's software. *The Ecology of Games: Connecting Youth, Games, and Learning,* 89–116.

Jenkins, H. (2006). *Fans, bloggers, and gamers: Exploring participatory culture.* New York: New York University Press.

Kellner, D., & Kim, G. (2010). YouTube, critical pedagogy, and media activism. *The Review of Education, Pedagogy, and Cultural Studies, 32*(1), 3–36. doi:10.1080/10714410903482658

Koh, C. (2014). Exploring the use of Web 2.0 technology to promote moral and psychosocial development: Can *YouTube* work? *British Journal of Educational Technology, 45,* 619–635. doi:10.1111/bjet.12071

Kramer, A. D. I., Guilloory, J. E., & Hancocck, J. T. (2014). Experimental evidence of massive-scale emotional contagion through social networks. *Proceedings of the National Academy of Science of the United States of America, 111*(24), 8788–8790.

Lange, P. G. (2014). *Kids on YouTube: Technical identities and digital literacies.* Walnut Creek, CA: Left Coast Press.

Lewinski, P. (2015). Don't look blank, happy, or sad: Patterns of facial expressions of speakers in banks' YouTube videos predict video's popularity over time. *Journal of Neuroscience, Psychology, and Economics, 8*(4), 241–249. doi:10.1037/npe0000046

Mihailidis, P. (2014). *Media literacy and the emerging citizen: Youth, engagement and participation in digital culture.* New York: Peter Lang.

Navarrete, R. D. L. C. B. (2017). The negative impact of technologies in adolescents and young people. *Medimay, 23*(2), 173–178.

Peterson, C., & Seligman, M. E. (2004). *Character strengths and virtues: A handbook and classification* (Vol. 1). Oxford: Oxford University Press.

Pew Research Center. (2014, February). *The web at 25*. Retrieved from www.pewinternet.org/2014/02/25/the-web-at-25-in-the-u-s

Reig, D. (2013). Describiendo al hiperindividuo, el nuevo individuo conectado. In D. Reig & L. F. Vílchez (Eds.), *Los jóvenes en la era de la hiperconectividad: tendencias, claves y miradas* (pp. 21–81). Madrid: Fundación Telefónica.

Reig, D., & Vilches, L. F. (2013). *Los jóvenes en la era de la hiperconectividad: tendencias, claves y miradas*. Madrid: Fundación Telefónica.

Rodríguez, D. (2013/2000). *Memecracia. Los virales que nos gobiernan*. Barcelona: Ediciones Gestión.

Sherman, L. E., Hernández, L. M., Greenfield, P. M., & Dapretto, M. (2016). The power of like in Adolescence: Effects of peer influence on neural and behavioral responses to social media. *Psychological Science*, 27(7), 1027–1035. doi:10.1177/0956797616645673

Strangelove, M. (2010). *Watching YouTube: Extraordinary videos by ordinary people*. Toronto, ON: University of Toronto Press.

Vella-Brodrick, D. A. (2016). Positive interventions that erode the hedonic and eudaimonic divide to promote lasting happiness. In J. Vittersø (Ed.), *Handbook of eudaimonic well-being* (pp. 395–406). Switzerland: Springer International Publishing.

29

AESTHETICS, USABILITY, AND THE DIGITAL DIVIDE

An Approach to Beauty, UX, and Subjective Well-Being

Juan-Ramón Martín-Sanromán, Fernando Suárez Carballo, Fernando Galindo Rubio, and Daniel Raposo

Introduction

Since the dawn of time, human beings have strived to steadily better their levels of well-being. Either under a classic approach of problem-driven design or of possibility-driven design (Desmet & Hassenzahl, 2012), first artisans, and later designers have always endeavored to manufacture items to solve the people's problems, to make their life easier, and even to try to achieve greater levels of happiness (Yang, Aurisicchio, Mackrill, & Baxter, 2017).

As technology has become more complex, humans have developed different strategies to make it more usable. Or in other words, to adapt its interface to the type of target user and to the context in which it supposedly will be used. Therefore, all the knowledge generated by the human computer interaction (HCI) has been developed, leading, among many other things, to the ISO 9241 standard, which defines usability. It should be noted that usability must not be interpreted as ease-of-use in general. For example, a complex interface, such as the one used in the steering wheel by a Formula 1 driver, may be defined as usable if it is appropriate for its target users (racing drivers) and to the context of user (ergonomic adaptation in the minimum space and decision-making in the shortest possible time).

However, products aimed at mass consumption, such as the majority of the digital devices that we use today (computers, smartphones, tablets, or wearables) must have an interface that does not require a steep learning curve for most people if they want to succeed in the marketplace. Thus, the majority of devices have developed the most user-friendly interface as possible, with a predominantly visual environment (helped by sound and haptic stimuli) and with an input system based on a touch screen or on the traditional keyboard and mouse/trackpad.

Beyond the design of the operating systems by the leading hardware companies, the need to design interaction systems both in the form of native apps and web applications or sites for desktops or mobiles has become widespread in recent years. Thus, there are increasingly more products and services that can be consumed digitally and more companies that need to offer them through this channel. In this regard, the media are no exception, but rather quite the contrary. Therefore, the need to create usable digital products for the general public is no longer something exclusive to hardware manufacturers, resulting in a true need for nearly each company or organization and consequently, in a learning requirement for many target groups that had up so far avoided using them and preferred the traditional channels (for example, the personal contact with the points of sale and customer service or the traditional access to the media).

The problem is that many of the digitalization processes have not managed to reach everyone, so that a digital divide has been created between those people who are capable of using the technology and those who cannot. That is where usability really acquires its importance not to leave behind the target audiences who turn their back on technology as they find it difficult to use (Martín San-Román, Suárez Carballo, Raposo, Galindo Rubio, & Rivas Herrero, 2015).

What we argue in this text is that beauty plays an important role to soften the learning curve of the interface systems, making the use experience more pleasurable and achieving a greater degree of acceptance by the target audiences. However, beauty would be based not only on the more formal aspect (*look and feel*), but also on the information structure and on the logical order of the interaction processes. In other words, it would go beyond what is usually known as *visual design* as Garrett (2011) understood it and affect the whole design of the product. It is here where the different professional profiles and skills converge toward a single objective. *Visual Design* (in charge of the aesthetics), along with *Information Architecture* (in charge of structure), *Data Visualization* ,or Human *Computer Interaction* (in charge of usability) professionals must work together. This big picture is the one defended by the user experience (UX), where a good use experience would lead to a high degree of acceptance by users. In this light, the importance of beauty in the user experience needs to be highlighted, along with renewing the ethical approach of designers in their mission to reduce the digital divide.

Having reached this point, and using the framework of positive design put forward by (Desmet & Pohlmeyer, 2013b), beauty would not only be a source of pleasure in the experience of use (Design for Pleasure), but rather would become essential for digital products to be able to help the majority of people to achieve their personal goals (personal meaning) or to become better people from the moral point of view (design for virtue). Of course, beauty would not guarantee happiness, but would be a means to become part of the initial decision by the users to accept or reject, at first, a specific technology, and, furthermore, to avoid the frustration from a possible feeling of social exclusion or of being beaten by a maze that is impossible to solve.

Accessibility, Usability, and Digital Divide

In terms of the Digital Divide, the problem that we pose is that of the difficulty for certain people to be able to access the technology. That collective can be divided into two main groups: those who suffer a disability and those who are patently unable to understand how certain devices work, reject them, or merely use the technology below the average for the rest of the population.

In the first group, the focus would be on the terms of accessibility of interactive systems, in line with that put forward by ISO (ISO, 2016): "usability of a product, service, environment or facility by people with the widest range of capabilities." Or rather an accessible web, if we follow the W3C (W3C, 2015): "whatever their hardware, software, language, culture, location, or physical or mental ability." However, and even though these definitions cover a wide variety of cases, the term "accessibility" is usually used in the professional context to refer to problems relating to people with some type of disability.

As regards the second group of people, the focus would rather be on usability and user experience, and the difficulties of accessing or rejecting the use of technology would derive from issues relating to age, education, gender, or socioeconomic level (Kontos, Blake, Chou, & Prestin, 2014; Korupp & Szydlik, 2005; Niehaves & Plattfaut, 2014; Rogers, 2016). These circumstances are leading to situations of inequality between different collective both as regards access or capacity to search for information, and in the creation of contents in Internet. In this regard, the study by Kontos et al. (2014) on the use of and access to digital services offered by the public health system in the USA is particularly revealing.

This is where improving usability in its different dimensions (ease of learning, efficiency, attribute of being remembered, effectively, and satisfaction) becomes highly relevant and where a good user experience (UX) defined from the initial design of the product, from its conception, could help to reduce the gap. For example, the widespread use of apps in smartphones with very simple features has meant that a sector of the population that does not use the computer is now able to harness the benefits of having an Internet-connected device. The mainstreaming of the Internet of Things will mean that solutions will soon appear outside the mobile devices appear that are accessible to the majority of people. Proposals such as the *Nest* thermostat app or the mainstreaming of the emergency call systems used by the elderly who live alone may be proof of this.

Thus, the naturalization of the way in which we interact with the technology may, undoubtedly, help to reduce the digital divide, at least with respect to ease of use.

The Role of Beauty in Improving the UX

The user experience (UX) combines different areas based on product design. However, we will focus on the view proposed by Garrett (2011) in his well-known *The Elements of User Experience* diagram as an initial approach. Garrett proposes something that is very common among professionals coming from software design, which consists of separating what they call "visual design" from the rest of the process. This distinction is particularly striking for many information design professionals, used to participating in the whole process, but is widespread in the software industry. Following the premises, beauty could be understood to only lie in the *visual design*, with the other elements/stages of the user experience process not being included. However, any designer knows that the aesthetical perception of the product will depend (and a great deal) not only on the colors, shapes, or font chosen, but also how the elements are arranged on screen, along with the way in which the information is structured. The interaction design and the information architecture are therefore responsible for the final aesthetical outcome of the experience as the visual design itself. In short, usability, as part of the UX, is an important part of that aesthetical perception.

While acknowledging that many more elements than the mere aesthetical perception come into play in the acceptance of a product (for example, as can be seen on the scale of Van Der Laan, Heino, & De Waard, 1997), it is a fact that beauty plays a fundamental role in that acceptance and in the perception of the ease of use of that system is part of its users (Ahmed, Al Mahmud, & Bergaust, 2009; Ben-Bassat, Meyer, & Tractinsky, 2006; David & Glore, 2010; Kurosu & Kashimura, 1995; Lavie & Tractinsky, 2004; Tractinsky, 1997, 2004; Tractinsky, Katz, & Ikar, 2000).

That being said, it is clear that the aesthetics perceived by the users in an interface system fulfills a mission that not only embraces the aesthetic enjoyment—in other words, from an exclusively hedonistic perspective, but also a functional aspect that improves access, experience, and use of that interface. And from that point of view, it can help to reduce the digital divide.

Positive Design, Hedonia, and Eudaimonia

According to Desmet and Pohlmeyer (2013a), the ultimate goal of the design process in positive design must be to design products that help their users to achieve a prosperous life: "It's design for human flourishing." This current, based on positive psychology, is not immune to only 10 percent of happiness being determined by external factors (such as money or living conditions), whereas 40 percent is determined by how we think and act in everyday lives (Lyubomirsky, King, & Diener, 2005), yet it argues that design has a role to play in this regard.

What the Delft School proposes is to approach the design process right from the start with the ultimate goal of improving the subjective well-being of the users with what is designed. A framework is therefore put forward based on three goals toward which the designer must focus each project: design for pleasure, design for personal significance and design for virtue (Desmet & Pohlmeyer, 2013a; Jiménez, Pohlmeyer, & Desmet, 2015). In this regard, both the design of the products and the experiences with them could help to achieve better levels of happiness (they use happiness and subject well-being as synonyms). This would certainly be in a range from "reducing sources of discomfort and ill-being to crafting digital and physical solutions that intentionally promote well-being" (Anna E. Pohlmeyer, 2017). In the first case, and based on Huta (2015), we would be facing a more modest objective, that of reducing frustration, meeting needs, perhaps closer to a hedonic approach or to a hedonic low negativity, and in the second case, of improving happiness in a more ambitious sense. Thus, if we take the four categories of definitions of well-being put forward by (Huta & Waterman, 2014) (orientations, behavior, experience, and functioning), we observe that positive design could work under any of their umbrellas, but even from the most modest, it would helping to improve the well-being of the users to some extent.

In this regard, the proposal of Huta (2015) is highly useful and organizes the different types of experiences used in previous studies into subjective well-being around four factors: eudaimonic; positive hedonic; low negative hedonic, need satisfaction; and personal expressiveness. It is interesting to discover in which way each of these experiences is part of each factor and how some of them share hedonic and eudaimonic factors. As the author points out, happiness is not only about hedonism or eudaimonia, but rather about both:

> People who pursue both hedonia and eudaimonia have higher degrees of well-being than people who pursue only one or the other (Anić & Tončić, 2013; Huta & Ryan, 2010; Peterson, Park, & Seligman, 2005). And people who score high on both hedonic and eudaimonic outcomes have higher degrees of mental health than other individuals (Keyes, 2002).
>
> *(Huta, 2015, p. 19)*

This approach dispels two doubts: 1) That, if this is the case, the experiences generated by the design that are essentially hedonic also help to improve the well-being; and 2) That not only hedonic, but also eudaimonic factors come into play in some of the experiences, as can be seen in Table 29.1.

However, even though the scope of the aforementioned study by Huta (2015) and of the previous one by Huta and Ryan (2010) seems not to cast doubts, studies such as the one by Mekler and Hornbæk (2016) question whether there is such a high correlation between the eudaimonic and hedonic experiences, meaning that, yet again, it needs to be continued in future works.

Table 29.1 Experiences related with digital divide

EXPERIENCES RELATED WITH DIGITAL DIVIDE. HUTA (2015)	Eudaimonic	Positive Hedonic	Low Negative Hedonic, Need Satisfaction	Personal Expressiveness
Negative Affect (Bradburn, 1969)	−.15	−.06	**−.82**	−.04
Negative Affect (Diener & Emmons, 1984; Lyubomirsky et al., 2005)	−.05	−.28	**−.80**	.01
Competence (Gagné, 2003)	.36	.21	**.65**	.07
Life Satisfaction (Diener, Emmons, Larsen, & Griffin, 1985)	**.48**	.38	**.44**	.04
Autonomy (Gagné, 2003)	.33	.25	**.48**	−.03
Carefreeness (Huta & Ryan, 2010)	.15	**.78**	.12	.09
Pleasure (Vittersø, Dyrdal, & Røysamb, 2005) (Vittersø & Søholt, 2011)	.38	**.74**	.39	.17
Positive Affect (Diener & Emmons, 1984)	.36	**.74**	.37	.17
Positive Emotions (Kern & Butler, 2013)	.36	**.66**	.34	.07
Positive Experience (Diener et al., 2009; Lyubomirsky et al., 2005)	.25	**.66**	.39	.08
Positive Affect (Bradburn, 1969)	**.47**	**.48**	.23	.17
Life Satisfaction (Diener et al., 1985)	.48	.38	.44	.04

(source: Huta, 2015).

A Framework to Research into Aesthetics, UX, Digital Divide, and Subjective Well-Being (Hedonic and Eudaimonic)

Considering the experiences analysed by Huta (2015), we can list those that, according to the authors, are closer related to the digital divide and to well-being. They are therefore set out in Table 29.1, which also scores the factor of each of the experiences used by the different authors, and checks how some of them depict hedonic and eudaimonic factors on a level playing field.

An analysis of Table 29.1 shows how the experiences related to aesthetic perception, and its impact on reducing the digital divide, are first related, and in an extraordinarily clear way, with the "Low Negative Hedonic, Need Satisfaction" factor, second, with "Positive Hedonic" and, third, with "Eudaimonic," and not including "Personal Expressiveness":

- Experiences clearly related with satisfying needs such as negative affect (Bradburn, 1969; Diener & Emmons, 1984), where they score-.82 and-.80 respectively
- Experiences clearly aimed at meeting needs, but with appreciable scores in Eudaimonic, such as Competence (Gagné, 2003); Life Satisfaction (Diener et al., 1985) and Autonomy (Gagné, 2003)
- Experiences that clearly score highly in Positive Hedonic, such as Carefreeness (Huta & Ryan, 2010), Positive Affect (Diener & Emmons, 1984), Positive Emotions (Kern & Butler, 2013) and Positive Experience (Diener et al., 2009).
- Experiences relating to the effects of the interaction design that could have a key impact both on Positive Hedonic and on Eudaimonic, as would be the case of Positive Affect (Bradburn, 1969) or Life Satisfaction (Diener et al., 1985), with doubts regarding whether or not that is the case with the latter.

Table 29.2 Partial correlations for eudaimonia and hedonia related with digital divide

PARTIAL CORRELATIONS FOR EUDAIMONIA AND HEDONIA RELATED WITH DIGITAL DIVIDE	VARIABLE	EUDAIMONIA	HEDONIA	t-value
AFFECT	Positive Affect	.50★★	.22★★	3.61★★
	Self-Assurance	.49★★	.20★	3.60★★
NEEDS	Competence	.58★★	-.12	8.63★★
	Security	.40★★	.13★	3.56★★
	Self-Actualization	.47★★	.20★	3.33★★
PRODUCT	Pragmatic Quality	.21★★	.02	1.88

(source: Mekler and Hornbæk (2016).

The study by Huta (2015) allows light to be shed regarding the relationship between certain type of experiences and their pre-eminently hedonic or eudaimonic quality. However, it raises new doubts when relating experiences such as "competence" and "autonomy," with the "Low negative Hedonic" factor and not to such an extent with eudaimonia, as Pohlmeyer had proposed two years earlier: "Eudaimonia relates less to a specific outcome, but more to a way of (virtuous) living and flourishing, e.g. pursuing intrinsic values and goals as well as meeting basic psychological needs of relatedness, competence, and autonomy" (Pohlmeyer, 2013, p. 542).

The more recent paper by Mekler and Hornbæk (2016), which specifically addresses user experience, is in that same line. This study 1) places variables such as Positive Affect, Self-Assurance, Competence, Security, and Self-Actualization much closer to eudaimonic than to hedonic experiences (Table 29.2) and 2) it also shows the high correlation existing between eudaimonia and the experience known as Pragmatic Quality, which in the words of the authors "suggesting that the interactive technology helped users to successfully strive toward their personal goals by being practical and manageable to use."

In short, and at first glance, we find two apparently divergent ways. On the one hand, the one set by Huta (2015) including the positive psychology and, on the other hand, the one put forward from positive design (Mekler & Hornbæk, 2016; Pohlmeyer, 2013) with specific studies. However, this apparent division of opinions may only result from there still being much work to be done as regards experimental research in this field, or that the selections of experiences performed by the authors should be reviewed. Further research may clarify this matter.

Conclusions and Future Lines of Work

Taking into account the role of aesthetics in improving usability and user experience of the interactive user interfaces, it is now time to also assess its responsibility regarding the subjective well-being of those users. Therefore, identifying the specific experiences relating to the digital divide must be soon addressed if future research relating digital divide, aesthetics, and subjective well-being is to be conducted. Thus, the consequences of modifying the aesthetics variable regarding well-being could be identified by means of observing the performance of the different experiences related to the digital divide and to thus establish its specific responsibility regarding hedonic or eudaimonic factors.

Thus, the paper by Mekler and Hornbæk (2016) is of particular interest, as it puts aside the traditional distinction between hedonic and utilitarian or instrumental aspects, by showing, for example, how: ". . . eudaimonic experiences also often mentioned instrumental qualities, such as being able to install some software without help due to easy controls and good usability."

If similar conclusions appear in future research, it could be emphatically argued that beauty, also by means of this channel, would be fostering the happiness of people, both from a hedonic and eudaimonic perspective. It would only remain to be discovered how it is done and if it is to be done in the same way, for example, when taking into account the cultural differences of the users. Several lines of research thus open.

It would also remain to be specified what the role of information architecture or the interaction design is in the aesthetic experiences, which could be another independent line of work.

As regards the research techniques, it would be time to consider whether the neuroscience techniques would also allow some of those types of experiences to be studied reliably. In this regard, the advances made in recent years in the field of neuroaesthetics (Kawabata, 2004; Pearce et al., 2016) could reinforce the reliability of the data-gathering in this type of studies.

References

Ahmed, S. U., Al Mahmud, A., & Bergaust, K. (2009). Aesthetics in human-computer interaction: Views and reviews. *Lecture Notes in Computer Science (Including Subseries Lecture Notes in Artificial Intelligence and Lecture Notes in Bioinformatics), 5610 LNCS(PART 1),* 559–568. https://doi.org/10.1007/978-3-642-02574-7_63

Anić, P., & Tončić, M. (2013). Orientations to happiness, subjective well-being and life goals. *Psihologijske teme, 22,* 135–153.

Ben-Bassat, T., Meyer, J., & Tractinsky, N. (2006). Economic and subjective measures of the perceived value of aesthetics and usability. *ACM Transactions on Computer-Human Interaction, 13*(2), 210–234. https://doi.org/10.1145/1165734.1165737

Bradburn, N. M. (1969). *The structure of psychological well-being.* Chicago, IL: Aldine-Atherton.

David, A., & Glore, P. (2010). The impact of design and aesthetics on usability, credibility, and learning in online courses. *Proceedings of World Conference on E-Learning in Corporate, Government, Healthcare, and Higher Education 2010,* (2004), 42. Retrieved from www.editlib.org/p/35507%5Cnwww.westga.edu/~distance/ojdla/winter134/david_glore134.html

Desmet, P., & Hassenzahl, M. (2012). *Towards happiness: Possibility-driven design* (pp. 3–27). Berlin & Heidelberg: Springer. https://doi.org/10.1007/978-3-642-25691-2_1

Desmet, P., & Pohlmeyer, A. E. (2013a). *Positive design.* Retrieved from https://repository.tudelft.nl/islandora/object/uuid:db7d0dbc-ef9b-404f-801a-2f0a19bb4d14/?collection=research%0Ahttps://repository.tudelft.nl/islandora/object/uuid%3Adb7d0dbc-ef9b-404f-801a-2f0a19bb4d14/datastream/OBJ/view

Desmet, P., & Pohlmeyer, A. E. (2013b). Positive design: An introduction to design for subjective well-being. *International Journal of Design, 7*(3), 5–19. https://doi.org/10.1108/10878571011029028

Diener, E., & Emmons, R. A. (1984). The independence of positive and negative affect. *Journal of Personality and Social Psychology, 47*(5), 1105–1117. https://doi.org/10.1037/0022-3514.47.5.1105

Diener, E., Emmons, R. A., Larsen, R. J., & Griffin, S. (1985). The satisfaction with life scale. *Journal of Personality Assessment, 49*(1), 71–75. https://doi.org/10.1207/s15327752jpa4901_13

Diener, E., Wirtz, D., Tov, W., Kim-Prieto, C., Choi, D. W., Oishi, S., & Biswas-Diener, R. (2009). New well-being measures: Short scales to assess flourishing and positive and negative feelings. *Social Indicators Research, 97*(2), 143–156. https://doi.org/10.1007/s11205-009-9493-y

Gagné, M. (2003). The role of autonomy support and autonomy orientation in prosocial behavior engagement. *Motivation and Emotion, 27*(3), 199–223. https://doi.org/10.1023/A:1025007614869

Garrett, J. J. (2011). *The Elements of User Experience User-Centered Design for the Web and beyond Second Edition* (New Readers Publishing, Ed.) (2nd ed.). Retrieved from www.jjg.net/elements/

Huta, V. (2015). An overview of hedonic and eudaimonic well-being concepts. *Handbook of Media Use and Well-Being,* 14–33. https://doi.org/10.4324/9781315714752

Huta, V., & Ryan, R. M. (2010). Pursuing pleasure or virtue: The differential and overlapping well-being benefits of hedonic and eudaimonic motives. *Journal of Happiness Studies, 11*(6), 735–762. https://doi.org/10.1007/s10902-009-9171-4

Huta, V., & Waterman, A. S. (2014). Eudaimonia and its distinction from hedonia: Developing a classification and terminology for understanding conceptual and operational definitions. *Journal of Happiness Studies, 15*(6), 1425–1456. https://doi.org/10.1007/s10902-013-9485-0

ISO. (2016). *ISO/DIS 9241–11.2 ergonomics of human-system interaction, Part 11: Usability: Definitions and concepts.* Retrieved from www.iso.org/obp/ui/#iso:std:iso:9241:-11:dis:ed-2:v2:en

Jiménez, S., Pohlmeyer, A. E., & Desmet, P. (2015). *Positive design reference guide.* Delft: Delft University of Technology. Retrieved from www.simonjj.com/positive-design-guide/

Kawabata, H. (2004). Neural correlates of beauty. *Journal of Neurophysiology, 91*(4), 1699–1705. https://doi.org/10.1152/jn.00696.2003

Kern, M. L., & Butler, J. (2013, June). *The PERMA-profiler: A brief multidimensional measure of flourishing.* Poster presented at the Third World Congress on Positive Psychology, Los Angeles, CA.

Keyes, C. L. M. (2002). The mental health continuum: From languishing to flourishing in life. *Journal of Health and Social Behavior, 43,* 207–222. doi:10.2307/3090197

Kontos, E., Blake, K. D., Chou, W. Y. S., & Prestin, A. (2014). Predictors of ehealth usage: Insights on the digital divide from the health information national trends survey 2012. *Journal of Medical Internet Research, 16*(7), 1–14. https://doi.org/10.2196/jmir.3117

Korupp, S. E., & Szydlik, M. (2005). Causes and trends of the digital divide. *European Sociological Review, 21*(4), 409–422. https://doi.org/10.1093/esr/jci030

Kurosu, M., & Kashimura, K. (1995). Apparent usability vs. inherent usability: Experimental analysis on the determinants of the apparent usability. *Proceedings of the ACM Conference on Human Factors in Computing Systems,* 292–293. https://doi.org/10.1145/223355.223680

Lavie, T., & Tractinsky, N. (2004). Assessing dimensions of perceived visual aesthetics of web sites. *International Journal of Human-Computer Studies, 60*(3), 269–298.

Lyubomirsky, S., King, L., & Diener, E. (2005). The benefits of frequent positive affect: Does happiness lead to success? *Psychological Bulletin, 131*(6), 803–855. https://doi.org/10.1037/0033-2909.131.6.803

Martín San-Román, J.-R., Suárez Carballo, F., Raposo, D., Galindo Rubio, F., & Rivas Herrero, L. A. (2015). Positive design: Beauty and usability for a better technology environment, (March), 61–65. *Proceedings of the First International Conference for Positive Communication,* Sevilla: Universidad Loyola Andalucía.

Mekler, E. D., & Hornbæk, K. (2016). Momentary pleasure or lasting meaning? *Proceedings of the 2016 CHI Conference on Human Factors in Computing Systems: CHI, 16,* 4509–4520. https://doi.org/10.1145/2858036.2858225

Niehaves, B., & Plattfaut, R. (2014). Internet adoption by the elderly: Employing IS technology acceptance theories for understanding the age-related digital divide. *European Journal of Information Systems, 23*(6), 708–726. https://doi.org/10.1057/ejis.2013.19

Pearce, M. T., Zaidel, D. W., Vartanian, O., Skov, M., Leder, H., Chatterjee, A., & Nadal, M. (2016). Neuroaesthetics: The cognitive neuroscience of aesthetic experience. *Perspectives on Psychological Science, 11*(2), 265–279. https://doi.org/10.1177/1745691615621274

Peterson, C., Park, N., & Seligman, M. E. P. (2005). Orientations to happiness and life satisfaction: The full life versus the empty life. *Journal of Happiness Studies, 6,* 25–41. doi:10.1007/s10902-004-1278-z

Pohlmeyer, A.E. (2013). Positive design: New challenges, opportunities, and responsibilities for design. In: A. Marcus (Ed.): *Design, user experience, and usability, Part III,* HCII 2013, LNCS 8014, pp. 540–547. Berlin: Springer-Verlag.

Pohlmeyer, A. E. (2017). How design can (not) support human flourishing. In *Positive psychology interventions in practice* (pp. 235–255). Cham, Switzerland: Springer International Publishing. https://doi.org/10.1007/978-3-319-51787-2_14

Rogers, S. E. (2016). Bridging the 21st century digital divide. *TechTrends, 60*(3), 197–199. https://doi.org/10.1007/s11528-016-0057-0

Tractinsky, N. (1997). Aesthetics and apparent usability: Empirically assessing cultural and methodological issues. In *Conference on human factors in computing systems* (pp. 115–122). New York: ACM.

Tractinsky, N. (2004). "Toward the study of aesthetics in information technology" *ICIS 2004 Proceedings.* 62. https://aisel.aisnet.org/icis2004/62

Tractinsky, N., Katz, A. S., & Ikar, D. (2000). What is beautiful is usable. *Interacting with Computers, 13*(2), 127–145. https://doi.org/10.1016/S0953-5438(00)00031-X

Van Der Laan, J. D., Heino, A., & De Waard, D. (1997). A simple procedure for the assessment of acceptance of advanced transport telematics. *Transportation Research Part C: Emerging Technologies, 5*(1), 1–10. https://doi.org/10.1016/S0968-090X(96)00025-3

Vitterso, J., Dyrdal, G. M., & Roysamb, E. (2005). Utilities and capabilities: A psychological account of the two concepts and their relation to the idea of a good life. Paper presented at the 2nd Workshop on Capabilities and Happiness. Milan, Italy.

Vitterso, J., & Soholt, Y. (2011). Life satisfaction goes with pleasure and personal growth goes with interest: Further arguments for separating hedonic and eudaimonic well-being. *The Journal of Positive Psychology*, 6(4), 326–335. https://doi.org/10.1080/17439760.2011.584548

W3C. (2015). *Accessibility: W3C*. Retrieved October 9, 2017, from www.w3.org/standards/webdesign/accessibility

Yang, X., Aurisicchio, M., Mackrill, J., & Baxter, W. (2017). On the products and experiences that make us happy. *Proceedings of the International Conference on Engineering Design, ICED, 8*(DS87–8).

30

POPC AND THE GOOD LIFE

A Salutogenic Take on Being Permanently Online, Permanently Connected

Frank M. Schneider, Annabell Halfmann, and Peter Vorderer

What makes a good life? How can we live well? Achieving and sustaining the perhaps most fundamental human aspirations has been a longstanding endeavor in the humanities and in the social sciences (e.g., Delle Fave, 2013; Keyes & Haidt, 2007). Although the various conceptualizations are diverse, most of them share some central characteristics (Park & Peterson, 2009). Seligman (2011), for instance, proposes positive emotions, engagement, relationships, meaning, and accomplishment in his PERMA model as building blocks of well-being. Ryan, Huta, and Deci (2008) characterize living well as eudaimonic living that can be achieved by satisfying the intrinsic needs of autonomy, competence, and relatedness. And Ryff and Singer (1998) emphasize leading a life of purpose and quality connections to others but also include self-realization, personal growth, and mastery.

But how is achieving these goals feasible in a digital world with its constant demands and opportunities? In times of being permanently online and permanently connected (POPC) via ubiquitous mobile devices (Vorderer, Hefner, Reinecke, & Klimmt, 2018; Vorderer et al., 2016), it is a pressing question if such a POPC lifestyle benefits or impairs a good life (Vorderer, 2016). As permanently using instant messengers (IM) and social network sites (SNS) are the main activities carried out on smart devices (e.g., Mihailidis, 2014; Vorderer et al., 2016) and provide the most striking examples of a POPC mindset (Klimmt, Hefner, Reinecke, Rieger, & Vorderer, 2018), research on these topics is integrated and used synonymously with being POPC. POPC is defined as both "1) an overt behavior in the form of protracted use of electronic media and 2) as a psychological state of permanent communicative vigilance" (Vorderer et al., 2016, p. 695). On the one hand, this definition refers to the neutral observation that our daily life is interspersed with digital (online) behavior which per se is neither bad nor good. On the other hand, given the fact that human cognitive capacity is limited, a POPC mindset (Klimmt et al., 2018) may distract us from focusing on what is important to live well (e.g., by losing ourselves to the manifold affordances of mobile devices) and even lead to stressful experiences (e.g., Hefner & Vorderer, 2017). However, it may also facilitate fulfilling basic human needs (e.g., by intensifying and maintaining meaningful connections to others; e.g., Trepte & Oliver, 2018).

To elaborate on this notion, we want to cast light on an approach that has been acknowledged in the health literature but received little attention with regard to positive psychology and positive communication thus far: Drawing on the general idea of salutogenesis (Antonovsky, 1979, 1987)—not focusing on what makes us ill but on how we stay healthy—we therefore offer a new perspective that takes health-supportive and preventive aspects of being POPC into account. Throughout the chapter, we use *salutogenic* or *salutogenesis* rather as umbrella terms that comprise the health-promoting aspects of individuals and society and not specifically as parts of the "model of salutogenesis" (Antonovsky, 1987).

A Salutogenic Perspective

Most of the research on POPC has focused on (1) the negative aspects of POPC, conceiving digital media as pathogenic stressors that are directly related to negative effects on well-being or on (2) positive aspects of POPC like social support or need satisfaction that help us to cope with pathogenic stressors outside the mobile media realm (e.g., Vorderer et al., 2018). From a saluto-genic perspective, however, "stressors" are not seen as necessarily negative but as internal or exter-nal stimuli that may promote health and well-being. The medical sociologist Aaron Antonovsky developed the salutogenesis approach in the 1970s and 1980s as a counter-perspective to the then dominant pathogenic orientation in medicine (Antonovsky, 1979, 1987). He proposed that the human system should not be conceived as usually well-functioning and balanced unless it is torpedoed by pathogenic stressors but as a system that is continuously exposed to unpreventable environmental stimuli. This permanently dealing with ubiquitous stressors leads to tensions. These tensions, however, are only transformed into negative forms of stress, if they are not successfully managed. And managing these tensions mainly depends on internal and external (resistance) resources. Moreover, the human system can rather be located on an "ease—dis-ease continuum" than classified into a health—disease dichotomy (Antonovsky, 1996). Consequently, Antonovsky (e.g., 1996) argues that the concentration on risk factors and pathogenic stressors has to be replaced by focusing on salutary factors (i.e., factors that "actively promote health rather than just being low on risk factors," Antonovsky, 1996, p. 14).

A central concept and resistance resource in the salutogenic framework is the *sense of coher-ence* (SOC, Antonovsky, 1987). SOC has been found to be a positive predictor of general health and quality of life outcomes (e.g., Sagy, Eriksson, & Braun-Lewensohn, 2015), consists of three facets—comprehensibility, manageability, and meaningfulness—and is defined as

> a global orientation that expresses the extent to which one has a pervasive, enduring though dynamic feeling of confidence that (1) the stimuli deriving from one's internal and external environments in the course of living are structured, predictable, and expli-cable; (2) the resources are available to one to meet the demands posed by these stimuli; and (3) these demands are challenges, worthy of investment and engagement.
>
> *(Antonovsky, 1987, p. 19)*

How can such a salutogenic perspective be applied to the notion of being POPC? We think it is crucial to examine the connections between POPC and the sense of coherence and its facets. To understand these links, it is initially helpful to briefly summarize the research on positive and negative effects of POPC.

Does POPC Serve the Good Life and If Yes, How?

Nearly every new medium was accused of having negative effects on its users (e.g., reading books and novels in the 18th century, watching TV, playing video games, etc.). Internet, social media, smartphones are today's targets of the ever-recurring debate of pathological and pathogenic media use. And indeed, the research on negative effects of these media seems to underscore the worst fears: The permanent use of media may create iDisorders (i.e., clinical symptoms of psy-chiatric personality and mood disorders; Rosen, 2012). Admittedly, many researchers critically discuss their correlational and cross-sectional findings as not being evidence for causal relationships. However, what remains is the impression that especially social media use may have large-scale negative consequences, although first meta-analyses revealed only very small effects, for instance, on psychological well-being (e.g., Huang, 2017).

On the other hand, Internet, social media, and mobile phone use have also been found to have positive effects on individuals' well-being (e.g., Reinecke, 2018). Being POPC may serve simple hedonic functions that help to regulate emotions and moods and put its users in a happy state; it may also facilitate the encounter with more complex forms of entertainment that include meaningful communication (Trepte & Oliver, 2018; see also in this volume Oliver & Raney, 2018; Hofer & Rieger, 2018).

In sum, the amount of seemingly contradictory findings suggests that the effects of being POPC rather depend on the media content and features that are used and how they are used, more than on the medium itself and how frequently or long this medium has been used (e.g., Verduyn, Ybarra, Résibois, Jonides, & Kross, 2017; Vogel & Rose, 2016). More specifically, Vorderer (2016) described the current POPC lifestyle as janiform: On the one hand, we have many opportunities to fulfill fundamental human needs such as belongingness, autonomy, meaningfulness that support a good life (cf. Park & Peterson, 2009). On the other hand, "[t]he affordances of new technologies seem to have shifted . . . from an opportunity to an obligation" (Vorderer, 2016, p. 7). However, whether these affordances are perceived as (pathogenic) stressors, supporting resources or salutary challenges, depends on many boundary conditions.

What Are the Conditions Under Which Being POPC Serves the Good Life?

A branch of literature reviews and empirical studies have proposed boundary conditions and processes under which being POPC leads rather to positive or to negative effects. For instance, Verduyn and colleagues (2017) suggested distinguishing between active SNS use that seems to enhance well-being via social capital and connectedness, and passive SNS use that rather undermines well-being via upward social comparison and envy. In a similar vein, Vogel and Rose (2016) argued that other-focused activities on SNS (e.g., visiting the overly positive self-presentations of others) may be detrimental to one's well-being, whereas self-focused activities (e.g., watching and editing one's own SNS profile) may be self-affirming and self-enhancing, and thus beneficial.

Particularly with regard to a salutogenic perspective, Reinecke's (2018, pp. 239–241) thoughts about the role of autonomy-enhancing and autonomy-inhibiting features of POPC merit further consideration. He argues that all kinds of online communication can be seen as "self-determined and intrinsically motivated forms of behavior" (Reinecke, 2018, p. 439) and proposes that users with a POPC mindset (Klimmt et al., 2018) may act online in a natural, autonomously motivated way. Consequently, being POPC may in fact facilitate expressing oneself and accomplishing goals, thereby fostering well-being. However, online communication may also result from internal and external pressures (e.g., Reinecke et al., 2017). In these cases, being POPC could fuel the negative effects of heteronomously motivated online communication on well-being (Reinecke, Vorderer, & Knop, 2014). Reinecke (2018, p. 240, emphasis in original) concludes that

> the chances and risks of living in the "always on" society not so much depend on *whether* an individual is POPC but *how* and *why*. On the one hand, being POPC offers intriguing opportunities for enhanced well-being, particularly when it represents a form of intrinsically motivated, self-determined, and autonomy-enhancing behavior. On the other hand, POPC may increase the vulnerability of Internet users and result in impaired well-being when it is driven by external forces or internal fears and thus represents an externally motivated and autonomy-impeding behavior.

In fact, a current study found that engaging in mobile communication due to external pressure to be available reduced users' autonomy, which, in turn, lowered their well-being and fueled their stress perception (Halfmann, Rieger, & Vorderer, 2017). Although more empirical evidence is still needed, these are intriguing assumptions that are in line with self-determination theory and related approaches to well-being (Deci & Ryan, 2000). To delineate the "hows" and "whys" of being POPC, we would like to go one step further and expand on Reinecke's (2018) ideas. With the facets of the salutogenic concept of SOC—comprehensibility, manageability, and meaningfulness—in mind, we think that three concepts are of crucial importance to this endeavor: mindfulness, self-control, and meaningfulness.

Mindful POPC

Mindfulness can be defined as "a receptive attention to and awareness of present events and experience" (Brown, Ryan, & Creswell, 2007, p. 212; see also in this volume Jones & Youngvorst, 2018). Research provides evidence that mindfulness not only supports autonomous regulation as a predecessor for well-being (e.g., Schultz & Ryan, 2015) but also directly affects psychological health (Keng, Smoski, & Robins, 2011).

Weissbecker and colleagues (2002, p. 299) elaborated on the similarity between mindfulness and the sense of coherence:

> SOC has been described as viewing the world as manageable and understandable, and mindfulness may promote a sense of manageability of the world by fostering more adaptive responses to stress. Mindfulness practice could also enhance SOC because moment-to-moment awareness may facilitate openness and making sense of experiences. Mindfulness may promote a sense of life meaning by simply allowing space for the exploration of meaning. Defined in such terms, mindfulness may bear a striking similarity to SOC, and systematic mindfulness practice might be expected to enhance SOC.

A recent empirical study from Grevenstein, Aguilar-Raab, and Bluemke (2018), who found a high correlation between mindfulness and SOC, support this similarity. Further studies underline this connection too (e.g., Glück, Tran, Raninger, & Lueger-Schuster, 2016) and report that mindfulness-based intervention programs succeeded in positively altering the SOC (e.g., Gimpel et al., 2014; Weissbecker et al., 2002).

Can mindfulness be achieved while being POPC and will it positively affect users' well-being? Research on these questions is scarce but first findings seem to hint into this direction. Mindful instant messaging (IM), for instance, was directly and positively related to well-being, and also enhanced well-being indirectly via fostering the autonomous motivation to use IM (Bauer, Loy, Masur, & Schneider, 2017). Social media use at the workplace was related to positive health outcomes, when users were mindful (Charoensukmongkol, 2016). Mindful awareness was also negatively related to problematic Internet use (Ataşalar & Michou, 2017; Gámez-Guadix & Calvete, 2016).

Self-Controlled POPC

Like mindfulness, trait self-control is related to more conscious mobile media use (Bayer, Dal Cin, Campbell, & Panek, 2016) and shows similarities with the sense of coherence. Self-control refers to "the ability to override or change one's inner responses, as well as to interrupt undesired behavioral tendencies and refrain from acting on them" (Tangney, Baumeister, & Boone, 2004,

p. 275). This requires that individuals deliberately reflect on their goals and values (Hofmann, Friese, & Strack, 2009). Researchers have linked self-control with the manageability facet of sense of coherence: By exerting self-control, individuals may successfully manage interpersonal tensions (emotional self-control; e.g., Nilsson, Starrin, Simonsson, & Leppert, 2007) as well as tensions between behavioral tendencies and endorsed goals (impulse control; e.g., Cederblad, Dahlin, Hagnell, & Hansson, 1994). Indeed, previous studies indicate that both facets of self-control are positively related to sense of coherence (e.g., Forsberg-Wärleby, Möller, & Blomstrand, 2001; Pålsson, R Hallberg, Norberg, & Björvell, 1996). Moreover, results from a longitudinal study revealed that good impulse control in childhood increases people's capacity for manageability (Cederblad et al., 1994). Overall, from a salutogenic perspective, self-control should function as resource for coping with stressors (Antonovsky, 1996), including those resulting from a POPC mindset.

At the same time, however, this mindset challenges users' situational self-control. As explicated above, mobile media permanently provide users with various immediate gratifications, which frequently lead to "situations that demand the resolution of goal conflicts resulting from media temptations" (Hofmann, Reinecke, & Meier, 2017, p. 216). Nevertheless, previous research suggests that, on average, users only sometimes fail to self-control their mobile media use (e.g., Meier, 2017). Moreover, users with high level in trait self-control are more successful in controlling their media use (e.g., Panek, Bayer, Dal Cin, & Campbell, 2015), which Hofmann and colleagues (2017) regard as a precondition for positive effects of the ability to be POPC on users' well-being.

Does self-control enhance a self-determined POPC lifestyle? According to Ryan and Deci (2006), uncontrolled behavior jeopardizes individuals' autonomy, because they do not reflect upon whether this behavior meets their needs: "Some habits and reactions are ones we would experience as autonomous; others seem alien, imposed, or unwanted" (Ryan & Deci, 2006, p. 1573). Self-control should thus enable individuals to prevent externally motivated behavior. With regard to being POPC, social pressure to be available to others seems to be a strong external force that determines users' mobile media use (e.g., Ling, 2012). This pressure may even result in uncontrolled usage, with potentially negative long-term consequences for its users (e.g., reduced accomplishments; Meier, 2017). Importantly, current research suggests that individuals high in self-control are less prone to engage in mobile communication due to this pressure (Halfmann et al., 2017). Consequently, trait self-control may indeed contribute to a more autonomous mobile media usage behavior.

Meaningful POPC

A sense of meaning in life is an important facet of the good life (e.g., Hooker, Masters, & Park, 2018)—maybe even the most important—and seems to be crucial for SOC as well (e.g., Antonovsky, 1987; Grevenstein, Aguilar-Raab, and Bluemke (2018). Recently, Trepte and Oliver (2018) elaborated on the notion of meaningful POPC. In a nutshell, being POPC

> provides users with broad opportunities for meaningfulness, in other words, for the opportunity to tackle meaning-in-life questions. . . users permanently and vigilantly produce and read content that supports them in their need for interconnectedness; they learn from other peoples' lives and stories with the aim of living a fulfilling life; they stay in touch with others to find answers for questions of virtue and wisdom.
>
> *(Trepte & Oliver, 2018, p. 107)*

Given these connections between mindfulness, self-control, meaningfulness, and POPC, we argue that, on the one hand, being POPC may contribute to the development of a strong SOC during socialization, thereby promoting well-being sustainably. The absence of mindful, self-controlled, and meaningful POPC, however, does not necessary lead to a weak SOC because other sources may provide these experiences (e.g., family, community). On the other hand, a strong SOC may work as a buffer against negative forms of stress throughout one's lifespan. Individuals with a strong SOC should perceive less stress, even if they are POPC.

Conclusion

Using a salutogenic perspective, we outlined that the challenges resulting from being POPC are not inherently negative but can be consciously, deliberatively, and meaningfully managed in such a way that they may even promote health and well-being. Instead of propagating the effects of supposedly pathogenic stressors, we encourage future research to focus more strongly on investigating which resources enable mobile media users to stay healthy and experience the constant demands of a POPC lifestyle as salutary.

According to the WHO (1986),

> [h]ealth promotion is the process of enabling people to increase control over, and to improve, their health. To reach a state of complete physical, mental and social well-being, an individual or group must be able to identify and to realize aspirations, to satisfy needs, and to change or cope with the environment. Health is, therefore, seen as a resource for everyday life, not the objective of living. Health is a positive concept emphasizing social and personal resources, as well as physical capacities. Therefore, health promotion is not just the responsibility of the health sector, but goes beyond healthy life-styles to well-being.

Being POPC provides lots of opportunities for individuals to increase their mindful, self-controlled, and meaningful behavior to live well. Like a toolkit, smart mobile devices do not only include means of repairing and fixing broken things but also means of constructing and building new things or deconstructing and rebuilding old ones. Being POPC can be seen as an amplifier (Reinecke, 2018) or as a catalyst for such processes. However, this promotes health only if users are in control and aware of these processes, if they are autonomously motivated to use mobile media to its full advantage (Reinecke, 2018) and to realize meaningful experiences. If individuals, however, use such devices but do so in a non-purposely and non-mindfully way, they run the risk of losing control and being motivated rather heteronomously.

In sum, we believe that mobile media use can establish a sense of coherence and meaning in life. Being POPC may also force individuals to permanently reflect their goals and aspirations and make them wonder if their activities serve their intrinsic needs. Or to cite Gui, Fasoli, and Carradore (2017, p. 166): "in the long term and at a deeper level of analysis, being able to channel digital media toward individuals' personal and professional goals becomes relevant for a full self-realization in life" (Ryff & Singer, 1998). We believe that developing appropriate skills should be a central aspect of media literacy and competence in general as using mobile media in a mindful, self-controlled, and meaningful way may be more important these days than ever before.

References

Antonovsky, A. (1979). *Health, stress, and coping.* San Francisco, CA: Jossey-Bass Publishers.
Antonovsky, A. (1987). *Unraveling the mystery of health: How people manage stress and stay well.* San Francisco, CA: Jossey-Bass Publishers.
Antonovsky, A. (1996). The salutogenic model as a theory to guide health promotion. *Health Promotion International, 11*, 11–18. https://doi.org/10.1093/heapro/11.1.11

Ataşalar, J., & Michou, A. (2017). Coping and mindfulness: Mediators between need satisfaction and generalized problematic Internet use. *Journal of Media Psychology*. Advance online publication. https://doi.org/10.1027/1864-1105/a000230

Bauer, A. A., Loy, L. S., Masur, P. K., & Schneider, F. M. (2017). Mindful instant messaging: Mindfulness and autonomous motivation as predictors of well-being and stress in smartphone communication. *Journal of Media Psychology, 29*, 159–165. https://doi.org/10.1027/1864-1105/a000225

Bayer, J. B., Dal Cin, S., Campbell, S. W., & Panek, E. (2016). Consciousness and self-regulation in mobile communication. *Human Communication Research, 42*, 71–97. https://doi.org/10.1111/hcre.12067

Brown, K. W., Ryan, R. M., & Creswell, J. D. (2007). Mindfulness: Theoretical foundations and evidence for its salutary effects. *Psychological Inquiry, 18*, 211–237. https://doi.org/10.1080/10478400701598298

Cederblad, M., Dahlin, L., Hagnell, O., & Hansson, K. (1994). Salutogenic childhood factors reported by middle-aged individuals: Follow-up of the children from the Lundby study grown up in families experiencing three or more childhood psychiatric risk factors. *European Archives of Psychiatry and Clinical Neuroscience, 244*, 1–11. https://doi.org/10.1007/BF02279805

Charoensukmongkol, P. (2016). Mindful Facebooking: The moderating role of mindfulness on the relationship between social media use intensity at work and burnout. *Journal of Health Psychology, 21*, 1966–1980. https://doi.org/10.1177/1359105315569096

Deci, E. L., & Ryan, R. M. (2000). The "what" and "why" of goal pursuits: Human needs and the self-determination of behavior. *Psychological Inquiry, 11*, 227–268. https://doi.org/10.1207/S15327965PLI1104_01

Delle Fave, A. (Ed.). (2013). *The exploration of happiness: Present and future perspectives.* Dordrecht, NL: Springer.

Forsberg-Wärleby, G., Möller, A., & Blomstrand, C. (2001). Spouses of first-ever stroke victims: Sense of coherence in the first phase after stroke. *Journal of Rehabilitation Medicine, 34*, 128–133. https://doi.org/10.1161/01.STR.32.7.1646

Gámez-Guadix, M., & Calvete, E. (2016). Assessing the relationship between mindful awareness and problematic Internet use among adolescents. *Mindfulness, 7*, 1281–1288. https://doi.org/10.1007/s12671-016-0566-0

Gimpel, C., Scheidt, C. von, Jose, G., Sonntag, U., Stefano, G. B., Michalsen, A., & Esch, T. (2014). Changes and interactions of flourishing, mindfulness, sense of coherence, and quality of life in patients of a mind-body medicine outpatient clinic. *Forschende Komplementarmedizin, 21*, 154–162. https://doi.org/10.1159/000363784

Glück, T. M., Tran, U. S., Raninger, S., & Lueger-Schuster, B. (2016). The influence of sense of coherence and mindfulness on PTSD symptoms and posttraumatic cognitions in a sample of elderly Austrian survivors of World War II. *International Psychogeriatrics, 28*, 435–441. https://doi.org/10.1017/S104161021500143X

Grevenstein, D., Aguilar-Raab, C., & Bluemke, M. (2018). Mindful and resilient? Incremental validity of sense of coherence over mindfulness and big five personality factors for quality of life outcomes. *Journal of Happiness Studies, 19*(7), 1883–1902. https://doi.org/10.1007/s10902-017-9901-y

Gui, M., Fasoli, M., & Carradore, R. (2017). "Digital well-being": Developing a new theoretical tool for media literacy research. *Italian Journal of Sociology of Education, 9*, 155–173. https://doi.org/10.14658/pupj-ijse-2017-1-8

Halfmann, A., Rieger, D., & Vorderer, P. (2017). Who determines your mobile communication? The effects of social pressure on self-control, need satisfaction, well-being, and perceived stress. *Manuscript in preparation.*

Hefner, D., & Vorderer, P. (2017). Digital stress: Permanent connectedness and multitasking. In L. Reinecke & M. B. Oliver (Eds.), *The Routledge handbook of media use and well-being* (pp. 237–249). New York, NY: Routledge.

Hofer, M., & Rieger, D. (2018). On being happy through entertainment: Hedonic and non-hedonic entertainment experiences. In J. A. Muñiz-Velázquez & C. Pulido (Eds.). *The Routledge handbook of positive communication* (pp. 120–128). New York, NY: Routledge.

Hofmann, W., Friese, M., & Strack, F. (2009). Impulse and self-control from a dual-systems perspective. *Perspectives on Psychological Science, 4*, 162–176. https://doi.org/10.1111/j.1745-6924.2009.01116.x

Hofmann, W., Reinecke, L., & Meier, A. (2017). Of sweet temptations and bitter aftertaste: Self-control as a moderator of the effects of media use on well-being. In L. Reinecke & M. B. Oliver (Eds.), *The Routledge handbook of media use and well-being* (pp. 211–222). New York, NY: Routledge.

Hooker, S. A., Masters, K. S., & Park, C. L. (2018). A meaningful life is a healthy life: A conceptual model linking meaning and meaning salience to health. *Review of General Psychology, 22*(1), 11–24. https://doi.org/10.1037/gpr0000115

Huang, C. (2017). Time spent on social network sites and psychological well-being: A meta-analysis. *Cyberpsychology, Behavior, and Social Networking, 20*, 346–354. https://doi.org/10.1089/cyber.2016.0758

Jones, S. M., & Youngvorst, L. J. (2018). Supportive and mindful communication. In J. A. Muñiz-Velázquez & C. Pulido (Eds.), *The Routledge Handbook of Positive Communication* (pp. 89–97). New York, NY: Routledge.

Keng, S.-L., Smoski, M. J., & Robins, C. J. (2011). Effects of mindfulness on psychological health: A review of empirical studies. *Clinical Psychology Review, 31*, 1041–1056. https://doi.org/10.1016/j.cpr.2011.04.006

Keyes, C. L. M., & Haidt, J. (Eds.). (2007). *Flourishing: Positive psychology and the life well-lived* (4th print). Washington, DC: American Psychological Association.

Klimmt, C., Hefner, D., Reinecke, L., Rieger, D., & Vorderer, P. (2018). The permanently online and permanently connected mind: Mapping the cognitive structures behind mobile internet use. In P. Vorderer, D. Hefner, L. Reinecke, & C. Klimmt (Eds.), *Permanently online, permanently connected: Living and communicating in a POPC world* (pp. 18–28). New York, NY: Routledge.

Ling, R. (2012). *Taken for grantedness: The embedding of mobile communication into society.* Cambridge, UK: MIT Press.

Meier, A. (2017, May). *Neither pleasurable nor virtuous: Procrastination links smartphone habits and messenger checking behavior to decreased hedonic as well as eudaimonic well-being.* Presentation at the 67th Annual Conference of the International Communication Association (ICA), San Diego, CA.

Mihailidis, P. (2014). A tethered generation: Exploring the role of mobile phones in the daily life of young people. *Mobile Media & Communication, 2*, 58–72. https://doi.org/10.1177/2050157913505558

Nilsson, K. W., Starrin, B., Simonsson, B., & Leppert, J. (2007). Alcohol-related problems among adolescents and the role of a sense of coherence. *International Journal of Social Welfare, 16*, 159–167. https://doi.org/10.1111/j.1468-2397.2006.00452.x

Oliver, M. B., & Raney, A. A. (2018). Positive media psychology: Emerging scholarship and a roadmap for emerging technologies. In J. A. Muñiz-Velázquez & C. Pulido (Eds.), *The Routledge handbook of positive communication* (pp. 111–119). New York, NY: Routledge.

Pålsson, M.-B., R Hallberg, I., Norberg, A., & Björvell, H. (1996). Burnout, empathy and sense of coherence among Swedish district nurses before and after systematic clinical supervision. *Scandinavian Journal of Caring Sciences, 10*, 19–26. https://doi.org/10.1111/j.1471-6712.1996.tb00305.x

Panek, E. T., Bayer, J. B., Dal Cin, S., & Campbell, S. W. (2015). Automaticity, mindfulness, and self-control as predictors of dangerous texting behavior. *Mobile Media & Communication, 3*, 383–400. https://doi.org/10.1177/2050157915576046

Park, N., & Peterson, C. (2009). Achieving and sustaining a good life. *Perspectives on Psychological Science, 4*, 422–428. https://doi.org/10.1111/j.1745-6924.2009.01149.x

Reinecke, L. (2018). POPC and well-being: A risk-benefit analysis. In P. Vorderer, D. Hefner, L. Reinecke, & C. Klimmt (Eds.), *Permanently online, permanently connected: Living and communicating in a POPC world* (pp. 233–243). New York, NY: Routledge.

Reinecke, L., Aufenanger, S., Beutel, M. E., Dreier, M., Quiring, O., Stark, B., . . . Müller, K. W. (2017). Digital stress over the life span: The effects of communication load and internet multitasking on perceived stress and psychological health impairments in a German probability sample. *Media Psychology, 20*, 90–115. https://doi.org/10.1080/15213269.2015.1121832

Reinecke, L., Vorderer, P., & Knop, K. (2014). Entertainment 2.0? The role of intrinsic and extrinsic need satisfaction for the enjoyment of Facebook use. *Journal of Communication, 64*, 417–438. https://doi.org/10.1111/jcom.12099

Rosen, L. D. (2012). *iDisorder: Understanding our obsession with technology and overcoming its hold on us.* New York, NY: Palgrave Macmillan.

Rosen, L. D., Whaling, K., Carrier, L. M., Cheever, N. A., & Rokkum, J. (2013). The media and technology usage and attitudes scale: An empirical investigation. *Computers in Human Behavior, 29*(6), 2501–2511.

Ryan, R. M., & Deci, E. L. (2006). Self-regulation and the problem of human autonomy: Does psychology need choice, self-determination, and will? *Journal of Personality, 74*, 1557–1585. https://doi.org/10.1111/j.1467-6494.2006.00420.x

Ryan, R. M., Huta, V., & Deci, E. L. (2008). Living well: A self-determination theory perspective on eudaimonia. *Journal of Happiness Studies, 9*, 139–170. https://doi.org/10.1007/s10902-006-9023-4

Ryff, C. D., & Singer, B. (1998). The contours of positive human health. *Psychological Inquiry, 9*, 1–28. https://doi.org/10.1207/s15327965pli0901_1

Sagy, S., Eriksson, M., & Braun-Lewensohn, O. (2015). The salutogenic paradigm. In S. Joseph (Ed.), *Positive psychology in practice: Promoting human flourishing in work, health, education, and everyday life* (2nd ed., pp. 61–79). Hoboken, NJ: Wiley.

Schultz, P. P., & Ryan, R. M. (2015). The "why," "what," and "how" of healthy self-regulation: Mindfulness and well-being from a self-determination theory perspective. In B. D. Ostafin, M. D. Robinson, & B. P. Meier (Eds.), *Handbook of mindfulness and self-regulation* (pp. 81–94). New York, NY: Springer.

Seligman, M. E. P. (2011). *Flourish: A visionary new understanding of happiness and well-being.* New York, NY: Free Press.

Tangney, J. P., Baumeister, R. F., & Boone, A. L. (2004). High self-control predicts good adjustment, less pathology, better grades, and interpersonal success. *Journal of Personality, 72,* 271–324. https://doi.org/10.1111/j.0022-3506.2004.00263.x

Trepte, S., & Oliver, M. B. (2018). Getting the best out of POPC while keeping the risks in mind: The calculus of meaningfulness and privacy. In P. Vorderer, D. Hefner, L. Reinecke, & C. Klimmt (Eds.), *Permanently online, permanently connected: Living and communicating in a POPC world* (pp. 107–115). New York, NY: Routledge.

Verduyn, P., Ybarra, O., Résibois, M., Jonides, J., & Kross, E. (2017). Do social network sites enhance or undermine subjective well-being? A critical review. *Social Issues and Policy Review, 11,* 274–302. https://doi.org/10.1111/sipr.12033

Vogel, E. A., & Rose, J. P. (2016). Self-reflection and interpersonal connection: Making the most of self-presentation on social media. *Translational Issues in Psychological Science, 2,* 294–302. https://doi.org/10.1037/tps0000076

Vorderer, P., & Kohring, M. (2013). Permanently online: A challenge for media and communication research. *International Journal of Communication, 7,* 188–196.

Vorderer, P. (2016). Communication and the good life: Why and how our discipline should make a difference. *Journal of Communication, 66,* 1–12. https://doi.org/10.1111/jcom.12194

Vorderer, P., Hefner, D., Reinecke, L., & Klimmt, C. (Eds.). (2018). *Permanently online, permanently connected: Living and communicating in a POPC world.* New York, NY: Routledge.

Vorderer, P., Krömer, N., & Schneider, F. M. (2016). Permanently online: Permanently connected: Explorations into university students' use of social media and mobile smart devices. *Computers in Human Behavior, 63,* 694–703. https://doi.org/10.1016/j.chb.2016.05.085

Weissbecker, I., Salmon, P., Studts, J. L., Floyd, A. R., Dedert, E. A., & Sephton, S. E. (2002). Mindfulness-Based Stress Reduction and sense of coherence among women with fibromyalgia. *Journal of Clinical Psychology in Medical Settings, 9,* 297–307. https://doi.org/10.1023/A:1020786917988

WHO. (1986). *The Ottawa Charter for health promotion.* Retrieved from www.who.int/healthpromotion/conferences/previous/ottawa/en/

31

WEARABLES FOR HUMAN FLOURISHING

David Varona and Javier Nó-Sánchez

Introduction

If there is one form of technology that perfectly defines the state of technical evolution experienced by advanced societies at the height of 2017, it is wearable technologies. Efforts to bring computing to the most trivial areas of life and to the most intimate and most important; efforts to connect any object capable of generating relevant information for a network; and the spirit of miniaturizing device and rendering connected devices more powerful are contained in wearable technologies. Such tools are increasingly becoming more present in the lives of individuals and even those who are not particularly fond of electronic gadgets or of the digital domain.

When we speak about wearable technologies, we must start by focusing on the so-called Internet of Things (IoT), which according to Xia, Yang, Wang, and Vinel (2012, p. 1101) "refers to the networked interconnection of everyday objects, which are often equipped with ubiquitous intelligence." Among these everyday connected objects, wearables are devices that are worn. They can be glasses, watches, accessories (including jewelry), shoes and clothes. They are according to Canhoto and Arp (2017, p. 50) "machine to human IoT devices, embedded with Internet connectivity, and with the capability of colleting, storing and transmitting data."

The constant proliferation of these wearable devices greatly promotes the expansion of the Internet of Things itself, constituting one of its main growth vectors and expanding the digital ecosystem. In fact, private devices are expanding the most. Consultant Gartner (2017) estimates that 8.4 billion connected devices are being used as of 2017 (20 billion for 2020), of which 5,2 billion or 63 percent are objects owned by end users.

Therefore, the IoT and wearable devices not only expand, but they do especially thanks to the momentum of individual users, who largely recognize their utility and potential. It should therefore be noted that this form of technology is being adopted in a decided manner by the public, a conclusion also made by authors such as Castro and McQuinn (2015, p. 22) and Deacon (2014).

In addition, there are some areas in which wearable technologies are already being used on a regular basis. One area of note, for example, is medical use. In the field of medicine, devices of this type have been used for a long-time to improve the conditions of patients. In fact, it is this field together with psychology that has generated the most scientific literature on wearables, including a very recent paper by Wang, Markopoulos, Yu, and Chen (2017) on the use of wearables for the rehabilitation of patients, Ajami and Teimouri's (2015) work on the use of biosensors, and Matthews and colleagues's (2015) work on the use of wearable cameras for the treatment of dementia.

These are only recent works, as countless articles have addressed this form of technology in the field of medical sciences and psychology while relatively few have addressed the area from other disciplines such as communication.

Despite this lack of attention and given the emergence of this form of technology, it is worth asking what its effects will be on society and regarding our approach to the phenomenon what its effects will be on the welfare of people. We are interested in understanding whether wearable technologies can have beneficial effects on individuals and thus whether wearables can be considered positive technologies. We are also interested in determining this from the field of communication and based on the rich digital ecosystem generated by new information and communication technologies, which are also understood as happiness and positive digital technologies.

Positive technologies and especially those of communication have already been widely described by Riva (2012); Botella et al. (2012) and especially by Riva, Ban, Botella, Wiedehold, and Gaggioli (2012, p. 70), who note that these technologies seek "to manipulate and enhance the features of our personal experience with the goal of increasing wellness, and generating strengths and resilience in individuals, organizations, and society."

The works of Riva and his colleagues are related to those of Seligman (2002) and they endorse the "three pillars" of the "good life": the pleasant life, the engaged life and the meaningful life. From this frame of reference, they classify positive technologies as hedonic, eudaimonic, and social/interpersonal "according to their effects on these three features of personal experience" (Riva, 2012, p. 71).

Here, we are especially interested in discussing Riva et al.'s eudaimonic technologies, which are "used to support individuals in reaching engaging and self-actualizing experiences" (Riva, 2012, p. 71). That is, such technologies allow human beings to achieve full, conscious, and decisive happiness and personal fulfillment (see also in this volume Riva, Serino, Chirico, & Gaggioli, 2018). The concept is also associated with the psychological well-being and growth of a person as a human being (Hefferon & Boniwell, 2011, p. 88) and with the notion that the arrival of wearable technologies could forge a new path in the quest for eudaimonic happiness.

Wearable Technologies for Information and Knowledge

Can we say that wearables are positive technologies that contribute to eudaimonic happiness? A priori, not all devices or uses contribute to this goal. Some are more oriented toward hedonic happiness while others contribute more to the social/interpersonal approach. However, some cases exemplify how these devices can contribute to the development of eudaimonic happiness.

The development of eudaimonic happiness is related to an orientation toward virtue. Without having to resort to classical notions of virtue, we can find a frame of reference for this value from Peterson and Seligman (2004), who established a classification of six virtues and 24 character strengths that allow us to aspire toward eudaimonic happiness, a classification that is addressed by other authors of this same manual.

Later Seligman evolved his concepts to discuss "human flourishing" (Seligman, 2011, p. 24), an idea that is based on what he calls the PERMA model, which involves the union of five elements among which positive emotions, commitment, and positive relationships are at the forefront. Seligman believes that true well-being and therefore true happiness are achieved by serving an end greater than oneself and by remaining aware of the relevance of achievements: "to set motivating goals to continue growing vitally" (Muñiz-Velázquez, 2015, p. 51). That path toward flourishing complements the hedonic and eudaimonic visions of happiness, which converge in an integrated vision wherein strengths of character are used fully at the service of achieving well-being that is full happiness.

From this frame of thought and taking strengths into account, we find several areas to which wearable technology could contribute or at least serve as a mediator of this process.

If we take the strengths of wisdom and knowledge, which include creativity, curiosity, the openness of mind, love of knowing, and perspective (Peterson & Seligman, 2004, p. 93) into account, we can find related applications of wearable technologies and especially in the field of communication. We also identify the environment of happiness and positive digital technologies described above to better frame this observation.

According this approach, curiosity and love of knowing are the strengths most enjoyed through the emergence of this new technology. Our example is recurrent but illustrative: Google Glass. These and other glasses connected to the Internet allow one to retrieve information in a simple manner through voice commands while keeping one's hands free to engage in any other activity. Information is projected onto the pupils of the user, who can read, see photographs or videos, consult maps, etc. A device of this type used permanently before the user's eyes exponentially multiplies possibilities to satisfy one's curiosity, to inform oneself and to acquire knowledge on any issue.

In the same vein, connected watches or smartwatches offer such opportunities, although interactions with the interface differ greatly from those offered by headset-type devices such as glasses. However, access to information and knowledge is also immediate and thus these connected watches help satisfy one's curiosity and the need to know something at any time.

Creativity, another strength of wisdom and knowledge, is implicit in the development of applications for wearable technology. However, devices can stimulate it. In the case of children, for example, a wearable device (a watch or bracelet) can be a wonderful playmate that proposes challenges or complements toys through a child's pedagogical mission.

Even intrapersonal communication (Muñiz-Velázquez, 2015, p. 63) can benefit from the emergence of such technologies: they provide information that can be immediately incorporated into "self-talk" as discussed by authors such as Puchalska-Wasyl (2015, p. 444).

Such gadgets are relatively simple; wearables such as watches or bracelets do not offer much more than what smartphones already provide. They offer different functions as shown below, and their ways of interacting with information are already known. However, future advances will lead to transcendent advances in the ways that we relate to wearables. This is the case for eye lenses. Several manufacturers such as Samsung are already developing contact lenses that will offer connectivity and the capacity to display and record information.

With devices of this type, the power of wearables is transformed. They completely free the user and are virtually invisible to others and allow one to receive information in an intimate manner that enters the realm of biology. Just a few steps away are biotechnological solutions that will allow us to use implants connected to our bodies. Contact lenses constitute a gateway to this bionic technology that promises access to knowledge that is much more personal, complex, and efficient.

Wearables and Other Character Strengths

Let us now examine other strengths such as courage, which includes bravery, persistence, integrity, and vitality (Peterson & Seligman, 2004, p. 198). Here again we can find aspects and uses through which wearable technologies can reinforce such values. For example, in the field of sports, wearables are being used extensively. Athletes of any discipline support their training with wristbands, watches, and even connected shirts and slippers. These objects are able to monitor their physical condition and sports performance. With this information, such wearables become ideal assistants for setting objectives and for encouraging the athlete to achieve them, encouraging persistence that is at the core of courage.

They serve in the same vein to support vitality. This strength is closely linked to the subjective experience of feeling alive and energetic. The information provided by wearables on the physical state of the user can reinforce this feeling. Information on good health and body functioning can be perfectly known using wearable devices and so the user has more reasons to notice this vitality and to use it in the service of well-being and happiness.

Peterson and Seligman (2004) also speak of the strengths of humanity, such as love, social intelligence, and goodness; strengths of justice such as citizenship, impartiality, and leadership; strengths of temperance such as clemency, humility, prudence, and self-regulation; and strengths of transcendence such as the appreciation of beauty, gratitude, hope, humor, and spirituality.

In this case, wearables have a narrower scope of action, but they have much to offer. Indeed, already in 1997 Picard and Healey spoke of "affective wearables." Their work noted that "equipped with special sensors and tools from signal processing and pattern recognition, a wearable computer can potentially learn to recognize physical and psychological patterns, especially those which correspond to affective states—such as when you are fearful, stressed, relaxed, or happily engaged in a task" (Picard & Healey, 1997, p. 90).

Wearables have changed considerably since the works of Picard and Healey. However, the notion that machines can identify the moods of people is still very much alive. In medical applications it is common to use such devices to monitor the physical and mental conditions of patients; however, more attractive uses linked to well-being are beginning to become known.

Using clothes and gadgets such as bracelets or even jewelry, one can determine the emotional state of a person. One can even determine whether someone is afraid or stressed. This information can also be combined with other more common data on weather or traffic patterns. In addition, information from social networks can be obtained in addition to knowledge of content that a user has published.

All in all, it is possible to very precisely determine the state that a person occupies and to allow connected devices to make decisions (load a specific list of music into a car, illuminate a house in a way that synchronizes with the mood of the person who arrives, modify refrigeration temperatures, etc.). That is, improved conditions that support self-regulation, humor or even social intelligence can be reinforced.

The case of social intelligence allows us to go one step further: through contact, wearables can warn other users that their owners are sad, angry, nervous, or scared. With this information, it is easier to approach a person and empathize with him or her, to help him or her and to better understand what has happened to him or her as social intelligence advocates.

In this same line of work there are fields in which this knowledge of a user's mood is combined with the acquisition of knowledge or with the enjoyment of content in a very intelligent manner. For example, beyond being used to select a playlist or movie that betters the mood of a person, content can respond to a given mood. There is already talk of reactive content (Alcalá, 2015) that changes as a user reacts to it.

The production of reactive content can function based on different itineraries and levels so that depending on the mood of a user or spectator, various routes are proposed. For example, if one is watching a frightening movie on television and one's wearable detects excessive levels of stress and fear, it can inform the television, which can select a variant of the movie that produces less fear. This necessitates extra effort when creating products, but it supports consumer experiences that are much more pleasant for users, thus their curiosity, persistence, self-regulation and even humor.

Ethical Considerations

As we show, wearables can help people in countless ways, from facilitating leisure to promoting health. Further, it seems that they can contribute to the reinforcement of important strengths of character. However, it is also important to draw attention to the ethical implications of these devices and to their potential misuses.

Many authors have already noted ethical problems that can result from the use of wearable technologies. Perhaps the most contested devices are connected glasses due to their ability to take photos and videos without anyone noticing, which for many constitutes an attack on users' privacy.

Castro and McQuinn (2015) have investigated the fears that some technologies produce and note that wearables are feared most after behavioral advertising and facial recognition technologies (2015, p. 20). The same authors note that in the case of glasses and specifically for Google Glass, there have been opposing reactions even through "over the last decade, we have been able to interact positively with them" (Castro & McQuinn, 2015, p. 23). Other authors are far more pessimistic, like Wagner (2013, p. 490) who argues that "as the use of Google Glass becomes widespread, people will be hard-pressed to go anywhere in public without being recorded by a Google Glass device. This will allow data aggregators to turn the current state of 'big data' into 'massive data' with minimal costs."

Wagner's dark—and for now unfulfilled—prediction reveals one of the great ethical problems that underlie the field of wearables, that of big data. Beyond aggressions on privacy that the cameras of connected glasses can entail, there is a growing preoccupation with what happens to data collected through these devices. This information is stored in wearables in large volumes and is offered to the user to use from other devices such as smartphones or computers. However, does anyone else have access to these data? In many cases, users do not know.

This issue is delicate, as much data that wearables collect on users are private. Information is stored on one's health, moods, routines, and even habits. All of this information is very valuable and allows companies of all forms to use the personal data of users, to make personalized and unwanted offers and to offer or deny services. In an extreme case, an insurer may deny life insurance to a person based on what they know of their health thanks to information obtained from a wearable.

Therefore, privacy, in many of its expressions, can be threatened by wearables and this must be taken into account in the development and use of technologies. Ethical conditions must have as much presence in the design and production of wearables as issues of security, for example. In fact, some works point in this direction and equate security constraints of hardware with those of privacy.

Even in academic research these reflections have already been made and several authors have focused on the ethical implications of using wearables. This is the case for Mok, Cornish, and Tarr (2014) and for Shipp, Skatova, Blum, and Brown (2014), who warn of this problem in pointing to ethical problems that the use of wearable cameras can create for research and especially for research conducted in the medical and psychological fields. Furthermore, as is the case for the Shipp team, means to minimize the impacts of wearables on research subjects are proposed (Shipp et al., 2014, p. 5).

Wearables as Positive Technologies

We show here what wearable devices are, roles they play in the so-called IoT and their impacts on the current digital ecosystem with a special emphasis on new forms of communication and information. In regard to strengths of character, we have seen examples through which such technologies can help or mediate in the reinforcement of these strengths and in this way contribute to "human flourishing" of which Seligman spoke (2011).

This contribution is especially evident from so-called strengths of wisdom, but we have also found applications to other forms of strength. We have even taken into account ethical considerations that affect wearable devices, which should also be considered when evaluating such technologies.

Therefore, and although the forced brevity of this chapter does not allow us to explore the matter fully, we believe it is pertinent to conclude that wearables are positive technologies. Their rational, conscious, and ethically oriented use allows the user to reinforce and exercise several fundamental strengths in the construction of eudaimonic happiness and flourishing as outlined at the beginning of this paper.

We argue that these devices can also facilitate the development strengths that a user may not have fully deployed in working on traits of empathy or persistence. Concepts such as resilience can also be linked to this type of apparatus.

Positive technologies are becoming more prominent with the emergence of such tools, which are easily linked to other tools such as virtual and augmented reality devices or smartphones. In the future, research on corresponding positive effects on individuals and perhaps on societies should be conducted. It will be necessary to analyze if such positive technologies are improving the well-being of people and helping them achieve eudaimonic happiness.

References

Ajami, S., & Teimouri, F. (2015). Features and application of wearable biosensors in medical care. *Journal of Research in Medical Sciences, 20*(12 OP—*Journal of Research in Medical Sciences, 20*(12), 1208–1215 (2015)), 1208. http://doi.org/10.4103/1735-1995.172991

Alcalá, N. (2015, November). *Contenido Reactivo.* Innovación Audiovisual. Retrieved from https://innovacionaudiovisual.com/2015/11/02/contenido-reactivo/

Botella, C., Riva, G., Gaggioli, A., Wiederhold, B. K., Alcañiz, M., & Baños, R. M. (2012b). The present and future of positive technologies. *Cyberpsychology, Behavior and Social Networking, 15*(2), 1–7.

Canhoto, A. I., & Arp, S. (2017). Exploring the factors that support adoption and sustained use of health and fitness wearables use of health and fitness wearables. *Journal of Marketing Management, 33*(1–2), 32–60. http://doi.org/10.1080/0267257X.2016.1234505

Castro, D., & Mcquinn, A. (2015). *The privacy panic cycle: A guide to public fears about new technologies.* Washington, DC. Retrieved form www2.itif.org/2015-privacy-panic.pdf?_ga=2.75258706.119499753.149 7265936-929027762.1497265936

Deacon, H. (2014). *Smartwatches and smart bands dominate fast-growing wearables market.* Retrieved from www.ccsinsight.com/press/company-news/1944-smartwatches-and-smartbands-dominate-fast-growing-wearables-market

Gartner. (2017). *Garnert says 8.4 billion connected "things" will be in use in 2017, up 31 per cent from 2016.* Retrieved from www.gartner.com/newsroom/id/3598917

Hefferon, K., & Boniwell, I. (2011). *Positive psychology: Theory, research and applications.* Maidenhead: McGraw-Hill.

Matthews, J. T., Lingler, J. H., Campbell, G. B., Hunsaker, A. E., Hu, L., Pires, B. R., & Schulz, R. (2015). Usability of a wearable camera system for dementia family caregivers. *Journal of Healthcare Engineering, 6*(2 OP—*Journal of Healthcare Engineering, 6*(2), 213–238 (2015)), 213. http://doi.org/10.1260/204 0-2295.6.2.213

Mok, T. M., Cornish, F., & Tarr, J. (2014). Too much information: Visual research ethics in the age of wearable cameras. *Integrative Psychological and Behavioral Science, 49*(2), 309–322. http://doi.org/10.1007/s12124-014-9289-8

Muñiz-Velázquez, J. A. (2015). La Comunicación Eudaimónica: Confluencias entre la Comunicación y la Felicidad. *Comunication & Social Change, 3*(1), 48–76. http://doi.org/10.17583/csc.2015.1775

Peterson, C., & Seligman, M. E. P. (2004). *Character strengths and virtues: A handbook and classification.* Washington, DC: American Psychological Association.

Picard, R. W., & Healey, J. (1997). Affective wearables. Digest of Papers. *First International Symposium on Wearable Computers,* 90–97. https://doi.org/10.1007/BF01682026

Picard, R. W., & Healey, J. (1997). Affective wearables. *Personal Technologies,* 1 (4) 231–240.

Puchalska-Wasyl, M. M. (2015). Self-talk: Conversation with oneself? On the types of internal interlocutors. *Journal of Psychology, 149*(5), 443–460. http://10.1080/00223980.2014.896772

Riva, G. (2012). What is positive technology and its impact on cyber psychology. In B. K. Wiederhold & G. Riva (Eds.), *Annual review of cybertherapy and telemedicine 2012: Advances technologies* (pp. 37–41). Amsterdam: IOS Press.

Riva, G., Ban, R., Botella, C., Wiedehold, B., & Gaggioli, A. (2012). Positive technology: Using interactive technologies. *Cyberpsychology, Behavior and Social Networking, 15*(2), 69–77. http://doi.org/10.1089/cyber.2011.0139

Riva, G., Serino, S., Chirico, A., & Gaggioli, A. (2018). Positive technology: From communication to positive experience. In J. A. Muñiz-Velázquez & C. Pulido (Eds.). *The Routledge Handbook of Positive Communication* (pp. 267–277). New York, NY: Routledge.

Seligman, M. E. P. (2002). *Authentic happiness: Using the new positive psychology to realize your potential for lasting fulfillment.* New York: Free Press.

Seligman, M. E. P. (2011). *Flourish: A visionary new understanding of happiness and well-being.* New York: Simon and Schuster.

Shipp, V., Skatova, A., Blum, J., & Brown, M. (2014). *The ethics of wearable cameras in the wild.* Proceedings of the IEEE 2014 International Symposium on Ethics in Engineering, Science, and Technology, Chicago.

Wagner, M. (2013). Google glass: A preemptive look at privacy concerns. *Journal on Telecommunications & High Technology Law, 11,* 477–492.

Wang, Q., Markopoulos, P., Yu, B., & Chen, W. (2017). Interactive wearable systems for upper body rehabilitation: A systematic review. *Journal of NeuroEngineering and Rehabilitation, 14*(20), 1–22. http://doi.org/10.1186/s12984-017-0229-y

Xia, F., Yang, L. T., Wang, L., & Vinel, A. (2012). Internet of things. *International Journal of Communication Systems, 25,* 1101–1102. http://doi.org/10.1002/dac

32

DIGITAL ALTRUISM

It Is Good to Be Good Also in Social Media

Andrés del Toro and Purificación Alcaide-Pulido

Web 2.0: The Democratization of Content

Aiming to make a preliminary analysis of the role of Internet users and the nature of their digital interactions, it is fundamental to go deeper into the implications of the Web 2.0 phenomenon, which allowed subsequent development of social media. At the same time, we must study users' relationship with digital content and how they manage their identity on the Internet, direct effects of the emergence of Web 2.0 and social media.

If we focus on the Web 2.0 phenomenon, first, we must review the concept and its implications with regard to content. One concept, that of a participatory Web or Web 2.0, which for various authors (Romaní & Kuklinski, 2007; Kaplan & Haenlein, 2010; Hernández, Ramírez-Martinell, & Cassany, 2014; Orenga-Roglá & Chalmeta, 2016) represents one of the main revolutions in the sphere of social communication.

We should point out that the Web 2.0 concept was stimulated by O'Reilly in 2004 and subsequently, as stated by Romaní and Kuklinski (2007, p. 15), it was "popularized thanks to its most representative applications: Wikipedia, YouTube, Flickr, WordPress, Blogger, MySpace, Facebook, etc." As indicated by Hernández et al. (2014, p. 114) thanks to this term, O'Reilly managed to identify the change in network users: "the step from a closed web (. . .) to a participatory web (. . .) in which users had the possibility of interacting with others, sharing and collaborating in the creation of content."

If we analyze the Web 2.0 concept, we can state that, on one hand, it groups a set of new technologies applied to the Internet. On the other, it refers to a change in the social order that implies multiple possibilities for collaboration and exchange between users (Romaní & Kuklinski, 2007; Alcaide-Pulido & Herrero-Diz, 2013). That is to say, the Web 2.0 concept implies that the Internet is no longer simply a display of contents, but has been transformed into an open platform based on user participation (Álvarez & Gallego, 2014). This is a characteristic that will mark the impact of Web 2.0 on social communication and the evolution of the consumer's position in social media.

Following this line, Kaplan and Haenlein (2010) point out that Web 2.0 is the platform where contents are no longer created by a small group of individuals, but are modified and elaborated by users as a whole in collaboration. Similarly, Ritzer and Jurgenson (2010) claim that in Web 2.0 contents are generated by the user, compared to the traditional 1.0 web, where these come from a provider. In turn, Dhar and Chang (2009) indicate that this new Internet has brought an end to the hegemony of the more traditional content creators as primary sources of knowledge. In the same way, García Aretio (2014, p. 2) speaks of collaborative learning as that which favors "group work and cultivating social attitudes; allows learning with others, from others and to others through exchanging ideas and tasks, and that learning develops with greater or lesser orientation (cooperation)."

Briefly, given these reflections, we can state that Web 2.0 represented one of the phenomena with greatest impact on social communication, since besides a set of technological tools, it brings new forms of collaboration and human participation. Consequently, a democratization of content has taken place. That is, for the first time in history, everyone has the possibility of creating, modifying, and sharing information and contents simply with the vast community of Internet users (Hernández et al., 2014).

Social Media in the Web 2.0 Context

The Web 2.0 phenomenon we have just analyzed assumes a necessary previous technological step that allowed the subsequent development of social media. Here, Kaplan and Haenlein (2010, p. 61) speak of the Web 2.0-based origin of the social media phenomenon, defining this as "a group of Internet-based applications that build on the ideological and technological foundations of Web 2.0, and that allow the creation and exchange of User Generated Content."

Similarly, Kietzmann, Hermkens, McCarthy, and Silvestre (2011, p. 241) conclude that, "Social media employ mobile and web-based technologies to create highly interactive platforms via which individuals and communities share, co-create, discuss, and modify User Generated Content (UGC)." In this connection, Martínez Estremera (2012, p. 9) states that social media are "a social instrument of communication, where information and contents in general are created by the users themselves."

These conceptualizations have two fundamental elements in common. First, consideration of social media as a set of technological applications where users interact. In relation to this element, authors such as Tomé (2011) recommend deep understanding of users' needs in social media to be able to contribute content of value. Second, these definitions introduce the concept of User Generated Content (UGC), which we will analyze further on, as the resulting element of use and interactions in these applications.

The leading role the user attains in relation to those interactions in social media is fundamental. A user who creates content—UGC—or who carries out any other activity made available by this social web. Therefore, and based on various authors, Hays, Page, and Buhalis (2013) detect that social media refer to those online "participative," "familiar," and "fluid" online communities, centered on users and the content they generate. Similarly, Tomé (2011, p. 220) mentions that "social media are spaces created for interaction between people that, due to the easy publication afforded by digital tools, allow their users to give opinions, enter into dialogue and share content."

From all these reflections, we can conclude that social media, despite being relatively recent technological tools born with Web 2.0, imply human communication in its most essential conception. That is, digital social media are platforms that allow, facilitate, and extend people's capacity to participate, create, share, collaborate, or connect, just as the communicative nature of human beings demands. Therefore, the importance of content, how that content is generated, and how people facilitate that content in one way or another in these media, are fundamental for this study.

The Importance of Content: Prosumer and UGC

Bearing the above in mind, we can state that one of the main characteristics of the changes taking place with the rise of social media is the great leading role of content. As we already saw in the analysis of the Web 2.0, the democratization of content is one of the particular features of this phenomenon, and UGC is the best exponent of this phenomenon. Content, which through social media, stimulates even more this idea of Web 2.0 and transforms how society creates and consumes information (Hays et al., 2013).

As a generator of content, the user assumes the role of *prosumer* (Galera & Valdivia, 2014; Hernández et al., 2014), a term derived from joining the two words: producer and consumer. A concept anticipated by McLuhan and Nevitt in 1972, when they indicated that new technologies would allow the consumer to take on the roles of producer and consumer of contents at the same time (Islas & Arribas, 2010; Galera & Valdivia, 2014), and elaborated what the authors define as UGC.

However, it was Alvin Toffler who expressly proposed the term in 1980 with his book *The Third Wave*, arguing that these prosumers acquire growing importance in defining the direction of the "invisible economy" (Ritzer & Jurgenson, 2010; Castrillo, 2014; Galera & Valdivia, 2014). According to Alvin and Heidi Toffler, the term refers to the fact that we create goods, services or experiences for our own use or enjoyment, rather than to sell or exchange them (Islas & Arribas, 2010; Hajli, 2014).

As we see, although the concept of prosumer is not something new, it is something that takes on new relevance with the rise of social media (Berthon, Pitt, Plangger, & Shapiro, 2012; Johnson et al., 2014). These prosumers are protagonists in developing Web 2.0 (Islas & Arribas, 2010; Hernández et al., 2014) and technological platforms allow massive participation, becoming the main facilitators of *"prosumption"* (Ritzer & Jurgenson, 2010).

As for the term UGC, according to Kaplan and Haenlein (2010, p. 60), it may be considered as "the sum of all ways in which people make use of Social Media." In turn, the OECD— Organization for Economic Cooperation & Development—specifies that UGC must fulfill three basic requirements: it must be published on a public website or on a social network accessible to a specific group of people; it must show a certain creative effort; and must have been created outside professional routines and practices (quoted in Kaplan & Haenlein, 2010).

UGC represents a major part of the interactions users or *prosumers* carry out through social media. An example of this are the blogs and social networks that let users publish and access information in a simple way, according to Dhar and Chang (2009) and Hajli (2014). According to these authors, the consequence is that the proportion of content that has been generated by Internet users increases progressively, covering practically all possible topics.

Although certainly it is individual people who contribute mostly to creating this UGC, increasingly we find relevant examples of groups of people who work in collaboration, as in the case of wikis (Ransbotham, Kane, & Lurie, 2012). For Castrillo (2014, p. 53) UGC: "has created a strong impact on the economic sector which has seen new business models emerge based on growing collaboration between consumers and producers."

Through the content they generate, together with their interactions, consumers take on a new position of power. A situation that from a positive point of view can help extend the projection of marketing and communication actions thanks to their ability to influence other users (Hanna, Rohm, & Crittenden, 2011; O'Hern & Kahle, 2013). But on the other hand, the information and content created by users implies exhaustive assessment and control of organizations' activities, with possible negative consequences for the latter. In short, thanks to Web 2.0 and the presence of social media in this digital context, individuals become the true protagonists of marketing and communication strategies.

Finally, it is worth pointing out that this relationship between *prosumer* and content we have been analyzing is enhanced by electronic word-of-mouth communication, or eWOM. A concept that explains the *prosumer's* influence on the opinion and behavior of other users, and where digital altruism is fundamental. Indeed, for some authors there is a direct link between UGC and eWOM. As for Ransbotham et al. (2012), who conclude that a great part of UGC on the Internet is directed to influencing other consumers' purchasing decisions through opinions, product tests and recommendations. More specifically, Smith, Fischer, and Yongjian (2012) claim that UGC can be considered a form of eWOM. Nevertheless, we must clarify that they are not identical concepts, since not all UGC can be considered eWOM, although certainly eWOM often implies the creation of content by users, meaning that these concepts overlap in much research.

Management of the User's Digital Identity

Users who acquire the role of *prosumers* are not only characterized by generating content but also act as opinion leaders. They are proactive and well-informed, listen to other users and try to go one step ahead (Mejía Llano, 2013). From this consciousness users have of the consequences of their participation on the Internet, Labrecque, Markos, and Milne (2011) state that this management of digital identity and the information provided by users implicitly constructs personal brands. A concept that, due to its importance in people's digital presence, we will examine next.

The concept of personal branding was first proposed by Peters (1997) when stating that anyone, due to the labor context we are part of, should be aware of the importance of self-management of their own brand and identity, just as organizations do. This concept of personal branding implies, therefore, a transfer of knowledge coming from the organizational domain—marketing, corporate communication, branding, etc.—to management of professionals (Lair, Sullivan, & Cheney, 2005). The main object of that management is, specifically, the personal brand—a personal brand that similarly to traditional ones implies the positioning, differentiation, and values that a person builds around themselves through their interactions, actions, use of social media, etc. (Schawbel, 2011; Arda & Fernández, 2012; Pérez, 2013).

The proposition of personal branding has witnessed an important rise in recent years. Various methods have been developed and established thanks to numerous authors who, via books, web pages, chats, courses, and consultancy services, have generalized the concept (Shepherd, 2005). Indeed, management of people as brands has become something accessible and commonplace for any professional (Groskop, 2008).

Simultaneously, due to the major development of digital social media previously referred to, personal branding has become more prevalent (Rampersad, 2009). Something which among other reasons is due to the great accessibility of digital platforms and their great potential for management of individual identity (Shepherd, 2005). Anyone with a minimum of means can build a personal brand thanks to these tools (Pérez & Arias, 2007), without any economic barrier to entry (Roca, 2009).

The synergies generated between both phenomena—personal branding and digital social media—have meant that in the most recent proposals digital platforms acquire great leading role in personal branding activities (Dasilva, 2013). Indeed, research has highlighted that users of social media usually optimize and manage their identity through the use of distinct techniques such as selection of the images they share, the handling of language, and the choice of contents they spread or by connecting to specific users, among others (Chou & Edge, 2012).

According to Kaplan and Haenlein (2010), self-management of one's presentation online corresponds to a twin motivation. On one hand, users aim to influence others to obtain rewards. On the other, they seek to project a coherent and authentic image to achieve consistency between their digital identity and their own personality. These rewards, as we shall see, are generated from the altruistic activity of *prosumers*, which creates bonds with users to share images and contents.

In addition, this identity or personal brand created thanks to the Internet and social media is potentially massive, as concluded by Castells (2007) when coining the term "mass self-communication." In this connection, Arda and Fernández (2012) state that currently inter-personal communication is often mass communication, and therefore undefined. This means we tend to create brands of ourselves aiming to stand out as different. In this context, the mass self-communication phenomenon increases exponentially the possibilities of projecting users' personal brand, since a potentially global target public is available.

In this digital personal brand, relationship networks with other users are fundamental. There-fore, and as argued by Arqués (2012, p. 76), "when we make an appearance, the platform shows our connection with other members, how many people we know and what they are involved in (. . .) on the Internet our contacts contribute to defining our identity." So, it is important to build a good digital identity, because on it will depend the image others have of us. When we share information on social media, our image, our personal brand will determine the credibility we project in our profiles, and will affect the connections and relationships we form. Furthermore, as we will analyze next, the content we generate and share will be fundamental in managing this digital identity.

Digital Altruism: The Role of Relevance in Digital Communication

As a result of the popularity gained by effective management of online identity, but especially the success of digital personal branding, various authors have analyzed and proposed the key fac-tors for successful management of the personal brand (Montoya & Vandehey, 2002; Rampersad, 2009). Among these factors, *relevance* stands out particularly, in the sense of contributing what is important or of value for the target public to whom users' activities are directed in managing their digital identity or personal brand. Here, McNally and Speak (2003, p. 21) conclude that successful personal brands are characterized by their relevance, i.e., "what they defend is related to what the other person considers important."

If we consider the role of content analyzed previously, this *relevance* can play an even more important role when we speak of personal branding in the social media context, since here the content the professional brings to the target public has a crucial role in successful management of the personal brand (Del Toro Acosta, 2015). That is, we should bring content that is relevant for the target public—content of value—because as argued by Tomé (2011, p. 96), "only through relevant content will be able to connect with our audience." This author adds: "we have to be where our customer is, carefully assess their deep reasons for being there and what they would expect from us to be able to make contact with them adapting forms and messages" (Tomé, 2011, p. 106).

As a direct consequence of this need for *relevance* in digital personal branding, people who want to take advantage of the possibilities offered by social media center their strategy on man-agement and elaboration of content of value for other users (Del Toro Acosta, 2015). In this way, they prioritize the user community's needs and demands in their digital activities. In other words, these people make a great effort to offer their knowledge and work in an altruistic and accessible way in the form of relevant digital content.

Furthermore, if we think about interactions between users, this altruism is important because it stimulates loyalty, interdependence, and commitment to long-term prosperity. Not just that, but besides setting the necessary conditions for the beginning of interpersonal relationships, it helps to solve difficulties related to the complicated process of exchanging knowledge (Ma & Chan, 2014).

Consequently, a user who concentrates on this altruism in their social media presence will draw benefits, by being valued and rewarded by other users. This leads to our statement about the positive consequences of a person "being good" also on the Internet. As we will see next, this action, sharing knowledge altruistically brings happiness and well-being.

Altruism, Well-Being, and Happiness

Post (2005) argues that helping others is returned in the form of well-being. Indeed, this author makes the close relationship between help and benevolence. That is, helping behavior could be directly related to that altruistic behavior, without looking for benefits, the *prosumer* shows when sharing knowledge on social media. In this context, we can refer to the concept of altruism, a phenomenon that Reimers, Magnuson, and Chao (2017, p. 116) define as a form of disinterested motivation, where actions are carried out voluntarily and intended to benefit others without expecting any reward (Powers & Hopkins, 2006; Corral-Verdugo, Mireles-Acosta, Tapia-Fonhiem, & Fraijo-Sing, 2011).

In this connection, in this study we define digital altruism as that in which individuals take advantage of the possibilities offered by the Internet to direct their efforts and knowledge toward voluntarily and intentionally helping others. Digital altruism performed without expecting a direct reward, although due the very nature of social media that individual will receive recognition from other users.

The altruist is therefore someone who offers a result-oriented toward the future and who benefits society as a whole (Lee & Holden, 1999; Kim, Yeonshin, & Choi, 2005; Kim, 2011). For Park, Peterson, and Seligman (2004, p. 603), the altruistic individual generates better living environments, where human strengths and positive experiences are the central standards. In addition, this is reflected in one way or another on our well-being, since the impact of altruistic attitudes influences psychological well-being, positive emotions, and satisfaction with life (Kahana, Bhatta, Lovegreen, Kahana, & Midlarsky, 2013).

As a conclusion of the above, we can state that also on the Internet "it is good to be good." In a context such as the one we are experiencing, where the digital environment has evolved to Web 2.0, and social media are the new platforms for transmitting ideas, knowledge, information, etc., consumers are active rather than passive subjects. *Prosumers* who generate content, UGC, and who must build a strong digital identity to project a personal brand that positions them on the Internet. An environment where it is good that *prosumers* show altruistic attitudes in their activity on social media.

Certainly, on the Internet it is good to share content and knowledge that other consumers consider relevant, without expecting anything in return. In the words of Cialdini (2001), digital altruism can be observed as a principle of reciprocity regarding content, since if we offer content of quality, which is useful, well structured, and what is more, free, it will be much easier for the receiver, or the social community, to respond more satisfactorily. Because, in addition, that attitude in the digital environment leads us to happiness and well-being.

References

Alcaide-Pulido, P., & Herrero-Diz, P. (2013). Comunicación institucional en Twitter para la gestión de marca en las universidades andaluza. In *La sociedad ruido: entre el dato y el grito: actas*. La Laguna (Tenerife): Sociedad Latina de Comunicación Social.

Álvarez, M., & Gallego, D. J. (2014). *Capacitación y gestión del conocimiento a través de la Web 2.0*. Madrid: Dykinson.

Arda, Z., & Fernández, C. (2012). Social media, autoimagen e imagen de la marca. *Ad Comunica, 3*, 231–234.

Arqués, N. (2012). *Y tú, ¿qué marca eres? 14 claves para gestionar tu reputación personal*. Barcelona: Planeta (GBS).

Berthon, P. R., Pitt, L. F., Plangger, K., & Shapiro, D. (2012). Marketing meets Web 2.0, social media, and creative consumers: Implications for international marketing strategy. *Business Horizons, 55*(3), 261–271. https://doi.org/10.1016/j.bushor.2012.01.007

Castells, M. (2007). Communication, power and counter-power in the network society. *International Journal of Communication, 1*(1), 29.

Castrillo, C. F. (2014). Prácticas transmedia en la era del prosumidor: Hacia una definición del Contenido Generado por el Usuario (CGU). *Cuadernos de Información y Comunicación, 19*, 53–67.

Chou, H. G., & Edge, N. (2012). "They are happier and having better lives than I am": The impact of using Facebook on perceptions of others' lives. *Cyberpsychology, Behavior, and Social Networking, 15*(2), 117–121.

Cialdini, R. B. (2001). *Influence: Science and practice.* Boston, MA: Allyn and Bacon.

Corral-Verdugo, V., Mireles-Acosta, J., Tapia-Fonhiem, C., & Fraijo-Sing, B. (2011). Happiness as correlate of sustainable behavior: A study of pro-ecological, frugal, equitable and altruistic actions that promote subjective well-being. *Human Ecology Review, 18*(2), 95–104.

Dasilva, J. A. (2013). Las empresas en Facebook y Twitter. Situación actual y estrategias comunicativas. *Revista Latina de Comunicación Social, 68*(6), 20–30.

Del Toro Acosta, A. (2015). *Marca personal en medios sociales digitales: propuesta de un modelo de autogestión* (Diss.). Universidad Complutense de Madrid. Retrieved July 24, 2016, from http://eprints.ucm. es/31130/1/T36220.pdf

Dhar, V., & Chang, E. (2009). Does chatter matter? The impact of user-generated content on music sales. *Journal of Interactive Marketing, 23*(4), 300–307.

Galera, M. C. G., & Valdivia, A. N. (2014). Prosumidores mediáticos.: Cultura participativa de las audiencias y responsabilidad de los medios. *Comunicar: Revista científica iberoamericana de comunicación y educación, 43*, 10–13.

García Aretio, L. (2014). Web 2.0 vs web 1.0. *Contextos Universitarios Mediados, 14*(1).

Groskop, V. (2008). *Brand me! New statesman.* Retrieved from www.newstatesman.com/north-america/ 2008/08/personal-branding-obama

Hajli, M. N. (2014). A study of the impact of social media on consumers. *International Journal of Market Research, 56*(3), 387–404.

Hanna, R., Rohm, A., & Crittenden, V. L. (2011). We're all connected: The power of the social media ecosystem. *Business Horizons, 54*(3), 265–273. https://doi.org/10.1016/j.bushor.2011.01.007

Hays, S., Page, S. J., & Buhalis, D. (2013). Social media as a destination marketing tool: Its use by national tourism organizations. *Current Issues in Tourism, 16*(3), 211–239.

Hernández, D., Ramírez-Martinell, A., & Cassany, D. (2014). Categorizando a los usuarios de sistemas digitales. *Pixel-Bit. Revista de Medios y Educación, 44*, 113–126.

Islas, O., & Arribas, A. (2010). Comprender las redes sociales como ambientes mediáticos. In A. Piscitelli, I. Adaime, & I. Binder (Comps.), *El proyecto facebook y la posuniversidad. Sistemas operativos sociales y entornos abiertos de aprendizaje* (pp. 147–161). Madrid: Fundación Telefónica.

Johnson, M., Mozaffar, H., Campagnolo, G. M., Hyysalo, S., Pollock, N., & Williams, R. (2014). The managed prosumer: Evolving knowledge strategies in the design of information infrastructures. *Information, Communication & Society, 17*(7), 795–813. https://doi.org/10.1080/1369118X.2013.830635

Kahana, E., Bhatta, T., Lovegreen, L. D., Kahana, B., & Midlarsky, E. (2013). Altruism, helping, and volunteering: Pathways to well-being in late life. *Journal of Aging and Health, 25*(1), 159–187. doi:10.1177/0898264312469665

Kaplan, A. M., & Haenlein, M. (2010). Users of the world, unite! The challenges and opportunities of social media. *Business Horizons, 53*(1), 59–68.

Kietzmann, J. H., Hermkens, K., McCarthy, I. P., & Silvestre, B. S. (2011). Social media? Get serious! Understanding the functional building blocks of social media. *Business Horizons, 54*(3), 241–251. https://doi. org/https://doi.org/10.1016/j.bushor.2011.01.005

Kim, Y. (2011). Understanding green purchase: The influence of collectivism, personal values and environmental attitudes, and the moderating effect of perceived consumer effectiveness. *Seoul Journal of Business, 17*(1), 65.

Kim, Y., & Choi, S. M. (2005). Antecedents of green purchase behavior: An examination of collectivism, environmental concern, and PCE. *NA-Advances in Consumer Research, 32*, 592–599.

Labrecque, L. I., Markos, E., & Milne, G. R. (2011). Online personal branding: Processes, challenges, and implications. *Journal of Interactive Marketing, 25*(1), 37–50.

Lair, D. J., Sullivan, K., & Cheney, G. (2005). Marketization and the recasting of the professional self: The rhetoric and ethics of personal branding. *Management Communication Quarterly, 18*(3), 307–343.

Lee, J. A., & Holden, S. (1999). Understanding the determinants of environmentally conscious behavior. *Psychology and Marketing, 16*(5), 373–392.

Ma, W. W. K., & Chan, A. (2014). Knowledge sharing and social media: Altruism, perceived online attachment motivation, and perceived online relationship commitment. *Computers in Human Behavior, 39*, 51–58.

Martínez Estremera, J. I. (2012). Introducción a los medios sociales (social media). *Community Manager: gestión de comunidades virtuales, 8*.

McNally, D., & Speak, K. D. (2003/2000). *Sea su propia marca: destacando entre la multitud.* Barcelona: Gestión.

Mejía Llano, J. C. (2013). *La guía del Community Manager. Estrategia, táctica y herramientas.* Madrid: Anaya.

Montoya, P., & Vandehey, T. (2002). *The personal branding phenomenon*. Santa Ana: Peter Montoya.

O'Hern, M. S., & Kahle, L. R. (2013). The empowered customer: User-generated content and the future of marketing. *Global Economics and Management Review, 18*(1), 22–30.

Orenga-Roglá, S., & Chalmeta, R. (2016). Social customer relationship management: Taking advantage of Web 2.0 and Big Data technologies. *SpringerPlus, 5*(1), 1462.

Park, N., Peterson, C., & Seligman, M. E. P. (2004). Strengths of character and well-being. *Journal of Social and Clinical Psychology, 23*(5), 603–619.

Pérez, A. (2013). *Te van a oír*. Barcelona: Alienta.

Pérez, A., & Arias, T. M. (2007). ¿Quién teme al Personal Branding? *Capital humano: revista para la integración y desarrollo de los recursos humanos, 20*(210), 94–106.

Peters, T. (1997). The brand called you. *Fast Company, 10*(10), 83–90.

Post, S. G. (2005). Altruism, happiness, and health: It's good to be good. *International Journal of Behavioral Medicine, 12*(2), 66–77.

Powers, T. L., & Hopkins, R. A. (2006). Altruism and consumer purchase behavior. *Journal of International Consumer Marketing, 19*(1), 107–130.

Rampersad, H. (2009). *Tu marca personal*. Madrid: LID Editorial Empresarial.

Ransbotham, S., Kane, G. C., & Lurie, N. H. (2012). Network characteristics and the value of collaborative user-generated content. *Marketing Science, 31*(3), 387–405.

Reimers, V., Magnuson, B., & Chao, F. (2017). Happiness, altruism and the Prius effect: How do they influence consumer attitudes towards environmentally responsible clothing? *Journal of Fashion Marketing and Management: An International Journal, 21*(1), 115–132. https://doi.org/10.1108/JFMM-07-2016-0053

Ritzer, G., & Jurgenson, N. (2010). Production, consumption, prosumption the nature of capitalism in the age of the digital "prosumer". *Journal of Consumer Culture, 10*(1), 13–36.

Roca, J. (2009). *Revolución LinkedIn: la red profesional del management 2.0 del siglo XXI*. Barcelona: Planeta (GBS).

Romaní, C. C., & Kuklinski, H. P. (2007). *Planeta Web 2.0: Inteligencia colectiva o medios fast food*. Barcelona: Uvic.

Schawbel, D. (2011). *Yo 2.0: Guía para aprovechar el potencial de los medios sociales en la promoción persona*. Barcelona: Conecta.

Shepherd, I. D. H. (2005). From cattle and coke to Charlie: Meeting the challenge of self marketing and personal branding. *Journal of Marketing Management, 21*(5–6), 589–606. http://dx.doi.org/10.1362/0267257054307381

Smith, A. N., Fischer, E., & Yongjian, C. (2012). How does brand-related user-generated content differ across YouTube, Facebook, and Twitter? *Journal of Interactive Marketing, 26*(2), 102–113. https://doi.org/https://doi.org/10.1016/j.intmar.2012.01.002

Tomé, P. (2011). *Conecta! La empresa en la red social*. Barcelona: Libros de Cabecera.

33

HAPPINESS AND DIGITAL ETHICS

Don Heider

As discussed by other authors in this volume (see Hervás & Chaves, 2018), eudaimonia is a quest for satisfaction or a sense of accomplishment that helps us feel a sense of purpose in our lives. On the other hand, digital realms have been locales where often people can feel disconnected, disoriented, even attacked. Thus, our quest is to help both people and organizations have an ethical framework by which to understand digital technology and make decisions regarding that digital technology. Because the better we behave online, the better chance for eudaimonia in these spaces.

Although many organizations and associations have codes of ethics, codes are just guidelines for us. Doing ethics is truly about a mindset, a thought process and a way to help us make decisions about situations, especially situations where there are decisions to be made about how to behave or what action to take. We can all think of situations where we are faced with moral dilemmas; should I do A or B? Should I lie to my friend or tell them an unpleasant truth? Would we use violence to prevent violence? There's one parachute and three people in a plane that's bound to crash; who gets the parachute? Ethics is the process of weighing competing moral claims. In these tough situations, there are often good reasons for the different choices; often good moral reasons for each choice. So, someone trained in ethics can help consider and weigh the options, so that in the end an informed decision is made.

Of course, difficult decisions and ethics have been around since humans could speak and think, but the digital revolution has added some new wrinkles. Many online forums offer users anonymity, which for some people must feel like permission to behave badly. The Internet also allows people some unprecedented access to people that might not have previously been aware of, had access to, or had any dealings with. In many ways this can be positive, exposing people to a wider array of opinions and perspectives. But for others it seems to have a detrimental effect, encouraging attacks. Other considerations are that in communication via technology there is often less nuance and fewer social cues (Baym, 2006). Researchers have also described the detachment behavior of trolls, who often speak of themselves and their actions in the third person (Phillips, 2011).

Spending time systematically observing people in online settings over the past fifteen years, I have also come to understand that because the Internet does not reside in one particular place, there is often a sense of lawlessness. Freeing in one way, but also in another way often even encouraging a sentiment of anarchy. Another interesting factor regarding our new digital world is that messages can be disseminated much more quickly and more widely than ever before. An unfortunate tweet can be seen by millions of people in a matter of minutes now. This kind of breath and speed, one can argue, do not lead to calmer heads and thoughtful reflection.

All these factors and more have led to many researchers' and citizens' concern about technology's influence on human behavior. My stance is that any technology is neither inherently good nor evil, but what is interesting is how humans use that technology. Equally important is how that technology might enhance, or diminish certain kinds of behavior, especially in regard to communication.

Most of us currently have no choice about whether or not we use technology, thus having some help in thinking about and using that technology I believe will help us become eudaimonic users of technology, using these tools to focus on helping ourselves and others. We want, as best we can, to keep our lives focused on happiness and well-being, rather than some of the negative behavior we see in digital spaces.

At Present Digital Ethics Issues Fall Into a Number of Different Categories

Privacy is most commonly defined as the right to be free from being observed or disturbed by other people. Digital technology has allowed much more profound ways in which our privacy may be invaded. From a drone hovering over your house or workplace, to someone intercepting your text messages, digital technology provides us with interesting new ways to communicate but also threatens our ability to protect our privacy. The revelations of Edward Snowden revealed one government's willingness to even break laws in the name of security and surveillance. US Supreme Court Justice Louis Brandies was prescient when he wrote in 1928: "Discovery and invention have made it possible for the government, by means far more effective than stretching upon the rack to obtain disclosure in court of what is whispered in closet. The progress of science in furnishing the government with means of espionage is not likely to stop with wiretapping."

It's not just the government gathering your whispers. Who owns your browsing history? How long does your information live on the Internet? Do you *ever* have the right to be forgotten? Every time you type a search term or click a link, some organization is gathering and recording that information, whether you know it or not, and whether or not you think you have given consent for them to do it. They, in turn, may sell or give that information to others. For each of us, what is a reasonable expectation of privacy? In the UK there are over six million surveillance cameras peering into public spaces. What's the expectation of privacy in a public space? Shoshana Zuboff (2015) argues persuasively about the new form of surveillance capitalism designed and implemented to generate huge revenues at the expense of our privacy, as Google and others monetize each choice we make while online.

An ethical approach to privacy would include at least three elements; notice of when our privacy is being violated (when our data is captured, our picture being taken, our words and sounds being recorded), some type of choice in that surveillance, and if no choice is given and our privacy is violated, some type of redress. Without these, how can one have any peace of mind when using any digital technology?

Another area concerns **content sharing**. From Napster, to Spotify to Bit Torrent, questions arise of when is it legal and ethical to file share. An estimated seventy million people engage in file sharing, most of it illegal. How can we acknowledge, respect, and even compensate content creators for their work?

There are questions as well even about legal sharing services such as Spotify and iTunes as to whether these outfits fairly compensate artists for their creative work. How can we enjoy art and music and other creations in digital spaces and yet be sure the artist is recognized and rewarded for what they have done?

As well, in this new sharing economy, companies like Uber have been accused of multiple ethical violations, from discrimination and harassment against women who work for the company, to how the company records and shares data on people's riding habits. In addition, to be able to skirt regulations, the company has claimed to be a technology and not a transportation company. Is it legal and ethical to allow companies to define which regulations they do and do not fall under?

Airbnb, which allows people to lease their houses and apartments, has been accused of designing a platform that gives owners the opportunity to systematically discriminate against people of color. Often with new technology, there are unintended consequences. What responsibility should companies take for such consequences?

Most of Us by Now Are Aware of the Use of Robots and Artificial Intelligence

Whether chatting with someone online or by phone, is it ethical to have artificial intelligence mimic humans, tricking us into believing we are conversing with a person, when really it's a bot? How much control should we give over to machines, even if we think we can program them to protect our best interests?

When it comes to forms of artificial intelligence there are a number of concerns. Who designs the AI and what particular point-of-view or bias is it programmed with? Can the AI stand up to manipulation? Can the AI be hacked? It's not difficult in the case of AI to see how things can easily go wrong. For instance, Cathy O'Neill (2016) has demonstrated how algorithms can be used to systematically discriminate against the poor and disenfranchised. In this case the programming and math might be fine, but the intent has a disastrous outcome.

From robotic hamsters to sex robots, there are serious questions about whether programmed devices will ultimately help or harm us, many of which are raised eloquently by Sherry Turkle in *Alone Together: Why We Expect More from Technology and Less from Each Other* (Turkle, 2011). Since Isaac Asimov developed three laws of robotics in 1942 as part of a science fiction novel (Asimov, 1950) both scientists and ethicists have debated what might be contained in a robot code of ethics.

Of all the digital ethics topics, digital behavior is perhaps the area that gets the most attention in news media. Cases of online bullying and various online attacks seem to be rampant. There have been myriad cases of mob behavior in digital spaces, where people attack others by releasing their personal information, a form of cybervigilantism, where we see cases of doxing and swatting and flaming. These are brutal attacks that are difficult to understand and almost never in proportion to the issue at hand. This is the world of anonymous behavior where people feel free to do things they would never do face-to-face or in the light of day. This is the place online where we find griefers and trolls. Psychologist John Suler (2004) has described some of this behavior as the online disinhibition effect, wherein social restrictions and inhibitions which are normally present in face-to-face encounters are somehow loosened or forgotten. Look at the comments section of many websites. People write often horrific things one would imagine they would never, ever say to another person face-to-face.

A chronic problem with the Internet that has come into sharp focus in recent times is the abundance of inaccurate information, which some have labeled fake news. We live in a world where creating fake news sites and spreading complete lies can be profitable. We live in a world where making utterly false claims is a political strategy to distract the public from real issues.

Given that, it makes one wonder what an ethics of accurate information might look like. The social media companies, often conduits for false information and fabricated stories, have washed their hands of responsibility. We ask how technology companies can be more responsible for the posts they carry on their platforms. Is it enough to ask news organizations and others to police their sites? Digital ethics helps us think about online behavior, such as knowingly passing on false information, and what true credibility might look like in these new online environments.

We propose a form of digital citizenship, wherein participants in and creators of digital technology not only can exercise the tremendous freedoms which currently exist, but also understand that with these freedoms come responsibilities. In this sense, there are certain ethical principles that may transcend boundaries and cultures and apply to the digital realm as well as our physical realm. These would include transparency, avoiding harm, preserving people's autonomy, justice, and privacy.

The principle of transparency asks people and organizations to share information with users freely, and not to conceal crucial facts. So, for instance, when an app or program or device is collecting a person's data, that should be disclosed clearly and people should have the opportunity to opt out of that data collection. Too often, this information is collected discreetly and then used for purposes the individual might not ever approve of, including surveillance. Honoring transparency would also, for instance, require companies to shorten and simplify terms of service, those long documents full of legal language that are so arduous few people read them and even fewer can understand exactly what they say. An organization committed to the ethical principal of transparency would offer shorter, clearer versions of terms of service so consumers understand exactly what they are agreeing to. Philosopher Sissela Bok argues that when we stop short of full disclosure, we are failing to treat others with dignity and respect (1999). This insight is rooted in Immanuel Kant's moral system (Kant, 1991), wherein communication is crucial for human respect. When we keep information from people, it is an inherent form of disrespect.

Perhaps the most universally accepted ethical idea is that we should do no harm to others. John Stewart Mill argued that "The only purpose for which power can be rightfully exercised over any member of a civilized community, against his will, is to prevent harm to others" (Mill, 1999, p. 51). Mill distinguish physical harm from other types of harm, but argued that almost all actions impact people beyond the individual, and that we are accountable for how we impact others. In the digital world, we see attacks on a routine basis, where people try to harm others through bullying, hurling insults, releasing personal information, and more. A digital code of ethics would ask people to treat one another with respect and dignity.

Autonomy is the idea that we want to preserve people's ability to make their own independent decisions and govern themselves. As Isaiah Berlin (1969, p. 131) wrote; "I wish to be a subject, not an object; to be moved by reasons, by conscious purposes, which are my own, not by causes that affect me, as it were, from the outside." In operating on digital platforms, how much autonomy do we have? How many of our decisions have been predetermined or limited by a programmer? Other philosophers have also postulated that with autonomy comes responsibility in how we act. One goal of digital ethics would be to have autonomous individuals take ownership of their behavior online.

Also common in ethics discussion is the consideration of justice. John Rawls (1971) has argued that society should be structured in a way to ensure the greatest amount of liberty for every citizen. Do we have a just and ethical digital space when many people have no access or extremely limited access to digital technology? The digital divide may be diminishing a bit, but there's little doubt it still exists. Even with access to technology such as the Internet, there's a gap between those of us who can control the Internet, those of us who can code or structure the net and those of us who are merely users. Does digital technology offer maximum liberty when women and people of color are still routinely marginalized or victimized? What would an Internet committed to justice look like? Can we imagine it? From the perspective of those of us who endorse digital ethics, justice, and fairness would have to be part of the consideration of any technology.

The newest right has to do with our personal privacy. This is the idea that we should be able to live our lives without public scrutiny. In most places, this right is still being defined. Would we consider private things we do or say in public? What about things you say or do in your own home? What about things you say or do via the Internet or other digital technology? Who owns our data, the footprints and data point we leave as a trail when we surf the Internet or make a phone call on cell phone? Does the government have the right to record this and use this information? Along with this comes the idea of a right to be forgotten. Even if we post something through social media, should that posting be forever associated with us, or should there be some statute of limitations on what we post? An ethical approach to digital technology would include ways in which individuals could preserve their privacy; companies and governments and organizations would be required to give users a clear understanding of what data is being collected and give the opportunity to opt out.

A framework of eudaimonia would help us to see the larger picture of using digital technology, including how these tools can be used for good, and in what ways the use of these tools may also harm people. A eudemonic framework would also encourage individuals and organizations to be authentic, to be the same online and offline, and to be transparent, honest, and open.

As we began the digital revolution decades ago there were two common reactions to these large technological changes both in the popular press and among academics. One reaction came in the form of a utopian view. From this perspective, new technology would give us an opportunity to usher in a new era of cooperation, pluralism, and communication. Some believed the Internet would level the playing field, taking away power from legacy media and turning it over to normal, everyday citizens. Social networks were seen as a way of allowing people with like interests to connect and organize. Mobile phones would allow the masses to have access to technology in a way the world had never seen before.

The other reaction was framed in a fear of new technology. In the dystopian view technology would lead to a world of Big Brother, where we would be in a constant state of being surveilled, where technology would be used as a weapon, and where artificial intelligence would eventually outwit humans and take over the world. Although today you can still see evidence of both views, our lived experience has shown us the reality of a world that exists something in between these two views.

Technology thus far has ushered in neither a utopian word world nor a dystopian world. To understand technology, we must understand who created it and for what purpose, and then exactly how it is being used and what the implications and impacts are from the technology once launched. Some technology may indeed be designed with evil Internet, other technology may be designed with good Internet or even no particular intent, yet used for evil or harmful purposes. The crucial factors are the designer and the user. These are humans. We know that humans can be and often are both good and evil. What digital ethics does is help us question intent and effect. It provides a way of thinking and even perhaps a framework by which we can examine technologies, or situations that arise from technology, to try to determine possible harm and the other considerations I have outlined here.

Another crucial consideration will be what steps technology companies and technology providers are willing to take toward becoming ethical organizations, considering it is the use of their products which at times help or hurt human beings. I have called (Heider, 2017) for technology firms to hire ethicists to help guide decision-making, though thus far the call has seemingly gone without response. Given the power and influence these companies have, I believe we must continue to call for accountability from these organizations as well.

Whether for organizations or individuals, the eudemonic approach to me is very much line with an ethical approach and would include striving for excellence and defining high values and ideals, which could mean behaving with civility, trying to encourage others to be civil, and also helping us as we strive to be the best version of ourselves possible, whether represented in digital spaces or not.

References

Asimov, I. (1950). *I, Robot*. Greenwich, CT: Fawcett Publications.

Baym, N. (2006). Interpersonal life online. In L. A. Lievrouw & S. Livingstone (Eds.), *The handbook of new media* (Student ed., pp. 35–54). Thousand Oaks, CA: Sage Publications.

Berlin, I. (1969). Two concepts of liberty. In *Four essays on liberty*. Oxford: Oxford University Press.

Bok, S. (1999). *Lying: Moral choice in public and private life*. New York: Vintage.

Heider, D. (2017, Jan. 8) Why Facebook should hire a chief ethicist, *USA Today*. (Retrieved from https://www.usatoday.com/story/opinion/2017/01/08/facebook-ethics-fake-news-social-media-column/96212172/)

Hervás, G. & Chaves, C. (2018). What can science can tell us about human happiness (and why and how should we disseminate it)? In J. A. Muñiz-Velázquez, & C. M. Pulido (Eds.), *The Routledge Handbook of Positive Communication* (pp. xx–xx). New York: Routledge.

Kant, I. (1991). *The metaphysics of morals*. (M. Gregor, Trans.) Cambridge, England: Cambridge University Press. (Original work published 1797).

Mill, J. S. (1999). *On Liberty*. London: Longman, Roberts & Green. (Original work published 1869).

Olmstead v. United States, 277 U.S. 438 (1928): Wiretaps: Brandeise, Dissenting Opinion.

O'Neil, C. (2016), *Weapons of math destruction: How big data increases inequality and threatens democracy*, New York, NY: Crown Publishing Group.

Phillips, W. (2011) LOLing at tragedy: Facebook trolls, memorial pages, and resistance to grief online. *First Monday*, 16(12), http://dx.doi.org/10.5210/fm.v16i12.3168.

Rawls, T. (1971). *A Theory of Justice*. Cambridge, MA: Harvard University Press.

Suler, J. (2004). The online disinhibition effect. *Cyberpsychology & behavior*, 7(3), 321–326.

Turkle, S. (2011). *Alone together: Why we expect more from technology and less from each other*. New York, NY: Basic Books.

Zuboff, S. (2015). Big other: Surveillance capitalism and the prospects of an information civilization. *Journal of Information Technology*, 30(1) 75–89.

PART VI

Happiness at School

Positive Communication and Education

34

POSITIVE EDUCATION

Promoting Well-Being at School

Diego Gomez-Baya and Jane E. Gillham

The Emergence of Positive Education

Positive education has been developed as an application of positive psychology to the scientific study of the optimal functioning of the human being in the educational contexts. The recognition that good mental and physical health consists not only in the absence of pathologies but also in the presence of well-being, has encouraged the implementation of interventions to promote well-being and resilience in the different settings in which human development happens, such as the school (Norrish, Williams, O'Connor, & Robinson, 2013). Positive education is based on the premise that the purpose of education is to help students flourish in a variety of ways, not only academically, but also to develop the skills that allow them to succeed in work and in life, and to become productive citizens who contribute to making society better. Seligman (2011) defines positive education as the union between traditional education focused on the development of academic skills with interventions that nourish well-being and promote better mental health. Although positive education has relevance throughout the lifespan, the focus of this chapter is on children and adolescents at elementary through high school education.

Positive education is relevant to all aspects of education, from interactions between individual teachers and students to classroom interventions to school building level policies to public policy. Peterson noted that positive psychology interventions should not only be applied at the individual level, but also at the institutional level, with the goal of building institutions that allow the optimal development of both students and professionals. Peterson (2006) coined the term "The Good School," which refers to educational institutions in which, in addition to academic pursuits, students are encouraged to share and develop values and strengths that allow them to contribute to the society in which they live. In this "Good School," teachers have a privileged position, both for their psychological and pedagogical training in the instruction of psychosocial skills, and for being a crucial model of attitudes and behaviors that promote greater psychological well-being. While most work in positive education focuses on children and adolescents and their teachers, positive education also aims to develop skills that promote optimal functioning in school administrators, coaches, and other staff members who work in schools and in youths' parents and caregivers (Boniwell, 2013).

Well-Being Outcomes and Character Strengths as Roots to Well-Being

Positive education emerges especially as a response to a problem consistently shown by research on the well-being of children and adolescents in developed countries. Many students report low levels of well-being. For example, findings from the California School Climate, Health, and Learning Survey (Health and Human development program, 2011) indicated that students report low levels of caring relationships and meaningful engagement in school. Epidemiological studies reveal that the prevalence of depression among children and adolescents has been alarming for decades (Costello, Erkanli, & Angold, 2006). Positive education aims to address such challenges by promoting personal qualities and skills and social contexts that foster resilience and well-being (Gillham, Abenavoli, Brunwasser, Reivich, & Seligman, 2013). Positive education has two major overlapping areas of focus. First, it aims to reduce and prevent downward spirals by promoting resilience, the capacities for adapting to stressors and challenges. Second, it aims to promote upward spirals by cultivating character strengths and capacities for creating and experiencing positive emotions, positive relationships, and meaning. In positive education, the focus is primarily on these upward spirals, that is, on directly building positive outcomes such as positive emotion, engagement, good relationships, and meaning (e.g., Seligman, 2017).

Positive education is concerned with a broad range of well-being outcomes. For example, Seligman (2011) proposed a multidimensional approach to well-being, identifying five core areas that comprise the PERMA model. These include *positive emotions* (hedonic feelings of happiness), *engagement* (psychological connection to activities or organizations, i.e. interest, curiosity, and absorption), *relationships* with others (including feeling socially integrated and satisfied with social connections), *meaning* (defined as the believe that one's life is valuable and is connected to something which goes beyond one's own life, e.g., contributing to other people and the good development of the whole community), and *accomplishment* (by reaching meaningful outcomes and developing a feeling of achievement and self-efficacy). In its whole school approach to positive education, Geelong Grammar School has expanded Seligman's model to also include health (i.e. PERMA+H model, which is composed of these outcomes: positive emotions, positive engagement, positive accomplishment, positive purpose, positive relationships with others, and the promotion of positive health; Norrish et al., 2013). Other models of well-being also have been proposed. For example, Ryff and Keyes (1995) defined a six-component-model for optimal well-being, composed of autonomy, environmental mastery, personal growth, positive relations with others, purpose in life, and self-acceptance.

There are many different routes to these well-being outcomes. Positive education focuses particularly on increasing students' attitudes, beliefs, and behaviors, and on building habits and skills that promote flourishing. A central pathway in positive education is the cultivation of character strengths. According to Seligman (2011), strengths are important for each area of area well-being in PERMA. Much of the work in positive education incorporates the Character Strengths and Virtues (CSV) framework proposed by Peterson, Seligman, and their colleagues (Dahlsgaard, Peterson, & Seligman, 2005; Peterson & Seligman, 2004; Peterson, 2006). Unlike many existing frameworks for character education that focus on promoting a few specific strengths, the CSV framework celebrates the diverse range of strengths and virtues that have been consistently valued across time and across culture. The six general virtues are: humanity (composed of the character strengths of love, kindness, and social intelligence), wisdom and knowledge (composed by creativity, curiosity, open mind, love of learning, and perspective), courage (integrated by courage, perseverance, integrity, and vitality), justice (integrated by citizenship, sense of justice, and leadership), moderation (composed of forgiveness, modesty, prudence, and self-control), and finally transcendence (formed by the appreciation of beauty and excellence, gratitude, hope, sense of humor, and spirituality). Peterson and Seligman propose that each of us has signature strengths, a few top strengths that are closely connected to our deepest values and reflect who we are at our core. According to the CSV model, then, a major goal of character education is to promote well-being by helping students identify and apply their signature strengths.

Evidence That Positive Education Processes Also Matter for Academic Achievement

The development of positive education has been supported by the research on the role of emotions in the teaching and learning processes. Ryan and Deci (2001) explained in their Self-determination Theory how learning is fostered when the students find enjoyment in the academic tasks, especially when these tasks are configured to promote children's and adolescents' feelings of autonomy and competence and to allow for the construction of knowledge in the interaction with peers. Csikszentmihalyi's theory of Flow proposes that engagement, enjoyment, and performance increase when students are appropriately challenged. Thus, as students' skills develop, increasing the level of challenges helps to maintain this flow state and hence optimal engagement and learning (Shernoff & Csikszentmihalyi, 2009). Research on Fredrickson's Broaden and Built theory has demonstrated that positive emotions broaden students' attention and promote more creative thinking and problem-solving (Fredrickson & Branigan, 2005). Programs that aim to increase social support and skills such as self-regulation and persistence, promote better achievement and completion of school (Zins, Weissberg, Wang, & Walberg, 2004). Similarly, grit, defined as perseverance and passion for long-term goals, predicts students' educational attainment over and beyond IQ and conscientiousness (Duckworth, Peterson, Matthews, & Kelly, 2007). Similarly, optimism predicts students' educational attainment over and above their past academic performance (Schulman, 1995). Some positive education programs target specific pathways to well-being such as positive emotion (e.g., savoring and attending to positive events), and specific strengths (e.g., gratitude, self-control or GRIT) (e.g., Eskreis-Winkler, Shulman, Beal, & Duckworth, 2014; Froh, Miller, & Snyder, 2007).

Overlap with Other Traditions

Kristjánsson (2012) has challenged scholars in positive education to consider whether positive psychology (or positive education) makes any unique contribution to the field of education. Many philosophical and educational traditions have emphasized the promotion of engagement, character, and well-being as central goals of education (Cohen, 2006; Palmer, Bresler, & Cooper, 2001). Positive education overlaps with approaches such as character education, positive youth development, and social and emotional learning. Positive education also overlaps with psychosocial approaches to preventing anxiety, depression, and other mental health problems in youth. At a very broad level, all of these approaches aim to promote youths' social and emotional well-being (one or more aspects of PERMA). All promote character strengths or attitudes, beliefs, and behaviors that are closely related to character strengths. For example, social and emotional learning programs aim to promote several competencies such as awareness of self and others (e.g., awareness of feelings, management of feelings, perspective taking), positive attitudes and values (e.g., personal responsibility, respect for others, and social responsibility), responsible decision-making (e.g., adaptive goal setting and problem-solving), and social interaction skills (i.e. active listening, cooperation, negotiation, and help seeking) (Durlak, Weissberg, Dymnicki, Taylor, & Schellinger, 2011). These competences are closely related to CSV strengths such as self-control, social and emotional intelligence, fairness, teamwork, and critical thinking. Similarly, positive youth development focuses on engaging young people within their developmental contexts and enhances their strengths, to build positive outcomes, i.e. competence, confidence, character, connection, and caring (Catalano, Berglund, Ryan, Lonczak, & Hawkins, 2004; Lerner, Almerigi, Theokas, & Lerner, 2005). School-based programs that aim to prevent psychological difficulties such as anxiety and depression often focus on increasing emotional awareness, optimism, social skills, assertiveness, and problem-solving, as well as the ability to confront difficult experiences (e.g., through exposure). These skills and strategies are similar to character strengths such as social and emotional intelligence, optimism, critical thinking, and courage. As Kern and Kaufman (2017) have argued, the boundaries of positive education are unclear.

Positive education's contribution is, arguably, its emphasis on a broad spectrum of well-being. Much of the work in prevention and in social and emotional learning, for example, has focused on teaching skills for handling difficult emotions and responding adaptively to interpersonal stressors and conflicts. Positive education recognizes the importance of such skills but also aims to promote youth's capacities to experience positive emotions and to develop and sustain caring relationships. Like positive psychology, positive education explicitly focuses on teaching skills that directly promote positive experiences and relationships.

Much of the research in prevention, character education, social and emotional learning, and positive youth development has focused on reducing negative outcomes (e.g., substance use, teen pregnancy, dropping out of school). Positive education stresses the importance of positive outcomes as well. In fact, positive education programs typically focus primarily on helping students to flourish. While this is arguably positive education's primary contribution, it is not new. Scholars and practitioners in these other fields have noted the importance of attending to a wider range of skills and experiences. For example, Karen Pittman, a leading scholar of positive youth development, has argued for the power of focusing on youth's strengths rather than their deficits, noting that "problem-free isn't fully prepared" (Pittman, Martin, & Yohalem, 2006). Still, reviews have noted that empirical evaluations of positive youth development programs focus on reductions in negative outcomes (e.g., Catalano, Berglund, Ryan, Lonczak, & Hawkins, 2004). One of positive psychology's greatest contributions to education may be the development of tools for assessing strengths and positive aspects of well-being, including measures of PERMA (Kern, Waters, Adler, & White, 2015).

Like social and emotional learning, character education, and positive youth development, positive education includes a wide range of interventions and approaches from school curriculum, to after school programming, to whole school approaches, to education policy although, to date, most work has focused on school curricula. Positive education is relevant to all ages, from preschool (and before) to high school (and beyond). Positive education can be taught in a variety of ways—explicitly through curriculum for example; implicitly through modeling. Moreover, professional development/support for teachers and mentors is essential within positive education—for effective teaching, support, and modeling of skills. Positive education focuses primarily on school and other educational settings, including co-curricular activities, while traditionally positive youth development has also focused after school and out of school programs.

Evidence for Positive Education

Experiences in positive education can be classified into curriculum programs and whole school interventions. Curriculum programs consist in the explicit performance of concrete activities during school time, both included in the formal subjects and developed apart from those subjects, with the aim of recognizing and using character strengths and competences to promote well-being. Whole school interventions involves the explicit and implicit learning of character strengths and competences related to well-being in the classroom and throughout many aspects of school life. In whole school approaches, positive education principles and practices become part of the school culture, affecting many aspects of the students' and teachers' experience. Below we briefly describe a few examples of positive education practices (curricula and whole school approaches) that have been examined in published research. We focus on those that illustrate positive education's origins in positive psychology.

Curricula and Classroom Programs

High School Positive Psychology Curriculum

The High School Positive Psychology Curriculum (aka Strath Haven Positive Psychology curriculum) is one of the first positive education programs developed that is based on positive psychology (Seligman, Ernst, Gillham, Reivich, & Linkins, 2009). The curriculum was originally designed for ninth-grade students (the first year of high school) in the United States and consists of 20–25 lessons delivered throughout the school year. It includes three major units, roughly following Seligman's (2002, 2011) model of well-being, which focused on three aspects of PERMA: positive emotions, engagement (through strengths), and meaning. The first unit is designed to help students increase positive experiences and emotions (e.g., through savoring, counting blessings, gratitude letters). The second unit focuses on increasing engagement through character strengths. The unit emphasizes the positive psychology approach of helping students to identify and use signature strengths. However, it also encourages students to work another (non-signature) strengths that they value. The third unit focuses on understanding and increasing meaning. Each lesson lasts about 80 minutes and includes activities related to positive psychology and setting up a homework activity that involves practicing a relevant skill or behavior. Students write reflections about their experiences. Each meeting opens with a discussion of students' experiences applying positive psychology in their lives. The curriculum includes many activities that have since become common components of positive psychology and positive education interventions. For example, activities included writing a positive experiences journal (writing about three good things that have happened during the day), writing and delivering a gratitude letter, and developing and implementing strengths action plans (plans to apply a strength to a new situation). In addition to the three units, teachers are encouraged to infuse concepts from the positive education course in their teaching of other academic topics. For example, the curriculum was originally implemented in the context of language arts classes. Teachers were encouraged to bring positive psychology concepts (e.g., positive emotions, character strengths, and meaning and purpose) to their discussions of literature with their students. For example, in discussing the *Odyssey*, teachers might encourage students to think about the characters' signature strengths and also to consider other strengths that could have helped the character to face challenges more effectively.

This curriculum has been evaluated in a randomized controlled study with approximately 350 ninth-grade students. Students were randomly assigned to language arts classes that included the positive psychology curriculum or to language arts as usual. The positive psychology lessons and activities replaced language arts lessons that focused on shorter works of literature. Findings indicated that the positive psychology curriculum increased students' social skills and engagement in learning, compared with controls. These effects endured for two years following the program. No significant intervention effects were found for positive emotions or for feelings of depression and anxiety (Seligman et al., 2009; Gillham et al., 2013).

Strengths Gym

This character strengths-based intervention aims to encourage students to build their strengths, learn new strengths, and to recognize others' strengths, on the basis of 24 lessons (one lesson for each character strength in the CSV model) during three levels of implementation, i.e. Year 7, 8, and 9 in British curriculum (Proctor et al., 2011). Each lesson focuses on one character strength. The teacher describes the strength, engages the class in two exercises designed to build this strength, and assigns a follow-up activity that encourages students to practice using the strengths. For example, the first lesson in each course is "love of beauty" and students are invited to remember a time when they or someone they know showed this strength and then to write down a story of love of beauty in action. As a challenge, students are encouraged to look for beauty on their way to school and then tell a friend or family member what they noticed.

This intervention program was evaluated in two secondary schools in Great Britain using a quasi-experimental design. Students in the intervention condition were compared to a control group of students, who attended their scheduled class as normal without the inclusion of Strengths Gym activities. Both groups of students completed self-report measures of life satisfaction, positive, and negative affect, and self-esteem before and after the intervention phase. Proctor et al. (2011) found that, following the intervention, the students in the intervention condition reported higher life satisfaction than students in the control group. No significant differences were found for affect or self-esteem, although there was a non-significant tendency for intervention participants to report greater positive affect than controls.

Positive Education in Bhutan, Mexico, and Peru

Adler and colleagues developed positive education interventions in three countries: Bhutan, Mexico, and Peru (Adler, 2016). In each country, the interventions targeted 10 life skills: mindfulness, empathy, self-awareness, coping with emotions, communication skills, interpersonal relationships, creative thinking, critical thinking, decision-making, and problem-solving. The teachers and the principals were trained to practice and teach the ten life skills to infuse positive education into existing academic subjects (e.g. math, reading, science). For example, in Literature classes, students were invited to identify strengths and virtues in characters from novels and encouraged to use those strengths in their daily lives. The interventions also emphasized students' active and meaningful engagement in learning. Students performed botanic practices, by planting, growing, and harvesting plants in organic gardens. As well as learning about biological concepts, they had the opportunity to reflect on the role of food in local and national economic systems, and to practice skills such as critical thinking and problems solving. Intervention teachers also learned strategies for incorporating positive psychology principles in their work with students. For example, teachers were encouraged to include feedback on what students were doing well.

Adler and colleagues evaluated this positive education approach in each country using randomized controlled designs. In each country, the positive education program focused on the 10 skills but was adapted to fit the local cultural and educational context. The positive education program was delivered over at 15-month period. The average age of students was between 15 and 17. Students in positive education curriculum were compared to students in a placebo control condition that met for a similar amount of time. In which students were taught principles of nutrition, psychology, and human anatomy but did not include the positive education components. The research program began in Bhutan, with replications in Mexico and Peru. In Bhutan, a total of 8,385 students (grades 7 through 12) participated in the study from 18 secondary schools, which were randomly assigned to treatment (11 schools) and control group (7 schools). Bhutan is the first country to nationally implement positive education, as a part of a wider political approach toward Gross National Happiness (GNH), the primary indicator Bhutan uses to assess national progress. In Mexico, a total of 68,762 students (grades 10 to 12) participated. These students came from 70 secondary schools (35 secondary schools in the intervention group and other 35, in the control group). In Peru, a total of 694,153 students (grades 7 to 12) participated. These students came from 694 secondary schools which were randomly assigned to the intervention or control groups.

Students' well-being was assessed using a measure of the positive outcomes in PERMA, called EPOCH (Kern et al., 2015). This instrument was composed of 20 items that assess engagement, perseverance, optimism, connectedness, and happiness. The researchers also examined students' performance on academic achievement tests. Students in the intervention schools reported higher well-being and showed better performance in standardized national exams after the intervention ended, compared to control groups. These benefits endured for 12 months in Bhutan (follow-up information was not yet available for the other countries). An important implication of this intervention is that well-being can be taught in schools on a large-scale in a variety of social, economic, or cultural contexts.

Whole School Approach

Geelong Grammar School (GGS) in Australia has implemented a whole school approach to positive education (Norrish, 2015). Norrish and colleagues (2013) developed a practice-oriented model, which foster strengths of character, following the definition by Peterson and Seligman (2004), as the processes to promote well-being, as proposed PERMA + H model (Norrish et al., 2013). This model has been followed by many schools and practitioners to guide practice in positive education. Geelong's approach emphasizes four levels of implementation of positive education concepts and skills. These are: 1) Learn it (educators learn the positive education concepts and skills); 2) Live it (educators learn to apply what is learned in daily life and in work in the school context; educators who "live it" are better able to engage in the other levels of performance); 3) Teach it (educators help students to learn skills through explicit instruction (i.e. structured lessons) and through implicit instruction (i.e. by integrating skills into routine during academic life and transversally in other subjects); and 4) Embed it (which refers to implementing the learning outcomes in every day practices). The processes of "learn it," "live it," "teach it," and "embed it" are additive, synergetic, and dynamic, and create a whole school culture and community for well-being (Bott, 2017; Norrish et al., 2013). Thus, this model provides "a sustainable and flexible framework for moving towards flourishing school communities" (Norrish et al., 2013).

Geelong Grammar School was the first school to use a whole school approach to positive education. Seligman and colleagues conducted workshops with staff and then two experts in positive education resided in Geelong during the first year of implementation. Thus, the staff had the opportunity to learn live positive psychology strategies and apply them to their lives before teaching those to students. A positive education curriculum was developed to provide explicit instruction to students at several grades. The curriculum component incorporated Strath Haven Positive Psychology Curriculum (described earlier) and the Penn Resilience Program (Gillham et al., 2013), a program that is designed to promote resilience through teaching skills for handling common stressors during adolescence. School staff also embedded positive education into academic subjects, sports, music classes and pastoral counseling. For example, in geography class students are invited to reflect on the measure of well-being of the nations and why criteria among cultures may be different. Positive education was embedded into school policies and practices to affect the overall school climate, for example by starting the class of each day asking "what went well?"

Vella-Brodrick, Rickard, and Chin (2014) have evaluated Geelong Grammar School's approach with a total of 383 participants enrolled at Years 9, 10, and 11. Using a quasi-experimental design, these students were compared to a control group of 138 students from other private schools in the Melbourne area, with similar socioeconomic status. Students in both groups were surveyed at two times, approximately 10 months later. At each assessment, they completed measures of mental health and well-being and strengths. Moreover, within the intervention group, a smaller group of 50 students at Year 9 provided reports by tablet devices (by experience sampling methodology, with daily reports of strategies used and the subsequent outcomes), and 79 students at Years 9 and 10 also participated in focus groups in which they responded to questions about positive education program content and delivery.

Although the design of this study includes a three-year follow-up, some preliminary findings after the first year have been reported (Vella-Brodrick et al., 2014). Quantitative findings indicate increases in mental health and well-being and strengths knowledge in GGS Year 9 students compared to Year 9 controls (Vella-Brodrick et al., 2014). It is important to note that Year 9 is a special year at GGS. In addition to teaching positive education, Year 9 students participate in the Timbertop program, a full academic year that focuses heavily on outdoor education, responsibility, and cooperation in addition to academic subjects. While Timbertop itself is arguably consistent with positive education, it is difficult to separate out the contributions of positive education instruction from the larger Timbertop experience. In focus group and experience sampling reports, GGS students reported applying many of the positive education skills. Saint Peter's College in Adelaide has also implemented a whole school approach to positive education for several years (e.g., White & Waters, 2015). Both schools are actively involved in sharing positive education practices with educators throughout the world.

Discussion

Despite its recent development, many schools around the world have begun to implement positive education practices from stand-alone curricula to whole school approaches. These practices are strongly rooted in positive psychology. They focus less on reducing and preventing difficulties and more on building upward spirals and helping youth to thrive. Many positive education approaches focus on a full range of outcomes included in PERMA (or PERMA+H). They often include activities designed to promote positive emotions, to deepen relationships, and to increase meaningful engagement. Character education, especially identifying and applying strengths, is a core component of these programs.

Research suggests that positive education approaches benefit students' social and emotional well-being (e.g., Adler, 2016; Seligman et al., 2009). Studies have found that, compared with school as usual, positive education programs increase positive social skills (e.g., empathy and leadership), optimism, and happiness. While school teachers and administrators often worry that devoting time to well-being initiatives detracts from students' academic attainment, findings from these studies indicate the opposite. Positive education enhances students' engagement in school and achievement (e.g., Adler, 2016; Seligman et al., 2009). These findings are consistent with recent meta-analytic reviews examining the effects of social and emotional learning programs (e.g., Durlak et al., 2011; Zins et al., 2004). Whole school approaches are more difficult to evaluate using rigorous randomized studies; however, quasi-experimental and qualitative studies of whole school approaches suggest an improvement in mental well-being and strengths knowledge (Vella-Brodrick et al., 2014; White & Waters, 2015). Multi-year, whole school approaches are likely to have even greater impact that curriculum or classroom-only approaches. Several schools are implementing multi-year programs. For example, Geelong Grammar School includes positive education activities in elementary through high school. The recently developed Happy Classrooms program provides positive education exercises for children ages 3 to 18 (Arguis, Bolsas, Hernandez, & Salvador, 2010). When positive education is embedded into the very fabric of the school over many years, it is likely to affect children's development, engagement, and well-being in a deep and lasting way.

Positive education, like learning, is a process. For each educator and each school, it involves increasing knowledge, skills, and strategies to move along a continuum. Noble and McGrath (2013) have identified several conditions or characteristics that educational interventions must bring together to promote well-being. Interventions should: 1) be incorporated into the school as a whole; 2) be taught by teachers and integrated into normal academic learning; 3) be accepted by students and also accepted by teachers; 4) be universal, involving all students; 5) last several years; and 6) use a multi-strategic approach in which different "active ingredients" in children's education may incorporate elements of cognitive-behavioral therapy and other evidence-based teaching strategies. However, not all schools are ready or able to implement whole school and multi-year approaches. In moving toward a world in which schools promote well-being broadly (e.g. social and emotional well-being in addition to academic achievement), each school can progress along this path. For some schools, the next step will be training teachers and other staff to use these skills/ideas in their own lives, while in for other schools, it may be embedding positive education throughout their programming implementing a few programs or only implementing a few programs. To enable this training, adequate planning and implementation within the academic curriculum and agenda is needed in schools (White & Waters, 2015). The application of practices in positive education should start from the specific school realities and assume that the time and the efforts of the teachers are limited, so that it would be necessary to prioritize and distribute the tasks properly toward this new roadmap. This is another area in which collaboration with other fields is useful. We can learn about the practices that support effective professional development, training, and implementation. We can learn about the approaches that allow successful programs to be sustained, to thrive, and to grow. We can also share this knowledge, when developed within positive education as several schools are already doing (e.g., Bott, 2017; White & Kern, 2017).

Despite this progress, positive education has yet to mature as a field. Most programs focus on a fairly narrow range of interventions (many are adapted from positive psychology practices with adults). More studies are needed with rigorous designs, including randomized controls, longitudinal designs, and measures that go beyond self-report. It will be important to determine whether positive education produces long-term benefits and how these benefits compare to those found for other types of interventions (e.g., social and emotional learning, character education). It will be important to determine which positive education approaches are most beneficial for which outcomes.

A definition of positive education is needed. A broad and integrative definition may state that positive education aimed to integrate both concrete interventions, curriculum design, and whole-organization programs performed in school context to promote psychological well-being by developing character strengths, adaptive coping, positive thought, and different social and emotional skills. As well as the promotion of well-being, these interventions are expected to improve school adjustment, peer relationships and general health. Still, questions remain. Is positive education simply positive psychology applied in schools, or is it more than this? The field needs to address concerns expressed by Kristjánsson, Kern, Kaufman, and others and clarify whether and how positive education differs from other closely related fields such as positive youth development, social and emotional learning, and character education, for example. What makes an intervention a "positive education" intervention as opposed to an intervention from one of these other fields? Does positive education provide unique contributions to understanding the development and promotion of well-being in young people? If not, positive education's contribution is likely to be limited and short-lived.

A child of positive psychology, positive education has largely been reared in isolation from these close cousins. Scholars and practitioners in positive education have a great deal to learn from the large bodies of relevant work in these other fields. Important directions for future theoretical, empirical, and applied work are to identify/clarify areas of overlap as well as unique contributions of each field. Thus, rather than working toward the same purpose in isolation, we underline the need of more collaboration across the different fields. Ultimately, collaboration across these fields will allow us to achieve our common goal of helping schools to promote well-being in youth.

As Kristjánsson argues, even if it turns out that positive education is not new, it could still make a helpful contribution to education. At a minimum, positive education has invigorated this area of work as shown by publications, international conferences, and the increasing number of schools and governments that are embracing this approach. Positive education has provided measures and specific intervention approaches. And positive education continues to grow. Examples of recent initiative include the creation of an education division within the International Positive Psychology Association, and the creation of the International Positive Education Network (www.ipositive-education.net/). These organizations are providing opportunities for educators and researchers who are interested in positive education to share and learn from each other. Thus, positive education has just begun and still has to solve many issues. Important and exciting work remains to address these challenges so that positive education can meet its aim of helping schools promote well-being and academic performance on a wide-scale, ultimately enabling all children and adolescents to thrive.

References

Adler, A. (2016). *Teaching well-being increases Academic performance: Evidence from Bhutan, Mexico, and Peru*. Publicly Accessible Penn Dissertations. 1572. Retrieved from http://repository.upenn.edu/edissertations/1572

Arguis, R., Bolsas, A., Hernandez, S., & Salvador, M. (2010). *The "Happy Classrooms" programme: Positive psychology applied to education*. Retrieved July 18, 2017 from http://educaposit.blogspot.pt/p/free-programme-download.html

Boniwell, I. (2013). Introduction to positive education. In S. A. David, I. Boniwell, & A. Conley Ayers (Eds.), *The Oxford handbook of happiness* (pp. 535–539). Oxford, UK: Oxford University Press.

Bott, D. (2017). Geelong Grammar School, Victoria, Australia. In E. E. Larson (Ed.), *The state of positive education* (pp. 12–16). Retrieved from www.ipositive-education.net/ipens-state-of-positive-education-report/

Catalano, R. F., Berglund, M. L., Ryan, J. A., Lonczak, H. S., & Hawkins, J. D. (2004). Positive youth development in the United States: Research findings on evaluations of positive youth development programs. *The Annals of the American Academy of Political and Social Science, 591*(1), 98–124.

Cohen, J. (2006). Social, emotional, ethical, and academic education: Creating a climate for learning, participation in Democracy, and well-being. *Harvard Educational Review, 76*(2), 201–237.

Costello, J. E., Erkanli, A., & Angold, A. (2006). Is there an epidemic of child or adolescent depression? *Journal of Child Psychology and Psychiatry, 47*(12), 1263–1271.

Dahlsgaard, K., Peterson, C., & Seligman, M. E. (2005). Shared virtue: The convergence of valued human strengths across culture and history. *Review of General Psychology, 9*(3), 203–213.

Duckworth, A. L., Peterson, C., Matthews, M. D., & Kelly, D. R. (2007). Grit: Perseverance and passion for long-term goals. *Journal of Personality and Social Psychology, 92*(6), 1087–1101.

Durlak, J. A., Weissberg, R. P., Dymnicki, A. B., Taylor, R. D., & Schellinger, K. B. (2011). The impact of enhancing students' social and emotional learning: A meta-analysis of school-based universal interventions. *Child Development, 82*(1), 405–432.

Eskreis-Winkler, L., Shulman, E. P., Beal, S. A., & Duckworth, A. L. (2014). The grit effect: Predicting retention in the military, the workplace, school and marriage. *Frontiers in Psychology, 5*, 1–12.

Fredrickson, B. L., & Branigan, C. (2005). Positive emotions broaden the scope of attention and thought-action repertoires. *Cognition & Emotion, 19*(3), 313–332.

Froh, J. J., Miller, D. N., & Snyder, S. (2007). Gratitude in children and adolescents: Development, assessment, and school-based intervention. *School Psychology Forum, 2*, 1–13.

Gillham, J., Abenavoli, R., Brunwasser, S., Linkins, M., Reivich, K., & Seligman, M. (2013). Resilience education. In S. David, I. Boniwell, & A. Conley Ayers (Eds.), *The Oxford handbook of happiness* (pp. 609–630). Oxford: Oxford University Press.

Health and Human Development Program. (2011). *Workbook for improving school climate.* Los Alamitos: WestEd.

Kern, M. L., & Kaufman, S. B. (2017). Research in positive education. In E. E. Larson (Ed.), *The state of positive education* (pp. 29–34). Retrieved from www.ipositive-education.net/ipens-state-of-positive-education-report/

Kern, M. L., Waters, L. E., Adler, A., & White, M. A. (2015). A multidimensional approach to measuring well-being in students: Application of the PERMA framework. *The Journal of Positive Psychology, 10*(3), 262–271.

Kristjánsson, K. (2012). Positive psychology and positive education: Old wine in new bottles? *Educational Psychologist, 47*(2), 86–105.

Lerner, R. M., Almerigi, J. B., Theokas, C., & Lerner, J. V. (2005). Positive youth development a view of the issues. *The Journal of Early Adolescence, 25*(1), 10–16.

Noble, T., & McGrath, H. (2013). Well-being and resilience in education. In S. A. David, I. Boniwell, & A. Conley Ayers (Eds.), *The Oxford handbook of happiness* (pp. 563–578). Oxford, UK: Oxford University Press.

Norrish, J. M. (2015). *Positive education: The Geelong Grammar School journey.* Oxford Positive Psychology Series.

Norrish, J. M., Williams, P., O'Connor, M., & Robinson, J. (2013). An applied framework for positive education. *International Journal of Well-Being, 3*(2), 147–161.

Palmer, J., Bresler, L., & Cooper, D. E. (Eds.). (2001). *Fifty major thinkers on education: From Confucius to Dewey.* New York: Psychology Press.

Peterson, C. (2006). *A primer in positive psychology.* New York, NY: Oxford University Press.

Peterson, C., & Seligman, M. (2004). *Character strengths and virtues: A handbook and classification.* Oxford: Oxford University Press.

Pittman, K. J., Martin, S., & Yohalem, N. (2006). Youth development as a "big picture" public health strategy. *Journal of Public Health Management and Practice, 12,* S23–S25.

Proctor, C., Tsukayama, E., Wood, A. M., Maltby, J., Eades, J. F., & Linley, P. A. (2011). Strengths gym: The impact of a character strengths-based intervention on the life satisfaction and well-being of adolescents. *The Journal of Positive Psychology, 6*(5), 377–388.

Ryan, R. M., & Deci, E. L. (2001). On happiness and human potentials: A review of research on hedonic and eudaimonic well-being. *Annual Review of Psychology, 52*(1), 141–166.

Ryff, C. D., & Keyes, C. L. M. (1995). The structure of psychological well-being revisited. *Journal of Personality and Social Psychology, 69*(4), 719–727.

Schulman, P. (1995). Explanatory style and achievement in school and work. In G. M. Buchanan & M. E. P. Seligman (Eds.), *Explanatory style* (pp. 159–171). Hillsdale, NJ: Lawrence Erlbaum Associates.

Seligman, M. E. P. (2002). *Authentic happiness.* New York: Free Press.

Seligman, M. E. P. (2011). *Flourish.* London: Nicholas Brealey Publishing.

Seligman, M. E. P. (2017). One leader's account: Introduction and history of positive education. In E. E. Larson (Ed.), *The state of positive education* (pp. 5–10). Retrieved from www.ipositive-education.net/ipens-state-of-positive-education-report/

Seligman, M. E. P., Ernst, R. M., Gillham, J., Reivich, K., & Linkins, M. (2009). Positive education: Positive psychology and classroom interventions. *Oxford Review of Education, 35*(3), 293–311.

Shernoff, D. J., & Csikszentmihalyi, M. (2009). Cultivating engaged learners and optimal learning environments. In R. Gilman, E. S. Huebner, & M. J. Furlong (Eds.), *Handbook of positive psychology in schools* (pp. 131–145). New York: Routledge.

Vella-Brodrick, D., Rickard, N., & Chin, T.-C. (2014, August). *An evaluation of positive education at Geelong Grammar School: A snapshot of 2013.* The University of Melbourne, Vic, Australia. Retrieved from www.ggs.vic.edu.au/ArticleDocuments/889/Research%20Report-GGS-August2014.pdf.aspx

White, M. A., & Kern, M. L. (2017). St. Peters's College, Adelaide, Australia. In E. E. Larson (Ed.), *The state of positive education* (pp. 17–22). Retrieved from www.ipositive-education.net/ipens-state-of-positive-education-report/

White, M. A., & Waters, L. E. (2015). A case study of "The Good School": Examples of the use of Peterson's strengths-based approach with students. *The Journal of Positive Psychology, 10*(1), 69–76.

Zins, J. E., Weissberg, R. P., Wang, M. C., & Walberg, H. J. (2004). *Building school success through social and emotional learning.* New York: Teachers College Press.

35

THE REAL HAPPINESS IN EDUCATION

The Inclusive Curriculum

Isabel Lopez-Cobo, Inmaculada Gómez-Hurtado, and Mel Ainscow

Currently, the discourse that proposes taking actions to ensure students are happy in schools is becoming more prevalent. This discourse has provoked numerous reactions among academics. In certain educational contexts, a misunderstanding has arisen concerning happiness because the latter has been restricted to a single expression, namely, hedonic happiness. This restriction has caused schools, with good intentions but mistaken means, to promote the segregation of students based on race, disability, or academic performance. This separation is justified by appealing to the assumption that students must be happy, while often neglecting eudemonic happiness, which is associated in contrast with functions of a higher-order and achieved in the long-term.

The literature supports the understanding that such discriminatory practices, as well as this way of understanding education and organizing the educational system, cause serious damage to the strengths of the human being that were recognized by Peterson and Seligman (2004). Hence, the alternative agreed on by the scientific community is the use of school inclusion to facilitate the development of all students.

Throughout this chapter, we demonstrate the intimate link between the principles of the inclusive school and the cultivation of the strengths of the human being. Based on scientific evidence, we defend a curriculum that enhances these strengths in the classroom and improves academic performance through a commitment to an inclusive curriculum based on inclusive principles that encourage students to achieve true happiness by harnessing their own potentialities (Seligman et al., 2009).

Inclusive Education

School inclusion emphasizes the positive value of differences, which are considered to further human development. It also values diversity as enriching for students. We require an educational model based on respect of differences and for human rights, a model that effectively embeds a culture of diversity within a framework of democracy, coexistence, and humanization (López Melero, 2004).

As Murillo and Hernández (2011) observe, the concept of school inclusion or inclusive education has undergone great advances since its inception. Thus, whereas the inclusion process was initially associated with integrating students with disabilities into the general classroom, it has been enriched with a new vision focusing on the differences of students in educational processes, whether the differences derive from race, gender, social class, ability, language, or belonging to a cultural minority.

Currently, happiness and common well-being are commonly spoken about, but achieving them entails a commitment to social and educational inclusion that includes all individuals in our society. O'Brien (2010) states: "Sustainable happiness is happiness that contributes to individual, community, or global well-being without exploiting other people, the environment, or future generations." To achieve this goal, we must fight for more equitable educational systems that defend non-exclusive policies and practices and attend to the characteristics of all students (Ainscow, 2016a); that is, we must aspire to build schools that offer everyone a place and that can develop the strengths of the human being to achieve the common goal of happiness.

Thus, a key challenge for 21st-century schools is providing appropriate educational responses to address the diversity of skills, cultures, or motivations of students (Durlak, Weissberg, Dymnicki, Taylor, & Shellinger, 2011). Such a response should be coupled with inclusive practices aimed at addressing the requirements of all students, regardless of their characteristics, and fostering communication links between all parties involved in teaching-learning processes, namely, students, teachers, families, and communities.

Inclusive education is supported by the principles of the Declaration of Salamanca (Booth, Ainscow, & Dyson, 1998). It seeks to mitigate the influence of exclusionary tendencies and negative assessments of difference by adopting a perspective based on the belief that methodological and organizational changes can provide a twofold answer, specifically, helping students with difficulties and improving the abilities, expectations, and social skills of all other students (Ainscow, 2006). The benefits of inclusive education are numerous and affect classroom diversity. To name a few benefits, we can highlight benefits most closely linked to the social field, such as the foundation of the development of human strengths, similar levels of self-esteem among the entire student body (Ntshangase, Mdikana, & Cronk, 2008), and improved participation and interaction in the classroom (De Boer, Timmerman, Pijl, & Minnaert, 2012). Such benefits do not affect only students because, according to Ortiz González and Lobato Quesada (2003), the concept of an inclusive school has positive repercussions in three areas: the conception of individual differences, the quality of education, and the social development of students. Therefore, school inclusion is not neutral and is achieved through the full consideration of all stated factors (e.g., organization, culture, community). Thus, its principles must be present at its core to propel the organization and operation of the inclusive school, promoted by individuals who exercise leadership functions and direct teamwork with all individuals who belong to the school (Ainscow, 2001b), as well as create collaborative networks between schools that increase educational attainment and reduce the achievement gap between struggling students and their classmates Ainscow (2009).

These ideas are considered a paradigm of organization (Ainscow, 2001a; Dyson & Millward, 2000) that supposes a new perspective centered on analyzing barriers within school's systems that block student participation and learning (Booth & Ainscow, 2002), a phenomenon that Ainscow, Booth, and Dyson (2006) call "school improvement with attitude."

Thus, school inclusion is defined as a process designed to respond to the diversity of characteristics and needs of all students, toward establishing quality education for all (Murillo & Hernández, 2011, p. 17). Undoubtedly, in many countries, inclusion remains associated with the inclusion of students with special educational needs. However, a diversity of students is increasingly assumed (Ainscow, 2007), and policies, cultures, and educational practices that promote any type of exclusion are rejected (Parrilla & Susinos, 2004, p. 196). Therefore, we assume a philosophy based on effective education for all (Arnáiz, 2002), premised on an educational model that goes beyond school integration because this philosophy implies adopting a new attitude toward all students (Jiménez Martínez & Vilà Suñé, 1999, p. 171).

Numerous investigations support the development of inclusive schools for achieving more equitable systems that address student needs and guarantee the universal right of all children to receive a quality education (Ainscow, 2016a, 2016b; Ainscow & Messiou, 2016; Ainscow, Dyson, Goldrick, & West, 2016; Ainscow, 2015; Echeita & Navarro, 2014; Ainscow, Dyson, Goldrick, & West, 2013; Dison, 2007).

We advocate a new type of school, concerned with educating all students and interested in their development according to their personal characteristics and the qualities of their environment. This type of school would be open to diversity and would be the fruit of the commitment and reflection of the members of the entire educational community who intervene and work in it (Pujolàs Maset, 2001). Such a school would help students attain happiness.

Principles of the Inclusive School

Based on the theoretical foundations discussed above, we understand the inclusive school as embodying the following necessary and sufficient principles to direct education (Ainscow, 2009, p. 1):

- Increase student participation, reducing student exclusion in the curriculum, culture, and local communities of the school.
- Restructure school cultures, policies, and practices to ensure they respond to the diversity of the students.
- Encourage the presence, participation, and self-realization of all students vulnerable to exclusion, understanding that inclusion does not apply only to students with special educational needs.

Ainscow (1999) argues that progress toward more inclusive educational systems requires shifting from educational practices based on traditional perspectives of special education to perspectives focused on developing "effective schools for all."

Hence, we consider that becoming inclusive is an uninterrupted process (Booth, Ainscow, & Dyson, 1997, 1998; Booth, 1996; Ainscow et al., 2006; Ainscow, 2009) in which different factors, such as educational policies, the organization of supports, and the leadership of the center, interact.

We also emphasize the importance of considering the following characteristics or assumptions when understanding what we mean by inclusive education (Ainscow, 2012, p. 40):

- Inclusion applies to all children and young people in the school.
- Inclusion emphasizes presence, participation, and school outcomes.
- Inclusion is an ongoing process.
- Inclusion and exclusion are closely linked such that inclusion implies an active struggle against exclusion.

Therefore, an inclusive school should continuously change because the inclusive framework activates a process that demands continuous vigilance (Ainscow, 2012, p. 40). Muntaner, Rosellón, and De la Iglesia (2016, p. 36) consider that inclusive schools promote the consolidation of inclusive practices that imply a series of indicators, namely, understanding difference as natural to each person (the positive value of difference); recognizing the richness of diversity; and managing heterogeneous groups and inclusive practices that satisfy at least three conditions: guaranteeing the presence, participation, and learning of all students.

Inclusive Education for Achieving Happiness

Positive education is considered by Seligman et al. (2009) as not only an educational model that strives for habitual competences in the educational system but also a pedagogy exemplifying a broader perspective on fostering the happiness of the individual.

If we analyze different investigations, we will find that the main contribution of positive psychology coincides with several basic principles of inclusive education. For example, positive psychology considers that achieving happiness and well-being requires prioritizing the construction of the strengths and virtues of the human being (Peterson & Seligman, 2004; Sheldon & King, 2001; Seligman & Csikszentmihalyi, 2000). Similarly, the foundations of the inclusive school confer a positive value on the characteristics of all students and promote the realization of the student's potential (Muntaner et al., 2016; Ainscow, 2005; Arnáiz, 2003).

Peterson and Seligman (2004) set forth a classification of strengths and virtues involving 24 strengths that are divided into six virtues considered universal. These strengths, with their corresponding virtues, can be cultivated in schools (Seligman et al., 2009) to establish an inclusive curriculum that fulfills the needs of all students, thus improving resources (Ainscow, 2012) and favoring the development of an inclusive school.

Seligman et al. (2009) introduce positive education in schools to strengthen different competences through a common inclusive curriculum premised on building strengths because the authors consider three important reasons that justify this type of education.

Bahona, Sánchez, and Urchaga (2013) praise the possibilities of Positive Psychology in the educational field and share their experiences concerning programs implemented with favorable results by Seligman et al. (2009), such as the Pen Resilience Program (PRP) and the Strath Haven Positive Psychology Curriculum, in addition to the ongoing Geelong Grammar School project, as well as programs created in Spain, namely, the Happy Classrooms Program (Programa Aulas Felices) (Arguís Rey et al., 2011) and the Educational Program for emotional and moral growth (Programa educativo de crecimiento emocional y moral, PECEMO) (Alonso & Iriarte, 2005). Apart from these programs, Bahona, Sánchez, and Urchaga (2013) also cite other researchesthat corroborates solidly the claim that well-being improves learning and that positive attitude increases attention, creative thinking, and holistic thinking capacities.

To delve more deeply into analyzing the points of contact between positive education and the inclusive school, we could start with the lessons of Ainscow (2012, pp. 39–49) to review the lessons of each educational model and confirm that they share a dual objective that becomes one: to admit diversity to find happiness. The first lesson is specifying the components of inclusive education to develop inclusive schools and create policies and practices to achieve this goal in the school environment. Likewise, we must emphasize the necessity of developing human strengths in the classroom so that the curriculum proposed by the school administration is not reduced to academic content but admits all components that can support the overall development of students.

Another basic task to promote an inclusive school entails revitalizing available human resources and changing the attitudes of professionals to overcome barriers to participation and learning. Valverde, Fernández, and Revuelta (2013), supported by Nias (1996), defend this ideal based on their study of the importance of teachers' emotions in constructing teaching and learning processes (Zembylas, 2005). In this way, teachers would exhibit a more positive attitude as they develop more of their strengths, which would in turn directly impact learning.

The third lesson, consistent with Ainscow (2012), involves using different forms of evidence available in the classroom. That is, the application of different methods, didactic and organizational, and resources would be another effective way to encourage teachers to develop more inclusive practices. Hence, to include programs in the classroom that cultivate the strengths and virtues identified by Seligman (2002) would not constitute merely another initiative or teaching method to improve learning but would imply teachers developing their own content, none other than the strengths themselves (Seligman et al., 2009).

The use of additional pedagogical support for addressing students' needs requires careful planning by and adequate training of the individuals committed to this task. This lesson links the importance of developing specific programs that help promote the strengths of the human being to happenings in the classroom. Crucially, all professionals must be involved with students to perform these programs.

Inclusive schools may assume different forms, but they all embrace an organizational culture that positively values student diversity, a feature compatible with Positive Education, which seeks to develop the strengths of the human being and abandon ideas that adopt negative perspectives of the person (Peterson & Seligman, 2004).

Finally, in inclusive schools, the role of school leaders is to collaborate to promote an inclusive culture, which involves considerable effort in communication and interrelation with our remaining classmates. Hence, a high degree of well-being is necessary, as well as strengths and virtues for developing an inclusive leadership (Ryan, 2003, 2006). Thus, Essomba (2007) believes that inclusive leadership implies that the leader situates human relationships at the center of action, above strategies and resources. The leader must also perceive the educational community as an open system of interdependent and complex relationships to guide transformation toward the social environment, so it does not remain confined to the classroom.

Likewise, relations between schools and the community, networking, social networks, and the mass media greatly influence the implementation and effects of emotional education (Bisquerra, 2016). Additionally, Seligman (2002) states that positive emotions should predominate in every educational space, thereby promoting feelings of gratitude, forgiveness, enjoyment, and optimism, among others. To foster inclusive schools that address the diversity of student requirements, we must, as Seligman (2002) asserts, promote positive emotions, which demand positive attitudes that favor an educational model that enlists all children, as they all have a right to education. Attitudes are, therefore, fundamental factors for developing inclusive schools (Jiménez Martínez & Vilà Suñé, 1999).

In 2010, Bisquerra noted that happiness in education is more interesting as a process than as a product, with the priority being to discern how, through learning, one can learn to be happy. To achieve this discernment, the school must aim at the happiness of the student by focusing on well-being, understanding it as not only an antidote to depression but also a means to increase life satisfaction, an aid for stimulating learning and creative thinking (Seligman et al., 2009)—in other words, human flourishing.

Finally, we must remember that language "is essentially involved in all academic subjects" and that communication provides the basis for all other actions and achievements. Therefore, incorporating a diversity of voices into the classroom would help improve the acquisition of the desired language and tone. Further developing this idea, we can note that effective communication is the main means of conducting a dynamic assessment of shared understanding because communication entails more than using language to exchange information. In fact, communicating involves interpreting emotions, understanding contexts, combining and adjusting ideas, as well as cultivating creativity through listening and interpreting the *other's* message. The inclusion of dialogue in the classroom therefore facilitates the appropriation, co-construction and transformation of one's thoughts, helping individuals grow as people and with the community (Mercer, 2013). In this sense, we can also speak of fully positive communication in the classroom.

In 1978, Vygotsky had already highlighted that the level of potential development is determined by the ability to solve problems under the guidance of an adult or in collaboration with peers. The benefits of interactions with diverse students in the classroom extend beyond cognitive improvements, positively influencing emotional development and well-being (Whitebread, 2012).

The brain's sociality (RSA, 2010) enables a constant orientation toward the *other* and toward meaning-making during the interaction to improve the student's abilities. Starting from the theory of the mind, we can observe that the brain not only allows us to make predictions regarding our or *another's* emotional state but also helps us make assessments about the type of knowledge we share with another person, enabling us to judge their levels of understanding. Interaction with different students helps continuously refine one's judgments, values, and knowledge, but above all, it encourages the understanding of the *other* (Jeong & Chi, 2007), which affects the comprehension, in brief, of oneself, which is greatly relevant to eudemonic happiness.

In summary, inclusive education and enhancing quality dialogs between equals are not only useful for acquiring skills and improving academic performance. They also form a backbone in the development of human strengths and therefore in helping students achieving hedonic and eudemonic happiness, students who, as adults, can live a full and flourishing life.

References

Ainscow, M. (1999). Understanding the development of inclusive schools. In R. Slee (Ed.), *Studies in inclusive education series*. London: Falmer Press.

Ainscow, M. (2001a, Autumn). Developing inclusive schools. *Journal of Educational Change, 26,* 1–7.

Ainscow, M. (2001b). *Desarrollo de escuelas inclusivas. Ideas, propuestas y experiencias para mejorar las instituciones escolares*. Madrid: Narcea.

Ainscow, M. (2005). Developing inclusive education systems: What are the levers for change? *Journal of Educational Change, 6*(2), 109–124.

Ainscow, M. (2006). Towards a more inclusive education system: Where next for special schools? In R. Cigman (Ed.), *Included or excluded? The challenge of the mainstream for some SEN children*. London: Routledge.

Ainscow, M. (2007). Taking an inclusive turn. *Journal of Research Special Education Needs, 7*(1), 3–7.

Ainscow, M. (2009). Local situations for local contexts: The development of more inclusive education systems. In R. Rasmus (Ed.), *Den inkluderende skole I et ledelsesperspektiv. (Leadership perspectives on the inclusive school)*. Frydelund: Copenhagen.

Ainscow, M. (2012). Haciendo que las escuelas sean más inclusivas: lecciones a partir del análisis de la investigación internacional. *Revista de Educación Inclusiva, 5*(1), 39–49.

Ainscow, M. (2015). *Towards self-improving school systems: Lessons from a city challenge* (1st ed.). London: Routledge.

Ainscow, M. (2016a). Collaboration as a strategy for promoting equity in education: Possibilities and barriers. *Journal of Professional Capital and Community, 1*(2), 159–175.

Ainscow, M. (2016b). Diversity and equity: A global education challenge. *New Zealand Journal of Education Studies, 51*(2), 143–155. doi:10.1007/s40841-016-0056-x

Ainscow, M., Booth, T., & Dyson, A. (2006). Inclusion and the standards agenda: Negotiating policy pressures in England. *International Journal of Inclusive Education, 10*(4), 295–308.

Ainscow, M., Dyson, A., Goldrick, S., & West, M. (2013). Promoting equity in education. *Revista de investigación en educación, 3*(11), 32–43.

Ainscow, M., Dyson, A., Goldrick, S., & West, M. (2016). Using collaborative inquiry to foster equity within school systems: Opportunities and barriers. *School Effectiveness and School Improvement, 27*(1), 7–23. doi: 10.1080/09243453.2014.939591

Ainscow, M., & Messiou, K. (2016). Learning from differences: A strategy for teacher development in respect to student diversity. *School Effectiveness and School Improvement, 27*(1), 45–61. doi:10.1080/09243453.2014.966726

Arguís Rey, R. A., Valero, A. P. B., Paniello, S. H., & Monge, M. D. M. S. (2011). Aulas felices puesta en práctica. *AMAzônica, 6*(1), 88–113.

Alonso, N., & Iriarte, C. (2005). *Programa educativo de crecimiento emocional y moral: PECEMO*. Málaga: Aljibe.

Arnáiz, P. (2002). Hacia una educación eficaz para todos: La educación inclusiva. *Educar en el 2000, 5*, 5–19.

Arnáiz, P. (2003). *Educación inclusiva: una escuela para todos*. Málaga: Ediciones Aljibe.

Bahona, M. N., Sánchez, A., & Urchaga, J. D. (2013). La Psicología Positiva aplicada a la educación: el programa CIP para la mejora de las competencias vitalesen la Educación Superior. *Revista de Formación e Innovación Educativa Universitaria, 6*(4), 244–256.

Bisquerra, R. (2010). *Educación emocional y bienestar.* Madrid: Wolters-Kluwer.

Bisquerra, R. (2016). Educación emocional. *I Jornadas del Máster en Resolución de Conflictos en el Aula,* Valencia, junio. Retrieved from https://online.ucv.es/resolucion/jornadas-de-resolucion-de-conflictos/

Booth, T. (1996). A perspective on inclusion from England. *Cambridge Journal of Education, 26*(1), 87–99.

Booth, T., & Ainscow, M. (2002). *Index for inclusion* (2nd ed.). *Developing leaning and participation in schools* (2nd ed.). Manchester: CSIE [trad. Guía para la evaluación y mejora de la educación inclusiva. Madrid: Consorcio Universitario para la Educación Inclusiva].

Booth, T., Ainscow, M., & Dyson, A. (1997). Understanding inclusion and exclusion in the English competitive education system. *International Journal of Inclusive Education, 1*(4), 337–354.

Booth, T., Ainscow, M., & Dyson, A. (1998). England: Inclusion and exclusion in a competitive system. In T. Booth & M. Ainscow (Eds.), *From them to us: An international study of inclusion in education.* London: Routledge.

De Boer, A., Timmerman, M., Pijl, S. J., & Minnaert, A. (2012). The psychometric evaluation of a questionnaire to measure attitudes towards inclusive education. *European Journal of Psychology of Education, 27*(4), 573–589. doi:10.1007/s10212-011-0096-z

Dison, A. (2007). National policy and the development of inclusive school practices: A case study. *Cambridge Journal of Education, 37*(4), 473–488.

Durlak, J. A., Weissberg, R. P., Dymnicki, A. B., Taylor, R. D., & Shellinger, K. B. (2011). The impact of enhancing students' social and emotional learning: A meta-analysis of school-based universal interventions. *Child Development, 82*(1), 405–432.

Dyson, A., & Millward, A. (2000). *School and special needs: Issues of innovation and inclusion.* Londres: Paul Chapman.

Echeita, G., & Navarro, D. (2014). Educación Inclusiva y desarrollo sostenible: una llamada urgente a pensarlas juntas. *Edetania: estudios y propuestas socio-educativas, 46,* 141–162.

Essomba, M. A. (2007): "Estrategias de innovación para construir la escuela intercultural", in J. L. Álvarez & L. Batanaz (Eds.). *Educación intercultural e inmigración. De la teoría a la práctica* (pp. 177–212), Madrid: Biblioteca Nueva.

Jeong, H., & Chi, M. (2007). Knowledge convergence and collaborative learning. *Instructional Science, 35,* 287–315. doi:10.1007/s11251-006-9008-z

Jiménez Martínez, P., & Vilà Suñé, M. (1999). *De educación especial a educación en la diversidad.* Málaga: Ediciones Aljibe.

López Melero, M. (2004). *Construyendo una escuela sin exclusiones. Una forma de trabajar en el aula con proyectos de investigación.* Málaga: Ediciones Aljibe.

Mercer, N. (2013). The social brain, language, and goal-directed collective thinking: A social conception of cognition and its implications for understanding how we think, teach, and learn. *Educational Psychologist, 48*(3), 148–168.

Muntaner, J., Roselló, M. R., & De la Iglesia, B. (2016). Buenas practicas en Educación Inclusiva. *Educatio Siglo XXI, 34*(1), 31–50.

Murillo, F. J., & Hernández, R. (2011). Una dirección escolar para la inclusión. *Revista de Organización y Gestión Educativa, 1,* 17–21.

Nias, J. (1996). Thinking about feeling: the emotions in teaching. *Cambridge Journal of Education 26*(3), 293–306.

Ntshangase, S., Mdikana, A., & Cronk, C. (2008). A comparative study of self-esteem of adolescent boys with and without learning disabilities. *International Journal of Special Education, 23*(2), 75–84.

O'Brien, C. (2010). Sustainability, happiness and education. *Journal of Sustainability Education, 1.* Retrieved from www.jsedimensions.org/wordpress/content/2010/04

Ortiz González, M. C., & Lobato Quesada, X. (2003). Escuela inclusive y cultura escolar: algunas evidencias empíricas. *Bordón: Revista de Pedagogía. Monográfico: Más allá de la Educación Especial, 55*(1), 27–40.

Parrilla, A., & Susinos, T. (2004). El desafío de la educación inclusiva a las exclusiones en los sistemas y comunidades educativas. In J. López Yañez, M. Sánchez Moreno, & P. Murillo Estepa (Eds.), *Cambiar con la sociedad, cambiar con la sociedad. 8° Congreso Interuniversitario de Organización de Instituciones educativas* (pp. 195–200). Sevilla: Secretariado de Publicaciones. Universidad de Sevilla.

Peterson, C., & Seligman, E. P. (2004). *Character strengths and virtues: A handbook and classification.* Oxford: Oxford University Press.

Pujolàs Maset, P. (2001). *Atención a la diversidad y aprendizaje cooperativo en la educación obligatoria.* Málaga: Ediciones Aljibe.

RSA. Royal Society of Arts. (2010). *Royal society of arts education seminars: Curriculum and the social brain.* Retrieved from www.thersa.org/projects/education/education-seminars-2010/curriculum-and-the-socialbrain

Ryan, J. (2003). *Leading diverse schools*. Dordrecht: Kluwer.

Ryan, J. (2006). Inclusive leadership and social justice for schools. *Leadership and Policy in Schools, 5*, 3–17.

Seligman, M. E. P. (2002). *La auténtica Felicidad*. Barcelona: Ediciones B.

Seligman, M. E. P., & Csikszentmihalyi, M. (2000). Positive psychology: An introduction. *American Psychologist, 55*(1), 5–14.

Seligman, M. E. P., Ernst, R. M., Gillham, J., Reivich, K., & Linkins, M. (2009). Positive education: Positive psychology and classroom interventions. *Oxford Review of Education, 35*(3), 293–311.

Sheldon, K. M., & King, L. (2001). Why positive psychology is necessary. *American Psychologist, 56*, 216–217.

Valverde, J., Fernández, M. R., & Revuelta, F. I. (2013). El bienestar subjetivo ante las buenas prácticas educativas con TIC: su influencia en profesorado innovador. *Educación XX1, 16*(1), 255–280. doi:10.5944/educxx1.16.1.726

Vygotsky, L. S. (1978). *Mind in society*. Cambridge, MA and London: Harvard University Press.

Whitebread, D. (2012). *Developmental psychology and early childhood education*. London: Sage Publications.

Zembylas, M. (2005). Discursive practices, genealogies, and emotional rules: A poststructuralist view on emotion and identity in teaching. *Teaching and Teacher Education, 21*(8), 935–948.

36

MUSIC EDUCATION AND HAPPINESS

Susan Hallam and Francisco Cuadrado

Introduction

Being happy is one of the main aims of every human being. Despite this, education systems have not typically made the promotion of happiness or well-being one of their aims. According to the authors of the "Happy Classrooms" program, "teachers think that students' well-being is something that will develop in the future and that education will provide them with the knowledge, skills and attitudes that one day will produce results, and allow them to find a job and a high standard of living so that, eventually, they can be happy" (Arguís, Bolsas, Hernández, & Salvador, 2012, p. 5). As set out in other chapters in this volume, there is a growing interest in education from the positive psychology movement.

Positive education has provided a framework for the development of initiatives and programs that contribute to the enhancement of well-being and happiness through education. As Seligman argues, "positive education is defined as education for both traditional skills and for happiness. The high prevalence worldwide of depression among young people, the small rise in life satisfaction, and the synergy between learning and positive emotion all argue that skills for happiness should be taught in school" (Seligman, Ernst, Gillham, Reivich, & Linkins, 2009, p. 293).

Since the development of positive psychology, different pioneering educational initiatives have been proposed by Seligman and his collaborators. A successful programme has been developed in "Strat Haven" High School in Philadelphia (started in 2002), which focuses on enhancing positive emotions, the identification and use of personal strengths and giving meaning to students' lives. The programme "Bounce Back!" was developed to enhance well-being and resilience (McGrath & Noble, 2011), and "Strong Planet" combines a number of strategies to reinforce students, specifically the positive elements within students' character (Fox, 2008).

Music education across the world is typified by a diversity of approaches. What constitutes music education in one national context, state, or locality does not necessarily apply elsewhere (Cox & Stevens, 2017). Formal provision of music education is not universal. Apart from the music taught in schools as part of the wider curriculum, there are different opportunities to learn music skills and participate in a range of musical activities, in formal or informal contexts, including movement, singing, playing an instrument, listening, appraising, improvising, composing, acquiring musical knowledge, and understanding the national culture.

There is considerable evidence that music education, particularly education by means of music (Elliot, 1995) can contribute to the enhancement of well-being and happiness throughout the lifespan. This conception involves the teaching and learning of music with the focus on direct goals such as brain development, accelerated learning, and the improvement of health and spiritual well-being (Michels, 2001).

This chapter will consider that evidence in terms of the model proposed by Seligman (2002, 2011), which sets out 24 character strengths defined as positive traits that are reflected in thought, feelings, and behavior (Park, Peterson, & Seligman, 2004, p. 603), grouped in terms of six universal virtues derived from a eudaimonic conception of happiness. The six universal Virtues in Action (VIA) are: wisdom and knowledge (curiosity, love of learning, open-mindedness, creativity, perspective); courage (bravery, persistence, authenticity, vitality); humanity (love, kindness and generosity, social intelligence); temperance (self-regulation, prudence, humility and modesty, forgiveness); justice (citizenship, fairness and equity, leadership) and transcendence (appreciation of beauty and excellence, gratitude, hope, spirituality, playfulness).

In this chapter, thirteen strengths identified by Seligman and colleagues that have particular relevance for music education will be considered (Park et al., 2004, p. 606). These have been grouped into five areas as they relate to the ways that music education might support their development:

1. Listening and appraisal: appreciation of beauty and excellence.
2. Improvisation and composition: open-mindedness, creativity, and playfulness.
3. Developing musical skills and performance: self-regulation, persistence, prudence, and bravery.
4. Ensemble activities: citizenship, leadership, and social intelligence.
5. Musical engagement: vitality, well-being, positive self-beliefs.

Table 36.1 sets out the characteristics, alongside their definitions and the behaviors which illustrate them in general and specifically in relation to music. The chapter will set out how the

Table 36.1 Relationship between character strengths and music

Character strength	Musical applications
Appreciation of beauty and excellence (awe, wonder, elevation)	Engaging with music involves evaluating and appraising which in part includes appreciation of beauty
Curiosity (interest, novelty-seeking, openness to experience)	Improvisation, composition, open to learning new genres
Open-mindedness is defined in relation to judgment and critical thinking.	Evaluating and appraising: musical compositions (own and others), performance, and progress in learning
Creativity (originality, ingenuity)	Improvisation and composition, novel interpretations of existing music
Playfulness	Ability to explore sounds playfully in the process of composition or improvisation
Self-regulation (self-control)	Being disciplined about instrumental practice; self-regulating practice in relation to progress.
Persistence (perseverance, industriousness)	Persisting in learning to play an instrument and in learning new music; continuing to practice when progress is slow.
Prudence	Care in performance preparation to ensure overlearning to secure good performance.

(Continued)

Table 36.1 Continued

Character strength	Musical applications
Bravery (valor)	These skills are required in undertaking any kind of public musical performance.
Citizenship (social responsibility, loyalty, teamwork)	The skills required for ensemble performance.
Leadership	The skills required in ensemble rehearsal and performance.
Social intelligence (emotional intelligence, personal intelligence)	Skills required for ensemble rehearsal and performance
Vitality (zest, enthusiasm, vigor, energy)	Actively making music with others provides motivation, music itself can be energizing, success enhances self-belief which protects against depression.

(source: own elaboration)

development of each of these might be supported through music education. The focus will be on children and young people. There is much research in relation to the way that music education can develop these characteristics from neuroscience, psychology, sociology, and education (for reviews see Hallam, 2014; Creech et al., 2013; Papageorgi, Hallam, & Welch, 2007).

Listening to Music and Appraisal: Appreciation of Beauty and Excellence

Music is a means of communication between the composer, the performer, and the listener. The performer interprets the composer's meanings and communicates directly with the audience, who in turn communicate through the feedback they give. For this communication to be successful, all parties need to be able to listen. The skills related to listening, appraisal, and evaluation are crucial to music making at every level. Listening is central to all musical activity. Responses to music can be physiological, through movement, intellectual, aesthetic, and emotional, although in education the focus has tended to be on aesthetic and intellectual responses (Hallam, 2010). The very powerful effects that music can have on the emotions (Gabrielsson, 2010) tend not to be taken into account. This is despite the fact that when young people are encouraged to appraise music not only analytically but also using figurative language including similes, analogies, and metaphors (O'Brien, 1990) and references to emotion (Bula, 1987) they consistently score higher on attitudinal and conceptual understanding, unless they reactive negatively to the musical genre. Familiarity plays a role in our liking and appreciation of music. The more familiar we are with a piece of music, the more we like and value it, although over familiarity may lead to boredom or even dislike (North & Hargreaves, 1997). This suggests that musical preferences can be changed through prolonged exposure (Shehan, 1987).

These activities are crucial to music making at every level, professional, amateur, expert, or novice. The process of appraising involves listening and making comparisons (implicit or explicit) with already acquired internal representations of music. Even quite young children are able to articulate ideas about their listening and as they get older they are able to predict, compare, evaluate, express preferences, reflect, recognize, and make judgments about music (Bundra, 1993). Musically trained children demonstrate similar skills to adults including classifying, elaborating, comparing, predicting, and evaluating (Richardson, 1996) suggesting that the ability to think critically while listening to music is related to experience with music rather than age.

Improvisation and Composition: Creativity, Playfulness, Open-Mindedness

It has become increasingly common for class music lessons to include opportunities for improvisation and composition. The nature of these activities varies depending on the age of the learner. For instance, in the early years and during elementary education compositions may be undertaken with the whole class working together, perhaps adding musical accompaniment to a story or creating music around a specific topic. For older children, creative activities may be undertaken in small groups with the teacher acting as a facilitator (Hallam, Creech, & McQueen, 2016). However these activities are undertaken, they require musical communication between the participants as they listen and respond to the sounds created by others.

Children's creative music activities are supported by evidence that they are open-eared. They are willing to listen to and engage with all kinds of music (Hargreaves, 1982). However, as they become older, they tend to become less tolerant of a broader range of music in favor of popular music. Music education, where a range of different genres is included, can prevent this (McKoy, 2003). The extent of time actively making music in childhood is also associated positively with more general openness-to-experience (John, Naumann, & Soto, 2008).

Composition is usually viewed as requiring the highest levels of creativity, in part, perhaps, because of its greater permanence in comparison with improvisation. In education, however, the distinction between composition and improvisation is frequently blurred. The early stages of children's composing can be conceptualized as free improvisation. Very young children can improvise and do so spontaneously usually in the form of songs (see Azzara, 2002 for a review). The process of composing is remarkably similar for children, young people and professional composers (Folkestad, 2004). The process consists of interactions between the participant's musical experiences and competences, their cultural environment, the available tools and instruments, and the instructions that they are given. Externally imposed constraints, the professional composer's commission, and the instructions given to learners by the teacher provide the framework. There are also common elements to each creative act, early formulations suggested four main stages (see Table 36.2). Each of these stages satisfies some of the elements of the criteria for happiness.

Music technology has the potential to break down the barriers between composer, performer, and listener providing extensive opportunities for non-musicians to undertake creative musical activities, as well as to explore, create, and manipulate sounds through a variety of processes. In a field study of 220 musicians from 38 different countries, Cuadrado (2015) concludes that the use of a Digital Audio Workstation has clear and positive effects on musicians and their creative processes and improves productivity. Crow (2006) describes how children can develop creative skills through using DJ remixing software which allows the user to control and alter the music in a number of different ways. Some software provides the opportunity to record and mix musical performances which enables the creation of original compositions. Furthermore, participating in

Table 36.2 Four stages of creativity

Creativity Stage—Wallas (1926)	
Preparation	Gathering of relevant information
Incubation	Time to mull over the problem
Illumination	Derivation of a solution
Verification	Formalization and adaptation of the solution

(source: own elaboration)

musical activities develops creativity beyond musical activities in pre-schoolers (Kalmar, 1982), first graders (Wolff, 1979), and second, fourth and sixth graders (Kiehn, 2003). However, where children are offered opportunities for participating in creative musical activities the effects are stronger (Koutsoupidou & Hargreaves, 2009).

Developing Musical Skills and Performance: Persistence, Self-Regulation, Prudence, and Bravery

Much learning in music is focused on developing musical skills and the communication skills required in performing. Particularly important in instrumental practice is the development of self-regulation and persistence. These skills once developed in musical contexts seem to transfer to other activities.

Evaluations of El Sistema (the Venezuelan youth orchestra program for social development of children through musical learning and performance) and related programmes have shown that participation enhances children's determination and persistence (Creech et al., 2013). The experience of flow during practice may support this (Butkovic, Ullen, & Mosing, 2015). People who experience flow typically report higher levels of well-being, with positive emotions and moods (Csikszentmihalyi, 1988). A sense of accomplishment may also support commitment to practice.

Self-regulation skills are crucial in learning to play an instrument. Participating in formal early learning education classes has been shown to impact positively on self-regulation in three- to four-year-olds (Winsler, Ducenne, & Koury, 2011) and also on children engaging in music therapy with their parents (Malloch et al., 2012), in terms of inappropriate speaking to others (Galarce, Berardi, & Sanchez, 2012) and emotional regulation (Brown & Sax, 2013).

Closely related to research on self-regulation is exploration of whether actively making music impacts on executive functions, i.e. working memory; the conscious control of action, thoughts, emotions; and general abilities such as planning, the capacity to ignore irrelevant information, to inhibit incorrect automatic responses and to solve problems, skills which are required for musical communication. Executive functions also include cognitive flexibility—the ability to adjust to novel or changing task demands. Playing a musical instrument requires many of these sub-skills. Formal music practice involves cognitive challenge, controlled attention for long periods of time, keeping musical passages in working memory or encoding them into long-term memory and decoding musical scores and translating them into motor programmes. These activities draw on complex cognitive functions that have been illustrated in brain imaging research (Stewart et al., 2003).

One element of playing an instrument or singing is performance, the communication of musical meaning. This requires bravery but also elements of prudence. For some performance is an exhilarating and joyful experience but for some any pleasure that may be derived from it is minimal because of stage fright (Hallam et al., 2016). The physiological changes which accompany performance anxiety are accompanied by behavioral indicators which can result in loss of concentration and attention, heightened distractibility, memory failure, distorted thinking, and misreading of the musical score (Steptoe, 2001). Performing in public or for examinations or competitions requires courage to overcome these challenges.

Preparing for performance requires prudence in the sense that the performer must be well prepared (Papageorgi, 2007). The key elements to overcoming the maladaptive effects of performance anxiety include appropriate preparation (technical and psychological) and the acquisition of appropriate coping strategies, for instance, maintaining a positive attitude to the performance, reducing its perceived level of importance, and focusing on communication of the music to the audience.

Ensemble Work: Citizenship, Leadership, and Social Intelligence

Music provides many opportunities for developing skills relating to citizenship. Where music making occurs with others, it can play a major role in developing team working. In the El Sistema programme intensive ensemble activities are seen as a rich opportunity for nurturing positive citizenship skills, including "respect, equality, sharing, cohesion, team work, and, above all, the enhancement of listening as a major constituent of understanding and cooperation" (Majno, 2012, p. 58). The evidence from such programmes has shown that children develop strengthened friendships with peers and learn to work and communicate in teams (Creech et al., 2013). Group music making provides an ideal vehicle for developing prosocial, communication, and team-working skills across a range of different groups of children and young people (see Hallam, 2014 for a review). There is also evidence that music making can be used to teach leadership skills to children in elementary and secondary schools (Hallam, 2017) where they learn to communicate verbally and musically with other children.

Group music making in school can contribute to feelings of social inclusion (Rinta, Purves, Welch, Stadler Elmer, & Bissig, 2011), as can extra-curricular activities (Almau, 2005). Music is used with refugee children to support acculturation and integration (Marsh, 2012), with a range of disengaged students to support team working, learning to trust peers and the development of negotiation skills (Dillon, 2010) and with those in the criminal justice system to promote self-efficacy and self-esteem (Daykin, Moriarty, Viggiani, & Pilkington, 2011). Musicalizatech, a project that promoted musical creativity in secondary and high school students showed a clear impact on participants in relation to the development of social and emotional skills; problem-solving and team working; the development of technological skills, and improvement in creative processes (Cuadrado, López-Cobo, Valverde, & Varona, 2017). There is also some evidence that engagement with music is related to positive attitudes toward school and better attendance.

Particularly important in relation to citizenship is the way that participating in group music making can encourage tolerance and the development of social ethics, for instance, there is evidence that music participation can increase acceptance of children with intellectual impairments (Humpal & Wolf, 2007). Concern with wider community issues may also be enhanced. Miszka (2010) investigated the relationships between participation in a range of musical ensembles and community ethics in a very large sample of pupils in over 600 schools. Music participation was related to community ethics including having strong friendships, helping people in the community and working to correct social and economic inequalities.

Members of musical groups have to pay attention to the actions and intentions of the other players and their physical and emotional states. They have to be able to communicate their emotions and respond to those of others (Cross, Laurence, & Rabinowitch, 2012). This is one of the main aspects that connects music activity with communication, especially in a positive sense. As scientists from the Max Plank Institute for Human Development in Berlin have demonstrated, interbrain networks do emerge when making music together, connecting areas of both brains that previously have been associated with social cognition and music production (Sanger, Müller, & Lindenberger, 2012). This is key to developing empathy. Musical participation can enhance empathy in children (e.g. Rabinowitch, Cross, & Burnard, 2013). Active music making may also have the capacity to increase emotional sensitivity. For instance, Resnicow, Salovey, and Repp (2004) found that there was a relationship between the ability to recognize emotions in performances of classical piano music and measures of emotional intelligence that required individuals to identify, understand, reason with, and manage emotions using hypothetical scenarios. The two were significantly correlated which suggests that identification of emotion in music performance draws on some of the same skills that make up everyday emotional intelligence.

Musical Engagement: Vitality, Well-Being, and Self-Beliefs

The concept of vitality in terms of zest, enthusiasm, vigor, and energy is diametrically opposed to the concept to depression. Having no sense of purpose in life can cause depression and a lack of vitality (Seligman, 2011). There is considerable evidence, throughout the lifespan, that active engagement with music enhances vitality, motivation, and enthusiasm for life and also protects against some mental health issues.

Music plays a major role in people's lives. Listening to music can generate feelings of well-being, can facilitate working through difficult emotions, and is frequently linked to spirituality (Juslin & Sloboda, 2010). It is widely used for exploring and regulating emotions and moods and can be effective in inducing positive affective states and also for coping with negative moods and emotions (e.g. Shifriss & Bodner, 2014). In adolescence, music is seen as a source of support when young people are feeling troubled or lonely, acting as a mood regulator, helping to maintain a sense of belonging and community (e.g. Schwartz & Fouts, 2003).

The impact of music on psychological well-being and subsequently good health is largely, although not exclusively, through the emotions it evokes which can be wide ranging (for a review see Juslin & Sloboda, 2010). Music elicits emotions and changes moods through its stimulation of the autonomic nervous system. Bodily responses related to emotion include changes in dopamine, serotonin, cortisol, endorphin, and oxytocin levels (see van Eck, Berkhof, Nicolson, & Sulon, 1996). As oxytocin plays a central role in the formation of social attachment and relationships in humans, music making have an important influence on social relationships.

Making music can also enhance self-esteem which in turn increases feelings of well-being. Enhanced self-beliefs in music can also transfer to other areas. For instance, Degé et al. (2014) showed that the number of music lessons experienced by 12- to 14-year-olds contributed significantly to the prediction of academic self-concept scores. There was a significant positive association between music lessons and academic self-concept even when confounding variables were controlled for. In an intervention study, Rickard and colleagues (2013) studied the impact of Kodaly or instrumental classes on young children and found that the musical activities prevented a decline in global self-esteem measures as experienced by the control group. Overall, however, there is mixed evidence regarding the impact of active engagement with music on self-beliefs. This is not surprising as self-belief systems depend on feedback received from others. If feedback about the development of musical skills and performance is positive then self-beliefs will be enhanced. If this is not the case then no enhancement will occur. If feedback is critical then there could be a negative impact.

Conclusions

As the evidence presented in this chapter confirms, there is a strong relationship between different kinds of musical activity and the virtues and strengths associated with a positive psychological approach to education. The evidence further supports the approach to education proposed in relation to multiple intelligences. From this perspective, musical activity can be seen as offering a pathway toward the personalization of learning, helping to develop different intelligences in every child.

Finally, in relation to lifelong learning, musical activity contributes to the development and maintenance of cognitive, social, and emotional skills, including those that relate to musical and other forms of communication. Music education can therefore be viewed not only for the purposes of musical development but as enriching lives and experiences that support and complement the virtues that relate to all humanity. In this respect, it is no accident that music has always been one of the key foundations in every society and culture. As Philip Balls concludes, "cultures without writing are known and even without visual arts, but there are none that do not produce some kind of music" (2010, p. 14).

References

Almau, A. (2005). Music is why we come to school. *Improving Schools, 8*(2), 193–197.

Arguís, R., Bolsas, A. P., Hernández, S., & Salvador, M. D. M. (2012). *The "Happy Classrooms" programme.* (S. H. P. and M. del M. S. M. Ricardo Arguís Rey, Ana Pilar Bolsas Valero, Ed.) (2nd ed.). Creative Commons. http://doi.org/10.1073/pnas.0703993104

Azzara, C. D. (2002). Improvisation. In R. Colwell & C. Richardson (Eds.), *The new handbook of research on music teaching and learning.* Oxford: Oxford University Press.

Ball, P. (2010). *The music instinct.* New York: Oxford University Press.

Brown, E. D., & Sax, K. L. (2013). Arts enrichment and preschool emotions for low-income children at risk. *Early Childhood Research Quarterly, 28*, 337–346.

Bula, K. (1987). The participation of the verbal factor in perception of musical compositions. *Bulletin of the Council for Research in Music Education, 91*, 15–18.

Bundra, J. (1993). *A study of music listening processes through the verbal reports of school-aged children* Dissertation Abstracts International, UMI No. 9415701.

Butkovic, A., Ullen, F., & Mosing, M. A. (2015). Personality related traits as predictors of music practice: Underlying environmental and genetic influences. *Personality and Individual Differences, 74*, 133–138.

Cox, G., & Stevens, R. (2017). *The origins and foundations of music education: International perspectives* (2nd ed.). London: Bloomsbury Academic.

Creech, A., Gonzalez-Moreno, P., Lorenzino, L., & Waitman, G. (2013). *El Sistema and Sistema-Inspired Programmes: A literature review of research, evaluation and critical debates.* San Diego, CA: Sistema Global.

Cross, I., Laurence, F., & Rabinowitch, T.-C. (2012). Empathetic creativity in music group practices. In G. McPherson & G. Welch (Eds.), *The Oxford handbook of music education* (pp. 337–353). Oxford: Oxford University Press.

Crow, B. (2006). Musical creativity and the new technology. *Music Education Research, 8*(1), 121–130.

Csikszentmihalyi, M. (1988). *Optimal experience.* Cambridge: Cambridge University Press.

Cuadrado, F. (2015). The use of sequencer tools during the composition process: A field study. *Journal of Music, Technology and Education, 8*(1), 55–70. doi:10.1386/jmte.8.1.55_1

Cuadrado, F., López-Cobo, I., Valverde, B., & Varona, D. (2017). Musicalizatech: A collaborative music production project for secondary and high school students. *Journal of Music, Technology and Education, 10*(1), 93–115. doi:10.1386/jmte.10.1.93_1

Daykin, N., Moriarty, Y., Viggiani, N., & Pilkington, P. (2011). *Evidence review: Music making with young offenders and young people at risk of offending.* Bristol and London: University of West of England/Youth Music.

Degé, F., Wehrum, S., Stark, R., & Schwarzer, G. (2014). Music lessons and academic self-concept in 12- to 14-year-old children. *Musicae Scientiae, 18*(2), 203–215. https://doi.org/10.1177/1029864914523283

Dillon, L. (2010). *Looked after children and music making: An evidence review.* London: Youth Music.

Elliott, D. (1995). *Music matters: A new philosophy of music education.* Oxford: Oxford University Press.

Folkestad, G. (2004). A meta-analytical approach to qualitative studies in music education: a new model applied to creativity and composition. *Bulletin of the Council for Research in Music Education* (161/162), 83–90.

Fox, J. (2008). *Your child's strengths: Discover them, develop them, use them.* New York: Viking.

Gabrielsson, A. (2010). Strong experiences with music. In P. N. Julsin & J. A. Sloboda (Eds.), *Handbook of music and emotion: Theory, research, applications* (pp. 547–604). Oxford: Oxford University Press.

Galarce, E., Berardi, L., & Sanchez, B. (2012). *OASIS, OAS Orchestra programme for youth at risk in the Caribbean—Music for social change: Final report.* Washington, DC: Organization of American States.

Hallam, S. (2010). Music education: The role of affect. In P. N. Juslin & J. A. Sloboda (Eds.), *Handbook of music and emotion: Theory, research, applications* (pp. 791–818). Oxford: Oxford University Press.

Hallam, S. (2014). *The power of music: A research synthesis of the impact of actively making music on the intellectual, social and personal development of children and young people.* London: iMERC.

Hallam, S. (2017). *Evaluation of the young music leader programme.* London: VCM Foundation.

Hallam, S., Creech, A., & McQueen, H. (2016). What impact does teaching music informally in the classroom have on teachers, and their pedagogy? *Music Education Research.* http://dx.doi.org/10.1080/1461 3808.2015.1122749

Hallam, S., Creech, A., Papageorgi, I., Gomes, T., Rinta, T., Varvarigou, M., & Lanipekun, J. (2016). Changes in motivation as expertise develops: Relationships with musical aspirations. *Musicae Scientiae*, first published on February 23, 2016as. doi:10.1177/1029864916634420

Hargreaves, D. J. (1982). The development of aesthetic reaction to music. *Psychology of Music*, Special Issue, 51–54.

Humpal, M. E., & Wolf, J. (2007). Music in the inclusive classroom. *Young Children, 58*(2), 103–107.

John, O. P., Naumann, L. P., & Soto, C. J. (2008). Paradigm shift to the integrative big-five trait taxonomy: History, measurement, and conceptual Issues. In O. P. John, R. W. Robins, & L. A. Pervin (Eds.), *Handbook of personality: Theory and research* (pp. 114–158). New York: Guilford Press.

Juslin, P. N., & Sloboda, J. A. (Eds.). (2010). *Handbook of music and emotion: Theory, research and applications.* Oxford, UK: Oxford University Press.

Kalmar, M. (1982). The effects of music education based on Kodaly's directives in nursery school children: From a psychologist's point of view. *Psychology of Music*, Special Issue, 63–68.

Kiehn, M. T. (2003). Development of music creativity among elementary school student. *Journal of Research in Music Education, 51*(4), 278–288.

Koutsoupidou, T., & Hargreaves, D. (2009). An experimental study of the effects of improvisation on the development of children's creative thinking in music. *Psychology of Music, 37*(3), 251–278.

Majno, M. (2012). *From the model of El Sistema in Venezuela to current applications.* Annals of the New York Academy of Sciences, The Neurosciences and Music IV: Learning and Memory (1252).

Malloch, S., Shoemark, H., Cmcec, R., Newnham, C., Paul, C., Prior, M., & Burnham, D. (2012). Music therapy with hospitalised infants: The art and science of communicative musicality. *Infant Mental Health Journal, 33,* 386–399.

Marsh, C. (2012). The beat will make you be courage: The role of a secondary school music program in supporting young refugees and newly arrived immigrants in Australia. *Research Studies in Music Education, 34*(2), 93–111.

McGrath, H. & Noble, T. (2011). *BOUNCE BACK! A wellbeing & resilience program.* Melbourne: Pearson Education.

McKoy, C. (2003). A review of research on instructional approach and world music preference. *Update: Applications of Research in Music Education, 22*(1), 36–43.

Michels, P. (2001). *The role of the musical intelligence in whole brain education* (Doctoral Thesis). Hatfield, Pretoria: University of Pretoria.

North, A. C., & Hargreaves, D. J. (1997). Experimental aesthetics and everyday music listening. In D. J. Hargreaves & A. C. North (Eds.), *The social psychology of music.* Oxford: Oxford University Press.

O'Brien, W. (1990). *The effects of figurative language in music education instruction.* Paper presented at the conference of the Music Educators National Conference, Washington.

Papageorgi, I. (2007). *Understanding performance anxiety in the adolescent musician. Unpublished PhD thesis.* London: Institute of Education, University of London.

Papageorgi, I., Hallam, S., & Welch, G. F. (2007). A conceptual framework for understanding musical performance anxiety. *Research Studies in Music Education, 28*(1), 83–107.

Park, N., Peterson, C., & Seligman, M. E. P. (2004). Strengths of character and well-being. *Journal of Social and Clinical Psychology, 23*(5), 603–619.

Peterson, C., & Seligman, M. E. P. (2004). *Character strengths and virtues: A classification and handbook.* New York: Oxford University Press/Washington, DC: American Psychological Association.

Rabinowitch, T. C., Cross, I., & Burnard, P. (2013). Long-term musical group interaction has a positive influence on empathy. *Psychology of Music, 41*(4), 484–498.

Resnicow, J. E., Salovey, P., & Repp, B. H. (2004). Is recognition of emotion in music performance an aspect of emotional intelligence? *Music Perception, 22,* 145–158.

Richardson, C. P. (1996). A theoretical model of the connoisseur's musical thought. *Bulletin of the Council for Research in Music Education, 128,* 15–24.

Rickard, N. S., Appelman, P., James, R., Murphy, F., Gill, A., & Bambrick, C. (2013). Orchestrating life skills: The effect of increased school-based music classes on children's social competence and self-esteem, *International Journal of Music Education, 31*(3), 292–309.

Rinta, T., Purves, R., Welch, G., Stadler Elmer, S., & Bissig, R. (2011). Connections between children's feelings of social inclusion and their musical backgrounds. *Journal of Social Inclusion, 2*(2), 35–57.

Sanger, J., Müller, V., & Lindenberger, U. (2012). Intra-and interbrain synchronization and network properties when playing guitar in duets. *Frontiers in Human Neuroscience, 6,* 312–331. doi:10.3389/fnhum.2012.00312

Schwartz, K. D., & Fouts, G. T. (2003). Music preferences, personality style, and developmental issues of adolescents. *Journal of Youth and Adolescence, 32*(3), 205–213.

Seligman, M. E. P. (2002). *Authentic happiness: Using the new positive psychology to realize your potential for lasting fulfilment.* New York: Free Press.

Seligman, M. E. P. (2011). *Flourish: A visionary new understanding of happiness and well-being.* New York: Free Press.

Seligman, M. E. P., Ernst, R. M., Gillham, J., Reivich, K., & Linkins, M. (2009). Positive education: Positive psychology and classroom interventions. *Oxford Review of Education, 35*(3), 293–311. Philadelphia: Taylor Francis.

Shehan, P. K. (1987). Stretching the potential of music: Can it help reduce prejudices? *Update, 5,* 17–20.

Shifriss, R., & Bodner, E. (2014). When you're down and troubled: Views on the regulatory power of music. *Psychology of Music, 43*(6), 793–807. doi:10.1177/0305735614540360

Steptoe, A. (2001). Negative emotions in music making: The problem of performance anxiety. In P. N. Juslin & J. A. Sloboda (Eds.), *Music and emotion: Theory and research.* Oxford: Oxford University Press.

Stewart, L., Henson, R., Kampe, K., Walsh, V., Turner, R., & Frith, U. (2003). Becoming a pianist: An fRMI study of musical literacy acquisition. *Annals of the New York Academic Sciences, 999,* 204–208.

van Eck, M., Berkhof, H., Nicolson, N., & Sulon, J. (1996). The effects of perceived stress, traits, mood states, and stressful events on salivary cortisol. *Psychosomatic Medicine, 58*(5), 447–458.

Wallas, G. (1926). *The art of thought.* London: Watts.

Winsler, A., Ducenne, L., & Koury, A. (2011). Singing one's way to self-regulation: The role of early music and movement curricula and private speech. *Early Education and Development, 22,* 274–304.

Wolff, K. (1979). The non-musical outcomes of music education: A review of the literature. *Bulletin of the Council for Research in Music Education, 55,* 1–27.

37

AUDIOVISUAL AND MEDIA LITERACY FOR SOCIAL CHANGE

Emma Camarero, Alexander Fedorov, and Anastasia Levitskaya

Introduction

We are currently immersed in a world where there is continuous learning of digital contexts. This learning, which can be induced or autonomous, exponentially leads society to the search for information in a space where the most recently developed communication and information content is stored, which is none other than the Internet. It is not a matter of age, sex, or nationality; the reality is that with the exception of some sectors at the top of the population pyramid, no one escapes the spell of the Net.

The growing importance of digital contexts in our lives is a matter of particular concern, especially due to the increasing amount of time we spend linking our cognitive activity to the digital medium and to what the screens of our computers and smartphones transmit to us. The skills and abilities that we develop socially in the coming years and that will lead us to become more or less happy and to articulate positive social changes will be directly linked to our ability to interact with, understand, assimilate, or reject information we receive through the Internet. Hence, the creation of policies and strategies that support good practices linked to the so-called media and audiovisual literacy is essential.

Traditionally, information and media literacy have been considered as two separate and different spheres. However, UNESCO (2014) brings them together in a single category of competencies, knowledge, and attitudes that they consider necessary for the proper development of the personal and professional spheres of individuals: *media literacy*. This concept recognizes the fundamental role of information and media in our daily lives. In it lies the freedom of expression and information, as it enables citizens to understand functions of the media and of other information providers, to critically evaluate their content and to make informed decisions as users and producers of information and media content.

Media contents can be in very different formats and can range from simple text to more complex forms of virtual reality. However, without a doubt, one of the formats that has experienced the most development and that will continue to develop in the coming years is the audiovisual format. According to the report titled "Consumo Audiovisual a través de la Red. Hábitos, modelos de negocio y casos de éxito" [Audiovisual consumption through Net habits, business models and success stories] published in 2014 by Eiken-*Basque Audiovisual and Digital Content* (Observatorio Estratégico del Cluster Eiken, 2014), global data consumption was estimated to grow by 400 percent by 2015, mainly from the production of and demand for online videos.

This figure has only increased over the last two years, and all signs indicate that the same trend will continue in the medium term.

Therefore, user data and the production and consumption of online videos leave no room for doubt: such content is some of the most important content of all media communication processes. Users, companies, and institutions converge in an amalgam of roles in which all are simultaneously incipient producers and mass consumers of videos produced by other parties.

According to experts, this growth in audiovisual data traffic will continue over the next few years as a trend of exponential growth, with a profound change to take into account: videos most widely consumed today and those that will generate the most traffic in the immediate future will not be those produced by traditional protagonists of the sector (producers, agencies, and media), but those produced by consumers themselves. Users already lead the creation of the most widely used audiovisual content, creating a new communication language through which the roles of audiovisual creators and consumers are confused.

Bearing in mind that the audiovisual format is increasingly present in communication and information processes, the weight and importance of this format and the need to learn how to use this format as a tool for personal development and positive social change is evident. The correct use of audiovisual media in social relations offers a series of advantages derived both from the ability for such media to reach a larger number of individuals and from the effectiveness of this format in disseminating a message or information. Among these advantages, three must be highlighted:

- Communicative Democracy. The generalization of personal computers and especially of mobile devices and connections coupled with the emergence of numerous low-cost tools that are simple to use have caused limitations on the production and diffusion of audiovisual content to disappear. Anyone anywhere in the world can create videos and disseminate them with greater or lesser impacts on users.
- Reach and diffusion potential. The capacity to broadcast video on the Internet across all population groups is incredibly influential. The power of such videos to transmit messages with more proximity and to offer a more human account imbues a stronger image of credibility among audiences. Creative democratization also encourages peer-to-peer exchange, as audiovisual messages created and disseminated by other users are considered part of a communal experience that unites and promotes socialization through the Internet.
- Production economy. One of the main advantages of online videos is that such videos do not require large investments to produce. A video camera or computer is no longer necessary to own. Virtually any mobile device is capable of recording, editing and disseminating quality audiovisual content. The existence of platforms and social networks available to all users (YouTube, Vimeo, Facebook, etc.) that already allow for live broadcasting have millions of users, and they continue to grow unstoppably.

Audiovisual and Media Literacy for Social Change: Formal and Informal Models of Positive Learning

From its considerable development and ability to transport messages, the correct use of audiovisual content for education is essential. With this we are not only referring to the adaptation of teaching strategies by teachers or to a more concentrated use of this form of content as part of the learning process. The introduction of audiovisual content to the classroom both in formal and informal education is a basic tool to guarantee young people the skills they need to function in today's world. Proper learning for the creation and/or understanding of video content entails the acquisition of positive communication skills. Linking these skills to the acquisition of specific knowledge linked to the realities surrounding students (tolerance, respect for others, climate change, food sovereignty, etc.) offer concrete benefits to students that promote citizen participation and positive social change. According to a report produced by the Autonomous University of Barcelona on the use of audiovisual material in the classroom (Gabinete de Comunicación de la Universidad Autónoma de Barcelona, 2015), there are clear advantages of using this format for teaching:

1. Such content favors the observation of reality, as audiovisuals allow one to accurately represent or record real events.
2. Such content facilitates understanding and analysis, as audiovisual content, interactive animations and graphics allow one to not only observe reality but to also visualize structures, processes and relationships between factors that can be described and captured with simplicity and ease.
3. Such content offers an element of motivation and attraction for students, as students are attracted to both its ease of understanding and realism, including its spectacularity.
4. Such content complements the didactic value of oral and written language, as it is accustomed to linguistic convergence, which is typical of most communications of our time. This encourages complex critical thinking that can inspire attitudes for social change.
5. Such content improves the effectiveness of teaching activities, as audiovisual storytelling improves performance, helps teachers explain concepts, and is more effective in terms of adhering to specific needs beyond those of exhibition.
6. Using audiovisual content in class favors the adaptation and integration of young people in the contemporary world and especially facilitates their acquisition of skills to express themselves through audiovisuals.
7. The use of audiovisuals also entails developing creativity, taking charge of new technological production systems, and acquiring teamwork or problem-solving skills.
8. Such content encourages the use of and access to banks of shared resources and the use of Internet platforms that accelerate the creation and dissemination of audiovisual materials.
9. Such content allows for the introduction of aesthetic and creative evaluation criteria, as audiovisual content can not only be used a representation of reality but also as a form of artistic expression that allows one to value and better understand specific products of cinema and television besides those that are merely digital.

The ways in which we must learn to use new multimedia technologies and to acquire skills that allow us to understand media messages and act for social change are two essential points of scientific discussions held in the field of media and audiovisual literacy, and this is the view of the leading experts. For American thinker Renée Hobbs, one of the great theorists of *media literacy* and the founder and director of the *Media Education Lab*, media literacy covers a much more complex learning process involving skills and abilities that must necessarily involve the ability to create audiovisual content. An adequate use of language, images, sounds, and new digital tools and technologies should reflect behaviors and communicative behaviors based on the application of social responsibility and ethical principles and on the adoption of individual or collective social action for sharing knowledge and solving problems in the familial, labor or territorial environment as members of a community (Hobbs, 2010).

The need for education on the creation and dissemination of audiovisual content is also highlighted by a survey that we conducted using 65 experts of media literacy from 20 countries (Ignacio Aguaded, Ben Bachmair, Frank Baker, Richard Cornell, Tessa Jolls, Laszlo Hartai, W. James Potter, Alexander Sharikov, Silverblatt Art, and Kathleen Tyner among others); the experts are all actively involved in media literacy processes occurring in schools, universities, and other educational institutions and have also published a significant number of scientific papers in this field (Fedorov, Levitskaya, & Camarero, 2016). The experts described the main challenges and difficulties associated with the implementation of audiovisual literacy and of its curricular design. Most experts agreed that are major challenges in five main areas:

1. The resistance of different organisms of state administration to the gradual implementation of learning strategies involving the use of audiovisual tools and content.
2. An excess volume of educational content included in classroom curricula concerning the acquisition of skills and abilities.
3. A lack of initial and ongoing teacher training on audiovisual content.
4. A need to develop critical thinking on the media and audiovisual production in the short and medium term.
5. The development of research proposals and quality curricula on audiovisual literacy.

These challenges identified by experts on audiovisual and media literacy show that in formal education contexts, the volume of video content used and its correct use are issues that are marginalized in most educational settings. This situation is particularly pronounced in terms of the scope of national or regional policies, according to which education lacks curricular projects on effective audiovisual literacy adapted to the current times. This often forces us to create audiovisual literacy strategies outside of classroom or regulated training settings. Employing informal educational settings and especially in socioeconomic environments at risk of exclusion is positive, as they promote more active forms of learning for subjects, are more motivating in that they are directed by what individuals want or need to learn, and are more interactive in facilitating collective exchange between learning communities (Ribeiro Pessoa, Hernández Serrano, & Muñoz Rodríguez, 2015).

David Buckingham (2015), who is considered by many researchers as one of the "fathers" of *media literacy*, affirms that learning contexts have changed as technological tools have changed, that channels of dissemination have been broadened with the Internet revolution and, therefore, that opportunities to use video to promote social change have expanded. Years ago, one needed to have access to complex technological tools accessible only to a few to edit a video; now, a phone in one's pocket allows one to create a video, edit it, and send it, and this constitutes a substantial change and a unique opportunity. This opportunity is not always valued by public policies that promote audiovisual literacy, and therefore, it is worrisome that society is advancing faster than the academic curriculum. This fact is especially grave for developing countries, where audiovisual literacy could play an essential role in the training of young people and in preparing them to become agents of social change through educational projects through which positive audiovisual communication could be given more attention.

The reality is that at the moment, formal education does not in most countries deploy concrete policies on audiovisual literacy in the short and medium term. Therefore, experiences have arisen and are emerging outside of the classroom through non-formal education, which could be considered at the forefront of future educational policies that consider audiovisual content as an essential facet of the curriculum and as a tool for identifying values and concepts that promote positive change. Numerous informal media literacy initiatives have been launched in the last decade and especially in developing countries, and many have been aimed at groups at risk of exclusion (Peguerer-Caprino & Martínez-Cerdá, 2016; Pyles, 2016; Ribeiro Pessoa et al., 2015; Reid, 2013; Soep, 2006). These initiatives aim to empower populations through media and/or audiovisual education as a global educational objective of the *Grunwald Declaration on Media Education* (UNESCO, 2014). In addition, several recent studies have analyzed the need to combine formal and informal media education applied in different contexts and collectives as a training strategy for achieving higher levels of citizen commitment to social change (Martens & Hobbs, 2015; Vraga & Tully, 2015). Especially when speaking about young people, the joint implementation of formal and informal educational experiences can help develop knowledge and skills associated with civic commitment and with the development of positive attitudes through interpersonal communication. All of this is closely linked to subjective and psychological well-being through the application of human strengths (Peterson & Seligman, 2004).

Even when audiovisual literacy finally comes to a head in formal education, informal projects and initiatives are still absolutely necessary in most contexts. This conclusion is drawn, for example, by Damiana Gibbons Pyles (2016) from their study on the documentary productions of young people from rural areas of the Appalachian region, one of the poorest regions in the United States with an index of school failure so high that 60 percent of the population does not complete high school. Through an analysis of a corpus of documentaries produced by young people, the author analyzed how these students participate in media literacy practices by creating documentary videos about themselves and their communities.

Such an experience reflects an audiovisual literacy practice that respects the knowledge, identities, and values of local and rural areas. The young people did not imitate other documentary videos through their productions; instead, they used documentary video editing tools to adopt their own arguments on issues that concern them as a result of their rural environment. This work offers an important example of how audiovisual literacy is encouraged in rural areas, where rural inhabitants themselves teach young people how to create stories about their communities and about themselves and where young people are responsible for telling their own stories through documentary videos. As a result of this initiative, young people of this community began to actively participate in local processes, addressing issues of social isolation. Rural youth then began to find their place in the community through their exploration and videographic representations of members of their community. In learning to represent their own community ties, they better understood themselves and their place in society, fostering a more positive view of their surrounding reality. By increasing their sense of belonging, they also increased their involvement in initiatives to improve their own communities and, through this, their views of themselves.

Another initiative linked to non-formal media literacy with a strong audiovisual component and with interesting results is analyzed by Pegurer-Caprino and Martínez-Cerdá (2016) who focus on the current state of media literacy in Brazil from the perspective of informal education. Their study quantifies this situation by examining a sample of projects and organizations that have formulated activities according to the three main dimensions of internationally recognized media education (access/use, critical understanding, and the production of media content) and that are aimed at different communities of citizens based on different levels of segmentation (age, place, social situations, social groups, and professional fields of application). Likewise, and based on the literature and the diagnosis made, a model from which to study media education projects developed in the field of informal education is proposed. The analysis shows the following: a preponderance of audiovisual content production activities over any other linked to media literacy and how these become tools for the extension of the rights and communication skills of certain people who are generally excluded from traditional media. Audiovisual content production does not always result in citizen empowerment as a tool for social change, but this study confirms that when NGOs focus on critical comprehension activities linked to videographic productions, they manage to articulate proposals offering medium to high potential for empowerment. Thus, the 107 NGOs analyzed were classified into four groups according to the following objectives:

- Democratize access to one of the following resources: communication, education, culture, and technology;

- Work for social change, the transformation of society, and social inclusion;
- Encourage the socioeconomic insertion of recipients; and
- Guarantee and fight for human rights, citizenship, and the rights of populations at risk of social exclusion.

The need to develop media literacy in young people via the use of audiovisual production as a tool for empowerment, participation and/or the exercise of citizenship, and social change is claimed by most of the great researchers of *media literacy*. In this way, media education in the non-formal sphere also complements communicative training aimed at the socioeconomic integration of recipients through the provision of skills, abilities, and useful skills to function as citizens and to act directly through social environments to bring about positive social change.

In a national environment that is completely different from the Brazilian one and in formal educational contexts, for the United States, experiences and studies that value the need for media literacy have multiplied in contrast to those contending that young people do not need special training in the creation and distribution of digital content, as they control the medium (the Internet) and accessible audiovisual technologies. For Martens and Hobbs (2015), media education for young people is necessary if we want them to contribute to civic engagement. To corroborate this theory, the authors conducted an investigation of 400 American high school students. This study investigated the relationship between media literacy programs and greater or lesser academic capacity, frequency in the use of the Internet, skills in the search for information and finally interest in social commitment. The results show that students who had participated in these media literacy programs exhibited substantially higher levels of media knowledge and superior news analysis, audiovisual content creation and advertising analysis skills than students who had not participated. These results confirm that initiatives that instruct on the correct use of online media content can encourage the participation of young people in civic life, as communicative exchange that occurs on the Internet is considered by young people as a pre-eminent facet of their social environment, which when well oriented can foster a tangential avenue for citizen participation and personal involvement by allowing such individuals to play an active role in positive social change.

There have also been experiences of media literacy and informal audiovisual content in supranational contexts. This has been the case for the Interactive Social Media for Integration, Skills Bartering, Empowerment, Informal Learning (ISABEL) project carried out in its experimental phase by 10 organizations from 6 countries: Italy, the United Kingdom, Spain, Turkey, Hungary, and Germany (Ribeiro Pessoa et al., 2015). The project uses the logic of interactive media to enhance the acquisition of skills and social participation and interactivity on the Internet through the reticular articulation of communities or social networks through which subjects in addition to being recipients of information become content producers and protagonist of the processes of social interaction that they promote, thus resembling community reporters. It is an initiative that not only involves young people as the target population but that also has multiple recipients in targeting disadvantaged and/or marginalized groups (the mentally ill, immigrants, the elderly, the unemployed, at-risk women, etc.). Consequently, the objective should be to optimize social and labor conditions and to facilitate the acquisition of skills to enable participation in society and community life.

In short, the project encourages participation, empowers individuals to achieve social inclusion through media literacy and offers training to encourage active participation among citizens who can make their voices heard while remaining connected and integrated in an effective way. According to researchers who have analyzed the results on the experimental phase of the ISABEL project, the project has developed innovative educational approaches that facilitate the integration of at-risk groups through the acquisition of media literacy competencies. In turn, the project affords recipients with personal development and with a strong sense of personal achievement through a flexible virtual environment wherein all types of people learn from one another, thus decreasing their vulnerability.

Finally, we must mention the NICA project initiative, which has facilitated informal audiovisual literacy. Since 2011, through its different phases, more than 200 young people without access to vital resources and people at risk of social exclusion have participated from countries such as Nicaragua, Honduras, Ecuador, or El Salvador. The general objective of this training project and of other actions linked to this initiative (which is still ongoing in other social contexts and countries) is the acquisition of professional knowledge of audiovisual technologies that prepares participants for better employment in a particularly precarious socio-labor context while also contributing to an awareness of collective problems. The results obtained from various analysis tools and publications (Camarero, Cuadrado, & Herrero, 2015; Camarero & Varona, 2016) confirm that training in audiovisual literacy for those belonging to low-income communities can serve as an effective tool for empowerment that prevents social exclusion and that favors social change. It is a flexible training initiative that is based on a proactive learning methodology that is designed to teach from one's knowledge of surrounding realities and that can adapt to the media literacy needs for social change of different groups at risk of exclusion and of communities of developing countries and especially those in Latin America. The results of the NICA project confirm that training activities of this initiative have improved social-labor conditions and have encouraged citizen commitment from young people and participants in general, for whom the creation of audiovisual content and knowledge of the use of social networks can prevent social exclusion while allowing individuals to become spokespersons for their communities and to commit to social change.

Conclusions

In linking audiovisual and/or media literacy, empowerment, and social change, the participatory and civic use of digital tools (and especially when learning leads to the creation or management of such resources) minimizes the existing digital divide affecting vulnerable groups and those at risk of exclusion. Social change is no longer tied exclusively to old paradigms of economic development but is, rather, also materialized through other ways in which societies evolve. Users can create digital content to communicate and to participate in society while achieving empowerment.

The immediate future tells us that digital environments and audiovisual content will be central to future societies. For this reason, it is vital to establish policies and educational initiatives that promote audiovisual literacy as a tool for societal and individual development and that encourage positive social change. The challenge now is to force institutions and organizations to create formal or informal learning spaces in accordance with what society demands from its citizens. Individuals from a community who have received the necessary training to manage their network resources through audiovisual literacy will undoubtedly develop the skills and abilities required to create and disseminate audiovisual content, thus forming digital societies that can interact with other communities and that can manage their communicative needs with a high probability of success.

References

Buckingham, D. (2015). Defining digital literacy: What do young people need to know about digital media? *Nordic Journal of Digital Literacy*, *4*, 21–34.

Buckingham, D., Fedorov, A., & Vrabec, N. (2016). Is media literacy still one of the priorities for policy makers? *Communication Today*, 7(2), 100–107.

Camarero, E., Cuadrado, F., & Herrero, P. (2015). Media literacy focused on social change: Promoting a model of empowerment and employability in Nicaraguan poor communities. *Journal of Media Communication, 2,* 54–61. Retrieved from http://oaji.net/articles/2015/2113-1433918646.pdf

Camarero, E., & Varona, D. (2016). Life story as a research technique for evaluating formation processes in media literacy for social change: Approaching a case of success of the educational project "training, education and innovation in audiovisual media to raise awareness of hunger in Nicaraguan". *International Journal of Media and Information Literacy, 1*(1), 4–10. doi:10.13187/ijmil.2016.1.4

Fedorov, A., Levitskaya, A., & Camarero, E. (2016). Curricula for media literacy education according to international experts. *European Journal of Contemporary Education, 17*(3), 324–334. doi:10.13187/ejced.2016.17.324

Gabinete de Comunicación de la Universidad Autónoma de Barcelona. (2015). *El uso del audiovisual en las aulas. La situación de España.* Retrieved from https://goo.gl/4nG661

Hobbs, R. (2010). *Digital and media literacy: A plan of action.* Washington, DC: The Aspen Institute Communications and Society Program. Retrieved from https://goo.gl/7STM47

Martens, H. & Hobbs, R. (2015) How Media Literacy Supports Civic Engagement in a Digital Age, Atlantic *Journal of Communication, 23*(2), 120–137, DOI: 10.1080/15456870.2014.961636

Observatorio Estratégico del Cluster Eiken. (2014). *Consumo Audiovisual a través de la Red. Hábitos, modelos de negocio y casos de éxito.* Retrieved from https://goo.gl/7KGxC5

Pegurer-Caprino, M., & Martínez-Cerdá, J. F. (2016). Alfabetización mediática en Brasil: experiencias y modelos en educación no formal. *Comunicar, 24*(49), 39–48. http://dx.doi.org/10.3916/C49-2016-04

Peterson, C., & Seligman, M. E. (2004). *Character strengths and virtues: A handbook and classification.* New York: Oxford University Press and Washington, DC: American Psychological Association.

Pyles, D. G. (2016). Rural media literacy: Youth documentary videomaking as a rural literacy practice. *Journal of Research in Rural Education, 31*(7), 1–15.

Reid, J. A. (2013). Rural boys, literacy practice, and the possibilities of difference: Tales out of school. In M. Corbett & B. Green (Eds.) *Rethinking rural literacies* (pp. 135–153). New York: Palgrave Macmillan.

Ribeiro Pessoa, M. T., Hernández Serrano, M. J., & Muñoz Rodríguez, J. M. (2015). Aprendizaje Informal, alfabetización mediática e inclusión social. Descripción de una experiencia. *Profesorado. Revista de curriculum y formación del profesorado, 19*(2), 75–91.

Soep, E. (2006). Beyond literacy and voice in youth media production. *McGill Journal of Education, 41,* 197–214. Retrieved from www.ugr.es/~recfpro/rev192ART5.pdf

UNESCO. (2014). *Declaration on media and information literacy in the Digital Era.* Retrieved from https://goo.gl/nKu0XW

Vraga, E., & Tully, M. (2015). Effectiveness of a non-classroom news media literacy intervention among different undergraduate populations. *Journalism & Mass Communication Educator, 71*(4), 440–452. https://doi.org/10.1177/1077695815623399

38

CARING ETHICS AND MEDIA LITERACY PRACTICE

Megan Fromm and Paul Mihailidis

Contemporary media literacy pedagogy—a critical facet of both communication research and practice in the 21st century—emphasizes issues of inquiry, agency, citizenship, and engagement. Historical explorations of media literacy trace its evolution from simple responses to propaganda and misinformation forward to today's emphasis on "crap detection" (Hobbs & McGee, 2014, p. 57; Rheingold, 2012) and critical processes for identifying manipulation, bias, and what many now refer to as "fake news." With its emphasis on critical analysis and evaluation of facts, sources, and credible information, media literacy has not necessarily adapted to meet the demands of new technologies that increasingly blur lines between fact and fiction. Nor has media literacy practice adequately responded to a culture where mobile phones, algorithmic design, and homophilous networks continuously lessen the ability for people to be in direct dialog with each other. In their recent work on civic imagination and new youth activism, Jenkins, Shresthova, Gamber-Thompson, Kligler-Vilenchik, and Zimmerman (2016) propose more agency-based and participatory models for media literacy education, arguing those empowered to create meaning through media production are better positioned to create and deploy media for personal and collective action taking, especially in relation to politics. Jenkins' team found "that the most highly motivated youth—those most eager to change the world—are taking advantage of any and every available media channel to tell their stories" (2016, n. p.). This attention to the intersection of well-being, media empowerment, and media skepticism represents a unique shift in how researchers and educators come to understand the role of media literacy education in classrooms and communities.

In exploring questions of agency and well-being, for example, Scharrer, Sekarasih, and Olson (2017; Mihailidis, 2009) question whether specific media literacy interventions not only diminish negative media effects but also increase potential for positive media effects, ultimately feeding into current trends of distrust of media institutions as a whole (Edelman, 2017). What do media literacy interventions look like that promote media as a means of "being in the world with others toward a common good?" (Gordon & Mihailidis, 2016). And can media literacy initiatives premised on the critique of media messages and deconstruction of text realistically enable a more positive disposition to media as having the capacity for human agency?

In this chapter we argue for an approach to media literacy that embraces an ethic of care. As a means to designing media literacy pedagogy and practice, care ethics allow us to focus on the relational aspects of media literacy, shifting the locus of inquiry from critical analysis to critical consciousness, and the processes of media that put us in the world with others. Building on scholarship in caring ethics, and critical consciousness, this chapter frames media literacy practice as an appropriate process for developing a relational approach to caring, where critiquing and creating media supports a sense of personal and collective responsibility to act in relation to the betterment of others. In this sense, media literacy supports inclusion and civility in a digital culture increasingly defined by distrust and division.

Media Literacy and Caring

The landscape for digital media and community engagement is in flux. The same large-scale connective networks that were once championed as having the potential to embrace democratic engagement and the collective capacity of citizens are now seen as places for increasing divisiveness, partisanship, and vitriol. The commodification of networks like Facebook, Twitter, Google, and Instagram (Taplin, 2017) have led to tools and platforms that fracture communities by emphasizing differences just as often as they bring communities together under the auspices of shared visions or communal values. The same tools that, for example, helped to organize and launch the Arab Spring also facilitated #Gamergate (Massanari, 2017). In many ways, these tools are optimized for structural capacity building but not necessarily for social good; because these tools and platforms are value-neutral, the key difference lies in whether, and then *how*, those using the tools embrace notions of bringing people together in support of social good. We argue that the prosocial position for social networks supports and is supported by caring ethics, and such ethics are central to the ability for large-scale connectivity to embrace more positive civic engagement.

Media literacies positioned as mechanisms for *caring* emerge from the work of education scholar Nel Noddings, who developed a feminist perspective on care where humans care and are cared for in a relational context, centered on their ability to co-exist. Here we aim to connect the work of caring ethics to media literacy. Media literacy practice framed by caring ethics focuses on media inquiry and application to support "a state of being in relation, characterized by receptivity, relatedness and engrossment" (Noddings & Shore, 1984, p. 112). In their support of agency and self-fulfilment, literacies of caring rely on dispositions that advance critical consciousness (Freire, 1973). In capacities for community-building, literacies of caring resemble attitudes of collaboration, investment, and advocacy in social and civic life. Media literacies often assume that learners come to a space of caring through the media inquiry process. But caring is not emphasized or even located in media literacy pedagogy or practice. We argue here that a caring ethic can position media literacy as a means of bringing learners together through what Gordon and Mugar (2018) call "caring practice." By exploring caring ethics, critical consciousness, and action taking, we will put forward an argument for media literacies that bring people together to support collective efficacy and action taking.

Approaching a Caring Ethic

Caring ethics, or those standards that build positive relationships from a moral standpoint, have been applied to education and pedagogy in many ways, especially as a means for interpersonal understanding and connection. Caring ethics are most readily studied among teacher and education scholars who seek to improve the student-teacher dynamic. Noddings distinguishes caring ethics from the ethics of *caregiving*. The former, and the approach relevant here, refers to a "rapidly developing normative moral theory (. . .) concerned with how, in general, we should meet and treat one another" (2013, p. 11). In this way, we ask specifically "how can I best care for the one before me without damaging other relations in the web of care and without engaging in deceptions that eventually might undermine future encounters?" (Noddings, 2013, p. 14). Such a disposition requires intentional and focused receptivity to others and their messages, a critical component of media literacy. Building on Noddings' work, education scholar Muffet Trout (2012) positions caring ethics within the teacher-student relationship because of its rich focus on Noddings' two levels of care: caring for others and helping them learn to care. Trout finds "caring facilitated the learning process because, for the most part, we did not close off doors to avoid difficult issues" (p. 6). While Trout's studies specifically explore her dynamics educating student teachers about the craft, the lessons gleaned from her research are especially applicable to media literacy practice, in which open communication and engaging in dialog across differences are central. In particular, Trout argues that top-down experiences of care, which flow from teacher to student, also have potential to flow outward as students enact these mechanism within their own peer, family, and community relationships. The intellectual requirements of the caring ethic should not be underestimated; while moral caring is rooted in questions of power, emotion, and authority, the intellectual and interpersonal skills required to uphold and enact a caring ethic are significant. Hansen (2001) articulated the work involved, which, among other aspects, requires "fueling rather than draining students' sense of agency and confidence" while "deepening rather than rendering more shallow students' engagement with the larger world they inhabit" (p. 10). Through moments of educational care and caring vis-a-vis the teacher-student relationship, emotional lessons become intellectual as they are applied in new contexts and for novel ends. Here, students experience the evolution from natural caring (that which arises from love) to ethical caring (that which arises out of duty). In doing so, they open the door to potential for increased critical consciousness.

Critical Consciousness and Caring

The moral imperative and intellectual duty to care for others aligns with important methodologies of critical literacy and critical consciousness (Freire, Ramos, & Macedo, 2014). Additionally, concepts of individual agency and action are reshaped when considered through an ethical caring framework. To Noddings this shift occurs between thoughts of "I must do something" and "something must be done," which removes an individual from a list of potential actors through which change can occur (2013, p. 97). The moral imperative to act, which compels someone into a capacity for caring, is at once an exemplification of the intersection of agency and critical consciousness. Simply put, "in caring, we accept the natural impulse to act on the present other" (p. 99). While Freire envisioned critical consciousness as a means of helping those oppressed by inequality to understand the structures of oppression and work toward liberation from those structures, the process of critical consciousness can also be seen as an extension of the caring ethic. Once one has observed or experienced structures of oppression against themselves or others, one becomes obliged to act toward remedying the injustice. This transference of position to power is reflected in ideas of critical pedagogy (Giroux, 2011), which prioritizes "producing citizens who are critical, self-reflective, knowledgeable and willing to make moral judgments and act in a socially responsible way" (p. 3). To position oneself within this place of social responsibility and moral judgment requires understanding power structures, ideas of privilege, and examples of inequality. Traditional media literacy pedagogies acknowledge this need but stop short of suggesting a moral imperative to others or society writ large. In this capacity, media literacy as practiced without a sense of critical consciousness, has the potential to become only self-serving instead of outward-looking. On the other hand, applied critical consciousness to the highest taxonomies of media literacy-evaluation and engagement-positions individuals to consider the bigger picture, a community and society-oriented application of those literacies.

Education which begins with a caring ethic, and then which establishes a sense of agency and critical consciousness, requires a final, imperative step: action taking. Linking the former concepts shows a distinct need for improvement or change of conditions (conditions which might be absent a caring ethic, critical consciousness, or both). Here, approaches to action taking and participatory culture can provide direction for how to close the caring-action loop. When education and literacy are focused on and embrace community involvement, students begin to shift their focus from individual expression to culture- and community-oriented dialogue (Jenkins, 2006). Because educational institutions have inherent obligations to cultivate responsible citizens, realigning expression literacies to this goal can have lasting impacts and can minimize the participation gap (Losh & Jenkins, 2012). This participation gap, or the absence of meaningful opportunities to participate in community and culture, widens when young adults have neither the ethic or sense of agency to involve themselves in civic and community spaces or issues. On the other hand, viewing media literacies as stepping stones to creating meaningful community participation experiences opens the door for individuals to become advocates, to express their agency, and to act within a caring ethic for those around them.

Caring Literacies in Action

The intersection of these fields of study is reflected in two contemporary case studies which we explain in brief below. These case studies exemplify citizens, politicians, and corporations whose actions embody traditional media literacy cues to think critically about the impact of media in the world. However, in these cases, the subjects of the case studies move beyond analysis, criticism, and even engagement with the media to consider both a real and presumed "other" which meaningfully pivots their responses toward an ethic of digital caring.

1. Conversations with People Who Hate Me

Dylan Marron, a 29-year-old YouTuber, created a new platform for discussion after receiving criticism and vitriol for his "Unboxed" series—podcasts that explore issues such as police brutality and sexual violence. In his new series, "Conversations with people who hate me," which launched July 31, 2017, Marron hosts discussions with those who have reacted critically to his shows, those who demonstrate what he has called "fear of other" (O'Brien, 2017). In a video promoting the new series, Marron narrates that he sees "this podcast as a way to take hateful jabs online and turn them into productive conversations offline" ("Podcast," n. d.). Marron exemplifies robust media literacy skills layered with a caring ethic and disposition to improve civic dialogue. To begin, Marron's production skills allow him to practice media literacy skills including message creation and dissemination, and his successes show he understands issues of audience. That he has built a well-known media company from the ground up reflects a sense of self-direction and agency evident in his work. Most significantly, however, is Marron's expression of a caring ethic through his desire to understand those who most aggressively disagree with him. By inviting others to the digital table for conversations that are often rude, uncomfortable, and even offensive, Marron displays an investment in making sure others are truly heard to facilitate more positive relationships via online communities. In doing so, Marron pushes his podcasts beyond merely an exercise in media literacy—the creation of a media response to critical voices—and places them as a unique tool for community-building and cultural participation. The podcast series has shown significant outcomes in collaboration and dialogue, the very results media literacy and civic action pedagogies hope to create. After one conversation on LGBTQ issues, a former hostile guest changed his opinion: "I no longer hate you, Dylan" (Mallenbaum, 2017). What's more, Marron's platform and approach circumvents traditional media gatekeepers covering these sensitive issues, giving both himself and his guests digital space to further important conversations that often exist online only as sound bites or caricatures of groupthink.

2. The Push for Social Media Accountability Against Hate Speech

Media literacies of caring are also becoming evident at the institutional level as governments around the world consider whether hate speech is appropriate content for social media platforms. Following a formal inquiry between 2016–2017, the United Kingdom's Commons home affairs committee recommended the government devise a series of escalating sanctions for social media companies who do not remove illegal content, including hate speech and child pornography (Commons home affairs committee report, 2017; Bowcott, 2017). The committee's report found "[t]he biggest and richest social media companies are shamefully far from taking sufficient action to tackle illegal and dangerous content, to implement proper community standards or to keep their users safe. Given their immense size, resources and global reach, it is completely irresponsible of them to fail to abide by the law, and to keep their users and others safe." The committee's stance reflects central tenets of both media literacy and caring ethics. First, the committee's initial concern resonates with central media literacy beliefs, including: media messages can have potential consequences, not all media messages are appropriate for all audiences, and media messages create and perpetuate systems of power that can be both asymmetrical and abused. That the committee focuses on the need for social media companies to "keep their users safe" shows a wide-scale, political application of caring ethics that places concern for others, especially marginalized others, within the mainstream consciousness. In the United States, social media users and media experts are similarly calling for renewed responsibility to curtail online hate speech, violence, and marginalization. After a race rally turned violent in Charlottesville, Virginia, Facebook said it was removing pages of white supremacists on its social network (Wong, 2017). In these examples in particular, embracing a caring ethic through regulatory or corporate actions demonstrates a potentially utopian application of the premise, that those with the most political and social capacity to affect change do so with a mindset to protect those with the least.

A Normative Approach to Media Literacies of Caring

Implementing caring ethics in media literacy education may represent an uncomfortable shift for some educators toward more explicit advocacy of societal and communal norms; presupposing an obligation to others regarding how one consumes and creates media indeed contradicts person-centric educational philosophies that prioritize individual needs, message deconstruction, and media creation. Educators should embrace this discomfort as a way to highlight the caring gap itself and to help citizens better understand the construction and perpetuation of power through media. Citizens are already co-opting communal media narratives as a means of participatory politics. For instance, social media users who chose a photo filter that placed a red equal sign on their profile pictures to support same-sex marriage went beyond mere symbolic communication and "slacktivism" to participate in an aggregate form of protest and advocacy (Penney, 2015). When these narratives are shaped through an ethic of caring and aimed at greater societal improvement, the efficacy of media literacy processes is amplified because those involved implicitly accept shared responsibility for what happens next and to whom.

The growing cannon of media literacy scholarship seeks to understand how citizens can engage with myriad media content in ways that are informative, empowering, and even entertaining without relegating the audience to the status of passive consumers. Well-regarded approaches to media literacy education emphasize a learner progression from simple description of media to more critical steps of analysis, evaluation, creation, and ultimately, engagement with the world through media texts. In general, these approaches prioritize an individual interaction with media in a highly personal, self-directed way and in support of outcomes that are largely user-centric.

In response, we argue a caring ethics approach to media literacy does the following:

- Emphasizes outward-looking and community-focused media engagement that closes the participation gap;
- Reinforces agency and critical consciousness;
- Cultivates concern for others amid structures of oppression and injustice; and
- Pre-supposes the "present other" without necessitating an in-person relationship.

Somewhere, on the other side of an image, phrase, or sound bite, are both the subject of media content and fellow recipients, a community of consumers pre-morally united in their shared consumption. Thus, the caring ethic supersedes relationships that are physically or spatially organized by imploring the consumer to act on behalf of others who may not be moved to act or capable of acting on their own. While traditional media literacies have placed a premium on deep engagement with media and a civic responsibility to care about truth, fact, and context, placing a caring ethic within these boundaries also requires those who develop those literacies to act on behalf of those who have not yet been so fortunate.

References

Bowcott, O. (2017, May 1). Social media firms must face heavy fines over extremist content—MPs. *The Guardian.* Retrieved September 2, 2017 from www.theguardian.com/media/2017/may/01/social-media-firms-should-be-fined-for-extremist-content-say-mps-google-youtube-facebook?CMP=share_btn_tw

Commons home affairs committee report (2017). *Hate crime: Abuse, hate and extremism online.* Retrieved September 2, 2017 from https://publications.parliament.uk/pa/cm201617/cmselect/cmhaff/609/60904.htm#_idTextAnchor012

Edelman Group. (2017). *Annual global report.* Retrieved October 28, 2017 from www.edelman.com/executive-summary/

Freire, P. (1973). *Education for critical consciousness.* New York: Seabury Press.

Freire, P., Ramos, M. B., & Macedo, D. (2014). *Pedagogy of the oppressed.* New York and London: Bloomsbury Academic.

Giroux, H. A. (2011). *On critical pedagogy. [electronic resource].* New York: Continuum.

Gordon, E., & Mihailidis, P. (Eds.). (2016). *Civic media: Technology, design, practice.* Cambridge, MA: MIT Press.

Gordon, E., & Mugar, G. (2018). *Civic Media Practice. Identification and Evaluation of Media and Technology That Facilitates Democratic Process.* Boston: Emerson College.

Hansen, D. T. (2001). *Exploring the Moral Heart of Teaching: Toward a Teacher's Creed.* New York: Teachers College Press.

Hobbs, R., & McGee, S. (2014). Teaching about propaganda: An examination of the historical roots of media literacy. *Journal of Media Literacy Education, 6*(2), 56–66.

Jenkins, H. (2006). *Confronting the challenges of participatory culture: Media education for the 21st century.* John D. and Catherine T. MacArthur Foundation. Retrieved September 16, 2017 from http://files.eric.ed.gov/fulltext/ED536086.pdf

Jenkins, H., Shresthova, S., Gamber-Thompson, L., Kligler-Vilenchik, N., & Zimmerman, A. (2016). *By any media necessary.* New York: New York University Press. Retrieved September 16, 2017 from http://connectedyouth.nyupress.org/book/9781479899982/

Losh, E., & Jenkins, H. (2012). Can public education coexist with participatory culture? *Knowledge Quest, 41*(1), 16–21.

Mallenbaum, C. (2017, August 8). Podcast pick: Dylan Marron has candid "conversations with people who hate me". *USA Today.* Retrieved August 31, 2017 from www.usatoday.com/story/life/entertainthis/2017/08/08/podcast-dylan-marron-conversations-people-who-hate-me/543865001/

Massanari, A. (2017). #Gamergate and the Fappening: How Reddit's algorithm, governance, and culture support toxic technocultures. *New Media & Society, 19*(3), 329–346. doi:10.1177/1461444815608807

Mihailidis, P. (2009). Beyond cynicism: Media education and civic learning outcomes in the university. *International Journal of Media and Learning, 1/3*, 1–13.

Noddings, N., & Shore, P. J. (1984). *Awakening the Inner Eye Intuition in Education*, New York: Columbia Univeristy- Teachers College.

Noddings, N. (2013). *Caring: A relational approach to ethics & moral education.* Berkeley, CA: University of California Press.

O'Brien, S. (2017, August 23). *One man's approach to confront his online harassers: Empathy.* Retrieved September 2, 2017 from www.news8000.com/news/money/one-mans-approach-to-confront-his-online-harassers-empathy/611371332

Penney, J. (2015). Social media and symbolic action: Exploring participation in the Facebook red equal sign profile picture campaign. *Journal of Computer-Mediated Communication, 20*, 52–66. doi:10.1111/jcc4.12092

"Podcast" (n.d.). Retrieved from www.dylanmarron.com/podcast/

Rheingold, H. (2012). *Net Smart: How to Thrive Online.* Cambrigde, MA: MIT Press.

Scharrer, E., Sekarasih, L., & Olson, C. (2017). Media, youth, and well-being: What are the outcomes of media literacy education? In L. Reinecke & M. B. Oliver (Eds.), *The Routledge handbook of media use and well-being: International perspectives on theory and research on positive media effects* (pp. 250–261). New York, NY, US: Routledge/Taylor & Francis Group.

Taplin, J. (2017). *Move fast and break things: How Facebook, Google and Amazon cornered culture and undermined democracy.* New York, NY: Little, Brown and Company.

Trout, M. (2012). *Making the moment matter: Care theory for teacher learning.* Rotterdam and Boston: Sense Publishers.

Wong, Q. (2017, August 16). How Facebook is tackling hate speech after the Charlottesville rally. *San Jose Mercury News (CA).*

39

SEEKING EUDAIMONIA IN ONLINE EDUCATION

Beatriz Valverde and Erica C. Boling

Aiming to define new goals in the practice of professions, Martin Seligman, one of the most public faces of "positive psychology," and Mihaly Csikszentmihalyi, predicted in 2000 that "the next century will see a science and profession that will come to understand and build the factors that allow individuals, communities, and societies to flourish" (Seligman & Csikszentmihalyi, 2000, p. 5). In their view, psychology, since World War II, had focused on pathology, weakness, and damage, becoming a science about healing, neglecting the factors that lead to people's well-being. The time has come, however, for psychology to concentrate on the positive features that make people's lives worth living (Peterson & Seligman, 2004). Bearing this idea in mind, then, positive psychology cannot be considered just a branch of medicine; on the contrary, it concerns "work, education, insight, love, growth, and play." (Seligman & Csikszentmihalyi, 2000, p. 7) This new focus offered by the field of positive psychology must be considered at three main levels:

> at the subjective level is about valued subjective experiences: well-being, contentment, and satisfaction (in the past); hope and optimism (for the future); and flow and happiness (in the present). At the individual level, it is about positive individual traits: the capacity for love and vocation, courage, interpersonal skill, aesthetic sensibility, perseverance, forgiveness, originality, future mindedness, spirituality, high talent, and wisdom. At the group level, it is about the civic virtues and the institutions that move individuals toward better citizenship: responsibility, nurturance, altruism, civility, moderation, tolerance, and work ethic.
>
> *(Seligman & Csikszentmihalyi, 2000, p. 5)*

In its eudaimonic reading, positive psychology aims at fostering in young people, at an individual level, the virtues and character strengths of a flourishing life, which include courage, curiosity, love of learning, self-regulation, perseverance, creativity, social intelligence, fairness, and the capacity for flow and insight (Seligman & Csikszentmihalyi, 2000).

Applied to the world of learning, positive education means teaching students the skills of well-being without compromising the traditional skills of achievement (Seligman, Ernst, Gillham, Reivich, & Linkins, 2009). In this sense, positive education advocates for a holistic view of the process of character formation (Romero & Pereira, 2011). In addition to teaching the tools of accomplishment, educators therefore need to identify and nurture their students' strongest qualities, helping them find spaces in which they can best exercise these strengths and flourish in the process. Well-being should be taught for three main reasons: it helps fight depression and boredom, a malaise so widespread among Western adolescents (Larson, 2000), it increases the level of self-satisfaction, and more importantly, *"more well-being is synergistic with better learning"* (Seligman et al., 2009, p. 294; emphasis in original). Introducing activities such as "WWW" (What went well?) at the beginning of the first-class session every day, students seem to learn with more eagerness, without displacing any content to be taught in the lesson (Seligman et al., 2009).

As we are seeing education change and evolve in a 21st Digital Age society where increasingly more university programs are going online (Bell & Federman, 2013; Luyt, 2013; Moller, Foshay, & Huett, 2008; Rezaei, 2009), the effectiveness of these programs is being questioned, both by experts in the field and also by the general public. For example, in a survey carried out in the USA in 2011 with a representative sample of over 2,000 adults, only 29 percent of them thought that online courses are as helpful in the learning process as courses taught in a traditional face-to-face classroom (Bell & Federman, 2013). As larger numbers of higher education programs become available online, educators face unique challenges implementing positive education in online learning environments. Instead of creating online learning spaces that nurture students and provide them with opportunities to flourish, deploying their highest strengths to meet the challenges they come across, studies show many students find online learning to be dissatisfying due to reasons such as their own lack of technology skills and confidence (Bell & Federman, 2013), low level of interaction, which makes the learning process impersonal, and insufficient or delayed feedback (Luyt, 2013). Although promoting positive psychology and eudaimonic teaching practices faces additional challenges when instruction occurs online, it is not an impossible task to achieve, especially when instruction is grounded in teaching practices that encourage curiosity, creativity, bravery, perseverance, self-regulation, and a love of learning in students. There is evidence that using the principles and practices of heutagogy, a theory of self-determined learning, to drive teaching practice can indeed result in such eudaimonic experiences (Boling, Dudley, & Sachdeva, 2017).

The purpose of this chapter is therefore to show possibilities and to offer suggestions for altering the online learning experience by creating spaces that promote students' well-being while at the same time pursuing excellence. We do this by organizing the chapter into the following sections:

1. Unique challenges that instructors and students face when instruction goes online and how this presents additional challenges for eudaimonic teaching practices.
2. A new vision for online teaching and learning and how heutagogy, a form of self-determined learning, can help individuals overcome challenges described above.
3. Implications and recommendations for designing instructional practices in ways that promote students' well-being through eudaimonic teaching and learning practices.

Challenges to Promoting Well-Being in Online Education

As Terras and Ramsay (2015) have described, "Technological advances, particularly Web 2.0, have brought major transformations in the delivery of education" (p. 472). Focusing on one of the most recent developments in online higher education, massive open online courses (MOOCs), these researchers analyze the main challenges presented in online based learning, based on the psychological determinants of learner behaviors relevant to online courses. According to them, these challenges fall into three main categories: "(1) individual differences in skills, preferences and cognitive profile; (2) engagement, motivation, learning and performance; and (3) the ability to monitor and appropriately respond to the demands of both the external and internal contexts of learning" (Terras & Ramsay, 2015, p. 480).

Considering learners' skills, the fact that online education involves a technology-mediated learning environment seems crucial; lack of skills in using the Internet and Learning Management Systems (LMS) are major factors affecting students' engagement and achievement in online courses (Sowan & Jenkins, 2013). Therefore, to build online spaces effectively designed and supported, an essential element is to understand how learners use technology to learn, which leads us to identify the main psychological barriers in the context of technology-enhanced learning (Terras & Ramsay, 2015). In this line of thought, Beaven, Hauck, Comas-Quinn, Lewis, and de los Arcos (2014) have identified that the main challenge for online course organizers is to have realistic expectations about learners' capabilities. Many learners are intimidated by technology or show low confidence working with technology; as a consequence, if the organizer's or instructor's assumptions do not match learners' capabilities, the percentage of drop-out increases significantly (Beaven et al., 2014). In addition, one must consider challenges surrounding the digital divide where proficiency in digital literacy skills and access to technology are not equal for everybody. As higher education increases its offerings in online education, it is imperative that institutions "address digital divides in terms not only of students' access to technology but also of their technology skills and literacy" (Bell & Federman, 2013, p. 179).

Another identified main factor in the high drop-out rate in online courses is the lack of sufficient support in the learning process, a key element in students' learning process related to engagement and motivation. This lack of support has been shown to have a negative influence on student performance (Terras & Ramsay, 2015). In online education, there is a shift to more learner autonomy and control when compared to traditional face-to-face learning. This shift can cultivate the character strengths of self-regulation, bravery, and persistence. Learners with sound self-regulatory skills, including self-monitoring and self-evaluation, are then more motivated and have higher possibilities of achievement and course completion (Bell & Federman, 2013). In connection to this, having sufficient support becomes fundamental. In a traditional face-to-face system of education, students are provided with individualized support by their instructor and can receive immediate and continuous feedback on their performance. Hence, the issue of personalizing the learning experience becomes another key challenge in online education to prevent students from feeling that online learning is impersonal and less effective.

If, as we have seen, instructor's support is fundamental in the students' autonomous learning process, instructors need to face new challenges involved in online education. Moller et al. (2008) argue that educators in online programs "are faced with new pedagogical issues surrounding student interactions, course content design and delivery" (as cited in Boling et al., 2011, p. 1). First, they need to consider what their new role is in online programs: they must leave behind their traditional role of providers of content and assume a greater role as designers, guides, mentors, and facilitators. In addition, they need to be technologically literate and keep up-to-date in technological advances applied to education. Concerning their area of expertise, instructors must realize that transfer of knowledge is insufficient: they must help their students acquire thinking and emotional skills, together with cognitive strategies that allow them to organize and make meaningful use of the knowledge they have access to through the Internet (Gillespie, 1998). As many instructors are still not familiar with these competences, they can feel insecure and anxious when having to teach online courses.

Closely related to needing support is also the importance of interaction in online programs. According to Desai, Hart, and Richards (2008), for learners to have a positive attitude and show satisfaction, strong interaction is necessary. To create this interaction online, instructors need to continuously guide and interact with learners enrolled in their courses for them to be effective and efficient instructors. As Desai et al. (2008) stated, interaction plays a "huge role in establishing a sense of community over the web for the learner given there is no physical setting" (p. 332). As a result, the online instructor's support and guidance becomes fundamental to nurture the aforementioned strengths of self-regulation, perseverance, and bravery in their students, which are essential when seeking eudaimonia in online education.

Social presence, together with instructor-learner interaction, is another relevant factor to consider in online education since it "is a strong communication component that reduces isolation between the distant learner and other learners and instructor. Lack of social presence might affect learner's performance and outcomes during the instructional transaction" (Desai et al., 2008, p. 328). Social presence is especially relevant for learners who possess a firm social intelligence character strength. As research shows, one of the main challenges of computer-mediated interaction is the lack of social cues; when relational cues are filtered out, communication becomes more "task oriented, cold and less personal than face-to-face communication" (Walther, Anderson, & Park, 1994, as cited in Boling, Hough, Krinsky, Saleem, & Stevens, 2012, p. 119). Consequently, one of the major current challenges for e-learning is "to provide a sense of community with constructive feedback and provide open forthcoming communications as well as recognizing membership and feelings of friendship, cohesion, and satisfaction among learners" (Desai et al., 2008, p. 333). Researchers and practitioners of online education need to therefore develop good practice appropriate to the new technological advances applied to education (Sowan & Jenkins, 2013) and seek approaches "grounded upon social, authentic, and community-based learning experiences, where presence, communication, interaction, and collaboration are valued" (Veletsianos, 2010, p. 317).

A New Vision for Online Education

Although moving instruction fully online brings its own unique set of challenge, it does not mean that it is impossible to seek eudaimonia in online education. There are indeed ways to personalize the learning experience, increase intrinsic motivation, and build nurturing, online learning communities that foster courageous action, mindfulness, hope, and trust, promoting as a consequence, students' well-being. One of the ways to do this, we argue, is by using heutagogy to inform teaching practice.

Heutagogy, a term first used by Hase and Kenyon (2000), is a study of self-determined learning "with practices and principles rooted in andragogy" (Blaschke, 2012, p. 56). At the heart of self-determined learning is that "the learner is at the centre of the learning process" (Hase, 2014, p. 2). In heutagogical teaching practices, learners take on an active "rather than passive role in their individual learning experiences" (Blaschke, 2012, p. 62). There is also an emphasis on reflective practice (Hase, 2009). A key concept in heutagogy "is that of double-loop learning and self-reflection (Argyris & Schön, 1996, as cited in Hase & Kenyon, 2000)" (Blaschke, 2012, p. 59).

> In double-loop learning, learners consider the problem and the resulting action and outcomes, in addition to reflecting upon the problem-solving process and how it influences the learner's own beliefs and actions (see Figure 1). Double-loop learning occurs when learners "question and test one's personal values and assumptions as being central to enhancing learning how to learn."
>
> *(Argyris & Schön, 1978, as cited in Hase, 2009, pp. 45–46)*

Citing the work of Merriam (2001) and Mezirow (1997), Blaschke states, "The goals of self-directed learning include helping learners develop the capacity for self-direction, supporting transformational learning, and promoting 'emancipatory learning and social action' (Merriam, 2001, p. 9)" (Blaschke, 2012, p. 58). Research reveals how grounding teaching practices in heutagogy can lead to self-directed, intrinsically motivated learners who exhibit individual traits such as self-efficacy, creativity, positive values, and confidence in themselves and their capabilities (Blaschke, 2012; Hase & Kenyon, 2000; Kenyon & Hase, 2010). As seen here, designing online instruction around heutagogical teaching practices can indeed promote more eudaimonic practices in online education.

Course design elements that support a heutagogical approach to teaching include first and foremost "*learner-centeredness* in terms of both learner-generated contexts and content" (Blaschke, 2012, p. 64). Other design elements, as described by Blaschke (2012), include learning contracts that are defined by the learner, a flexible curriculum, learner-directed questions, and "negotiated and learner-defined assessments" (p. 65). In addition, reflective practice, an essential component of heutagogy, can be promoted through learning journals, action research, personalized assessment, and collaborative learning (Blaschke, 2012).

In one study conducted by Boling et al. (2017), a university instructor used project-based learning and heutagogical practices to inform her Digital Storytelling teacher education course. Using a heutagogical approach to teaching and learning that included all of the design components described above, the study revealed how "creating digital stories was challenging to students yet resulted in personal transformations" (p. 335). Students in the course gave examples of how such transformation impacted them on both a personal and professional level. One student, for example, described how participating in the course "transformed her personal identity and how she saw herself as a teacher" to the point where she saw herself as being more creative, more open-minded, and more confident than when she first began the course (Boling et al., 2017, p. 337). This same student explained how completing the digital storytelling project in the course through project-based learning helped her take more responsibility for her own learning and "gave her confidence to engage in the world around her in new ways, and she began to see that not always having the answers and not always having a person there telling you what to do could be a very positive thing in one's life" (Boling et al., 2017, p. 338). This student was not alone in her experience.

There were other students in the course who also described how they began the semester feeling overwhelmed, intimidated, and uncertain about their ability to complete the final digital story project. By the end of the semester, however, they saw increased confidence in themselves and their ability to confront unexpected challenges both inside and outside the classroom (Boling et al., 2017). According Seligman et al. (2009),

> *More well-being is synergistic with better learning.* Increases in well-being are likely to produce increases in learning, the traditional goal of education. Positive mood produces broader attention [...], more creative thinking [...], and more holistic thinking [...].
> *(pp. 294–295; emphasis in original)*

If educators can help students shift their feelings of fear, inability, and inadequacy to confidence, excitement, and passion, then we are well on our way to better supporting the well-being of our students and seeking eudaimonia in education. Findings such as those found by Boling et al. (2017) and by other educators who ground their work in heutagogy (Ashton & Newman, 2006; Bhoryrub et al., 2010; Blaschke, 2012) give us hope and practical strategies for bringing eudaimonia into online education.

Implications and Recommendations for Teaching and Research

Online education based on heutagogy-informed teaching practices can transform learning through self-reflection, creative thinking, and collaborative work (Blaschke, 2012; Boling et al., 2017). This, in turn, can give students online spaces where they can exercise the character strengths that are strongest in them. Positive education advocates for a holistic view of the learning process, teaching students the skills of well-being without compromising the traditional skills of achievement (Seligman et al., 2009). Consequently, it is fundamental to consider that positive education is not just about teaching the traditional tools of accomplishment. It is about helping meet the emotional and social needs of students, nurturing their strongest qualities, and helping them flourish in the process. This means giving students opportunities to interact with one another and encouraging them to form connections with classmates through ongoing inter- actions and collaborative work. It also means celebrating students' successes and supporting them when they lack confidence or are fearful as well as guiding them when working collaboratively, interacting, and learning online (Boling et al., 2017).

Additionally, for online programs to be successful in achieving eudaimonia, we must human- ize the online learning experience, developing an environment of openness, honesty, trust, and personal sharing. Students need teacher's guidance through continuous interaction between stu- dent and instructor. As explained above, a heutagogic approach promotes a learner-centered experience where students' autonomy plays a fundamental role; however, this does not mean simply promoting self-paced, isolated learning. It means having interactivity, collaboration, and room for creativity if we want to promote student well-being. Learning and feedback must be personalized, helping students see their strengths while also supporting them in becoming, as both positive education and heutagogy advocate, more self-determined, self-directed, and reflective learners.

Implementing a heutagogical approach to teaching can be powerful and transformative for both instructors and students; however, it is not always easy (Boling et al., 2017). For some instructors, releasing control and choice to students can be unnerving. It seems essential then that educators come to terms with the concept of heutagogical-informed teaching practice and its relevance to online education. This means that online instructors must "take on roles such as mentors, coordinators, and facilitators of learning rather than conveyors of information (Bower & Hardy, 2004; Smolin & Lawless, 2003)" (Boling et al., 2012, p. 118). In this sense, learning becomes "an activity that students do for themselves in a proactive way rather than as a covert event that happens to them in reaction to teaching" (Zimmerman, 2002, p. 65). Research must be carried out on how university faculty can best acquire the technological skills, philo- sophical outlook, and pedagogical strategies necessary to build more effective, heutagogically driven, online learning experiences.

In addition, students who are used to a more traditional model of teacher-centered instruction might resist heutagogical teaching approaches (Boling et al., 2017). These students will need more support and scaffolding than others when instructors ground their work in self-determined practices; thus, these practices may need to be combined with alternative directive methods so that students struggling with their self-direction abilities can achieve specific learning outcomes (Hase, 2014; Timmins, 2008). Research is needed to determine the effectiveness of different types of online scaffolds and the diverse ways they can be used (Boling et al., 2011).

Nurturing the character strength of self-regulation is essential in online education (Zim- merman, 2002), and we argue that it is also needed to promote students' well-being in online programs. When exercising self-regulation, students can become aware of their own strengths and limitations and take a proactive role in their learning process. However, instructors' additional guidance when setting goals, engaging in task-related strategies, and attempting to effectively structure their time and effort is still fundamental. As students receive this guidance through instructor support, their self-satisfaction and motivation can increase as they continue reflecting on the ways in which they learn (Zimmerman, 2002). In this sense, project-based learning where students are encouraged to follow their passions has proven to be successful in creating transform- ative learning experiences (Boling et al., 2017).

Effective online teaching and learning is more than just pushing content out to students. We want them to acquire new knowledge and skills, but even more powerful in this day and age is helping them become more independent, self-directed, lifelong learners. We want to instill lifelong learning so that the benefits of learning go beyond the classroom and beyond formal educational contexts. This involves "advising and teaching while students learn to put their strengths to work in learning and social situations" (Knoop, 2016, p. 460). This type of teaching and learning could be the most powerful and beneficial to students in today's world. However, the ability to confront challenges during self-determined learning and our ability to deal with uncertainty can greatly vary from one person to another. Cultural and individual factors can influence our ability to deal with uncertainty (Frambach, Driessen, Chan, & van der Vleuten, 2012). Better understanding of these differences and their impact on individual learning could help us develop a deeper, more informed understanding of heutagogy, its role in online learning contexts, and how it can help achieve eudaimonia in online education.

References

Argyris, C., & Schön, D. A. (1978). *Organizational learning: A theory of action perspective.* Reading, MA: Addison-Wesley.

Argyris, C., & Schön, D. A. (1996). *Organizational learning II: Theory, method and practice.* Reading, MA: Addison-Wesley.

Ashton, J., & Newman, L. (2006). An unfinished symphony: 21st century teacher education using knowledge creating heutagogies. *British Journal of Educational Technology, 37*(6), 825–840.

Beaven, T., Hauck, M., Comas-Quinn, A., Lewis, T., & de los Arcos, B. (2014). MOOCs: Striking the right balance between facilitation and self-determination. *Journal of Online Learning and Teaching, 10*(1), 31–43.

Bell, B., & Federman, J. (2013). E-learning in postsecondary education. *The Future of Children, 23*(1), 165–185.

Bhoryrub, J., Hurley, J., Neilson, G. R., Ramsay, M., & Smith, M. (2010). Heutagogy: An alternative practice based learning approach. *Nurse Education in Practice, 10*(6), 322–326.

Blaschke, L. M. (2012). Heutagogy and lifelong learning: A review of heutagogical practice and self-determined learning. *International Review of Research in Open and Distance Learning, 13*(1), 56–71.

Boling, E. C., Dudley, K., & Sachdeva, K. (2017). Enhancing preservice teachers' digital literacy skills through the making of digital documentaries. In O. M. Alegre & L. M. Villar (Eds.), *Research on university teaching and faculty development-international perspectives* (pp. 329–343). Hauppauge, NY: Nova Science Publishers, Inc.

Boling, E. C., Holan, E., Horbatt, B., Hough, M., Jean-Louis, J., Khurana, C., Krinsky, H., & Spiezio, C. (2011). Using online tools for communication and collaboration: Understanding educators' experiences in an online course. *The Internet and Higher Education, 23*, 48–55.

Boling, E. C., Hough, M., Krinsky, H., Saleem, H., & Stevens, M. (2012). Cutting the distance in distance education: Perspectives on what promotes positive, online learning experiences. *The Internet and Higher Education, 15*(2), 118–126.

Bower, B. L., & Hardy, K. P. (2004), From correspondence to cyberspace: Changes and challenges in distance education. *New Directions for Community Colleges,* 5–12. doi:10.1002/cc.169

Desai, M. S., Hart, J., & Richards, T. C. (2008). E-learning: Paradigm shift in education. *Education, 129*(2), 327–334.

Frambach, J. M., Driessen, E. W., Chan, L., & van der Vleuten, C. P. M. (2012). Rethinking the globalization of problem-based learning: How culture challenges self-directed learning. *Medical Education, 46,* 738–747.

Gillespie, F. (1998). Instructional design for the new technologies. *New Directions for Teaching and Learning, 76,* 39–52.

Hase, S. (2009). Heutagogy and e-learning in the workplace: Some challenges and opportunities. *Impact: Journal of Applied Research in Workplace E-Learning, 1*(1), 43–52.

Hase, S. (2014). An introduction to self-determined learning (Heutagogy). In L. M. Blaschke, C. Kenyon, & S. Hase (Eds.), *Experiences in self-determined learning* (pp. 1–19). San Bernardino, CA: Blaschke, Kenyon & Hase.

Hase, S., & Kenyon, C. (2000). From andragogy to heutagogy. *ultiBASE* (Faculty of Education Language and Community Services, RMIT University). Retrieved May 16, 2017 from www.psy.gla.ac.uk/~steve/pr/Heutagogy.html

Kenyon, C., & Hase, S. (2010). Andragogy and heutagogy in postgraduate work. In T. Kerry (Ed.), *Meeting the challenges of change in postgraduate education* (pp. 165–177). London: Continuum Press.

Knoop, H. (2016). The eudemonics of education. In J. Vittersø (Ed.), *Handbook of eudaimonic well-being* (pp. 453–471). Switzerland: Springer International Publishing.

Larson, R. (2000). Toward a psychology of positive youth development. *American Psychologist, 55*(1), 170–183.

Luyt, I. (2013). Bridging spaces: Cross-cultural perspectives on promoting positive online learning experiences. *Journal of Educational Technology Systems, 42*(1), 3–20.

Merriam, S. B. (2001) *Qualitative research and case study applications in education.* San Francisco: Jossey-Bass Publishers.

Mezirow, J. (1997) Transformative learning: Theory to practice. *New Directions for Adult and Continuing Education, 74,* 5–12. http://dx.doi.org/10.1002/ace.7401

Moller, L., Foshay, W., & Huett, J. (2008, July/August). The evolution of distance education: Implications for instructional design on the potential of the Web. *TechTrends, 52*(4), 66–70.

Peterson, C., & Seligman, M. (2004). *Character strengths and virtues: A handbook and classification.* Washington, DC: Oxford University Press.

Rezaei, M. (2009). Challenges of developing online learning in higher education in Iran. *The Turkish Online Journal of Distance Education, 10*(4), 80–90.

Romero, C., & Pereira, C. (2011). El enfoque positivo de la educación: aportaciones al desarrollo humano. *Teoría De La Educación, 23*(2), 69–89.

Seligman, M., & Csikszentmihalyi, M. (2000). Positive psychology: An introduction. *The American Psychologist, 55*(1), 5–14.

Seligman, M., Ernst, R., Gillham, J., Reivich, K., & Linkins, M. (2009). Positive education: Positive psychology and classroom interventions. *Oxford Review of Education, 35*(3), 293–311.

Smolin, L. I., & Lawless, K. A. (2003). Becoming literate in the technological age: New responsibilities and tools for teachers. *Reading Teacher, 56*(6), 570. Retrieved from https://www.learntechlib.org/p/96280/.

Sowan, A., & Jenkins, L. (2013). Designing, delivering and evaluating a distance learning nursing course responsive to students' needs. *International Journal of Medical Informatics, 82*(6), 553–564.

Terras, M., & Ramsay, J. (2015). Massive Open Online Courses (MOOCs): Insights and challenges from a psychological perspective. *British Journal of Educational Technology, 46*(3), 472–487.

Timmins, F. (2008). Take time to facilitate self-directed learning. *Nurse Education in Practice, 8*(5), 302–305.

Veletsianos, G. (2010). *Emerging technologies in distance education.* Edmonton: AU Press.

Walther, J. B., Anderson, J. F., & Park, D. W. (1994). Interpersonal effects in computer-mediated interaction: A meta-analysis of social and antisocial communication. *Communication Research, 21*(4), 460–487. https://doi.org/10.1177/009365094021004002

Zimmerman, B. (2002). Becoming a self-regulated learner: An overview. *Theory into Practice, 41*(2), 64–70.

40

SUSTAINABLE HAPPINESS AND LIVING SCHOOLS

Repurposing Education with a Vision of Well-Being for All

Catherine O'Brien and Sean Murray

Education and communication can play significant roles in establishing new narratives that support individual and collective transitions toward healthier, sustainable lifestyles and livelihoods. Given the time sensitive environmental challenges that we face, locally and globally, it is imperative to recognize how interdisciplinary discussions and collaboration are advancing this change process. Exploring positive education and communication is just one example. Understanding the potential of integrating sustainability *with* happiness and well-being holds even greater promise. As noted by the Danish Happiness Research Institute "it is no longer possible to imagine a future where the pursuit of happiness is *not* somehow connected to sustainability. As the human species continues its quest for happiness and well-being, more emphasis must be placed on sustainability and the interaction between sustainability and happiness" (Happiness Research Institute, 2015, p. 16). This poses considerable challenges for education because sustainability education and positive education are not a central focus of mainstream curricula and pedagogy. Additionally, even though it would be widely accepted that student well-being is important, as Falkenberg (2014) writes,

> the well-being of students has always been a concern in school education. However, such concern seems often more implicit than explicit, seems grounded in a more narrow rather than a more comprehensive and holistic conceptualization, and is generally not seen as the overarching goal of school education.
>
> *(p. 77)*

Nor will it suffice to simply add positive education, sustainability education or well-being education to existing approaches to schooling. Rather, we need to embrace an education vision of well-being for all, sustainably (Hopkins, 2013) and discover what that means in practical terms.

Conventional education is criticized for being outdated, stuck in patterns that were suitable for the Industrial Age (Hargreaves & Shirley, 2012; Robinson & Aronica, 2009; Zhao, 2012), too limited in our integration of technology (C21 Canada, 2012), or stifling creativity and innovation (Robinson, 2011; Wagner, 2012). Creativity, innovation, and entrepreneurship have risen to the top of many education transformation discussions. Proponents of 21st-century learning (C21, 2012; P21, 2011) have recognized the value of developing competency or skills relevant to these three interrelated areas. National prosperity figures strongly as a rationale, though individual well-being is also an anticipated outcome (Kelly, 2012; Kelley & Kelley, 2013; Robinson, 2011; Wagner, 2012; Zhao, 2012).

A key phrase above is "stuck in patterns that were suitable for the Industrial Age." Unearthing these patterns, revealing the underlying assumptions, and reflecting on which ones to keep and which ones are keeping us moored to "old school" narratives is essential. Otherwise, striving to infuse creativity into systems that, by their very nature, stifle creativity will lead to limited success. Furthermore, given the extensive "system makeover" (Fullan, 2013) that is required, simply adding a few more ingredients to the mix would be grossly inadequate. A more holistic vision is needed that gets at the very purpose of education, one that is relevant for this era. Hopkins (2013) has offered a recommendation to repurpose education with a vision that contributes to *well-being, for all, forever.* In support of this view, O'Brien (2016) writes,

> This embraces well-being—individually and collectively, for all people and the "other than human" life on our planet. It is an inclusive vision that recognizes that our well-being is important both now and in the future and that our well-being is intertwined with that of other people and the natural environment.
>
> *(O'Brien, 2016, p. 9)*

A similar perspective is embedded in O'Brien's work on sustainable happiness that is defined as happiness that contributes to individual, community, or global well-being without exploiting other people, the environment, or future generations (O'Brien, 2010).

Realizing a Vision of Well-Being for All

While the notion of realizing a vision of *well-being for all* through education might seem desirable but daunting to achieve in practice, we have found that there are pockets of excellence, schools around the world that demonstrate what is already possible. O'Brien and Howard (2016) refer to these organizations as Living Schools. These are schools that are successfully integrating sustainability education, "new" pedagogies, such as inquiry learning, real-world project-based learning, land-based learning, mindfulness, yoga, "Genius Hour"-when educators allocate 20 percent of the day, of a week, or a unit of study, etc., to student-centered and student-directed learning activities where the student's passions drive the direction of inquiry (Juliani, 2015; Krebs & Zvi, 2015; Wettrick, 2014), and 21st-century competencies. They "bring life to education and education to life" (William & Brown, 2012). Pioneering examples of such schools are the Barefoot College in India and Green School Bali (O'Brien & Howard, 2016). While neither institution identifies as a Living School, they both reflect the attributes that have been outlined by Howard and O'Brien (2017) in the figure below. Note the reference to positive communication in the column under Health and Well-Being.

Living Schools

A superb example of a Living School can be found in Sigurbjorg Stefansson Early School located in Gimli, Manitoba (Canada). About seven years ago, the principal of Sigurbjorg Stefansson, Rosanna Cuthbert, invited her staff to join her on an exploration of the Reggio Emilia student-centered approach to teaching and learning. The local school district had already made a commitment to Education for Sustainable Development (ESD), in line with the province of Manitoba's commitment to sustainability education: "Education for Sustainable Development (ESD) entails a reorienting of education to guide and motivate people to become

Values and Vision
School community members are committed to:

- Engaging with the world
- Developing a cultural awareness of other's world views and identities
- Demonstrating and modeling care for plants, other animals, and the rest of the natural world
- Developing compassion for oneself, other people and all living things as well as skills to address positive change
- Promoting the health and well-being of students, staff, the wider community, natural environment
- A solution focused growth mindset when facing challenges and opportunities
- Creating trusting and respectful relationships in the school community
- Respecting indigenous world views and traditional ways of knowing

Leadership
Organizational structures are characterized by:

- Ensuring teachers, students have voice and agency
- Developing strong collaborative relationships with staff, parents, guardians, and community
- Creating opportunities for professional development for transformative learning
- Cultivating an ethos of equity, inclusion and diversity
- Explicit support for sustainability education and well-being
- Encouraging risk taking to explore new ways of living, learning, and working in a safe environment

Teaching and Learning
Pedagogical practices are influenced by:

- Collaborative processes
- Holistic approaches to teaching and learning
- A commitment to inquiry-based strategies to affect real world change
- A spirit of inclusion, student centred and differentiated learning
- The development of creativity and creating a climate for risk taking and student agency
- Modeling healthy and sustainable lifestyles
- Authentic assessment of and for learning practices

Nature and Place Based Orientation
Schools reflect a commitment to:

- Using natural, social, built environments, including the school envelope to foster learning
- Incorporating outdoor learning relative to location of school
- Developing ecological literacy of students and teachers
- Incorporating furniture, light, classroom resources sustainably and to promote well-being
- Developing strong ties to community and commitment to active citizenry

Health and Well-Being
School community demonstrates practices designed to:

- Develop emotional, physical and spiritual well-being of students, staff, and teachers
- Support the principles of health promoting schools
- Explore the links between human health and the natural world
- Explore the relationships between sustainability, happiness, and well-being for all
- Support positive communication in the classroom, at school and with the wider community

Figure 40.1 Living School Attributes and Practices
(Source: Howard & O'Brien, 2017)

responsible citizens of the planet. It addresses the interrelationships among the environment, the economy, and society" (IISD, 2016, p. 5). Cuthbert's vision was that the staff and students were launching a co-learning journey. Skipping forward to the present day, every classroom in the school has a Wonder Wagon that is used daily on outdoor excursions to carry supplies and transport "wonders" (sticks, rocks, plants, etc.) that students collect. There are no desks in the classrooms but rather an assortment of surfaces at varying levels. In addition to natural light, lamps, strings of lights, and light tables provide illumination that is calming and aesthetically pleasing. Curriculum outcomes are met in an interdisciplinary, multi-age process that draws on student curiosity. For example, as one of the primary students entered the classroom on a rainy day he declared, "I made friends with the rain today!" From that statement, his teacher designed a learning sequence that covered English language arts, science, and math. Another teacher chose to build on this in a music class.

In the structured world of education, there are designated outcomes that teachers are expected to cover. An entirely student-directed program might not be guaranteed to meet all of these outcomes so Sigurbjorg Stefansson teachers use "provocations" to nudge students toward further inquiries if needed.

As a visitor to the school, one is treated to an atmosphere where it is clear that student and staff well-being are attended to explicitly. Students are engaged, focused, energetic, excited to share their learning, and kind to one another. Sigurbjorg Stefansson has successfully realized what the founder of Reggio Emilia, Malaguzzi, described in 1998 with his view that saw schools as a "living organism . . . schools as interconnected living systems that require sustenance, nurturing, room to move, grow, and house the pulse of life, instead of as institutions for the production of knowledge based in bureaucratic processes of regulation" (in Wien, 2008, p. 7).

Living Campus

At a higher education level, Dawson College, in Montreal uses the term Living Campus to denote their focus on sustainability and well-being. The college's 2016 strategic plan makes a commitment to *well-being for all.*

> Dawson College as a Living Campus, and through its commitment to well-being for all, sustainably, departs from the most troublesome and dated components of traditional education and enters a transformative period that will help implement what the UN Earth Charter International (2009) clearly states as one of its aspirations:
>
> > *Let ours be a time for awakening of a new reverence for life, the firm resolve to achieve sustainability, the quickening of the struggle for justice and peace, and the joyful celebration of life.*
>
> Dawson is boldly attempting to be one of the leaders for educational change that many researchers write about, students hope for, and society needs to address 21st century issues.
>
> *(Dawson College, 2016)*

Living Campus utilizes the college grounds, building envelope and infrastructure as learning spaces and has developed integrated projects that redefine existing academic and organizational boundaries. In essence, they are changing the conventional education narrative. Through Living Campus, first-hand experience in and with Nature (we follow the recommendation of the Earth-values Institute to capitalize the word "Nature," see www.earthvalues.org/v1/put_in_nature. php) is encouraged, as is the use of technology to build learning capacity.

Living Campus (see O'Brien & Adam, 2016) projects include:

Ecological Peace Garden

Established after the tragic school shooting at Dawson in 2006, this centerpiece of life within an urban setting now contains thousands of plants and attracts insects, butterflies, birds, and people.

Biodiversity Zones

Nine micro-habitats are planned, with five currently established, where students can study natural areas on campus. These include a forest floor, dry and wet meadow, pond, monarch butterfly nursery, and a decomposition zone. These zones supplement the Peace Garden and create enough on-site habitat to support some full life cycle insect populations.

Monarch Tagging

Every year, several hundred monarch butterfly caterpillars are adopted by teachers, departments, students, and children of staff and reared until they emerge from their chrysalis. The butterflies are tagged and released in the Ecological Peace Garden to begin their flight to Mexico. This activity brings out the wonder of the natural world, stimulates conversation throughout the college and brings out a passion for life that is contagious.

Carbon Neutral Campaign

Dawson continuously strives to reduce its ecological footprint. Carbon credits are being purchased through an organization that creates long-term employment for farmers by reforesting marginal land in Nicaragua.

Rooftop Honey Bee Project

Several honey bee hives are placed on Dawson's rooftop. Healthy living connections are also being made with the bee hives. The Dawson Campus Life & Leadership team organizes a yearly health challenge that involved over 200 teams of teachers and students in 2015. Any team or individual that completed the physical activity equivalent of 1249 kilometers (the distance 12 female bees fly to make one teaspoon of honey) received a special prize—1 teaspoon of Dawson College Ecological Peace Garden honey. The challenge is aptly named the "1249 Club."

Dawson Rooftop Gardens

Several rooftop gardens have been established that grow vegetables in self-watering containers or raised beds. Student volunteers maintain the gardens and harvest produce for sale at the college market.

Teacher Project Room With Living Wall

In 2016, the college inaugurated a Teacher Project Room with a two-story living wall containing over 500 plants. The room was designed by faculty specialists as a place that encourages collaboration, imagination, and creativity.

Living Campus and Well-Being

Living Campus demonstrates how living schools engender individual and organizational well-being in a multitude of ways. Through discussions with Dawson faculty and staff, the following themes emerged as indications of how Living Campus reflects a vision of *well-being for all*, sustainably.

1. *Living Campus fosters hope.* Students, staff, faculty, and visitors to Dawson are encouraged by the positive activities that demonstrate how sustainability can enhance well-being. Living Campus affirms that change is possible. The Monarch Tagging program is especially uplifting in an urban environment.

2. *Forging new relationships.* Living Campus fuels projects and events that involve interaction of management, support staff, teachers, and students across departments. It challenges these educational stakeholders to blur course and job description boundaries and model inter-disciplinary cooperation. The conversations that emerge tend to be growth oriented and solution-focused.

3. *Encouraging collaboration.* It requires considerable collaboration to plan and implement some of the Living Campus projects. This can prompt discussions about how to troubleshoot potential problems, drawing staff and students together to explore options. For instance, placing bees on an urban roof raises questions about the weight load on a hot tar roof. There are security issues with moving bees through the school building. Managing the care of the hives must be addressed as well as preventing the bees from entering the ventilation system.

4. *Modeling and fostering systems thinking.* Living Campus nurtures interdisciplinary conversations and prompts individuals to draw connections between such things as climate change and the butterflies they nurture through the butterfly tagging program.

5. *Supporting sustainable, healthy living.* Even when education policies and practice model sustainability with respect to energy, recycling, water use, and so on, this does not automatically mean that students are consciously aware of the relevance to their own well-being and the well-being of others. Projects such as Dawson's health challenge (1249 Club) and the rooftop garden model sustainable living, making the learning more explicit and enjoyable.

6. *Nature-connectedness and positive emotions.* Connecting with Nature is associated with positive emotions (Nisbet, 2014) and Living Campus reinforces opportunities for such connections. Dawson staff recounted how they gladly came into work on a weekend to check on their butterflies. Some staff even named the butterflies before their release!

7. *Living campus is inclusive.* Most models of well-being address human well-being, often over-looking how this can be interconnected with the well-being of other species. Living Campus makes this interconnection explicit.

8. *Choice-makers and change-makers.* Through Living Campus students and staff contribute to positive change and build their capacity as choice-makers and change-makers. They experience the sense of well-being that arises from contributing to positive change and Living Campus also models sustainable, healthy choices. Understanding that making such choices can also be enjoyable is one of the many contributions that Living Campus makes to sustainable happiness and *well-being for all.*

Edible Campuses

Edible Campuses, with their particular focus on food, could be viewed as a subset of Living Campus as well as a transformative model for sustainability practices in post-secondary education. Edible Campuses as defined by Murray (2017):

> Edible Campus is defined as food production on the campus of post-secondary institutions. Food production on post-secondary campuses is frequently cultivated in under-utilized spaces such as rooftops. However, food production can also take place

in a multitude of locations such as classrooms, greenhouses and converted lawn space. Multiple food production projects on one campus are captured within the term Edible Campus.

The term Edible Campus is not inclusive of livestock or medicinal plant life that is inedible. The term Edible Campus could be expanded to include campus beekeeping if the honey is used as a food product and/or if the bees benefit the surrounding food production.

Edible Campuses have moved beyond a few pilot projects to diverse and expansive projects across Canada. For example, Ryerson University's Urban Farm is a rooftop farm in the heart of Toronto generating income, employment, and local food for the surrounding community. The University of British Columbia (UBC) has a 24 hectre farm that grows over 200 fruits and vegetables that are sold through the UBC farmers' market, wholesale, and Centre for Sustainable Foods program.

We will consider how Living Schools and Living Campus advance our understanding of positive communication after a brief discussion of positive communication and education.

Positive Communication and Education

Positive communication is born from a growing body of research rooted in positive psychology and communication studies. Pitts and Socha (2013) begin *Positive Communication in Health and Wellness* with a comparison of positive communication and the definition of health. The World Health Organization (WHO) famously defined "health" as a state of complete physical, mental, and social well-being and not merely the absence of disease or infirmity (WHO, 2006). Similarly, Pitts and Socha suggest that positive communication cannot be characterized as simply the absence of negative verbal and nonverbal communication, "but rather the presence of positive, enhancing, and facilitative talk and gestures" (p. 1). They also emphasize that positive communication is intended to contribute to positive relationships and institutions to help us to thrive.

In relation to education, positive communication has the tremendous potential to influence the well-being of teachers, student, and staff. Seligman's (2011) framework for well-being considers how positive communication can contribute to positive emotions, healthy relationships, deepening one's experience of meaning and accomplishment, summarizing this with the acronym PERMA. Carney's well-being model (2015) has been developed for schools and places strong, caring relationships at the center of a Venn diagram with three intersecting spheres that support these relationships: resilient, active, and flourishing. The Resilient sphere outlines skills and attributes to solve problems, cope with challenges, bounce back from adversity, and reach out to new opportunities. Within the Flourishing sphere, this includes experiences of enjoyment, engagement, meaning, competence, and connection. The Active sphere incorporates lifestyle balance through fitness, adequate sleep, good nutrition, meeting spiritual needs and connections with others. (Carney, 2015, p. 7)

We might apply Carney's model by considering how the school environment promotes a growth mindset that builds skills and attributes for resilience. The concept of a growth mindset was introduced by Carol Dweck of Stanford University (2006). It involves having the belief or mindset that an individual has qualities that can be strengthened and "grow" rather than believing that those qualities are fixed and will not change. Claxton builds upon Dweck writing that "the language of 'work'" can create/reinforce the idea that "learning is drudgery, and of the value of the product over the satisfaction of the process" (2013, p. 152). He provides the example of one school where the teachers stopped using the word "work" and found that student engagement rose. He also discusses the difference between "could be" and "is" language. Claxton recounts

Table 40.1 Positive Communication Self-Assessment

- What percentage of questions are generated by students, and what percentage come from you?
- Are your questions more likely to be open-ended or closed questions? (closed questions usually result in a yes or no answer)
- Are you more likely to use Could Be language or Is language?
- How does the physical configuration of the class create a culture of shared communication and equality?
- When you are asked a question by a student and don't know the answer how do you respond? i.e. would you be more inclined to state that you don't know the answer, invite the student to find the answer with you, reinforce the question as a good question that has you stumped? Some other response?
- How many of your questions invite personal reflection on the part of your students?
- Are students always required to raise their hand (suggesting you are the authority who controls communication) or are there times when communication is more free flowing?
- Do your written and oral assessments of students reflect a growth mindset suggesting areas for further development?
- Do you portray yourself as a visible learner?
- Do you and your students practice active listening?
- Does any of your verbal or nonverbal communication reinforce the view that education is primarily about "getting a job"?
- How often are students responsible for their own assessment and learning goals?
- Is your school reflecting health-promoting schools' practices?
- How are "failures" viewed in your classroom? Are these seen as learning opportunities?
- Do you use a generic "he" when referring to all genders?
- Are your examples in classroom discussion and worksheets gender inclusive?

(source: O'Brien and Murray in O'Brien, 2016)

many examples of teachers making small changes to language and finding that this leads to much greater positive outcomes than they would have predicted.

Extending this work, O'Brien and Murray developed the *Positive Communication Self-Assessment* (O'Brien and Murray in O'Brien, 2016, pp. 113–114) to help guide teachers with implementing positive communication for well-being (see Table 40.1).

Physical Environment and Positive Communication

One's physical environment can significantly impact communication. Imagine having a conversation about sexuality in several different locations and ask yourself how the conversation would/ could change because you are influenced by these diverse contexts. For example, picture having that conversation in a classroom, in a place of worship, or in a forest. The physical structure and location of our classrooms shapes what we learn, how we learn, and the language that we use in that process. Imagine how lessons may change if they were outside, as they are at the Green School Bali or in the Peace Garden of Dawson College.

Fostering Positive Communication through Living Schools and Living Campus

Rob Cassidy, associate dean in the office of Academic Development at Dawson College, eloquently captured how Living Campus generates positive communication and transformation.

> When it comes to Living Campus it's a difficult realization and I think that's one of the important things about it too. If it were easy it would be done and I like how difficult

it is because if it were easy it wouldn't be anything of substance. It wouldn't be real change.

. . . I feel that it provides a stage for very meaningful conversations to take place that otherwise don't take place and very meaningful conflict to take place that may not take place . . . there is a tremendous value in its ability to focus our discussions in a way that change, and improvement and development would be at the other end, or not. It provides a framework for having meaningful discussions that are ultimately small-scale instances of what needs to happen on a global scale. That to me is very powerful.

(Robert Cassidy, Dawson College, personal communication, November 6, 2015)

As educators are introduced to the concept of Living Schools, we are discovering that they are highly receptive and readily appreciate how this holistic view of education can be transformative and contribute to *well-being for all*. Pascal Carrara, a high school teacher in British Columbia, Canada describes it like this:

I find the word itself, "Living" very appealing. It puts learning for students into a visible and real form beyond what is only the theoretical. It feels true to learn through something that is alive. It feels as if we are part of something. Something real. I close my eyes and picture vertical gardens, and perhaps micro habitats around the school. I see interconnections that bring local insects, plants, and animals, that brings with it a natural flow of information. I don't picture a quiet space. . . . I picture movement and flow, a flourishing place that I want to be. We all feel more inspired to be there.

(Carrara, 2017)

Grade one teacher, Angela Neufeld, makes the connection between Living Schools, creativity, innovation, well-being, and sustainable happiness.

I think that Living Schools support healthy relationships because a Living School lends itself to more partnerships instead of power-based relationships. With more collaboration, skills in problem solving and coping grow as they are needed more frequently. Since Living Schools encourage creativity, innovation and sustainable happiness, staff and students are given opportunities to flourish. No longer trapped within restrictive expectations, everyone in the building can experience joy, engagement and meaning as they follow their interests and find deeper meaning in their learning.

(Neufeld, 2017)

Ryan Smithson, a high school physical education teacher, provides the perspective that Living Schools create an overarching theme and purpose.

When taking part in sustainability initiatives around the school, I sometimes ask myself "what is the endgame?" Although the staff and students at our school have taken part in several sustainability initiatives such as gardens, naturalization zones, bike repair clubs, composting programs, etc. I still can't help but feel as though they are all just somewhat random initiatives working independently of one another. That is not to say that it is a bad thing, but I feel that [Living Schools has] helped me realize a potential goal, "end game" if you will, of unifying our sustainability initiatives and organizing them all under the same umbrella.

(Smithson, 2017)

Conclusion: Future of Living Schools

The testimonies from educators assembled in this chapter support the position that Living Schools are at the forefront of education transformation. They represent practical examples that realize a vision of *well-being for all* and extend discussions of positive communication, positive education, and well-being to incorporate sustainability and sustainable happiness. For instance, Carney's (2015) well-being model is evident in the reference to Sigurbjorg Stefansson school where we noted that "students are engaged, focused, energetic, excited to share their learning, and kind to one another." Both Living Schools and Living Campus emphasize relationships with the natural world which is a perspective that is often overlooked in well-being models and education transformation literature.

The chapter utilizes testimonies from educators on Living Schools as there is no empirical research on this emerging field that explicitly explores positive communication and well-being for all. Future research should survey students, educators, and staff on their experiences with developing and working in a Living School as well as documenting the potential benefits of doing so. Furthermore, the attributes of Living Schools developed by Howard and O'Brien (2017) could be used as a foundation for developing research questions that focus on the connections between positive communication, positive education, Living Schools, and well-being for all.

Smithson and Mays are high school teachers in Winnipeg, Manitoba (Canada) who have just begun the process of visualizing how that want to incorporate the Living School concept and they articulate their experience of the transformation with considerable enthusiasm:

> The future at our school will be an exciting one. We view the Living School concept as a journey rather than a final objective. Ideally, there is no end in sight and we will continue to grow and add to our initiatives. By doing so, we hope to provide our students with useful deep pedagogical practices that promote lifelong learning through real-world education and experiences.
>
> *(Smithson & Mays, 2017)*

Living Schools represent a viable model for the imagined education reforms proposed by leaders in education, sustainability, and communication. The overwhelmingly positive testimonials from educators who are working in, or transforming their schools, into Living Schools supports the need for further research to expedite and support future Living School initiatives.

References

C21 Canada. (2012). *Shifting minds: A 21st century vision of public education for Canada.* Retrieved from www.c21canada.org

Carney, P. (2015). *Well aware: Developing resilient, active, and flourishing students.* Don Mills, Canada: Pearson.

Carrara, P. (2017, June 16). *Living it up. [Sustainability, happiness, and well-being course online forum discussion].* Sydney: Cape Breton University.

Claxton, G. (2013). *What's the point of school? Rediscovering the heart of education.* London: Oneworld.

Dawson College. (2016). *Living campus and well-being for all, sustainably.* Retrieved from www.dawsoncollege.qc.ca/sustainable/wp. . ./Well-Being-for-All-interactive.pdf

Dweck, C. S. (2006). *Mindset: The new psychology of success.* New York, NY: Random House.

Earth Charter International. (2009). *A guide for using the Earth Charter in education.* Retrieved from www.earthcharterinaction.org/invent/images/uploads/EC_Education_Guide_new_format.pdf

Falkenberg, T. (2014). Making sense of Western approaches to well-being for an educational context. In F. Deer, T. Falkenberg, B. McMillan, & L. Sims (Eds.), *Sustainable well-being: Concepts, issues, and educational practices* (pp. 77–94). Winnipeg, MB: ESWB Press. Retrieved from www.ESWB-Press.org.

Fullan, M. (2013). *Stratosphere: Integrating technology, pedagogy, and change knowledge.* Toronto, ON: Pearson.

Happiness Research Institute. (2015). *Sustainable happiness report: Why waste prevention may lead to an increased quality of life*. Copenhagen: Happiness Research Institute and Danish Ministry of the Environment.

Hargreaves, A., & Shirley, D. (2012). *The global fourth way*. Thousand Oaks, CA: Corwin.

Hopkins, C. (2013). Educating for sustainability: An emerging purpose of education. *Kappa Delta Pi Record, 49*, 122–125.

Howard, P., & O'Brien, C. (2017, May 17). *Living school attributes and practices*. [Weblog]. Retrieved from http://sustainablehappiness.ca/sh-extra/attributes-of-a-living-school/

IISD [International Institute for Sustainable Development]. (2016). *Guide for sustainable schools in Manitoba*. Winnipeg, Canada. Retrieved from www.edu.gov.mb.ca/k12/esd/pdfs/sustainable_guide.pdf

Juliani, A. (2015). How 20% time changed the world. In *Inquiry and innovation in the classroom: Using 20% time, genius hour, and PBL to drive student success*. New York: Routledge.

Kelley, T., & Kelley, D. (2013). *Creative confidence: Unleashing the creative potential within us all*. New York: Crown Business.

Kelly, R. (Ed). (2012). *Educating for creativity: A global conversation*. Calgary: Brush Education.

Krebs, D., & Zvi, G. (2015). Introducing genius hour to your class. *The genius hour guidebook: Fostering passion, wonder, and inquiry in the classroom*. New York: Routledge.

Murray, S. (2017). *Growing an edible campus* (unpublished masters thesis). Ryerson University, Toronto.

Neufeld, A. (2017, June 15). *Well-being and living schools. [Sustainability, happiness, and well-being course online forum discussion]*. Sydney: Cape Breton University.

Nisbet, E. (2014). *Canadians connect with nature and increase their well-being: Results of the 2014 David Suzuki Foundation 30x30 nature challenge*. Trent University. Retrieved from www.davidsuzuki.org/publications/DSF%2030x30%20report.pdf

O'Brien, C. (2010). Sustainability, happiness and education. *Journal of Sustainability Education, 1*. Retrieved from www.jsedimensions.org/wordpress/content/2010/04/

O'Brien, C. (2016). *Education for sustainable happiness and well-being*. New York: Routledge.

O'Brien, C., & Adam, C. (2016). Sustainable happiness, living campus, and well-being for all. *International Journal of Innovation, Creativity, and Change, 2*(3), 57–70.

O'Brien, C., & Howard, P. (2016). The living school: The emergence of a transformative sustainability education paradigm. *Journal of Education for Sustainable Development, 10*(1), 115–130.

P21. (2011). *Partnership for 21st century learning: P21 common core toolkit*. Retrieved from www.p21.org/storage/documents/P21CommonCoreToolkit.pdf

Pitts, M., & Socha, T. (2013). Positive communication in creating healthy lives, healthy relationships, and healthy institutions. In M. Pitts & T. Socha (Eds.), *Positive communication in health and wellness* (pp. 1–25). New York: Peter Lang.

Robinson, K. (2011). *Out of our minds: Learning to be creative*. Chichester, UK: Capstone.

Robinson, K., & Aronica, L. (2009). *The element: How finding your passion changes everything*. New York: Viking.

Seligman, M. (2011). *Flourish*. Toronto, ON: Free Press.

Smithson, R. (2017, June 18). *The road to a living school. [Sustainability, happiness, and well-being course online forum discussion]*. Sydney: Cape Breton University.

Smithson, R., & Mays, M. (2017, June). Leading change project: The living school. [Weblog]. Retrieved from https://educ6108lcp.wordpress.com/next-steps/

Wagner, T. (2012). *Creating innovators: The making of young people who will change the world*. Toronto, ON: Scribner.

Wettrick, D. (2014). There is no plan. In *Pure genius: Building a culture of innovation and taking 20% time to the next level*. San Diego: Dave Burgess Consulting.

Wien, C. A. (2008). *Emergent curriculum in the primary classroom: Interpreting the Reggio Emilia approach in schools*. New York, NY: Teacher's College Press.

Williams, D., & Brown, J. (2012). *Learning gardens and sustainability education*. New York: Routledge.

WHO [World Health Organization]. (2006). *Constitution of the World Health Organization: Basic documents* (45th ed.), Supplement, October. http://www.who.int/about/mission/en/

Zhao, Y. (2012). *World class learners: Educating creative and entrepreneurial students*. Thousand Oaks, CA: Corwin.

41

POSITIVE COMMUNICATION AND EDUCATION

Applying Character Strengths in Schools

Mathew A. White

Introduction

Defined as an evidence-based approach to teaching well-being in schools the growth of the positive education movement has been well documented over the past ten years (Waters, 2011; Rusk & Waters, 2013; White & Murray, 2015; White, Slemp, & Murray, 2017; White, Loton, Slemp, & Murray, 2017). However, examples of whole school approaches are limited to a handful of cases, and more rare are examples of theoretical models of how teachers communicate with students during positive education lessons. Moreover, White (2016) explores the barriers many institutions face when implementing positive education. In many settings, positive education is characterized as a series of lessons taught as an overarching program at different year levels in schools.

With the growth of the positive education movement, the integration of Peterson and Seligman's (2004) Values-in-Action (VIA) classification system of character strengths has become a favorite way for school leaders and teachers alike to commence well-being approaches. This chapter explores two applications of character strengths in educational settings 1) as a theoretical framework and 2) as integrated educational programs. In exploring these applications, the chapter will propose a conceptual model will be proposed on the Peterson and Seligman's (2004) classification, which aims to promote positive communications within a school culture.

Schools as Positive Communities

White and Waters (2014) note Peterson's argument that positive psychological approaches and interventions should not only take place at the individual level but also at the societal or institutional level. In particular, Peterson argued that schools were well placed to integrate well-being interventions to support preventative mental health strategies and foster a student's search for the meaningful life. Peterson's claim extended Seligman and Csikszentmihalyi's (2000) original introduction to positive psychology which proposed that positive psychology or the scientific study of what goes right in life, should be explored at the individual and the collective level and specifically refer to schools and education. Peterson (2006) asserted that by adopting a systematic approach to the integration of positive psychological interventions schools could become what he described as enabling institutions. Significantly, Peterson did not paint an overly simplistic view of education. He recognized that for many students' significant negative experiences that many students experienced at schools such as bullying and other harmful behaviors were just as real as positive ones (White & Waters, 2014, p. 69).

Character Strengths

Howard Gardner hailed the development of Character Strengths Classification by Christopher Peterson and Martin Seligman as "One of the most important initiatives in the psychology of the past half century" (Peterson & Seligman, 2004). Brdar and Kashdan (2010) define character strengths as "pre-existing qualities that arise naturally, feel authentic (and) are intrinsically motivating to use" (White & Waters, 2014). Peterson and Seligman's (2004) classification of character strengths provides an overarching theoretical approach for the possible integration of strengths in teacher communications. Developed in the early 2000s by Peterson and Seligman the VIA framework was developed after consulting many experts in the fields of philosophy, psychology, history theology.

Summarized in Table 41.1 Values-in-Action (VIA) classification system of character strengths Peterson and Seligman established six virtues and 24 strengths. Significantly, Peterson and Seligman claimed that it was possible to measure the 24 strengths. The virtues and strengths were classified as wisdom (creativity, curiosity, judgment, love-of-learning, perspective); courage (bravery, honesty, perseverance, zest); humanity (kindness, love, and social intelligence); justice (fairness, leadership, teamwork); temperance (forgiveness, humility, prudence, self-regulation); and transcendence (appreciation of beauty, gratitude, hope, humor, spirituality).

But can the language of character strengths act as the catalyst build positive school communities? One of the most popular starting points for many educators in schools hoping to promote well-being is the language from the integration of Peterson and Seligman's (2004) Values-in-Action Classification system. Yet, the greatest challenge for school leaders is how to achieve a consistency of integration of this vocabulary and an intellectual and behavioral level. Despite the growth in popularity for a positive education approach much work needs to be done to highlight the impact of such applications (Waters, 2011; White & Murray, 2015; White, Slemp, & Murray, 2017; White, 2017a).

There are few published theoretical models, which explicitly outline how to integrate character strengths into communications strategies, and many focus on activity rather than impact (Niemiec, 2017; Waters, 2011; White, 2017a, 2017c). In some instances, the integration of this vocabulary across schools can be described at best as ad hoc rather than systematic. A recent study by Malin, Liauw, and Damon (2017) considered the developmental relations between purpose and three other key character strengths that emerge during early adolescence: gratitude, compassion, and grit. Data analyses showed small but significant correlations between purpose and each of the other three character strengths under investigation.

Table 41.1 Values-in-Action (VIA) classification system of character strengths.

Virtue	Strengths
Wisdom	Creativity, curiosity, judgment, love-of-learning, perspective
Courage	Bravery, honesty, perseverance, zest
Humanity	Kindness, love, and social intelligence
Justice	Fairness, leadership, teamwork
Temperance	Forgiveness, humility, prudence, self-regulation
Transcendence	Appreciation of beauty, gratitude, hope, humor, spirituality

Weber, Wagner, and Ruch (2016) note that character strengths showed an important relationship to school achievement in a study of 196 children taking the VIA Youth Survey. Here the strengths of, zest, love of learning, perseverance, and social intelligence showed the strongest positive relations to school-related positive affect while teamwork, hope, self-regulation, and love showed the strongest negative correlations with negative affect at school. Bates-Krakoff, McGrath, Graves, and Ochs (2016) outline another example. In this article, a strengths program is discussed that is implemented in public schools. It also considers strategies for the gifted classroom setting to apply, balance, and appropriately match character strengths in the right situation.

In a pioneering article White and Waters (2014) outline a systematic approach to the integration of character strengths in a school. In the paper, the authors discuss five character strengths examples. Four of the strengths were integrated into existing school experiences such as English curriculum, school sport, student leadership, and counseling. The fifth initiative involved a brand new program, which introduced Positive Education Curriculum for years Kindergarten to Year 10. Similar applications were later expanded by White and Murray (2015) and White, Slemp, & Murray (2017). Another recent example by White (2017b) considers the integration of character strengths analysis in theology and its possible implications for education. The integration of character strengths vocabulary is also explored from various perspectives by Ambler, Anstey, McCall, and White (2017).

Defining Positive Communications

Positive communications is defined as the systematic application of Values-in-Action (VIA) classification system of character strengths within educational settings. It focuses on the pedagogical process adopted by teachers to integrate strengths in their daily interaction with students and the teams of teachers with whom they collaborate. It is characterized as a whole school approach. This means that the vocabulary of the strengths classification is integrated into leadership, teacher practice, the change process, policy, and programs at all levels of a school. Many schools have introduced well-being approaches, and many appear to have overlooked the need to adopt a strategic and whole school approach in particular to the opportunity for systematic use of strength-based vocabulary. In failing to adopt a systematic approach to the integration of well-being theory and positive education programs, many educators have overlooked the significant part communications plays in creating a culture of well-being within school communities.

An Application of Positive Communications: A Theoretical Framework

Communications and vocabulary are the building blocks of education. To teach is to lead discussion, debate, and interrogate ideas, text, and concepts. From the earliest years of education students are placed at the center of a conversation about knowledge and understanding. Advances in neuroscience and education demonstrate that teachers talk more in classes than they realize. Often this is to communicate subject content. For example, in the literature classroom, this could be to analyze text, and the cultural content of a novel, poem, or play.

In a recent study of Australian teachers, Weldon and Ingvarson (2016, p. 9) claim that a "[. . .] full-time primary teachers averaged 52.8 hours per week and full-time secondary teachers averaged 53.2 hours per week. Leading teachers worked a slightly longer week, averaging about 55 hours per week. Proportionally, teachers spent just under 80 percent of their time on teaching and teaching-related tasks, or about 41 hours per week. Just over one-fifth of their time, or about 11 hours per week, was spent on other activities." But *how* these teachers are communicating during these hours is one of the most challenging questions in education.

Given the number of hours, the average teacher spends with young people the opportunity for the integration of a strength-based approach in education appears to be endless. From teaching, sports coaching, coaching the school debating team, or providing feedback in drama productions, the possibilities seem endless. However, the justification used by school leaders to integrate positive education into school offerings appears to be as diverse as the schools claiming to offer this style of education. These goals can include preventative mental health programs, increasing the level of happiness and resilience in student, or to educate young people in the skills for human flourishing.

An approach school leaders and teachers can adopt outlined in Table 41.2. Positive communications in education: a theoretical framework. In this framework, teachers are invited to complete the VIA survey and reflect on the results. At this first stage, teachers are encouraged to consider how they use their strengths inside and outside the classroom. Moreover, teachers are invited to reflect on how and when they lean on particular strengths when faced with specific pedagogical challenges. The second step is to share this reflection with teaching teams and to practice catching each other using their strengths as a team.

For example, it might be preparing a whole year level for a series of challenges pieces of assessment, which requires the ingenuity of the teaching team to work together coherently and know and understand each other strengths well before engaging with the challenge ahead. Once this has been completed, and individual teacher and teams can reflect and spot other team members using their strength the teacher's focus should turn to the student. At this stage, the student is introduced to the vocabulary of the VIA strengths classification and invited to complete the survey (if the students are aged over 11 years old).

Following this when the students have finished the strengths survey they are asked to compare and contrast how they used their strength to approach the task. This reflection will be particularly critical given that teachers have also undertaken the test and should be able to share their

Table 41.2 Positive communications in education: a theoretical framework.

Teaching stages	Explanation
Self	Individual teachers start by discovering and reflecting on how they use their strengths-based on the Values-in-Action (VIA) classification system of character strengths. Also consider how their strengths might hinder the learning process.
Teaching Team	Teaching teams discover and reflect on how they use their strengths-based on the Values-in-Action (VIA) classification system of character strengths. For example, is there a cluster of strengths in the team.
Individual Students	Students are invited to explore the vocabulary of the Values-in-Action (VIA) classification system of character strengths. In particular discussions could include the type of strengths shown in texts, or by characters. If over the age of 13 they might be invited to take the survey.
Class	Classes are invited to explore the vocabulary of the Values-in-Action (VIA) classification system of character strengths.
School	Students are invited to consider what the signature strengths of the school could be based the vocabulary of the Values-in-Action (VIA) classification system of character strengths.

results with the student and explore the question of when and how often they have used their signature strengths.

At the class level, the benefit of the VIA classification become very clear, as individual students can form groups and teams to be able to tackle assessment tasks and projects to achieve educational objectives. For example, it might be found that a class needs a higher degree of self-regulation to tackle a task to the best of their ability. The discussion between the teacher and the student and the student and student about what strengths they can use at different points means that students have access to a higher degree of vocabulary to be able to master the self-regulation required to complete a task. This is particularly useful for students who have difficulty articulating how they approach their learning.

This then raises the question, "what do school or institutional strengths look like and how to student articulate the strengths of their schools?" Many would like to think that a love of learning is the dominant strength. However, it might be found that aligning the strengths with the existing values of the school means that they have a greater emphasis on the values of fairness, leadership, and teamwork or the strengths of bravery, honesty, perseverance, and zest. Each institution will have a variety of values that could be strengthened by the adoption of the VIA classification to sharpen the institutional intentions for students.

How Can Positive Communications Be Integrated into Existing Educational Programs?

In discussing how positive communications might be integrated into existing educational programs subject areas commonly taught in schools, positive communications focus on the process and way that each teacher interacts and communicates with her students to achieve learning and social goals. As one of the founders of the field, Christopher Peterson (2006) argued, "positive psychology is not a spectator sport." To integrate strength-based approaches with students it is imperative that teachers become aware of their strengths, when and how they use these, and moreover become aware of when their strengths can inhibit the learning process. While this sounds simple in principle, in practice and behavior it requires teachers to become genuinely reflective in their approach to learning and teaching, as summarized in Table 41.3 (examples of positive communications process integrated into existing educational programs). This means that a teacher engages in the subject discipline will teach (for example, reading, writing, and arithmetic) they will adopt the strength-based approach. The difference between positive communications as an approach and other processes is that with positive communications teachers are asked to reflect on their strengths before they consider the discipline content they are required to teach, and the strengths of the students in their class. This stage is an essential step in the process. Teachers are invited to become aware of their signature strengths, and the dominant way they will approach learning and teaching. By internalizing strength-based vocabulary teachers can become more aware of when, and how often they will employ their strengths. Further examples of the application of positive communications in requires more exploration.

Applications of Positive Communications in Literature

Teaching literature is one of the natural homes for a positive communications approach in education. Literature teachers focus on the study of text, characters, and their development, poetry, and drama to name a few examples of writing. In each instance teachers are inviting students to consider the individual motivation and objectives of character and why they make the decisions they do books. However, with a positive communications approach, teachers are inviting students to consider their strengths first before jumping in to examine the strengths of other characters. For example, as teachers encourage students to explore the decision for a significant character in a book, they invite students to first think about their strengths first and then to consider the presence or absence of these strengths in the character they are examining. Teachers should encourage students to integrate the vocabulary acquired in the reflection to the strengths illustrated by characters. The outcome of the reflection should be a richer interpretation of the characters' motivations in the novel being discussed. In particular, with positive communications approach teachers should be able to ask how their strengths enabled the class discussion to flow and move in particular areas as well to help students to make the link between and across the theory of strengths and practical examples in the novels being examined.

Applications of Positive Communications in Second Language

The application of strengths as part of the process of positive communications in second language acquisition is a fertile area for potential. In particular, it raises the natural cross-cultural question about strengths. When discussing strengths for example in Chinese, or French and German are we talking the same thing? This is a vibrant discussion in particular for the teacher to engage senior students on to consider how strengths may differ between and across cultures and that some cultures might have a greater emphasis on some strengths rather than others. In the practical terms of actually learning another language, positive communication is a very rich area. For example, if the teachers first consider how they use their strengths of creativity, curiosity, judgment, love of learning, self-regulation to master new vocabulary and phrases this will be unable a discussion with students to link these strengths with the particular acquisition of the second language. One of the critical strengths is self-regulation and perseverance of this subject area. A student can then also consider how they are using their strengths to be able to learn the new language, making cross-cultural links between and across the strengths and how they might manifest in other languages. This is a crucial stage in the development of greater empathy between and across individuals and groups in society.

Applications of Positive Communications in History and Economics

Positive communications raise fascinating learning opportunities in history; geography and economics given these social sciences are traditionally seen as deficit-oriented fields. In all three areas, what will benefit teachers and students in the applications of strength-based approach is the ability to know and understand how their strengths might hinder or help in the analysis being undertaken. For example, a strength-based interrogation by the teacher of their strengths might demonstrate that the potential that historians have to present a biased or subjective perspective of the past. Students could be invited to consider how by focusing on particular strengths could blind historians for specific views. Here, a productive conversation could take place in the class about how historians write history and the perspectives that they adopt might be a reflection of the strengths. Students could also be invited to consider how their own strengths could negatively influence the way they consider how history is written and the motivation various historical characters could have. In economics, a potential application could be for students to consider how the strengths of an economist lead to the discovery and implementation of economic theory to be able to understand the communities of the world of business finance and the economy.

Applications of Positive Communications in Biology, Physics, and Chemistry

While it might not seem immediately obvious how to apply strengths in the study of the sciences, like literature it is here where there can be significant application that integrates not only the strengths-based qualities needed to apply the scientific method and to "do" science, it is also the opportunity to invite students to consider the qualities that are required by scientists as they tackle one of the most challenging questions. For example, when students are asked to undertake scientific experiments and learn about the scientific method of falsification, there is an excellent opportunity for the class to discuss the strengths needed to observe and apply the stages at each step during an experiment. These strengths are critical in helping to encourage students to become more reflexive in their approach.

Applications of Positive Communications in Mathematics

Positive communications can potentially play a significant role in helping students to know and understand their strengths, those of the peers and which strengths are required in particular to be able to develop stronger skills in mathematics. For example, the teacher can openly discuss with students the qualities and characteristics of great mathematicians and what strengths are required to be able to master particular mathematical challenges. Herein, students who struggle with mathematics can also find use in the diversity of strengths as they tackle a question. For example, students could find that the strengths of creativity, curiosity, judgment, and perspective can help them to address particular challenges. Also, this might serve as a unifying language to help students and teachers align more closely with their learning objectives.

Applications of Positive Communications in the Arts: Music, Drama, and Visual Arts

Like literature applications of strength-based conversations in the arts appear to have limitless possibilities. From the perspective of the teacher, there is the question how will I bring my strengths to teach this class? But there is also the question, how will I use my strengths to be able to bring out the best possible strengths in an orchestra, a play or as students paint. Here, the strengths of creativity, curiosity, judgment, and appreciation of beauty can be used by the teacher to be able to inspire students to develop new understandings about the possibilities in creativity. Moreover, the student can be invited to consider the particular strengths that a composer, playwright, or musician are required to be able to perform a concert or play or mount an exhibition. Here, teacher, taught, and the subject matter discussed can show endless possibilities of the interaction between the vocabularies of strengths required to create such works of art.

Conclusions and Future Possibilities

The possibilities of the use of positive communications in education are significant. It has been defined as the systematic application of Values-in-Action (VIA) classification system of character strengths within educational settings. This aspect of positive education remains an emergent field, and we need examples of the application of the VIA to help more teachers understand that aside from the content of positive education lessons there is the need to focus more closely on the process. This chapter makes a contribution to the growth of the field and explores potential applications across a variety of subject areas to help document and overarching theoretical frameworks.

Table 41.3 Examples of positive communications process integrated into existing educational programs.

Discipline Area	Teachers step	Example	Student's step
Literature		Study of a Shakespearian play	Students are asked to reflect on their strengths and the strengths they can spot in the main character of the play being studied. They are also invited to consider when and how they might call of these strengths in real life.
Second Language		Learning about a social issue in contemporary China and acquiring new vocabulary	Students are asked if they think that strengths are culturally universal, and if they think that strengths manifest themselves differently across the world and why this might be the case.
History, Geography, Economics	Teachers are invited to reflect on their strengths before engaging with the discipline content. The teacher then shares with the class their signature strengths and discuss how they believe their strengths intersect with their teaching	Learning about the Causes of the First World War	Students are invited to consider their own strength in relation to the historical events being uncovered in the class and how they might react in the same situation. Also what strengths are required to undertake the study of history.
Biology, Physics, Chemistry, and Information Technology		Undertaking an scientific experiment linked to the course syllabus	Students are asked to write a crucial reflection of the strengths they used during the application of the scientific method.
Mathematics		Learning a new formula	Students are asked to write a reflecting of the strengths they used to tackle mathematical questions. For students who struggle with mathematics this could be a very powerful approach to maintain a level of engagement.
The arts: music, drama, and visual arts		Preparing for a concert, play or major exhibition	Students consider how they will use their strengths to be able to tackle a particular creative challenge. In particular in the ability to respond to feedback from teachers when undertaking rehearsal for musical and plays. Herein the use of the strength vocabulary could be very helpful for students in drama.

References

Ambler, G., Anstey, A., McCall, T., & White, M. (2017). *Flourishing in faith: Theology and positive psychology.* Eugene, OR: Cascade Books, Wipf and Stock Publishers.

Bates-Krakoff, J., McGrath, R. E., Graves, K., & Ochs, L. (2016). Beyond a deficit model of strengths training in schools: Teaching targeted strength use to gifted students. *Gifted Education International.* doi:10.1177/0261429416646210

Brdar, I., & Kashdan, T. (2010). Character strengths and well-being in Croatia: An empirical investigation of structure and correlates. *Journal of Research in Personality, 44,* 151–154. doi:10.1016/j.jrp.2009.12.001

Hopkins, C. (2013). Educating for sustainability: An emerging purpose of education. *Kappa Delta Pi Record, 49,* 122–125.

Malin, H., Liauw, I., & Damon, W. (2017). Purpose and character development in early adolescence. *Journal of Youth and Adolescence.* Np. http://dx.doi.org/10.1007/s10964-017-0642-3

Fullan, M. (2013). Stratosphere: Integrating technology, pedagogy, and change knowledge. Don Mills, Ont.: Pearson.

Niemiec, R. (2017). *Character strengths interventions: A field guide for practitioners.* Toronto, ON: Hogrefe.

O'Brien, C. (2010). Sustainability, happiness and education. *Journal of Sustainability Education, 1.* Retrieved from www.jsedimensions.org/wordpress/content/2010/04/

O'Brien, C. (2016). Education for Sustainable Happiness and Well-Being. New York: Routledge.

O'Brien, C., & Howard, P. (2016). The living school: The emergence of a transformative sustainability education paradigm. *Journal of Education for Sustainable Development, 10*(1), 115–130. https://doi.org/10.1177/0973408215625549

Peterson, C. (2006). *A primer in positive psychology.* New York, NY: Oxford University Press.

Peterson, C., & Seligman, M. E. P. (2004). *Character strengths and virtues: A handbook and classification.* New York, NY: Oxford University Press.

Rusk, R., & Waters, L. (2013). Tracing the size, reach, impact, and breadth of positive psychology. *The Journal of Positive Psychology, 8*(3), 207–221.

Seligman, M., & Csikszentmihalyi, M. (2000). Positive psychology: An introduction. *The American Psychologist, 55*(1), 5–14.

Waters, L. (2011). A review of school-based positive psychology interventions. *The Australian Educational and Developmental Psychologist, 28*(2), 75–90.

Weber, M., Wagner, L., & Ruch, W. (2016). Positive feelings at school: On the relationships between students' character strengths, school-related affect, and school functioning. *Journal of Happiness Studies, 17,* 341–355. doi:10.1007/s10902-014-9597-1

Weldon, P., & Ingvarson, L. (2016). *School staff workload study final report to the Australian Education Union—Victorian branch* (pp. 1–85, Publication). Melbourne, Victoria: The Australian Council for Educational Research Ltd (ACER).

White, M. (2016). Why won't it stick? Positive psychology and positive education. *Psychology of Well-Being: Theory, Research & Practice, 6*(1), 1. doi:10.1186/s13612-016-0039-1

White, M. (2017a). Impact of activity: Future direction of positive education. In M. White, G. Slemp, & S. Murray (Eds.), *Future directions in wellbeing: Education, organizations and policy* (pp. 27–33). Cham, Switzerland: Springer.

White, M. (2017b). Mary—Theotókos: Fulfilment of God's grace and embodiment of virtues: A strength-based reading. In G. Ambler, A. Anstey, T. McCall, & M. White (Eds.), *Flourishing in faith: Theology and positive psychology* (pp. 34–54). Eugene, OR: Cascade Books, Wipf and Stock Publishers.

White, M. (2017c). Welfare to wellbeing: Australian education's greatest challenge. *Australian Educational Leader, 31*(1), 18–22.

White, M., Loton, D., Slemp, G., & Murray, S. (2017). Positive education overview. In M. White, G. Slemp, & S. Murray (Eds.), *Future directions in wellbeing: Education, organizations and policy* (pp. 1–5). Cham, Switzerland: Springer.

White, M., & Murray, S. (2015). Building a positive institution. In M. White & S. Murray (Eds.), *Evidence-based approaches to positive education in schools: Implementing a strategic framework for well-being in schools* (pp. 1–26). Cham, Switzerland: Springer. Series Editor Ilona Boniwell. doi:10.1007/978-94-017-9667-5_1

White, M., Slemp, G., & Murray, M. (Eds.) (2017). *Future directions in wellbeing: Education, organizations and policy* (pp. 27–33). Cham, Switzerland: Springer.

White, M., & Waters, L. (2014). A case study of "The Good School": Examples of the use of Peterson's strength-based approach with students. *The Journal of Positive Psychology,* 1–8.

INDEX

Note: Page numbers in italic indicate a figure and page numbers in bold indicate a table on the corresponding page